	DIVISION	CLASS	SUBCLASS	ORDER
(Algae)	Cyanophyta *(Blue-green Algae)*	Cyanophyceae		Chroococcales Chamaesiphonales Dermocarpales Oscillatoriales
	Pyrrophyta	Dinophyceae *(Dinoflagellates)* Cryptophyceae *(Cryptomonads)*		
	Chrysophyta	Chrysophyceae *(Golden Algae)* Bacillariophyceae *(Diatoms)*		Biddulphiales *(Centrales)* Bacillariales *(Pennales)*
	Phaeophyta *(Brown Algae)*	Phaeophyceae		Ectocarpales Dictyotales Chordariales Desmarestiales Dictyosiphonales Sphacelariales Cutleriales Laminariales Fucales
	Rhodophyta *(Red Algae)*	Rhodophyceae	Bangiophycidae Florideophycidae	Porphyridiales Goniotrichales Bangiales Nemalionales Gelidiales Cryptonemiales Gigartinales Rhodymeniales Ceramiales
	Euglenophyta *(Euglenids)*	Euglenophyceae		
	Xanthophyta *(Xanthophytes)*	Xanthophyceae *(Yellow-green Algae)* Chloromonadophyceae *(Chloromonads)*		
	Chlorophyta *(Green Algae)*	Chlorophyceae Charophyceae		Volvocales Tetrasporales Chlorococcales Ulotrichales Schizogoniales Cladophorales Codiales Siphonocladales Dasycladales Zygnematales Oedogoniales
(Bryophytes)	Bryophyta	Hepaticae *(Liverworts)* Anthocerotae *(Hornworts)* Musci *(Mosses)*		Calobryales Jungermanniales Met~~zo~~riales M~~o~~~~n~~eales ~~Sphaerc~~carpales ~~M~~~~archa~~ntiales ~~Anthoce~~rotales

Buxbaumiidae
Bryidae

PLANT DIVERSITY:
An Evolutionary Approach

THE WADSWORTH BOTANY SERIES

William A. Jensen and Leroy G. Kavaljian, *Series Editors*

PLANT PHYSIOLOGY: *Salisbury and Ross*

AN EVOLUTIONARY SURVEY OF THE PLANT KINGDOM: *Scagel, Bandoni, Rouse, Schofield, Stein, and Taylor*

PLANT DIVERSITY: AN EVOLUTIONARY APPROACH: *Scagel, Bandoni, Rouse, Schofield, Stein, and Taylor*

Fundamentals of Botany Series

Jensen: THE PLANT CELL

Cook: REPRODUCTION, HEREDITY, AND SEXUALITY

Doyle: NONVASCULAR PLANTS: FORM AND FUNCTION

Salisbury and Parke: VASCULAR PLANTS: FORM AND FUNCTION

Billings: PLANTS, MAN, AND THE ECOSYSTEM

Baker: PLANTS AND CIVILIZATION

Bell: PLANT VARIATION AND CLASSIFICATION

Banks: EVOLUTION AND PLANTS OF THE PAST

PLANT DIVERSITY:

ROBERT F. SCAGEL
ROBERT J. BANDONI
GLENN E. ROUSE
W. B. SCHOFIELD
JANET R. STEIN
T. M. C. TAYLOR

The University of British Columbia, Canada

An Evolutionary Approach

WADSWORTH PUBLISHING COMPANY, INC.
Belmont, California

PLANT DIVERSITY: An Evolutionary Approach

by Scagel, Bandoni, Rouse, Schofield, Stein, and Taylor

L. C. Cat. Card No.: 69–14779

Printed in the United States of America

5 6 7 8 9 10 — 80 79 78 76 75

Preface

Plant Diversity: An Evolutionary Approach is designed for the plant diversity section of an introductory botany or biology course, the new plant organisms course that many schools are now offering, and, of course, for the one-semester plant morphology course. *Plant Diversity* is written for the average student but at the same time will provide additional material to further stimulate his interest and curiosity. Students who wish to go even further in their reading should consult *An Evolutionary Survey of the Plant Kingdom,* which also contains extensive additional references at the end of each chapter.

To broaden the conceptual perspective of the book, we have included such topics as algal ecology and provided a liberal integration of recent work from the fields of physiology, cytogenetics, and electron microscopy; and we have emphasized, uninterrupted, the overall trends in evolution and phylogeny. These trends, in addition, help maintain the continuity of treatment. We have attempted throughout to apply the findings of paleobotany directly to the living representatives in order to gain perspective on these two complementary aspects of botanical science.

To a certain extent, the text is a condensed and revised version of *An Evolutionary Survey of the Plant Kingdom,* which was designed for a year (two semester) survey of the plant kingdom. Its wide use in schools, colleges, and universities offering a variety of programs in the life sciences demonstrated the need for a text covering similar material with a more conceptual or principles emphasis which can be encompassed reasonably within a single quarter or semester.

Moreover, as in the earlier text, we feel that the collaboration of several specialists in one book makes a unique contribution to students of the plant kingdom, providing a more satisfactory coverage of each of the groups than is often achieved in a book written by one author. We have standardized our terminology throughout the text as far as is practical, and eliminated some technical terms for the sake of simplicity. A comprehensive glossary, including terms used throughout the text, is included at the end of the text preceding the index.

For constructive criticism and valuable recommendations concerning the preparation of the book, we are especially indebted to Dr. H. G. Baker, University of California, Berkeley; Dr. Peter Dixon, University of Washington; Dr.

vii

Mason E. Hale, Smithsonian Institute; Dr. Richard Korf, Cornell University; Dr. Johannes Proskauer, University of California, Berkeley; Dr. K. R. Sporne, Cambridge University. Although their comments and criticisms contributed to our preparation, the authors take full responsibility for the final product.

As in the earlier book, our individual contributions in our respective fields of specialization are as follows: bacteria, slime molds, and fungi (R. J. Bandoni); lichens and bryophytes (W. B. Schofield); algae (Robert F. Scagel and Janet R. Stein); lower vascular plants (Glenn E. Rouse); and flowering plants (T. M. C. Taylor). But, again, since we have consolidated our efforts and consulted closely with each other in the interests of uniformity and continuity, it is impossible to define completely the limits of each person's contribution.

Many of the original drawings prepared by Mr. Ernani Meñez, Dr. Frank Lang, and Mrs. P. Drukker Brammall for *An Evolutionary Survey of the Plant Kingdom* have been reproduced in *Plant Diversity: An Evolutionary Approach;* some of their drawings have been regrouped, redrawn, or reduced. In addition, some new drawings have been added to the figures; these were prepared by Mrs. Margaret (Dean) Jensen and Mr. John C. Andrews. The following figures were prepared by Mrs. Jensen: 3–3D, 3–4A,B, 3–5C–G, 3–6G,H, 3–7A–C, 3–8A,B, 3–9A,B, 4–3, 5–3, 5–5C, 6–1, 6–11, 7–1, 7–3, 7–5, 7–7, 7–10, 7–12, 7–14, 7–15A,B, 7–27, 7–43D, 7–48, 7–55, 7–70, 7–75A,C, 7–78B,D, 7–81A, 8–2H, 8–3G,H, 8–4D,H, 8–5E,G,L,M,O, 8–10B,C,H, 8–11B,F, 8–12A–C, 8–13E, 9–1A, 9–2C, 9–5B,E, 9–6G, 9–8F, 9–10A,B, 9–11D, 9–14, 9–22C, 9–23C, 10–2A,B,D,F, 10–4F, 10–6A, 11–1E,G, 11–3A, 11–4A,D,E, 11–5A,C,G, 11–6A–D, 11–7A–D, 11–8D, 11–9, 11–11C,D,M, 11–13A,D, 11–14A,B, 11–15, 11–16A,E, 11–17A, 12–1E,K, 12–2F,L, 12–4A–C, 12–6B, 12–7A,B, 12–8C,E, 12–9A, 12–10D, 12–11D,E, 12–14B,C, 12–16E, 12–17F. Mr. Andrews prepared the following figures: 12–2A, 13–1, 13–2, 13–3, 15–16A, 15–27, 17–1, 18–7, 18–8, 20–7, 20–8, 20–11A, 20–17A, 20–25, 21–4B,C, 23–3, 23–4, 23–5, 23–6.

We are indebted to individuals and publishers who loaned original illustrations and photographs, and who gave permission to copy or redraw figures; these are acknowledged in the appropriate captions. We are especially grateful to our colleague Dr. Thana Bisalputra for providing us with a number of original electron micrographs; also to Dr. R. M. Schuster, University of Massachusetts, and Dr. G. A. M. Scott, University of Dunedin, who generously provided preserved material of a number of bryophytes.

Finally, we wish to acknowledge the assistance provided by the Department of Botany, The University of British Columbia.

Contents

NONVASCULAR PLANTS

x

VASCULAR PLANTS

xi

CONTENTS

xii

PLANT DIVERSITY:
An Evolutionary Approach

1 / Introduction

The plant kingdom is the most dominant and essential aspect of man's environment. Well over a quarter of a million species can be distinguished among living plants, and the fossil record reveals many others. This diverse array can be studied from many aspects, depending on the special interest of the investigator. In this book, *organic evolution* is the theme linking the representatives of the various taxa.

In this text we start with the primitive divisions, the members of which are perhaps closest to their ancestral morphology, and proceed to the divisions that show the greatest amount of evolutionary change. Each division contains primitive and advanced members, and some trends appear to be leading to an evolutionary dead end. There are also isolated groups, whose affinities with living and fossil plants are still obscure; their origin may always remain a matter of speculation. This situation has led to the picture of an evolutionary tree with a central trunk—the main line of evolutionary development—with many branches, large and small, emerging from it. Most botanists agree that, in light of the evidence available, this very unsatisfactory model is not only grossly oversimplified but inaccurate. We feel that the "family tree" is really best represented by a three-dimensional network of branches and twigs—a truly complicated picture.

There is general agreement among biologists that evolution has taken place and is still proceeding in both plants and animals. There is also much agreement on the mechanisms involved; biologists recognize that while inherited changes may be brought about in many ways, the methods are essentially all variations on a limited number of themes. Charles Darwin recognized more than a century ago that variation was the biological basis for evolution. But he could not explain how variability arises in a population or how it is transmitted from generation to generation. His theory that evolution is an outcome of natural selection had no experimental support, but was a conclusion based on a large number of shrewd observations made in many parts of the world. The work of numerous other investigators, starting with Gregor Mendel, has made it possible for us to understand at least the broad outlines of the process.

THE EVOLUTIONARY APPROACH

Evolution, the main theme of this book, provides a common thread for examining the development of the plant kingdom.

Certain botanical investigators try to determine phylogenetic relationships among

1

organisms, and evolution undoubtedly holds the key to this understanding. Thus, evidence that sheds light on evolutionary development will also shed light on phylogeny. For this reason fossil evidence, where available, has been included in this book for each group of plants.

Almost certainly the bacteria, fungi, and algae were the earliest groups of plants to evolve. They have the oldest fossil record, and their members appear closer to the presumed single-celled ancestral form of multicellular plants. Although the bryophytes have a meager fossil record, they are generally considered to have evolved at approximately the same time as vascular plants—that is, some time during the Paleozoic Era. We know that vascular plants are recorded with certainty from the middle of the Paleozoic, but they may have had a beginning earlier in that era. Since they have the most complete fossil history of all plants, their evolution can accordingly be traced much more certainly. It is now generally held that the bryophytes and vascular plants evolved from green algae of the chlorophycean line, but the exact time and manner are still in question.

In the present volume, space limits us to only a few basic considerations of organic evolution. For details and summaries, consult the writings of Stebbins, Dobzhansky, Huxley, Grant, and others. The remainder of this chapter will review general biological topics and relate them to the evolution of plants.

ALTERNATION OF GENERATIONS

There is little doubt that the same general biological principles apply just as validly to evolution in the algae as in the flowering plants. Certain features are common to the life cycle of all organisms that reproduce sexually: (1) *syngamy,* in which two gamete nuclei fuse to form a zygote, and (2) *meiosis,* the special form of nuclear division in which haploid meiospores are produced from diploid spore mother cells. As a rule, syngamy and meiosis

are inseparable; if one is present in a cycle, the other must be also.

In the plant kingdom it is convenient to distinguish between the two generations that intervene between syngamy and meiosis, one normally diploid and the other haploid. The diploid generation is often spoken of as the sporophyte and the haploid as the gametophyte. These follow one another in the sexual life cycle and constitute alternation of generations. These generations are defined as follows: the sporophyte generation begins with the zygote, while the meiospore is the first cell of the gametophyte. The last cell, or the last ontogenetic stage of the sporophyte, is the meiospore mother cell, and the corresponding terminal stage of the gametophyte is the gamete. Relative sizes and photosynthetic nature of the sporophyte and gametophyte are details relevant only to a particular kind of organism.

The next step is to consider the biological implications and importance of the life cycle. When a phenomenon is widespread among living organisms of both the plant and animal kingdoms, it is probably biologically very significant. Since sexual reproduction is the obvious feature of the life cycle, one must look for its biological significance. The answer lies in an understanding of cytology and genetics. Sexual reproduction makes possible the chance fusion of two gametes. In this way two sets of chromosomes and their genes are brought together in the zygote nucleus.

One should consider the significance of meiosis and what is involved in a meiotic division. The meiotic division is the transition between the sporophyte and the gametophyte, and involves the division of a diploid nucleus. However, instead of thinking of the number of chromosomes in the sporophyte as $2n$ in the ordinary algebraic sense, it should be regarded as n pairs, which in fact it is. In the first phase of meiosis, chance alone determines how the chromosomes of each pair will move. This provides a mechanism for segregation—i.e., the breaking up of combinations of chromosomes and genes. Meiosis is biologically important as a mechanism for segregating chromosomes, and consequently genes, in a random fashion. In contrast, syngamy provides a mechanism for the *reassortment* of genes—bringing together genes in new or different combinations.

BIOLOGICAL IMPORTANCE OF SYNGAMY AND MEIOSIS

Sexual reproduction, followed by meiosis, produces heterozygous populations—populations of genetically dissimilar individuals. Populations with genetic variability have a much better chance of survival than uniform populations. In an environmental crisis, such as a severe frost, individuals of a heterozygous population do not respond to the same degree. Some may be killed, whereas others survive. Genetically alike individuals would all survive or all die. Also important, as a result of the crisis the proportion of advantageous genes increases and that of the disadvantageous genes decreases.

A heterogeneous population is the raw material from which natural selection produces new forms. However, if natural selection operates for a sufficiently long time, the population will tend to become homogeneous again; unfit individuals (and their genes) will be eliminated from the population, and evolution would finally come to a stop. But there is no evidence that this happened—in fact, quite the contrary. For example, the algae were present at least 2 billion years ago; the ferns and bryophytes had their origin 300 million years ago; and both are still with us, still apparently varying and hybridizing. The flowering plants, which first appear in the geological record over 100 million years ago, are certainly still evolving.

The majority of animals are unisexual, but plants for the most part are bisexual. Plants have an inherent possibility for self-fertilization; this is biologically undesirable since it tends to produce homozygous populations. But, through natural selection, there has been a definite evolutionary trend away from self-fer-tilization. Species in which individuals are cross-fertilized have a genetic advantage over those that are self-fertilized. During evolution of the plant kingdom, many ingenious devices have developed to ensure cross-fertilization.

MUTATIONS

In the course of time, even populations with prevalent cross-fertilization will tend to become more or less uniform, because neither syngamy nor meiosis can add anything new to the gene pool of a species. If evolution is to continue, new characteristics must be added to populations; these characteristics, when they occur, are due to mutations, of which there are several kinds.

Even where sexual reproduction is lacking, certain mutations do result in some, though more limited, genetic flexibility. Although the progeny are all of the same genotype, this can produce a population peculiarly well adapted to certain environmental conditions and so be very successful. Many weedy Compositae (e.g., dandelion) fall into this category.

THE TIME SCALE

Mutations, variation, and natural selection require considerable periods of time for their fullest expression. Latest estimates place the age of the earth at 5 to 6 billion years; the first recorded fossils are about 2 billion years old. Between the formation of the earth and the appearance of these early fossils, life evolved. Although the record of plants is meager until some 400 to 600 million years ago, prior to this time evolution must have been proceeding rapidly.

To help us comprehend periods of several thousand million years, a useful concept is to represent the age of the earth as a calendar year, beginning on January 1. Prorating times, the first fossils would not be recorded until about September 1. Many of the algal groups

3

and primitive animals would not appear until November 30; undoubted vascular plants not until December 7; and the first flowering plants not until about December 25!

The fossil remains of several groups of plants guide paleobotanists in studying evolution and in reconstructing plants of the past. Reconstructing and interpreting fossil plants also is important for an understanding of the origin and relationships of living plant groups. Where the fossil record is relatively well known, as in the vascular plants, the evolutionary history and relationships are best understood. Groups with inadequate records, such as the fungi and bryophytes, cannot be related with nearly the same satisfaction. In such groups, it is necessary to estimate the probable course of evolution and to suggest relationships on the basis of similar morphology, anatomy, biochemistry, or ecology.

ENVIRONMENTAL EFFECTS

The growth and structure of a plant, although basically controlled by genetics, is also strongly influenced by environment. The phenotype of an individual is the result of environment acting upon its genotype. The same genotype, exposed to different environmental conditions, may exhibit differing phenotypes correlated with the environmental differences. This is particularly conspicuous in some amphibious flowering plants. In the pond weed *Potamogeton* the submerged leaves are thin, often linear, lack a cuticle, and possess no stomata. The emergent leaves, floating on the surface of the water, are thicker, usually elliptic, and possess stomata and a cuticle (Fig. 1–1A). The north temperate water crowfoot *Ranunculus aquatilis* (Fig. 1–1B) is an even more striking example. On this plant the submerged leaves are deeply dissected while the aerial leaves are merely lobed. Such phenotypic plasticity provides the plant with a wider range of environmental tolerance and assures it of more certain survival.

Environmental variation has produced plants whose morphology and other characteristics permit them to survive and reproduce. Knowledge of the gross morphology of plants helps to generalize about climates. An area can be described as possessing a particular spectrum of life forms—a spectrum that results from the climate of the region. The life-form spectrum in arctic regions is quite different from that of desert climates, since natural selection sorts out a different array of morphological types.

The interaction of morphology and environment, as well as other factors, has led to the evolution of the vegetational patterns of the world. Similarly, gross morphology largely determines the role each plant will take in the development of a plant community. The first plants to occupy a newly available site differ conspicuously from later plants. Although it is not the only factor involved, morphology does give some indication of the physiological tolerances of many species.

NUTRITIONAL RELATIONSHIPS

Plants may be grouped according to nutritional requirements. Most autotrophic plants need only inorganic substances and an energy source for growth. If the energy source is sunlight, the plants are called photoautotrophs; if the energy is derived from chemical reactions, the plants are called chemoautotrophs. Chemoautotrophs obtain energy through oxidation-reduction reactions of various inorganic substances, such as hydrogen sulfide, ammonia, and hydrogen. Autotrophic plants assimilate carbon dioxide and, for the most part, obtain hydrogen from inorganic donors. However, a few photosynthetic bacteria may use organic acids as hydrogen donors.

In contrast, heterotrophic plants must have external supplies of one or more organic substances. These organic compounds serve as oxidizable substrates; they are both an energy and a carbon source. Some heterotrophic plants

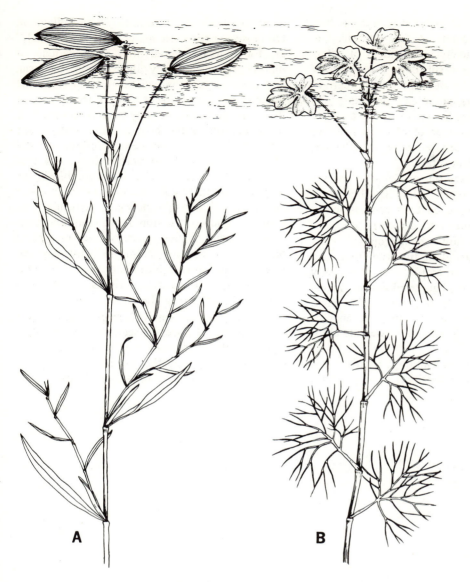

FIGURE 1–1 Differences in phenotypic response correlated with environmental differences, showing floating and immersed leaves. A, *Potamogeton gramineus,* ×0.5; B, *Ranunculus aquatilis,* ×0.5.

5

assimilate small amounts of carbon dioxide, but they must have additional carbon and organic compounds. If these are derived from dead plant or animal remains, the organisms are called saprophytes or saprobes. Parasitic heterotrophs obtain their requirements from living hosts. Some parasitic plants are obligate parasites; they must have a living host. Facultative parasites can exist either saprophytically or parasitically.

Most of the algae, bryophytes, and vascular plants are photoautotrophic. Although photoautotrophic, certain algae and bacteria can exist on dissolved organic materials in the environ-

INTRODUCTION

ment. These may be considered facultative heterotrophs, or mixotrophs. A few phototrophic algae are not completely independent of external supplies of organic substances; such auxotrophs are incapable of synthesizing certain substances (such as vitamins) necessary for growth. Although they belong primarily to autotrophic groups, a number of plants are either parasitic (dodder), semiparasitic (mistletoe), or saprophytic (Indian pipe).

None of the bacteria or fungi possesses chlorophylls of the types found in other plant groups. However, some bacteria possess somewhat similar pigments and do carry on photosynthesis; others are chemotrophic. Most bacterial species and all of the true fungi and myxomycetes are heterotrophic. Of these, only the myxomycetes are phagotrophs—i.e., ingest solid food particles. A few unicellular algal species are phagotrophic, although the characteristic is uncommon in species possessing chlorophyll.

The interrelationships among organisms are often important in their nutrition. A single plant or animal body is not necessarily an individual. On close examination many such "individuals" are found to be aggregations of individuals of different species. Many algae, fungi, bacteria, and other organisms can be isolated from the inner portions or bark of a single tree. Some of these are parasites, or may become parasitic if the condition of the host permits. Others are saprophytes, living on dead portions of the plant. Still others form partnerships of a sort with the host plant. The term symbiosis, as originally applied by De Bary, was used to cover any such relationship between dissimilar organisms. The term is now more commonly applied to what is best described as reciprocal parasitism. Examples of this in plants are the relationships between algae and fungi in lichens, and in mycorrhizal relationships where both partners benefit from the association.

Nutrition and symbiosis might seem at first glance to be of little consequence in morphological studies. However, form and function go hand in hand, and the evolution of diverse groups of organisms is sometimes linked.

6

2 / Classification

As in other branches of learning, the body of scientific knowledge contains a large number of unrelated facts. For this reason scientists have devised special methods of organizing information, and many of these methods have been refined into formal schemes or classifications. Some of these, based arbitrarily on a limited number of criteria, are termed *artificial classifications;* others, based on a large number of characteristics, are referred to as *natural classifications*. In some instances these may show evolutionary relationships, either phenetic or phylogenetic.

PHENETIC AND PHYLOGENETIC SYSTEMS

In both phylogenetic and phenetic systems of classification the biologist attempts to arrange plants or animals according to the lines that they appear to have followed in evolution. Thus, for any grouping of species, biologists select characteristics believed to have phylogenetic significance. The criteria vary greatly, depending on the particular group of plants and on the level of classification. Phylogenetic systems include evidence from fossil ancestors, whereas phenetic systems are based only on in-

formation derived from extant plants (see Chapter 23). In both systems, characteristics or criteria may be anatomical, if they concern cellular arrangement or the organization of cells of similar form and function in tissues, or morphological. They may concern fundamental biochemical or physiological characteristics, such as the nature of the cell wall, food reserves, and pigments. They may deal with reproductive organs and the arrangement of parts or motile reproductive cells of these organs. Or they may concern cytological details, such as chromosome number or genetic characteristics. To be useful, a criterion must be reasonably constant. Thus, to classify plants satisfactorily, one must observe and evaluate many different characteristics, usually in considerable detail.

THE NEED FOR PLANT IDENTIFICATION

In certain aspects botany is descriptive. Just as the physicist and chemist employ ergs, degrees, electrons, and grams, the botanist has a fundamental unit—the species. However, in contrast to the exact units of the physicist and the chemist, species are not so readily defined, and few biologists define them in precisely the same way. This is mainly because species are living evolutionary units subject to genetic change and their fluctuations sometimes produce overlapping in essential features. This blurring of boundary lines often makes the determination of species somewhat arbitrary. The system of classification must be modified as more information is gained about species and as significant differences appear in species because of evolution.

In the more exact aspects of botany dealing with physiological and biochemical processes, conclusions must be related to particular species or genera. If certain fundamental processes are attributed to a given species, one must use individuals of that species each time experimental work is performed. Ideally, one should be certain that the plants used are morphologically and genetically similar. Certain morphologically similar organisms may be quite different genetically and physiologically; other morphologically and physiologically similar organisms may be genetically quite different.

LEVELS OF CLASSIFICATION

Any classification system is subject to man's interpretation of nature, his current understanding of natural processes, and his interpretation of the evolutionary history of plants from the fossil record. For this reason, many different classification systems have been developed, particularly for the higher levels of classification. Botanists differ in their opinions and have evaluated the same evidence from living and fossil data with different degrees of emphasis.

The main categories generally used in plant classification are as follows:

Plant Kingdom
Division
Class
Order
Family
Genus
Species

This book's system of classification, with the names of groups, is outlined on the front and back endpapers.

NOMENCLATURE

The internationally accepted method for naming plants is based on a *binomial system of nomenclature*. Our modern practice stems from the works of Linnaeus published in 1753, although the system was not entirely original with him. Genera are divided into species and the name of each species consists of two words —the generic name followed by a specific epithet. The names and epithets are chosen largely from words with Greek or Latin roots, and are descriptive in many instances. Using this procedure, Linnaeus coined hundreds of binomials for plants and animals, many of which are still in use.

The major advantage of the Latin binomial is that it can be understood and applied by people anywhere in the world. Latin and Greek are ancient and well-established languages, and are sufficiently versatile to allow an almost endless number of combinations. This is preferable to any system that employs local, provincial, or national names. Such *common* names usually have little significance to people in other countries, or even in different parts of the same country, and are often confused with names applied to different organisms elsewhere.

The binominal is simply a name—a means of referring to a plant. It has no phylogenetic significance other than indicating the genus to which a species belongs. Thus, if a plant has been correctly identified and properly named, it will always bear the same binomial; and no other plant can bear that binomial.

SEQUENCE OF PLANT DIVISIONS

Botanists have used different characteristics for subdividing the plant kingdom. In the 18th century, Linnaeus established a class Cryptogamia for plants lacking flowers, or what were interpreted as flowers. The name refers to what he considered the concealed reproductive structures. Almost 100 years later, the flowering plants were grouped together by Brongniart into the Phanerogamae, which really includes all extant seed-bearing plants. These names are still used, and hence one often finds references to "Cryptogamic" and "Phanerogamic" botany. In this text Chapters 4 to 12 include the "cryptogams" and Chapters 13 to 22 the "phanerogams."

About 1830 Endlicher proposed a division of the plant kingdom into two large categories: the Thallophyta, or plants not differentiated into roots and stems; and the Cormophyta, or plants with roots and stems. The thallophytes can also be characterized as plants that typically have unicellular reproductive structures. The cormophytes were later restricted by Braun to include only vascular plants that do not produce seeds.

Another method of dividing the plant kingdom is based on the presence or absence of photosynthesis. This system segregates from all other plants the fungi, slime molds, and most bacteria which are nonphotosynthetic. The remaining plants are further subdivided into two groups: those that are green and grow on land; and those that grow in moist to aquatic environments and often possess pigments masking the green of chlorophyll. In adapting to the terrestrial habitat, green land plants appear to have evolved a life history in which a multicellular embryo is produced on the parent plant. The term Embryophyta was proposed late in the 19th century by Engler for those plants which produce a multicellular embryo. This resulted in the recognition of two major divisions of plants: the embryo-producing plants (Embryophyta) and the nonembryo-producing plants (Thallophyta). The latter include the nonphotosynthetic organisms.

Any of the above systems is acceptable for organizing and classifying plants. The choice of system is arbitrary, depending on which characteristics are considered most important. This text generally follows a system proposed by de Candolle in 1819; primary emphasis is on the presence or absence of a conducting system containing specialized cells for the movement of water (xylem) and food materials (phloem). Those plants possessing a conducting or vascular system are vascular; those without are nonvascular. The plant groups are separated into these two categories—each category containing several divisions—and are arranged in what we consider a phylogenetic system.

9

NONVASCULAR PLANTS

3 / Nonvascular Plants

The nonvascular plants, which include the bacteria, slime molds, fungi, algae, and bryophytes, are a diverse assemblage of organisms in which regular water- and food-conducting systems are generally lacking. Many of the nonvascular plants consist of cells that are almost identical throughout the plant body or thallus. In these morphologically simple plants there is little differentiation or divison of labor. Thus, every cell is able to function either as a vegetative or reproductive cell. Because of this morphological simplicity, biochemical and physiological characteristics are of fundamental importance in classifying some groups of nonvascular plants.

The nonvascular plants may be separated into two groups on the basis of ultrastructural cellular detail, as clearly shown by the electron microscope (see Fig. 3–1). The first, the prokaryotic group (Fig. 3–1B), lacks membrane-limited cellular organelles such as a nucleus, mitochondria, plastid, or vacuoles. This group consists of only the bacteria (Division Schizomycophyta) and the blue-green algae (Division Cyanophyta), both of which contain photosynthetic and nonphotosynthetic representatives. The second group has organelles separated from the cytoplasm by a unit membrane (Fig. 3–1A), the eukaryotic group (Fig. 3–1C).

This group contains the majority of nonvascular plants, all vascular plants, and includes both photosynthetic and nonphotosynthetic organisms.

CELL STRUCTURE

The prokaryotes lack internal membranes that separate the nuclear material, the respiratory enzymes, and the photosynthetic apparatus (when present) from the rest of the protoplast. The protoplast is circumscribed by a plasma membrane. However, there is present nuclear material, or deoxyribonucleic acid (DNA), in the form of very small fibrils (0.0025 microns or 25 Å), often near the center of the cell. The respiratory enzymes are scattered throughout the cell, although they are sometimes concentrated near the cell surface. The photosynthetic pigments are located within or on individual photosynthetic lamellae distributed peripherally in the cytoplasm.

In the eukaryotes, the DNA is in chromosomes within a well defined nuclear membrane, and nuclear division is regularly by mitosis. Some of the respiratory enzymes are within the membrane-limited mitochondria. The photo-

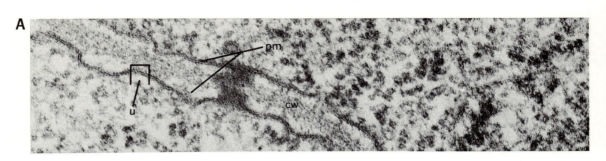

A

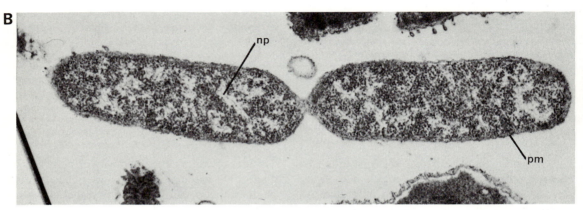

B

14

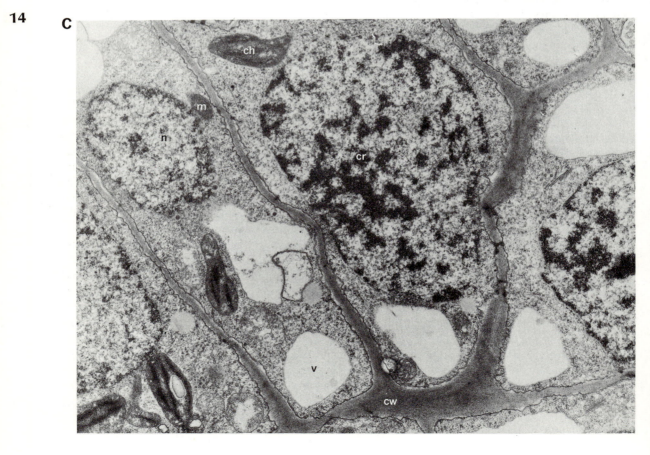

C

synthetic pigments and enzymes are contained within a chloroplast envelope. In this text the term chloroplast is used for all chlorophyll-bearing plastids with membrane-limited, lamellar structure.*

Some of the nonvascular plants are motile in the vegetative, or assimilative, stage (in particular, some bacteria, fungi, slime molds, and algae). But many nonvascular plants have motile reproductive cells with one or more hair-like organelles, the flagella. The prokaryotic flagellum (which occurs only in bacteria) differs from all others, as it consists of one to several fibrils (Fig. 3–2A). In all other plants and animals, the flagellum is composed of nine pairs of fibrils surrounding two central fibrils contained within a membrane (Fig. 3–2B) that is continuous with the plasma membrane. The outer membrane is either smooth and referred to as a whiplash flagellum (Fig. 3–2C); or it has thin hairs along its length (Fig. 3–2D) and is then termed a tinsel flagellum. The base of the flagellum is the basal body, and anchored to it are the flagellar rootlets (Fig. 3–2E). The location and number of the flagella remain constant for a given cell, or for a reproductive stage of a given species, as shown in Figure 3–3.

The nature of the cell wall in the nonvascular plants is almost as diverse as the organisms. Some have no cell wall, whereas others have a wall throughout for all or for only a part of the life history of the organism. The cell wall of the prokaryotes differs from that of the eukaryotes. The wall is generally composed of organic compounds, and it sometimes contains inorganic materials such as silica, magnesium, or calcium carbonate. However, in some of the smaller, microscopic nonvascular plants the cell covering is only a membrane, which can be composed of scales of silica, calcium carbonate, or undetermined organic compounds.

The food reserves, or storage products, of the nonvascular plants are also diverse, especially in the algal groups. These reserves are carbohydrate, protein, or fat and oil; they vary somewhat depending upon environmental conditions. Most information concerning storage products deals with the carbohydrates present, some of which are similar to the cell wall components. Starch and starch-like carbohydrates are the most commonly occurring carbohydrates. Some groups of nonvascular plants also store large amounts of another carbohydrate, laminarin, and laminarin-like compounds.

REPRODUCTION

In a large number of the nonvascular plants, reproduction can be vegetative, or asexual. This involves simple fission (Fig. 3–4A), budding (Fig. 3–4B), fragmentation, development of specialized deciduous parts of the plant, termed gemmae, or the production of special reproductive structures termed spores (Fig. 3–5). The spores, generally produced in sporangia (Fig. 3–5A, B), are usually unicellular and may or may not have a cell wall. Spores that are motile by means of flagella are planospores, or zoospores (Fig. 3–5C, D). Nonmotile spores are aplanospores, or sporangiospores (Fig. 3–5E, F). In some organisms, a heavy wall surrounds the protoplast, and this cell serves as a resting stage (Fig. 3–5G). All prokaryotic organisms reproduce extensively by asexual means; for many this is apparently the exclusive means of reproduction.

Sexual reproduction is not known for all of the nonvascular plants. In eukaryotic forms in

---

* Some botanists use the term chromatophore for nongreen photosynthetic plastids; however, in current usage the chromatophores include nonphotosynthetic or nonlamellar structures.

FIGURE 3–1 Electron micrographs of general cell types. A, plasma membranes (*pm*) and cell wall (*cw*) of young sunflower cell showing two-layered nature of unit membrane (*u*), ×80,000; B, dividing prokaryotic cell (bacterium) showing nucleoplasm (*np*), and lack of organelles other than plasma membrane (*pm*), ×90,000; C, eukaryotic cell (sunflower) showing presence of organelles, ×15,000 (*ch*, chloroplast; *cr*, chromatin; *cw*, cell wall; *m*, mitochondrion; *n*, nucleus; *v*, vacuole). (A, C, courtesy W. Walker; B, courtesy T. Bisalputra.)

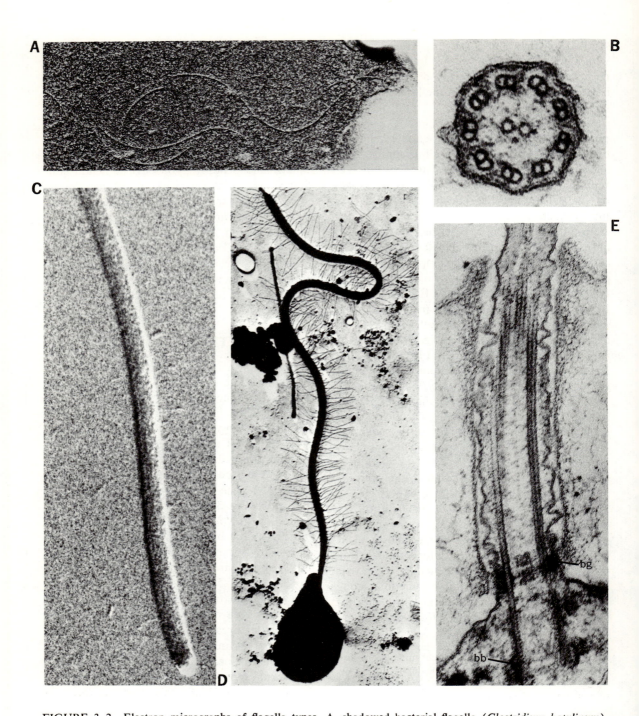

FIGURE 3–2 Electron micrographs of flagella types. A, shadowed bacterial flagella (*Clostridium botulinum*), ×17,600; B, cross section of eukaryotic cell (*Volvox*) showing nine peripheral pairs of fibrils surrounding two central fibrils, ×90,000; C, whiplash flagellum (*Chlamydomonas*), shadowed with platinum and gold, ×17,600; D, shadowed tinsel flagellum (*Dictyota*), ×5,700; E, longitudinal section showing basla granule (*bg*) and basal body (*bb*), ×90,000. (A, courtesy L. L. Veto; B, E, courtesy T. Bisalputra; C, courtesy J. M. Gerrath; D, from Manton, Clarke and Greenwood with permission of *Journal of Experimental Botany*.)

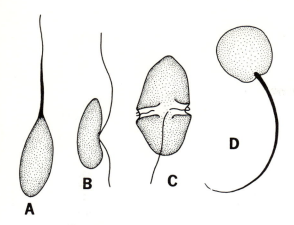

FIGURE 3–3 Types of flagellar arrangement. A, anterior attachment; B, C, lateral attachment; D, posterior attachment.

which it is known, there is a great diversity in the morphology of the gametes (Fig. 3–6, 7) and in the relative time and location of syngamy (gamete fusion) and meiosis (reduction division) in the life history of an organism (Fig. 3–8, 9). In the prokaryotes there is a unidirectional transfer of genetic material between the cells instead of an alternation of syngamy and meiosis. This results in genetic recombination but should not be regarded as sexual reproduction.

In most eukaryotes, the gametes are produced in specialized structures, the gametangia (Fig. 3–6G, H). In the fungi and algae these gametangia are usually unicellular (Fig. 3–6G), whereas in the bryophytes they are multicellular (Fig. 3–6H). The gametes are either identical in appearance (isogamous, Fig. 3–6A, D) or dissimilar (anisogamous, Fig. 3–6B, E). Both gametes may be motile, only one, or neither. If one gamete is large and nonmotile, and the other is markedly smaller (motile or not), sexual reproduction is oogamous (Fig. 3–6C, F). The larger gamete is regarded as the female (egg) and the smaller as the male (sperm). In some species the nuclei alone function as the gametes, moving by means of a fertilization tube that develops after contact of the gametangia (Fig. 3–7A). Another modification of sexual

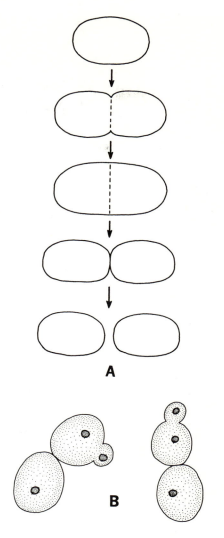

FIGURE 3–4 Asexual reproduction in nonvascular plants. A, fission in bacteria; B, budding in yeast.

reproduction, known as conjugation, occurs through the fusion of whole protoplasts or gametangia (Fig. 3–7B, C). For most organisms exhibiting conjugation, male and female gametes cannot be distinguished, because they are of similar form and size. However, if only one protoplast moves, it is usually considered male.

The time of syngamy relative to meiosis determines the type of alternation of generations, as well as whether the predominant

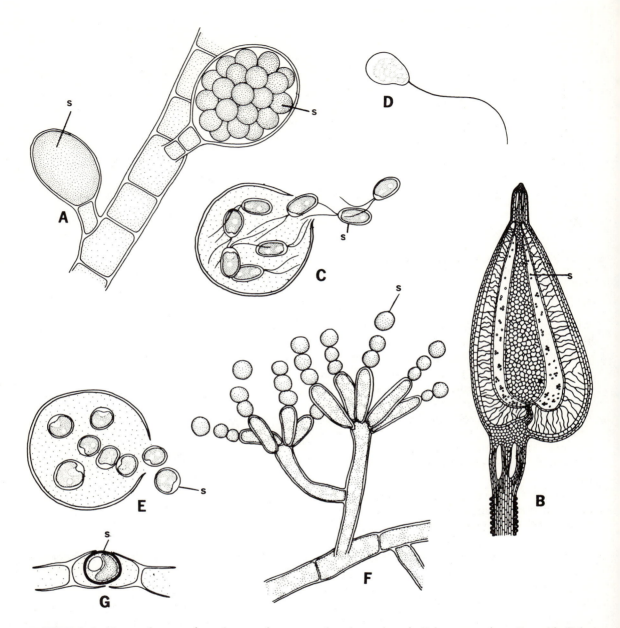

FIGURE 3–5 Types of sporangia and spores in nonvascular plants. A, unicellular sporangium; B, multicellular sporangium; C, D, zoospores; E, aplanospore; F, aplanospore (sporangiospore); G, resting spore. *s*, spore.

phase is haploid (*n*) (Fig. 3–8A), diploid (2*n*) (Fig. 3–8B), or both are equal (Fig. 3–9A). In some fungi, syngamy is divided into two phases: plasmogamy where there is fusion of only the cytoplasm; and karyogamy where there is nuclear fusion. After plasmogamy, the paired nuclei divide mitotically into binucleate cells that are either of limited duration or persist indefinitely, producing the dikaryon (*n* + *n*) stage (Fig. 3–9B). Eventually many of the nuclear pairs fuse, and meiosis usually follows immediately, restoring the haploid phase.

NONVASCULAR PLANTS

18

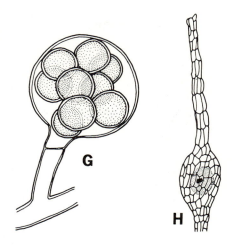

FIGURE 3–6   Types of sexual reproduction and gametangia. A–F, types of sexual reproduction; G, unicellular gametangium; H, multicellular gametangium.

INTERRELATIONSHIPS AMONG LOWER PLANTS AND ANIMALS

Among the lower plants, several groups are closely related to lower groups of animals. For example, certain algae (as treated here) are often considered protozoa by zoologists. Some of the fungus-like taxa are also often incorporated in the animal kingdom by zoologists. It will probably never be possible to assign many of these lower groups to either the plant or animal kingdom to the complete satisfaction of both botanists and zoologists. If the principle of organic evolution is accepted, one should not be surprised at this close relationship. One should expect it, since the earliest evolutionary forms were almost certainly not sharply differentiated from one another. The important point is that some organisms have both plant-like and animal-like characteristics. With equal justification such organisms can be referred to as plants with animal-like affinities or as animals with plant-like affinities. Groupings of organisms (Protista and Monera) distinct from both plant and animal kingdom have been proposed by some investigators to encompass this heterogeneous group.

PROKARYOTIC DIVISIONS

The Schizomycophyta (bacteria) and Cyanophyta (blue-green algae) are the only prokaryotic organisms. In addition to the similarities in cellular structure, morphology, and reproduction discussed earlier, these plants have some common physiological attributes. Both divisions lack the organic compounds known as sterols. Each division has representatives capable of fixing atmospheric nitrogen, living in thermal areas (45–85°C), and colonizing bare surfaces of rock and soil. Present-day Cyanophyta and Schizomycophyta are descendants of the earliest form of life, recognizable in rocks approximately 2 billion years old; a recent report shows alga-like fossils in rocks over 3 billion years old.

Bacteria

In the bacteria (Division Schizomycophyta), structure and reproduction are simple, and there are few morphological features to be used for identification within the group (see Chapter 4). Bacteria are unicellular or

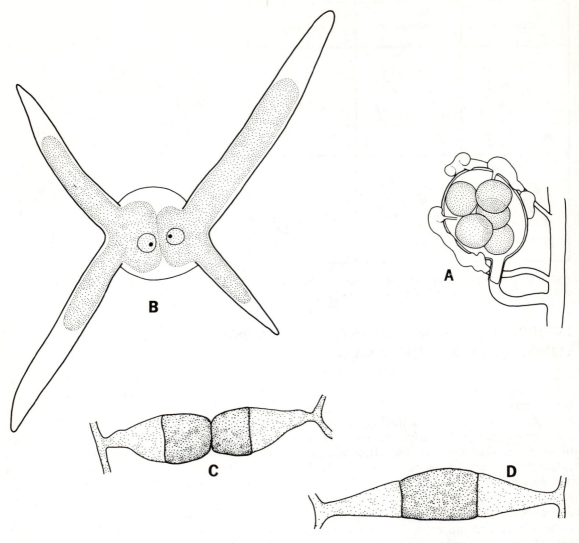

FIGURE 3–7 Types of sexual reproduction. A, fertilization tubes; B, protoplast conjugation; C, D, gametangial conjugation.

colonial, and the cells are either spheres, straight rods, curved rods, or filaments. The cells range in size from 0.5 to 500 microns. Most of the bacteria reproduce vegetatively, although some have a type of genetic recombination that is different from that reported for eukaryotic organisms. Physiologically, the bacteria are complex and diverse. They are important in nutrient cycles, decay, and disease production. The majority of bacteria are hetero-

trophic, requiring an external supply of organic compounds for both energy and carbon assimilation. However, some bacteria can utilize either inorganic compounds or light as energy sources and carbon dioxide for a carbon source. The photosynthetic bacteria contain the pigments bacteriochlorophyll and chlorobium chlorophyll, with photosynthesis occurring only under anaerobic conditions. Oxygen is neither released nor used in bacterial photosynthesis.

The reserve foods are usually stored as the carbohydrate glycogen, which is similar to starch.

Bacteria are classified according to morphology and physiology, as outlined in Chapter 4. Most bacteria are included in the class Schizomycetes, which is divided into several orders based primarily on morphology. A second class (Microtatobiotes) is often designated for the rickettsias, viruses, and mycoplasma (pleuropneumonia) organisms, most of which are parasitic.

Blue-Green Algae

Morphologically some of the blue-green algae (Division Cyanophyta) resemble bacteria. However, most are larger and there are many more filamentous representatives (as outlined in Chapter 5). Almost all contain the photosynthetic pigment chlorophyll *a*. In contrast to the bacteria, photosynthesis in the blue-green algae occurs under aerobic conditions with oxygen as the by-product. Reserve products are starch-like compounds. Classification within the blue-green algae is based on morphological features, since at present very little is known of the biochemical activities of this group. There is only one class, the Cyanophyceae, with several orders delimited by morphological and reproductive characteristics.

EUKARYOTIC DIVISIONS—
NONPHOTOSYNTHETIC
ORGANISMS

Some recent workers treat the Myxomycota (slime molds) and the Eumycota (fungi) as a single division, the Mycota. However, differences in morphology, cell structure, and method of securing food separate these two divisions (as discussed in Chapters 6 and 7). All slime molds are characterized by naked food-absorbing stages, and many are capable of feeding phagotrophically—i.e., ingesting solid food particles. The fungi, on the other hand, are

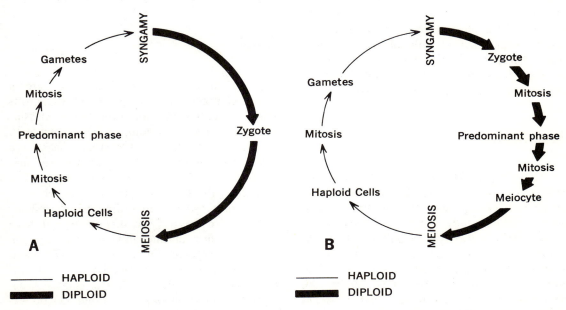

FIGURE 3–8 Types of alternation of generations. A, zygotic meiosis (predominantly haploid); B, gametic meiosis (predominantly diploid).

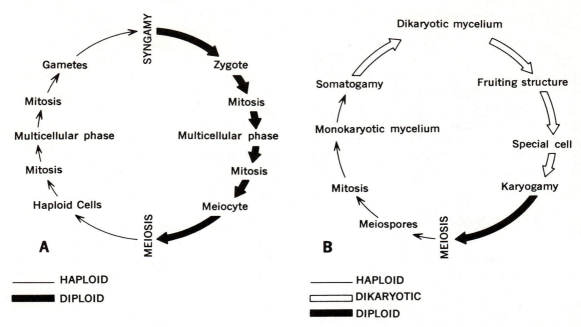

FIGURE 3–9 Types of alternation of generations. A, sporic meiosis (haploid alternating with diploid); B, dikaryon.

primarily filamentous, although some are unicellular, and generally they have a rigid cell wall for most of the life history. The fungi cannot ingest food phagotrophically; instead, they secrete exoenzymes capable of digesting materials. Subsequently the breakdown products are absorbed. Food reserves of the fungi are generally glycogen, lipids, and sugars.

Slime Molds

The slime molds (Division Myxomycota) include organisms of two very distinct types: the Class Myxomycetes, or true slime molds; and the cellular slime molds, consisting of two classes, the Acrasiomycetes and the Labyrinthulomycetes (see Chapter 6). The cellular slime molds do not appear closely related to each other or to the true slime molds. All Myxomycota have naked assimilative stages and reproduce by spores. The assimilative body, which is multinucleate in the true slime molds and uninucleate in the cellular slime molds, generally ingests solid food particles.

Fungi

The fungi (Division Eumycota) are a large heterogeneous assemblage of organisms which presents formidable problems in classification. No system is completely acceptable to all mycologists. In this text four classes are recognized on the basis of morphology and reproduction (see Chapter 7 for details). The first class, the Phycomycetes, is relatively simple morphologically and often has flagellated reproductive stages. The life history, in most instances, has plasmogamy immediately followed by karyogamy without a dikaryon stage. Also, macroscopic reproductive or "fruiting" structures are rarely found. The classes Ascomycetes and Basidiomycetes often exhibit extensive development of a dikaryon stage and of a macroscopic reproductive structure. The haploid spores formed by meiosis immediately after karyogamy occur within a sac-shaped (ascus) structure in the Ascomycetes and on a club-shaped (basidium) structure in the Basidiomycetes. The fourth class, known as the Fungi Imperfecti (or sometimes, as the Deuteromycetes), contains species in which only asexual reproduction (the imperfect stage) is known. This class is primarily a receptacle for incompletely understood species of uncertain relationships.

Lichens

These organisms have often been treated as a separate division; however, most workers consider them as part of the fungi (see Chapter 7). The lichen association, with algal (phycobiont) and fungal (mycobiont) partners, is one of the most intriguing in biology. The lichen fungi differ little from other parasitic fungi except that the fungal filaments and algal cells associate to produce a single "plant." The lichen reproductive structures are similar to those of fungi, and lichen classification is, therefore, essentially fungal classification. Only recently has it been possible to secure sexual reproduction of the mycobiont in culture, with or without the phycobiont. The phycobiont rarely reproduces sexually while in the lichen association.

EUKARYOTIC DIVISIONS—PHOTOSYNTHETIC ORGANISMS

Algae

At one time the organisms referred to as algae were grouped in one category. With increasing knowledge, resulting from studies of biochemistry, physiology, and morphology, it is now apparent that such a grouping is artificial and comprises a number of parallel lines of evolution. At present, the algae are classed in several divisions (see Chapters 8 to 11). Typically, algae possess chlorophyll *a* and produce oxygen as a by-product of photosynthesis. Often the chlorophyll *a* is masked by other chlorophylls or by other pigments such as the fat-soluble, yellow-to-orange carotenoids (carotenes and xanthophylls) or the water-soluble, red or blue phycobiliproteins (phycocyanin and phycoerythrin). As in the bacteria (although not as noticeable), there is some diversity in metabolic characteristics for a given group, and this diversity is used to help separate the algal divisions. Storage products appear to be mostly carbohydrates in the form of starch or laminarin and laminarin-like compounds.

The algae are unicellular or multicellular. The multicellular species are small (10 microns) and simple, consisting of a few cells, or as large as 50–100 meters, containing several different cell types. An important morphological characteristic used in classification of the algae is the nature and location of the flagella. The extent of variation within the algae is indicated in Table 3–1, where the major pigments, storage products, and flagellar types are summarized.

Bryophytes

This last group of nonvascular plants encompasses the mosses and the moss allies (Division Bryophyta, Chapter 12). The pigments, cell walls, and storage products are the same as for most of the green algae (Division Chlorophyta) and the vascular plants. However, the Bryophyta are an isolated group apparently not closely related to other plants, and probably not ancestral to any other group. Some authors consider the bryophytes as part of the large group of green terrestrial plants because of their habitat, the multicellular complexity of their reproductive structures, and the dependence of the embryo on the parent plant. Similarly, because of their gross morphology the bryophytes are placed by some botanists near

NONVASCULAR PLANTS

TABLE 3–1
Major Distinguishing Characteristics of Algal Divisions *

DIVISION (COMMON NAME)	MAJOR PIGMENTS	MAJOR STORAGE PRODUCTS	TYPICAL FLAGELLATION
Rhodophyta (red algae)	Chlorophyll *a* Phycobiliproteins	Starch-like	None
Phaeophyta (brown algae)	Chlorophyll *a, c* Xanthophylls	Laminarin	Lateral, 2, unequal, longer tinsel
Chrysophyta (golden algae including diatoms)	Chlorophyll *a, (c)* Xanthophylls	Laminarin-like	Apical, 1, 2, equal or unequal, whiplash and/or tinsel
Xanthophyta (yellow-green algae)	Chlorophyll *a* Xanthophylls	Laminarin-like	Apical, 2, unequal, longer tinsel
Pyrrophyta (dinoflagellates and cryptomonads)	Chlorophyll *a, c* Xanthophylls Phycobiliproteins	Starch	Lateral, 2, unequal, whiplash or tinsel
Euglenophyta (euglenids)	Chlorophyll *a, b*	Laminarin-like	Apical, 1, 2, unequal, tinsel
Chlorophyta (green algae)	Chlorophyll *a, b*	Starch	Apical, 2, 4, ∞, equal, whiplash

* Blue-green algae are considered in the prokaryotic group (see p. 19).

the vascular plants. In both morphology and anatomy, the Bryophyta are structurally simpler than vascular plants; the gametophyte and sporophyte are relatively conspicuous, each with distinctive features.

The Bryophyta are generally divided into three classes: Hepaticae (liverworts), Anthocerotae (hornworts), and Musci (mosses). The smallest are nearly microscopic, and the largest erect forms are less than 60 cm high, but some of the creeping forms are more than a meter long. Most bryophytes are strictly terrestrial and grow in humid environments; however, some grow in arid sites and a few are aquatic.

24

4 / Division Schizomycophyta

The bacteria, once classified with the true fungi, appear to be most closely related to blue-green algae (Division Cyanophyta, Chapter 5). The Schizomycophyta and Cyanophyta are prokaryotic organisms; their nuclear material is not surrounded by a nuclear membrane, and they lack both the nucleoli and the chromosomal organization of other organisms. Prokaryotic cells also lack plastids, mitochondria, vacuoles, and other organelles characteristic of the eukaryotic cells of higher plants. In addition, the cell walls of bacteria and blue-green algae contain substances not found in the walls of other plant groups.

DISTRIBUTION

Bacteria are predominantly heterotrophs; most require a supply of ready-made organic substances. The saprobic species obtain organic nutrients from dead plant or animal remains. Such bacteria are common in soil, water, sewage, and many foods; they are responsible for much of the process of decay. Parasitic bacteria obtain their nutrients from living organisms of many kinds, i.e., they live at the expense of a host. Many bacteria also form the symbiotic relationship known as mutualism, from which both partners benefit. These bacteria are abundant in the digestive tracts and on the mucous membranes and skins of animals; similar bacteria occur on or in many kinds of plants.

The autotrophic bacteria inhabit soil and water. Bacterial photosynthesis occurs only under anaerobic conditions, and molecular oxygen is neither liberated nor consumed in the process. Because of this, and because of the absorption range of their photosynthetic pigments (circa 4,000–9,000Å), bacteria carry on photosynthesis where other plants cannot. Chemosynthetic bacteria obtain energy through a variety of oxidation-reduction reactions and usually require only carbon dioxide as a carbon source. Such bacteria are abundant in habitats with a supply of the necessary oxidizable substrates, such as hydrogen sulfide, methane, ammonium and nitrate ions, and carbon monoxide.

CELL FORM AND STRUCTURE

The bacteria show relatively little variation in morphological and cytological features. Perhaps the most conspicuous features visible with light microscopy are the cell shape and size.

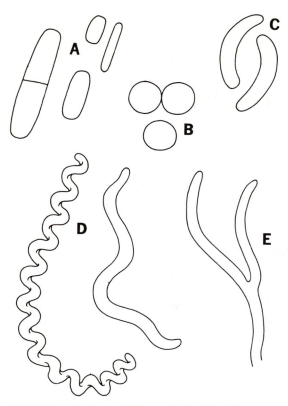

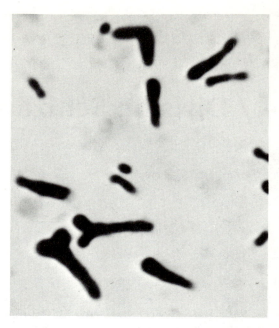

FIGURE 4–2 *Rhizobium* cells from a root nodule, ×2,000. Note variation in form.

FIGURE 4–1 Bacterial form. A, bacillus; B, coccus; C, vibrio; D, spirillum; E, coenocytic filament.

The commonly encountered forms (Fig. 4–1) are spheres and straight or curved rods. Spheroidal bacteria are called cocci, and straight rod-shaped bacteria are designated bacilli. The curved bacterial cells are spirilla, if helically coiled, and very short curved rods are vibrios. Certain bacteria, e.g., *Streptomyces,* produce filaments similar to the hyphae of true fungi but of smaller diameter.

Cell shape is relatively constant in most bacterial species. However, some variation may be found in old cultures or under unusual culture conditions, e.g., when penicillin is added to the medium. Some bacterial species are of variable form, an example being *Rhizobium* cells from legume root nodules (Fig. 4–2).

Bacilli of some species may measure less than 0.5 micron in diameter and 1.0 micron in length. The longest bacterial cells, other than those forming hyphae, sometimes reach 500 microns in length. In most species having cells of the bacillus type, the size range is 1 to 5 microns in length and 0.5 to 1.0 micron in diameter. Cocci usually attain a diameter of about 0.5 to 1.0 micron.

Structures common to many bacterial species are shown in Figure 4–3, composite diagram of a cell. A rigid wall surrounds the protoplast of most bacterial species; this wall is of one or more layers and is less than 0.1 micron thick. Walls, as well as other cell fractions, can be obtained by first crushing the cells, then subjecting them to differential centrifugation. Analysis of the wall fragments has shown that they contain a complex polymer called mucopeptide or mucocomplex. Mucopeptide is composed of chains of alternating molecules of acetyl muramic acid and acetyl glucosamine. Short peptide side chains are attached to each acetyl muramic acid unit.

__AGA____AMA____AGA____AMA__
          | |
   Peptide   Peptide

The peptides are long chains composed of alanine, glutamine, and either lysine or diaminopimelic acid. The amino-sugar, muramic acid, is ubiquitous in, and possibly unique to, the cell walls of bacteria. Diaminopimelic acid is known as a wall constituent only in bacteria and blue-green algae. In addition to mucopeptide, some bacterial cell walls contain other polymers, proteins, polysaccharides, and lipids.

Mucopeptide appears to impart rigidity to most bacterial cell walls. This substance can be removed from the wall by treatment with the enzyme lysozyme. If this is done with bacilli, the cells lose their form and become spherical. These naked protoplasts are subject to osmotic rupture if formed in very dilute solutions. Thus the rigid component of the wall is responsible for cell form and for protection of the cell against osmotic damage.

The chemistry of the cell wall varies among the different bacterial groups. The most noteworthy variations of this type are those between Gram-positive and Gram-negative bacteria. The Gram stain, originally devised to stain bacterial cells in animal tissues, has long been used as an aid in bacterial identification. Bacterial smears are fixed by heating, stained with crystal violet, and then mordanted with an iodine solution. The smear is next treated with an organic solvent, such as ethyl alcohol. Gram-positive bacteria retain the iodine-stain complex; the ethyl alcohol quickly destains cells of Gram-negative species.

Walls of Gram-positive bacteria contain relatively large amounts of mucopeptide and, in some instances, other polymers. Those of the Gram-negative bacteria are more complex, consisting of several distinct layers, the innermost of which is mucopeptide. Here the wall contains large amounts of lipids, proteins, and polysaccharides. In the Gram stain procedure, the organic solvent removes lipid from the cell wall; the iodine-stain complex is then readily leached away by the solvent. The thicker mucopeptide layer of Gram-positive bacteria is thought to form a barrier to the removal of the stain.

The effectiveness of penicillin as an antibiotic is in part related to its interference with incorporation of muramic acid into mucopeptide. As might be expected from this fact and from the wall composition, pencillin is very effective against most Gram-positive bacteria, but not usually against Gram-negative species.

A slime layer of varying thickness may be present outside the cell wall. If this layer is of relatively constant thickness and is sharply defined, it is called a capsule (Fig. 4–4). In some species, the slime layer is either very thin and inconspicuous or it is composed of soft material which dissolves or is lost in the surrounding medium.

The slimes and capsules of most bacteria are composed of polysaccharides, or of poly-

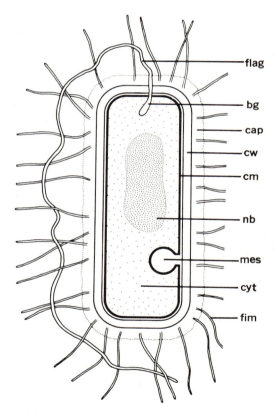

FIGURE 4–3 Bacterial structure (*bg*, basal granule; *cap*, capsule; *cm*, cell cytoplasmic membrane; *cyt*, cytoplasm; *cw*, cell wall; *fim*, fimbriae; *flag*, flagellum; *mes*, mesosome; *nb*, nuclear body).

DIVISION SCHIZOMYCOPHYTA

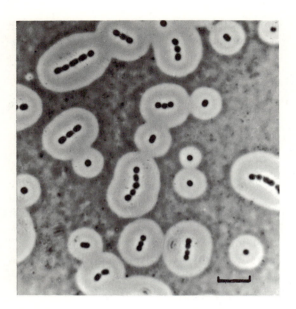

FIGURE 4–4 Photomicrograph showing an encapsulated bacterium mounted in India ink (scale line shown is 10 microns). (Photograph courtesy E. Juni, after Taylor and Juni, with permission of *Journal of Bacteriology*.)

28

saccharide complexes with proteins and other substances. The exact chemical composition of the capsule is known to vary even among the strains of a given bacterial species. Environmental and nutritional factors can markedly affect capsule formation. Among such factors are the types of carbohydrate, phosphorus, and nitrogen compounds supplied in the medium, and the carbon dioxide concentration.

The presence of a capsule is correlated with pathogenicity in some bacterial species. For example, virulent strains of the pneumococcus *Diplococcus pneumoniae* are normally encapsulated. They produce smooth glistening colonies in culture and are referred to as S-forms. In cultures of S-forms, one may find occasional colonies of roughened appearance, called R-forms, with cells that lack capsules.

FIGURE 4–5 Electron micrograph of a thin section through a bacterial cell, × 30,000 (*cm*, cell membrane; *cw*, cell wall; *cyt*, cytoplasm; *nb*, area of nuclear body; *mes*, mesosome). (Photograph courtesy of T. Bisalputra.)

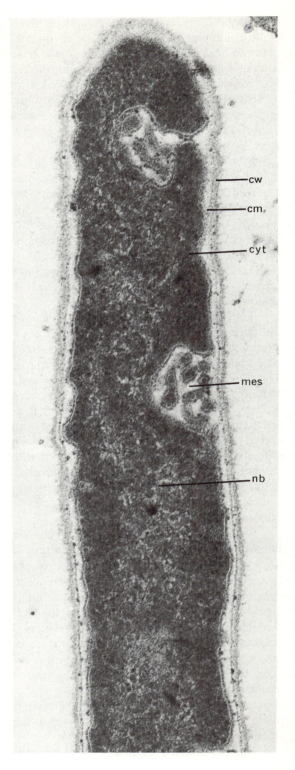

The R-forms are much less virulent than S-forms, but they may again become encapsulated and virulent through transformation (see p. 34) or mutation. The capsule appears to protect parasitic bacterial cells against engulfment by white blood corpuscles in some instances.

THE PROTOPLAST

As in other organisms, a cytoplasmic membrane surrounds the bacterial protoplast. This membrane is composed of proteins and lipids, and it controls movement of materials into and out of the cell. It has also been suggested that certain respiratory enzymes are located on the cytoplasmic membrane or on extensions of it. Some bacterial cells have membranous structures called mesosomes; they appear to be an internal continuation of the cytoplasmic membrane. In photosynthetic bacteria, a complex network of invaginations and tubules forms in the interior of the cell. These, like mesosomes, appear to be extensions of the cytoplasmic membrane and are thought to bear the photosynthetic pigments.

The cytoplasm forms a relatively homogeneous matrix within the cytoplasmic membrane. No vacuoles are present, but several kinds of granules may be seen if the bacteria are stained. The most common of granular substances present are volutin (metachromatic bodies) and glycogen. Starch-like materials and fat bodies or globules are found in some bacteria. Mitochondria of the type found in eukaryotic cells are not known in bacteria; their function possibly is taken over by mesosomes, by the cytoplasmic membrane, or by some of the small granules in the cytoplasm.

THE NUCLEAR BODY

Nuclear structure in the bacteria has been the subject of much controversy. Until relatively recently, it was widely believed that the bacterial cell either lacked a nucleus or contained a "diffuse nucleus." It is now known that bacterial cells have one or more nuclear bodies (Fig. 4–5, 6). Although many cells have a single nuclear body, several often are present when nuclear division is more rapid than cellular division.

Nuclear bodies of bacteria lack nuclear membranes, nucleoli, and the chromosome organization found in true nuclei. In stained preparations, the nuclear body appears globoid, dumbbell-shaped, or sometimes helical. The dumbbell shape is characteristic of dividing nuclear bodies, and helical forms occur during endospore formation in some species.

The nuclear body consists of a strand of DNA embedded in a matrix that appears to be continuous with the cytoplasm of the cell. Genetic and electron microscope studies suggest that the DNA strand is continuous, i.e., it is ring-shaped. This strand may be considered analogous to the chromosomes of higher organisms, although true chromosomes are not present in the bacterial cell. The DNA strand bears the hereditary units, or genes, and therefore is functionally similar to a chromosome.

29

FLAGELLA

Many bacterial species exhibit either swimming or gliding types of movement. In most swimming types, motility depends upon flagella (Fig. 4–7). Flagella may occur singly or in tufts, and are variously placed upon the cells. There may be a single flagellum at one end of the cell, a single flagellum at each pole of the cell, a tuft at one or both poles, or flagella located over the entire cell surface.

The end of each flagellum is embedded in the cytoplasm where it is bent and terminated by a basal granule. This granule, consisting of two discoid structures in some bacteria, possibly corresponds in function to the basal granule or blepharoplast of eukaryotic organisms. The flagellum itself is simpler in structure than that of other flagellated cells; it consists of one to several minute strands instead of the nine-plus-two arrangement common to other organisms. The flagellar strands are composed of flagellin, a muscle-like protein. Bacterial flagellar strands can be dissolved and reformed in the absence of bacterial cells. Their stranded nature therefore appears to be a result of macromolecular structure, and the strands should not be considered homologous to individual strands in the nine-plus-two flagella of other organisms.

The bacterial flagellum is about 12 millimicrons in diameter, the length varying with the species. Because of the small diameter, these flagella can be seen by light microscopy only after mordanting and staining. Mordanting precipitates substances around the flagellum, greatly increasing its diameter. Stains having an affinity for the mordant are then applied, and the flagellum becomes visible.

Some bacteria, e.g., spirochaetes and slime bacteria, are motile without flagella. Motility in these organisms is thought to depend upon flexing of the cells.

Some motile and nonmotile bacteria possess flagellum-like appendages called fimbriae. Fimbriae are shorter than flagella; they radiate from all of the cell surface and are much more numerous than are flagella. The function of fimbriae is uncertain, but possibly these structures help adhere bacterial cells to cells of other organisms.

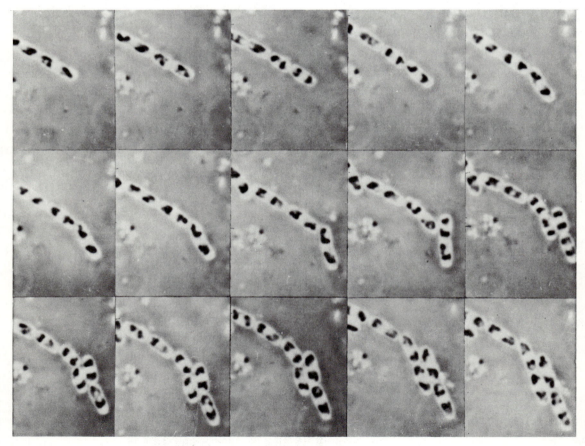

FIGURE 4–6 Nuclear division and growth in single group of living cells of *Escherichia coli*. Sequence of phase contrast photographs taken over period of 78 minutes, ×1,800. (Photographs courtesy D. J. Mason, from Mason and Powelson, with permission of *Journal of Bacteriology*.)

ENDOSPORES AND CYSTS

Many bacilli produce endospores or, less commonly, cysts. Endospores are found primarily in the genera *Clostridium* and *Bacillus*.

The shape and position of the endospore vary with the species. The endospore is a thick-walled resistant structure formed within the parent cell wall. The first observable stages in endospore formation involve the nuclear body. It has been reported that, at the time of en-

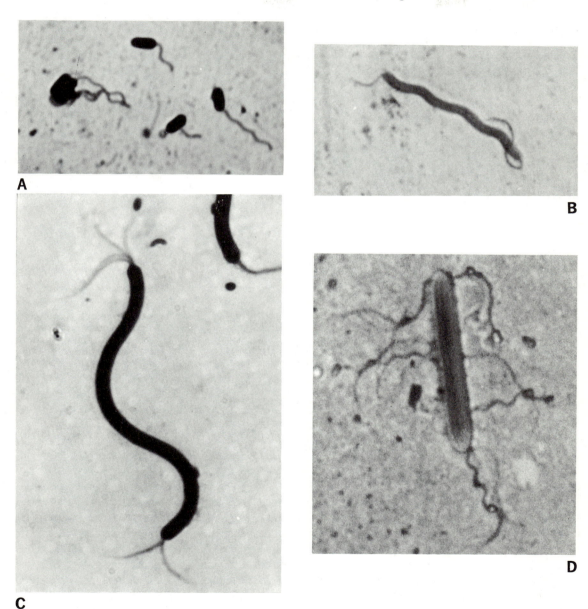

A

B

C

D

FIGURE 4–7   Bacterial flagella. A, single anterior flagellum; B, single flagellum at each pole of the cell; C, tufts of flagella at each pole; D, flagella located on both the poles and the sides of the cell. A, ×2,400; B, ×2,300; C, ×2,000; D, ×2,000.

DIVISION SCHIZOMYCOPHYTA

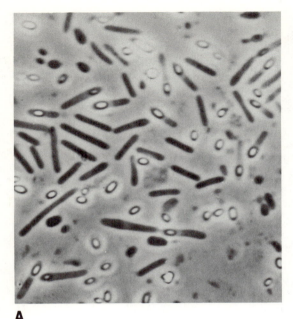

A

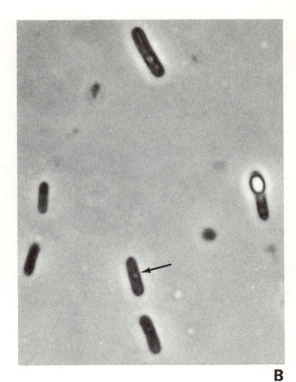

B

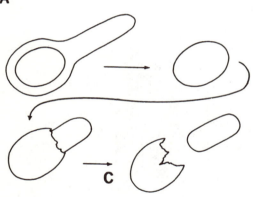

C

FIGURE 4–8 Bacterial endospores. A, heavily sporulating culture showing numerous mature and released endospores, ×2,000; B, single cell with mature endospore and a second cell with clear area indicating endospore formation (arrow), ×2,000; C, endospore germination following release from parent cell, ×2,000.

dospore formation, two nuclear bodies in the cell fuse. The nuclear material then elongates, assuming a rod-shaped or helically curved mass which then fragments into several smaller parts. During this process, granular food reserves accumulate around the nuclear body. One of the nuclear body fragments moves into the area to be occupied by the endospore and, together with some cytoplasm, becomes surrounded by a membrane system. A complex wall is then deposited around this material, forming the endospore. It has been suggested that meso-somes function in wall deposition during endospore formation.

With light microscopy and ordinary staining techniques, only a small part of the above process is visible. The first visible stage is the appearance of a clear area in the cytoplasm. This clear area becomes highly refractile as the endospore wall is formed (Fig. 4–8A, B).

The endospore wall differs in composition from the parent cell wall; enzymes in the endospore also differ and are fewer in number than in the vegetative cells. Endospores have a

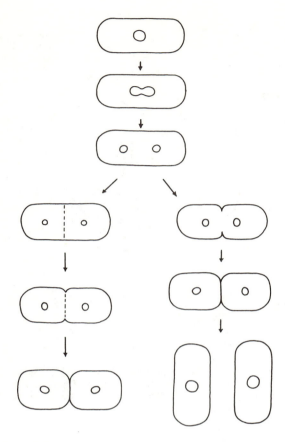

FIGURE 4–9 Binary fission. Top, division of nuclear body; below, left, division involving deposition of delicate septum (dotted line) followed by wall formation; right, alternative method of division in which the wall constriction is not preceded by formation of a membranous septum.

Conditions favorable for endospore formation seem to vary among species; in some species they form regularly under what appear to be ideal conditions. The culture medium, the age of the culture, and various environmental factors influence endospore formation. When an endospore germinates (Fig. 4–8C), it gives rise to a single vegetative cell. No increase or decrease in numbers of individuals is associated with endospore production.

Cysts are formed by cells of genus *Azotobacter* and in the slime bacteria, e.g., *Myxococcus* and *Chondromyces*. In cyst formation, the entire vegetative cell rounds up and becomes surrounded by a thick, multilayered wall. Cysts, like endospores, eventually germinate to give rise to a single vegetative cell. The cyst can also survive conditions that would kill vegetative cells.

REPRODUCTION

Reproduction in most bacteria is by binary fission (Fig. 4–9). In one type of division the nuclear body first divides; then a wall develops from the periphery inward, dividing the protoplast. The newly formed transverse wall splits as these two daughter cells separate. A delicate membranous septum forms prior to the appearance of the wall. In a second type of division the cell wall appears to constrict as the nuclear body divides; a membranous septum is not formed in this type of division.

Under ideal conditions, cell division can occur as frequently as once every 20 minutes. The increase in numbers of individuals under these conditions could theoretically result in immense masses of bacterial cells. Fortunately, various factors prevent such an increase. In nature, depletion of nutrient supplies, competition with other organisms, accumulation of respiratory by-products, and moisture and temperature changes help to regulate bacterial growth rates.

In addition to fission, or in place of it, reproduction in some bacteria is by budding,

33

very low water content and a relatively high calcium content. One of their constituents, dipicolinic acid, increases as water content decreases. This substance is not known in the vegetative cells.

The endospore is extremely resistant to heat, chemicals, desiccation, and other unfavorable conditions. In some species, endospores have been reported to withstand two hours of boiling and chemicals that rapidly kill vegetative cells. They may retain their viabilty for more than 50 years.

conidia, fragmentation, or other means. These methods of reproduction are discussed under the groups for which they are characteristic.

CELL AGGREGATES AND COLONIES

Cocci frequently produce loose aggregations of cells that may correspond to colonies in some algal groups. These aggregates are relatively constant in form and are characteristic for a given species (Fig. 4–10). When division of cocci occurs consistently on a given plane, the cells may adhere in pairs or chains. Such pairs are found in the genus *Diplococcus,* and chains are characteristic of the genus *Streptococcus.* In other genera, division on two or three opposing planes results in the formation of tetrads or packets of cells. *Staphylococcus* species are characterized by grape-like clusters of cells, with division on many different planes. Cell division occurs only at right angles to the long axis in rod-shaped cells. Thus, short chains or filaments are characteristic of some bacilli.

The masses of cells called colonies that develop on solid culture media help characterize bacterial species. A few of the variations found in the colony are illustrated in Figure 4–11. Colonies also differ from one another in texture, in the presence or absence of pigments, and in the nature of pigments.

GENETIC RECOMBINATION

Sexual reproduction, as found in other plant groups, is not known to occur in the Schizomycophyta. However, several phenomena result in genetic recombination; these involve a unidirectional transfer of genetic material, rather than syngamy and meiosis. The phenomena are conjugation, transformation, and transduction.

Conjugation was first observed in the bacterium *Escherichia coli.* In this process, a

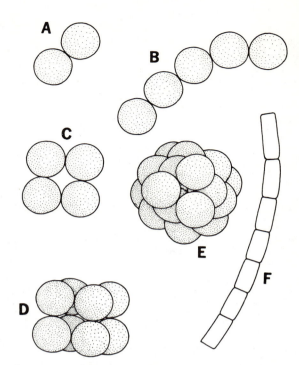

FIGURE 4–10 Cell aggregates. A–E, pairs, chains, packets, and clusters of cocci; F, chain of bacilli. The patterns of such aggregates depend upon the plane or planes of cell division.

bridge is formed between two compatible cells, called donor and recipient. By analogy, these haploid cells can be considered comparable to male and female, respectively. During conjugation, genetic material moves through the bridge from the donor to the recipient cell (Fig. 4–12). It can be shown that the amount of genetic material transferred varies, and that this amount depends upon the length of time for which the bridge is maintained. Typically, only a portion of the donor's "chromosome" is transferred to the recipient. Following conjugation, the recipient cell contains duplicate genes for a number of characteristics; it may therefore be considered a partial diploid. Generations of cells arising from the recipient typically are completely haploid, however. Such offspring frequently exhibit characteristics of both the donor and recipient strains.

In transformation (Fig. 4–13), soluble DNA from donor cells initiates inheritable changes in recipient cells. The DNA, released or extracted from dead bacterial cells, is genetically effective in very small amounts. In transformation experiments, pure DNA extracts are prepared from dead bacterial cells. This DNA is then added to cultures of living recipient cells. Transformation typically involves only one trait, although several may be acquired independently in this way.

Transduction (Fig. 4–14) involves bacterial viruses, called bacteriophages or simply "phages." Phage particles infect a bacterial cell, inducing the cell to form more phage particles. In some instances, defective phage particles are formed, incorporating in their structure part of the bacterial genetic code. When such a defective virus infects another bacterial cell, the

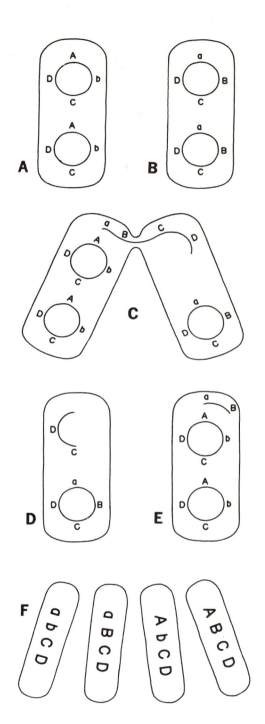

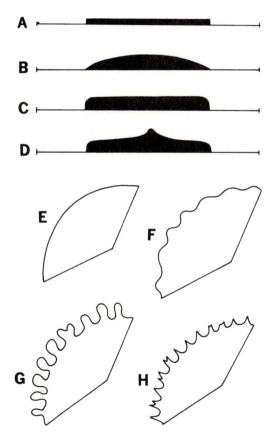

FIGURE 4–11 Colony form. A–D, profiles. A, flat; B, convex; C, raised; D, umbonate; E–H, margins. E, entire; F, undulate; G, lobate; H, erose.

FIGURE 4–12 Bacterial conjugation. A, B, recipient and donor cells, each with two nuclear bodies; C, transfer of genetic material from donor to recipient; D, E, cells after conjugation; F, possible types of descendants from recipient cell E.

35

DIVISION SCHIZOMYCOPHYTA

bacterial code it carries may be reproduced or copied in the recipient cell. Simultaneous transfer of several characteristics has been reported to occur in this manner, but a single characteristic is involved in most instances. As with conjugation and transformation, changes brought about through transduction are inheritable changes, and may be passed on to descendants of the recipient cell.

Conjugation, transformation, and transduction all involve a unilateral transfer of genetic material. They differ from sexual reproduction in that no zygote is formed and meiosis does not occur. The transferred material, i.e., a portion of the donor's DNA, may or may not be copied or incorporated into the genome of the recipient cell.

CLASSIFICATION

Because of the simplicity of bacterial structure, it is necessary to use features other than morphology to identify and classify them. For example, parasitic species can be identified in part by their serological reactions, by the identity of the host, and in some instances, by the symptoms produced. Among both parasitic and saprobic species, the ability to utilize specific substrates and any special nutritional requirements (such as amino acids or vitamins) are of value in classification and identification. Temperature, pH, oxygen requirements, and the end products of respiration, e.g., gases and acids, help characterize some species. The most widely used system of classification of bacteria is that found in Bergey's *Manual of Determinative Bacteriology*. The following discussion includes only a few of the recognized bacterial orders treated in the *Manual*.

Orders Eubacteriales and Pseudomonadales (True Bacteria or Eubacteria). The eubacteria include most of the economically important bacteria, such as many pathogenic species, the nitrogen-fixing bacteria, and the majority of those used in industrial processes. The introductory discussion of structure and

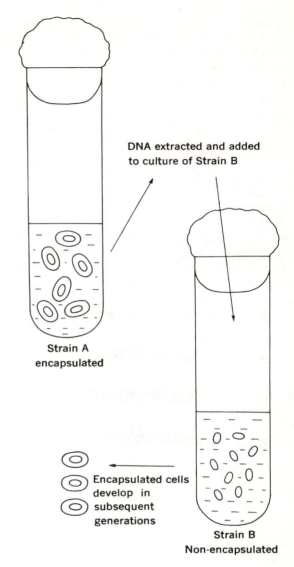

FIGURE 4–13 Bacterial transformation.

reproduction in bacteria is based primarily on studies of eubacteria. For this reason, the following account is concerned primarily with activities of some true bacteria.

Many eubacteria are abundant in soil, water, sewage, decaying plant and animal materials, food, and the atmosphere. Others exist as parasites in the bodies of animals or plants, or form mutualistic symbiotic relationships with other organisms. The group is of great eco-

36

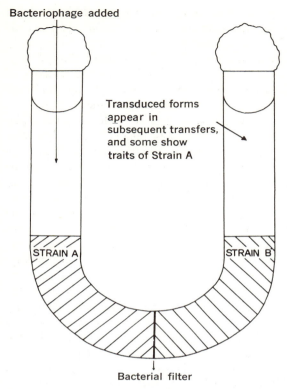

Bacteriophage added

Transduced forms appear in subsequent transfers, and some show traits of Strain A

STRAIN A   STRAIN B

Bacterial filter

FIGURE 4–14 Apparatus used in demonstrating transduction (the bacterial filter prevents mixing of strains A and B, but allows free passage of the bacteriophage).

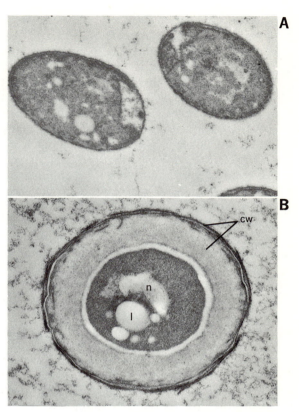

A

B

cw

n

l

FIGURE 4–15 Vegetative cells (A) and thin section of cyst (B) of *Azotobacter*, A, ×24,500; B, ×27,500 (*cw*, wall layers; *l*, lipid gobule; *n*, nuclear material). (After Scolofsky and Wyss, with permission of *Journal of Bacteriology*.)

37

nomic importance because of both beneficial and detrimental activities.

Species capable of fixing atmospheric nitrogen are found in several families of true bacteria. Among these are species of *Azotobacter, Rhizobium,* and *Clostridium.* The species of *Azotobacter* and *Clostridium* are free-living organisms common in soil; *Rhizobium* occurs either as a free-living organism in soil or in symbiotic associations within the roots of legumes. The cells of *Azotobacter* are varied in form, being more or less rod-shaped and frequently occurring in pairs or short chains. They do not form endospores, but develop resistant cysts (Fig. 4–15). The azotobacters live in well-aerated neutral soils, obtaining carbohydrates from the surrounding environment and nitrogen from the atmosphere. The species of

Clostridium also are soil inhabitants and almost all are saprobes. The nitrogen-fixing clostridia live predominantly in the poorly drained, acidic soil of bogs; they are therefore less important agriculturally as nitrogen fixers than is *Azotobacter.* The clostridia are anaerobic, endospore-producing bacilli. *C. botulinum* and *C. tetani,* causing botulism and tetanus, respectively, produce extremely powerful toxins. Because of the resistance of its spores and its anaerobic respiration, *C. botulinum* has long presented problems in the preservation of food. One species of *Clostridium* is used commercially in the production of butyl alcohol.

In addition to the variable form exhibited by vegetative cells of *Rhizobium,* motile reproductive cells have been reported. *Rhizobium* does not utilize atmospheric nitrogen when grown in culture; it is therefore assumed that nitrogen fixation requires the presence of both the legume and bacterial cells.

Rhizobia live in the soil and infect root hairs of developing legume plants. Characteristic root nodules, containing many bacterial cells, are formed after infection. The quantity of nitrogen fixed is in part dependent upon the strain of *Rhizobium* and the species of legume. In some instances, roots and *Rhizobium* strains form a combination which results in no nitrogen fixation; these strains can be considered parasites. It is now common agricultural practice to dust seeds of legumes with appropriate strains of *Rhizobium* at planting, ensuring an immediate nitrogen-fixing association.

Probably the most important bacterial activity in the soil and elsewhere is in decay. This process, while detrimental in some instances, is absolutely essential in nature. Through decay, elements incorporated into plant and animal bodies are eventually released, and can serve in the growth of others. Among the important chemical processes involved are those which transform nitrogen into a form usable by higher plants. When proteins decay, some of the nitrogen present is converted to ammonia. Nitrifying bacteria, such as *Nitrosomonas* and *Nitrobacter,* oxidize ammonia to nitrite, then nitrate. During oxidation, these chemotrophic bacteria obtain energy that functions in the generation of high-energy phosphate bonds and in the reduction of carbon dioxide. Other bacteria in the soil can carry on denitrification, converting nitrate to free nitrogen.

The photosynthetic eubacteria constitute three distinct groups of true bacteria. These are the purple sulfur bacteria, the purple nonsulfur bacteria, and the green sulfur bacteria. The purple bacteria contain a photosynthetic pigment called bacteriochlorophyll, and in the green sulfur bacteria two chlorobium chlorophylls are found. All of these pigments, while related chemically to chlorophylls of other plant groups, have their absorption maxima in the near-infrared portion of the spectrum. This enables the phototrophic bacteria to carry on

photosynthesis in the absence of visible light. As with true chlorophylls, carotenoid pigments are associated with the bacterial chlorophylls. Plastids are lacking in bacteria, and the pigments appear to be borne upon a network of membranous invaginations or tubules connected with the cytoplasmic membrane.

Although the bacterial photosynthetic pigments are chemically related to those of other plants, the photosynthetic process differs in a number of respects. Carbon dioxide may be utilized, but oxygen is not released in bacterial photosynthesis. This process is carried on only under anaerobic conditions. In the purple sulfur bacteria, reduced sulfur compounds—often hydrogen sulfide—serve as hydrogen donors, and free sulfur accumulates within the cells. Green sulfur bacteria carry on a similar process, but the sulfur is deposited externally. The purple nonsulfur bacteria are versatile organisms that utilize organic substances, e.g., ethanol or acetic acid, as both a carbon and hydrogen source. They carry on photosynthesis in the light, but can also live heterotrophically in the absence of light.

A large flora of bacteria, including many eubacteria, inhabits the intestine of animals. Some of these bacteria are potential pathogens; others are essential to the well-being of their host. For example, cellulose eaten by ruminants is digested by bacteria and other microorganisms. The ruminant derives much of its nutriment in the form of fermentation products of bacteria, e.g., fatty acids, and most of the remainder by the digestion of microbial cells. In this way, the ruminant obtains essential amino acids and vitamins; other mammals must obtain these from an external source.

Man also is host to both beneficial and detrimental species of eubacteria. The skin, mucous membranes, and digestive tract all have their characteristic bacterial flora.

Some true bacteria are important in food processing and in food spoilage. In manufactured food products such as butter, cheeses, yogurt, sauerkraut, pickles, and cocoa, processing involves bacteria. The bacteria utilized in butter and cheese production, e.g., *Lacto-*

bacillus, *Streptococcus,* and others, are common in dung and in soil; they often cause spoilage of fresh milk. Species of *Clostridium* and *Staphylococcus* often are responsible for food poisoning. Some eubacterial diseases, such as undulant fever and salmonellosis (gastroenteritis), are regularly transmitted in meat, eggs, and dairy products.

A morphologically distinctive group of eubacteria are the stalked bacteria, *Caulobacter* and *Gallionella.* In the genus *Caulobacter* (Fig. 4–16A), the cells are curved rods; they are attached to the substrate by a protoplasmic stalk. Reproduction is by means of transverse fission of the curved cell; the unattached daughter cell is polarly flagellate. These flagellated cells swim to a new location, settle down, and produce stalks. The cells typically occur in rosette-like aggregates.

In *Gallionella* (Fig. 4–16B, C) the cells are reniform and have a laterally attached stalk. The spirally twisted stalk, secreted continuously by each cell, contains ferric hydroxide; it is thought to be nonliving.

Order Chlamydobacteriales (*Sheathed Bacteria*). Cells of the sheathed bacteria are similar in form and structure to those of eubacteria. However, many cells are enclosed in a cylindric sheath, forming a long filament. Within the sheath, the rod-shaped or coccoid cells reproduce by fission. Ferric hydroxide or manganese hydroxide often is deposited in the sheath, giving it a yellow-brown color. In *Sphaerotilus* (Fig. 4–17), the cells are rod-shaped; the filaments are attached by one end to the substrate. Flagellated cells are released from the open end of the sheath. The sheathed bacteria are aquatic organisms, some of which are responsible for the deposition of "bog iron ore." *Sphaerotilus* is found in water rich in organic matter, such as sewage, and is often used as an indicator of pollution.

Order Beggiatoales (*Gliding Bacteria*). The gliding bacteria are aquatic organisms that bear a close resemblance to certain of the blue-green algae. *Beggiatoa* (Fig. 4–18) is a filamentous chemoautotroph that oxidizes sul-

39

FIGURE 4–16 A, *Caulobacter vibrioides.* Rosette of stalked cells, ×3,600. B, C, electron micrographs of *Gallionella ferruginea.* B, stalk secreted by several cells, two of which are visible at the stalk tip, ×75,000; C, branched stalk, each branch terminated by a single ghost-like cell, ×65,000. Note that each stalk is composed of a number of separate strands. (A, photograph courtesy E. A. Grula, with permission of *Journal of Bacteriology;* B, C, photographs courtesy R. S. Wolfe, after Vatter and Wolfe, with permission of *Journal of Bacteriology.*)

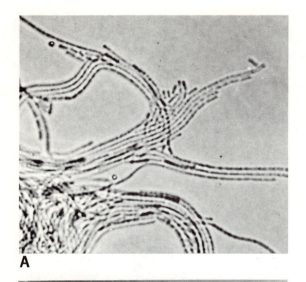

A

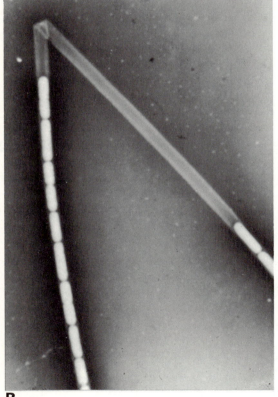

B

FIGURE 4–17 *Sphaerotilus.* A, mass of filaments in colony, ×650; B, single filament enlarged to show detail, ×2,500. (Photographs courtesy J. L. Stokes with permission of *Journal of Bacteriology.*)

fides to sulfur; as in the purple sulfur bacteria, free sulfur accumulates in cells. Filaments of *Beggiatoa* are free floating; they are capable of both gliding and flexing movements. The cells are not flagellated and motility cannot be ascribed to any mechanism known in other bacteria. However, the same types of movement are found in the blue-green alga *Oscillatoria* (see Chapter 5), which is morphologically very similar to *Beggiatoa*. In *Beggiatoa*, reproduction of filaments can occur through fragmentation; reproduction of cells is by fission.

Order Spirochaetales (Spirochaetes). The cells of spirochaetes are long, helically coiled, and motile. Unlike eubacterial spirilla, these cells lack flagella and have very thin, flexible walls. In some species, the cell length may reach 500 microns, but the diameter typically is less than 0.5 micron.

Motility in the spirochaetes is attributed to flexing movements of the spirally coiled cells. Although no flagella are present, each cell is provided with an axial bundle of filaments thought to be the homologs of bacterial flagella. The filament ends are firmly anchored within the cytoplasm, and the filaments appear to be located between the cell wall and the cytoplasmic membrane. The filaments, chemically similar to flagella, are contractile and apparently cause flexing of the cell.

The spirochaetes include both free-living and parasitic species. Of the latter, *Treponema pallidum* (Fig. 4–19), the cause of syphilis, and *T. pertenue,* the cause of yaws, are most important. Some species parasitize mammals, birds, shellfish, and other animals. The saprobic species are inhabitants of stagnant water, sewage, and similar habitats.

Order Myxobacteriales (Slime Bacteria). The slime bacteria have rod-shaped cells with very thin walls. No flagella are present, but the organisms are capable of individual or mass movement when in contact with a solid substratum. During gliding movement, they secrete masses of slime that tend to hold the cells together. Reproduction is by fission.

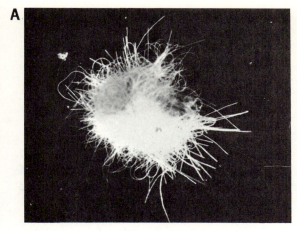

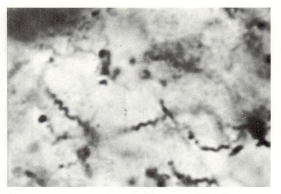

FIGURE 4–19 *Treponema*. Silver-impregnated cells in section of human liver tissue, ×5,000.

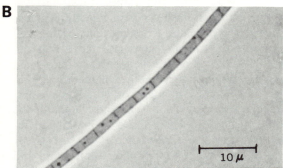

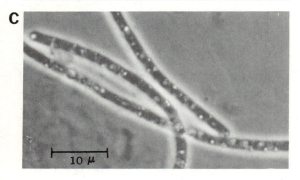

FIGURE 4–18 *Beggiatoa*. A, colony of filaments in water, photographed by reflected light, ×18. B, C, detail of filaments, dark phase-contrast. Crosswalls visible in dying filament (B): sulfur granules present in filaments (C) that have been exposed to atmosphere containing hydrogen sulfide. (Photographs courtesy R. S. Wolfe, from Faust and Wolfe, with permission of *Journal of Bacteriology*.)

The most remarkable feature of the slime bacteria is the production of communal fruiting bodies by certain genera. Many cells migrate together, producing a regular structure. In *Myxococcus* (Fig. 4–20), the masses of cells heap together into a pillow-shaped structure. Within the usually orange or yellow structure, individual cells encyst. The more complex fruiting bodies of *Chondromyces* (Fig. 4–21) are erect, branched, and shrub-like. Each branch is tipped by a large cyst-like structure within which are numerous encysted cells. The fruiting body stalk is composed of slime and dead bacterial cells. Upon germinating, each myxobacterium cyst gives rise to a single vegetative cell.

Not all of the slime bacteria form fruiting bodies. In some genera, cysts are formed but not fruiting bodies; in others, neither cysts nor fruiting bodies are produced.

Myxobacteria are abundant in certain types of soils, in dung or rotting vegetation, and in aquatic habitats. Some are capable of killing and digesting cells of other bacteria and fungi; a few are active in decomposition of cellulose. One species is responsible for a serious disease of fresh-water fish.

The life histories and habitats of slime bacteria and the Acrasiomycetes (Chapter 6) bear a remarkable resemblance to one another. Some of the slime bacteria and all of the acrasiomycetes feed upon other micoorganisms in their environment. The assimilative units—single cells in both groups—behave as individuals during assimilative growth, but work together to form complex fruiting bodies. In both

41

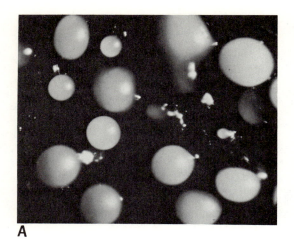

A

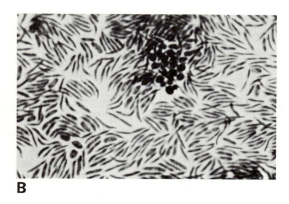

B

42

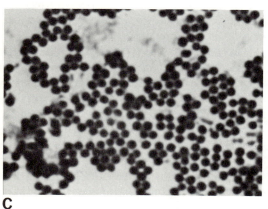

C

FIGURE 4–20 *Myxococcus*. A, mature fruiting bodies, ×30; B, cells fixed and stained at the time of cyst formation, ×1,100; C, stained, mature cysts, ×1,500. (A, B, photographs by N. A. Woods, after Henrici and Ordal, with permission of D. C. Heath and Company.)

groups, formation of communal fruiting bodies does not appear to lead to an increase in numbers of individuals, but probably makes dispersal more efficient. Obviously, the two kinds of organisms are not closely related and the similarities must be attributed to parallel evolution.

Order Hyphomicrobiales (Budding Bacteria). The budding bacteria are unique in structure, although budding has been reported for other groups of bacteria. *Rhodomicrobium* (Fig. 4–22) produces flagellated cells. After a motile period, the cell settles down and becomes attached to the substrate. A tubular filament then develops from the end of the cell opposite the attachment point, and a bud develops at the tip of this filament. The bud, when mature, may produce another filament and bud, and a branched network or colony develops. Septa are present in the filaments. Some of the buds develop into flagellated cells and are released to originate new colonies.

Rhodomicrobium is photoautotrophic and possibly is related to the purple nonsulfur bacteria.

Order Actinomycetales (Actinomycetes). The major distinguishing feature of most of the actinomycetes is their production of hyphae. These hyphae, usually less than 1.5 microns in diameter, are smaller than most fungal hyphae. Crosswalls are present in some genera, but are associated mainly with branching. The filaments thus are essentially coenocytic with many nuclear bodies.

In *Mycobacterium,* only a rudimentary mycelium develops, and it soon undergoes fragmentation into rod-shaped or branched segments. Each segment is capable of reproducing by fission, or it can develop into a new mycelium. *Mycobacterium tuberculosis* and *M. leprae* are pathogenic species, causing tuberculosis and leprosy respectively.

In *Streptomyces* and related genera, the mycelium is extensive and does not undergo

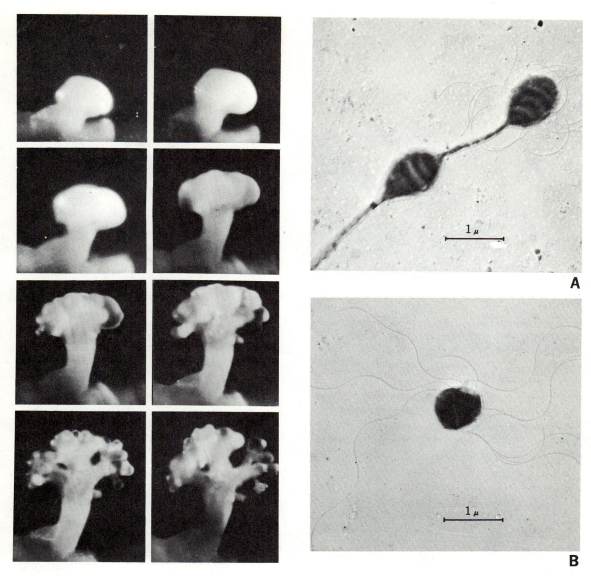

FIGURE 4–21 Successive stages in fruiting body development of *Chondromyces*, ×13.8. (Photograph courtesy John Tyler Bonner, from *Morphogenesis* by J. T. Bonner, by permission of Princeton University Press, copyright 1952.)

FIGURE 4–22 *Rhodomicrobium vanniellii*, A, cells attached to stalks; B, single flagellated cell. (After Douglas and Wolfe with permission of *Journal of Bacteriology*.)

fragmentation. Reproduction in these organisms is by special spores called conidia. *Streptomyces* forms conidia in chains on aerial branches of hyphae (Fig. 4–23); segments of the branch are cut off by septa and when

rounded off, develop a thickened, frequently spiny wall. Each conidium produces a germ tube that develops into a new hypha. These conidia are not very resistant to heat and other adverse factors, compared to endospores of the eubacteria.

DIVISION SCHIZOMYCOPHYTA

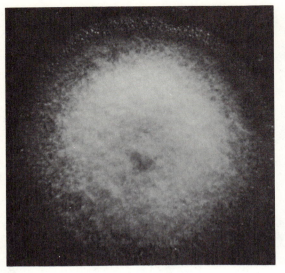

A

C

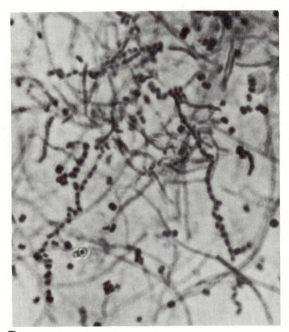

B

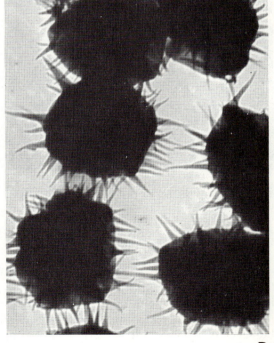

D

FIGURE 4–23 *Streptomyces.* A, young colony, ×50; B, stained mount of hyphae and conidial chains, ×1,000; C, electron micrograph of spores in chains, ×55,000; D, single spores, ×55,000. (C, D, photographs courtesy H. D. Tresner, from Tresner, Davis, and Backus, with permission of *Journal of Bacteriology.*)

44

Many of the actinomycetes are saprobic soil organisms; others occur in decaying vegetation, in water, and in other habitats. In addition to tuberculosis and leprosy, several less common diseases are caused by actinomycetes, e.g., nocardiosis and "lumpy jaw" of cattle and man. A number of these organisms produce antibiotics, such as streptomycin and actinomycin. Vitamin B_{12} is a by-product of antibiotic production of *Streptomyces* species.

Order Rickettsiales (*Rickettsias*). The rickettsias are obligate parasites of animal cells; they have been grown in culture only in tissue cultures and in chick embryos. Cells of rickettsias are similar in form to eubacterial cells but smaller. Their structure and the cell wall chemistry do not differ in any known way from those of true bacteria. Reproduction is by fission.

The rickettsias are responsible for a number of very important diseases of man, including typhus and Rocky Mountain spotted fever. Many live in the bodies of rodents and are transmitted to man by various arthropod vectors, e.g., ticks, fleas, and lice.

For a time, some bacteriologists considered the Rickettsiales to be intermediate between true bacteria and viruses. However, because of their close similarity to true bacteria, this concept now appears doubtful.

RELATIONSHIPS

Simplicity of cell structure and small size seem to separate bacteria from most other groups of organisms. The blue-green algae, however, appear to be closely related to certain bacteria. In both groups, the cells are prokaryotic and the predominant method of reproduction is binary fission. Other similarities are low degree of cellular differentiation and chemistry of the cell walls. The oldest known plant fossils, about 2 billion years, are of bacteria and blue-green algae.

Bacteria were once considered to be closely related to the true fungi. But fungi are eukaryotic, and differ markedly from bacteria in structure, reproduction, and cell wall chemistry.

Structural simplicity in the bacteria may not be due entirely to primitiveness. Some bacteria may be derived from more complex forms through regressive evolution.

45

DIVISION SCHIZOMYCOPHYTA

5 / Division Cyanophyta

There are over 150 genera with about 1,500 species in the single class Cyanophyceae of the Cyanophyta (*blue-green algae*). Current research indicates that this group is probably more closely related to the bacteria than to the algae. However, the affinities of the blue-green algae to other algal groups (especially the Rhodophyta, Chapter 8) cannot be overlooked.

CELL STRUCTURE

The blue-green algal cell wall is composed of at least two layers (Fig. 5–1A, 2). The layer next to the protoplast is similar to that present in some bacteria. External to this is a mucilaginous sheath which is often thick and intensely colored.

As noted before, the prokaryotic cell has very little of the type of differentiation characteristic of plants in general (Fig. 5–2). With the light microscope, the protoplast often appears as an inner colorless portion and an outer pigmented region. There is no central vacuole, no organized nucleus with nuclear envelope, and no nucleoli or mitochondria.

The pigments do not occur in definite plastids, but rather as photosynthetic lamellae (Fig. 5–2). Scattered throughout the cell are various granules and food reserves. The carbohydrate present is starch-like. Chlorophyll *a* is the only green pigment present. In addition, there are carotenoids and the phycobiliproteins. The presence of both chlorophyll *a* and the phycobiliproteins gives many of the Cyanophyta their typical blue-green color.

Under certain conditions small spherical or irregular gas vacuoles occur in the cell. They are not bounded by a unit membrane typical of eukaryotic plant cells. Gas vacuoles are particularly evident in free-floating species of such genera as *Microcystis* * (Fig. 5–4H, I). These sometimes serve as a flotation mechanism, permitting the alga to remain at or near the surface in optimum light conditions, or they can be indicative of unsatisfactory growing conditions. When placed under pressure, the gas vacuoles will collapse.

Cell division results from splitting of the protoplast by an ingrowth of the inner wall layer, pinching the cell in half and dividing the contents equally (Fig. 5–1B).

---

* The generic names used for the Cyanophyta are based upon usage by Smith (1950) and Prescott (1962). No attempt has been made here to use the taxa of Drouet and Daily (1956) and Drouet (1959).

Flagellated cells are never present, although in some filamentous species lacking a sheath, as in *Spirulina* and *Oscillatoria* (Fig. 5–5J, L), the thallus undergoes some movement. The movement is simple gliding or gliding combined with rotation around a longitudinal axis, somewhat similar to that of the Myxobacteriales (Chapter 4). The rate and direction of movement sometimes depend on light and temperature.

CLASSIFICATION AND MORPHOLOGICAL DIVERSITY

A number of systems of classification have been proposed for the Cyanophyta. Because these algae lack cellular differentiation and are simple in form, few characteristics clearly distinguish higher levels of classification. This is especially true at the ordinal level, where from three to five orders are generally recognized. Current work on classification of the blue-green algae is attempting to combine morphological and physiological characteristics. At present, two morphological lines of evolution can be distinguished: the filamentous and the nonfilamentous types (see Fig. 5–3). Morphologically, the simplest member of the division is a unicellular free-floating form, such as *Synechococcus* or *Chroococcus* (Fig. 5–4C, D). The unicellular *Chamaesiphon* is attached to the substrate, and there is a slight differentiation between the base and the apex (Fig. 5–4A). Some of the unicellular attached types form small clusters, as in *Dermocarpa* (Fig. 5–4B), on various substrates. From the unicellular, free-floating type colonial forms have probably developed. One line has led to the nonfilamentous (sometimes referred to as palmelloid) forms (Fig. 5–3B), and the other to the filamentous types (Fig. 5–3A). Both have arisen from the same primitive unicellular stock but along divergent lines.

The simplest type of colony is illustrated by *Gloeocapsa* and *Gloeothece* (Fig. 5–4F, G); the cells remain fastened after division and are embedded in a common mucilaginous sheath. The resulting colony usually fragments before more than four to eight cells are produced. In *Merismopedia* (Fig. 5–4J) the cells divide regularly in only two planes and form a single-layered sheet of cells. If regular divisions occur in three directions, a cubical colony such as *Eucapsis* is produced (Fig. 5–4E). In some instances the division planes appear irregular and the cells become oriented in a very diffuse manner, as in *Microcystis* (Fig. 5–4H, I). In this genus some species form spherical colonies (Fig. 4–4I) and others form large diffuse colonies containing thousands of cells (Fig. 5–4H). The cells are held together by the mucilaginous sheath and may be regarded as separate individuals since the colony is devoid of differentiation.

In the filamentous line of development there are simple, unbranched, and branched forms. Cell divisions in this series occur in only one plane in the unbranched forms (Fig. 5–5C, K, L) and occur throughout the filament. This is referred to as diffuse growth. Most of the filamentous genera are straight, but others, such as *Spirulina*, are helical (Fig. 5–5J). The filaments (consisting of the row of cells, termed a trichome, and the sheath) are free or aggregated into various types of macroscopic masses. In *Nostoc* (Fig. 5–5C) the unbranched filaments aggregate in a mucilaginous matrix and

47

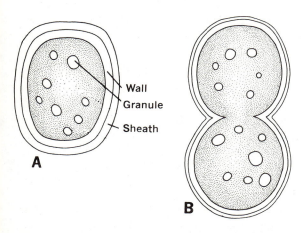

FIGURE 5–1 Typical Cyanophyta cell. A, vegetative phase, ×575; B, dividing phase, ×500.

DIVISION CYANOPHYTA

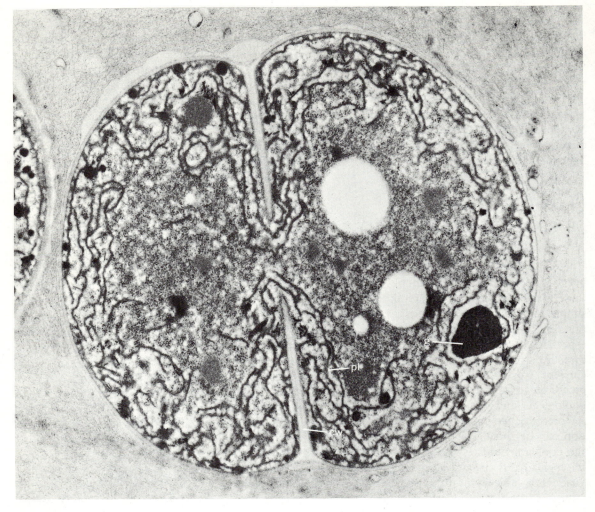

FIGURE 5–2 Electron micrograph of Cyanophyta cell (*Nostoc*) during division, showing absence of organelles (*cw,* cell wall; *g,* structured granule; *pl,* photosynthetic lamellae), ×25,000. (Courtesy T. Bisalputra.)

may produce a body of considerable size (Fig. 5–6). In *Schizothrix* (Fig. 5–5D) a filament is composed of several unbranched trichomes laterally aggregated into a common sheath. Although divisions are mainly in one plane in branched forms, the cells occasionally divide longitudinally in a second plane. Thus, either a uniseriate branched thallus, as in *Hapalosiphon* (Fig. 5–5B), or a multiseriate branched thallus, as in *Stigonema* (Fig. 5–5G, I) are produced. Branching of this type is referred to as true branching. In some of these, such as

Hapalosiphon (Fig. 5–5B), conspicuous protoplasmic or primary pit connections form between cells as a result of incomplete cell division by the ingrowing septa.

In the few genera where so-called false branching occurs (as in *Scytonema* and *Tolypothrix,* Fig. 5–5A, H), the trichome breaks at some point and one end (or both) at the point of fragmentation grows out of the sheath into a "branch." The break may result from death of an intercalary cell or from extensive growth of the trichome within its sheath.

NONVASCULAR PLANTS

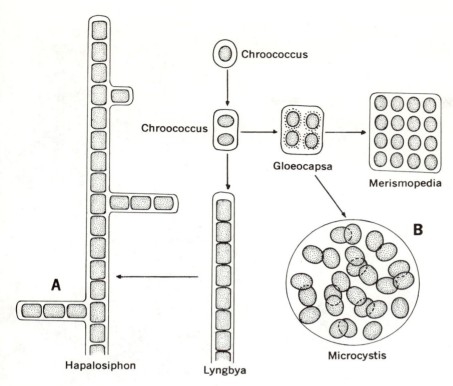

FIGURE 5–3 Diagram of possible evolutionary lines in Cyanophyta resulting from regular and irregular planes of cell division. A, filamentous; B, nonfilamentous.

In most of the filamentous forms, cell division and growth occur throughout the filament, but in some genera cell division is especially prevalent in the apical region, as in *Rivularia* and *Gloeotrichia* (Fig. 5–5E, F). These forms with localized growth can be regarded as having primitive types of intercalary meristems.

REPRODUCTION

The chief method of vegetative reproduction is by fragmentation. But in addition, various types of nonflagellated spores or spore-like bodies are produced. Reproduction by fragmentation can occur by a simple breaking apart of a thallus into two or more units, with each fragment capable of producing a new colony.

In some filamentous genera (*Oscillatoria,* Fig. 5–7C), hormogonia are common and develop into new plants. An intercalary cell dies, and the filament breaks to form a hormogonium. Such a place in a filament is biconcave because of a decrease in pressure in the adjacent cells (Fig. 5–7C). There is no conspicuous differentiation in the cells of the hormogonium, except terminal cells are rounded.

Another type of reproductive structure formed in certain filamentous genera is the spore-like akinete (Fig. 5–5K, 7B), a single cell that develops directly from differentiation of a vegetative cell. Usually the akinete is considerably larger than the ordinary cell, has a thickened external wall, and contains food reserves. On germination, the akinete develops into a new filament within the old cell wall. Akinetes can be extremely resistant to desiccation and high temperatures.

DIVISION CYANOPHYTA

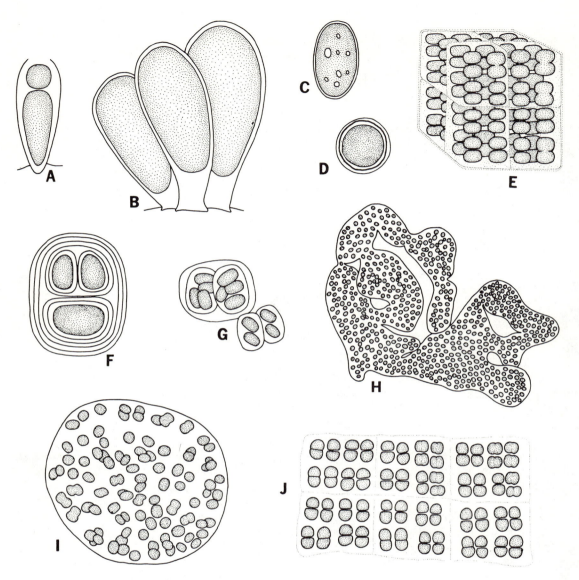

FIGURE 5–4   Unicellular and colonial Cyanophyta. A–D, unicellular Cyanophyta. A, *Chamaesiphon*, ×3,000; B, *Dermocarpa*, ×1,000; C, *Synechococcus*, ×630; D, *Chroococcus*, ×415. E–J, colonial and palmelloid Cyanophyta. E, F, J, regular planes of division; G–I, irregular planes of division. E, *Eucapsis*, ×690; F, *Gloeocapsa*, ×2,250; G, *Gloeothece*, ×1,235; H, a large diffuse species of *Microcystis*, ×325; I, a small compact species of *Microcystis*, ×555; J, *Merismopedia*, ×1,175.

Another specialized structure is the heterocyst, which is unique for several filamentous Cyanophyceae (Fig. 5–5C, E–H, 7A, B). There is some question whether all heterocysts behave in the same manner. However, the heterocyst is apparently a differentiated vegetative cell that can produce a new filament. Heterocysts are reported to have a higher rate of respiration than the vegetative cells of a filament. The contents of heterocysts are uniformly dense and appear clear when viewed with the light microscope, but electron micrographs reveal

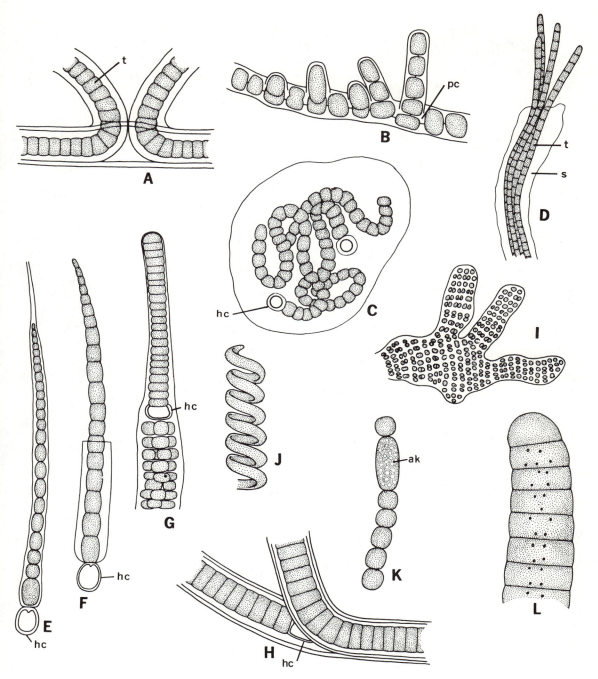

FIGURE 5–5 Filamentous Cyanophyta. A, H, false branching; B, G, I, true branching. A, *Scytonema,* ×570; B, *Hapalosiphon,* showing pit connection (*pc*), ×1,180; C, small colony of *Nostoc,* ×1,000; D, *Schizothrix,* showing several trichomes (*t*) with a single sheath (*s*), ×1,000; E, *Rivularia,* with basal heterocyst (*hc*), ×1,095; F, *Gloeotrichia,* with basal heterocyst, ×1,100; G, *Stigonema,* ×500; H, *Tolypothrix,* ×915; I, *Stigonema,* ×170; J. *Spirulina,* ×1,800; K, *Cylindrospermum,* showing large subterminal akinete (*ak*), ×880; L, *Oscillatoria,* ×2,355.

DIVISION CYANOPHYTA

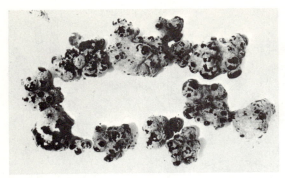

FIGURE 5–6 Macroscopic form of *Nostoc*, encrusted with soil, ×0.4.

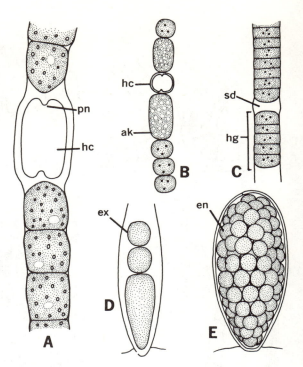

FIGURE 5–7 Reproductive structures in Cyanophyta. A, heterocyst (*hc*) with polar nodule (*pn*) in *Aphanizomenon*, ×2,890; B, akinete (*ak*) and heterocyst in *Anabaena*, ×1,800; C, hormogonium (*hg*) in *Oscillatoria*, showing separation disc (*sd*), ×1,800; D, exospores (*ex*) in *Chamaesiphon*, ×3,000; E, endospores (*en*) in *Dermocarpa*, ×1,000.

photosynthetic lamellae. A delicate protoplasmic connection passes through the pore of the heterocyst to the adjacent vegetative cell. In forms with both heterocysts and akinetes, the position of one is consistent and relative to that of the other.

Finally, true spore formation (by aplanospores) within a cell is present in certain genera. One type of true spore is the endospore (Fig. 5–7E). In certain forms such as the epiphyte *Dermocarpa,* the protoplast divides into a number of units. The wall of the parent cell eventually breaks down, liberating thin-walled spores which grow into new plants. Another aplanospore, the exospore, may be distinguished, although the distinction is not striking (Fig. 5–7D). Exospores are formed by transverse divisions of the protoplast at the distal end of an attached unicellular alga, as in *Chamaesiphon.*

Sexual fusion involving gametes, as known for most other algal groups, has not been observed in the blue-green algae. Recent reports of an exchange of genetic material have been questioned. Any sexuality in the Cyanophyta will probably be found to be similar to that reported in bacteria.

PHYLOGENY

The Cyanophyta are considered primitive. The extant Cyanophyta and Schizomycophyta have a great deal in common. The prokaryotic cell, as discussed in Chapter 3, occurs only in these two divisions. In addition, the bacteria and blue-green algae have similar types of DNA and ribosomes, have the same sensitivity to antibiotics, and lack sterols. Comparatively little is known about the physiology of the blue-green algae, but they are considered, along with the bacteria, to be the earliest of organisms and have probably undergone very little change since Pre-Cambrian time.

A number of fossil genera and species are reported from the Pre-Cambrian to the present. The oldest fossil algae are considered to be Cyanophyta. Most of the records from the Pre-Cambrian are extremely fragmentary and present no evidence of apparent phylogenetic significance. No heterocysts have been reported in the fossil condition. Many specimens are tubular and have been considered sheaths of blue-green algae. The significance of the Cyanophyta in the geologic past is probably great, judging from the ability of certain contemporary species to form calcium and magnesium carbonate deposits, the importance of some in reef formation today, and the ability of certain forms to fix nitrogen.

53

6 / Division Myxomycota

This chapter discusses three groups with uncertain affinities—the Myxomycetes, Acrasiomycetes, and Labyrinthulomycetes, often collectively referred to as *slime molds*. All have naked assimilative phases. Phagotrophic feeding by ingestion of solid food particles occurs in all Myxomycetes, Acrasiomycetes, and some Labyrinthulomycetes. However, the Myxomycetes, or *true slime molds,* have a multinucleate assimilative body, whereas that of the *cellular slime molds,* the Acrasiomycetes and Labyrinthulomycetes, is uninucleate. Reproduction in the true slime molds resembles that of the Eumycota in some features and differs markedly from that found in the cellular slime molds. Because of the numerous differences, each group is discussed separately in the following pages.

CLASS MYXOMYCETES
(True Slime Molds)

About 450 species of true slime molds are known, and many of these are universally distributed. They live in or on moist soil, wood, dung, or decaying vegetation and are of little direct economic importance.

All of the true slime molds have a naked, acellular assimilative body called a plasmodium, and all form fungus-like fruiting bodies. Within the fruiting body, numerous spores form and are eventually released. Under suitable conditions these spores germinate by the production of amoeboid or flagellated cells. The essential features of a myxomycete life history are shown in Figure 6–1.

Spores

The spores of myxomycetes (Fig. 6–3A, B) are similar in appearance to those of the true fungi. The spore wall, reported to contain cellulose, is often marked by a pattern of warts, spines, or ridges. Masses of such spores may appear violet, brown, rusty, reddish, or other colors, the pigment residing in the wall layers. The protoplast of the spore is provided with a cytoplasmic membrane, nucleus, mitochondria, and other organelles as shown in Figure 6–2 of *Fuligo septica*.

Myxomycete spores are long-lived, some retaining their viability after storage of more than 60 years. Spore germination (Fig. 6–3B) can be readily observed in some species if the spores are placed in water. Germination requires as little as 15 minutes in some species; in others, a week or more may elapse. At germination each spore liberates one or more naked photoplasts that can develop into either flagellated swarm cells or nonflagellate myxamoebae. Myxamoebae often develop flagella and, conversely, swarmers of some species can retract their flagella and become myxamoebae. Thus the two types of cells are interchangeable.

Swarm Cells and Myxamoebae

The swarm cell (Fig. 6–3C) is an anteriorly uniflagellate or sometimes biflagellate cell capable of both swimming and amoeboid movements. If two flagella are present, they may be either equal in length or of markedly different lengths. All flagella are of the whiplash type. Swarm cells typically are pear-shaped during swimming movement, but the form varies during amoeboid movement.

Myxamoebae lack flagella (Fig. 6–3D) and have only amoeboid movement. They are similar in appearance to the true amoebae (Protozoa).

Both swarm cells and myxamoebae ingest bacterial cells and absorb dissolved nutrients. Myxamoebae undergo fission; swarm cells apparently retract their flagella before dividing in this manner. Under unfavorable conditions, myxamoebae and swarm cells form resistant cysts.

Eventually, swarm cells or myxamoebae function as gametes. In most myxomycetes studied, syngamy occurs within two to eight days of spore germination. Syngamy can occur between two myxamoebae as in *Physarella oblonga,* or between two swarm cells as in *Physarum polycephalum* and *Fuligo septica.* The fusing gametes of some species are of distinct mating classes ($+$ and $-$ or a, a_1, a_2, etc.).

Zygote

The zygote may at first be flagellated or amoeboid, depending upon the gametes. If flagellated, the flagella are withdrawn and the zygote becomes amoeboid. Within a few hours, the zygote nucleus divides mitotically; thereafter, mitotic nuclear divisions occur synchronously as the zygote develops into a plasmodium. A plasmodium can develop from a single zygote. However, coalescence of several zygotes results in the production of small plasmodia in some species. In such cases, there is fusion of cytoplasm but not of the nuclei.

Plasmodium

The main assimilative or "vegetative" structure in the life history of a myxomycete is the plasmodium (Fig. 6–4). Plasmodia are multinucleate, acellular, and lack rigid walls. They remain microscopic in one group, but can form conspicuous protoplasmic sheets many centimeters in extent in others. Plasmodia of most

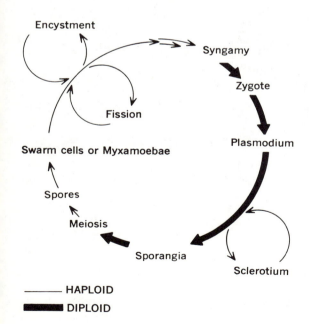

FIGURE 6–1 Outline of a myxomycete life history.

55

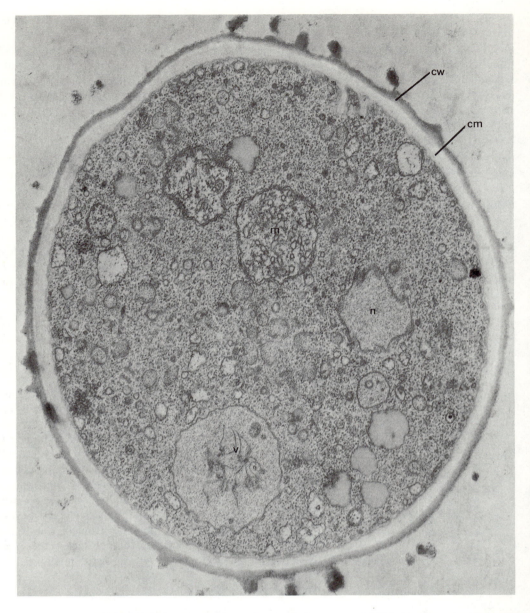

FIGURE 6–2 *Fuligo*. Thin section through spore, ×25,000 (*cm,* cytoplasmic membrane; *cw,* cell wall; *m,* mitochondrion; *n,* nucleus; *v,* vacuole). *Note:* only a small lobe of the nucleus is visible in this section. (Photograph courtesy of Nancy Corfman.)

species are colorless, white, yellow, or brown, less frequently violet or black.

Plasmodia of many myxomycetes are motile by means of a slow amoeboid movement. The plasmodium creeps in or on damp decay-ing wood, soil, leaves, or dung. As it moves, it ingests bacteria, mold spores, and other small particles in its path. The undigested debris picked up by a plasmodium is egested at its trailing end. This debris, together with slimy

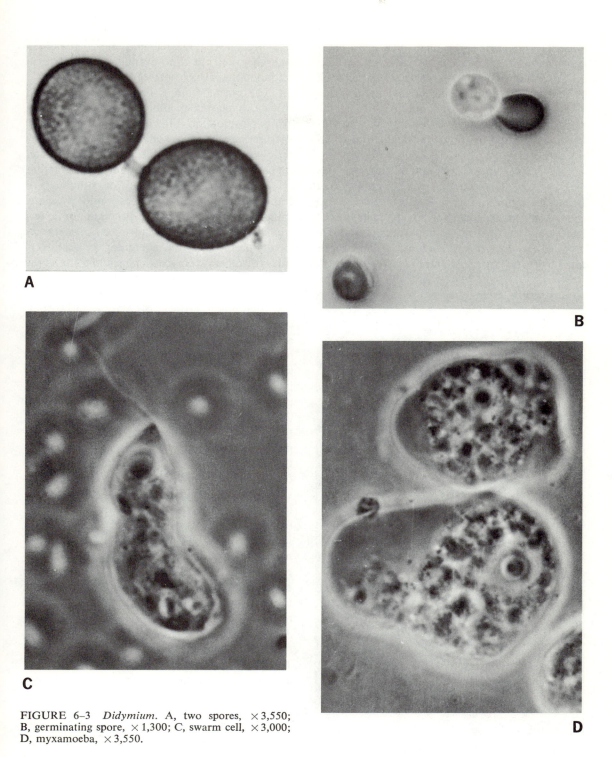

FIGURE 6–3 *Didymium*. A, two spores, ×3,550;
B, germinating spore, ×1,300; C, swarm cell, ×3,000;
D, myxamoeba, ×3,550.

57

material secreted by the plasmodium, forms a conspicuous trail. Plasmodia can also envelop and digest fruiting bodies of large fungi, such as mushrooms. Plasmodial movements are oriented responses; in the assimilative phase, the response generally is positive toward increasing moisture and dissolved nutrients, and negative toward light.

In form, the plasmodium is amoeba-like, slug-like, or of a changing pattern of vein-like strands or tubules (Fig. 6–4). In *Physarum* and related genera, the network is conspicuous; it is roughly fan-shaped in migrating plasmodia. Toward the posterior of such a fan, the strands are relatively large and infrequently branched.

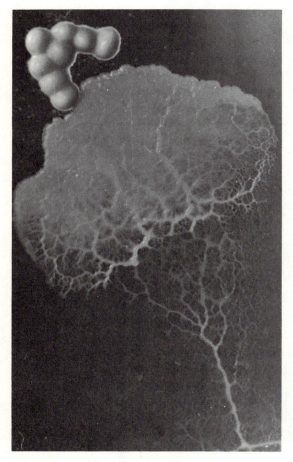

FIGURE 6–4 Small plasmodium of *Physarum* (plasmodium shown moving toward mass of yeast cells, upper left), ×3.

The branches are finer and more numerous anteriorly and, at the advancing margin, form a continuous layer of protoplasm.

The plasmodium is naked, being bounded only by a plasma membrane. If a strand of a living plasmodium of *Physarum* is examined microscopically, two zones can be seen. The peripheral layer of cytoplasm is transparent and appears to form a wall around the granular cytoplasm inside the strand or tubule. The granular cytoplasm undergoes rapid rhythmic streaming; it flows in one direction for a few seconds, slows, stops, and then reverses its direction. Cytoplasmic streaming is characteristic of all myxomycete plasmodia, but the movement is slow and irregular in some.

Electron microscope preparations show that the outer surface of plasmodial strands is irregular and has numerous deep indentations and striations. The outer clear layer of cytoplasm is generally devoid of organelles. The granular appearance of the inner cytoplasm is caused by nuclei, mitochondria, vacuoles, pigment granules, and other matter as well as by debris. In the peripheral cytoplasm, minute fibrils are present. These fibrils appear most commonly to be associated with the deep indentations or irregularities of the outer surface. Similar fibrils are present outside the plasma membrane, where they form a loose fibrillar sheath. The slime track, deposited by migrating plasmodia, also contains such fibrils. Some of the fibrils isolated from myxomycete plasmodia have physicochemical properties similar to those of the contractile protein of muscle, actomyosin. As with muscle protein, the contractile proteins of plasmodia undergo a reversible change in viscosity when treated with ATP. Direct treatment of the plasmodium with ATP has been shown to influence streaming. Thus, the evidence now available supports the concept that plasmodial streaming and motility are brought about through contractions of the fibrils.

Plasmodia of relatively few species have been isolated and grown in pure culture. In many instances, there appears to be a strong dependence of the plasmodium upon associated

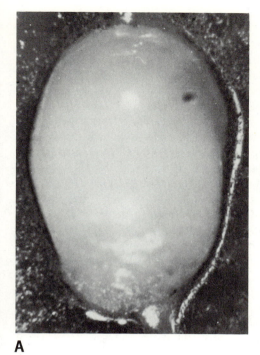

A

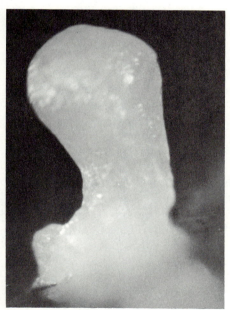

B

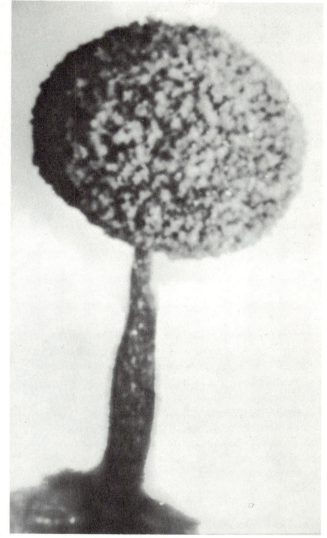

C

FIGURE 6–5 Sporangial development in *Didymium*. A, pillow-shaped thickening or primordium still attached to plasmodial strand, ×50; B, the primordium has assumed columnar form, ×66; C, mature sporangium, ×115.

bacteria. Only one species, *Physarum polycephalum,* has been grown in pure culture on a chemically defined medium. In such cultures, the plasmodium of *P. polycephalum* does not assume a fan shape as long as sufficient nutrient is available. It remains stationary, forming a thin compact disc that spreads over the surface of the culture medium. If plasmodia of this species are grown in agitated liquid cultures, they break up into numerous tiny fragments. Such fragments can coalesce to form again a single large plasmodium. Fragmentation also appears to be a common method of plasmodial reproduction in nature. A plasmodium sometimes fragments into two sections; the two sections may then form a single plasmodium again if they meet. While two fragments of the same plasmodium will readily coalesce to form a single large plasmodium, two different plasmodia of the same species do not always do so. In some species, a set of genetic factors controls compatibility, i.e., fusion or coalescence of plasmodia.

Sclerotium

If conditions remain favorable, the plasmodium takes in food and other materials and enlarges. Under certain conditions unfavorable to assimilation, e.g., drying or low temperatures, the plasmodium may be converted into a resistant structure called a sclerotium. Sclerotia are hardened masses of irregular form consisting of many cell-like compartments. Sclerotia retain their viability for several years, reforming a plasmodium with the return of favorable conditions.

Sporulation

Little is known concerning the factors that initiate sporulation in the myxomycetes. Changing environmental conditions, e.g., drying, decreasing food supply, or changes in pH, have been thought to induce sporulation in some species. In *Physarum polycephalum,* temperature, light, and pH have been implicated

in this process. Perhaps the factors vary from species to species or, as in *P. polycephalum,* several of the factors interact.

Before sporocarps (fructifications or fruiting bodies) are produced, the plasmodium creeps to an exposed position on the substrate. Some move up the stems or leaves of living or dead plants to positions more favorable to spore dispersal. There the plasmodium heaps up into one or more masses which soon assume the form of mature sporocarps.

In one genus, *Ceratiomyxa* (Fig. 6–7), spores are borne singly and externally on thread-like or columnar structures. The spores of all other genera are formed within the fructifications. The commonest type of sporocarp is called a sporangium, and typically a single plasmodium produces many sporangia. The plasmodium divides into a number of hemispherical protoplasmic portions or primordia (Fig. 6–5). In some species the primordia simply round up and are transformed directly into sporangia. In species with stalked sporangia, e.g., *Didymium iridis,* the primordia become columnar. Protoplasm moves upward within the column and a sporangium is formed at its apex.

Figure 6–6A illustrates structures in a myxomycete sporangium. An outer layer, the peridium, surrounds a mass of either spores alone or spores together with a capillitium. The capillitium is composed of thread-like strands, sometimes united to form a network, and interspersed with the spores. In some sporangia, a central columnar structure or columella is present. The columella of many stalked sporangia appears to be only a continuation of the stalk into the sporangium. A discoid hypothallus usually is visible at the base of the stalk.

In myxomycetes not producing sporangia, the plasmodium can form one to many sporocarps of other types. In the development of plasmodiocarps the major veins, or parts thereof, appear to be transformed directly into fructifications. Plasmodiocarps are sessile and usually of variable form (Fig. 6–6B). Those

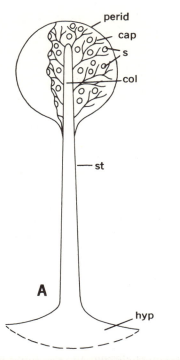

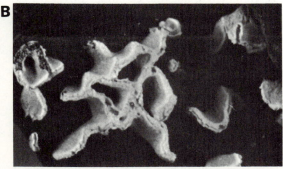

FIGURE 6–6 A, structure of sporangium (*cap*, capillitium; *col*, columella; *hyp*, hypothallus; *perid*, peridium; *s*, spores; *st*, stipe or stalk). B, plasmodiocarps of *Physarum bivalve*, ×5. C, aethalium of *Fuligo*, ×0.5.

of a single species are sometimes branched, donut-shaped, or simply elongate. In a third type of sporocarp, the aethalium (Fig. 6–6C), an entire plasmodium heaps up into one or a few pillow-shaped or rounded masses. Like sporangia, plasmodiocarps and aethalia have an outer peridium and may contain a capillitium in addition to the spores.

Some intergradation is found between the different types of sporocarps. Both plasmodiocarps and sporangia can be produced by a single plasmodium. The sporangia of some species are produced in crowded masses in which the individuals are partially or completely fused. Such masses closely resemble or are indistinguishable from aethalia.

Meiosis occurs during spore formation within the developing sporocarps or, less commonly, within the spores. The haploid nuclei and portions of the cytoplasm become surrounded by walls and mature into spores. At this time, the capillitial threads also are produced.

When the sporocarp is mature, the spores are unattached but are enmeshed in the capillitial network. Mature sporocarps open in one of several ways. In some myxomycetes, the peridium is very delicate and disappears soon after the fructification has matured. In others, the peridium splits either irregularly or along definite lines, exposing the spores. Following this, the capillitium may expand, forming a more open network.

Myxomycete Classification

The classification of the myxomycetes is based upon characteristics of the spores and of the mature sporocarps. Perhaps further studies of motile cells, plasmodia, and sporocarp development will alter the current taxonomic concepts for this group.

Ceratiomyxa fruticulosa, one of the commonest of temperate myxomycetes, produces an extensive system of columnar or branched

61

A

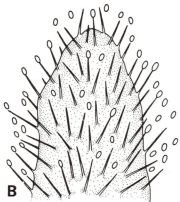

B

FIGURE 6–7 *Ceratiomyxa*. A, mature fructification, × 12.5; B, single branch showing attachment of spores, × 1,330.

thread-like strands referred to as a hypothallus (Fig. 6–7A, B). The spores of this species are borne singly on individual stalks on the surface of the hypothallus. It has been suggested that a single spore and stalk in *Ceratiomyxa* is equivalent to or homologous to an entire sporangium in other myxomycetes.

Sporangia of *Dictydium* do not have capillitia, but the peridium is composed of a net-work of delicate strands (Fig. 6–8A). The pallid spores gradually sift out through this delicate network. A related genus, *Lycogala* (Fig. 6–8B), produces large aethalia similar in appearance and function to the fructifications of some basidiomycetes (cf. *Lycoperdon*, p. 119). At maturity, an irregular opening develops at the top of the aethalium. The force of raindrops striking the flexible peridium produces a bellows-like action, and spores are blown out through the opening.

The sporangia of *Hemitrichia* and *Arcyria* are among the more brightly colored myxomycete fructifications. In *Hemitrichia* (Fig. 6–9A, B), the capillitial threads are marked by spiral bands; those of *Arcyria* have prominent cogs or spines (Fig. 6–9C, D). The spores are pale yellow or rosy in most species of *Arcyria* and *Hemitrichia;* the capillitium and peridium often are yellow, orange, or red.

Stemonitis and related genera produce brown to violet-brown spores. The sporangia are columellate and the capillitial threads arise as branches of the columella. No peridium is present on mature sporangia of *Stemonitis* (Fig. 6–10A), nor is lime (calcium carbonate) formed on the fructification. *Physarum* (Fig. 6–6B, 10B–D) and its allies have dark spores, as in *Stemonitis,* but lime is present in the capillitium or peridium, or both. Both sporangia and plasmodiocarps are formed in species of *Physarum;* in the related genus *Fuligo,* aethalia are produced. The aethalia of *F. septica* (Fig. 6–6C), a common species, sometimes reach 20 cm in diameter.

CLASS ACRASIOMYCETES
(Cellular Slime Molds)

The class Acrasiomycetes includes a group of organisms having an amoeba-like uninucleate assimilative phase. Reproduction occurs through fission of the amoeboid cells or myxamoebae. These myxamoebae also aggregate to form mold-like communal fruiting bodies and spores. Although sexual reproduction has been reported in *Dictyostelium discoideum,* other workers dispute these findings.

The acrasiomycetes are primarily soil-inhabiting organisms and are most abundant in forest soils. They are also found in dung and in other habitats where bacteria are abundant. The myxamoebae feed phagotrophically, ingesting bacteria, and are indistinguishable from soil amoebae classified in the Protozoa. The acrasiomycetes can easily be maintained in culture if grown with a suitable bacterial species. Some acrasiomycetes have also been grown on defined media in the absence of bacteria.

The life history of *Dictyostelium discoideum,* the most intensively studied acrasiomycete, is outlined in Fig. 6–11. Each spore releases one myxamoeba at the time of germination (Fig. 6–12A, B). The amoebae move over the substrate, feeding on bacterial cells and reproducing by fission. During this period, each amoeba acts independently of all others. The assimilative phase may go on indefinitely, if environmental conditions are favorable and if there is an adequate supply of food. Depletion of the food supply, changes in humidity, concentration of myxamoebae, and other factors affect the duration of this assimilative stage.

At the close of the assimilative phase, the myxamoebae enter an interphase period lasting from four to eight hours. During the interphase, the amoebae stop feeding and subsequent development is at the expense of reserve food. There is a decrease in size of the myxamoebae, food vacuoles disappear, and granular materials form in the cytoplasm. The myxamoebae still behave as a population of homogeneous and independent individuals. Aggregation, the next phase in the life cycle, involves convergence or movement of the cells toward a common point. The myxamoebae move together (Fig. 6–13A), forming branched streams, and produce a single heap at an aggregation center.

Movement of the cells toward the aggregation center is a chemotactic response to hormones called acrasins. The aggregation center is the point of maximum acrasin concentration. Acrasins are secreted by amoebae of all acrasiomycetes, the exact chemical composition varying from species to species. Little is known concerning the chemistry of acrasins, but present evidence suggests that they are steroid compounds.

A rounded papillate mass develops as myxamoebae heap up at the aggregation center (Fig. 6–13B). The mass tilts, elongates, and becomes a cartridge-shaped pseudoplasmodium

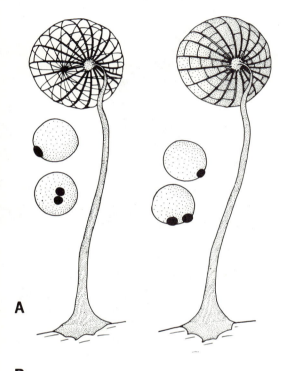

A

B

FIGURE 6–8 A, sporangia (×30) and spores (×2,800) of *Dictydium cancellatum;* B, aethalia of *Lycogala epidendrum,* ×6.

63

64

FIGURE 6–9   A, B, *Hemitrichia,* A, sporangia, ×45; B, capillitium and spores, ×550. C, D, *Arcyria.* C, sporangia, ×12; D, capillitium and spores, ×1,000.

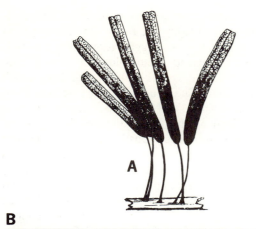

A

B

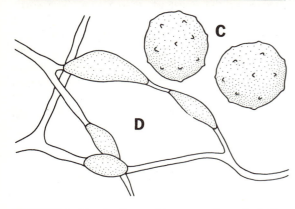

C

D

FIGURE 6–10 A, *Stemonitis* sporangia, ×8. B–D, *Physarum*. B, sporangia, ×30; C, spores, ×1,800; D, capillitium, ×875.

(Fig. 6–13C). Although the pseudoplasmodium appears to be a multicellular unit, it is actually composed of about 2,000 myxamoebae. If the pseudoplasmodium is placed in

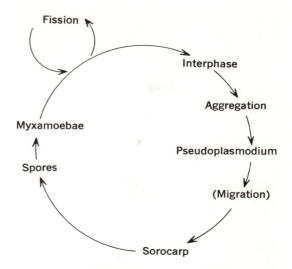

FIGURE 6–11 Life history outline of *Dictyostelium*.

water and shaken, the myxamoebae separate and resume individual activity.

The pseudoplasmodium of *D. discoideum* migrates away from the point of aggregation. The anterior portion of the pseudoplasmodium is light and heat sensitive; it responds positively toward both factors and controls the direction of migration. The pseudoplasmodium moves at a speed of 0.25 to 2.0 mm per hour, and migration may last for several hours. During this slow gliding movement, a slimy sheath is deposited and left behind the moving structure. The pseudoplasmodium may glide with its long axis parallel to the substratum, with the body flexed and only a portion in contact with the substratum, or standing erect on the posterior tip.

Cells in various regions of the pseudoplasmodium will eventually form specific portions of the fruiting body. Roughly one-third of the cells in the anterior portion of the pseudoplasmodium will produce the stalk; the remainder will form spores. Whether an amoeba becomes a prestalk or prespore cell must be determined after the cells have aggregated. If the anterior half of the pseudoplasmodium is excised and fruiting occurs immediately, the fruiting body will have a normal stalk bearing very few

65

spores. If the excised portion is kept in the migrating phase, there is redifferentiation of some amoebae and a normally proportioned fruiting body is formed.

The length of the migration period varies with environmental conditions, especially humidity and solute concentration in the substrate. If cultures are exposed to drying conditions, the next stage in the life cycle is soon initiated.

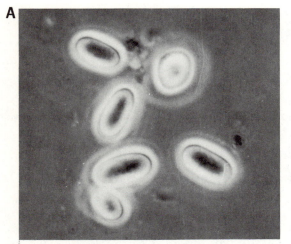

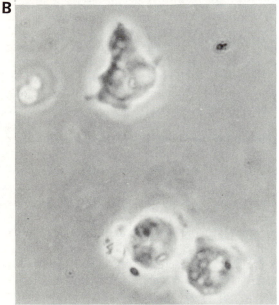

FIGURE 6–12 *Dictyostelium*. A, spores, ×2,000; B, myxamoebae, ×2,000.

Following migration, the pseudoplasmodium again assumes a form similar to that at the completion of aggregation (Fig. 6–14). Inside the pseudoplasmodium, a central core of stalk cells develops within a cellulose sheath or cylinder. These cells enlarge, secrete rigid cellulose walls, and then die. New stalk cells are added at the tip of the developing stalk. The prespore cells, constituting the remainder of the pseudoplasmodium, migrate upward around the stalk as it is being formed. At the tip of the completed stalk, or sorophore, each prespore cell secretes a wall and is transformed into a spore. The spherical mass of spores, called a sorus, and the sorophore constitute the fruiting body or sorocarp (Fig. 6–15A). Each spore is formed by the encystment of a single amoeboid cell; on germinating, the spore gives rise to a single myxamoeba. Thus, spore production here does not provide the potential increase in numbers of individuals that it does in the myxomycetes.

Not all of the acrasiomycetes have a life cycle as complex as that of *D. discoideum*. The migrating pseudoplasmodial stage is lacking in most of the group, and sorocarp formation occurs at the point of aggregation. The sorocarps of some genera, e.g., *Guttulinopsis,* have only slight differentiation between the stalk and spore cells. The stalk broadens upward and merges with the sorus. At the opposite extreme, species of *Polysphondylium* are characterized by complex branched fruiting bodies. Each sorocarp has a number of separate sori formed on whorled branches (Fig. 6–15B).

CLASS LABYRINTHULOMYCETES (Cellular Slime Molds)

The class Labyrinthulomycetes includes a group of little known fresh-water and marine aquatic organisms. None of the species has been sufficiently studied to provide a complete life history. Most of the species are parasites of algae or higher plants, but several have been grown in pure culture on laboratory media.

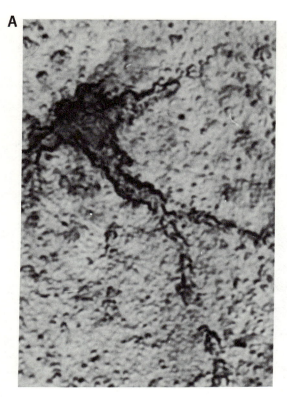

A

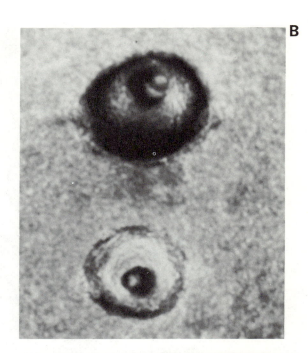

B

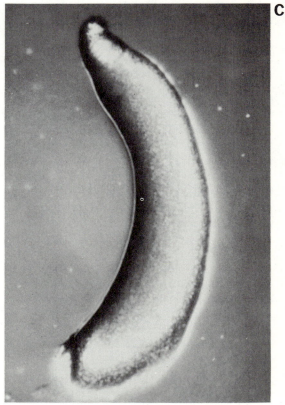

C

FIGURE 6–13 *Dictyostelium*. A, aggregation of myx-amoebae, ×35; B, two newly formed pseudoplasmodia at the end of aggregation phase, ×70; C, migrating pseudoplasmodium, ×125.

The assimilative stage of *Labyrinthula* consists of naked uninucleate cells (Fig. 6–16A, B). Each of these spindle- or oval-shaped cells secretes a collapsible slime tube. Although the slime tube is extracellular, electron micrographs show it to be at least partially covered by membranes. The assimilative cells glide within the tube, but the mechanism of movement is unknown. Slime tubes of a group of spindle cells form a network which, together with the naked cells, has been referred to as a "net plasmodium." However, there is little resemblance to either a true plasmodium of the myxomycetes or to the pseudoplasmodium of the acrasiomycetes.

The cells may divide mitotically to form two or four daughter cells. In *Labyrinthula*

DIVISION MYXOMYCOTA

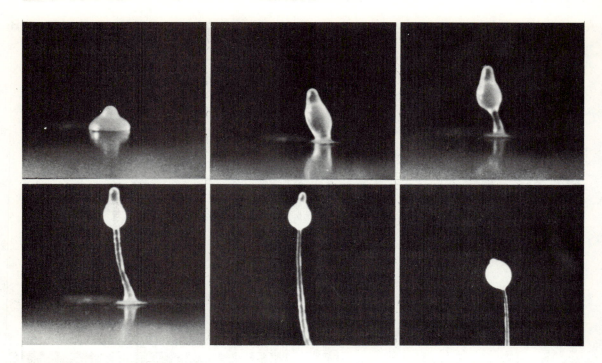

FIGURE 6–14 Culmination of migration and development of sorocarp of *Dictyostelium discoideum*, ×35.6. (Photograph by K. B. Raper, courtesy John Tyler Bonner from *The Cellular Slime Molds*, by permission of Princeton University Press, copyright © 1959.)

macrocystis, the spindle-shaped cells sometimes heap together and form a membrane-covered sorus within which spore-like bodies are produced. When released, each of the spores gives rise to a single spindle-shaped cell.

Anteriorly biflagellate swarm cells have been reported in one species of *Labyrinthula,* and multinucleate structures have been observed in another. The latter possibly represents a type of true plasmodium.

In *Labyrinthula,* the slime tubes are produced within and between cells of the host plant. *L. macrocystis* causes a serious disease of eel grass (*Zostera marina*).

RELATIONSHIPS OF THE SLIME MOLDS

The interrelationships of the three classes of Myxomycota, and their relationships to other groups of organisms, are unclear. The class Myxomycetes often is placed in the phylum Protozoa, following the treatment of the great German mycologist, De Bary. On the other hand, two of today's leading myxomycetologists, G. W. Martin and C. J. Alexopoulos, include Myxomycetes and true fungi in a single division, the Mycota. The myxomycete plasmodium, lacking rigid walls and with amoeboid movement and food ingestion, definitely is animal-like. However, the spores and sporocarps resemble those of fungi. Not all of the true fungi have rigid walls, and amoeboid movement has been reported for the cells of some species. Thus, the myxomycetes appear in certain respects to be intermediate between true fungi and protozoa.

The acrasiomycetes were at first placed with Myxomycetes because the pseudoplasmodium was thought to be a true plasmodium. The acrasiomycete myxamoebae are in most

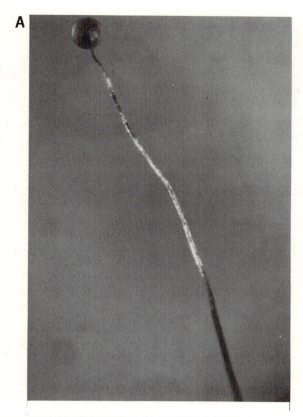

A

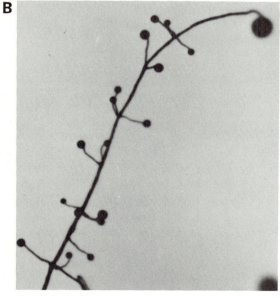

B

FIGURE 6–15   A, mature sorocarp of *Dictyostelium*, ×50; B, portion of a branched sorocarp of *Polysphondelium*, ×50.

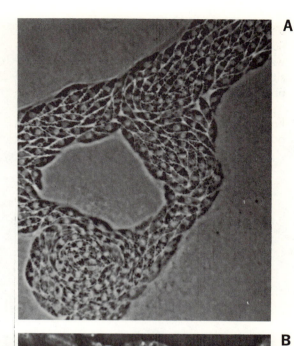

A

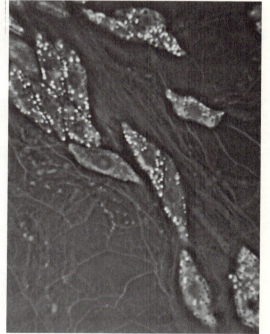

B

FIGURE 6–16   *Labyrinthula vitellina.* A, plasmodium-like mass of cells, ×300; B, cells and tracks, ×1,100. (Phase contrast photographs courtesy S. W. Watson, from *"Labyrinthula minuta* sp. nov." by S. W. Watson and K. B. Raper, *Journal of General Microbiology,* Vol. 17, 1957, with permission of Cambridge University Press.)

DIVISION MYXOMYCOTA

respects indistinguishable from amoebae classified in the Protozoa. Although cellulose in the walls of stalk cells and spores can be considered plant-like, some animals are known to produce cellulose.

The Labyrinthulales are as yet too poorly known to provide a basis for comparison with other organisms. A group of soil-inhabiting amoeboid organisms, the Protostelidae, has been described in recent years. Some of the protostelids appear to combine characteristics of true amoebae, acrasiomycetes, and possibly myxomycetes. Further studies of these organisms, and of the little known Labyrinthulomycetes, may provide clues about the interrelationships of various slime mold groups.

7 / Division Eumycota

The *true fungi,* or Eumycota, are an extremely large and diverse group of organisms. Approximately 100,000 species have already been described, and estimates of the total number range as high as 250,000 species.

Fungi occur in aquatic and terrestrial environments of many types. Like many of the myxomycetes, certain fungi are more or less cosmopolitan in their distribution. Fungi are most abundant in tropical regions, but many species occur in temperate and arctic zones. In general, moderate temperatures (20–30°C), moisture, and a supply of nutrients will provide for the growth of many kinds of fungi. However, some cold-tolerant species can carry on growth at temperatures slightly below freezing, while other fungi require a temperature in excess of 40°C for optimum growth or reproduction.

NUTRITION

All of the true fungi are heterotrophs, dependent upon living or dead organisms for certain organic nutrients. The saprobic species obtain these nutrients from decaying matter of many types. The symbiotic fungi form mutualistic or parasitic relationships with plants and animals or, in some instances, with other fungi. From such symbiotic associates, the fungus derives part or all of the nutrients it requires. In mutualistic associations, the fungus may provide nutrients for its partner, e.g., as in the relationship between fungi and plant roots. In this type of relationship, called mycorrhiza, the fungus is thought to provide nitrogen and possibly other mineral nutrients for its associate. The parasitic fungi may be either facultative or obligate parasites.

SOMATIC STRUCTURE

The assimilative body in the Eumycota is a uninucleate or, more commonly, multinucleate structure. The uninucleate thallus consists of a simple sphaeroidal cell or of such a cell together with an absorptive system of filaments called rhizoids. In the multinucleate types, the thallus typically is composed of hyphae. The hyphae of a few fungi are of determinate growth, but those of most fungi have potentially unlimited growth. In the latter group, the hyphae form a branching network collectively referred to as a mycelium. The hyphae of some fungi are coenocytic; only the reproductive structures are cut off by cross walls. However, most hyphae are divided into compartments by transverse septa. These septa typically are provided with a central pore which, in many instances, is large enough to permit passage of nuclei and other organelles from cell to cell.

The nuclei of fungal cells are similar to those of higher organisms; fungal cells also contain mitochondria, vacuoles, and other membrane-bounded organelles. Most of the Eumycota have rigid cell walls that contain cellulose, chitin, or both of these substances. Cellulose alone is found only in the walls of certain phycomycetes; chitin is usually found in the walls. However, in some yeasts cell walls contain large amounts of mannan but little detectable chitin. Fungal walls may also contain other polysaccharides, lipids, and proteins. As in most organisms with rigid walls, fungal walls maintain cell form and protect the cell against osmotic damage.

Those fungi having simple cells without apparent absorptive structures commonly occupy habitats in which they are bathed in a suitable nutrient medium. For example, some of the parasitic fungi of this type live within the cells of other organisms and absorb nutrients from the host protoplast. Another group of uninucleate, unicellular forms, the yeasts, lives on the surfaces of fruits, in nectaries of flowers, or other habitats, where they are surrounded by nutrient. If absorptive rhizoids are present on simple thalli, the main body of the fungus typically occupies a position outside the host cell or substratum.

If the thallus is mycelial, it may consist of both aerial and submerged hyphae. Fungal hyphae grow primarily through extension of the tip, the diameter remaining constant. Branches are initiated and septa are formed a short distance behind the growing tip. Within the cell wall, cytoplasmic streaming carries new protoplasm and building blocks to the growing point. Older regions of a growing hypha typically have thickened walls, and with age the

hyphal compartments become highly vacuolate and often contain large amounts of lipids. Still older compartments, some distance behind the growing tip, may be devoid of cytoplasm. As a hyphal tip grows through the substratum, it digests a pathway. Digestion is carried on by hydrolyzing enzymes located at the cell surface or secreted into the surrounding environment. The digestion products, and other materials in the surrounding medium, are absorbed and utilized by the hypha.

REPRODUCTION

In morphologically simple fungi, reproduction often involves the conversion of the entire fungus protoplast into reproductive units. In such fungi, there may be little change in the form of the cell when reproduction occurs. Differentiation is thus mostly or entirely internal. Most fungi produce special reproductive cells, e.g., sporangia or gametangia, within which the reproductive units are formed. The classification of the true fungi is based primarily upon the kinds of asexual and sexual reproductive structures or cells. The Division Eumycota is in this way divided into a number of classes, the characterstics of which are summarized as follows:

Class Phycomycetes. Thallus unicellular and uninucleate to multinucleate with coenocytic hyphae; asexual reproduction by motile or nonmotile sporangiospores; sexual reproduction by fusion of motile gametes, or by contact or fusion of gametangia; zygote often transformed into a thick-walled resistant spore or sporangium. This group of fungi is often divided into as many as six classes.

Class Ascomycetes. Thallus unicellular and uninucleate or, more commonly, composed of septate hyphae; asexual reproduction by spores called conidia or by budding; sexual reproduction through the formation of asci and ascospores, these in most instances being preceded by gametangia. The zygote nucleus

72

typically undergoes meiosis soon after it has been formed.

Class Basidiomycetes. Thallus typically of hyphae, the cells of which are uninucleate (monokaryotic) or binucleate (dikaryotic); asexual reproduction by conidia; sexual reproduction through the formation of basidia and basidiospores. As in the ascomycetes, meiosis occurs soon after karyogamy, or in some groups a diploid resistant phase is present.

Form Class Fungi Imperfecti. Uninucleate or filamentous forms; asexual reproduction through conidia or other structures; sexual reproduction unknown.

CLASS PHYCOMYCETES

The class Phycomycetes includes what are considered to be the most primitive fungi. They are relatively simple in structure, and many produce motile reproductive cells. Phycomycetes occur in both aquatic and terrestrial environments; they live either as saprobes or as parasitic or mutualistic symbionts. Cellulose, chitin and other substances serve as substrates for the saprobic species; the parasites attack many kinds of plants and animals.

The simplest phycomycete thallus is a uninucleate cell without rhizoids or other specialized absorptive structures. These may lack rigid walls when active assimilative growth is occurring, but walls typically envelop the mature thallus. In more complex forms, rhizoids are present, or the thallus may consist of an extensive mycelium. The assimilative hyphae of most phycomycetes are coenocytic. Specialized absorptive branches called haustoria are formed on the hyphae of some parasitic phycomycetes.

Asexual Reproduction

In most phycomycetes, asexual reproduction is by means of sporangiospores; these may be either planospores or aplanspores. Fungal planospores, commonly called zoospores, are naked uninucleate cells. They are incapable, as far as is known, of ingesting solid food particles and of dividing as do the swarm cells of myxomycetes. The aplanospores possess one or more nuclei and are surrounded by rigid walls.

Sporangiospores are formed through the cleavage of multinucleate sporangial protoplasts into one- or few-nucleate fragments. These then develop flagella, or walls, and are transformed into planospores or aplanospores.

The number, type, and insertion of flagella is important in determining the relationships of phycomycetous fungi. All of the motile cells of fungi have the nine-plus-two flagellar structure, but there are two distinct structural types (see Fig. 3–3): the whiplash flagellum and the tinsel flagellum. On the basis of the flagellar insertion the phycomycetes are divided into a series of classes or subclasses as follows:

Chytridiomycetidae
. . . . One posterior flagellum; whiplash.
* Hyphochytridiomycetidae
. . . . One anterior flagellum; tinsel.
Oomycetidae
. . . . Two anterior or lateral flagella; one tinsel, one whiplash.
* Plasmodiophoromycetidae
. . . . Two anterior flagella; both whiplash.
Zygomycetidae and * Trichomycetidae
. . . . No flagellated cells produced.

* Not discussed in this text.

Sexual Reproduction

In many phycomycetes, sexual reproduction involves fusion of motile gametes. The gametes typically are of the same form as zoospores of the same species. Where fusion of two motile gametes occurs, it usually is isogamous. However, anisogamy does occur in some fungi, for example in *Allomyces* (p. 77). Oogamy in the classical sense—fusion of a motile "sperm" with a large nonmotile egg—occurs only in one order. However, gametangial contact, where gamete nuclei are transferred

73

from an antheridium to an oogonium and fuse with nuclei of the latter, generally also is designated as oogamy. In other phycomycetes, e.g., the zygomycetes, sexual reproduction is by the fusion of entire gametangia (conjugation).

Life Histories

Complete life histories are known for relatively few phycomycetes. In one group, the Oomycetidae, the life history has recently been reported to be predominantly diploid, with the gametes forming the only haploid phase. In some species of the Blastocladiales and Chytridiales, there is an alternation of more or less equal haploid and diploid generations. However, the commonest type of life history in the class appears to be that in which the zygote develops into a thick-walled resistant spore or sporangium. Meiosis occurs at germination of such structures; the life history is therefore predominantly haploid (Fig. 7–1). In many phycomycetes, as in higher fungi, asexual reproduction occurs independently of the sexual cycle. Asexual reproduction may be the predominant means of maintaining and dispersing the species; in many instances, it is the only known type of reproduction.

Subclass Chytridiomycetidae

Order Chytridiales. The Chytridiales, or chytrids, are structurally simple fungi which parasitize other organisms or live as saprobes. Many algae, fungi, vascular plants, and protozoa are attacked by the parasitic species. The saprobes often are obtained by "baiting" water samples with cellophane, chitin, or hair.

Chitin is thought to be the rigid constituent of all chytrid cell walls. All of these simple fungi produce zoospores that possess a single posterior whiplash flagellum; the gametes, if formed, are similarly flagellated. The zoospore may be free swimming or have amoeboid move-

ment; the swimming often consists of erratic hopping or darting.

Sexual reproduction has been seen in only a small number of the many described species of chytrids. It can occur through fusion of motile isogametes, which are indistinguishable from zoospores of the species concerned. Sexual reproduction may also occur through the fusion of entire protoplasts of two adjacent thalli. The zygote develops into a thick-walled resistant spore or sporangium. Meiosis occurs within this structure; in most instances observed, zoospores are released upon germination of the resistant structure.

The species of *Rhizophydium* (Fig. 7–2) live either as saprobes or as parasites of other organisms. When a zoospore encysts upon a suitable host or substrate, the protoplast remains within the cyst wall. A small filament is produced, penetrating the host or substrate and developing into a system of rhizoids. The

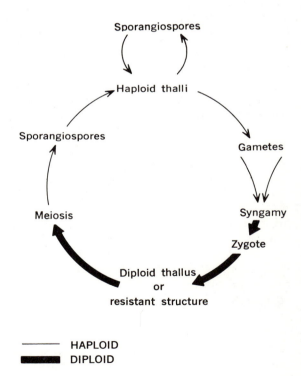

—— **HAPLOID**
▬▬ **DIPLOID**

FIGURE 7–1 Life history typical of many phycomycetes.

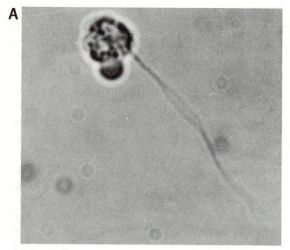

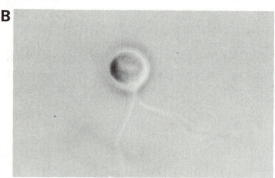

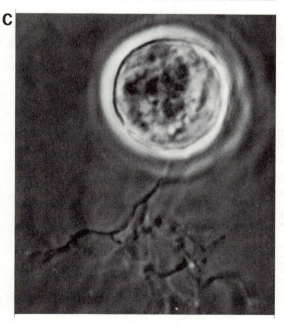

rhizoids presumably absorb materials and anchor the thallus. The cyst enlarges, eventually developing into a zoosporangium. The mature zoospores are released through a discharge pore and infect new hosts or substrates.

In most of the numerous species of *Rhizophydium,* only asexual reproduction has been observed. In one species, sexual reproduction occurs through fusion of the protoplasts of the two cysts (Fig. 7–3). Prior to sexual reproduction, zoospores swarm for a time, then settle on the host wall in compact groups. The adjacent ·encysted spores germinate and form rhizoids. A tube forms, connecting two adjacent cysts, and the entire protoplast of one cyst passes through this tube to merge with that of the second cyst. The latter continues to increase in size and eventually forms a thick-walled resistant sporangium. The emptied cyst shows no further development. Germination of the resistant cell has not definitely been observed, but it is thought to occur by the release of haploid zoospores.

Rhizophydium thalli have a single center of development, i.e., one infection point results in a single sporangium. Some chytrids, e.g., *Cladochytrium* (Fig. 7–4), develop a more extensive thallus. Here a system of rhizoids interconnects spindle-shaped swellings, sporangia, and thick-walled resistant structures. The spindle-shaped swellings frequently are transversely septate. The sporangia may be terminal or intercalary, and they often are provided with an elongate exit tube. The thick-walled resistant structures germinate to form sporangia similar to those borne directly upon the rhizoids. Sexual reproduction has not been observed in *Cladochytrium.*

Order Blastocladiales. Members of the Blastocladiales have uniflagellate zoospores resembling those of the chytrids. These fungi produce thick-walled resistant sporangia, the walls of which are pitted and mostly brown or

FIGURE 7–2 Asexual reproduction in *Rhizophydium.* A, zoospores, ×4,000; B, encysted zoospore with developing rhizoidal system, ×3,000; C, mature cyst and rhizoids, ×2,500.

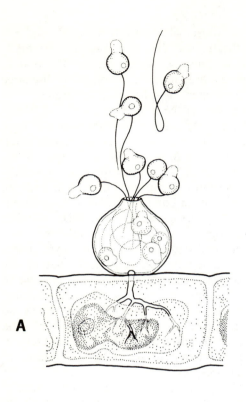

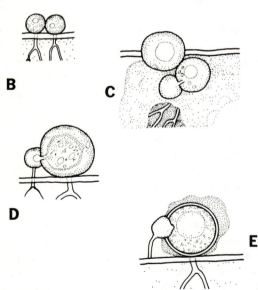

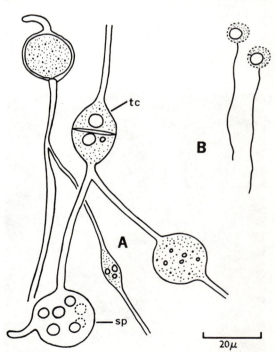

brownish. In contrast to the Chytridiales, resistant cells in this order are not the immediate products of syngamy.

The thallus of the Blastocladiales may be simple, as in the Chytridiales, but more often it is hyphal. Most of the species have rigid chitinous walls.

Sexual reproduction in the Blastocladiales is by fusion of motile iso- or anisogametes. In some instances, there is an alternation of isomorphic generations, a type of life history not common among filamentous fungi. Certain species of *Allomyces,* among the most intensively studied fungi in the Blastocladiales, have such life histories.

The diploid thallus of *Allomyces arbuscula* (Fig. 7–5) is filamentous with a basal system of rhizoids. The young hyphae are dichotomously branched; false septa, consisting of thickened rings, are present in the hyphae. Two types of sporangia are formed on the diploid thalli—thin-walled sporangia and thick-walled

FIGURE 7–3 Sexual reproduction in *Rhizophydium.* A, release of zoospores, × 1,035; B, young developing thalli, × 1,035; C, D, conjugation of adjacent thalli, × 1,035; E, thick-walled, resistant structure resulting after maturation of zygote, × 1,035. (After Sparrow, with permission of *Mycologia.*)

FIGURE 7–4 *Cladochytrium,* × 800. A, portions of two thalli bearing sporangia (*sp*) and turbinate cells (*tc*). B, zoospores. (After Richards with permission of *Transactions of British Mycological Society.*)

NONVASCULAR PLANTS

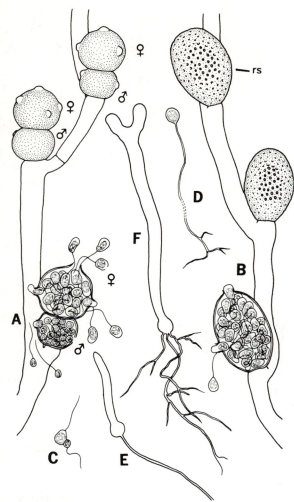

FIGURE 7–5 *Allomyces*. A, portion of mature haploid thallus showing gametangia and gametes, ×200; B, portion of diploid thallus bearing a thin-walled sporangium at the time of zoospore release and two resistant sporangia, ×200; C, syngamy, ×200; D–F, development of the thallus, ×200.

after a motile period, then germinate to form gamete-bearing thalli. The latter resemble the diploid thalli in all gross characteristics, but they produce male and female gametangia.

In *A. arbuscula,* the male gametangia are orange; they are borne below the slightly larger, colorless female gametangia. The gametes are anisogamous, the "female" being somewhat larger but morphologicaly similar to the "male." The male gametes are orange, as a result of carotenoid pigments. At the time of release, the male gametes often cluster around unopened female gametangia in response to a hormone, sirenin, secreted by the female gametes.

Studies of the related genera *Blastocladia* and *Blastocladiella* have revealed much information on morphogenesis. If cultures of one species of *Blastocladia* are grown in an atmosphere containing 99.5 per cent carbon dioxide, resistant sporangia develop. These are not formed under ordinary culture conditions, although they are produced together with thin-walled sporangia in nature. The natural habitats of some species of *Blastocladia* are polluted waters with low oxygen and high carbon dioxide content. The development of resistant sporangia has been more thoroughly studied in *Blastocladiella*. In this genus, the small thallus bears a single sporangium; this sporangium may be thin-walled and colorless or orange, or it is a thick-walled resistant structure. Incorporation of bicarbonate into the culture medium causes virtually all germlings but those destined to be orange to develop thick-walled resistant sporangia.

Subclass Oomycetidae

Order Saprolegniales. The Saprolegniales are aquatic or soil-inhabiting fungi. Most are saprobes, but a few parasitize plants or animals.

The zoospores produced by saprolegniaceous fungi are of two types: (1) primary zoospores that are anteriorly biflagellate; (2) secondary zoospores with laterally attached flagella. Both primary and secondary zoospores have a tinsel flagellum directed anteriorly and a trailing whiplash flagellum. The hyphae of

resistant sporangia. The resistant sporangia of *Allomyces* undergo a short dormancy period following formation. These thick-walled sporangia are more resistant to drying and high temperatures than are the hyphae and thin-walled sporangia. The thin-walled sporangia produce diploid zoospores that give rise to new sporangium-bearing thalli. Meiosis takes place within the brownish thick-walled sporangia, and these sporangia, upon germinating, release haploid zoospores. The haploid zoospores encyst

77

saprolegniaceous fungi have cell walls containing cellulose.

In the Saprolegniales, a series of simple forms parallels those in the Chytridiales. Only the more complex members (Saprolegniaceae) are discussed here.

Saprolegnia (Fig. 7–6, 7) and its relatives occur in fresh water and in soil. They possess an extensive coenocytic mycelium. Septa delimit only the reproductive structures and injured portions of the hyphae.

Sporangia are produced abundantly in most species; they are elongate, terminal, and of only slightly larger diameter than the hyphae which bear them. Cleavage of the multinucleate sporangial protoplast is followed by development of the primary zoospores. In *Saprolegnia,* these spores are released through a terminal pore that develops in the sporangial wall, and they swim about for a time and then encyst. In *Achlya* (Fig. 7–6E), primary zoospores are released from the sporangium, but they encyst just outside the discharge pore. *Dictyuchus* (Fig. 7–6F) derives its name from the netted appearance of its sporangia. This appearance results from the encystment of primary zoospores within the sporangium. Encysted zoospores of all three genera germinate to produce secondary zoospores. In these genera, the secondary zoospores swim for a time, then encyst again. A new filamentous thallus is developed upon germination of the encysted secondary spore.

The saprolegniaceous fungi produce distinguishable male and female reproductive structures but no motile gametes. Female gametangia, called oogonia, are generally formed on short lateral branches of the main hyphae. The oogonia are globose and contain the uninucleate "eggs" or oospheres. Male filaments may arise from the same branch or hypha as the oogonia or from a different thallus. At maturity, one or more antheridia lie in contact with the oogonium. From each antheridium, a simple or branched fertilization tube develops and grows to an oosphere. Nuclei are transferred from the antheridium and fuse with the oosphere nuclei. Following fertilization, each zygote de-

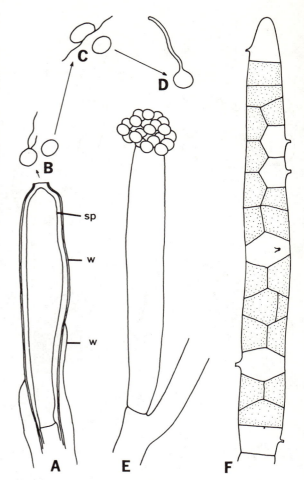

FIGURE 7–6 A–D, *Saprolegnia.* A, sporangium (*sp*) ensheathed by walls (*w*) of previously formed sporangia, ×415; B, primary planospore and cyst, ×415; C, secondary planospore and cyst, ×415; D, germination of encysted secondary planospore, ×415. E, sporangium of *Achlya* with apical cluster of encysted primary spores, ×415. F, sporangium of *Dictyuchus* containing encysted primary spores, ×860 (a few of the encysted cells have released secondary planospores).

velops a thick wall and is transformed into a resistant oospore. This type of sexual reproduction is called oogamy or gametangial contact.

The antheridia and oogonia commonly are borne on separate thalli in certain saprolegniaceous fungi, e.g., *Achlya bisexualis* and *A. ambisexualis.* Such thalli will not produce sexual structures if they are grown separately, but they do so when grown together in compatible

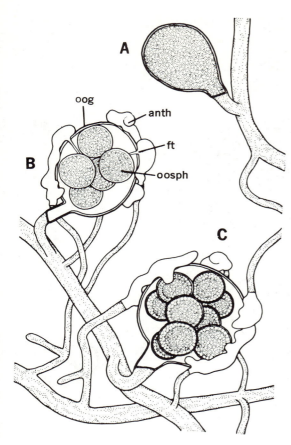

FIGURE 7–7 Sexual reproduction in *Saprolegnia*. A, hypha with young oogonium, ×60; B, oogonium following fertilization, ×60 (*anth*, antheridium; *oog*, oogonium; *ft*, fertilization tube; *oosph*, fertilized oospheres or zygotes); C, oogonium with mature oospores, ×60.

Raper performed a series of experiments demonstrating that this regular sequence is controlled by a number of hormones. The growth of antheridial filaments is initiated and regulated by four separate hormones—two produced by each thallus. Thereafter, each of the distinguishable stages of development is regulated by a separate hormone.

The oospores undergo a long resting period; the factors responsible for inducing germination are unknown. A short filament is produced upon germination of the oospore, and a typical sporangium is borne at the tip of this filament. Meiosis was long thought to occur at the time of oospore germination. However, recent studies indicate that meiosis possibly occurs in the gametangia in this order and in the Peronosporales.

Order Peronosporales. The Peronosporales are characterized by sexual reproduction of the type found in *Saprolegnia* and related genera. Asexual reproduction in the simpler Peronosporales also differs only in detail from that of the Saprolegniales. However, the more advanced members of the Peronosporales are terrestrial fungi with highly modified sporangia. The order includes a number of very important plant pathogenic species. The hyphae of the parasitic species often are intercellular and bear haustoria (Fig. 7–8A).

In *Plasmopara* (Fig. 7–8F), the elliptical or oval sporangia are borne upon specialized aerial branches, sporangiophores. One genus, *Albugo* (Fig. 7–8A–E), produces chains of sporangia; these are formed subepidermally in the host tissues. In *Albugo* and those genera with aerial sporangiophores, the sporangia are deciduous and function as disseminules; they may form either zoospores or a germ tube at germination. If sufficient moisture is present, zoospores are released in most instances. If water is not present, a germ tube is produced. In the few species that have apparently lost the ability to form zoospores, germination is only by germ tube. The latter function in much the same manner as asexual spores of higher fungi.

The gametangia of *Albugo* (Fig. 7–8D) and its relatives are similar to those of Sap-

pairs. J. R. Raper has studied reproduction in these species and has noted that a series of distinguishable stages can be observed in the reproductive process. These are: (1) production of antheridial filaments on the male thallus; (2) production of oogonial initials on the female thallus; (3) growth of antheridial filaments toward the oogonial initials and delimitation of the antheridia after contact of the initials; (4) delimitation of the oogonium and differentiation of oospheres; and (5) production of fertilization tubes and migration of antheridial nuclei through these to the oospheres.

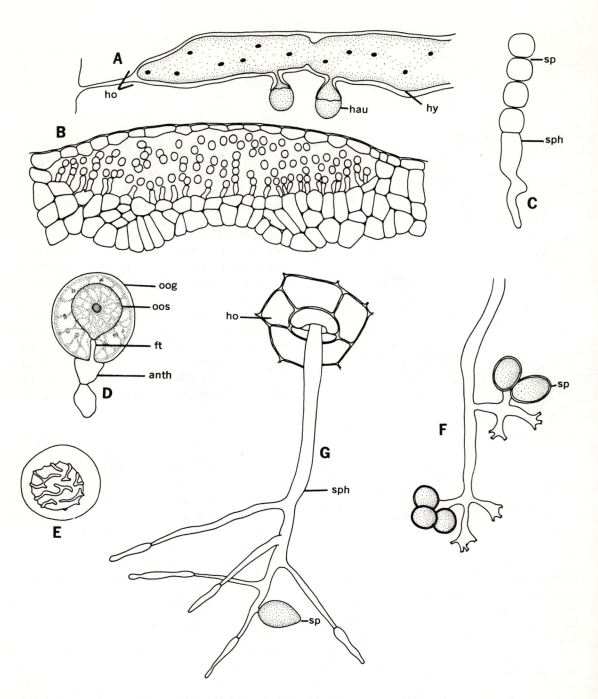

FIGURE 7–8 A–E, *Albugo*. A, hypha with haustoria penetrating host cell, ×1,080 (*hau,* haustorium; *ho,* host cells; *hy,* hypha); B, section through infected leaf showing sporangiophores and sporangia under host epidermis, ×215; C, enlarged sporangiophore and chain of sporangia, ×500 (*sp,* sporangia; *sph,* sporangiophore); D, sexual reproduction, ×500 (*anth,* antheridium; *ft,* fertilization tube; *oog,* oogonium; *oos,* oosphere); E, mature oospore, ×500; F, sporangiophore and sporangia (*sp*) of *Plasmopara,* ×585; G, sporangiophore and sporangia of *Phytophthora,* ×590; (*ho,* host epidermis; *sp,* sporangium; *sph,* sporangiophore).

rolegniales, but only one oosphere is present in the mature oogonium. Following fertilization, it develops into a thick-walled oospore. Germination of the oospore may be by germ tube or by the formation of zoospores.

One of the most destructive plant pathogens in the Peronosporales is *Phytophthora infestans* (Fig. 7–8G), the cause of late blight of potato. In the years 1845–46, this fungus caused the complete destruction of the potato crops in Ireland and many areas of Europe. Because of the resulting famine, death, and emigration, the population of Ireland dropped from about eight million to less than four million. Other species of the Peronosporales— e.g., in the genera *Plasmopara* and *Peronospora*—are also frequently responsible for serious crop losses.

Subclass Zygomycetidae

The remaining phycomycetes are characterized by the production of zygospores. These thick-walled spores are formed through conjugation, a process involving the fusion of entire gametangia. Unlike those of the Oomycetidae, the gametangia are typically identical in both form and size. Asexual reproduction occurs in most zygomycetes by the production of nonmotile sporangiospores or aplanospores. The sporangia, borne on sporangiophores, contain one to many spores. No flagellated cells are produced in this group. Chitin is present in the cell walls of most forms examined.

Order Mucorales. Most of the Mucorales are saprobes abundant in soil, dung, and decaying plant and animal materials. A few species can grow at temperatures near or below freezing and are often found on stored meat. Others are weak parasites of stored fruits and vegetables, and are responsible for much of the spoilage of these commodities. Some species parasitize vascular plants, animals, or other mucoraceous fungi; several have been reported to cause fatal infections of humans.

In the Mucorales, the mycelium usually consists of both aerial and submerged hyphae. The hyphae typically are coenocytic, although some species regularly have septa, and reproductive structures are cut off by cross walls. Where the hyphae are septate, the resulting compartments usually are multinucleate.

The terms heterothallism and homothallism were first used by the geneticist Blakeslee in his work with zygomycetous fungi. The heterothallic species produce two morphologically indistinguishable types of thalli. These thalli, designated as + and −, reproduce only by asexual means when grown separately. However, if two such thalli are grown together, they produce gametangia on special branches of the aerial hyphae. The + and − gametangia fuse, forming a large multinucleate cell, the coenozygote, that is transformed into a thick-walled spore, the zygospore. Sexual reproduction in homothallic species occurs in a similar manner, but the fusing gametangia are produced on branches of a single thallus. Thus, in homothallic forms, the thalli are all of a single type.

The species of *Mucor,* common in soil and dung, produce an extensive mycelium, much of which is embedded in the substratum. Short segments of the hyphae sometimes become delimited by cross walls and may be transformed into thick-walled chlamydospores (Fig. 7–9A). These nondeciduous spores commonly are intercalary; they can germinate to form a new mycelium after death of the parent hypha.

Sporangiophores of *Mucor* generally grow toward light; in other words, they exhibit positive phototropism. At the apex of the sporangiophore, a sporangium forms and becomes separated from the sporangiophore by a bulbous septum, the columella. Within the sporangium, the protoplast divides into numerous one-to-few nucleate segments. A wall is formed around each segment, transforming it into a spore.

When the sporangium is mature, the spores are released through deliquescence of the sporangial wall in *Mucor mucedo* (Fig. 7–9) and related species.

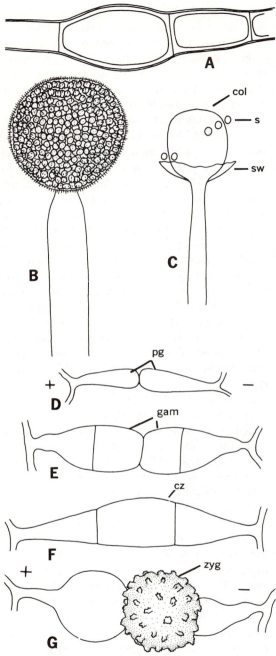

FIGURE 7–9 A, chlamydospores in hypha of *Mucor*, ×2,250; B, portion of sporangiophore bearing mature sporangium, ×835; C, sporangium after escape of spores; ×900 (*col*, columella; *s*, spore; *sw*, collar-like remnant of sporangial wall); D–G, sexual reproduction between + and − thalli, ×205 (*cz*, coenozygote; *gam*, gametangia; *pg*, progametangia; *zyg*, zygospore).

Mucor mucedo is a heterothallic species. When aerial hyphae of + and − strains approach one another, special reproductive branches are formed (Fig. 7–9D–G). The tips of these reproductive branches meet end to end and are called progametangia. A wall forms in each of the hyphae, and multinucleate gametangia are delimited. The end walls of gametangia in contact dissolve, and the two protoplasts become confluent. Within this cell, or coenozygote, pairs of + and − nuclei undergo karyogamy, then meiosis. A thick wall develops around the coenozygote, transforming it into a resistant zygospore. Germination of the zygospore typically results in the formation of a short sporangiophore and sporangium containing haploid spores.

Rhizopus stolonifer (Fig. 7–10), commonly called black bread mold, is similar to species of *Mucor* in most respects. It produces aerial hyphae that function similarly to the stolons of strawberries. These hyphae, also called stolons, grow from place to place over the substrate. At points of contact with the substrate, root-like rhizoidal systems are formed and, above the rhizoids, clusters of sporangiophores develop. The mature sporangial wall ruptures, exposing the dry, wind-dispersed spores.

Sexual reproduction in the heterothallic *R. stolonifer* is similar to that described in *Mucor mucedo*.

R. stolonifer frequently attacks stored fruits, especially the more succulent types such as peaches and strawberries. As with many other Mucorales, the growth of this species is rapid, and serious economic losses can occur.

The sporangia produced by germinating zygospores of heterothallic Mucorales contain all + spores, all − spores, or both types in some species. If a single type is present, the second presumably is lost through degeneration of nuclei following meiosis. Upon germinating, the spores give rise to new + or − mycelia.

The species of *Rhizopus* and *Mucor* just described have gametangia that are morphologically alike, i.e., members of a fusing pair are identical although produced by genetically distinct thalli. In *Zygorrhynchus moelleri*, on

NONVASCULAR PLANTS

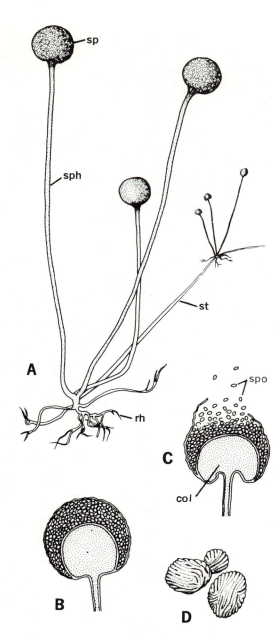

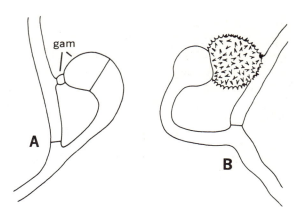

FIGURE 7–11 Conjugation in *Zygorrhynchus moelleri,* a homothallic species. A, early stage, ×520; note unequal size of gametangia (*gam*) and origin of these from single branch. B, mature zygospore, ×520.

one is invariably larger than its mate. The zygospores of *Zygorrhynchus* are like those of *Rhizopus* and *Mucor* in appearance and in function. In homothallic species of Mucorales, such as *Z. moelleri,* sexual reproduction regularly accompanies sporangiospore formation. In contrast to this, sexual reproduction of the heterothallic species appears to be relatively rare in nature.

The species of *Pilobolus* (Fig. 7–12) grow on the dung of herbivorous animals. Here the sporangium remains intact at maturity, and it is shot as a unit from the tip of the sporangiophore. As the sporangium matures, pressure is built up in the sporangiophore until a weakened zone at the sporangial base gives way. When this happens, a jet of liquid is emitted from the sporangiophore tip, and this jet carries the intact sporangium as far as 20 centimeters. The sporangium has a cutinized, waterproof layer on its upper surface and a mucilaginous hydrophylic zone at its base. If it and the accompanying liquid strike a nearby object, such as a plant, the sporangium bobs to the surface of the liquid, because of the waterproof layer. As the liquid dries, the sporangium becomes glued to the surface by the mucilaginous layer. If an herbivore then eats the plant, the sporangiospores pass unharmed through the digestive tract and germinate fol-

FIGURE 7–10 *Rhizopus.* A, habit sketch, ×50 (*rh,* rhizoids; *sp,* sporangium; *sph,* sporangiophore; *st,* stolon); B, C, sectional view of mature and ruptured sporangia, ×110 (*col,* columella; *spo,* sporangiospores); D, sporangiospores, ×1,000.

the other hand, distinctive gametangia (Fig. 7–11) are formed. Both gametangia arise from a single hypha in this homothallic species, but

DIVISION EUMYCOTA

lowing excretion. In *Pilobolus,* the sporangia typically develop over 24-hour cycles. Mature sporangia are shot from their sporangiophores in midmorning, and a new crop of sporangiophores and sporangia then starts to develop. This cyclic pattern is regulated by an internal "clock" and is referred to as a circadian rhythm.

Coemansia (Fig. 7–13) and certain other Mucorales produce one-spored sporangia. The wall of the single spore and that of the surrounding sporangium are more or less fused. However, the double nature of the wall is apparent at spore germination. Other Mucorales produce sporangia intermediate between those of *Coemansia* and the multispored sporangial types, such as *Mucor* and *Rhizopus.* Some biologists feel that the transition shown, from many spores to few spores to one spore, reflects an evolutionary trend toward reduction of the sporangium. According to this concept, the asexual spores called conidia may have evolved through reduction of sporangia to one-spored structures as seen in *Coemansia.*

Other Zygomycetes. Many of the remaining zygomycetes are associated in some way with animals. The species of *Entomophthora,* for example, are insect parasites. *E. muscae* (Fig. 7–14) infects the common housefly, growing within the body and assimilating the proteinaceous material there. The hyphae then grow out between the segments of the host exoskeleton and sporulation takes place. The spores, considered to be reduced sporangia, are

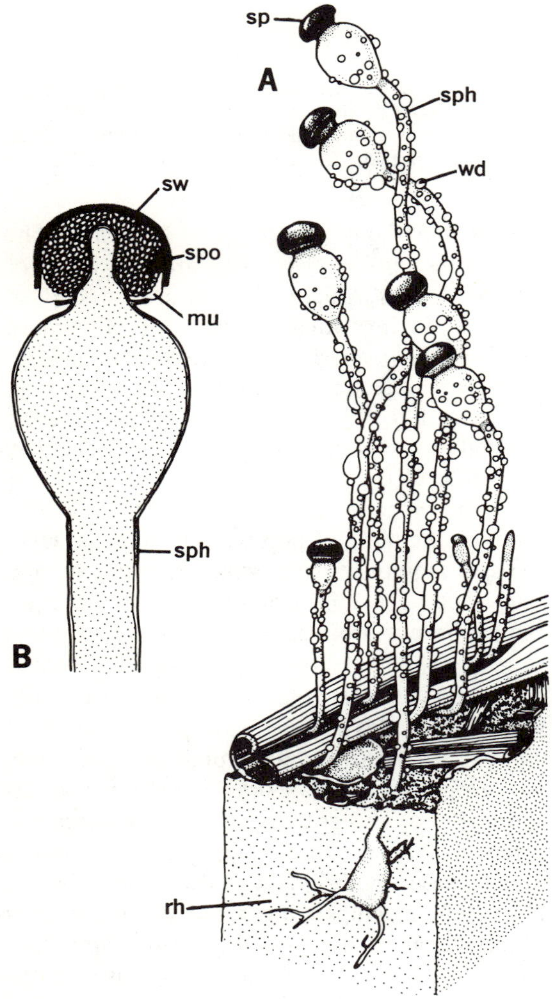

FIGURE 7–12 *Pilobolus.* A, habit sketch of sporangiophores and sporangia on excrement, ×15 (*rh,* rhizoid; *sp,* sporangium; *sph,* sporangiophore; *wd,* secreted water droplets); B, detail of sporangiophore and sporangium, ×70 (*mu,* mucilaginous zone; *spo,* sporangiospores; *sw,* sporangial wall).

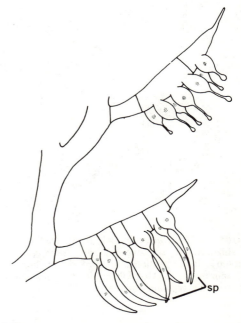

FIGURE 7–13 Portion of sporangiophore of *Coemansia* with two sporangium-bearing branches, ×1,575 (the lower branch bears a number of one-spored sporangia, *sp*).

84

shot from their sporangiophores at maturity. Infected flies often are found adhering to windows or walls and are surrounded by a whitish halo of spores. Sexual reproduction is unknown in *E. muscae*. However, conjugation similar to that of the Mucorales is characteristic of some species of *Entomophthora*.

Relationships of the Phycomycetes

The class Phycomycetes often is divided into several classes, e.g., Chytridiomycetes, Oomycetes, Zygomycetes, etc. This division reflects the current emphasis on flagellar structure and arrangement in determining relationships of fungi. According to this viewpoint, each group with distinctive flagellar structure and arrangement represents a separate evolutionary line. The morphological similarities observed between such groups are attributed to parallel evolution from distinct ancestral forms. The logical endpoint for dividing the phycomycetes in this manner might be to treat each such group as a separate division. However, although some phycomycetous fungi have been studied intensively, most of the species have not. Much more factual information is needed on the nature of the motile cells and the biochemistry of cell walls and other structures; even simple descriptive studies of structure and reproduction would be helpful.

One viewpoint, prevalent in the past and still held by some, is that the Phycomycetes arose from one or more groups of filamentous algae. The basis for this concept lies in the similarity in form and in reproduction found in certain members of the two groups. For example, the thalli of both *Vaucheria* (a yellow-green alga; see Chapter 10) and *Saprolegnia* are coenocytic and tubular; their sexual structures also resemble one another. The motile gametes of *Vaucheria* are kidney-shaped and laterally biflagellate, as are the secondary zoospores of *Saprolegnia*. An evolutionary link between *Vaucheria* and the Oomycetidae therefore appears to be possible. However, with this possible exception, the evidence now available does not indicate a close relationship between

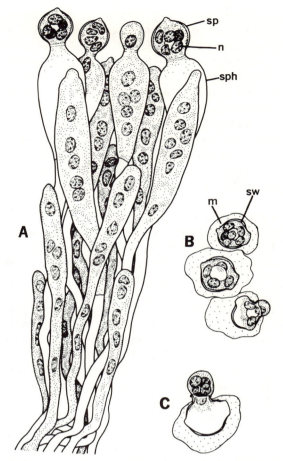

FIGURE 7–14 *Entomophthora*. A, cluster of sporangiophores with developing sporangia, ×700 (*n*, nuclei; *sp*, sporangium; *sph*, sporangiophore); B, three mature sporangia that have been fired from sporangiophores, ×700 (*m*, mucilaginous layer; *sw*, sporangial wall); C, germinating sporangium, ×700.

most of the phycomycetes and the algae. Many mycologists believe that the phycomycetes arose from protozoa-like ancestors. Amoeboid organisms reproducing by flagellated motile cells, and others have been suggested as the ancestral types from which the phycomycetes evolved.

CLASS ASCOMYCETES

The "sac" fungi or ascomycetes are a large and extremely varied group in which sexual reproduction involves the formation of a sac

85

or ascus containing ascospores. The ascus, which may or may not be preceded by development of recognizable male and female gametangia, is the site of both karyogamy and meiosis. The asci are produced within complex fruiting bodies or ascocarps in the majority of ascomycetes.

Both filamentous and unicellular ascomycetes are known, but the number of the latter type is relatively small. The filamentous types typically reproduce by one or more kinds of asexually produced spores called conidia. Most of the unicellular ascomycetes reproduce asexually by budding.

The ascomycetes are primarily terrestrial, but some species occur in fresh-water and marine habitats. The saprobic species grow on many substrates, including leaves, wood, keratinic materials such as feathers and hair, or dung, soil, and foods. Some species are parasites of plants and animals, including man, and many others occur in the symbiotic associations known as lichens (see p. 125).

The class Ascomycetes contains two distinctive subclasses, the Hemiascomycetidae and the Euascomycetidae. The hemiascomycetes, including yeasts and related fungi, do not produce ascocarps. Their asci are formed singly and scattered on the hyphae; or, if hyphae are lacking, they are formed by the direct transformation of assimilative cells. Asexual reproduction is primarily by budding in this group. In contrast, the euascomycetes produce their asci in groups within ascocarps. Ascus production is preceded by gametangial formation and by the development of specialized ascus-forming hyphae. All of the Euascomycetidae are filamentous and they reproduce asexually by conidia.

Subclass Hemiascomycetidae

Many hemiascomycetes occur in water, soil, on fruits, and in exudates from injured plants. Others exist either as parasites or as mutualistic symbionts in association with plants or animals.

Order Ascoideales. The fungi included in this order usually are associated with plants, often occurring in exudates from injured trees. In some instances, they also are associated with insects upon which their dispersal may depend.

The Ascoideales have septate hyphae, the cells of which may be either uninucleate or multinucleate. In *Dipodascus uninucleatus* (Fig. 7–15), the hyphal compartments are uninucleate. Sexual reproduction in this species occurs through conjugation, i.e., fusion of two adjacent cells in a hypha. Plasmogamy is followed by karyogamy within the resulting cell. This cell then enlarges, forming an elongate ascus within which meiosis is followed by a number of mitotic divisions. Each of the numerous nuclei becomes surrounded by a cell wall and is transformed into an ascospore. The ascospores are released through a rupture in the ascus tip, and they germinate by the formation of germ tubes.

Order Endomycetales. The ascospore-forming yeasts and related filamentous fungi are placed in the order Endomycetales. The yeasts do not typically produce hyphae, but short filaments are sometimes formed in old cultures or under certain cultural conditions. The cell walls of yeasts are composed of mannans, proteins, and other substances, including traces of chitin.

Saccharomyces cerevisiae, called baker's or brewer's yeast, might be considered one of the most important of domesticated organisms. In addition to its use in the baking and brewing industries, vitamin D, ephedrine, enzymes, and other substances are obtained from this species. Much effort is expended in isolating and developing suitable strains for each industrial process.

Asexual reproduction in *S. cerevisiae,* as in most yeasts, is by budding (Fig. 7–16A). In this process, a small protuberance forms, expands, and usually separates from the mother cell. The nucleus undergoes division during bud formation, and one daughter nucleus migrates into the developing bud. The nature of the nuclear division still is uncertain; the nuclear membrane apparently persists through the di-

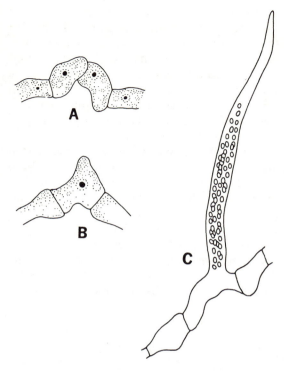

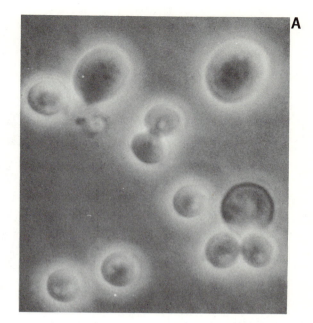

FIGURE 7–15 *Dipodascus.* A, B, conjugation; C, mature ascus containing ascospores. A, ×2,080; B, C, ×1,500.

viding process, and individual chromosomes are not visible.

S. cerevisiae is heterothallic, the two mating strains being referred to as *α* and *a* (or + and −) types. Fusion of two haploid cells (plasmogamy) is soon followed by karyogamy, but budding of the diploid zygote occurs and may continue indefinitely. Under certain conditions, a single diploid cell can function as an ascus; meiosis occurs and four ascospores develop (Fig. 7–16B). No special dehiscence mechanism is present, and the spores are eventually released by breakdown of the ascus wall. Buds are again produced when the ascospores germinate.

The cell form of budding yeasts, as well as details of the budding process, vary from species to species. However, the internal structure is essentially the same within cells of different species; that seen in the electron micrograph of *Hansenula* (Fig. 7–17) is typical.

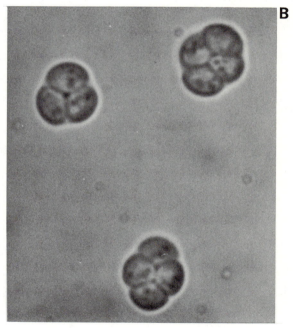

FIGURE 7–16 *Saccharomyces.* A, budding cells, ×2,000; B, asci and ascospores, ×2,300.

The haploid and diploid budding stages found in *S. cerevisiae* do not occur in all other yeasts. In some, conjugation occurs upon germination of the ascospores while they are still in the ascus. The diploid budding stage which follows is the only assimilative phase in the life histories of such yeasts. Cells of *Schizosaccharomyces* (Fig. 7–18) conjugate immediately before ascus formation, and the diploid phase is limited to the zygote. The yeasts in this genus are referred to as fission yeasts; the cells undergo fission, and budding does not occur.

Order Taphrinales. A single genus, *Taphrina,* is placed in the order Taphrinales; all species are plant parasites. *T. deformans,* causing peach leaf curl, is one of the common species (Fig. 7–19). The hyphae of *T. deformans* penetrate between cells of the host leaves, twigs, and other parts. Their presence typically induces abnormal growth of the host tissues. Some of the hyphae grow out between epidermal cells of the host and form asci on the surfaces of the leaves or other infected organs.

In ascus formation, karyogamy first occurs in the terminal cell of a hypha. A mitotic division follows, and the cell divides into two by a transverse wall. The outermost cell then functions as an ascus, its nucleus undergoing meiosis and mitosis. Eight ascospores are formed in each ascus, but because of budding, the asci often appear polysporous. Budding is the typical method of germination of *Taphrina* ascospores and budding colonies can be maintained indefinitely in culture. Conjugation has been observed in very few instances; it occurs by the formation of short tubes between two compatible cells. A septate mycelium then develops, each cell containing a pair of compatible nuclei. This dikaryotic condition is maintained until asci are produced. The mycelial phase apparently occurs only on or in the host; it has not been observed in culture.

Subclass Euascomycetidae

The euascomycetes produce their asci in complex ascocarps. All are mycelial and occur in both aquatic and terrestrial habitats. Parasitic Euascomycetidae infect many types of plants and animals; the saprobic species occur on wood, dung, soil, and other materials.

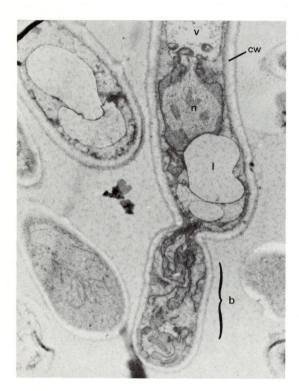

FIGURE 7–17 *Hansenula.* Electron micrograph of thin section through budding cell, × 10,000 (*b,* bud; *cw,* cell wall; *l,* lipid; *n,* nucleus; *v,* vacuole).

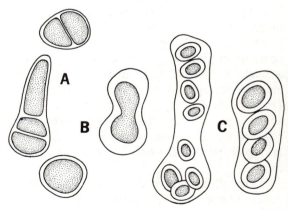

FIGURE 7–18 *Schizosaccharomyces.* A, three assimilative cells, two of which have undergone fission, × 2,300; B, conjugation of two cells, × 2,300; C, two mature asci with ascospores, × 2,300.

Assimilative Stage. Hyphae of euascomycetes are regularly septate with hyphal compartments that contain one or more nuclei. The septa have a small central pore, and the cytoplasm is thus continuous from cell to cell (Fig. 7–20). Nuclei and other organelles are sometimes carried from cell to cell by cytoplasmic streaming. The hyphal walls contain chitin in all species that have been examined.

Hyphae developing from a uninucleate spore generally contain nuclei of a single genetic type. In contrast, genetically different nuclei of several types can occur in a single thallus. This condition, heterokaryosis, is common in the hyphae of many higher fungi (Ascomycetes, Basidiomycetes, and Fungi Imperfecti. Heterokaryotic mycelia can arise in several ways, the commonest being fusion of hyphae that have developed from different spores. In a heterokaryotic mycelium, the different nuclei exist side by side in a common cytoplasm; each nuclear type increases by mitoses, and each type exerts its influence on the developing mycelium.

Asexual Reproduction. Asexual reproduction, common among the euascomycetes, typically occurs through formation of conidia. Conidia are essentially separable portions of hyphae or of specialized hyphal branches called conidiophores (Fig. 7–21A, B). Some conidia develop through hyphal fragmentation; others are budded off from the tips of conidiophores. The conidiophores of some euascomycetes are formed within flask-shaped structures called pycnidia (Fig. 7–21C) or in discoid structures called acervuli (Fig. 7–21D).

Conidial stages constitute a repeating or reinfecting stage in many parasitic ascomycetes, e.g., *Venturia inaequalis* and *Monilinia fructicola*. Conidia are produced in large numbers during the growing season of the host, and they infect new host plants. The sexual stage in many such species matures in the spring and initiates infection. The asexual stages often are those most commonly encountered in saprobic species.

Sexual Reproduction. The number of euascomycetes in which sexual reproduction has been thoroughly studied is relatively small.

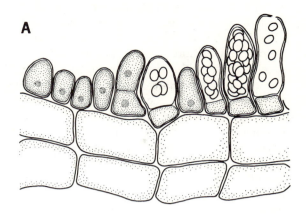

A

B

FIGURE 7–19 *Taphrina.* A, section through infected peach leaf showing asci in various stages of development, ×895; B, peach leaves infected by *Taphrina,* ×0.70 (note characteristic curling and distortion of leaf).

Typically, both male and female gametangia are formed on a single thallus. Such a thallus is designated as hermaphroditic and self-fertile if it can reproduce sexually by itself. Alternatively, in hermaphroditic and self-sterile species, cross fertilization by a genetically distinct but morphologically similar thallus is required.

89

The female gametangium, or ascogonium, is often somewhat larger than the antheridium (Fig. 7–22A). A tubular appendage, the trichogyne, may be present on the ascogonia. In species with antheridia, plasmogamy occurs through fusion of the antheridium with the ascogonium or with the trichogyne. Following plasmogamy, one or more nuclei are transferred from the antheridium through the trichogyne to the ascogonium. Compatible pairs of nuclei become associated within the ascogonium, but karyogamy does not occur. The pairs of compatible nuclei, called dikaryons, may undergo a series of mitotic divisions in which the two members of a pair divide side by side. The dikaryons move into hyphae, called ascogenous hyphae, that develop from the surface of the ascogonium (Fig. 7–22C). The ascogenous hyphae continue to grow, cross walls are deposited within them, and the compartments so formed are binucleate.

In species lacking antheridia but having cross fertilization, nuclear transfer may be brought about by spermatia. Spermatia are minute spore-like bodies; they are formed on specialized hyphal branches which grow either singly or in groups within pycnidium-like structures. Spermatia may be dispersed by insects, water, or air currents. When a spermatium comes in contact with a trichogyne, plasmogamy occurs and the spermatium nucleus migrates into the ascogonium. This process is followed by development similar to that in which antheridia are present.

As new cells are formed at the tips of ascogenous hyphae, crozier formation often takes place (Fig. 7–23A–D). The tip of an ascogenous hypha grows back upon itself, forming a broad crook. Following mitosis, two daughter nuclei lie in the curve, a third is near the hyphal tip, and the fourth is toward the base. Septa are then formed along each of the equatorial zones of the dividing nuclei, resulting in two uninucleate cells and one binucleate cell. Growth of the tip cell continues until it soon fuses with the basal cell. Crozier formation produces two daughter cells or compartments, each containing a pair of compatible nuclei.

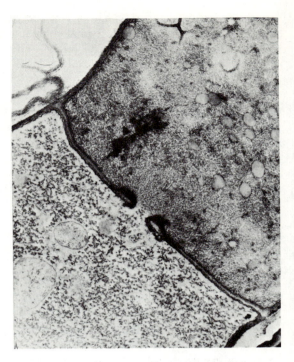

FIGURE 7–20 Ascomycete hypha and septum with central pore, ×12,000. (Photograph courtesy of G. C. Hughes and A. A. Bisalputra.)

Eventually, terminal cells of ascogenous hyphae function as ascus mother cells, developing into asci (Fig. 7–23E–I).

The Ascus. Within the ascus mother cell, the two haploid nuclei unite, the ascus mother cell enlarges, and meiosis occurs. Mitotic division usually follows meiosis and results in an eight-nucleate ascus. Cell walls are then formed around the nuclei, enclosing cytoplasm and other organelles as well, and the cells thus produced are ascospores.

The characteristics of asci are considered basic in determining relationships within this very large group of fungi (Fig. 7–24). In the majority of the Euascomycetidae, the asci appear to have a single wall, but in some forms the ascus wall obviously is two-layered. The asci open either by a minute lid or by a pore or irregular opening that develops at spore discharge. The ascospores are shot from the ascus in the majority of euascomycetes, but in some

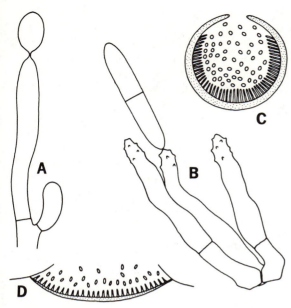

FIGURE 7–21 Asexual reproduction in the Euas-comycetidae. A, B, conidiophores and conidia; A, ×1,500; B, ×2,750. C, D, diagrams of pycnidium (C) and acervulus (D) containing numerous conidio-phores and conidia.

groups they are released through deliquescence or dissolving of the ascus.

Ascocarp Development. Ascocarp de-velopment typically commences a short time after plasmogamy. The ascocarp is formed from hyphae that grow up from hyphae bearing the antheridia and ascogonia. In the mature asco-carp, the individual hyphal elements often re-main identifiable. Alternatively, the hyphae lose their individuality, and the structure is then parenchyma-like (Fig. 7–25). The commonly encountered types of ascocarps (Fig. 7–26) are: (1) cleistothecia, (2) perithecia, (3) apothecia, and (4) variously shaped asco-stromata. The relative positions of ascogonia and antheridia within these ascocarp types also

FIGURE 7–22 A–C, sexual structures and plasmog-amy. A, ascogonium (*ascog*) with trichogyne (*tri*) and antheridium (*anth*); B, nuclei migrating from antheridium through trichogyne to ascogonium; C, pairs of nuclei, or dikaryons, moving into developing ascogenous hypha (*ah*).

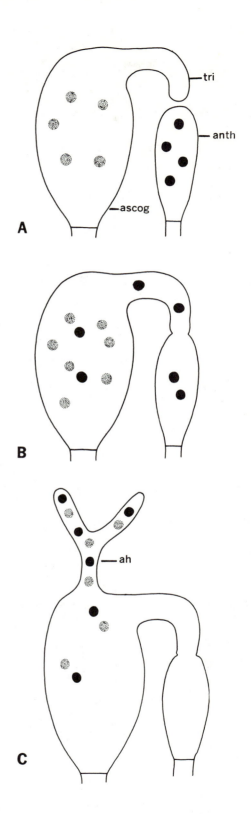

DIVISION EUMYCOTA

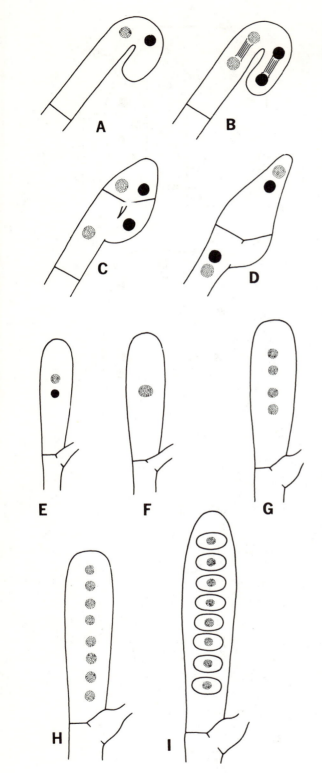

are indicated in Figure 7–26. Cleistothecia may have walls that either are formed of interwoven hyphae or are parenchyma-like. Within the cleistothecial wall, the ascogenous hyphae and asci are scattered at varying levels. Perithecia have parenchyma-like walls, and their asci usually occur in a basal tuft. Sterile hyphae, called paraphyses, frequently protrude up among the asci, and similar but shorter structures may line the ostiole. The apothecium has its asci in an exposed layer, the hymenium. Apothecia are commonly dish- or cup-shaped; they are stipitate in some species. The hymenium of some stipitate types is formed on a club-shaped structure, and in others it is borne on a saddle-shaped or convoluted structure clearly distinguished from the stipe. In the latter groups, the fertile upper portion of the ascocarp is referred to as the pileus.

A stroma is a variously shaped mass of fungus cells, or of fungus cells together with substrate materials. Typically it is formed of parenchyma-like fungal "tissue," and it is often rather dense. An ascostroma is a stroma in which ascus-containing chambers develop. These chambers, or locules, which often appear after stromatic development, are wall-less cavities.

Some nonascostromatic ascomycetes form perithecia that are embedded in, or superficial on, stromata. Others produce their ascocarps on stroma-like structures called sclerotia. Typically sclerotia are of definite and regular form, and function in most cases as overwintering structures.

Life History. Although there is a large amount of variation in structure and form in the euascomycetes, the life histories of these fungi often follow a similar pattern (Fig. 7–27). Those that produce conidia do not have an

FIGURE 7–23 A–D, crozier formation. A, hook with dikaryon; B, nuclear division; C, fusion of tip with hypha and septum formation; D, two dikaryotic cells with renewed growth of tip cell. E–I, ascus development. A, dikaryotic ascus mother cell; B, karyogamy; C, D, meiosis followed by mitosis, resulting in eight-nucleate ascus; I, each nucleus is surrounded by a wall to form ascospores.

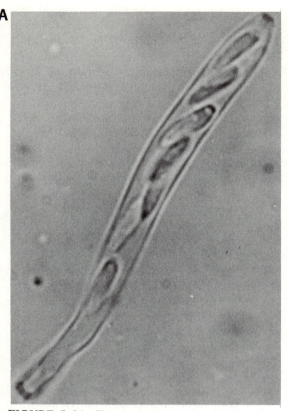

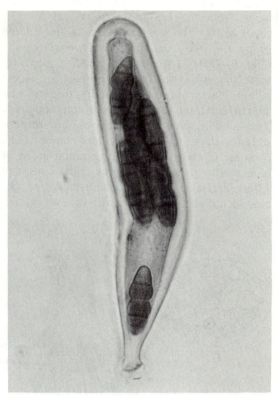

B

FIGURE 7–24   Two types of asci. A, single-walled ascus, with ascospore release through a terminal pore (pore area stained with iodine), ×1,000; B, double-walled ascus, ×2,000.

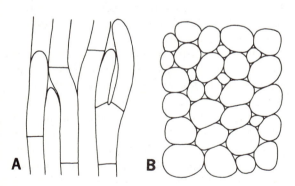

A   B

FIGURE 7–25   Cell form in ascocarps. A, hyphal; B, parenchyma-like.

obligate alternation of sexual and asexual phases. Instead, the two types of reproduction may occur simultaneously on a single thallus; or, more commonly, conidia are produced on a young thallus, which later produces ascocarps.

The subclass Euascomycetidae constitutes the largest group of true fungi. For the most part, the euascomycetes are poorly known, although some species have received intensive study. The orders discussed in the following pages represent the variety in ascocarp form and in ascomycete life histories.

Order Eurotiales. The Eurotiales includes a number of the most intensively studied fungi. Certain species produce antibiotics, organic acids, and other substances of great value. Others are responsible for destruction or deterioration of a variety of materials, e.g., stored foods, leather goods, and fine lenses. A few are implicated in human disease and in diseases of other mammals and birds.

The imperfect phase, or conidial state, of these fungi is the most commonly encountered. The conidiophores of *Talaromyces* are of the

Penicillium type (Fig. 7–28A) and derive their name from the Latin *penicillum,* meaning a small brush. The conidiophores of the related genus *Eurotium* are of the *Aspergillus* type (Fig. 7–28B), so named because of their resemblance to a holy-water sprinkler or aspergillum. Numerous minute conidia, dispersed by air currents, are formed on the conidiophores. The conidia, produced in chains, are responsible for the green or blue colors characteristic of many of the species. The common green or blue molds growing on citrus fruit, jams and jellies, bread, and other foods usually are species identifiable as *Aspergillus* or *Penicillium.*

Ascogonia and antheridia develop on separate hyphal branches of a single mycelium in *Talaromyces vermiculatis* (Fig. 7–29A–D). Hyphae grow up around the sexual structures, forming a cleistothecium with walls of interwoven hyphae. Ascogenous hyphae bear numerous asci within the wall, and the asci dissolve at maturity of the ascospores. The ascospores are eventually released by irregular dehiscence of the cleistothecial wall.

The ascocarps of *Eurotium* (Fig. 7–29E) develop as in *Talaromyces.* Here, however, the walls are composed of parenchyma-like cells.

Order Erysiphales. The "powdery mildews" are obligate parasites that infect many flowering plants. For the most part, these fungi cause little visible damage to infected plants. However, some species are extremely destructive if conditions are favorable for their spread and development. The mycelium of powdery mildews grows on the surfaces of leaves, twigs, and fruits of the host, producing haustorial branches (Fig. 7–30A) that penetrate the host epidermal cells or the cells adjacent to the epidermis.

Masses of conidia (Fig. 7–30B) impart a powdery white appearance to host surfaces infected by erysiphaceous fungi. These conidia, borne in chains on simple erect conidiophores, are wind-dispersed and bring about further infection of the host.

The ascocarps of powdery mildews also develop on the infected host surfaces; they appear late in the growing season of the host. These ascocarps are like perithecia in their development, but they lack an ostiole. The mature ascocarps have brown parenchyma-like walls that bear a series of radiating appendages (Fig. 7–31). The appendage tips are unbranched and hypha-like in *Erysiphe;* in other genera they are dichotomously branched, hooked, or coiled. This feature and the number of asci in the cleistothecium can be used to identify most genera of the powdery mildews. In certain genera, each ascocarp contains a single ascus, whereas in others, several asci are present.

The ascocarps of powdery mildews remain on fallen leaves and other plant parts over win-

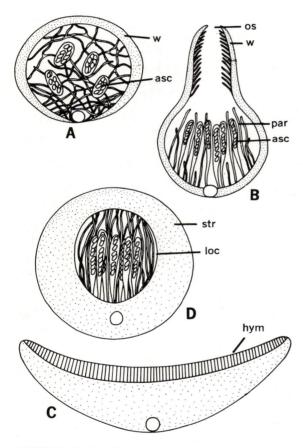

FIGURE 7–26 Common types of ascocarps. A, cleistothecium (*asc,* ascus; *w,* wall); B, perithecium (*asc,* ascus; *os,* ostiole; *par,* paraphyses; *w,* wall); C, apothecium (*hym,* hymenium); D, ascostroma (*loc,* locule; *str,* stroma). Note: clear circles indicate approximate positions of ascogonia and antheridia.

94

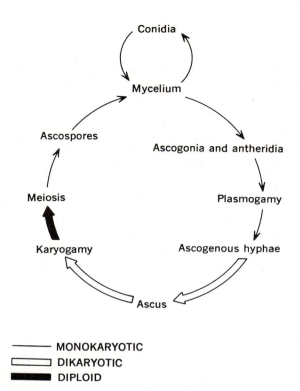

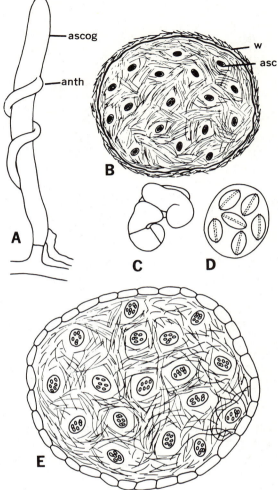

FIGURE 7–27   Typical euascomycetous life history.

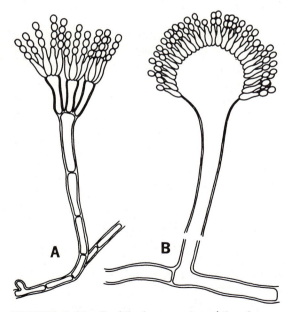

FIGURE 7–28   Conidiophores and conidia of euro-tiaceous fungi. A, *Penicillium,* ×1,250; B, *Aspergillus,* ×1,000.

95

FIGURE 7–29   A–D, *Talaromyces.* A, ascogonium and antheridium, ×2,000 (*anth,* antheridium; *ascog,* ascogonium); B, semidiagrammatic drawing of section through cleistothecium, ×1,000 (*asc,* ascus; *w,* wall); C, portion of ascogenous hypha with developing croziers, ×2,665; D, ascus and ascospores, ×3,000. E, section through cleistothecium of *Eurotium* showing parenchyma-like wall layer, ×1,220.

ter. In the spring, the ascocarp absorbs water, swells, and bursts, scattering the asci. The asci then burst and scatter the ascospores, which initiate infection of the hosts.

Order Xylariales.   Members of the Xylariales produce perithecia that have dark-colored, parenchyma-like walls. The perithecia of

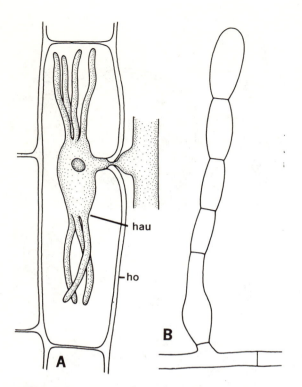

FIGURE 7–30 *Erysiphe.* A, haustorium in epidermal cell of host, ×1,500 (*hau*, haustorium; *ho*, host); B, aerial conidiophore and chain of developing conidia, ×1,000.

some species are embedded in the substratum or in a stroma.

Sordaria fimicola (Fig. 7–32) occurs on the dung of various animals and in the soil. This species reproduces only by ascospores; no asexual spores are formed. Ascogonia have been observed by several investigators, but there are conflicting reports concerning the antheridia. Within the perithecium, the asci and paraphyses form a basal tuft. The perithecium has a short beak-like extension or neck, the growth of which responds positively toward light. At maturity, a single ascus elongates until its apex extends a short distance through the ostiole. The ascospores are then shot from the ascus; the ascus collapses and retracts back into the perithecium. The process is repeated as other asci mature. The ascus tip, like the perithecial neck, shows a positive phototropic response.

Thalli of *S. fimicola* are self-fertile, and ascocarps are produced on a mycelium arising from a single ascospore. However, hyphal fusions will occur between two strains, with a subsequent transfer of nuclei from one to the other. Ascospores bearing characteristics of both parental strains may later appear in a single ascus. Thus, both cross fertilization and self-fertilization can occur in this species.

Neurospora, a genus closely related to *Sordaria,* has been utilized in numerous genetic studies. Much of our knowledge concerning biochemical aspects of genetics has been derived from studies of *N. crassa* and *N. sitophila.* In these hermaphroditic self-sterile forms, ascogonia with trichogynes develop in perithecial initials. Completion of development of the perithecial initials is dependent upon the transfer of compatible nuclei from spermatia or conidia. Both conidia and spermatia can either function as spermatizing agents or germinate to form new mycelia. Perithecia of *Neurospora* are similar to those of *Sordaria. N. sitophila,* sometimes called red bread mold, is often a nuisance in bakeries; once established, it is difficult to eradicate because of the numerous conidia formed.

In the species of *Xylaria* (Fig. 7–33A–D), large-stalked stromata are formed. During early development of the stroma, a layer of conidiophores and conidia is present on the stromatic surface. Mature stromata of *Xylaria* often have a hard black rind; the perithecia are embedded under this surface layer.

Order Hypocreales. Claviceps purpurea (Fig. 7–34), commonly called ergot, is a parasite of rye and other grasses. It infects the ovaries of these plants, the mycelium bearing numerous minute conidia. The conidia are exuded in a sticky liquid or "honey dew," which apparently attracts insects to the spore mass. Dispersal of the conidia is by insects or by the splashing of raindrops, and these spores infect adjacent plants.

The hyphae of *Claviceps* continue to grow within the host and form a hard purplish sclerotium. At maturity, the sclerotium has the form

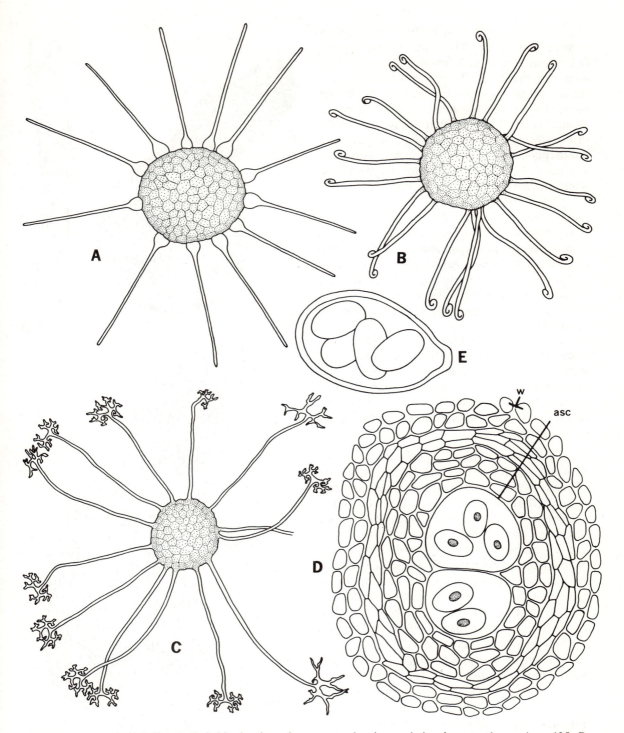

FIGURE 7–31 Erysiphales. A–C, habit sketches of ascocarps showing variation in appendages; A, ×125; B, ×400; C, ×200. D, E, *Erysiphe*. D, transverse section through ascocarp, ×940 (*asc,* ascus; *w,* wall); E, mature ascus and spores, ×200.

DIVISION EUMYCOTA

of a grain produced by a healthy ovary, but it is somewhat larger. The sclerotia or "ergots" fall to the ground and function there as overwintering structures. They retain their viability for several years, eventually germinating by the formation of one or more stalked stromata. Perithecia are formed within the swollen apices of the stromata. The thread-like ascospores are multiseptate and may fragment into numerous segments; they are released from the perithecia while susceptible hosts are in flower.

"St. Anthony's Fire," a serious type of intoxication caused by ergot, was once relatively common in humans. It usually resulted from eating rye flour contaminated by ergot and often was fatal. Cattle eating infected grain also are poisoned. Several important drugs are now extracted from ergots; the most valuable of these is used in controlling hemorrhage during childbirth.

Species of *Cordyceps* (Fig. 7–35) produce stalked stromata similar in structure to those of *Claviceps*. The brightly colored stromata, reaching a height of more than one foot in some species, arise from mummified bodies of insects or spiders, or from parasitized ascocarps of other fungi.

Order Pleosporales. In *Pleospora*, species of which are found on dead herbaceous stems of many types, small one-chambered ascostromata are formed (Fig. 7–36A–D). The asci of *Pleospora* and its relatives have walls that are distinctly two-layered. The brownish multiseptate ascospores are released through an ostiole-like opening that forms in the stroma. At ascospore release, the outer ascus wall ruptures and the inner layer becomes greatly distended. The ascospores are then shot out through an opening that develops in the apex of the inner ascus wall.

Venturia inaequalis (Fig. 7–36E, F), which causes a disease called apple scab, is

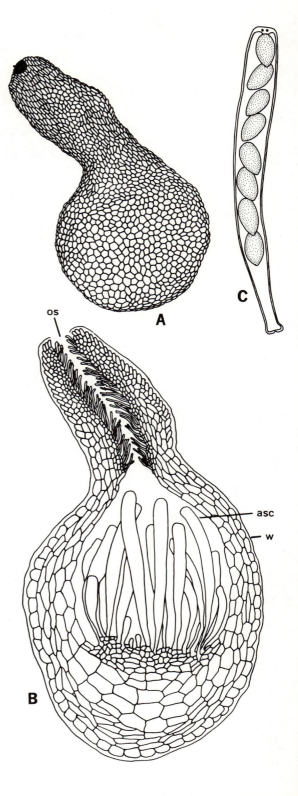

FIGURE 7–32 *Sordaria*. A, habit sketch of perithecium, × 190; B, section through mature perithecium, × 575 (*asc,* ascus; *os,* ostiole; *w,* perithecial wall); C, mature ascus with ascospores, × 560.

98

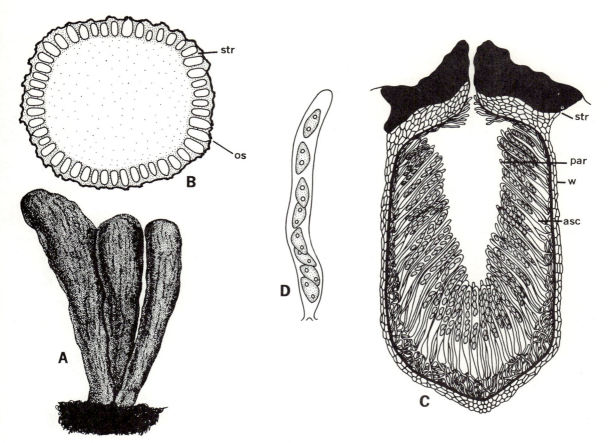

FIGURE 7–33 *Xylaria*. A, habit sketch of stromata, ×1; B, cross section through stroma showing embedded perithecia, ×4 (*os*, ostiole; *str*, stroma); C, section through single perithecium, ×150 (*asc*, ascus; *par*, paraphyses; *str*, stroma; *w*, perithecial wall); D, mature ascus and spores, ×600.

similar to *Pleospora* in most respects. Here the conidial stage is produced on the leaves and fruits of the host. Hyphae eventually penetrate into deeper tissues of infected structures and form there the sexual phase of this species. Ascostromata develop in the fall and spring, releasing ascospores early in the growing season of the host.

Order Helotiales. The Helotiales are mainly saprobic, but some species are important plant parasites. The asci of helotiaceous fungi open by a pore or irregular tear.

Most of the Helotiales produce small apothecia, those of *Calycella* (Fig. 7–37) usually reaching only 2–3 mm in diameter. The stipitate apothecia of *Calycella* and related species are formed of hyphae that retain their identity, i.e., they do not form parenchyma-like "tissue." The fertile zone, or hymenium, consists of asci and paraphyses.

Species of *Monilinia* are responsible for "brown rot" of various stone fruits. *M. fructicola* (Fig. 7–38) infects fruits and other plant parts, producing abundant conidia. Infected fruits rot and eventually are transformed into shriveled "mummies." The mummies, containing mycelia of the fungus, function as sclerotia and give rise to numerous stalked apothecia upon germinating. As with sclerotia, the mummies are overwintering structures and germinate early in the growing season of the host. The apothecia of *Monilinia* are similar in structure to those of *Calycella*.

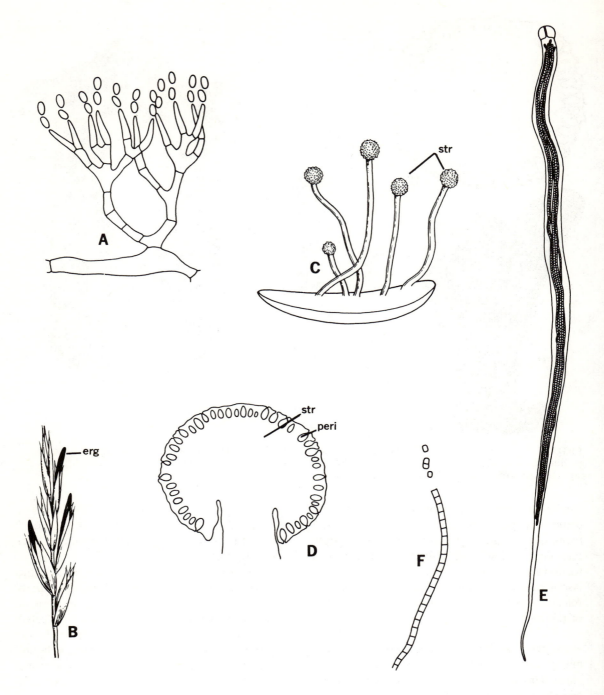

FIGURE 7–34 *Claviceps*. A, conidiophores and conidia from infected rye ovary, ×1,300; B, grass inflorescence with three sclerotia or ergots (*erg*), ×1; C, germinating sclerotium bearing four stalked stromata (*str*), ×5; D, section through a mature stroma showing arrangement of perithecia, ×25 (*peri*, perithecium; *str*, stroma); E, ascus with needle-shaped, septate ascospores, ×1,500; F, portion of single ascospore showing fragmentation, ×3,500.

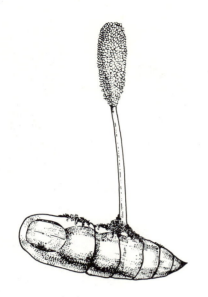

FIGURE 7–35 Stroma of *Cordyceps* arising from infected insect pupa, ×2.5.

In *Leotia* and related genera, the apothecia are stipitate and pileate. The pileus in *Leotia* (Fig. 7–39A) is essentially discoid, while that of *Geoglossum* (Fig. 7–39B, C) is spatulate with a fertile upper portion. *Leotia* and *Geoglossum* inhabit the soil.

Order Pezizales. The Pezizales have apothecia similar to those of the Helotiales, but in many instances they are much larger. The asci of this group open by a distinct lid when the spores are shot from the ascus. The Pezizales are primarily inhabitants of soil and dung; only a few species are found on dead plant parts.

The larger forms, e.g., *Aleuria* (Fig. 7–40), produce apothecia sometimes reaching 15–18 cm in diameter. In apothecia of these fungi, asci are arranged in a hymenium as in the Helotiales. The ascus tips bend toward light, and the ascospores are fired from the ascus. If an undisturbed apothecium is suddenly touched or blown upon, a cloud of spores may be released with an audible hiss.

A series of transitional forms connects the cupulate members of this group with pileate species (Fig. 7–41). In some species of *Helvella*, the pileus is obviously discoid, although

folded and saddle-shaped. In *Verpa*, the ridged pileus is bell-shaped and folded down over the stipe. In *Morchella* the hymenium lines numerous large pits on the pileus.

Relationships of the Ascomycetes

The Euascomycetidae are thought by some to have evolved from floridean algal ancestors (see Chapter 8). This evolutionary scheme is based upon certain similarities in reproduction and structure of the two groups. The simpler Hemiascomycetidae are considered in this concept to have developed through simplification or regression of euascomycetous forms.

A second commonly accepted theory derives the ascomycetes from phycomycetous (Zygomycetidae) ancestors. Certain filamentous hemiascomycetes are considered primitive, the euascomycetes being derived from them. The yeasts are treated as reduced forms, as in the scheme deriving the ascomycetes from red algae.

The ascomycetes are thought to be closely related to the remaining class, the basidiomycetes. Points of similarity shared by the two groups are: (1) dikaryotic hyphae; (2) early development of the ascus and basidium; and (3) crozier and clamp connection formation.

CLASS BASIDIOMYCETES

The basidiomycetes include many plant parasites as well as saprobes that occur on wood, soil, or dung. Virtually all of the known species grow in terrestrial habitats.

Assimilative Stage

Germination of basidiospores gives rise to a primary or monokaryotic mycelium in most heterothallic basidiomycetes. This mycelium consists of regularly septate hyphae with uni-

101

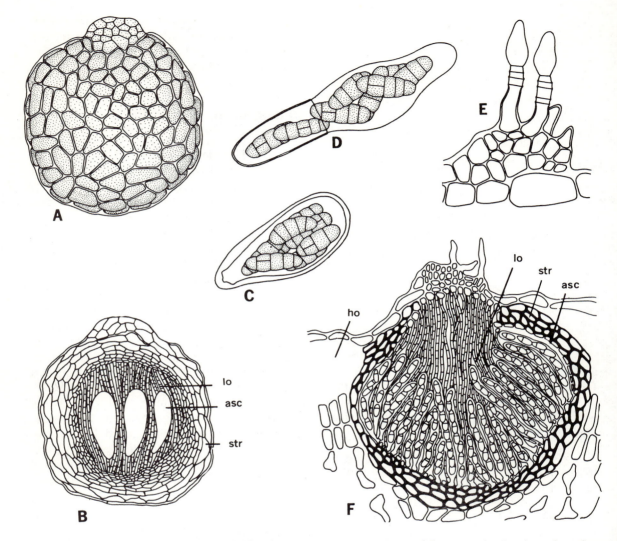

FIGURE 7–36 A–D, *Pleospora*. A, habit of ascostroma, ×250; B, semidiagrammatic drawing of section through ascostroma, ×250 (*asc*, ascus; *lo*, locule; *str*, stroma); C, ascus and ascospores, ×400; D, ascus after rupture of outer wall layer, ×400. E, F, *Venturia*. E, conidiophores and conidia, ×825; F, section through host leaf and ascostroma, ×500 (*asc*, ascus; *ho*, host; *lo*, locule; *str*, stroma).

nucleate cells; it may grow indefinitely in this form. Dikaryotization of a monokaryotic mycelium typically is accomplished either by fusion of hyphae or by spermatization followed by nuclear transfer. The dikaryotic or secondary mycelium grows indefinitely in many wood- and soil-inhabitating basidiomycetes. With only few exceptions, a dikaryon phase is a necessary prerequisite for basidiocarp formation. The dikaryotic mycelium of homothallic species arises upon germination of a single basidiospore.

The septa of dikaryotic hyphae are perforated, as in the ascomycetes, but the pore is more complex (Fig. 7–42). The monokaryotic hyphae also are provided with such septa. Chitin is present in the walls of most groups that have been examined.

During nuclear division in dikaryotic hyphae, structures called clamp connections are formed in many basidiomycetes (Fig. 7–43). The cytological events occurring in clamp connection formation are essentially the same as in ascomycetous crozier development. But the loop or clamp originates as a lateral branch in the basidiomycetes; in crozier formation the hyphal tip grows back upon itself.

Asexual Reproduction

Where known, asexual reproduction in the basidiomycetes is by means of conidia. Several distinct types of asexual spores are formed in the life histories of some primitive basidiomycetes, e.g., the Uredinales. However, in many of the more advanced forms, no conidial stages are known. Thus, asexual reproduction appears to play a less prominent dispersal role in basidiomycetes than in ascomycetes. The asexual spores are formed essentially as in the Euascomycetidae.

Sexual Reproduction

Plasmogamy, through fusion of hyphae or spermatization, can be considered the initial

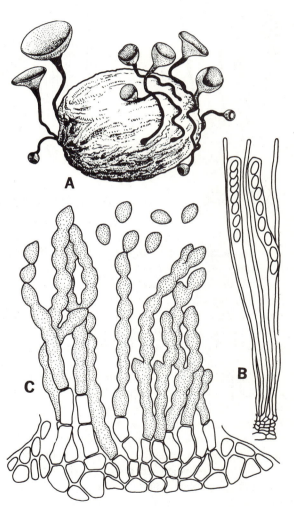

103

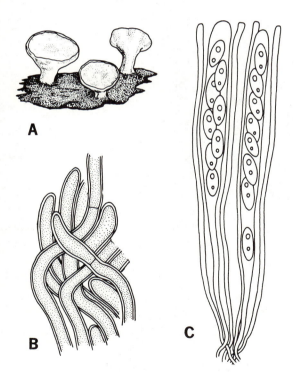

FIGURE 7–37 *Calycella.* A, habit sketch of apothecia, ×5; B, tissue from outer surface of apothecium, ×1,640; C, portion of hymenium showing asci and paraphyses.

FIGURE 7–38 *Monilinia.* A, mummified plum on which a number of apothecia have developed, ×1. B, asci and paraphyses, ×750. C, cluster of conidiophores arising from the surface of infected fruit, ×415.

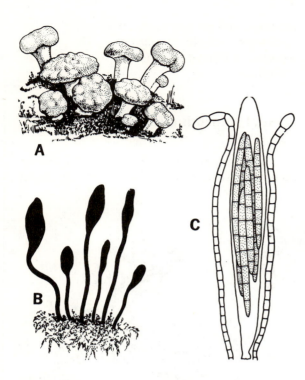

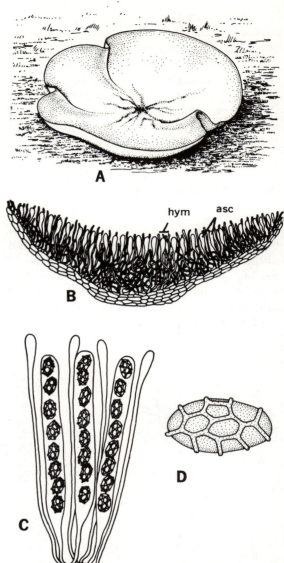

FIGURE 7–39 A, B, habit sketches. A, *Leotia*, ×1; B, *Geoglossum*, ×0.5. C, asci and paraphyses of *Geoglossum*, ×460.

step in sexual reproduction of heterothallic basidiomycetes. In the dikaryotic phase that follows, the pairs of compatible nuclei divide and increase greatly. The fusion of compatible nuclei does not occur until basidia are formed. Thus, plasmogamy and karyogamy are uniquely separated from one another by a prolonged assimilative phase.

Gametangium-like structures are known only in primitive basidiomycetes, such as the rusts. Few of the remaining heterothallic basidiomycetes produce spermatia and receptive hyphae, although conidia can function as spermatia in some species. Dikaryotization usually is accomplished through fusion of two compatible hyphae. The compatibility system may involve a single pair of factors, i.e., + and −, or A and a, as in the Uredinales and in ascomycetes. More commonly, complex compatibility systems regulate the formation of fertile dikaryotic mycelia.

FIGURE 7–40 *Aleuria*. A, habit sketch of apothecium, ×1; B, diagram of section through apothecium (*asc*, asci; *hym*, hymenium); C, asci and paraphyses, ×325; D, single ascospore showing reticulate pattern of ridges on spore wall, ×1,250.

Basidiocarp Development

A number of simple parasitic basidiomycetes produce no basidiocarps; their basidia

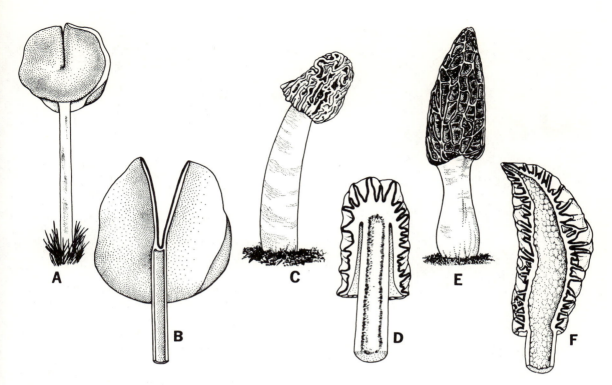

FIGURE 7–41 Habit and sectional views of ascocarps. A, B, *Helvella,* ×0.5; C, D, *Verpa,* ×0.5; E, F, *Morchella,* ×0.5. (Heavy lines in sections of ascocarps indicate extent of hymenium.)

are formed directly upon the dikaryotic mycelium, or they arise from thick-walled resistant spores. However, the majority of basiodiomycetes produce some type of basidiocarp. The formation of a fruiting body is not immediately tied to the establishment of the dikaryon phase, as it is in the Euascomycetidae. Here the dikaryon may grow indefinitely, producing either annual crops of basidiocarps or in some species, perennial basidiocarps. Once the mycelium has become sufficiently developed, the production of basidiocarps is controlled or initiated by environmental factors such as temperature, moisture, and light.

A dikaryotic mycelium typically grows out radially from its initial starting point. In perennial soil-inhabiting species, the buried mycelial thallus increases in diameter each year. Older parts of the mycelium—i.e., those in the center of the mat—die, and the thallus becomes ring-shaped. "Fairy rings" of basidiocarps indicate the presence of the buried ring-shaped thalli. By measuring the annual rate of increase in diameter of a fairy ring, an accurate estimate can be made of how long the mat has been growing. In some instances, this exceeds 500 years.

Basidiocarps are extremely varied in form; however, all share a few characteristics in addition to the presence of basidia. For example, the entire basidiocarp is composed of dikaryotic hyphae. Basidia are borne on or in the basidiocarp, either irregularly or in a definite hymenial layer.

The Basidium

The cytological events occurring in the developing basidium (Fig. 7–44) are similar to those in the ascus. However, meiosis is not

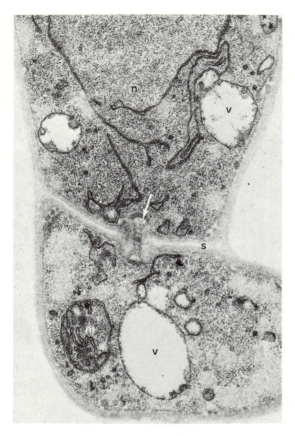

FIGURE 7–42 Basidiomycete septum, ×25,000 (*m*, mitochondrion; *n*, nucleus; *s*, septum; *v*, vacuole). Arrow indicates central pore. (Photograph courtesy A. A. Bisalputra.)

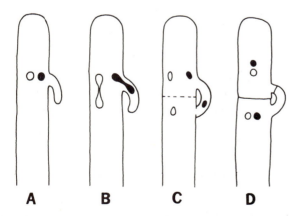

FIGURE 7–43 A–D, formation of clamp connections (compare with crozier formation, Fig. 7–23 A–D).

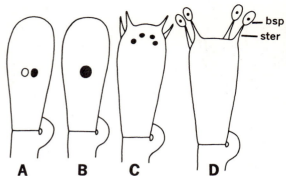

FIGURE 7–44 Basidial development. A, dikaryotic cell; B, karyogamy; C, meiosis; D, mature basidium with exogenous basidiospores (*bsp*) borne on sterigmata (*ster*).

followed by mitosis in most basidiomycetes, and consequently four basidiospores are usually produced. The spores of the majority of basidiomycetes are borne upon minute spicules, or sterigmata. One haploid nucleus and a portion of the basidial protoplast are transferred through the sterigmata into each developing spore. Mature basidiospores of many basidiomycetes are shot from the basidium (Fig. 7–45). Immediately before discharge, a bubble-like protrusion develops on the spore to one side of the sterigma attachment. The appearance of this bubble is thought to be associated with spore discharge, but the mechanism involved has not yet been explained satisfactorily. The basidiospores are shot away with a force sufficient to carry the spore a distance of ten to twenty times the spore length. Gravity and air currents then complete dispersal.

Classification

The class Basidiomycetes is divided into two subclasses, the Heterobasidiomycetidae and the Homobasidiomycetidae. These are distinguished from one another by basidial structure and other features. Basidia of the heterobasidiomycetes are septate or deeply divided, and they may arise from thick-walled resistant

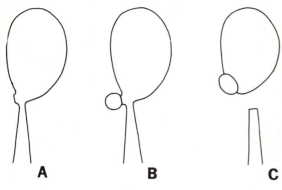

A   **B**   **C**

FIGURE 7–45   A–C, basidiospore discharge.

spores. Basidia of the homobasidiomycetes are typically club-shaped, nonseptate, and do not arise from resistant spores.

Subclass Heterobasidiomycetidae

The heterobasidiomycetes include two of the most important groups of vascular plant parasites, the rusts and the smuts. Other species live as saprobes or parasitize insects, fungi, and mosses.

Order Tremellales. Fungi in this order frequently are referred to as "jelly" fungi, a name derived from the gelatinous basidiocarp texture of many species. In *Tremella* and related genera, the basidiocarps are cushion-shaped to irregularly lobed (Fig. 7–46); they are composed of hyphae embedded in a gelatinous matrix. Most of the exposed surface is covered by a hymenium consisting only of basidia, or of basidia together with conidiophores and conidia. Karyogamy and meiosis are followed by division of the basidium into four compartments. An extension, tipped by a sterigma and basidiospore, then develops from each compartment. The spores are shot from the basidium.

Basidiospores of *Tremella* typically germinate by budding. The budding colonies so produced are similar to those of certain yeasts. If two compatible budding strains are brought

A

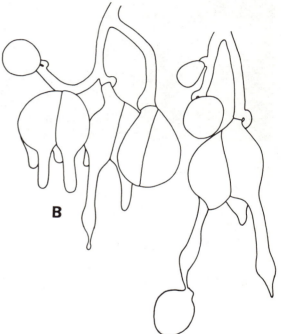

B

107

FIGURE 7–46   *Tremella*. A, young basidiocarp, ×2; B, portion of hymenium showing basidia in various stages of development, ×1,200.

together, conjugation occurs and a dikaryon is established.

The basidiocarps of *Dacrymyces* (Fig. 7–47B) are similar to those of *Tremella*. However, the basidia are nonseptate and deeply divided; they are sometimes referred to as "tuning fork" basidia. Mature basidiospores of *Dacrymyces* are septate and germinate by forming numerous small conidia (Fig. 7–47B).

Order Uredinales. No basidiocarps are produced by the rusts, although as many as five

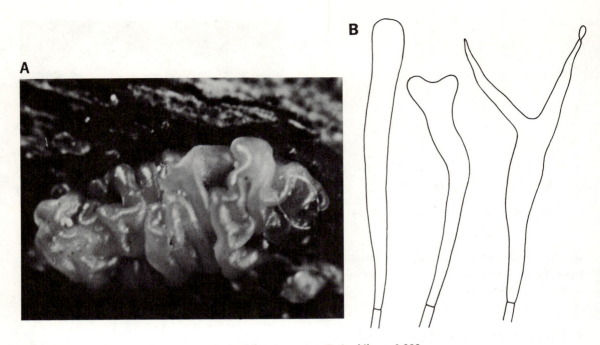

FIGURE 7–47 *Dacrymyces*. A, mature basidiocarp, ×3.5; B, basidia, ×2,000.

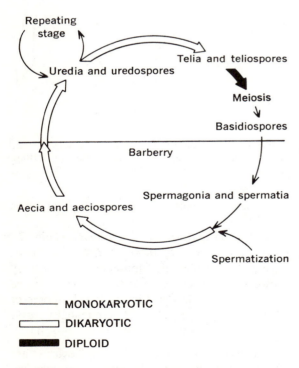

FIGURE 7–48 Life history of *Puccinia graminis*.

kinds of spores may be formed by a single species. The rusts all are obligate parasites with hyphae that are intercellular with haustoria. In recent years, some progress has been made in attempts to grow rusts on laboratory media. Some rusts require two different hosts in order to complete their life cycles; others complete their life history on a single host. The two hosts of a given rust always are from very different plant groups, e.g., a gymnosperm and an angiosperm or a gymnosperm and a fern.

One of the most intensively studied of the heterobasidiomycetes is *Puccinia graminis,* the cause of stem rust of wheat and other grasses. The life history of this rust (Fig. 7–48) is typical of the more complex rusts. Basidiospores are released in the early spring and infect leaves of the common barberry, *Berberis vulgaris.* Spermagonia and receptive hyphae are formed on the upper surfaces of the infected leaves (Fig. 7–49A). The spermagonium is perithecium-like in shape, and it contains many spermatia that are exuded in a sugary liquid called "honey dew." Receptive hyphae are

NONVASCULAR PLANTS

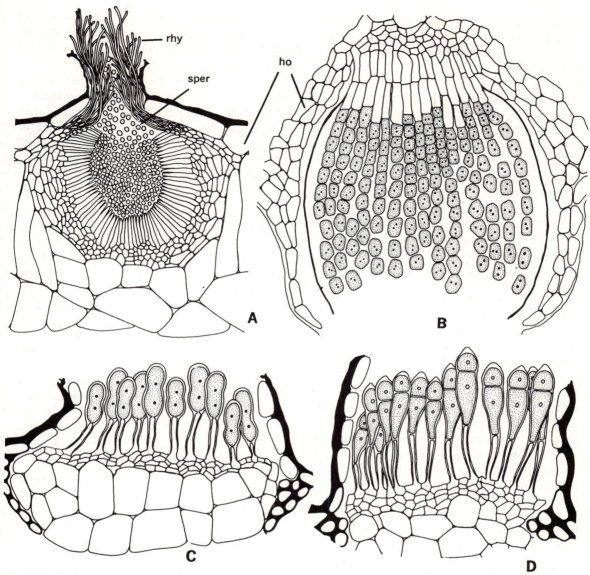

FIGURE 7–49 *Puccinia*. A, section through spermagonium and host leaf, ×550; B, aecium and aeciospores, ×450; C, uredium and uredospores, ×575; D, telium and teliospores, ×420. *ho*, host; *rhy*, receptive hyphae; *sper*, spermatia.

formed around the opening of the spermagonium.

Although portions of the life history of *P. graminis* have been known for almost a century, it was not until 1927 that J. H. Craigie discovered the function of the spermatia. He demonstrated that spermagonia of this species fall into two mating types, + and −. If a

+ spermatium is transferred to a − receptive hypha, or vice versa, the spermatium nucleus brings about dikaryotization of the thallus. Spermatia are transferred by insects attracted by the honeydew.

The second spore-producing stage on barberry consists of aecium and aeciospore formation. Aecia usually are formed on the under surfaces of the leaves and release dikaryotic aeciospores (Fig. 7–49B). The aeciospores infect wheat plants or related grasses, where a second binucleate spore-forming structure, a uredium (Fig. 7–49C), produces uredospores. The uredospores of *P. graminis* and other rusts are repeating spores, spreading the disease to other plants. In late summer, teliospores are formed (Fig. 7–49D); they are produced in telia or sometimes are mixed with uredospores. Teliospores remain attached to the host and are the resistant or overwintering spores. Soon after they are formed, karyogamy occurs within each of the two dikaryotic cells of the teliospore. In the spring, the teliospores germinate *in situ,* each cell producing a basidium and basidiospores (Fig. 7–50). Meiosis occurs during germination of the teliospore.

Because of its function as an alternate host for *P. graminis,* the common barberry has been systematically eradicated in North America. However, elimination of the alternate host has not prevented serious losses of grain through stem rust. The uredospores are sufficiently resistant to survive the mild winters in the southernmost wheat-growing regions of North America. Infection by these spores, and their dispersal by prevailing winds, have served to maintain the species. Furthermore, a cryptic genetic process provides for variation in the absence of the alternate host and sexual reproduction.

P. malvacearum, infecting malvaceous hosts, has a greatly reduced life history. This species produces teliospores similar to those of *P. graminis,* but they soon germinate and the basidiospores infect new host plants. Only those teliospores formed late in the growing season of the host function as resistant spores. The latter germinate, and the basidiospores initiate infection in the following spring. The dikaryotic mycelium of *P. malvacearum* is thought to develop following contact of two compatible monokaryotic mycelia.

Cronartium ribicola, called white pine blister rust, has a life history similar to that of *P. graminis.* This species produces its spermatia and aeciospores on various species of white pines. The uredial and telial stages occur on currant or gooseberry plants. The name "blister rust" is derived from the appearance of the aecia on branches of infected pines.

C. ribicola, a fungus native to Europe, was accidentally introduced into North America around 1900, on infected nursery plants. The fungus has spread over most of the range of both eastern and western white pine species. It threatens all native white pines, although some control is obtained through elimination of alternate hosts.

Order Ustilaginales. Smuts, like rusts, are all parasites of vascular plants. However, the haploid or monokaryotic phase of smuts can exist saprobically and is often grown in culture. All of the known species require only one host for completion of the life cycle, and all produce only one type of thick-walled resistant spore.

The resistant spore, called a teliospore, is thought to be homologous to that of the rusts. The teliospore is at first dikaryotic, then diploid; upon germinating, it produces a cylindric basidium similar to that of the rusts. In *Ustilago,* the largest genus of smuts, the usually four-celled basidium produces numerous ba-

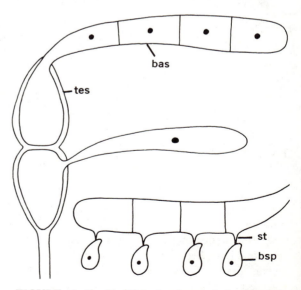

FIGURE 7–50 Basidial development in *Puccinia* (*bas,* basidium; *bsp,* basidiospore; *st,* sterigma; *tes,* teliospore).

sidiospores by budding (Fig. 7–51). This budding phase can be maintained in laboratory culture, where it results in yeast-like colonies. A stable dikaryon is formed if conjugation occurs on a suitable host, but this stage has been maintained in culture in only a very small number of species. Infection of the host by a monokaryotic hypha either does not occur or is of limited duration in most species.

The dikaryotic mycelium within the host is intercellular with haustoria; it commonly develops within meristematic tissues of the host and keeps pace with the developing meristem. In meristematic zones, infected ovaries, or other portions of the host, masses of teliospores are produced. The hyphae in the mass, or sorus, consist at first of numerous short dikaryotic cells (Fig. 7–52). Each cell becomes swollen, and a new wall is deposited within the old hyphal wall, forming a teliospore. Disintegration of the host parts eventually exposes the powdery mass of spores.

Smuts may infect the host plant in several ways. The teliospores of some species adhere to seeds of the host; they germinate and infect the seedling at seed germination. In other species, flowers of the host are infected by budding cells or by conidia. Some species of

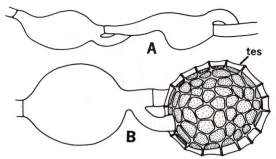

FIGURE 7–52 Teliospore development in a species of *Ustilago*. A, early development showing hyphal cells with clamp connection at septa, ×2,000; B, later stage with one mature teliospore (*tes*), ×2,000.

Ustilago infect developing embryos within the ovaries of host plants. An infection tube grows into the meristematic zone of the embryo and remains dormant there until the seed germinates.

The basidia of smuts are variable; frequently those of a single species of *Ustilago* have many different forms. The differences in basidia are to a certain extent used in classifying the smuts. For example, basidia of the genus *Tilletia* (Fig. 7–53) are cylindric and aseptate. The basidiospores are needle-shaped, borne at the basidial tip, and fired from the basidium at maturity. Conjugation of the basidiospores may occur while the spores are maturing on the basidium.

The smuts parasitize many economically important plants, especially the cereal grasses. Since they commonly infect the inflorescences or fruits, the yield and quality of such crops may be greatly reduced. Species of *Ustilago* and *Tilletia* are responsible for losses amounting to many millions of bushels of grain each year. *U. maydis* (Fig. 7–54) is, in some seasons, the most destructive of corn parasites. It accounts for more than one-fourth of the yield loss from all corn diseases.

111

Subclass Homobasidiomycetidae

Most of the large conspicuous fungi, such as mushrooms, puffballs, and bracket fungi, are

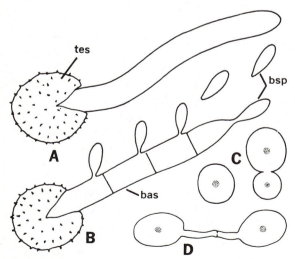

FIGURE 7–51 *Ustilago*. A, germinating teliospore (*tes*), ×2,600; B, mature basidium with basidiospores (*bas*, basidium; *bsp*, basidiospore); C, cells produced by budding of basidiospores; D, conjugation.

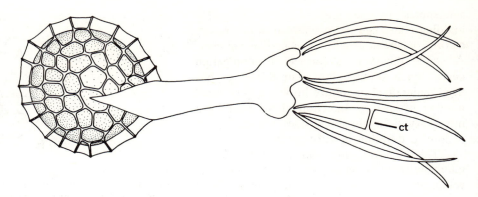

FIGURE 7–53 Teliospore and mature basidium of *Tilletia*. Note conjugation tube (*ct*) between two basidiospores.

homobasidiomycetes. Basidiocarps are formed by almost all species, and they are highly developed in many. The homobasidiomycetes are mainly saprobes, existing in soil, compost, dung, or wood. Their activity in the decay of such materials is beneficial and vital; but it also leads to great financial loss through decay of standing and sawn timber. A few species parasitize green plants; many form mycorrhizae.

Life Histories. The life histories of homobasidiomycetous fungi are relatively simple and uniform. The life history diagram in Figure 7–55 is typical of most heterothallic species; nearly all species investigated for sexuality have been heterothallic. The dikaryotic mycelium is considered the main assimilative phase in the life histories of most basidiomycetes; its growth in some soil- and wood-inhabiting species may continue for hundreds of years.

Conidia are formed on monokaryotic mycelia of some homobasidiomycetes and on the dikaryotic hyphae in others. In general, however, conidia do not appear to be as important in the life histories of these fungi as they are with the Heterobasidiomycetidae and the Euascomycetidae.

Classification. At present, no universally accepted system of classification exists for the majority of homobasidiomycetous fungi. Like the euascomycetes, these fungi have not been sufficiently studied to provide a sound basis for classification. The orders in the following discussion, therefore, are mostly unnatural assemblages, but they do illustrate some of the variation in form and in microscopic structure.

Order Polyporales. The Polyporales are mainly wood- or soil-inhabiting fungi. A few species are important as plant parasites, but the group is of much greater significance for their wood-decaying activity. They are most abundant in forested areas but occur in other habitats as well.

Basidiocarps of polyporaceous fungi may be fleshy, tough, corky, or woody; many can dry, then revive on wetting. The distinctions among the genera of polyporaceous fungi are based upon gross basidiocarp form, shape or configuration of the hymenium, and microscopic anatomy. The basidiocarps of many polyporaceous fungi consist of little more than a layer of fertile hyphae and a hymenium. Such effused basidiocarps, found in *Peniophora* (Fig. 7–56A) and related genera, usually are borne upon the undersurface of the substratum. The basidiocarps of *Stereum,* a closely related genus, are slightly more complex (Fig. 7–56B). In this genus, the basidiocarp is partially effused, but it has shelving or reflexed portions as well. The upper surfaces of shelving parts in these basidiocarps are sterile. In sessile pileate species, e.g., *Fomes* (Fig. 7–56C), the basidiocarps are laterally attached to the substratum, and the hymenium is limited to the lower surfaces. In *Fomes,* and in the stipitate

112

FIGURE 7–54 *Ustilago*. Infected kernels on upper portion of ear have ruptured, releasing powdery spores, ×0.75.

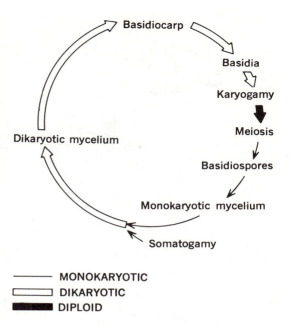

MONOKARYOTIC

DIKARYOTIC

DIPLOID

FIGURE 7–55 Typical homobasidiomycetous life history.

latter genus, the hymenium covers most of the exposed surface of the basidiocarp.

Basidiocarp texture varies with age, species, and moisture content. However, some of the texture variety can be attributed to differences in the hyphae that make up the basidocarp. In corky or woody forms, the basidiocarp may consist primarily of thick-walled hyphae (Fig. 7–60); those of softer consistency usually are composed of thin-walled, often inflated hyphae. Similar structural differences can be found in different parts of a single basidiocarp. For example, a distinct skin- or pellicle-like layer often is present on the upper surface of the basidiocarp, and other distinct zones or layers are sometimes visible.

The hymenial shape or configuration may be even as in *Stereum* and *Peniophora,* toothed as in *Hydnellum* (Fig. 7–57B), or poroid as in *Polyporus* and *Fomes.* The latter two configurations greatly increase surface area and, consequently, permit the formation of greater numbers of basidiospores. The hymenial type is not necessarily correlated with basidiocarp form.

species of *Polyporus* and *Hydnellum* (Fig. 7–57), the pileus usually possesses a substantial upper sterile zone, the context (Fig. 7–58). Finally, the basidiocarps of some Polyporales are erect and club-shaped or coralloidly branched, as in *Clavulina* (Fig. 7–59). In the

DIVISION EUMYCOTA

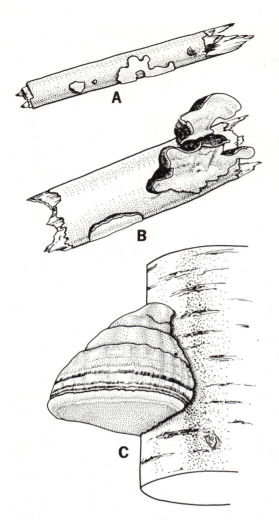

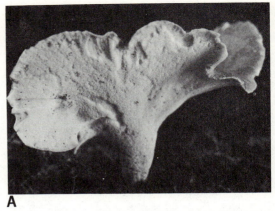

FIGURE 7–56 Basidiocarp form, habit sketches. A, resupinate or effused (*Peniophora*), ×1.5; B, effused-reflexed (*Stereum*), ×1; C, pileate, the pileus sessile and laterally attached to subtrate (*Fomes*), ×0.5.

FIGURE 7–57 Stipitate basidiocarps of *Polyporus* (A, × 81) and *Hydnellum* (B, ×0.75).

Thus, effused or reflexed basiocarps may have even, poroid, or toothed hymenia; the sessile or stipitate pileate basiocarps also may have any of the hymenial forms.

Although the hymenia of polyporaceous fungi appear upon casual microscopic examination to be rather uniform, they are relatively variable from species to species. The most significant differences are in the basidia (Fig. 7–61C, E) and in sterile elements in the hymenium (Fig. 7–62). Perhaps the commonest

of the latter structures are cystidia (Fig. 7–61A, B). Cystidia can be thick- or thin-walled; they are typically hyaline, somewhat larger than the basidia, and protrude beyond the basidia. The function of such sterile elements, if any, is not known in most instances.

The differences in basidiocarp and hymenial form may provide greater efficiency in spore production or in dispersal of spores. Wetting of the hymenial surfaces disrupts spore dispersal in basidiomyetes that violently discharge basidiospores. In erect coralloid types such as *Clavulina* and in many effused forms, the hymenium is directly exposed to falling

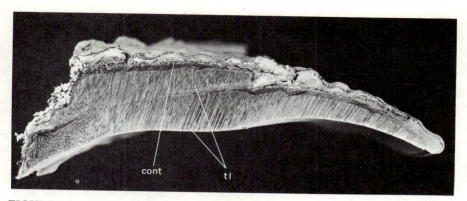

FIGURE 7–58 Vertical section through basidiocarp of *Fomes,* ×1 (*cont,* context; *tl,* tube layer or fertile zone).

rain. When the hymenium is wet in these, the basidiospores can be discharged but do not fall free. The hymenium is protected from rain in shelving and pileate species. Basidiocarps with poroid or toothed hymenia have the greatest hymenial area in proportion to basidiocarp size.

Order Agaricales. Most of the Agaricales have fleshy or tough-fleshy basidiocarps that do not revive after drying. All have pileate ba-

sidiocarps that are either sessile, as in *Pleurotus* (Fig. 7–63), or stipitate. The hymenium is borne upon lamellae in most of the genera, but in one group, the boletes, it is borne on pores or tubules.

The development of many agaric and bolete basidiocarps commences with the appearance of a hyphal knot or primordium either at or below the substrate surface. The con-

115

FIGURE 7–59 Coralloid basidiocarp of *Clavulina,* ×1.

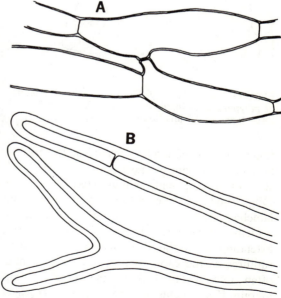

FIGURE 7–60 A, inflated, thin-walled hyphae typical of fleshy basidiocarps, ×1,400; B, thick-walled hyphae from leathery basidiocarp, ×350.

DIVISION EUMYCOTA

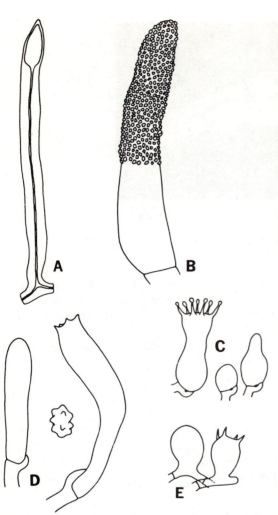

A

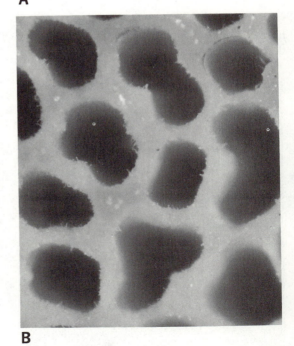

B

FIGURE 7–61 A, B, cystidia found in the hymenium of polyporaceous fungi; A, ×1,660; B, ×2,080. C–E, three types of basidia found in Polyporales, ×1,310.

FIGURE 7–62 Hymenial form. A, toothed or hydnoid, ×50; B, poroid, ×100. The hymenium covers the outer surfaces of the teeth in A and lines the tubes in B.

tinued growth of hyphae results in the formation of a miniature mushroom—the "button" stage of development, as illustrated in *Agaricus* (Fig. 7–64). In the buttons of *Agaricus,* the lamellae already are formed but are covered by a membranous layer, the partial veil. This veil, extending from the cap margin to the stipe, ruptures as the cap expands, and its remnants often remain attached to the stipe or cap margin. If it remains on the stipe, as in *Agaricus* and other genera, it is called an annulus. In the early stages of development, buttons of some

FIGURE 7–63 *Pleurotus.* Habit of laterally attached pilei, ×0.3.

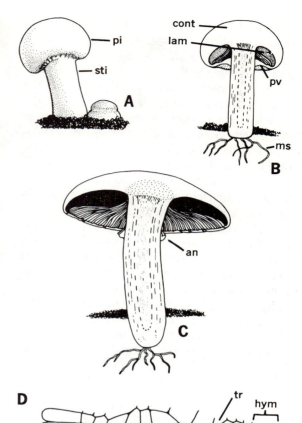

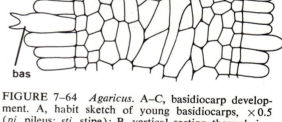

lamellate genera, e.g., *Amanita,* have another membrane, the universal veil, extending upward from the base of the stipe. This membrane also ruptures as the button expands, leaving a cup-like fragment or volva (Fig. 7–65) at the base of the stipe. Additionally, fragments of the universal veil frequently adhere as warty patches on the pileus surface. Only a universal veil is present in some genera; in many, neither a partial veil nor a universal veil is found. Mature basidiocarps of the latter type lack both the annulus and the volva.

As in the Polyporales, a sterile layer, the context, forms an often substantial portion of the mushroom pileus. On the undersurface of the pileus are the hymenium-bearing lamellae (Fig. 7–75) or tubules. During elongation of the stipe, responses to light and gravity help ensure that the cap is horizontal at maturity. The lamellae of some mushrooms also are gravity sensitive and become vertically oriented during growth.

Cystidia, similar to those in Polyporales, are frequently present in the hymenium, and they may also occur on the gill edges and on the surfaces of the cap and pileus. Other

FIGURE 7–64 *Agaricus.* A–C, basidiocarp development. A, habit sketch of young basidiocarps, ×0.5 (*pi,* pileus; *sti,* stipe); B, vertical section through immature basidiocarp, ×0.5 (*cont,* context; *lam,* lamellae; *ms* mycelial strands; *pv,* partial veil); C, vertical section through mature basidiocarp, ×0.5 (*an,* annulus). D, section through small portion of lamellae, ×1,000 (*bas,* basidium; *hym,* hymenium; *tr,* trama).

characteristics aid in delimiting genera of gill fungi—e.g., basidiospore color, the microscopic nature of the pileus surface and of sterile portions of the basidiocarp, and the gross features of the basidiocarp.

Perhaps the most complex of basidiocarps are those of the genus *Coprinus* (Fig. 7–66).

The lamellae often are very thin and numerous; their separation is maintained in some species by cystidia. The basidia of *Coprinus* mature in groups, starting at the lower edge of the gill and moving upward. Following discharge of the first basidiospores along the lower edge of the lamella, autodigestion of the spent portion of the lamella occurs. Another group of basidiospores is then discharged from the lower edge of the remaining portion of the gill, and autodigestion continues. In this manner, the lamellae are completely digested, producing an inky liquid as a result of the digestive process.

The Agaricales are mainly soil-inhabiting saprobes and wood-decay organisms. Many species are associated with specific vascular plants in mycorrhizae, and a few species parasitize vascular plants of economic importance. Others are edible mushrooms, among them being the cultivated market mushroom of North America and Europe, the Shii-take of Japan, and many wild species around the world. Numerous species contain toxins that cause illness or death. Among the more poisonous are *Amanita phalloides* and related species, often called "death angels" or "destroying angels."

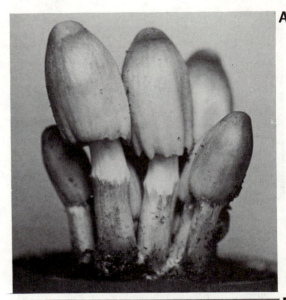

A

B

FIGURE 7–66 *Coprinus*. Two successive photographs of the same cluster of basidiocarps. A, just before the start of spore liberation, ×1; B, the lamellae of the larger basidiocarps have undergone autodigestion, ×0.75.

118

FIGURE 7–65 Pileate, stipitate basidiocarp of *Amanita*, ×0.5 (*an*, annulus; *lam*, lamellae; *pi*, pileus; *sti*, stipe; *vol*, volva).

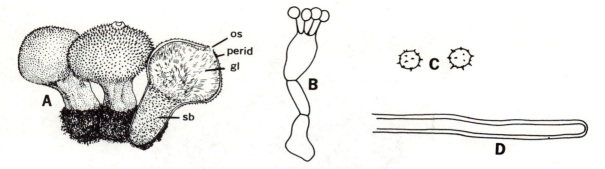

FIGURE 7–67 *Lycoperdon*. A, habit sketch of basidiocarps, one of which (at right) has been sectioned vertically, ×1 (*gl*, gleba; *os*, ostiole; *perid*, peridium; *sb*, sterile base); B, C, mature basidium and basidiospores; B, ×1,025; C, ×2,200; D, portion of capillitial strand, ×2,200.

The amanitas and other poisonous mushrooms cause numerous deaths in Europe each year. In North America, where relatively few wild mushrooms are gathered as food, the number of deaths through mushroom poisoning averages fewer than one per year.

Order Lycoperdales. Spore dispersal in the Lycoperdales, as in polyporaceous and agaricaceous fungi, is by air currents. However, violent spore discharge does not occur in the puffballs since the basidia are produced in closed fruiting bodies. The members of this order are primarily soil fungi, but some species form their basidiocarps on decayed wood.

Externally, the young basidiocarps of *Lycoperdon* and related fungi resemble the button stages of developing mushrooms. In section, however, little differentiation is visible in the young pear-shaped basidiocarps. An outer wall, the peridium, surrounds a soft fleshy inner mass, the gleba. Basidia are borne in small cavities within the gleba. The gleba undergoes autodigestion at maturity of the basidiospores; only the basidiospores and a mass of thread-like capillitial strands remain (Fig. 7–67). After autodigestion, drying occurs rapidly and the peridium becomes papery and flexible. An ostiole develops at the apex of the basidiocarp; any force applied to the flexible peridium, such as by raindrops or by animals, results in a bellows-like action. Spores are blown through the ostiole and are further distributed by air currents.

The genera *Bovista* and *Calvatia* (Fig. 7–68) are closely related to *Lycoperdon*. No ostiole is present in basidiocarps of these genera; their peridia crack irregularly. The basidiocarps of *Bovista* and of some species of *Calvatia* are weakly attached to the soil at maturity. They are easily blown free by wind and are tumbled along, scattering the basidiospores. The capillitium prevents rapid loss of the spores. The largest of *Calvatia* basidiocarps have been estimated to contain as many as 160 billion spores. In these, the basidiocarp may remain attached to the soil and the peridium falls away, exposing the spores to air currents.

Order Phallales. Stinkhorns are so called because the digestion of the gleba leaves a foul-smelling, slimy spore mass. The odor attracts insects, which effect spore dispersal.

In most instances, early stages in development of the basidiocarps are just below the soil surface or within the surface layer of litter. In the genus *Phallus* (Fig. 7–69A), the buttons are egg-like in appearance, and have a tough but flexible peridium. Immediately under the outer peridial layer is a thick layer of gelatinous material that helps store water. The gleba is borne on the upper surface of a cap-like pileus or receptacle. At maturity of the button, the stipe elongates and ruptures the peridial layers.

119

A

120

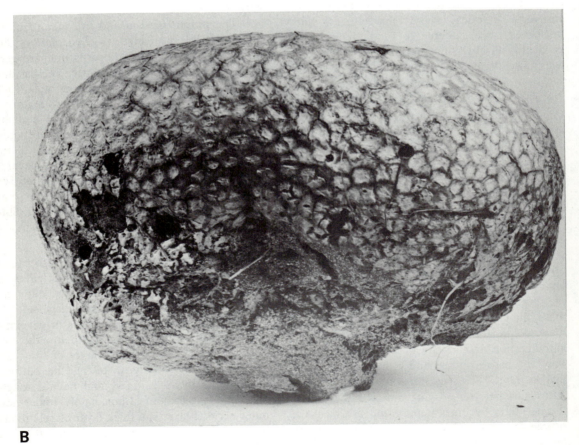

B

FIGURE 7–68 Mature basidiocarps (A, *Bovista,* ×0.75; B, *Calvatia,* ×0.3).

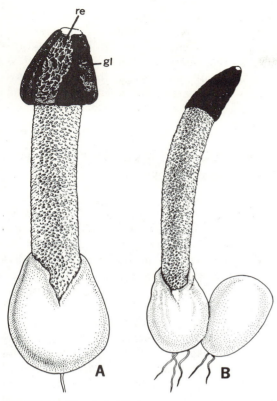

FIGURE 7–69 A, habit sketch of *Phallus;* portion of the gleba (*gl*) has been removed to show the pitted nature of the receptacle (*re*), ×1. B, *Mutinus,* ×1.

The slimy glebal mass then lies exposed on the upper surface of the pileus. Species of *Mutinus* (Fig. 7–69B) are similar in form, but the pileus is essentially continuous with the stipe, i.e., there is less differentiation of the spore receptacle than in *Phallus.*

Bright colors are common in the basidiocarps of the Phallales. These colors, together with the carrion-like odors, probably aid in the attraction of insects.

Order Nidulariales. Basidiocarps of the bird's nest fungi develop on wood, soil, or dung. The basidia are formed in hymenial layers that line cavities within the gleba. Each such cavity is lens-shaped and becomes surrounded by firm wall layers. The remaining glebal material undergoes autodigestion, exposing the lenticular peridioles. The thin, upper cover-like portion of the peridium breaks free, exposing the peridioles. In *Crucibulum* (Fig. 7–70), the peridioles are attached to the peridium by an elastic filament. The peridium of mature basidiocarps is more or less cupulate or funnel-shaped and contains a number of peridioles. The latter are dispersed when raindrops strike the bottom of the peridium and splash upward. The peridiole is then thrown from the cup, and the attachment cord tears away a small segment of the peridium. As the peridiole flies through the air, it functions as a small bolo, and the cord may become wrapped around objects such as nearby herbs or grass culms. The peridioles of bird's nest fungi can be carried more than a meter by the splashcup mechanism. Further dispersal can then take place when animals eat the herbage and attached peridioles.

Relationships of the Basidiomycetes

It is unlikely that the intricate basidiospore discharge mechanism found in many basidiomycetes is polyphyletic in origin. Thus, basidiomycetes with this mechanism—including both the heterobasidiomycetes and the homobasidiomycetes—are thought to have descended from the same ancestral forms. Species that lack violent spore discharge, e.g., the puffballs and stinkhorns, appear to have evolved from ancestors with this mechanism. The loss of violent discharge of basidiospores probably was associated with the development of closed basidiocarps.

The Heterobasidiomycetidae are now commonly accepted as the most primitive of basidiomycetous fungi. Assuming that this is so, the problem of their origin remains, and here the greatest diversity of opinion exists. Two suggested pathways of evolution are: (1) from red algal ancestors, either directly or through ascomycetous forms; and (2) directly from the ascomycetes, with no suggestion of a relationship with the red algae. The suggested relationship with red algae is based upon similarities in

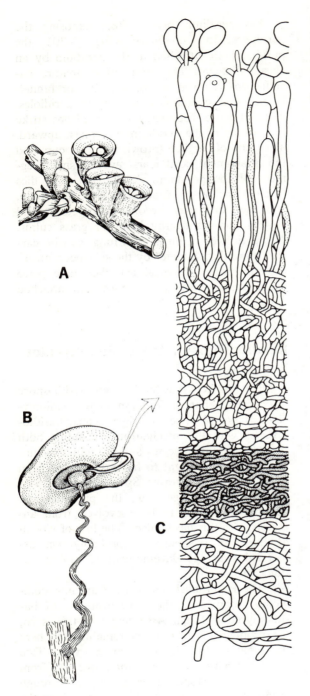

the life histories of certain red algae and the rusts or ascomycetes. Whatever their origin, the basidiomycetes appear to be closely related to the ascomycetes, judging by the presence of a dikaryotic stage, the probable homology of the clamp connection and crozier, and the similarity of asci and basidia.

FORM CLASS FUNGI IMPERFECTI (Deuteromycetes)

In many species of fungi, only asexual reproduction is known. The relationships of some such fungi are obvious, and these fungi are classified together with organisms in the Phycomycetes, Ascomycetes, or Basidiomycetes. However, a large group still cannot be placed on the basis of asexual structures. These are classified in the Form Class Fungi Imperfecti, a receptacle for incompletely known species of uncertain relationships. It was once thought that, as these fungi were studied, all would eventually be placed in natural classes. However, it now seems probable that some of these fungi have lost the ability to reproduce sexually, or perhaps they have never had such ability. The Form Class Fungi Imperfecti will not, therefore, be eliminated in the near future.

The Form Class Fungi Imperfecti is divided arbitrarily into form orders, form families, and form genera. In many known instances, similar asexual stages are produced by two or more sexually reproducing fungi of only distant relationship. Conversely, the asexual stages of two closely related species, as determined by the sexual stage, may be quite distinct. Thus, the form taxa in the Fungi Imperfecti, based upon asexual reproductive structures, must be treated only as assemblages, not as natural groups.

Based in the types of spore-bearing structures, four form orders are recognized: the Sphaeropsidales, Melanconiales, Moniliales, and Mycelia Sterilia. The Sphaeropsidales includes all imperfect fungi in which the asexual spores, or conidia, develop within pycnidia

FIGURE 7–70 *Crucibulum.* A, habit sketch of young and mature basidiocarps, ×1.5; B, single peridiole with attachment cord, ×20; C, small section through peridiole showing basidia and wall layers, ×950.

122

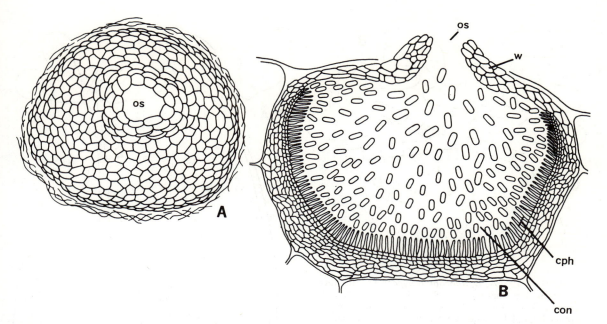

FIGURE 7–71 A, B, *Phoma*. A, habit sketch of pycnidium, ×1,050; B, section through pycnidium, ×1,230 (*con*, conidia; *cph*, conidiophores; *os*, ostiole; *w*, pycnidial wall).

(Fig. 7–71). *Phoma* and similar genera include many important parasites of crop plants. In this and other groups of Fungi Imperfecti, genera are distinguished from one another on the basis of spore color and septation, and on the nature of the conidiophores.

The Melanconiales, like the Sphaeropsidales, includes many species of plant parasites. Here the conidiophores are borne in saucer-shaped acervuli, characteristically formed subepidermally on plants. The acervuli may be produced on the leaves, stems, or other plant parts; they are responsible for plant diseases called anthracnose. One of the more important genera is *Pestalotia* (Fig. 7–72), which has short simple conidiophores that bear dark-colored, septate spores. Each spore bears a number of hyaline appendages.

Fungi placed in the Moniliales produce neither pycnidia nor acervuli. In some moniliaceous fungi, only yeast-like budding cells are known. Others, such as *Sporobolomyces* (Fig. 7–73A, B), form both buds and conidia. The conidia resemble basidiospores, in general appearance and in method of discharge. These

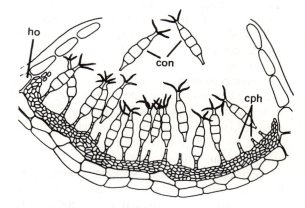

FIGURE 7–72 Acervulus of *Pestalotia*, ×550. *ho*, host tissue; *cph*, conidiophores; *con*, conidia.

conidia produce a mirror image of a colony on the lid of inverted cultures—thus the name "mirror yeasts," applied to this and related genera.

Some of the Moniliales reproduce through fragmentation of hyphae into spore-like segments. The species of *Geotrichum* (Fig. 7–73C, D), which reproduce in this manner, are important plant and human parasites. Most of the

DIVISION EUMYCOTA

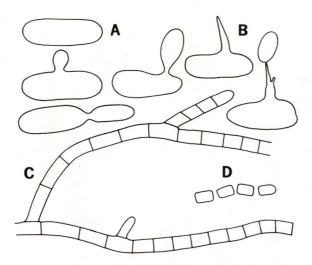

FIGURE 7–73   A, B, *Sporobolomyces*. A, cells, three
of which are budding, ×2,900; B, reproduction by
conidial formation, ×2,900. C, D, *Geotrichum*. C,
septate hyphal branches before fragmentation has occurred, ×3,000; D, after fragmentation, ×3,000.

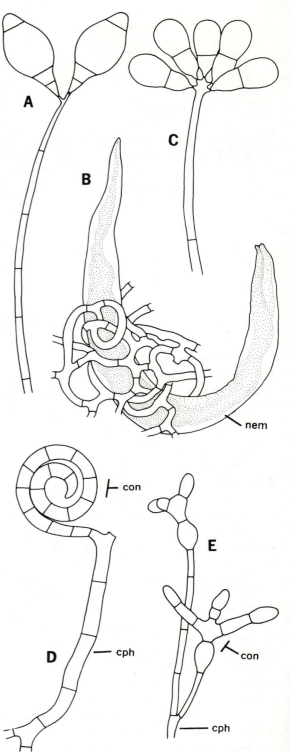

124

Moniliales bear their spores on definite conidiophores, as illustrated in *Dactylaria* (Fig. 7–
74A) and *Arthrobotrys* (Fig. 7–74C). These
genera, common in compost and dung, are of
special interest because of the nematode-trap-
ping snares formed on their hyphae (Fig. 7–
74B). Other genera trap small animals by means
of similar snares or adhesive structures. Once
captured, the bodies of such animals are pen-
etrated by special absorptive hyphae and are
utilized as nutrient.

Perhaps the most striking conidia are
those of certain aquatic Moniliales in which
the conidial form apparently is correlated with
the habitat type and probably is important in
dispersal. In one group, as illustrated by *Helicoma* (Fig. 7–74D), the spores are helically

FIGURE 7–74   A, B, *Dactylaria*. A, apex of conidiophore with two conidia, ×845; B, network of adhesive loops with entrapped nematode (*nem*), ×90.
C, portion of conidiophore of *Arthrobotrys* with terminal group of conidia, ×1,000. D, conidium (*con*)
and conidiophore (*cph*) of *Helicoma*, ×1,570. E,
conidiophore of *Clavariopsis* bearing two conidia,
×1,115.

coiled; in another, the spores are four-armed or tetraradiate, as shown in Figure 7–74E of *Clavariopsis*.

LICHENS

Although *lichens* are often treated as a separate plant division, lichenologists now consider them part of the fungi. More than 20,000 species of lichens have been described—more than 2,500 of these in North America. Lichen fungi differ little from other parasitic fungi, except that the lichen fungal hyphae and algal cells are so mutually dependent that the resulting association behaves as a single plant. Lichens probably illustrate the most perfect example of mutualistic symbiosis, in which each partner is dependent on the other for existence. This association (lichen) reproduces as an association rather than as an alga or a fungus. Indeed, the mycobiont, or fungal partner, usually cannot reproduce itself or live independently in nature. In most instances the algal partner is also unable to survive except as an algal component of a lichen and is rarely isolated in nature. Under pure culture conditions a large number of phycobionts (algal partners) have reproduced sexually and have thrived better than in the lichen association. Recently the cultured mycobiont has also been induced to reproduce sexually, rarely producing asexual reproductive structures.

Lichen taxonomy is essentially fungal taxonomy, since the mycobiont usually gives the lichen its gross morphology and does not exist in a nonlichenized state. More important, the sexual reproductive structures are strictly fungal.

Most lichens contain a single species of alga. In most lichens the phycobiont is a green alga (Division Chlorophyta)—in many instances it is a blue-green alga (Division Cyanophyta).

The mycobiont is generally an ascomycete; but a few tropical basidiomycetes, some deuteromycetes, and reportedly a single phycomycete lead a lichenized existence. Some workers suggest that the term lichen should be restricted to lichenized ascomycetes.

Gross Morphology

The lichen thallus may be unstratified or stratified (Fig. 7–75). In the unstratified type, the algal cells are scattered throughout. The growth form of the lichen thallus is constant for a given species and is highly important in classification. Several common growth forms are readily recognizable.

A crustose thallus may be unstratified or stratified (Fig. 7–76). In stratified crustose forms, the lichen is a thin crust closely adherent to the substrate. The hyphae in the upper portion of the crust form an upper cortex. These hyphae are usually tightly compacted and highly gelatinized. The cells of the algal layer, which underlies the cortex, are surrounded by a loose network of hyphae. Below the algal layer is a medulla of varying thickness composed of loosely arranged hyphae. The lowermost hyphae act as rhizoidal hyphae, attaching the thallus to the substratum. In some crustose forms, much of the thallus penetrates the outer layers of a relatively soft substrate.

The foliose thallus (Fig. 7–75, 76A, B, 81A) possesses an upper cortex, an algal layer, and a medulla. The thallus can be carefully peeled intact from the substrate. In some foliose lichens the thallus may be attached by a single bundle of hyphae, forming a central cord; the rest of the thallus expands over this single point of attachment. In others, the thallus is attached by a number of hyphal bundles. Depending upon the species, the foliose thallus may possess or may lack a lower cortex of densely packed hyphae beneath the medulla.

The squamulose thallus is structurally similar to the foliose type (Fig. 7–77A, B). However, the squamulose thallus is made up of many small lobes, which may be loosely attached to each other; in some species of *Cladonia*, these lobes (or squamules) form colonies in which each squamule is free of its neighbor.

The fruticose thallus is shrub-like, with cylindrical or flattened branches (Fig. 7–78).

125

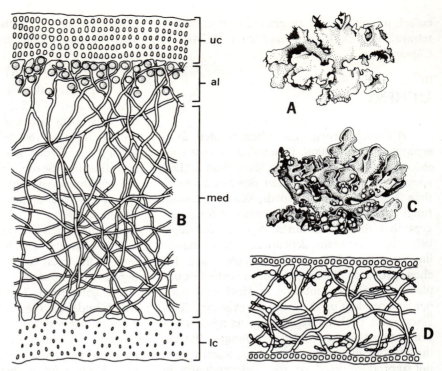

FIGURE 7–75 Foliose lichens, showing thallus structure. A, *Parmelia perlata*, habit, ×1.7; B, *P. perlata*, cross section showing stratified thallus with upper cortex (*uc*), algal layer (*al*), medulla (*med*), lower cortex (*lc*), ×450; C, *Leptogium tremelloides*, habit, ×1.8; D, *L. tremelloides*, cross section of thallus showing unstratified thallus, ×220. (B, D, after Schneider.)

Branching is either simple or very complex. The thallus may be stiffly erect or pendulous, some pendulous forms being more than 20 feet long (e.g., *Usnea longissima*). Most fruticose thalli are stratified, but stratification differs somewhat from the previously described types (Fig. 7–78A, C).

The gelatinous thallus is essentially unstratified, with a blue-green alga dominating the structure; the fungus is scarcely apparent. Most gelatinous lichens are black or bluish. The name is derived from the texture of the moist lichen.

Vegetative Structure

Some lichens bear coral-like outgrowths on the thallus. These isidia consist of rigid protuberances of upper cortex, plus algal and medullary layers of the thallus (Fig. 7–79).

Isidia readily break from the thallus and probably act as vegetative propagules.

In many lichens the upper or outer cortex ruptures and algal cells surrounded by fungal hyphae from the medulla erupt as loose, dusty masses on the surface of the thallus (Fig. 7–80). These dusty masses, termed soredia, are probably important in reproduction.

Some lichens have wart-like protuberances on the upper cortex. These cephalodia consist of an epiphytic lichen growing on the surface of another lichen thallus (Fig. 7–81). The algal cells of the cephalodia differ from those of the host lichen.

Reproductive Structures and Reproduction

Only 18 species of lichenized basidiomycetes are known, all from tropical regions.

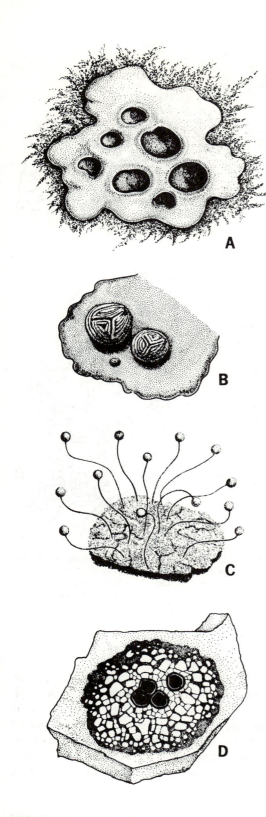

A

B

C

D

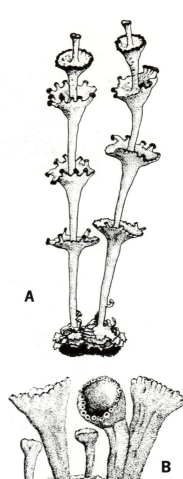

A

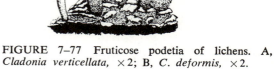

B

FIGURE 7–77 Fruticose podetia of lichens. A, *Cladonia verticellata*, ×2; B, *C. deformis*, ×2.

Their bracket-shaped fruiting bodies (Fig. 7–82) and method of reproduction through basidiospores are presumably the same as in other bracket basidiomycetes.

The ascomycetous lichens bear sexual ascocarps termed apothecia and perithecia

FIGURE 7–76 Morphology of lichen thalli. A, *Solorina saccata*, showing apothecia depressed in foliose thallus, ×2. B, *Umbilicaria polyphylla*, showing apothecia on foliose thallus, ×10. C, *Coniocybe furfuracea*, sorediate thallus with apothecia, ×10. D, *Rhizocarpon geographicum*, crustose thallus with apothecia, ×2.5.

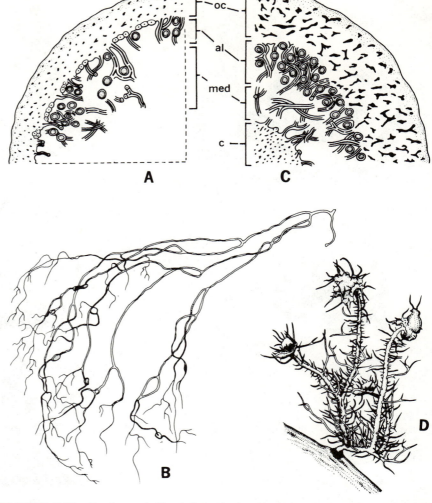

FIGURE 7–78 Fruticose thalli of lichens. A, *Alectoria,* cross section of thallus showing outer cortex (*oc*), algal layer (*al*), medulla (*med*), central strand (*c*), ×165; B, *Alectoria,* habit, ×0.75; C, *Usnea,* cross section of thallus showing anatomy, ×165; D, *Usnea,* habit, ×1.2. (A, C, after des Abbayes with permission of Paul Lechevalier.)

(Fig. 7–83). The apothecium is borne on the surface of the thallus, depressed within it, or raised high on a stalk. Several apothecia are generally produced on each thallus (Fig. 7–75C, 76, 77, 78B, D, 81A). The apothecium is small, its diameter seldom exceeding 1 centimeter and generally less than 5 millimeters. In *Cladonia,* the primary (first-formed) thallus gives rise to a secondary thallus of fruticose podetia (Fig. 7–77A, B), which usually bear many apothecia.

The anatomy of a common type of apothecium is shown in Figure 7–83A. The upper surface may be brightly colored and is frequently different in color from the rest of the thallus. Asci and paraphyses vary in shape, size, and morphology, depending on the lichen species. The asci may contain one, two, four,

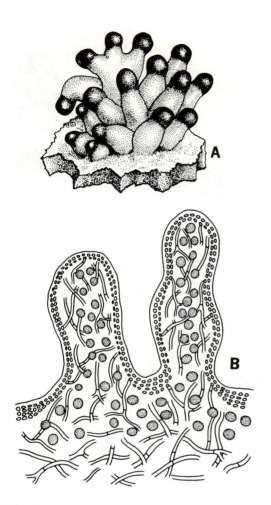

FIGURE 7–79 Isidia of *Lobaria pulmonaria*. A, isidia from upper surface of thallus, ×50; B, diagrammatic longitudinal section through isidia, ×200.

six, eight, or more spores—the number generally constant for a given species. The asci are inoperculate. Spores are released by bursting of the ascal wall when the thallus is moist; when the thallus becomes desiccated, spore discharge ceases. As in most discomycetous ascomycetes, the spores are shot from the asci.

The ascospores are morphologically characteristic of the lichen species. Ascospores are probably significant in lichen reproduction. The germinating spore must contact the appropriate phycobiont, and the spores are generally slow to germinate. Unlike most ascomycetous fungi,

many lichen apothecia retain spore-bearing capacity for several years.

Perithecia are urn-shaped and are partially or entirely immersed in the medulla of the thallus or substrate in which the lichen grows (Fig. 7–83B). They open through the upper cortex by an ostiole. In the perithecium the hypothecium is sharply delimited from the medulla. Perithecia are characteristic of many crustose lichens.

A number of asexual spores are also produced by lichens. Most lichens have pycnidia (Fig. 7–83A), superficially resembling perithecia but containing simple or branched hyphae that form asexual spores. Such spores are also produced in various other parts of some lichens but are often not restricted to a special organ-like portion. These spores vary in size and shape and their function is uncertain.

Most lichens appear to reproduce by simple fragmentation. When dry, most lichen thalli are exceedingly brittle; fragments are easily detached and carried to a new locality to produce a new thallus. This method is probably significant in all but the crustose forms, in which there is often no means of fragmentation. In many crustose forms, asexual reproductive bodies, such as soredia and isidia, are also lacking. Most crustose lichens produce an abundance of ascospores; and since many of these lichens are widely distributed, it is generally assumed that the ascospore is the means of dispersal. Only recently has success been attained in following the development of the lichen thallus from the spore. The general pattern of formation appears to be as follows:

1. The ascospore is released, carried by wind or water, and lands in a suitable environment. Suitable conditions vary considerably in light intensity, humidity, and temperature.

2. The ascospore germinates, producing a mass of hyphae. If no suitable algal partner is encountered, presumably the hyphae die. If a suitable alga is encountered, it is surrounded by the hyphae and lives within the new lichen. At this stage the lichen would resemble a soredium. If unlichenizable algae are encountered, they may be parasitized.

129

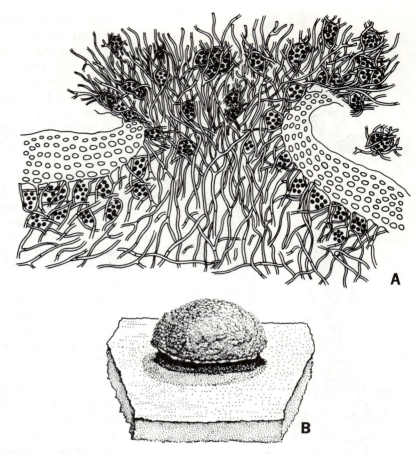

FIGURE 7–80 A mass of soredia of *Lobaria verrucosa*. A, cross section through thallus showing bursting mass of soredia, ×140; B, external view of sorediate mass on upper cortex of thallus, ×30.

3. The thallus expands and differentiates. It is estimated that one to two years elapse before a thallus forms that is visible to the naked eye.

4. Onset of dry conditions induces sexuality and ultimately apothecia result.

Growth

Growth of most lichens is very slow. In some crustose forms there is an annual increase in radius of from 0.1 to 2.0 millimeters, and in foliose types from 0.5–10.0 millimeters. In some fruticose forms annual growth varies from 2 to 4 centimeters. Crustose and foliose thalli grow chiefly at the margins; the center may degenerate with age and erode while the margin continues to grow. In foliose types, growth is similar. In fruticose types, growth is apical.

By determining the average radial growth of a thallus, and by measuring the diameter of the thallus, it is possible to calculate the approximate age of the lichen. Some crustose lichens have been estimated to be over 1,000 years old. In most lichens, however, growth rate is too erratic to aid in determining age with accuracy.

Physiology

In contrast with most fungi, most lichens are tolerant of extreme illumination and nearly complete desiccation. When wetted, the desiccated lichen simply absorbs water passively like a blotter. The dry thallus can absorb three to 35 times its own weight in water. Water loss is by simple evaporation and is rapid, so that little may be retained for growth and metabolism of the lichen.

The basic organic material on which the lichen fungus depends is produced by the phycobiont. Part of this is utilized by the phycobiont and part by the mycobiont. If the balance of usage is upset, one or both partners die. The metabolic products of the phycobiont are rapidly absorbed by the lichen thallus and are very slowly assimilated. Consequently, a reservoir of basic nutrients is built up in the lichen thallus under favorable conditions. This reserve may be drawn upon later by either mycobiont or phycobiont.

Minerals enter the thallus with rainwater and dew absorbed by the thallus. In crustose forms some dissolved minerals may be obtained from the substrate. Although the thallus has no means of eliminating minerals, they may accumulate in very high concentrations, but without apparent injury to the thallus.

The fungal cell walls in most lichens are largely of lichen starch, lichenin, which is iodine negative. Chitin is also present in many lichens. Both of these substances are absent in the phycobiont. Some of the organic products of the lichen are insoluble in water; these accumulate as crystals on the hyphal surfaces. Many of these substances—among them, the

131

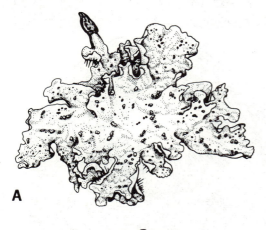

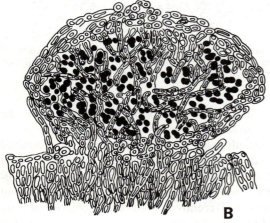

FIGURE 7–81 Cephalodia of *Peltigera aphthosa.* A, habit sketch of thallus with cephalodia on upper surface, ×1; B, longitudinal section through cephalodium, ×60. (C, after Galløe with permission of Ejnar Munksgaard.)

FIGURE 7–82 Habit sketch of a basidiomycetous lichen, *Cora pavonia,* ×1.

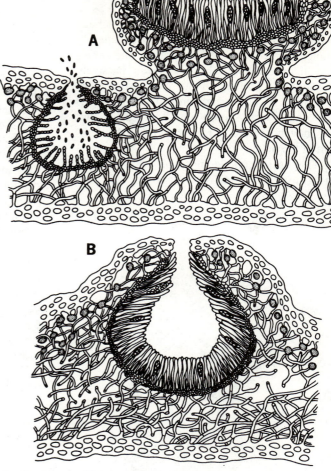

FIGURE 7–83 Apothecia, pycnidia, and perithecia of lichens. A, apothecium of *Lecanora* (right), and pycnidium (left), ×30; B, perithecium of unidentified lichen, ×30. (After Nienburg with permission of Gebrüder Borntraeger.)

lichenic acids—appear to be peculiar to lichens, but some have been found in nonlichenized fungi. The presence or absence of a particular lichenic acid is useful in distinguishing some species.

Synthesis

Given proper nutrient media, the phycobiont and mycobiont can be cultured inde-

pendently of each other. In most cases the cultured phycobiont thrives and reproduces sexually, which it seldom does in its lichenized state. The cultured mycobiont produces few of the lichenic acids that it produces in its lichenized state. In rare cases, it forms asexual spores. Recently a cultured mycobiont of *Cladonia*, in the absence of the phycobiont, has been induced to produce sexual reproductive structures but not sexual spores.

Attempts to isolate the phycobiont and mycobiont, culture them independently, and then resynthesize the lichen have met with varying success. In rare cases a thallus anatomically similar to that of the original lichen has been produced. In resynthesizing the lichen from its original component partners, growth conditions apparently do not highly favor either partner. In such cases the potential partners will dissociate and live independently. In the lichen association, balanced growth is necessary. Conditions that favor rapid growth of the alga are intolerable to the lichen fungus, while those that favor rapid growth of the fungus are intolerable to the alga. For the lichen association to be maintained, growth conditions must be poor for both partners; thus, growth is invariably slow.

Uses

Most lichens are nonpoisonous and may be used as food in an emergency. Rock tripe (*Umbilicaria*), for example, was used by early Arctic explorers to reduce scurvy. The extensive lichen pastures in the birch forests of Scandinavia and the lichen woodlands in subarctic Canada are important feeding areas for reindeer and caribou.

Lichens have long been used as a source of natural dyestuffs and medicine. A number of lichens possess antibiotic substances used in preparations for treating external wounds and burns.

Lichens are natural indicators of industrial pollution of the air. Since they cannot excrete the substances they absorb from the air, lichens accumulate quantities of industrial waste material. When this accumulation reaches a toxic level, the lichen dies. Some lichens are slightly more tolerant of industrial waste than others. The presence of particular tree bark lichens is a good indication that industrial waste entering the atmosphere is not excessive. One can estimate the degree of air pollution in industrial areas by sampling the lichen population at varying distances from the source of pollution.

Lichens and Plant Succession

A few workers consider lichens important in the breakdown of rock. Certainly crustose lichens are pioneers on newly exposed rock surfaces, but they grow and chemically break down the rock very slowly. Thus, lichens cannot be considered significant in initiating plant succession. The reindeer lichen (*Cladonia*) appears to require organic material as a basic substrate, although the initial colony will also expand and form a porous mat over inorganic material. Since such mats dry rapidly, they provide a poor substrate for other plants that might otherwise colonize the lichen-covered surface.

133

Distribution

Lichens will grow on well-illuminated areas on most substrates. They are best known from rocks and trees, or as mat formers on soil. Most lichen species are very specific in their substrate requirements.

Lichens are widely distributed. They are found on rocks in deserts as well as rocks at extreme altitudes and latitudes, where they do not compete for space with other organisms. Although lichens form the most conspicuous living terrestrial cover in Antarctica, in the high Arctic they are less conspicuous than bryophytes and vascular plants.

8 / Division Rhodophyta

The division Rhodophyta (*red algae*) is a large and diverse group of algae with almost 600 genera and nearly 4,000 species. This group is generally considered as one class, the Rhodophyceae, with two subclasses, the Bangiophycidae and the Florideophycidae.

As in the blue-green algae, there are no flagellated cells in the red algae. The Rhodophyta and Cyanophyta have similar pigment complexes (chlorophyll *a* and phycobiliproteins) and the same general class of storage products (*α*, 1–4, 1–6 linkage). As in the photosynthetic lamellae of the blue-green algae, the red algal chloroplast (Fig. 8–1) has unassociated photosynthetic lamellae. In the red algae, sexual reproduction is generally of regular occurrence and is oogamous. There is a regular alternation of syngamy and meiosis.

In the red algae the male gametangium is referred to as a spermatangium, and the nonmotile male gametes are called spermatia (Fig. 8–3H). The female gametangium, called a carpogonium, usually has an elongate, emergent, thread-like receptive portion called the trichogyne (Fig. 8–10H).

The male nucleus from the spermatium fuses with the female nucleus in the base of the carpogonium, forming the diploid zygote nucleus. Division in the zygote nucleus results directly or indirectly in the production of carposporangia, which produce carpospores (Fig. 8–3G). If the division is meiotic, the carpospores are haploid, and if the division is mitotic, they are diploid. Haploid carpospores give rise directly to gametophyte generations (Fig. 8–5, 12). Diploid carpospores give rise directly to a free-living sporophyte generation, the tetrasporophyte (Fig. 8–13D, 16K). The tetrasporophyte is generally morphologically similar to the free-living gametophytes in the life cycle, and it is in this diploid phase that meiosis occurs. The meiosporangium, or the tetrasporangium, produces four tetraspores, which then germinate into free-living gametophytes. Diploid carposporangia apparently occur only in members of the subclass Florideophycidae.

CELL STRUCTURE

The red algal cell wall is typically differentiated into an inner cellulose and an outer pectic layer. The polysaccharides agar and carrageenin may also occur in the cell wall and intercellular spaces of many of the more spe-

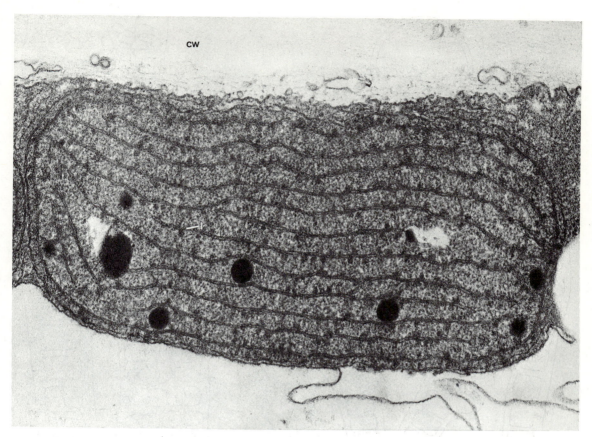

CW

FIGURE 8–1   Electron micrograph of Rhodophyta chloroplast showing double bands of unfused lamellae (*l*) and thick cell wall (*cw*), ×60,000. (Courtesy T. Bisalputra.)

cialized red algae. In certain genera, such as the coralline algae, there is a heavy calcification of the outer part of the cell wall.

The cells in simple forms are usually uninucleate. In the more advanced forms they are generally multinucleate, except for young or reproductive cells. The nuclei have a well-defined nuclear membrane and a nucleolus. Central or peripheral chloroplasts are also present. In some simple forms, there may be only one chloroplast, with or without pyrenoid-like structures. Generally the more complex forms have numerous small discoid chloroplasts in each cell, although irregular or band-like ones also occur. The chloroplast of the Rhodophyceae is characterized by single, unassociated lamellae (Fig. 8–1), which resemble the

photosynthetic lamellae of the Cyanophyceae (Fig. 5–2).

The red algae owe their characteristic reddish-purple color to the presence of the accessory phycobiliprotein pigments. The predominant ones are *r*-phycoerythrin, which is red; and *r*-phycocyanin, which is blue. These phycobiliproteins are very similar but not chemically identical to those of Cyanophyceae or Cryptophyceae. Accessory carotenoid pigments are also present, and include α-carotene and β-carotene and some xanthophylls. The green pigments include the universal chlorophyll *a* and possibly another reported in only a few red algae—chlorophyll *d,* which may be only a derivative of chlorophyll *a* and an artifact of the extraction techniques. The green

DIVISION RHODOPHYTA

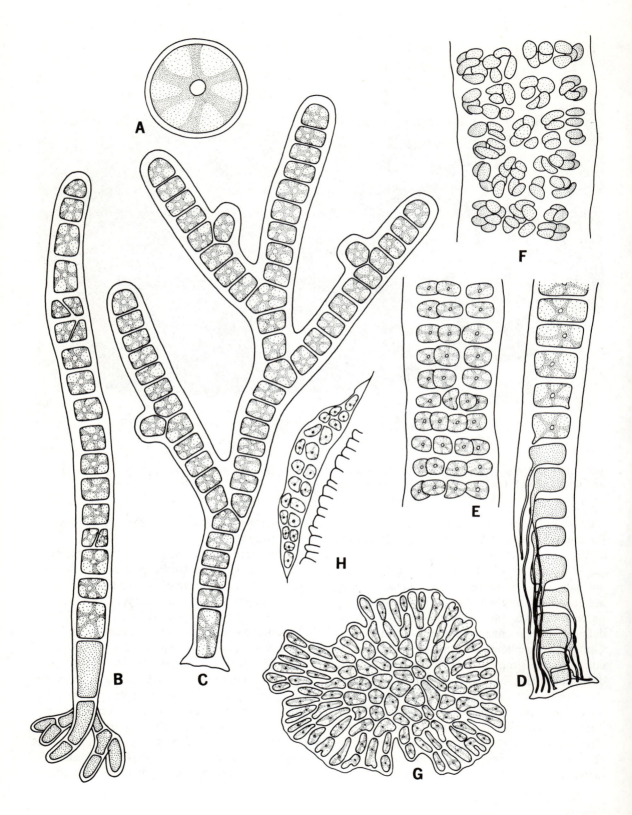

A

B

C

D

E

F

G

H

NONVASCULAR PLANTS

pigments are generally masked by the accessory pigments.

The main food reserve is floridean starch, composed essentially of the amylopectin fraction of starch. Other reserve substances of low molecular weight include the saccharides trehalose, floridoside, mannoglyceric acid, and sucrose. Several sterols present include cholesterol, sitosterol, and fucosterol. Most red algae are autotrophic.

Subclass Bangiophycidae

Classification and Morphological Diversity. The Bangiophycidae is a small subclass with fewer than 100 species in some 40 genera. These are the simplest of the red algae, and they exhibit a wide range in morphology. Many of them are marine.

The simplest type of thallus is unicellular (Fig. 8–2A). A number of the genera are filamentous. These may be erect, uniseriate unbranched (Fig. 8–2B), branched (Fig. 8–2C), or prostrate (Fig. 8–2G, H) forms. In others there may be a few regular divisions in the erect simple branches, indicative of parenchyma (Fig. 8–2D–F). The most advanced growth attained in the group is the parenchymatous, foliose type (Fig. 8–3A, D). The cells divide in two planes to form a monostromatic plant body (Fig. 8–3A–C), or rarely in three planes to form a distromatic thallus (Fig. 8–3D, E). The postulated lines along which these various types may have evolved are diagrammatically illustrated in Figure 8–4. It is possible to derive the upright parenchymatous thallus from a unicellular form (Fig. 8–4A) through either the upright filamentous forms (Fig. 8–4B–E) or the prostrate disc (Fig. 8–4F–M).

The thallus may be attached by a simple holdfast cell (Fig. 8–2C), by a few basal rhizoidal multicellular filaments (Fig. 8–2B), or by rhizoidal filaments sent out by a number of cells at the base of the thallus (Fig. 8–2D). There may be a very extensive production of nonseptate, rhizoidal processes aggregated to form a massive holdfast structure (Fig. 8–3F).

Life Histories and Reproduction. Vegetative reproduction by fragmentation is common. Various spore types are also formed. Sexual reproduction is unknown in the simpler forms, although it is well established in certain other genera.

The reproductive structures in the Bangiophycidae are generally differentiated vegetative cells, as illustrated in *Porphyra*. Characteristic of the Bangiophycidae is the production of many spermatia per spermatangium and many carpospores per carposporangium. In the spermatangium, a large number of almost colorless spermatia are formed by mitotic divisions (Fig. 8–3H, 5G). The female gametangium (the carpogonium) undergoes a slight modification to form a rudimentary trichogyne (Fig. 8–5D); the carpogonium is uninucleate. If a spermatium contacts the trichogyne, its nucleus passes into the cytoplasm of the carpogonium, fusing with the female nucleus (Fig. 8–5E). Immediately after fusion, it is believed that the zygote nucleus undergoes meiosis, followed sometimes by a number of mitotic divisions, forming a number of uninucleate haploid carpospores in each.

The carpospores may germinate and grow directly into new foliose multicellular gametophytes (Fig. 8–5A, B, H–J, N, O,). However, a number of alternatives are apparently possible. The carpospore may germinate, developing into a branched filamentous stage (Fig. 8–5K) which at maturity produces somewhat swollen cells. These function as monosporangia, each producing a single monospore (Fig. 8–5L) that is potentially similar to a carpospore in function.

137

FIGURE 8–2 Morphological diversity in Bangiophycidae. A, *Porphyridium*, unicellular form, ×1,750. B, C, unbranched and branched filamentous forms. B, *Erythrotrichia*, ×578; C, *Goniotrichum*, ×560. D–H, parenchymatous types. D–F, *Bangia*, ×350. D, basal region of thallus with rhizoidal cells; E, distal vegetative portion of parenchymatous region of thallus; F, fertile portion of thallus. G, H, *Erythrocladia*, ×700. G, unistratose species viewed from above. H, multistratose epiphytic species on algal substrate, viewed from side.

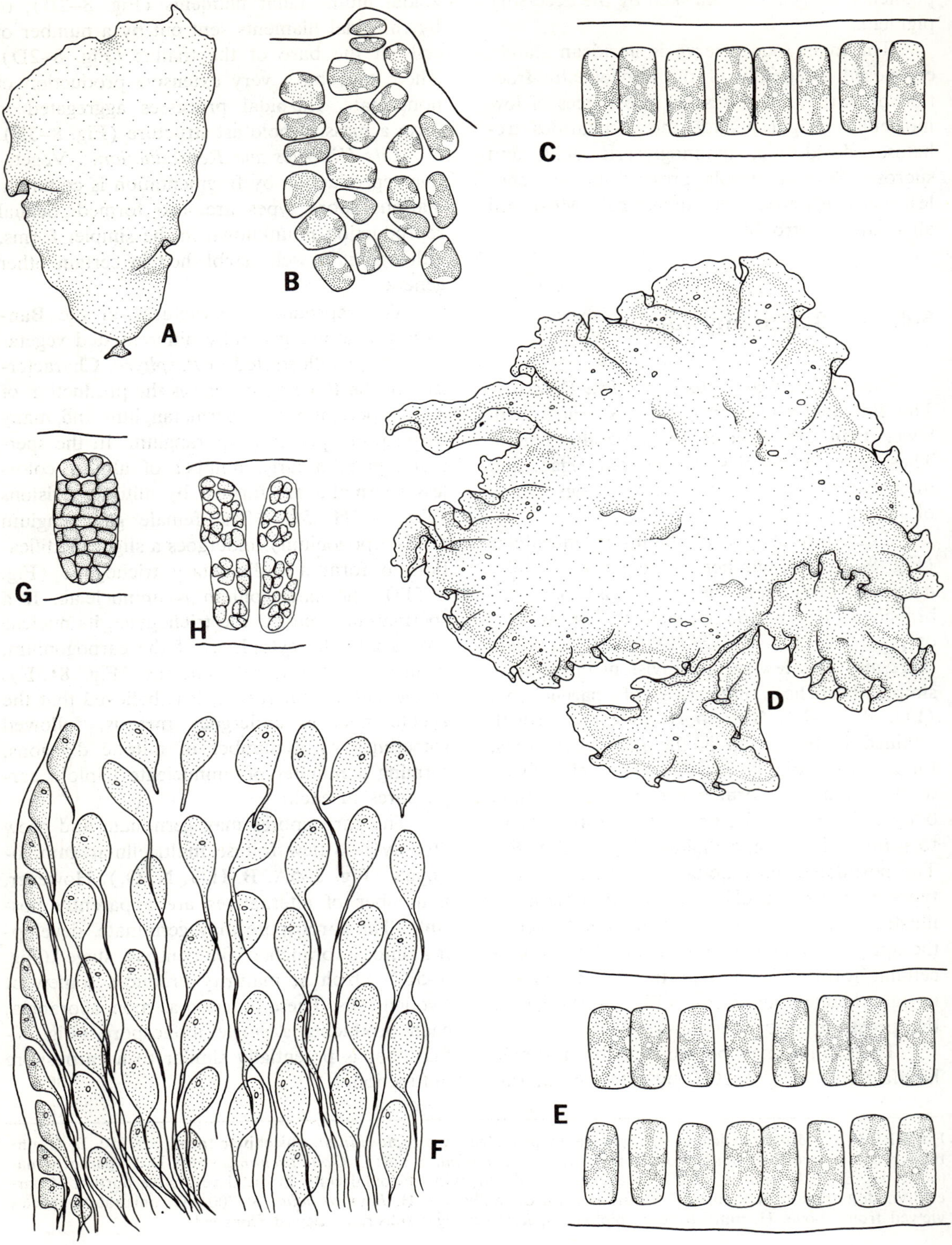
A
B
C
D
E
F
G
H

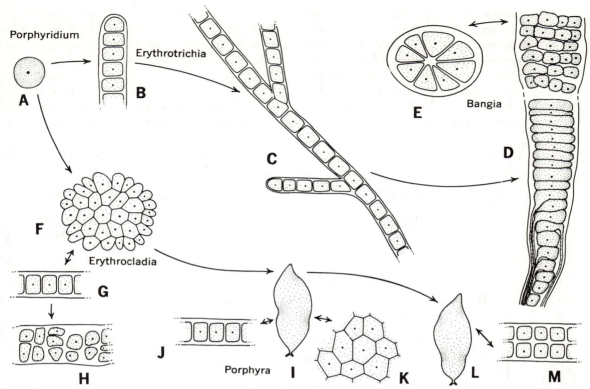

FIGURE 8–4 Possible evolution of growth types in Bangiophycidae, from unicellular (A) to parenchymatous types, through two possible lines: (1) filamentous (B–E) or (2) prostrate disc (F–M).

Although the cytological details have not yet been confirmed for all species, it has been suggested that alternate phases are not cytologically different and that meiosis occurs immediately following syngamy. Knowledge of the factors affecting the life history of *Porphyra* are important in the commercial farming of this alga (known as nori or purple laver) in Japan (Fig. 8–6A, B).

Subclass Florideophycidae

Classification and Morphological Diversity. The Florideophycidae is a large subclass with

over 3,500 species in about 500 genera. Most are marine, but a few genera with about 200 species occur in fresh-water habitats. The Florideophycidae are also vegetatively simple.

The Florideophycidae have primary pit connections (Fig. 8–7A–C) between adjacent cells, in contrast to the Bangiophycidae, where primary pit connections are uncommon. In more complex thalli, secondary pit connections may occur between adjacent cells in the same filament and between cells in adjacent filaments (Fig. 8–7D–H). The formation of secondary pit connections involves migration of a nucleus from one cell to another.

FIGURE 8–3 Morphological diversity and reproduction in parenchymatous Bangiophycidae (*Porphyra*). A–C, monostromatic species. A, habit, ×1.5; B, surface view of cells, ×500; C, transverse section through portion of thallus, ×500. D, E, distromatic species. D, habit, ×0.5; E, transverse section through portion of thallus, ×500. F, portion of basal attachment region of thallus in longitudinal section, showing rhizoidal cells, ×500. G, H, reproduction in a monostromatic species, ×600. G, carpospores within carposporangia; H, spermatia within spermatangium.

The subclass is composed of filamentous forms; there are no unicellular or truly parenchymatous members. The simplest are uniseriate, branched forms (Fig. 8–8A, E); the more complex forms have branches that are laterally fused, resulting in a pseudoparenchymatous thallus (Fig. 8–8B–D, 9). The pseudoparenchymatous and loosely branched forms may have either uniaxial (Fig. 8–8) or multiaxial (Fig. 8–9) growth. In the former the main axis consists of a single row of large cells. In multiaxial types the main axis is composed of a number of parallel or almost parallel filaments. The various lines of development of the uniaxial and multiaxial types are diagrammatically illustrated in detail in Figures

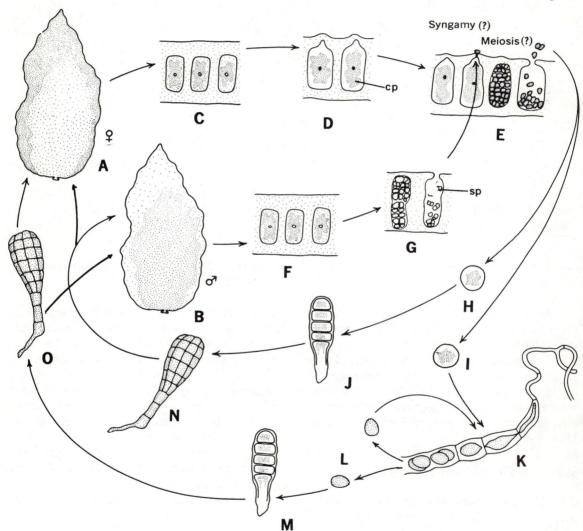

FIGURE 8–5 Life history of *Porphyra* (monostromatic species). A, female gametophyte with fertile margin; B, male gametophyte with fertile margin; C, F, vegetative gametophyte cells; D, carpogonium (*cp*) development; G, formation and liberation of spermatia (*sp*) from spermatangium; E, syngamy (left) and formation of carpospores (right) from zygote on female gametophyte; H, I, carpospore; J, germination of carpospore to form gametophyte; K, filamentous phase developed from germinated carpospore; L, monospore produced from K; M, germination of monospore to form gametophyte; N, O, young foliose gametophytes developing from monospore or carpospore. (For details and relative sizes of structures, refer to Fig. 8–3.)

A

B

FIGURE 8–6 Nori culture in Tokyo Bay, Japan. A, net (partly submerged) suspended from bamboo poles with meshes covered by growth of *Porphyra* plants; B, Japanese "fisherman" at low tide tending emergent nets covered with growth of *Porphyra* plants. (Photographs by A. Miura, courtesy S. Ueda.)

DIVISION RHODOPHYTA

8–8 and 8–9. The aggregation of filaments often results in an outer, compact, small-celled cortex and an inner medulla that is loose and filamentous (Fig. 8–11D) or large-celled (Fig. 8–11F). Growth of each axis of a filament and each branch is by means of a simple apical cell (Fig. 8–10D).

Life Histories and Reproduction. In many of the more complex Florideophycidae, vegetative reproduction is common and perennial from an undifferentiated base. A variety of mitospores are produced, especially in some of the simpler forms; they germinate, reduplicating the thallus that bore them.

Sexual reproduction is well established in the Florideophycidae, with usually an alternation of free-living generations. When a free-living tetrasporophyte occurs, it is usually vegetatively indistinguishable from the haploid gametophytes. Unlike the Bangiophycidae, each spermatangium gives rise to a single spermatium. Similarly, each carposporangium gives rise to only one carpospore. Following syngamy there is produced "parasitically" on the female gametophyte a diminutive phase, the carposporophyte. It is either haploid or diploid, and produces the carpospores. The carposporophyte comprises vegetative cells, the carposporophyte filaments, and the carposporangia.

In the simpler forms the life history is similar to that of some of the Bangiophycidae. For example, on *Batrachospermum* (Fig. 8–10C–K, 12) or *Nemalion* (Fig. 8–11A, B), the gametophyte is the conspicuous generation—the only diploid cell apparently being the zygote that is never liberated. The first division of the zygote nucleus is meiotic. On the male gametophyte, colorless spermatia are produced in spermatangia borne on the tips of filamentous branches (Fig. 8–10G, 12C). The carpogonia, also at the tips of filamentous branches, have a well-defined, diminutive trichogyne (Fig. 8–10H, 12D). The spermatium rests on the trichogyne (Fig. 8–12F), and the nucleus passes to the enlarged basal part of the carpogonium, where it fuses with the female nucleus (Fig. 8–12G, H). After meiosis of the zygote nucleus (Fig. 8–12I), daughter nuclei are cut off in

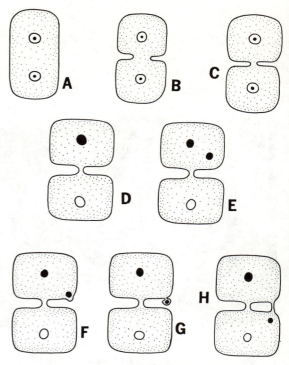

FIGURE 8–7 Formation of pit connections in Florideophycidae. A–C, formation of primary pit connection; D–H, formation of secondary pit connection.

cells, which then divide repeatedly, forming the carposporophyte filaments (Fig. 8–10J, 12J, K), which are thus haploid cells. The carposporophyte is exposed and the terminal cells develop directly into carposporangia (Fig. 8–12K), each of which produces a single haploid carpospore (Fig. 8–12L, M). The carpospores germinate and develop into free-living gametophytes (Fig. 8–12A, B, N–Q).

A few members of the Nemalionales have a more complex life history. For example, in *Bonnemaisonia* there are a large, free-living gametophyte plant (Fig. 8–13A) and a diminutive, free-living tetrasporophyte (Fig. 8–13D, *Trailiella*-stage). In *Bonnemaisonia,* meiosis apparently does not occur immediately after syngamy, and the carposporophyte is diploid, producing diploid carpospores (Fig. 8–13C). The carposporophyte produces tetrasporangia, and meiosis is believed to occur during tetraspore production (Fig. 8–13E). The liberated tetra-

142

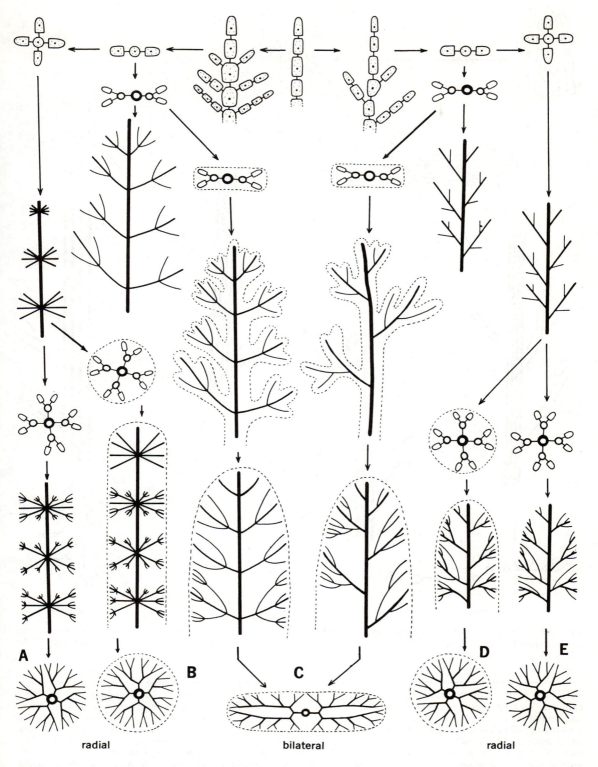

FIGURE 8–8 Growth types in uniaxial Florideophycidae, showing possible evolutionary lines leading to freely branched (A, E) and pseudoparenchymatous (B–D) types with radial (A, B, D, E,) and bilateral (C) symmetry.

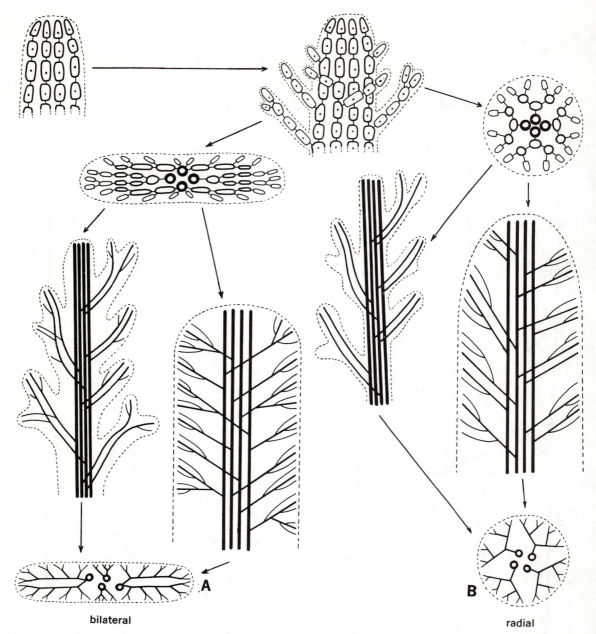

144

bilateral

B

radial

FIGURE 8-9 Growth types of multiaxial Florideophycidae, showing possible evolutionary lines leading to pseudoparenchymatous forms with varying amounts of fusion of filaments, and with bilateral (A) and radial (B) symmetry.

FIGURE 8-10 Morphology and reproduction in uniaxial Florideophycidae. A, B, *Antithamnion*. A, habit epiphytic on kelp stipe, ×0.5; B, terminal portion of thallus, showing uniaxial, loose, filamentous construction, and immature tetrasporangia (*tspn*), ×240. C–K, *Batrachospermum*. C, habit, ×1; D, apical region of thallus, showing apical cell (*ac*) and filamentous branches, ×475; E, portion of main axis, showing uniaxial construction and whorls of filamentous branches, ×165; F, more mature portion showing development of corticating filaments that cover the axial row of cells, ×165; G, branch bearing several mature spermatangia (*sp*), ×960; H, unfertilized carpogonium (*cp*), ×915; I, post-fertilization stage showing initiation of carposporophyte filaments (*cf*), ×915; J, later stage of carposporophyte filament development, showing chains of carposporangia (*cspn*), ×790; K, portion of thallus showing mature and empty monosporangia (*mspn*), ×790.

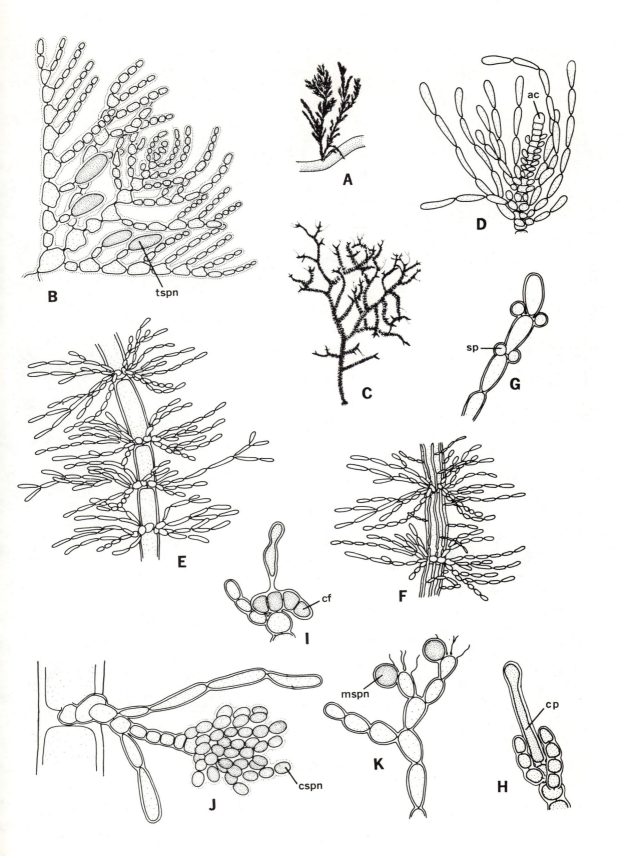

145

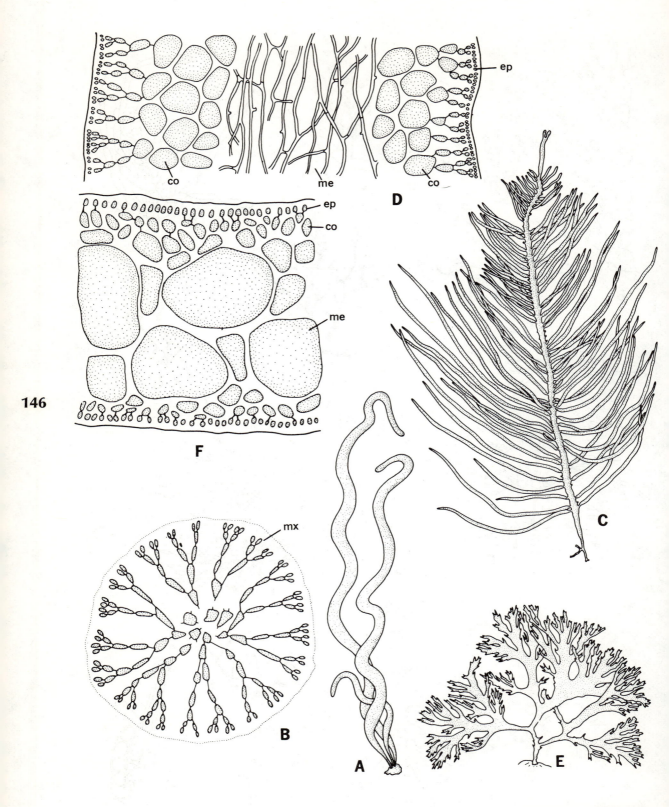

146

D

ep

co

me

co

ep

co

me

F

mx

B

A

C

E

NONVASCULAR PLANTS

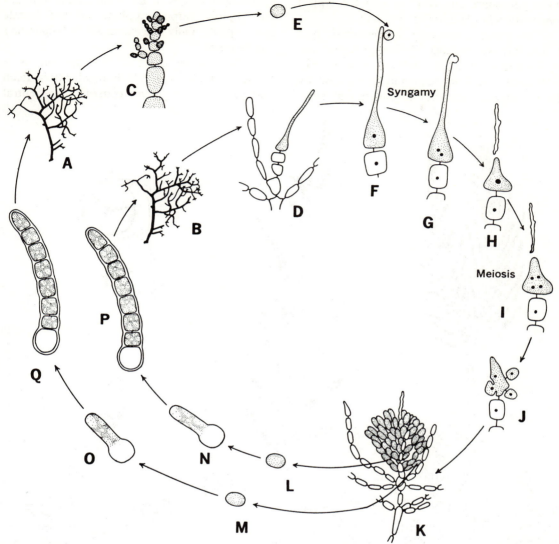

FIGURE 8–12 Life history of *Batrachospermum*. A, B, gametophytes; C, branch of male gametophyte with several spermatangia and one released spermatium (E); D, branch of female gametophyte with carpogonium; F, spermatium adjacent to trichogyne; G, spermatium nucleus in base of carpogonium; H, syngamy completed; I, after meiosis, trichogyne degenerates; J, initiation of carposporophyte filaments from fertilized carpogonium; K, mature carposporophyte with numerous carposporangia; L, M, carpospores; N, O, germinating carpospores; P, Q, filamentous germlings. (For details and representative sizes of comparable structures refer to Fig. 8–10C–K.)

FIGURE 8–11 Morphology of multiaxial Florideophycidae, A, B, *Nemalion*. A, habit of several plants, ×0.7; B, transverse section through thallus, showing multiaxial construction and organization of branched filaments embedded in mucilaginous matrix (*mx*), ×415. C, D, *Agardhiella*. C, habit, ×0.5; D, longitudinal section through portion of thallus, showing filamentous medulla (*me*), pseudoparenchymatous cortex (*co*), and epidermis (*ep*), ×60. E, F, *Callophyllis*. E, habit, ×0.5; F, transverse section through portion of multiaxial thallus, showing pseudoparenchymatous organization with compact large-celled medulla, small-celled cortex, and epidermis, ×150.

DIVISION RHODOPHYTA

spores germinate and develop into the typical *Bonnemaisonia* plants (Fig. 8–13A).

The most commonly encountered type of life history in the Florideophycidae has an alternation of isomorphic generations (Fig. 8–16) with free-living male and female gametophytes alternating with a free-living tetra-sporophyte and with an intermediate diminutive diploid carposporophyte on the female gametophyte. Only one example (*Polysiphonia*) will be cited.

The mature plant of *Polysiphonia* is a branched thallus with cells in regular tiers. Each mature tier, or segment, consists of a central

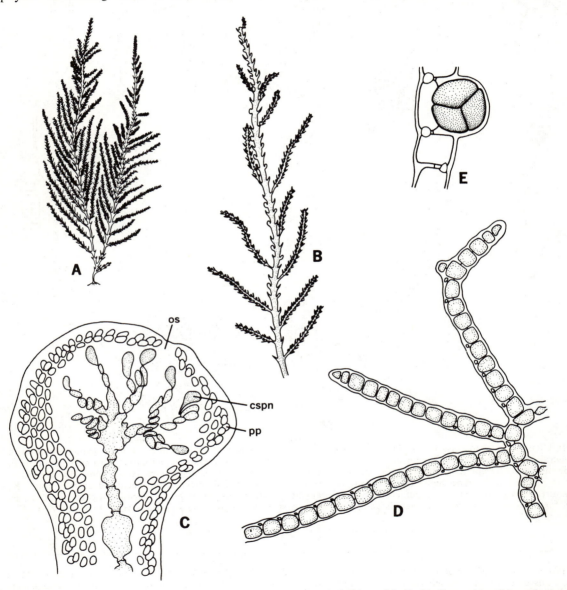

148

FIGURE 8–13 *Bonnemaisonia*. A, B, C, female gametophyte. A, habit, ×0.3; B, fertile portion of branch showing position of developing carposporophytes, ×1; C, carposporophyte shown within pericarp (*pp*), with ostiole (*os*), and elongate carposporangia (*cspn*). D, filamentous tetrasporophyte (*Trailiella*-stage), ×220; E, portion of filamentous thallus showing tetrasporangium with three of four tetraspores apparent, ×400.

NONVASCULAR PLANTS

cell surrounded by a number of pericentral cells of equal length. This is often referred to as a polysiphonous construction. Growth in *Polysiphonia* is strictly apical, and the apical cell cuts off cells from its posterior face, as summarized in Figure 8–14.

On the female branch the first segment above the basal one becomes fertile, and the last-formed pericentral cell in the fertile segment produces the carpogonial branch. Adjacent pericentral cells cut off series of vegetative cells. This filamentous series of haploid vegetative cells results in the formation of an urn-shaped ostiolate pericarp, which encloses the

developing female reproductive system (Fig. 8–15F).

Prior to fertilization, the fertile pericentral cell within the pericarp undergoes three primary divisions, with the remaining proximal portion becoming the supporting cell. Thus, there is produced a four-celled carpogonial branch borne on a supporting cell (Fig. 8–15E, 16E). The terminal cell of the branch develops into the carpogonium (Fig. 8–15E, 16E), which has a long narrow trichogyne that emerges through the pericarp ostiole.

On the male branch, there are formed a large number of spermatia. Several segments

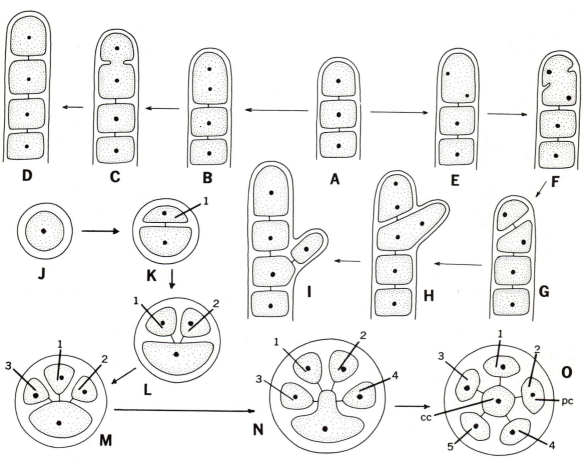

FIGURE 8–14 Apical growth and polysiphonous structure in *Polysiphonia*. A–D, stages in division of apical cell to produce nonbranch-forming segments; E–I, stages in division of apical cell (note position of nuclei in apical cell) to produce a branch-forming segment; J–O, divisions in segments (as seen in transverse section) cut off from the apical cell, resulting in polysiphonous structure of axis with central (axial) cell and several (in this example, five) pericentral cells. Sequence in division is indicated by number. *cc*, central cell; *pc*, pericentral cell.

DIVISION RHODOPHYTA

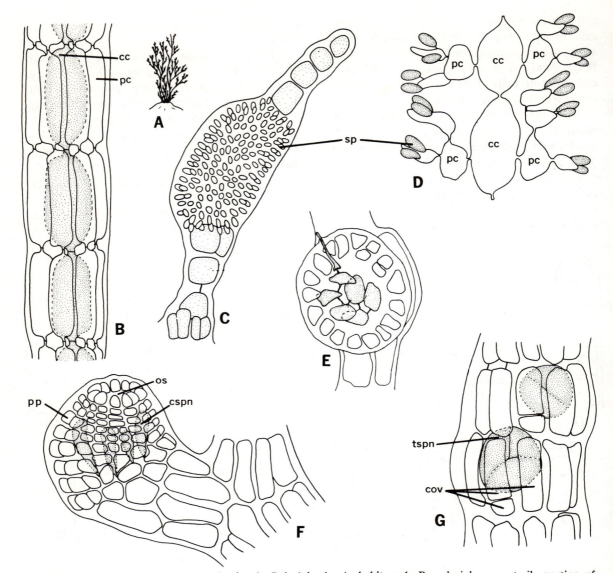

FIGURE 8–15 Structure and reproduction in *Polysiphonia*. A, habit, ×1; B, polysiphonous sterile portion of thallus, showing central series of cells (*cc*) surrounded by pericentral cells (*pc*), ×250; C, mature male branch, showing dense mass of spermatangia (*sp*), ×200; D, longitudinal section through two fertile segments of male branch, showing derivation of spermatangia from pericentral cells, and relationships to central cells, ×500; E, carpogonium, ×200; F, cystocarp, showing ostiole (*os*) and outer sterile pericarp wall (*pp*), through which some of fertile terminal carposporangia (*cspn*) of carposporophyte are shown, ×150; G, surface view of fertile portion of thallus, showing mature tetrasporangia (*tspn*) as seen through protecting cover cells (*cov*), ×250.

of the male branch divide to form a central cell and five pericentral cells. All five pericentral cells in each of these fertile polysiphonous segments become fertile (Fig. 8–15C, D, 16C). Each fertile pericentral cell under-

goes a number of transverse divisions to produce three or more spermatangial mother cells. In turn, each of these divides obliquely, cutting off two or more spermatangia, which at maturity liberate a single colorless naked spermatium

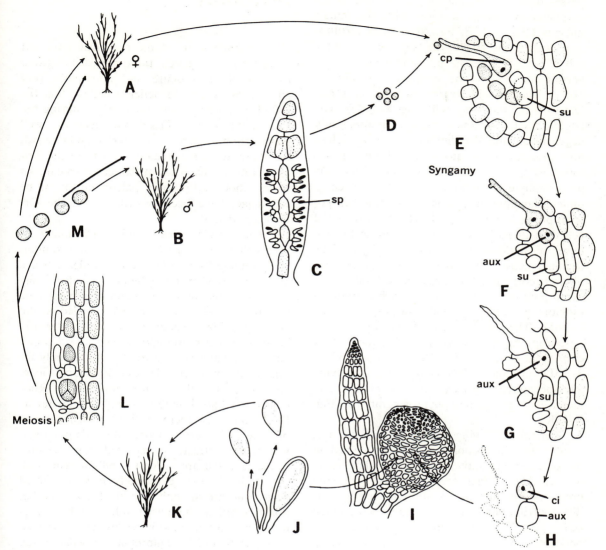

FIGURE 8–16 Life history of *Polysiphonia*. A, B, gametophytes; C, male branch with spermatangia; D, spermatia; E, fully developed carpogonium (*cp*) on carpogonial branch borne on supporting cell (*su*) (details of surrounding pericarp omitted); F, syngamy complete and auxiliary cell (*aux*) formed; G, movement of zygote nucleus into auxiliary cell (*aux*); H, formation of carposporophyte initial (*ci*); I, mature pericarp containing mature carposporophyte; J, carposporangia liberating carpospores; K, tetrasporophyte; L, fertile branch of tetrasporophyte with tetrasporangia forming (lowest tetrasporangium mature); M, tetraspores (meiospores). (For structural details and representative sizes of structures, refer to Fig. 8–15.)

(Fig. 8–15D). The mature male branch appears as a stalked club-shaped structure with a large number of small, almost colorless, refractive cells (the spermatangia) on its surface.

The spermatia come to rest on the receptive trichogyne (Fig. 8–16E).

When a spermatium makes contact with the receptive trichogyne, the male nucleus passes down the trichogyne to the base of the carpogonium, where it fuses with the female nucleus (Fig. 8–16E, F). As soon as fertilization occurs, the trichogyne degenerates and a cell is cut off from the upper end of the supporting cell. This is the auxiliary cell (Fig. 8–16F). The diploid zygote nucleus is transferred to the auxiliary cell (Fig. 8–16G). The haploid nucleus of the auxiliary cell apparently degenerates, and the diploid (zygote) nucleus now present in the auxiliary cell divides mitotically. The first true diploid cell of the carposporophyte generation is formed when a diploid daughter nucleus is cut off in the carposporophyte initial (Fig. 8–16H); this initial cell then divides repeatedly by mitosis to produce a multicellular carposporophyte. The terminal cells of the filamentous carposporophyte become much enlarged and develop into carposporangia. At maturity, each carposporangium liberates a single carpospore (Fig. 8–16J). The development of the diploid carposporophyte occurs within the haploid pericarp (Fig. 8–15F, 16I). The carpospore (Fig. 8–16J) germinates, developing into a free-living tetrasporophyte generation morphologically identical to the gametophyte generations (Fig. 8–16K).

On the free-living tetrasporophyte the tetrasporangia (meiosporangia) are produced in the ordinary vegetative axes of the plant (Fig. 8–15G, 16L). Each fertile segment generally produces one tetrasporangium, which arises indirectly from one of the pericentral cells. Three cells cut off from the outer face of the fertile pericentral cell serve as sterile cover cells (Fig. 8–15G). The tetrasporangium and the three cover cells are attached to the stalk cell. The tetrasporangium enlarges considerably, and its diploid nucleus divides meiotically to form four haploid nuclei. The cytoplasm then divides into four uninucleate portions (Fig. 8–15G, 16L). At maturity the tetraspores (meiospores) are liberated from between the cover cells. These meiospores germinate to develop into the free-living gametophyte generations (Fig. 8–16A, B).

PHYLOGENY

Although some of the red algae have left excellent fossil records, the origin of the group as a whole is obscure and apparently very ancient. Some phylogeneticists believe that the red algae probably had their origin during the Pre-Cambrian Era. Fossil red algae are well known from the Cretaceous Period and onward, but there are a few records also from the Triassic. Other somewhat questionable calcareous forms, thought by some paleobotanists to be red algae, have been recorded from the Ordovician Period.

The red algae are so different in many respects that they must be regarded as taxonomically remote from other groups of algae. It has been suggested that the blue-green algae may have given rise to some simple nonsexual type of red alga. This origin could have led to the Bangiophycidae, some of which apparently have no sexual reproduction. The Florideophycidae may have evolved from some sexually reproducing prototype in the Bangiophycidae. However, since the fossil history of the Rhodophyta is known with certainty only as far as the Cretaceous, there is little evidence for a phylogenetic series from the Cyanophyta, which, by contrast, are reported from the Pre-Cambrian, and are at least 2 billion years old.

Both divisions completely lack flagellated stages and are the only two algal divisions that do. In addition, there are similarities in the pigments and the main storage product. The lack of association of the chloroplast lamellae in the red algae is very similar to the distribution of the photosynthetic lamellae in the blue-green algae. In both divisions the thallus form ranges from unicellular to filamentous to parenchymatous types. However, in the Rhodophyta there is a greater elaboration of the filamentous form so that the uniaxial and multiaxial pseudoparenchymatous thallus is the most commonly encountered. Finally, pit connections have been reported in representatives of both divisions.

9 / Division Phaeophyta

The division Phaeophyta (*brown algae*), treated in this text as a single class, the Phaeophyceae, is a large group of algae containing about 240 genera and over 1,500 species, almost entirely restricted to the sea.

CELL STRUCTURE

In general, the cell wall is composed of a firm inner cellulose layer and an outer mucilaginous pectic or pectic-like layer. The pigments are present in one (Fig. 9–1A, C) or more (Fig. 9–1B) chloroplasts, which vary to some extent in size and shape. They are usually small and discoid (Fig. 9–1B); but they may be elongate, flattened, laminate (Fig. 9–1C), or reticulate (Fig. 9–1A). Pyrenoids are reported in some species. Electron micrographs (Fig. 9–4) show the chloroplasts to consist of three associated but unfused lamellae. The cells are generally uninucleate. The nucleus contains one or more nucleoli and is surrounded by a well-defined nuclear membrane.

The characteristic brownish color of these algae is due to the presence of the accessory xanthophyll pigment fucoxanthin. Other accessory carotenoid pigments such as β-carotene and additional xanthophylls are present in smaller amounts. The green pigments, which are masked by the brown fucoxanthin, are chlorophyll *a* and *c*.

A central vacuole (Fig. 9–1A) is usually present in the cell. The food reserves are stored outside the chloroplast primarily as the polysaccharide laminarin, which is composed of β, 1–3, 1–6 linked glucosides. An integral part of laminarin is the sugar alcohol mannitol, which oxidizes to produce the hexose sugar mannose. Numerous refractive vesicles, usually aggregated about the nucleus, contain a tannin-like substance, termed phaeophyte tannin, thought to be a waste product of metabolism. Fats and small amounts of other carbohydrates have been reported. Most of the brown algae are autotrophic.

MOVEMENT

None of the brown algae is motile although they produce motile cells (zoospores and gametes) which are almost always laterally biflagellate and usually somewhat bean-shaped, or pyriform. The flagella are usually unequal in length, with the longer one generally projecting anteriorly and the shorter posteriorly (Fig. 9–2A–C). However, in the Fucales the longer

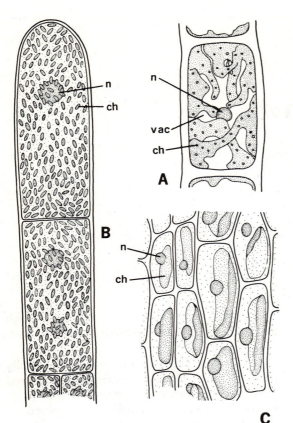

FIGURE 9–1 Chloroplast (*ch*) types in Phaeophyta. A, reticulate (*Ectocarpus*), ×1,500; B, discoid (*Sphacelaria*), ×320; C, laminate (*Scytosiphon*), ×300. *n*, nucleus; *vac*, vacuole.

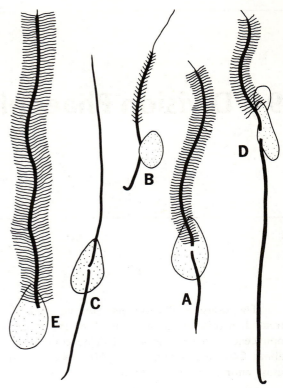

FIGURE 9–2 Arrangement of flagella in Phaeophyta (anterior end toward top of each diagram). A, B, zoospores. A, *Laminaria;* B, *Chordaria.* C–E, sperms. C, *Alaria;* D, *Fucus;* E, *Dictyota.*

flagellum trails and the shorter one projects anteriorly; the flagellated cell (sperm) is also somewhat bell-shaped (see Fig. 9–2D, 3A, B). And in the Dictyotales (Fig. 9–2E) one of the two flagella (the posterior one) is absent or rudimentary. In the brown algae the anterior flagellum is tinsel (Fig. 9–2, 3A, B), with two rows of mastigonemes, and the posterior flagellum is whiplash (Fig. 9–2A–D, 3A).

CLASSIFICATION AND MORPHOLOGICAL DIVERSITY

The orders of Phaeophyta can be placed in a number of evolutionary lines based on life history and alternation of generations, on vegetative construction (Fig. 9–5, 10), and on reproductive characteristics. The simplest organization is an unbranched or sparingly branched uniseriate filament (Fig. 9–5A, C, 10A). In the more specialized members, well developed tissues are present.

The simplest type of growth results from intercalary cell division in one plane and only occasionally in a second plane, resulting in a uniseriate, unbranched, or sparingly branched filament shown in the Ectocarpales (Fig. 9–5A, C, 6D, E, *Pylaiella*). Occasional divisions in a second plane may result in a freely branching series of uniseriate filaments, as in *Ectocarpus* (Fig. 9–5B, 6A). Erect unbranched filaments arising from a prostrate branched system are characteristic of some genera (Fig. 9–6J,

Myrionema). In some instances there may be an aggregation of only slightly branched filaments, which adhere laterally, forming a compact encrusting layer (Fig. 9–6H, I, *Ralfsia*). A pseudoparenchymatous thallus may be formed by an aggregation or intertwining of branched filaments, which may be loosely organized, as in the Chordariales (Fig. 9–5F, 7C, D, *Leathesia*), or densely compacted (Fig. 9–7A, B, *Heterochordaria*).

The ultimate in size and complexity in basically filamentous brown algae is achieved through a special type of intercalary cell division in a filament, as in the Desmarestiales (Fig. 9–8A, B). Cell divisions are confined to a localized subapical portion of the thallus apex at the base of hair-like, uniseriate filaments, resulting in trichothallic growth (Fig. 9–5D, E, 8C, D, *Desmarestia*). Despite the relative simplicity of this type of growth, a complex pseu-

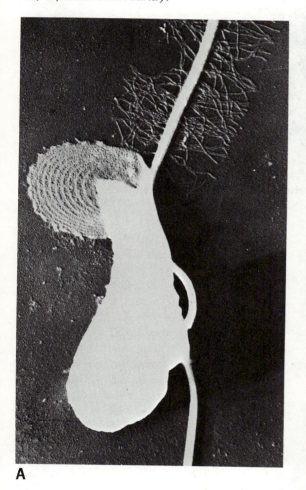

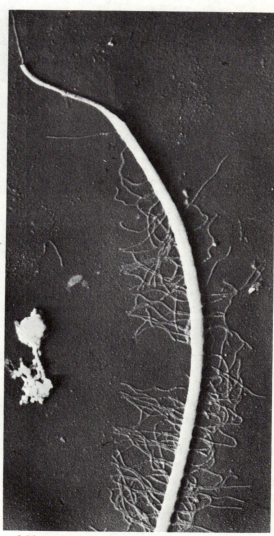

155

FIGURE 9–3 Electron micrographs of flagellar structure of Phaeophyta. A, B, sperm of *Fucus* showing (A) body of sperm and insertion of two flagella, and (B) distal end of tinsel flagellum, ×27,000. (A, from Manton and Clarke, with permission of *Annals of Botany;* B, from Manton and Clarke with permission of *Journal of Experimental Botany.*)

DIVISION PHAEOPHYTA

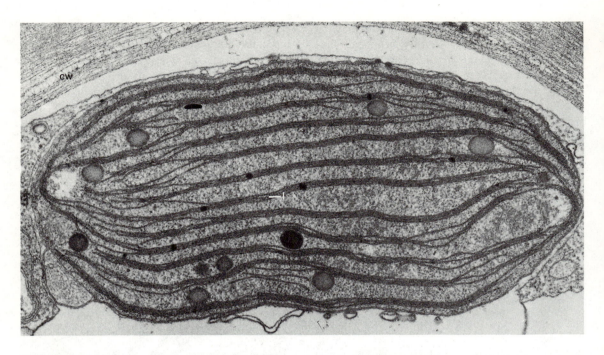

FIGURE 9–4 Electron micrograph of chloroplast structure of *Egregia* (Phaeophyta) showing unfused lamella (*l*) in groups of three or more and thickened cell wall (*cw*), ×26,000. (Photograph courtesy of T. Bisalputra.)

156

doparenchymatous organization results (Fig. 9–8E, F).

Intercalary cell divisions can also result in development of a parenchymatous thallus, as in the Dictyosiphonales. The diffuse growth occurs as a result of divisions only in surface cells. Divisons parallel to the surface in these cells increase the thickness of the thallus, and occasional perpendicular divisions permit the surface growth to keep pace with the increase in girth. The thallus may be a solid foliose one (as in *Phaeostrophion,* Fig. 9–9E, F), or it may become hollow (as in *Scytosiphon,* Fig. 9–9C, D).

Although growth is generally intercalary in several orders, there is often a marked apical development of a thallus. Cells of a primary uniseriate axis with growth from an apical cell (Fig. 9–10C, 11B) may divide more than once to produce a thallus suggesting parenchymatous development, as in the Sphacelariales (Fig. 9–10C–E, 11A, B, *Sphacelaria*). A similar situation occurs in the Dictyotales, which have either a single apical cell (Fig. 9–10F–H, 12A–C, *Dictyota*), or a margin of apical cells (Fig. 9–9A, B, 10K, L, *Syringoderma*).

The most highly developed type of parenchymatous thallus occurs in the kelps, or Laminariales (Fig. 9–10M–O, 13, 14, 15, 16), where growth is by specialized meristems. Differentiation is such that structures somewhat comparable to higher plant organs, but lacking a vascular system, may be distinguished. Morphologically these parts are leaf-like (lamina), stem-like (stipe), and root-like (holdfast and haptera) (Fig. 9–13, 14, 16A). Some regions of the stipe become hollow and develop into floats which hold the plant more or less erect in the water (Fig. 9–13, 14). There is a primary intercalary meristem, called the transition zone, located between the lamina and the stipe. In addition, surface meristematic activity occurs in the epidermal region, which is referred to as the meristoderm (Fig. 9–10M, 15A, E). Definite anatomical regions other than the meristoderm are the cortex and the innermost

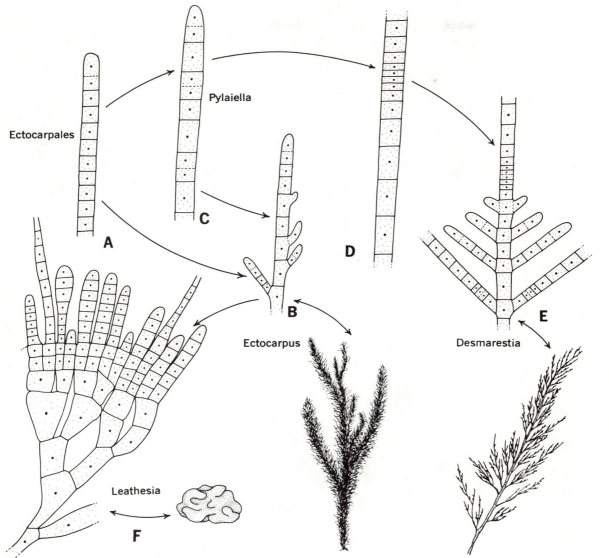

FIGURE 9–5 Growth types of filamentous and pseudoparenchymatous genera of Phaeophyta with possible evolutionary lines. A–C, unbranched and branched filamentous forms. A, B, with apical growth; C, with intercalary cell division in addition to apical growth. D, trichothallic growth. E, F, pseudoparenchymatous forms. E, trichothallic growth; F, apical growth.

medulla (Fig. 9–15A, B, E). The cortex contains pitted elements and mucilage ducts (Fig. 9–15A, 16C), whereas the medulla contains phloem-like elements (Fig. 9–15B, C, D). Morphologically and chemically the phloem-like elements are very similar to the sieve elements of vascular plants. Radioactive tracers show that these sieve-like elements function in conduction. Also, callose, present in sieve elements of higher plants, has been demonstrated (Fig. 9–15D).

A combination of a variety of different types of growth can also produce a macroscopic, complex thallus, as in the Fucales. The

157

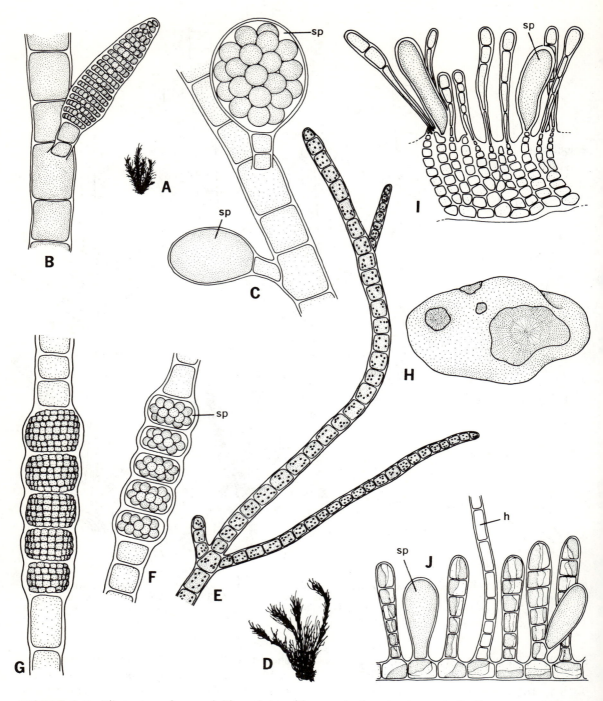

158

FIGURE 9–6 Filamentous forms of Phaeophyta with reproductive structures. A–C, *Ectocarpus*. A, habit, ×0.5; B, portion of filament bearing many-chambered structure, ×250; C, portion of filament showing immature (below) and mature (above) one-chambered meiosporangia (*sp*), ×250. D–G, *Pylaiella*. D, habit, ×0.5; E, vegetative portion of thallus, ×100; F, fertile portion of filament showing intercalary one-chambered meiosporangia, ×110; G, fertile portion of a filament, showing intercalary many-chambered structures, ×110. H, I, *Ralfisia*. H, habit showing several encrusting thalli growing on a rock, ×0.5; I, transverse section through portion of encrusting thallus, showing erect compacted filaments and two one-chambered meiosporangia, ×225. J, *Myrionema*, showing prostrate basal system, hair (*h*), erect vegetative filaments of cells, and two one-chambered meiosporangia, ×800.

surface cells of the embryo, which develops with a definite polarity (Fig. 9–17A–F, *Fucus*), continue to divide, but following the development of a prominent apical depression, trichothallic growth soon becomes established (Fig. 9–17I, J). This method of growth soon ceases, and establishment of the first apical cell (Fig. 9–17K) in the apical depression initiates apical growth, which continues throughout the life of the mature plant (Fig. 9–18A).

REPRODUCTION AND LIFE HISTORIES

The Phaeophyta have relatively simple reproductive structures, although sexual reproduction varies greatly. Typically there is an alternation of two multicellular generations.

Vegetative reproduction may occur by simple fragmentation of the thallus, or by some-

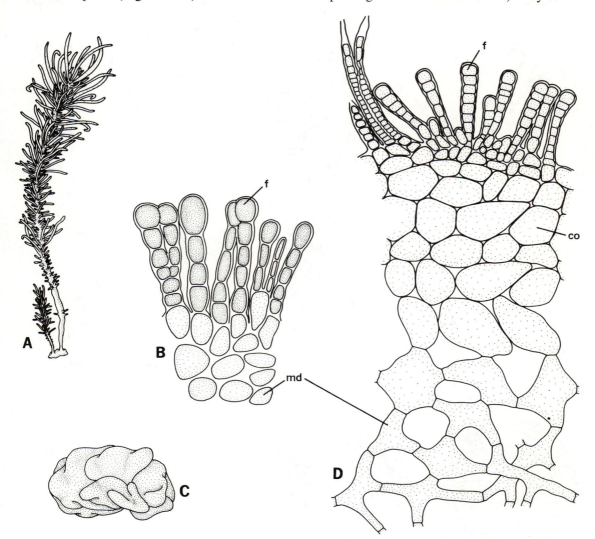

FIGURE 9–7 Pseudoparenchymatous forms. A, B, *Heterochordaria*. A, habit, ×0.5; B, transverse section through outer portion of thallus, showing pseudoparenchymatous medulla (*md*) and free surface filaments (*f*), ×300. C, D, *Leathesia*. C, habit, ×0.5; D, transverse section through outer portion of thallus showing loose filamentous medulla, pseudoparenchymatous cortical (*co*) region, and free surface filaments, ×115.

DIVISION PHAEOPHYTA

160

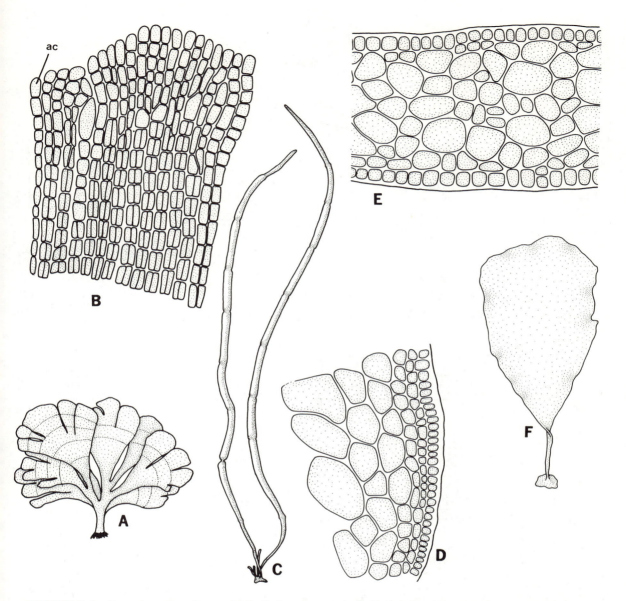

FIGURE 9–9   Parenchymatous forms. A, B, *Syringoderma*. A, habit of fan-shaped thallus, ×2.5. B, outer region of monostromatic thallus, showing marginal row of apical cells (*ac*), ×125; C, D, *Scytosiphon*. C, habit of hollow thallus, ×0.5; D, transverse section of outer portion of thallus, showing parenchymatous organization of cells, ×500. E, F, *Phaeostrophion*. E, habit, ×1; F, cross section through portion of thallus, showing parenchymatous organization, ×300.

FIGURE 9–8   Morphology and anatomy of pseudoparenchymatous form *Desmarestia* (Desmarestiales). A, habit of a flattened, strap-shaped species, ×0.3; B, habit of a terete species, ×0.3. C, D, juvenile sporophytes. C, filamentous phase, showing initiation of trichothallic growth (*tr*), ×150; D, more mature, showing trichothallic growth and pseudoparenchymatous habit (*ps*) of cortical filaments, ×110. E, enlarged longitudinal section of more mature portion of the thallus, showing axial row of cells (*ax*), ×250; F, transverse section of mature portion of plant, ×150.

DIVISION PHAEOPHYTA

162

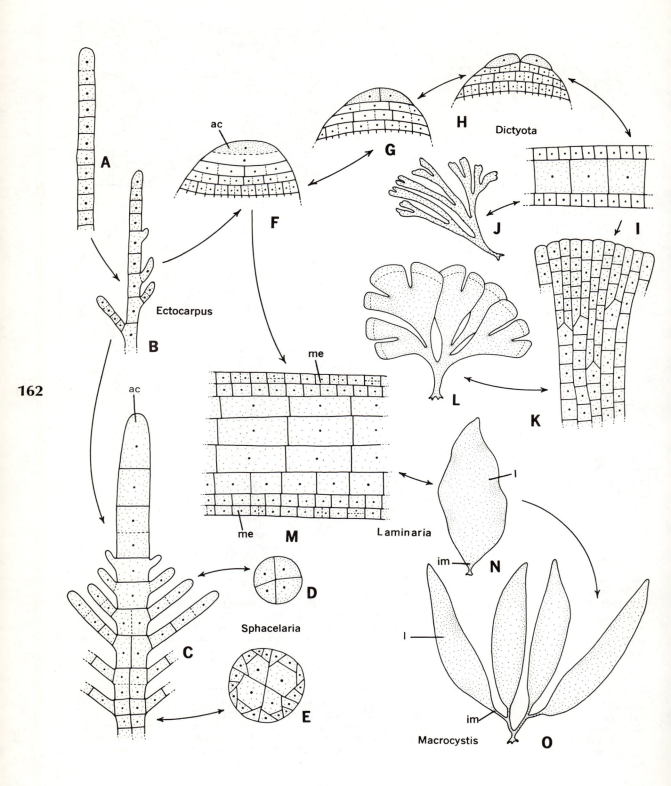

A

B

Ectocarpus

F

ac

ac

C

Sphacelaria

D

E

me

M

me

Laminaria

G

H

Dictyota

J

I

L

K

N

l

im

O

l

im

Macrocystis

NONVASCULAR PLANTS

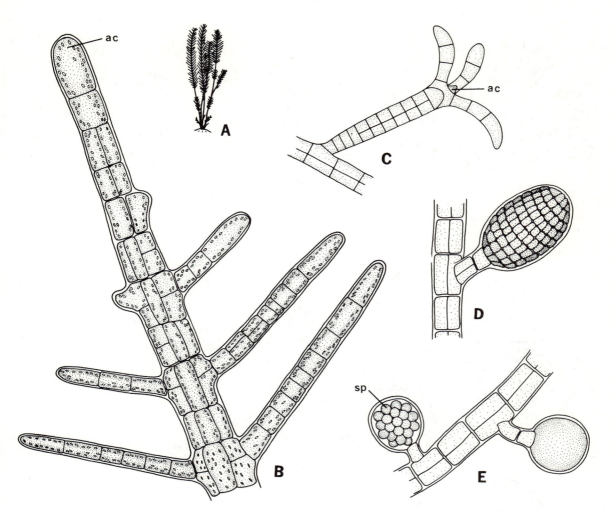

FIGURE 9–11 Morphology and reproduction of parenchymatous form with apical growth (*Sphacelaria*—Sphacelariales). A, habit, ×1; B, apical portion of thallus showing apical cell (*ac*), branches, and parenchymatous development of main axis, ×150; C, portion of axis showing asexual reproductive unit, the propagule, ×120. D, E, filaments with reproductive structures, ×180. D, many-chambered structure; E, immature (above) and mature (below) one-chambered meiosporangia (*sp*).

FIGURE 9–10 Growth types of parenchymatous genera of Phaeophyta with possible evolutionary lines from filamentous prototypes. A, B, filamentous forms. A, unbranched filament; B, branched filament. C–E, with a single apical cell (*ac*) at the tip of axis; F–J, also with a single apical cell, but with dichotomous branching as shown in J; I, transverse section of thallus showing three cell layers. C–L, apical growth followed by intercalary and parenchymatous cell divisions. D, E, transverse views of axis at points indicated in C by arrows; K, L, marginal row of apical cells; K, detail of portion of L. M–O, growth by meristoderm and intercalary meristem. M, detail of transverse section of lamina (*l*) of N or O showing intercalary meristem (transition zone) (*im*) and meristoderm (*me*).

DIVISION PHAEOPHYTA

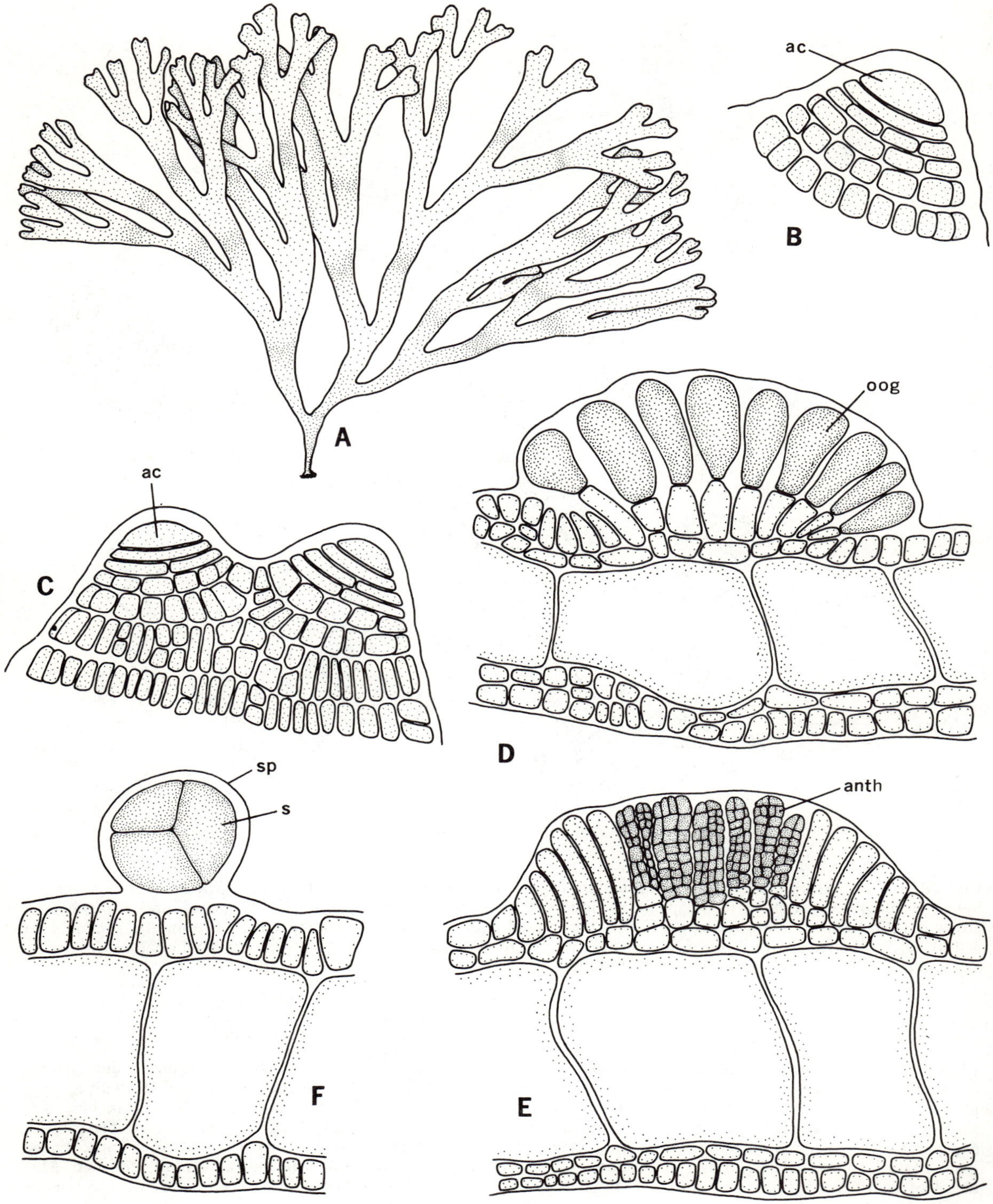

164

FIGURE 9–12 Morphology and reproduction of parenchymatous form with apical growth (*Dictyota*—Dictyotales). A, habit, ×0.5; B, apical region with apical cell (*ac*), ×300; C, apical region of branch showing dichotomous divisions, ×215. D–F, transverse sections through different thalli showing reproductive structures at surface. D, mature oogonia (*oog*), ×140; E, mature antheridia (*anth*), ×145; F, mature meiosporangium (*sp*), with three of four meiospores (*s*) visible, ×150.

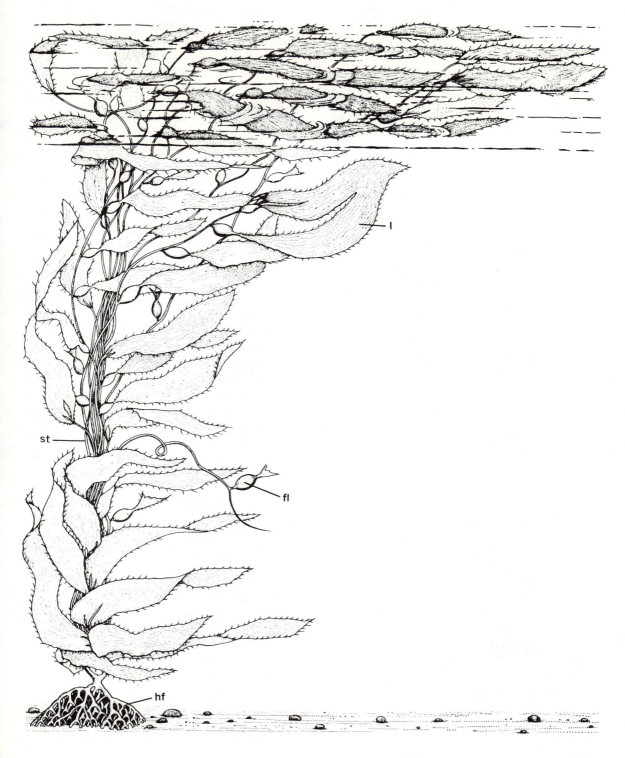

FIGURE 9–13 Habit view of *Macrocystis,* showing branched holdfast (*hf*) of root-like structures, and erect stalk-like structures (*st*) bearing leaf-like lamina (*l*) with basal floats (*fl*), ×0.01. (Modified after a drawing by M. Neushul.)

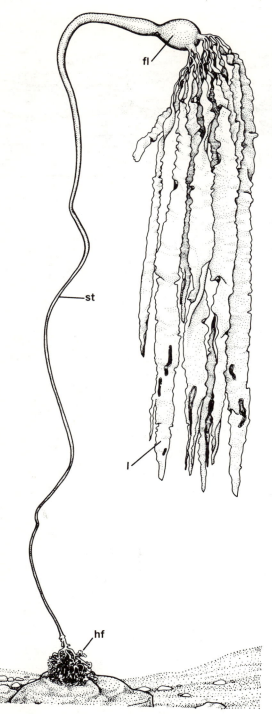

FIGURE 9–14 Habit view of *Nereocystis,* showing branched holdfast (*hf*) of root-like structures; erect, stalk-like structure (*st*); enlarged spherical float (*fl*); and dense clusters of terminal, blade-like laminae (*l*), ×0.1.

what specialized multicellular portions, such as the propagules of *Sphacelaria* (Fig. 9–11C). Fragmentation of the thallus is the only method of reproduction known in some free-floating species of *Sargassum* (Fig. 9–18B). Zoospores produced by mitosis occur as an accessory method of reproduction. These are produced in many-chambered mitosporangia (as in Fig. 9–6B). Meiosis occurs in an unpartitioned, one-chambered meiosporangium (Fig. 9–6C, F, I, J, 11E, 12F, 19A). The meiospores (zoospores or aplanospores) are produced by free-nuclear division followed by cytokinesis.

In sexual reproduction, plants with isogamy, anisogamy, and oogamy occur. Motile gametes are morphologically similar to the zoospores of brown algae (Fig. 9–2C–E). Generally syngamy occurs in the water away from the gamete-producing plants. However, an egg may remain fastened on the haploid female plant (Fig. 9–19G). In oogamous species (as in Dictyotales, Fig. 9–12D, E; Laminariales, Fig. 9–19D, G; Fucales, Fig. 9–23E, I), one to several eggs or sperms form in a gametangium. However, in some of the isogamous and anisogamous species (as in the Ectocarpales, Fig. 9–6B, G; Sphacelariales, Fig. 9–11D) the gametangia are subdivided into many compartments, each of which produces a single motile gamete. The sexual plants of brown algae generally produce either the male or the female gametangia.

All brown algae but the Fucales may have an alternation of free-living multicellular gametophytic and sporophytic generations. In some Phaeophyceae, as in the Ectocarpales and some Dictyotales, there is an alternation of isomorphic generations in which the haploid and diploid phases are morphologically identical and physiologically independent in the vegetative condition (Fig. 9–20).

In *Ectocarpus* the motile isogametes (Fig. 9–20E, F) produced by mitosis in many-chambered gametangia (Fig. 9–20C, D) fuse. The diploid zygote thus formed (Fig. 9–20H) immediately divides by mitosis to produce the diploid (sporophytic) generation (Fig. 9–20I, J). The sporophytic generation produces many-

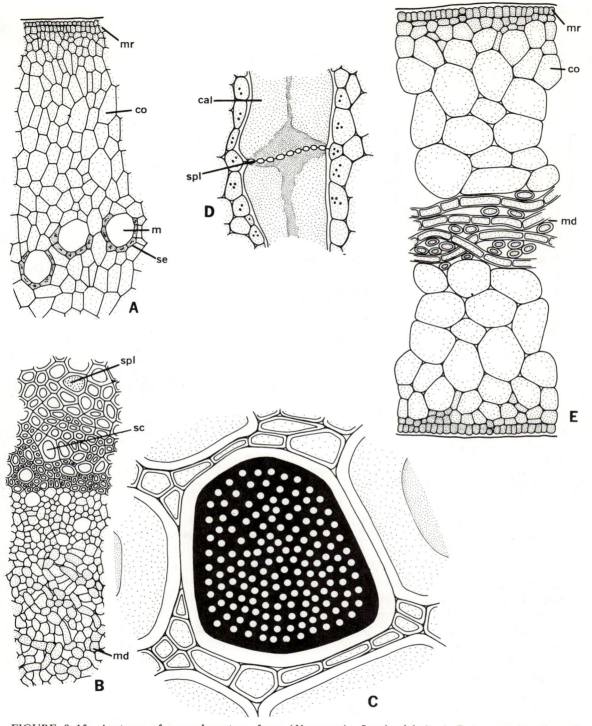

FIGURE 9–15 Anatomy of parenchymatous form (*Nereocystis*—Laminariales). A–C, transverse section of stalk-like region. A, outer portion showing surface meristoderm (*mr*), compact cortex (*co*), mucilage ducts (*m*), and secretory cells (*se*), × 150; B, inner portion showing thick-walled sieve cells (*sc*), filamentous medulla (*md*), and sieve plate (*spl*), × 150; C, enlarged transverse section of sieve plate × 1,200. D, longitudinal section through portion of stalk-like region, showing region of sieve plate and adjacent cells (note heavy deposit of callose (*cal*) in sieve cells), × 650; E, transverse section of lamina through a sterile region showing meristoderm, cortex, and medulla, × 350.

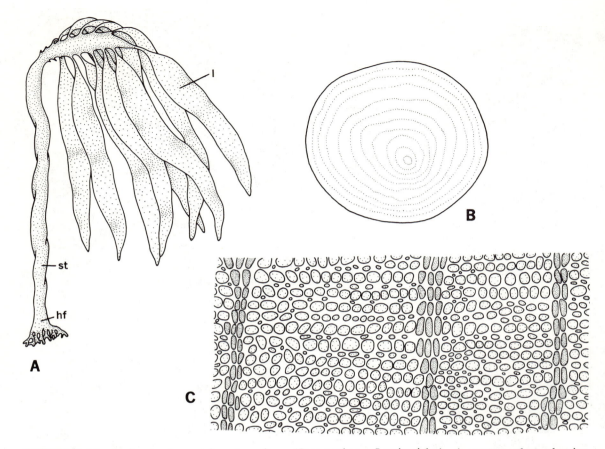

FIGURE 9–16   Anatomy of parenchymatous form (*Pterygophora*—Laminariales). A, mature plant, showing holdfast (*hf*), stalk-like region (*st*), and lamina (*l*), ×0.07; B, transverse section of stalk-like region showing "growth rings" formed by concentric rings of differentiated cells, ×0.5; C, enlarged view of a portion of stalk-like region showing distinct zones of differentiated cells, ×50.

chambered mitosporangia (Fig. 9–20T) that in turn produce diploid mitospores (Fig. 9–20U) capable of maintaining the diploid generation by asexual means (Fig. 9–20J, V). Meiosis occurs in one-chambered meiosporangia (Fig. 9–20K–M). The resulting motile meiospores (Fig. 9–20N, 0) grow into two types of haploid gametophytes (Fig. 9–20A, B, P–S), each producing one type of gamete (Fig. 9–20C–F). The life history of *Dictyota* (Fig. 9–12) is very similar to that of *Ectocarpus*. However, in this oogamous species (Fig. 9–12D, E), only four nonmotile meiospores are produced in the meiosporangium (Fig. 9–12F).

In the Laminariales (kelps), there is typically an alternation of heteromorphic genera-tions in which the haploid phase is a free-living, physiologically independent, diminutive (although multicellular) generation and the dip-loid phase is the conspicuous, relatively large, generation (Fig. 9–13, 14, 16A, 21J).

In the typical kelp, the haploid gameto-phytes are microscopic (Fig. 9–19D, F, 21A, B). The female gametophyte (Fig. 9–19F, G, 21B, D) produces one egg (per oogonium) which is held at the distal end of the oogonium. The male gametophyte (Fig. 9–19D, 21A) pro-duces many motile sperms (one per cell usually, Fig. 9–19E, 21C) which swim to the egg (Fig. 9–21E). The resulting zygote (Fig. 9–19H, 21F), as in the Ectocarpales, undergoes mitosis to form the embryo sporophyte (Fig. 9–19J–M,

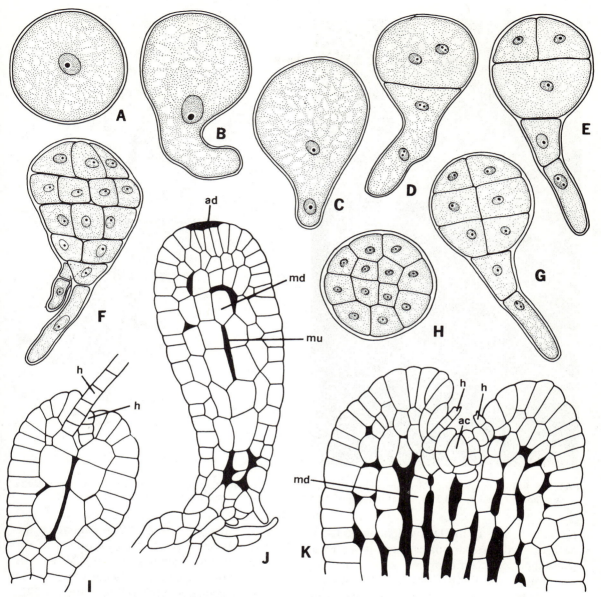

FIGURE 9–17 Early developmental stages of *Fucus* (Fucales). A, zygote, ×600; B–G, stages in development of juvenile thallus, showing nuclei, ×600; H, transverse sectional view of terminal portion of G, ×600; I, upper portion of more mature juvenile, showing two terminal hairs (*h*), ×325; J, juvenile plants, showing early development of apical depression (*ad*), filamentous medulla (*md*), and intercellular mucilage (*mu*), ×250; K, upper portion of more mature juvenile thallus, showing apical depression, remnants of terminal hairs (*h*), initiation of apical cell (*ac*), and medulla (*md*), ×325. (I, after Nienburg; J, K, after Oltmanns.)

21G–I). The sporophyte continues growing into the typical kelp plant (Fig. 9–13, 14, 16A, 19N, 21J). In specialized areas on the blade of the sporophyte (Fig. 9–21J), meiosis occurs in one-chambered meiosporangia (Fig. 9–19A, 21K). The motile meiospores (Fig. 9–19B, 21M, N) settle and by mitosis produce the two types of haploid gametophytes (Fig. 9–19C, D,

DIVISION PHAEOPHYTA

FIGURE 9–18   A, plant of *Fucus* growing in the intertidal zone, showing wart-like appearance of conceptacles on swollen receptacles, ×0.3; B, distal portion of *Sargassum,* showing leaflike branches and spherical floats, ×1.

F, G, 21A, B). In the Dictyosiphonales, Chordariales, and Desmarestiales there is a similar alternation of heteromorphic generations.

Only in the Fucales is the diploid generation the multicellular conspicuous phase, with the haploid generation reduced to single cells that become the gametes themselves (Fig. 9–22). In other words, meiosis occurs at gamete formation (Fig. 9–22K, M, 23B–F, G, H, J) in the diploid plant. Thus, the gametangia (Fig. 9–22A, B, 23E, F, I, J) are comparable to the unicellular (and one-chambered) meiosporangia of other brown algae.

In *Fucus,* at maturity, swollen tips on the thallus (Fig. 9–18A, 22H) produce numerous small cavities (Fig. 9–22I, 23A) in which the gametangia are formed. Meiosis occurs in the one-chambered oogonium (Fig. 9–22J, K, 23B–F), resulting in eight functional eggs; and in the one-chambered antheridium (Fig. 9–22L, M, 23I), resulting in 64 sperms.

In some brown algae, isogametes or anisogametes develop directly into haploid plants, thus behaving like mitospores. This suggests that vegetative reproduction is more primitive, that fusion of cells has occurred secondarily, and that sexuality is perhaps relative. For example, in some isogamous species of algae, both gametes are produced by the same plant; in other isogamous forms, the gametes fuse only

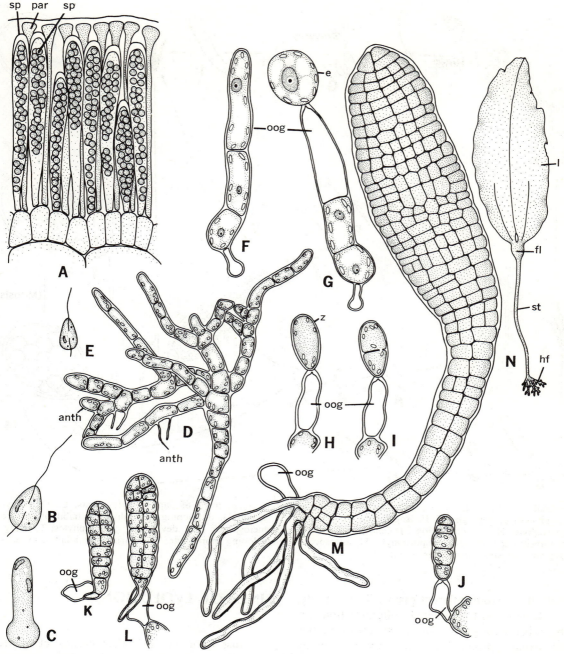

FIGURE 9–19   Stages in life history of *Nereocystis* (Laminariales). A, transverse section through outer fertile portion of lamina, showing almost mature one-chambered meiosporangia (*sp*) and sterile paraphyses (*par*), × 612; B, zoospore (meiospore), × 850; C, germinating zoospore, × 850; D, mature male gametophyte with immature and mature (empty) antheridia (*anth*), × 850; E, sperm, × 850. F, G, female gametophyte, × 850. F, with maturing oogonium (*oog*); G, mature, empty oogonium with discharged, unfertilized egg (*e*). H–J, zygote (*z*) and early divisions in young sporophyte attached to empty oogonium, × 850; K–M, stages in development of young sporophyte still attached to empty oogonium (K, L, ×680; M, ×340); N, later stage (macroscopic) of young sporophyte with holdfast (*hf*), stalk-like region (*st*), float (*fl*), and lamina (*l*), ×0.25.

DIVISION PHAEOPHYTA

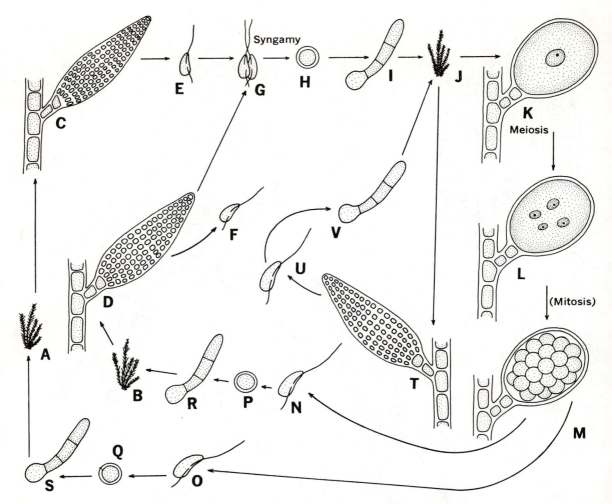

FIGURE 9–20 Life history of *Ectocarpus* (Ectocarpales). A, B, habit of gametophyte plants; C, D, many-chambered gametangia; E, F, isogametes; G, syngamy; H, zygote; I, developing sporophyte; J, habit of mature sporophyte; K–M, maturation of meiosporangium; N, O, meiospores; P–S, developing gametophytes; T, many-chambered sporangium on sporophyte; U, mitospore; V, developing sporophyte. (For structural details and relative sizes of structures, refer to Fig. 9–6A–C.)

with those from different plants. The next step in development of sexual differentiation was probably anisogamy. The most advanced type of sexual reproduction is oogamy. One of the advantages of oogamous sexual reproduction is that the large, nonmotile female gamete, or egg, can survive longer to be fertilized without exhausting its stored food reserves. Also, because of the stored food, the zygote can survive longer before developing.

LINES OF EVOLUTION

Just as in certain other groups of algae, we find a trend in the Phaeophyta from isogamy through anisogamy to oogamy. In the brown algae evidence indicates that this trend has occurred along two or three quite distinct lines of evolution, especially within the orders having an alternation of heteromorphic generations.

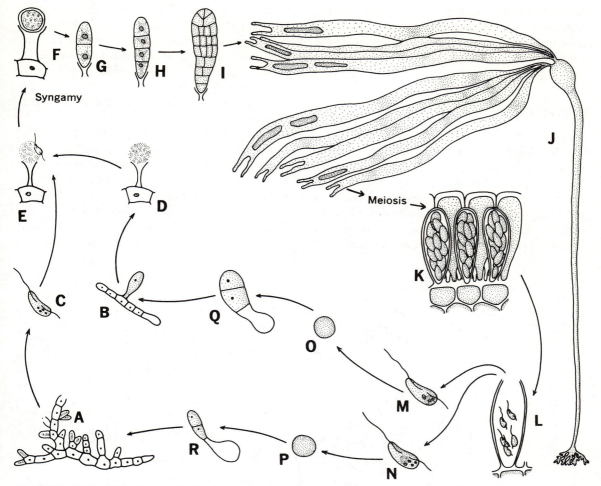

FIGURE 9–21 Life history of *Nereocystis* (Laminariales). A, male gametophyte with antheridia; B, female gametophyte with oogonium; C, sperm; D, unfertilized egg on oogonium; E, syngamy; F, zygote on empty oogonium; G–I, development of young sporophyte on female plant; J, mature sporophyte with dark, fertile sori on distal portion of lamina; K, meiosporangia; L, release of meiospores; M, N, meiospores; O–R, development of gametophytes. (For details and relative sizes of structures, refer to Fig. 9–14, 15A–F, 19.)

Three of these evolutionary series are particularly well distinguished.

In the Ectocarpales, *Ectocarpus* illustrates well the primitive features of the simplest brown algae and, at the same time, serves as a possible prototype from which all other groups of brown algae (with the possible exception of the Fucales) may be derived.

From the *Ectocarpus* type of life history (Fig. 9–20), forms with anisogamy and an alternation of isomorphic generations can readily be derived (as in *Sphacelaria,* Fig. 9–11). Similarly, a more advanced sexual reproduction, oogamy, still with an alternation of isomorphic generations (*Dictyota,* Fig. 9–12), is in a direct line of evolution from this basic group. Although vegetatively the kelps have a reduced *Ectocarpus*-like filamentous gametophytic stage (Fig. 9–19D, F, 21A, B), the sporophyte has become a massive, complex, and highly developed stage (Fig. 9–13, 14, 16A). The Fucales (Fig. 9–22), on the other hand, have the ultimate in reduction in the haploid phase, mainly the gametes, but also have a complex, highly developed diploid phase (Fig. 9–18A, B, 22G).

PHYLOGENY

No fossils can be referred to the brown algae with any degree of certainty from periods earlier than the Triassic, although fossils more or less resembling *Fucus* apparently occur in the early Paleozoic Period. Some phylogeneticists have suggested a possible origin for brown algae in the Proterozoic or late Pre-

Cambrian Periods. The brown algae are obviously not closely related to any other group of living algae. Most likely they are derived from some laterally biflagellate ancestral stock comparable to the characteristic motile cells of brown algae. The fact that there are no modern, free-living forms of unicellular flagellates referred to the Phaeophyta does not necessarily mean that they do not exist in the sea. However, our knowledge of the marine nannoplankton is still too fragmentary to preclude the possibility of finding a prototype for the brown algae among living flagellates. Because of the similarity in flagellation to some of the Chrysophyceae, a common ancestry has been suggested for the brown algae and the Chrys-

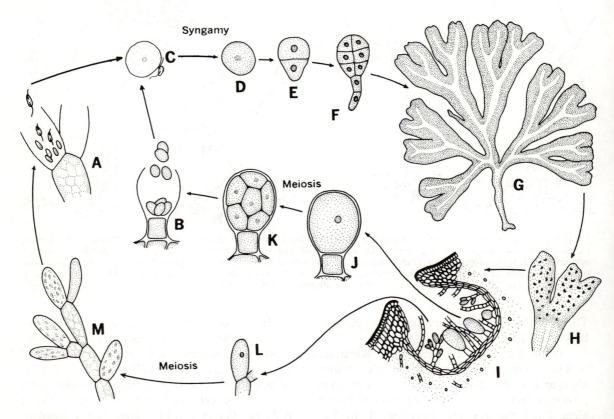

FIGURE 9–22 Life history of *Fucus* (Fucales). A, mature antheridium liberating sperms; B, mature oogonium liberating eggs; C, mature sperm and egg prior to fusion; D, zygote; E, F, early development of thallus; G, mature thallus; H, swollen fertile tips containing numerous cavities; I, cavity with immature male and female structures; J, K, development of oogonium and eggs within cavity; L, M, development of branch with several antheridia within the cavity. (For structural details and relative sizes of structures, refer to Fig. 9–17, 18A, 23.)

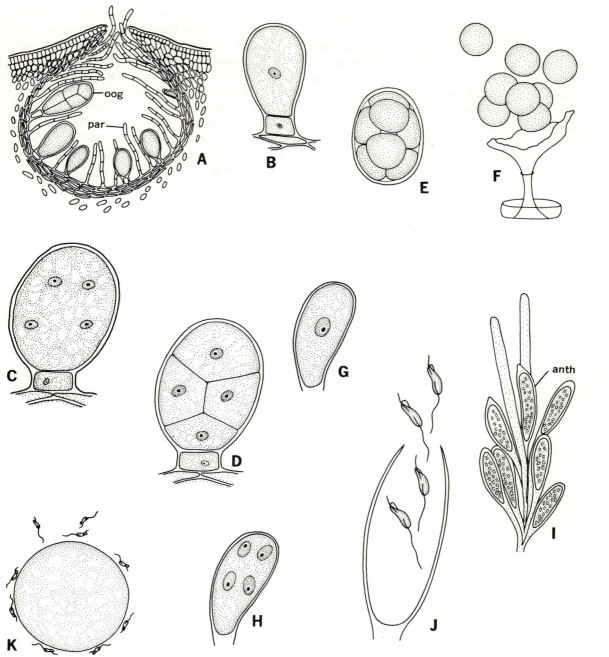

FIGURE 9–23   Reproduction in *Fucus*. A, transverse section of fertile portion of thallus, showing cavity containing immature and mature oogonia (*oog*) and paraphyses (*par*), ×125. B–F, stages in development and release of eggs in oogonium, ×500; K, sperms swimming about unfertilized egg, ×1,500; G–J, stages in development of antheridia and sperm release, ×1,800; I, branch bearing several antheridia (*anth*), ×800. (F, K, after Thuret.)

DIVISION PHAEOPHYTA

ophyceae. This suggestion is further supported by the presence of chlorophyll *c* and fucoxanthin in some Chrysophyceae and Bacillariophyceae. A more distant relationship of brown algae to the Pyrrophyta (see Chapter 10) has also been suggested because of the presence of chlorophyll *c* in the majority of the Dinophyceae. If these three divisions had a common origin, it is likely that the brown algae have had some pre-chrysophyte ancestor (see Fig. 23–5).

The most primitive order of brown algae is thought to be the Ectocarpales. From this assemblage or an *Ectocarpus*-like ancestry, all other orders of brown algae, with the possible exception of the Fucales, may have evolved. The strikingly different shape and flagellation of the sperms suggests a different origin for the order Fucales; but the biochemical characteristics, including pigment complex, support a common origin for the Fucales within the same division.

10 / Divisions Chrysophyta, Xanthophyta, Pyrrophyta, Euglenophyta

Several algal divisions contain a relatively small number of genera and species, although some representatives of these divisions occur in specific areas in large numbers. All of the divisions discussed in this chapter have motile as well as nonmotile genera. The motile forms are often considered Protozoa, and their animal-like nature cannot be ignored. The four divisions considered constitute approximately 30 per cent (or some 7,600 species in 500 genera) of the algae. Some of the divisions may have similar origins, as discussed at the end of this chapter; however, the grouping here is only for convenience.

DIVISION CHRYSOPHYTA

The division Chrysophyta (*chrysophytes*) is a grouping of golden or yellow-brown algae and alga-like organisms. In this text the Chrysophyta consists of only two classes, the Chrysophyceae (yellow-brown or golden algae) and the Bacillariophyceae (diatoms). Another class, the Xanthophyceae (yellow-green algae), generally placed in the Chrysophyta, is probably intermediate between the Chlorophyta and Chrysophyta.

The pigments characteristic of the Chrysophyta are similar to some of those of the Pyrrophyta and include chlorophyll *a*, sometimes chlorophyll *c*, as well as several xanthophylls. In the Chrysophyta, the food reserves are fats or oils and laminarin-like carbohydrates. In many forms the cell wall, when present, has scales or may consist of two overlapping halves and be impregnated with silicon, calcium, or organic material. Motile cells have flagella inserted apically or subapically.

CLASS CHRYSOPHYCEAE (Golden Algae)

Over 75 genera with about 300 species are referred to several orders in this class. They are predominantly fresh-water algae; however, a number of marine species are significant as marine nannoplankton.

Cell Structure

Many of the simpler unicellular forms are naked flagellates with a delicate periplast as in

Ochromonas and *Chromulina* (Fig. 10–1A, B). Some have a characteristic lorica (Fig. 10–1F). Cellulose may be present in the wall of certain species, whereas others may have superficial scales (Fig. 10–1C, D). The Chrysophyceae owe their characteristic golden or golden-brown color to the carotenoid pigments contained in one or two parietal smooth-edged chloroplasts. Chlorophyll *c* is not always present in representatives of this class. An eyespot may be present. The carbohydrate accumulates as a large refractive cytoplasmic granule posteriorly in the cell, and is never within the chloroplast envelope. The fats and oil are also present in the cytoplasm. The cells are uninucleate, and in the motile forms contractile vacuoles may be present near the flagellar insertion.

Most of the species are apparently photoautotropic, but many of those forms studied are auxotrophs. Colorless forms, which are saprobic or phagotrophic, are known. Some of the pigmented forms are also believed to be capable of ingesting particulate food.

Movement

In the motile cells, the one or two flagella are usually anteriorly inserted. In the biflagellate condition, one is generally tinsel and the other whiplash. If the two flagella are markedly unequal in length (Fig. 10–1A), the whiplash one is reduced; the reduction may be so complete that only the tinsel flagellum protrudes. Some biflagellate forms (*Chrysochromulina*, Fig. 10–1E) have a coiled attaching structure—the haptonema. The ultrastructure of the haptonema consists of six or seven fibers surrounded by three concentric membranes and thus differs from the flagellar structure (as shown in Fig. 3–2B).

Morphological Diversity

There is some diversity in form of the Chrysophyceae. Most of the members are motile, and include unicellular (Fig. 10–1A–C, E) and colonial (Fig. 10–1D) flagellates. Nonmotile forms include the palmelloid colonies (Fig. 10–1G, H), coccoid, and filamentous types.

Reproduction

In most forms zoospore production is common, with either one or two apical flagella present. In the motile genera, reproduction is by longitudinal cell division producng two zoospores. In the nonmotile forms, the zoospores generally resemble the biflagellate *Ochromonas* (Fig. 10–1A) or the uniflagellate *Chromulina* (Fig. 10–1B).

In many Chrysophyceae a resting cell called a statospore, or cyst, occurs. A single statospore is formed within a cell and may become heavily silicified throughout, except for a small opening containing a nonsiliceous plug that closes the statospore (Fig. 10–1I). Under favorable conditions the resting statospore germinates, generally liberating one or two motile cells (zoospores), which escape through the pore left after the plug is dissolved. Sexual reproduction is rare. It has been reported to be isogamous, with biflagellate gametes in some species.

CLASS BACILLARIOPHYCEAE (Diatoms)

About 190 genera with over 5,500 species are referred to this class. Some estimates, including fossil forms (which number about 70 genera), place the number of species as high as 10,000. The diatoms are conspicuous elements of both the present-day marine and freshwater environments as well as represented in the fossil record.

Cell Structure

The diatom cell is complex, consisting of two overlapping walls fitting together like two

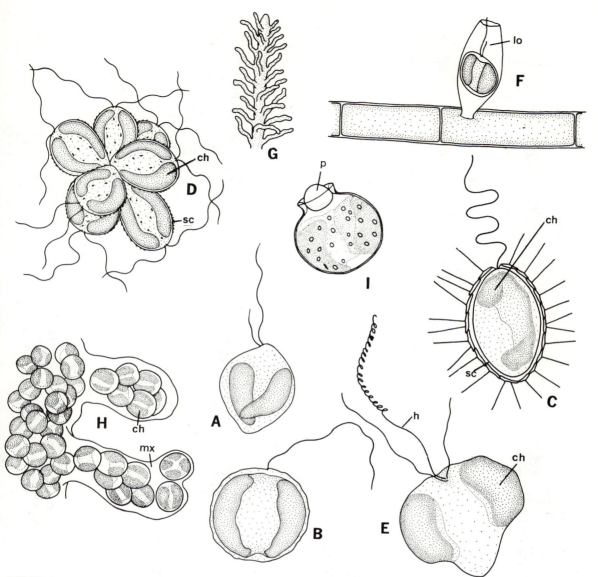

FIGURE 10–1   Morphological diversity in the Chrysophyceae. A–F, flagellate forms; A, *Ochromonas,* ×3,200; B, *Chromulina,* ×2,700; C, *Mallomonas,* with external organic scales and spines ×1,000; D, *Synura,* motile colonial form, with siliceous scales (*sc*), ×2,700; E, *Chrysochromulina,* with coiled apical attachment organelle (haptonema, *h*), ×700; F, *Epipyxis,* with lorica (*lo*) attached to algal filament, ×1,000. G–I, nonflagellate forms. G, H, *Hydrurus,* palmelloid form within matrix (*mx*). G, habit, ×50; detail of colony, ×1,000. I, *Chrysocapsa,* mature cyst or statospore, ×3,060. *ch,* chloroplast; *p,* plug.

halves of a box. These halves, called frustules, generally contain large amounts of silicon. The outer frustule that partially overlaps the other is the epitheca, whereas the inner frustule is the hypotheca (Fig. 10–2A). Each frustule consists of a flattened, or convex, valve with a connecting band attached along its edge. The overlapping walls form a girdle region and, when observed from the side, present the girdle view (Fig. 10–2A). Intercalated bands in the

DIVISIONS CHRYSOPHYTA, XANTHOPHYTA, PYRROPHYTA, EUGLENOPHYTA

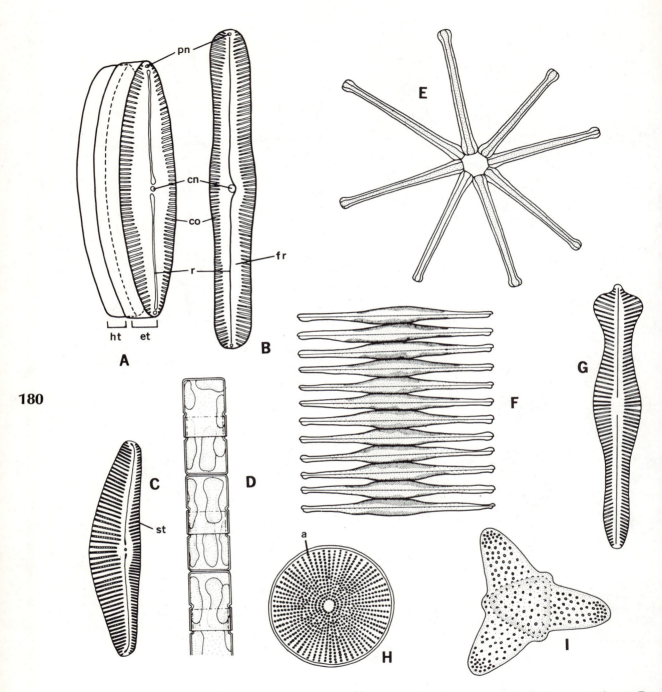

FIGURE 10–2 Morphological diversity and wall markings in Bacillariophyceae. A–C, E–G, pennate forms; D, H, I, centric forms. A, B, wall markings in *Pinnularia*, ×480. A, view showing valve and girdle to illustrate raphe (*r*), central (*cn*) and polar (*pn*) swellings, and relation of epitheca (*et*) and hypotheca (*ht*); B, valve view of frustule (*fr*). C, *Cymbella*, valve view, ×545; D, *Melosira*, girdle view, ×640; E, *Asterionella* colony, girdle view, ×1,000; F, *Fragilaria* colony, girdle view, ×750; G, *Gomphonema*, valve view, ×1,250; H, *Coscinodiscus*, showing aerolae (*a*) on the valve, ×125; I, *Triceratium*, valve view, ×545. *st*, stria; *co*, costum.

girdle may separate the two frustules and form a wide girdle area. The flat top or bottom surface of the cell is called the valve (see valve view, Fig. 10–2B).

The silicon is deposited within wall material often considered pectic. It varies in thickness and occurrence from one region to another, so that alternating thin and thick regions result in a definite pattern of pores or elongated ridges, especially on the valve (Fig. 10–3A, B).

The wall markings are of three types— aerolae, costa, and puncta. An aerola is a thin area bounded by ridges of siliceous material within which is an aggregation of fine pores and/or ingrowths. The punctum is a smaller, less complicated aerola. In many diatoms the puncta are in a linear order and so close together that they appear as a fine line, termed a stria (Fig. 10–2C). The stria may lie between well-defined ridges called costa (Fig. 10–2A, B). Generally most light microscope observations resolve only the large aerolae and striae, but sometimes puncta and costa can be seen. The whole cell or colony of cells is often enveloped in a mucilaginous material.

Those cells appearing round or triangular in valve view (radial symmetry) are classed as centric diatoms (Fig. 10–2D, H, I), and those appearing more rectangular in valve view (bilateral symmetry) are pennate diatoms (Fig. 10–2A–C, E–G). This classification based on symmetry is somewhat artificial.

In the majority of pennate diatoms there is a vertical unsilicified cleft or groove in the valve, the raphe (Fig. 10–2A–C, G), which may be straight, wavy, S-shaped, or lying in a canal. In the central region of the raphe and at each end of the groove there are spherical thickenings (Fig. 10–2A, B). The raphe seems to be intimately associated with movement. In those pennate diatoms lacking a raphe, a clear area between the rows of striae or costa is referred to as a pseudoraphe. Only the pennate diatoms containing a raphe are able to move. Their movement is somewhat jerky, or smooth and gliding. Rates of movement have been calculated at 0.2–25 microns/sec.

The cell has a central vacuole and one, two, or many yellow or golden-brown parietal chloroplasts. Centric diatoms generally have many chloroplasts, whereas pennate diatoms usually have only one or two. The green pigments, chlorophylls a and c, are masked by carotenoids, which are responsible for the characteristic color of the diatoms.

The uninucleate cells are apparently diploid in the vegetative condition. When cell division occurs, a new valve is secreted by each of the frustules at the point they were attached. Each frustule of the dividing cell becomes the outer frustule of the two daughter cells. In the centric diatoms motile uniflagellate or biflagellate cells interpreted as male gametes are produced.

The diatoms are chiefly autotrophic. In contrast to the golden algae, the majority of diatoms do not require an external source of vitamins. However, a number of the planktonic forms studied require vitamin B_{12}. Food reserves are stored as fats and oils, as well as a laminarin-like carbohydrate.

181

Classification and Morphology

The two orders of diatoms, the Biddulphiales (previously Centrales) and Bacillariales (previously Pennales), are separated on the basis of form, wall markings, chloroplast number, and presence of motility. The two main evolutionary types of diatoms are analogous to the two orders recognized. The Biddulphiales are radially symmetrical, usually with circular valves, as in *Coscinodiscus* (Fig. 10–2H), but sometimes they are triangular, as in *Triceratium* (Fig. 10–2I). The Biddulphiales usually have bilateral symmetry with elongate valves, as in *Pinnularia* (Fig. 10–2A, B), but sometimes they may be asymmetrical in valve view, as in *Cymbella* (Fig. 10–2C) and *Gomphonema* (Fig. 10–2G). In the Biddulphiales the sculpturing generally radiates out from a central point of the valve (Fig. 10–2H); in Bacillariales the valve markings occur in two longitudinal series on either side of a median line (Fig. 10–2

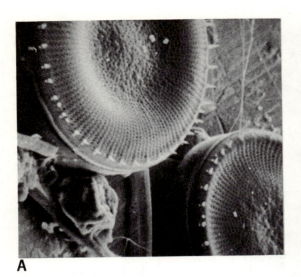

A

B

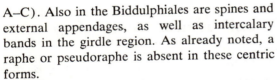

FIGURE 10–3 Electron micrographs (from scanning electron microscope) of centric Bacillariophyceae. A, two cells of *Stephanodiscus* in valve view, ×1,190; B, enlargement of A showing spines and punctae on valve (*v*) and wide girdle band (*gb*), ×2,750; C, valve view of *Cyclotella* from inside (right valve) and outside (left valve), ×2,350. (Photographs courtesy F. Round.)

A–C). Also in the Biddulphiales are spines and external appendages, as well as intercalary bands in the girdle region. As already noted, a raphe or pseudoraphe is absent in these centric forms.

Many diatoms occur individually; others are loosely aggregated in irregular filamentous chains, with adjacent cells interconnected by mucilaginous pads (Fig. 10–2D, F). Some genera form stalked, tree-like colonies, whereas others form colonies of different shapes (Fig. 10–2E). In some, the presence of long spine-like valve processes may assist in forming the filamentous colonies.

Reproduction

The chief method of reproduction in diatoms is vegetative, by cell division. The rapid rate of division under optimum conditions can result in dense blooms, which give the water a distinct brown color over an extensive area.

C

Silicon appears to be an absolute requirement for cell division in most diatoms. Since the two frustules of the parent cell act as the epitheca for the two resulting daughter cells, there may be a gradual diminution in the size of some of the cells in the population. However, in many diatoms the average size characteristic of the species is restored by fusion of two protoplasts (sexual reproduction) and production of new cells. Sexual reproduction may be isogamous, anisogamous, or oogamous, with the vegetative cell diploid and meiosis occurring during gametogenesis. The zygote, which is termed an auxospore, increases two to three times the size of the original gamete-producing cell. The auxospore tends to have the maximum cell dimensions of the species. Auxospore formation occurs only occasionally in a population, usually following a prolonged period of vegetative reproduction by cell division.

DIVISION XANTHOPHYTA

Until recently, members of this division (*xanthophytes*) have been considered part of the Chrysophyta. However, differences in pigmentation are significant enough to place the yellow-green algae (Xanthophyceae) in a division with affinities closer to the Chlorophyta. Also treated separately will be a class of uncertain systematic position, the Raphidophyceae (Chloromonadophyceae). The number of genera in this group of green monad forms is quite small, and there is little information about them.

CLASS XANTHOPHYCEAE
(Yellow-Green Algae)

There are over 75 genera with some 400 species referred to the class Xanthophyceae.

They occur predominantly in fresh-water habitats, including soil, but there are a few marine species.

Cell Structure

The cell-wall components are chiefly cellulose. One to several discoid, smooth-edged, green or yellow-green chloroplasts occur in a parietal location in the cells (Fig. 10–4A). A laminarin-like compound is the chief storage product and gives the chloroplast a smooth-edged appearance which is distinguishable from the granular chloroplast of the Chlorophyta. Most genera are uninucleate, but a few have a multinucleate, coenocytic thallus (as in *Vaucheria*, Fig. 10–5). Most of the members of this class are apparently autotrophic.

Movement

In motile forms or motile stages of non-motile species, the cells have two unequal anteriorly inserted flagella (Fig. 10–4F). The term heterokont is used to describe this unequal situation, and thus the Xanthophyceae are referred to as the heterokonts.

Morphological Diversity

Most genera of Xanthophyceae are unicellular, nonmotile forms, including *Chloridella* (Fig. 10–4C), which is free-floating; *Characiopsis* (Fig. 10–4B), which is attached, and *Ophiocytium* (Fig. 10–4A), which is either free-floating or attached. A few motile, biflagellate, unicellular forms occur as well as some unicellular amoeboid forms and palmelloid colonies, such as *Mischococcus* (Fig. 10–4G). The most commonly encountered yellow-green algae are the filamentous, unbranched, free-floating or attached, species of *Tribonema* (Fig. 10–4E) and the coenocytic, multinucleate species of

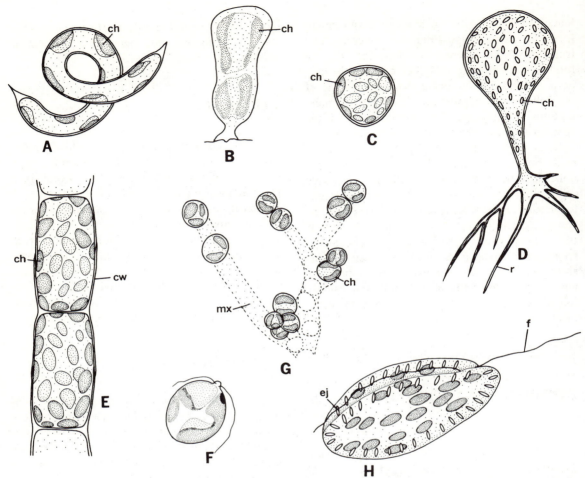

FIGURE 10–4 Morphological diversity in Xanthophyta. A–G, Xanthophyceae. A–C, coccoid forms. A, *Ophiocytium*, ×500; B, *Characiopsis,* attached on plant, ×1,800; C, *Chloridella,* ×940. D, coenocytic form, *Botrydium,* with rhizoids (*r*), ×250. E, F, filamentous form, *Tribonema*. E, vegetative plant, showing overlapping cell walls (*cw*), ×915, F, heterokont zoospore, ×400. G, palmelloid form with mucilaginous matrix (*mx*), *Mischococcus,* ×855. H, Raphidophyceae; *Gonyostomum,* showing groove on one side with forward and trailing flagella (*f*) and ejectosomes (*ej*) throughout entire cell, ×550. *ch,* chloroplast.

Botrydium (Fig. 10–4D) and *Vaucheria* (Fig. 10–5).

Reproduction

The chief method of reproduction is by cell division, but zoospore and aplanospore production occur. The zoospore has the unequal biflagellate characteristic of the Xanthophyceae (Fig. 10–4F), although that of *Vaucheria* is an exception (Fig. 10–5B, D). In this genus there is an unusual, large, multinucleate, and multiflagellate zoospore (Fig. 10–5B). The flagella are whiplash, arise in pairs, with one member of the pair slightly longer than the other (Fig. 10–5D). In the multicellular genera, fragmentation may also occur as a method of reproduction.

Sexual reproduction is not widespread in the group, although it is common in a few genera. It may be isogamous, anisogamous, or oogamous as in *Vaucheria* (Fig. 10–5E–G). In those forms studied, meiosis apparently occurs on germination of the zygote.

CLASS RAPHIDOPHYCEAE (CHLOROMONADOPHYCEAE) (Raphidophytes or Chloromonads)

This group of fewer than a dozen unicellular alga-like flagellates is very poorly known. The affinities to other algae are not clear, but they are placed with the Xanthophyceae on the basis of pigmentation.

Cell Structure

The cell is relatively large (50 to 100 microns) for a flagellate organism. The biflagellate cell is naked with a delicate periplast and is plastic in form. It may be somewhat circular in side view outline but is usually compressed; frequently there is a longitudinal groove in one surface (Fig. 10–4H). In many of the genera, ejectosomes (also known as trichocysts) occur in the outer cytoplasm, either throughout the cell (Fig. 10–4H) or in localized areas. These sensitive organelles are released as fine threads when the organism is disturbed. Numerous small discoid, bright green or yellowish-green chloroplasts are evident. The food reserves are thought to be oil.

Reproduction

Vegetative reproduction occurs by longitudinal cell division. Sometimes the cells become temporarily nonmotile; the flagella are lost and the cell rounds up, secreting a mucilaginous wall. Repeated cell division in this condition produces extensive palmelloid colonies with a copious mucilaginous matrix.

DIVISION PYRROPHYTA

This division of approximately 1,000 species in 125 genera contains many marine representatives. Most genera of *pyrrophytes* are unicellular motile flagellates; but some are nonmotile palmelloid forms, and a few are colonial or filamentous. The division has both colorless and pigmented forms, the latter being characteristically golden-brown or greenish-brown. In this text the flagellate cryptomonad group has been placed as a separate class, the Cryptophyceae. However, recent work concerning cytology and pigmentation indicates that the Cryptophyceae should probably be recognized as a separate division, the Cryptophyta. The remaining forms (the *dinoflagellates*) are placed in a single class, the Dinophyceae.

185

CLASS DINOPHYCEAE (Dinoflagellates)

Cell Structure

The cell is either naked with a firm periplast or provided with a cellulosic wall. The greatest diversity occurs in the motile forms that range in size from 25–500 microns. In the naked motile, or unarmored, forms such as *Gymnodinium* (Fig. 10–6A), the periplast may be smooth, striated, or ribbed. In armored forms, the cellulose layer may be composed of a number of discrete, articulated, sculptured plates cemented together tightly in a definite pattern. The plates are delicate, perforated with one or more pores (Fig. 10–6B), or strikingly ornamented with horns, spines, papillae, or wing-like processes (Fig. 10–7).

The cells are uninucleate with a highly organized nucleus, which characteristically con-

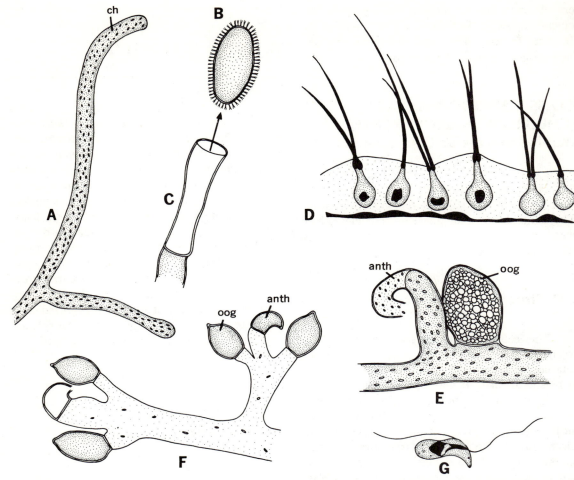

FIGURE 10–5 Reproduction in coenocytic *Vaucheria* (Xanthophyceae). A, portion of vegetative thallus, ×60. B–D, asexual reproduction. B, multiflagellate zoospore just released from empty sporangium shown in C, ×200; D, detailed structure of outer area of part of zoospore showing unequal whiplash flagella, ×1,240. E–G, sexual reproduction. E, F, two species showing relation of antheridium (*anth*) and oogonium (*oog*), ×150; G, sperm, ×1,240. *ch*, chloroplast. (D, G, redrawn by permission of William J. Koch and *Journal of Elisha Mitchell Scientific Society*.)

tains conspicuous bead-like threads of chromatin. Some of the motile forms also may have a pigmented eyespot considered to be light sensitive.

The photosynthetic forms are generally a greenish-brown or golden-brown. However, sometimes the organisms are a bright red. Usually two or more small, disc-shaped chloroplasts are present. The photosynthetic forms have two green pigments, chlorophyll *a* and *c,* as well as a number of carotenoid pigments.

The carbohydrate food reserves are stored in the form of starch, comparable to the starch of green algae and higher plants. The starch is formed outside the chloroplast and may be scattered in the cytoplasm. Fat or oil is also stored and may appear as bright red or yellow droplets.

Most types of nutrition are represented in the Dinophyceae. Those forms lacking photosynthetic pigments are saprobic or parasitic; some are phagotrophic. All autotrophic forms studied require an external source of vitamins and are therefore auxotrophs. Some pigmented species have also been reported to be phagotrophic, but this is rare.

Movement

The motile cells are biflagellate and consist of two morphologically dissimilar flagella usually inserted laterally close together (Fig. 10–6A, B). A broad ribbon-like flagellum encircles the cell in a transverse groove, the girdle. Within the expanded sheath of this flagellum there is, in addition to the 11 fibrils, a shortened striated strand. The second flagellum trails posteriorly, lying in a longitudinal groove, the sulcus.

Morphological Diversity

The unicellular, biflagellate type (Fig. 10–6A, B) is typical of the group and is by far the most common, although a few motile colonial forms, such as *Polykrikos* (Fig. 10–6C), occur in the marine phytoplankton. Some representatives occur in the tentacles of sea anemones (Fig. 10–8) and give the characteristic color to the animal. Nonmotile forms include palmelloid forms, coccoid forms such as *Cystodinium* (Fig. 10–6D), and multicellular filamentous types such as *Dinothrix* (Fig. 10–6E).

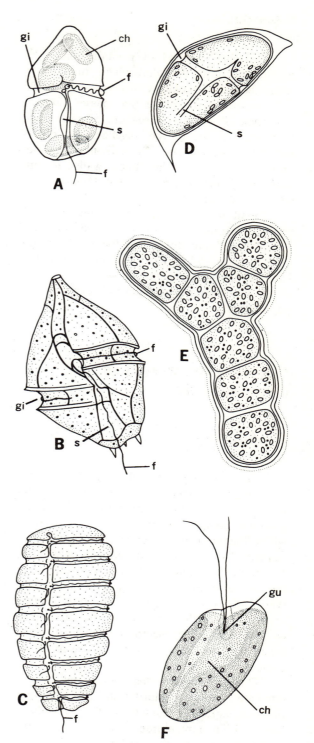

187

FIGURE 10–6 Morphological diversity in Pyrrophyta. A–E, Dinophyceae. A–C, motile forms viewed from ventral side to show orientation of flagella (*f*), sulcus (*s*), and girdle (*gi*). A, *Gymnodinium*, an unarmored form showing chloroplasts (*ch*), ×250; B, *Gonyaulax*, an armored form, ×750; C, *Polykrikos*, a colonial form, ×75. D, coccoid form *Cystodinium*, containing characteristic dinoflagellate cell showing girdle and sulcus, ×650; E, filamentous type, *Dinothrix*, ×750; F, Cryptophyceae; motile cell seen from ventral side showing flagella and gullet (*gu*), *Cryptomonas*, ×3,650. (A–C, after Schiller in Rabenhorst with permission of Akademische Verlagsgesellschaft, Geest and Portig K.–G., Leipzig.)

DIVISIONS CHRYSOPHYTA, XANTHOPHYTA, PYRROPHYTA, EUGLENOPHYTA

Reproduction

The chief method of reproduction is by longitudinal cell division, which may occur while the cell is motile. Cell division of motile cells occurs in the plane that passes through the point of flagellar insertion. Usually each half receives one of the flagella, soon differentiating a second one. The cells may also become encysted, forming thick walls. Recent work has shown that many fossil dinoflagellates are known in the encysted stage.

In all the nonmotile forms, motile unarmored reproductive cells are produced, with lateral flagellation typical of the motile forms (see Fig. 10–6A). Sexual reproduction has been reported as isogamous. Meiosis has been shown in some dinoflagellates to occur in zygote germination.

CLASS CRYPTOPHYCEAE (Cryptomonads)

Cell Structure

This relatively small class is composed of fewer than 100 species in 24 genera. The majority of Cryptophyceae are biflagellate, dorsiventrally compressed unicells (Fig. 10–6F), with a longitudinal furrow or gullet on the ventral side. Most forms are naked with only a firm membrane, or periplast. A few nonmotile genera are palmelloid or coccoid with motile cells typical of the motile genera. The gullet may be lined with small tuberculate, spindle-shaped cavities containing ejectosomes, whose exact function is unknown. In a few motile forms an eyespot is present.

The pigmented forms possess one or two laminate parietal chloroplasts. The storage product, starch, is formed outside the chloroplast, within a membrane that is part of the nuclear membrane. The chloroplast color varies

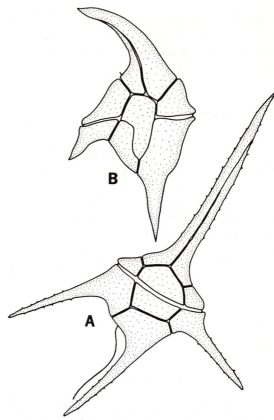

FIGURE 10–7 Variation in morphology of *Ceratium,* showing relative length of horns. A, a warm-water form, ×580; B, a cold-water form, ×465.

FIGURE 10–8 Tentacles of two sea anemones (*Condylactis*) containing symbiotic dinoflagellates. Upper, after exposure to darkness for 24 days; lower, after exposure to normal daylight for 24 days, ×0.8. (Photograph courtesy P. A. Zahl and J. J. A. McLaughlin, and permission of *Journal of Protozoology.*)

188

from yellowish-green to brown to blue-green to red. The pigment complex contains both chlorophyll *a* and *c,* and carotenoids. In addition, all genera investigated contain phycobiliprotein pigments which have properties different from those of the Cyanophyta and Rhodophyta.

The majority of the Cryptophyceae are photoautotrophs, although those few forms investigated carefully have been shown to be auxotrophs. Some saprobic and phagotrophic forms also occur.

Morphological Diversity

The unicellular motile form, *Cryptomonas,* is the most common morphological type (Fig. 10–6F). Some of these motile genera may enter a palmelloid condition at times. A few cryptophytes are typically palmelloid in the vegetative condition, liberating motile stages that have the typical flattened appearance and gullet of motile genera. There are also coccoid types with a thick wall containing cellulose.

Reproduction

The chief method of reproduction is vegetative by longitudinal cell division. The cell may divide in the motile condition or in a nonmotile condition where it becomes embedded in a mucilaginous matrix, forming a palmelloid mass by cell division. Sexual reproduction is doubtful and has not been confirmed in this class.

DIVISION EUGLENOPHYTA

There are almost 40 genera and 450 species of algae or alga-like organisms referred to this division (*euglenids*). Most of these genera are unicellular and motile; very few are sessile. This group has forms with both plant- and animal-like features. Only one class, Euglenophyceae, is recognized.

Cell Structure

The cell lacks a firm wall; the outer part of the protoplast is the pellicle, which is covered by the plasma membrane. The pellicle is flexible, with a plastic cell outline, as in *Euglena* (Fig. 10–10A–E); such a cell is said to exhibit euglenoid movement. Or the periplast may be more rigid with delicate diagonal or longitudinal striations, as in *Phacus* (Fig. 10–9D). In a few forms, such as *Trachelomonas* (Fig. 10–9A), the cell is within a firm lorica with only the flagellum projecting.

At the anterior end of the motile cell there is usually an invagination with a narrow tube-like portion and an enlarged posterior reservoir (Fig. 10–9B, C, E). From the base of the reservoir arise two flagella, one of which is always emergent beyond the invagination. In some of the colorless genera, as in *Peranema* (Fig. 10–9E), there are a special opening and rod-like structures lying parallel to the long axis of the invagination. These organelles are ingestion rods and function in obtaining particulate food. Near the base of the flagella within the flagellar membrane lies a swelling, the photoreceptor. Near the point of attachment of the flagella there may be a reddish eyespot, believed to be light sensitive (Fig. 10–9D). The eyespot is not within the chloroplast membrane (as it is in the green algae, Chapter 11).

The chromosomes remain condensed and stainable in interphase. Nuclear division is not like that typical of most algae. In some ways it resembles that of the Dinophyceae; however, there are some features unique to the Euglenophyceae.

The Euglenophyceae consist of both green (Fig. 10–9A, C, D, F, G) and colorless (Fig. 10–9B, E) forms. Many of the colorless genera are identical to the pigmented forms except for chloroplasts and eyespots. In pigmented forms, numerous bright green chloroplasts are irregularly scattered throughout the cytoplasm. Often the chloroplasts are most abundant at the posterior end of the cell. The pigments present are primarily chlorophyll *a* and *b* plus carotenoids. Several euglenids, including some species of *Euglena,* often contain numerous red granules referred to as hematochrome, which is a carotenoid.

The typical food reserve is paramylon, a laminarin-like polysaccharide. It is present in the form of granules of various shapes. In pigmented forms it is free in the cytoplasm or adjacent to the chloroplast but not enclosed in any membrane. Some of the Euglenophyta are truly autotrophic; however, many of the pigmented forms are auxotrophs and require vitamins for growth. The unpigmented euglenids are obligate heterotrophs and may be phagotrophic. Some of the pigmented forms are facultative heterotrophs (or mixotrophs).

Movement

The motile euglenids exhibit two basic types of movement. One is the well-known swimming movement, in which the flagellar action is helical or spiral. Thus, the cell moves forward as well as rotates on its long axis (Fig. 10–10H, I). The over-all result is that the organism moves in a spiral pathway. In the other basic movement, the euglenid creeps or glides, apparently because the flagellum is held in front of the cell rather than at an oblique angle (Fig. 10–10F, G); thus, no cell rotation occurs. If

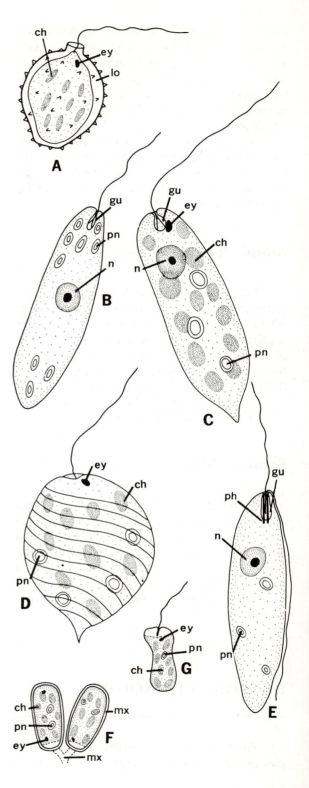

FIGURE 10–9 Morphological diversity in Euglenophyta. A–E, motile forms. A, *Trachelomonas,* showing surrounding lorica (*lo*), chloroplast (*ch*), and eyespot (*ey*), ×1,000; B, *Astasia,* colorless form showing nucleus (*n*), paramylon (*pn*), and gullet (*gu*), ×1,915; C, *Euglena,* ×1,550; D, *Phacus,* ×155; E, *Peranema,* showing colorless form, with pharyngeal rods (*ph*) at gullet, ×1,485. F, G, nonmotile form *Colacium.* F, vegetative stage with matrix (*mx*), ×800; G, zoospore, ×530.

190

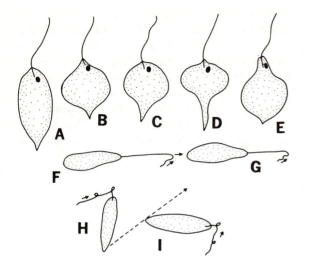

FIGURE 10–10 Swimming movements in Euglenophyta (arrows indicate direction of flagellar movement). A–E, metaboly in *Euglena;* F, G, direction of movement and flagellar position in *Peranema;* H, I, in *Euglena.* (F–I, adapted from T. L. Jahn, "Euglenophyta" in *Manual of Phycology—An Introduction to the Algae and Their Biology,* edited by Gilbert M. Smith, copyright 1951, The Ronald Press Company, New York.)

a long second flagellum is present, it trails the cell, beating only at the tip. Some euglenids constantly change shape or exhibit metaboly (Fig. 10–10A–E), probably because of a sliding of the semirigid rings composing the pellicle.

Morphological Diversity

The Euglenophyceae are generally divided into two or more orders. These may be based on morphological form (motile or palmelloid) or on mode of nutrition (phagotrophic or nonphagotrophic). Although the majority of Euglenophyceae are motile and unicellular, there is a single genus, *Colacium,* containing a nonmotile form. In the vegetative condition these cells are attached to the substrate by a mucilaginous stalk (Fig. 10–9F). In vegetative reproduction the cells (zoospores) become motile and are typically euglenid in form (Fig. 10–9G).

Reproduction

Reproduction in this group occurs by longitudinal cell division while the cell is actively motile. Two immediately motile daughter cells are produced. Under some conditions the cell becomes nonmotile, undergoing repeated division in a palmelloid condition. In unfavorable conditions a cell can encyst and accumulate large amounts of carotenoid.

Sexual reproduction is not well authenticated. Recently there has been a report of the occurrence of meiosis following a nonsexual process of self-fertilization. This is apparently rare and a response to unfavorable conditions.

RELATIONSHIPS

The treatment of the Chrysophyta, Xanthophyta, Pyrrophyta, and Euglenophyta in one chapter is not intended to indicate that these divisions are phylogenetically or phenetically closely related. The fossil evidence for the most part is lacking. Diatom frustules (Bacillariophyceae of the Chrysophyta) are known from at least the Jurassic Period and possibly from the Paleozoic. Cysts of the dinoflagellates (Dinophyceae of the Pyrrophyta) are reported from the Mesozoic primarily, but also occur in the Ordovician of the Paleozoic. However, these are only two of the seven classes considered in this chapter. Thus any argument for evolutionary relationships among the divisions is based on phenetic characteristics.

Actually, these groups have no one main characteristic in common. Yet there are overlapping relationships between these divisions and the Phaeophyta (Chapter 9). The Phaeophyta and Chrysophyta are probably the most closely related, since both contain chlorophyll *a* and *c,* similar carotenoids, similar flagellated cells (at least one tinsel flagellum), and have related storage products (laminarin and laminarin-like). Chlorophyll *a* and *c* also occur in the Pyrrophyta, but starch is present and the flagellation is quite different. Both the Xanthophyta and Euglenophyta have laminarin-like storage products and a tinsel flagellum, but the pigment complex differs. Thus, the phenetic relationship would place the Phaeophyta and Chrysophyta close together, and the Xanthophyta and Euglenophyta possibly closer to the Chlorophyta. The Pyrrophyta should be considered from the point of view of the two classes, the Dinophyceae and the Cryptophyceae. The Cryptophyceae are more like the Rhodophyta and Cyanophyta, because of the occurrence of phycobiliproteins and starch-like storage products. However, the presence in the Cryptophyceae of flagellated stages is possibly very important from an evolutionary standpoint. The Dinophyceae belong somewhere between the Cryptophyceae and the Phaeophyta-Chrysophyta complex and on a line of their own.

192

11 / Division Chlorophyta and Algal Ecology

The *green algae* are predominantly fresh-water forms; however, they are common and sometimes relatively conspicuous in marine environments. In general, the marine forms are much larger than the fresh-water; but macroscopic and microscopic green algae occur in both habitats. There are nearly 7,000 species of green algae in about 450 genera. Vegetatively, the Chlorophyta are relatively simple, but they exhibit a greater variety in life history and in reproduction than any other division of plants. There is some difference of opinion about the systematic arrangement of this group. The system followed here recognizes two classes: the Chlorophyceae, containing 11 or 12 orders, and the Charophyceae with one order (which is sometimes considered as an order in the Chlorophyceae).

The green algae are generally considered the progenitors of embryo-producing green plants and part of the main line of evolution to vascular plants. For this reason the Chlorophyta has been left for discussion until last among the algal divisions. The two classes will be considered together in the discussion of cell structure, but the morphology and reproduction in the Charophyceae are so distinct that they will be treated separately.

CELL STRUCTURE

Most of the green algae have a rigid cell wall composed of a firm inner cellulosic layer and an outer, less firm pectic layer. In some forms the cellulose may be partially replaced by xylan and mannan. The wall is impregnated with calcium carbonate in most Charophyceae and some marine representatives.

The cells of the green algae are uninucleate, and the nucleus contains one or more nucleoli. Motile cells may often have contractile vacuoles near the apex. The pigments of green algae occur in well-organized chloroplasts. When only one or two chloroplasts are present they may be shaped like a half-filled cup, a band, a ring, a net, a spiral, or a star (Fig. 11–1). They are parietal in the cell (Fig. 11–1A–C, E, F) or axile in position (Fig. 11–1D, G). When many chloroplasts are present, they are usually small, discoid, and often interconnected. Electron micrographs show bands of two to six fused lamellae that generally traverse the chloroplast (Fig. 11–2A, B). These resemble grana of higher plants, except the stacks of lamellae are longer in the chlorophytes. A pyrenoid may be associated with the chloroplast, and usually in a central position (Fig. 11–1, 2A). When present, the pyrenoid is an integral part of the chloroplast, often traversed by lamellae. In motile cells a single eyespot may occur at one side of the chloroplast. The ultrastructure of the eyespot has been shown to consist of three to eight rows of densely packed granules; these rows are intimately associated with the photosynthetic lamellae. No lens structure has been demonstrated.

The characteristic grass-green color of this group is due to chlorophyll *a* and chlorophyll *b*. In addition there are the carotenoid pigments, some of which are the same as in higher plants. In one order (Codiales), unique carotenoids are present.

Most of the green algae are autotrophic. Some of the photosynthetic species are nutritionally auxotrophic or mixotrophic. Carbohydrate reserves are stored as starch, and starch formation is usually intimately associated with the pyrenoids. The Chlorophyta is the only algal division in which the starch grains lie within the chloroplast and, when a pyrenoid is present, they surround it (Fig. 11–2A). The presence of starch gives the chloroplast a granular, rough appearance. Fats and oil similar to those in other algae may be present as a reserve in some green algae.

When present, motile cells are anteriorly biflagellate (or quadriflagellate). They are whiplash and equal in length (the isokont condition). In the order Oedogoniales and in *Derbesia* (Codiales), the motile cells always possess an anterior circlet of short flagella of equal length, termed stephanokont.

CLASS CHLOROPHYCEAE

Classification and Morphological Diversity

The Chlorophyceae are extremely diversified morphologically, ranging from unicellular motile or nonmotile forms to motile or nonmotile colonial forms; from multicellular

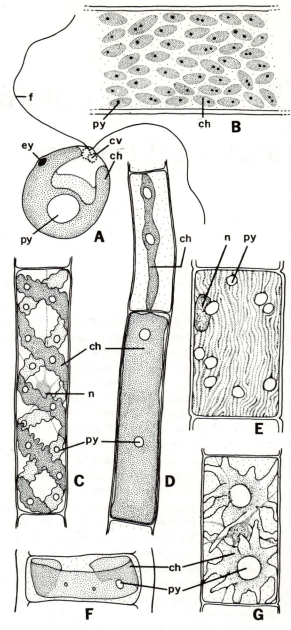

FIGURE 11–1 Chloroplasts of Chlorophyta. A, B, C, E, F, parietal in position; D, G, axile in position. A, cup-shaped (*Chlamydomonas*), ×2,750; B, discoid (*Bryopsis*), ×255; C, spiral-shaped (*Spirogyra*), ×530; D, band-shaped (*Mougeotia*), ×510; E, net-shaped (*Oedogonium*), ×280; F, band- or ring-shaped (*Ulothrix*), ×2,450; G, star-shaped (*Zygnema*), ×735. *ch*, chloroplast; *cv*, contractile vacuole; *ey*, eyespot; *f*, flagellum; *n*, nucleus; *py*, pyrenoid.

194

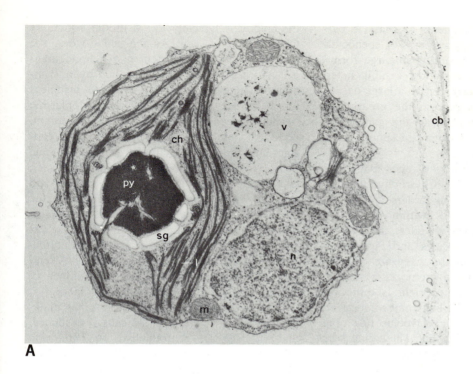

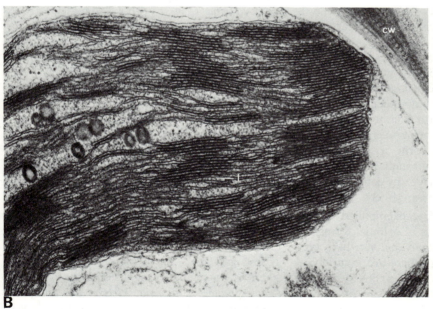

FIGURE 11–2 Electron micrographs of Chlorophyceae cells. A, section of *Volvox* cell showing chloroplast (*ch*) containing fused lamellae (*l*), pyrenoid (*py*), and starch granule (*sg*). Also present are mitochondrion (*m*), nucleus (*n*), vacuole (*v*), and boundary of colony (*cb*), ×12,000. B, chloroplast of desmid (*Bambusina*) showing stacks of fused lamellae and *cw*, cell wall, ×44,460. (A, courtesy T. Bisalputra; B, courtesy J. Gerrath.)

DIVISION CHLOROPHYTA AND ALGAL ECOLOGY

simple or branched filaments to massive parenchymatous types. Aggregations of coenocytic filaments also occur, resulting in large forms. Certain genera may regularly exhibit heterotrichy. Growth is intercalary to a large degree, and apical growth is rare in the group as a whole. In the Chlorophyceae the gametangia are freely exposed and often are simply metamorphosed vegetative cells.

There are three fairly distinct main lines of evolution within the Chlorophyceae, and with a few exceptions the orders can be arranged in phenetic series within these. The Oedogoniales and Zygnematales, and certain marine orders (Dasycladales and Siphonocladales), are so different that they are regarded as taxonomically remote from others in the green algae; their precise origin is quite obscure. The three general lines of evolution are usually referred to as the volvocine line (Fig. 11–3A), the tetrasporine line (including what is often termed the chlorococcine line, Fig. 11–3B, C), and the siphonous line (Fig. 11–3D).

The Volvocine Line. Vegetatively one of the simplest green algae is the unicellular motile form *Chlamydomonas* (Fig. 11–4C). This alga is representative of the primitive stock from which all other groups of green algae are thought to have evolved. *Chlamydomonas* is a biflagellate motile cell; but under certain conditions it may revert to a nonmotile state, become embedded in a gelatinous matrix, and divide vegetatively to form a dense amorphous mass, the palmelloid state. In these aggregations, the cells never have any connection with one another or definite arrangement.

In the volvocine line, exemplified by the order Volvocales, a series of colonial forms has evolved from the *Chlamydomonas*-like type (Fig. 11–3A). Although there are a variety of types, possibilities are limited; in the evolutionary sense, this line has apparently been a blind alley. In the colonial forms, each cell in the colony is typically like a motile vegetative *Chlamydomonas* cell. As the cell divides, the daughter cells are oriented in a definite manner and remain fastened together by a common mucilaginous matrix. In some instances the cells are interconnected by cytoplasmic strands. The colony is also termed a coenobium, since the number of cells in a colony is constant and does not change from the juvenile colony to the adult. In the simpler forms each cell of the colony is vegetatively similar and has the same reproductive potentiality. In the more advanced types, certain cells or groups remain vegetative, whereas others become differentiated and specialized for reproduction. Hence, in the volvocine series, there is a trend toward a gradual increase in the number of colony cells and some division of labor.

In *Gonium* (Fig. 11–4A, B) a flat plate-like colony of 4, 8, 16, or 32 cells is produced, and all cells are reproductive. In *Pandorina* (Fig. 11–4D) a spherical or ellipsoidal colony of 8, 16, or 32 tightly packed cells is formed. In *Eudorina* (Fig. 11–4E) a spherical colony of 16, 32, or 64 somewhat separated cells results; in some species the front tier of cells remains vegetative and the remaining cells become reproductive. *Pleodorina* (Fig. 11–4F) —sometimes not recognized as separate from *Eudorina*—is also a spherical colony of 32, 64, or 128 cells, in which the smaller cells are vegetative and the larger ones are reproductive. The ultimate in this line of evolution is *Volvox* (Fig. 11–3A, 10G), where 500 to 50,000 cells form a hollow spherical colony with only a few scattered reproductive cells. In sexual reproduction there is also an evolutionary series apparent. *Gonium* and *Pandorina* are isogamous and the gametes are *Chlamydomonas*-like. These gametes may be of different sizes, but there is no regularity in fusion of a large and small gamete. *Eudorina, Pleodorina,* and *Volvox* have oogamy with a small, ellipsoid, yel-

196

FIGURE 11–3 Habit types resulting from plane of cell and nuclear divisions in Chlorophyta. A, volvocine line; B, C, tetrasporine line culminating in two different plant types; D, siphonous line. (Flagella not included in motile forms; surface and transverse sectional views shown for parenchymatous series.)

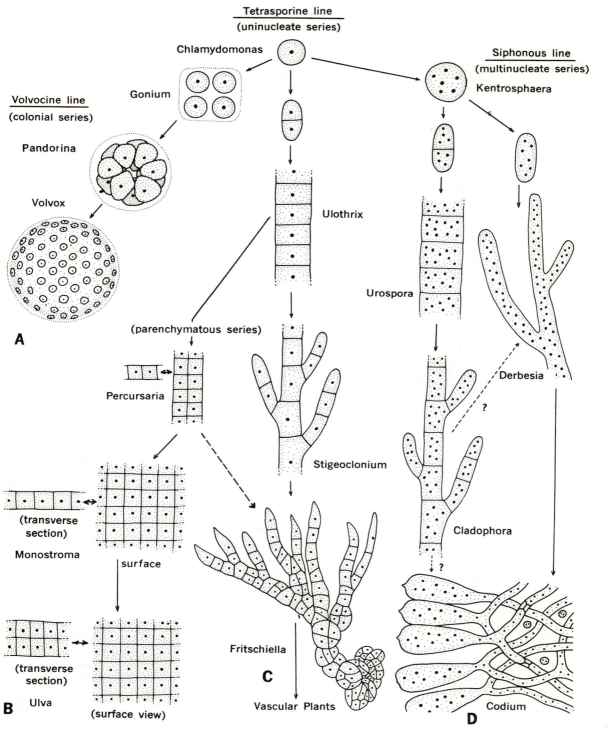

Tetrasporine line
(uninucleate series)

Chlamydomonas

Siphonous line
(multinucleate series)

Kentrosphaera

Volvocine line
(colonial series)

Gonium

Pandorina

Volvox

A

Ulothrix

Urospora

(parenchymatous series)

Percursaria

Derbesia

?

(transverse
section)

Monostroma

surface

Stigeoclonium

Cladophora

?

(transverse
section)

Ulva

(surface view)

Fritschiella

Vascular Plants

C

Codium

D

B

DIVISION CHLOROPHYTA AND ALGAL ECOLOGY

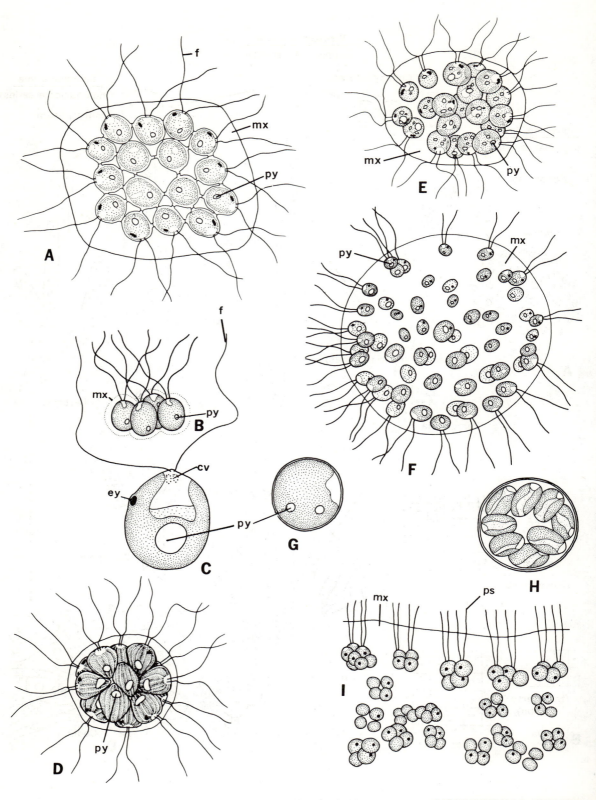

198

low-green sperm and a large round green egg.

The Tetrasporine Line. From the chlamydomonad prototype there are series of forms in the tetrasporine line ranging from the unicellular, nonmotile condition to more complex multicellular thalli (Fig. 11–3B, C). Motile cells similar to *Chlamydomonas* are produced but only during reproduction. In the tetrasporine line of evolution there are limitless possibilities, in contrast to the volvocine line. The main feature of the tetrasporine line is the uninucleate condition of the cells. The orders included are the Ulotrichales (in the broadest sense), the Ulvales, and part of the Chlorococcales.

The nonmotile vegetative cell is illustrated by *Chlorococcum* (Fig. 11–4G, H). An orderly series of vegetative divisions from a *Chlorococcum*-like cell leads to the filamentous colony. If a nonmotile cell divides and its derivatives continue to divide in the same plane, a simple uniseriate filament of cells results, as in *Ulothrix* (Fig. 11–5F). This is essentially a simple type of intercalary cell division. From the uniseriate, unbranched filament, repeated divisions in a second plane produce the monostromatic thallus typical of *Monostroma* (Fig. 11–5C–E). If cells divide regularly (but only once) in a third plane, a foliose thallus similar to that of *Ulva* is formed (Fig. 11–5A, B). If restricted divisions of cells in all three planes occur, the result is a partially parenchymatous thallus, as in *Fritschiella* (Fig. 11–6D). This division in three planes is the basis for true parenchymatous growth, making possible the development of complex tissues in higher plants.

If the regular division of the uniseriate type is supplemented by an occasional division of a cell leading to the branched uniseriate type of thallus, as seen in *Stigeoclonium* (Fig. 11–5G), this parallels the filamentous to parenchymatous lines of development (Fig. 11–3B) and creates

a heterotrichous plant, which is considered a precursor to certain characteristics of higher plants. In *Stigeoclonium* (Fig. 11–5G) both the prostrate and the erect systems are equally well represented. In *Fritschiella* (Fig. 11–6D) both systems also develop, and the prostrate portion is further differentiated into septate rhizoids, which anchor the plant in the mud. However, in other genera one or the other of these systems may be reduced or even completely eliminated. In *Draparnaldia* the basal system is completely suppressed (Fig. 11–6E), and in some species of *Coleochaete* the erect system is almost completely absent (Fig. 11–6A). In the very common *Pleurococcus,* which occurs generally on tree trunks, the filamentous form itself is somewhat suppressed, resulting in small packets of cells (Fig. 11–6B, C). As in the volvocine line, there is also an evolutionary series in sexual reproduction. Such forms as *Ulothrix, Stigeoclonium,* and *Fritschiella* are isogamous; *Ulva* may be isogamous or anisogamous; and *Coleochaete* is oogamous.

The Siphonous Line. Along a third line of evolution the multinucleate nature of the cell has resulted in several distinct series of green algae with the typically multinucleate nature of the cell an outstanding feature (Fig. 11–3D). Among the simple unicellular forms it is easy to imagine how a multinucleate genus such as *Kentrosphaera* (Fig. 11–7A–C) might have arisen, simply by failure of septa to form following one or more nuclear divisions. A simple filamentous multinucleate form, as in *Urospora* (Fig. 11–7H, I), would also result from regular septation. As in the filamentous uninucleate series, occasional divisions to produce branch initials result in a branched thallus of multinucleate cells (*Cladophora,* Fig. 11–7D). Another line from the *Kentrosphaera*-type, in which no septations are formed except when reproductive cells are formed, would produce

199

FIGURE 11–4 Morphological diversity in Chlorophyceae. A–F, motile unicellular and colonial forms (volvocine line). A, *Gonium,* surface view, showing flagellum (*f*), coenobial matrix (*mx*), and pyrenoid (*py*), ×1,215; B, *Gonium,* side view, ×1,215; C, *Chlamydomonas,* showing eyespot (*ey*), contractile vacuoles (*cv*), and flagella, ×2,810; D, *Pandorina,* ×2,000; E, *Eudorina,* ×1,075; F, *Pleodorina,* ×445. G–I, nonmotile unicellular and colonial forms (tetrasporine line). G, *Chlorococcum,* vegetative cell, ×1,040; H, *Chlorococcum,* daughter cell formation, ×1,040; I, *Tetraspora,* in mucilaginous matrix, ×625. *ps,* pseudocilia.

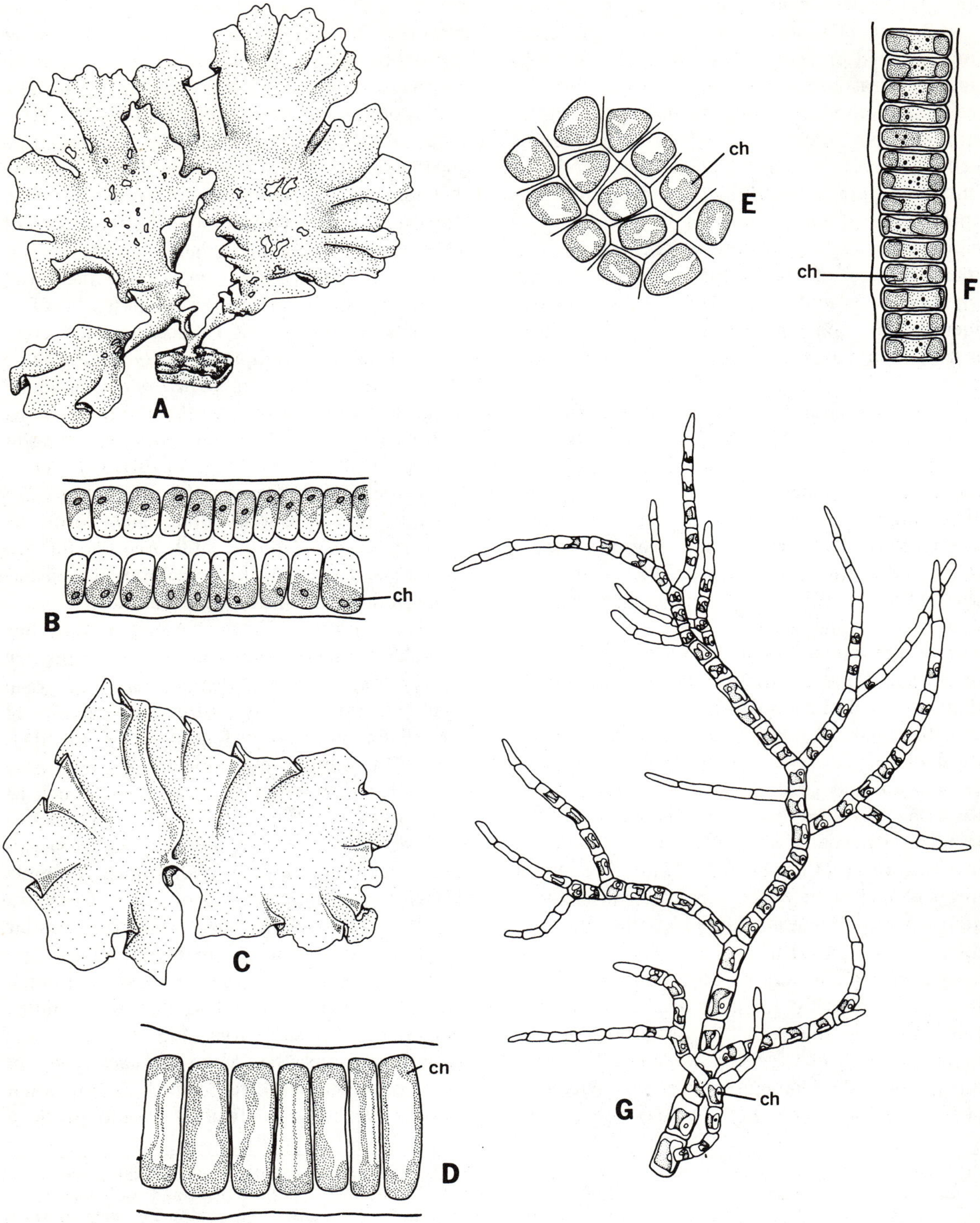

FIGURE 11–5   Morphological diversity in Chlorophyceae; filamentous and parenchymatous forms (tetrasporine line). A–E, parenchymatous forms. A, B, *Ulva* (A, habit, ×0.5; B, transverse sectional view, ×500); C–E, *Monostroma* (C, habit, ×0.5; D, transverse sectional view, showing chloroplast, ×530; E, cell arrangement in surface view, ×750). F–G, filamentous forms. F, *Ulothrix*, showing unbranched filament, ×560; G, *Stigeoclonium,* showing branched growth form, ×150. *ch,* chloroplast.

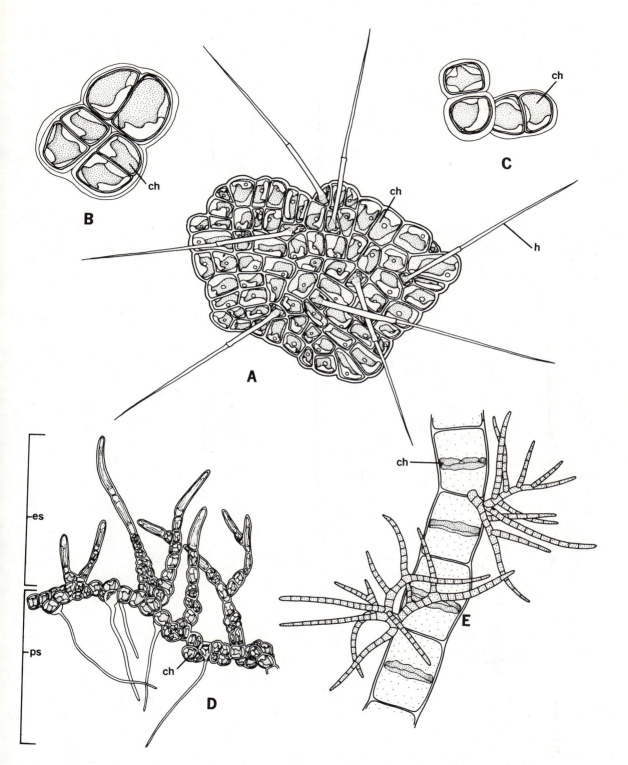

FIGURE 11–6 Morphological diversity in Chlorophyceae; filamentous and parenchymatous forms (tetra-sporine line). A, *Coleochaete,* a prostrate species showing hairs (*h*), ×435; B, C, *Pleurococcus,* showing reduced filamentous nature, ×2,150; D, *Fritschiella,* showing heterotrichy with prostrate (*ps*) parenchymatous and erect (*es*) filamentous regions, ×375; E, *Draparnaldia,* showing main axis of erect form, ×290. *ch,* chloroplast.

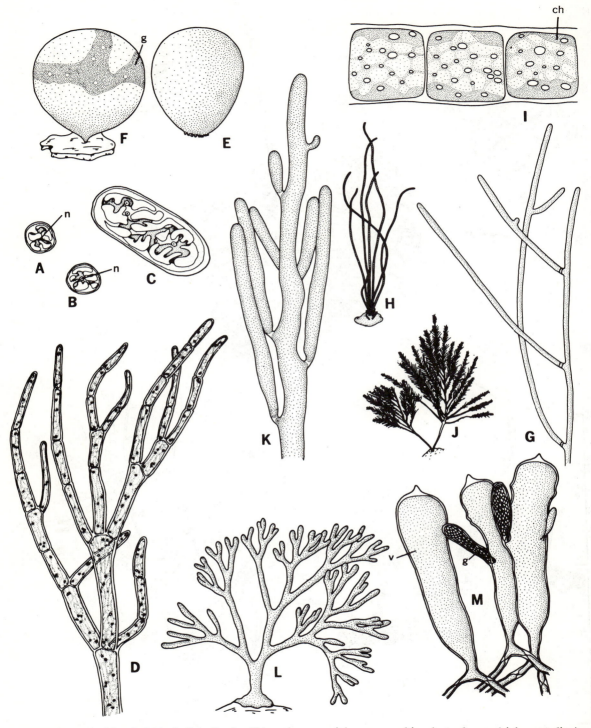

FIGURE 11-7 Morphological diversity in Chlorophyceae; siphonous, multinucleate forms (siphonous line). A–C, *Kentrosphaera,* showing change from uninucleate (A) to multinucleate (B, C) condition, ×460. D, *Cladophora,* ×74; E, *Valonia,* ×0.46; F, G, *Derbesia* (F, sac-like *Halicystis*-stage, showing differentiated gametangial region (*g*), ×4.6; G, filamentous *Derbesia*-stage, ×110); H, I, *Urospora* (H, habit, ×8.3; I, vegetative cells, showing chloroplast (*ch*); J, K, *Bryopsis* (J, habit, ×1.4; K, enlarged view of branch, ×110); L, M, *Codium* (L, habit, ×1; M, coenocytic vesicles (*v*) with gametangia, ×1,026). *n,* nucleus.

a coenocytic multinucleate thallus characteristic of the *Derbesia* sac-like stage (Fig. 11–7F)
or the elongate, filamentous stage (Fig. 11–
7G). Regularity in branching of the coenocytic
thallus results in forms such as *Bryopsis* (Fig.
11–7J, K), which also lacks septa and has
free branching. There may be an aggregation
of profusely branched filaments to form a dense
intertwined mass, as in *Codium* (Fig. 11–7L,
M), resulting in a massive thallus of definite
gross morphology.

As seen in Figure 11–3D, the siphonous
line is not a linear series. Rather, it probably
is composed of several parallel lines of evolution, resulting in a number of rather distinctive
orders—Cladophorales, Codiales, Dasycladales,
Siphonocladales, and part of the Chlorococcales. The last order has representatives that
fit also in the tetrasporine line. An evolutionary
sequence of sexual reproduction is not as evident in the siphonous series, although forms
exhibiting isogamy, anisogamy, and oogamy do
occur.

Reproduction and Life Histories

Vegetative reproduction occurs commonly
by fragmentation in multicellular forms and by
cell division in unicellular forms. Motile forms
may revert to a nonmotile, palmelloid phase
under certain circumstances and by repeated
cell division produce a large amorphous aggregation of nonmotile cells. Mitotic divisions
producing one to several aplanospores or zoospores occur throughout the Chlorophyceae.
The spores are usually produced within metamorphosed vegetative cells. In some of the
fresh-water forms, resting spores may be produced when the contents of an entire cell round
up and form a heavy wall.

Sexual reproduction is well established in
the Chlorophyceae as a whole. As noted earlier, reproduction includes isogamy (Fig. 11–
8B, C), as in *Gonium, Stigeoclonium,* or *Fritschiella;* anisogamy (Fig. 11–8E, F), as in
Eudornia, Bryopsis, Codium, or species of

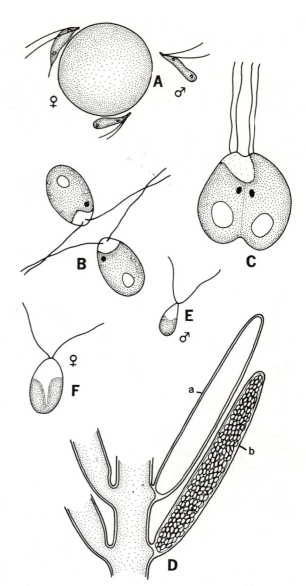

FIGURE 11–8 Sexual reproduction in Chlorophyceae. A, oogamy (*Volvox*), ×700; B, C, isogamy
(*Gonium*), ×1,150. D–F, *Bryopsis.* D, empty (*a*)
and immature (*b*) gametangia, ×50; E, F, anisogametes, ×1,250.

203

Ulva; and oogamy (Fig. 11–8A), as in *Volvox,*
or *Coleochaete.* In the genus *Chlamydomonas,*
different species illustrate all three types of
sexual reproduction. Gametes are produced in
metamorphosed vegetative cells or clearly differentiated gametangia. Both gametes can be

produced by one plant, or two separate plants may be necessary.

There is usually sexual reproduction and an alternation of generations in green algae. For the majority of genera the conspicuous generation is the haploid, with the zygote the only diploid cell in the life cycle, as in *Chlamydomonas* (Fig. 11–9). In fresh-water forms the zygote usually becomes a thick-walled resting structure; however, in marine forms it is usually a thin-walled structure germinating immediately. The first division of the diploid zygote is meiotic, and one or more viable haploid meiospores are formed.

An alternation of isomorphic generations also occurs in some marine and fresh-water forms. Hence, there may be one or two haploid gametophytes alternating with a morphologically similar but cytologically different diploid sporophyte, as in *Ulva* (Fig. 11–11). There are also certain pleomorphic genera, where the haploid and diploid phases are morphologically dissimilar (heteromorphic generations) as in *Derbesia*. In this genus the haploid generation

204

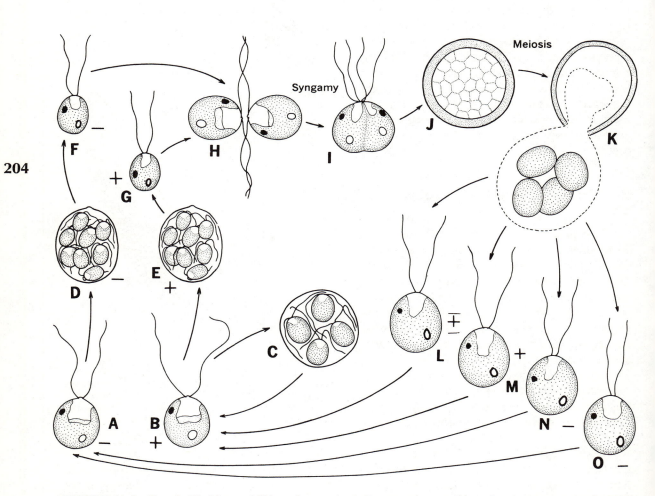

FIGURE 11–9   Zygotic life history (*Chlamydomonas*). A, B, vegetative condition; C, mitospore production; D, E, gamete production; F, G, gametes; H, fusion of isogametes (syngamy); I, planozygote; J, resting zygote; K, germinating zygote (after meiosis); L–O, meiospores. (+ and − indicate mating types.) (For magnification see Fig. 11–4C.)

is sac-like and was first known as a separate genus, *Halicystis* (Fig. 11–7F). The filamentous *Derbesia* plant is the diploid, or sporophytic, stage (Fig. 11–7G).

A third type of life history occurs, as in *Codium,* in which the diploid phase is the conspicuous generation (Fig. 11–12). Meiosis occurs at gametogenesis, and the gametes are the only haploid cells in the life cycle.

Representative Genera

The range of structure and reproduction is so great in the green algae that only a few examples will be considered in detail. The following types illustrate some of the fundamental characteristics of this class.

In the unicellular *Chlamydomonas,* vegetative reproduction takes place by cell division, often while the parent cell is in the motile condition, forming 4, 8, or 16 biflagellate daughter cells (mitospores, Fig. 11–9C). Although these are morphologically similar to the parent cell, they are smaller when liberated by parental-wall breakdown but grow to the characteristic adult size. The gametangium releases gametes, which then fuse (Fig. 11–9H). After syngamy, the zygote is motile for a brief period and possesses four flagella (Fig. 11–9I). The flagella soon disappear; the cell rounds up and secretes a heavy, often strikingly sculptured cellulosic wall (Fig. 11–9J). This resting zygote (or zygospore) is dormant, permitting the species to tolerate extreme changes in moisture and temperature. Under appropriate conditions of moisture, light, and temperature, the zygote germinates (Fig. 11–9K). The nucleus divides meiotically (and sometimes subsequently mitotically) to produce at least four biflagellate zoospores (meiospores) (Fig. 11–9L–O). When released, each zoospore enlarges to form a vegetative cell whose size and morphology is typical of the species. Although the mitospores and meiospores differ in the way they arise, they are both haploid and are otherwise similar in morphology and behavior. Genetically, however, they may differ—the result of recombination of genes during syngamy and segregation during meiosis.

Control of the sexual processes has been studied extensively in a few species of *Chlamydomonas*. The haploid stage may be maintained in a mineral medium in liquid or on agar. Cells grown on agar, when suspended in water and illuminated, become flagellated. Within two to four hours these motile cells behave like gametes; when they are mixed with gametes of the opposite type (plus or minus), mating occurs. At first the gametes clump in large groups; then gametes of opposite mating types pair. Fusion may occur very rapidly. If the resting zygote is placed in the dark within 24 to 48 hours of formation, germination may occur after one week. When the dark-matured zygote is transferred into the light on a fresh medium, meiosis occurs, with subsequent production of zoospores.

In the colonial forms—such as *Gonium, Pandorina,* and *Eudorina*—each cell of the colony is capable of producing daughter colonies identical to (although smaller than) the parental colony. In more advanced types, such as *Pleodorina* and *Volvox,* where division of labor occurs, only certain cells become reproductive. In all these volvocalean genera with a constant number of cells the colony is a coenobium.

In most of these colonial motile forms the cells of the developing daughter colony are oriented with the apical, or flagellar, end pointing inward. It is thus necessary for the entire daughter colony to turn inside out so the flagella are on the outside of the colony. This is best seen in the large colonies of *Volvox* (Fig. 11–10). After the daughter colony is formed, the new coenobium inverts, so that the flagella are ultimately on the outer surface of the colony (Fig. 11–10A–F). The mechanism involved may be similar to that of early gastrulation in animal embryos. After inversion, the daughter colony escapes from the mucilaginous matrix of the original cell and remains in the hollow center of the parent colony until the breakdown of the parental colony.

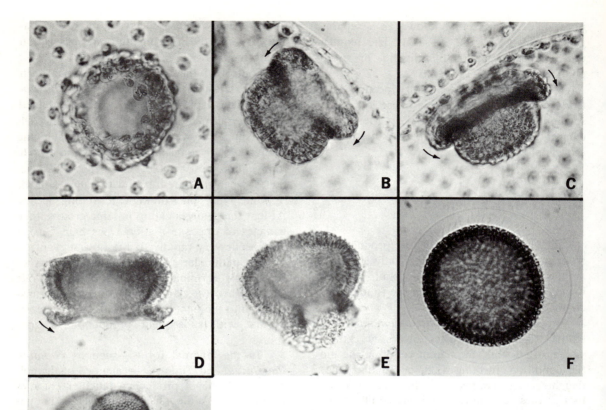

FIGURE 11–10 Daughter colony development in *Volvox aureus* showing one type of inversion. A, end view of young daughter colony to show opening through which colony will invert, × 504; B, beginning of inversion with daughter colony pushing through the opening, × 504; C–E, further stages in inversion (C, × 504; D, E, × 560); F, inversion complete with flagella extended, × 560; G, several daughter colonies with parental colony, × 112. (Photographs courtesy of W. H. Darden, with permission of *Journal of Protozoology*.)

In *Ulothrix* (Fig. 11–5F) each cell of the filament, except the basal holdfast cell, is capable of producing gametes or zoospores, and a resting zygote follows syngamy. In this genus and many others in the Ulotrichales, Ulvales, and Cladophorales, the zoospores are quadriflagellate and the gametes biflagellate.

In *Ulva* (Fig. 11–11), the juvenile vegetative thallus starts out as a uniseriate filament, but divisions in the second and third plane form a more complex thallus, consisting of two layers. At maturity there is close contact between the two cell layers, resulting in a flat foliose plant body. The basal cells of the plant are rhizoidal and are aggregated to form a compact holdfast. Vegetatively there is little morphological difference between the haploid gametophyte (male and female) plants and the diploid sporophytic plants. Except for the basal cells, which usually remain sterile, all cells are potentially capable of becoming fertile.

The uninucleate cells of the haploid game-

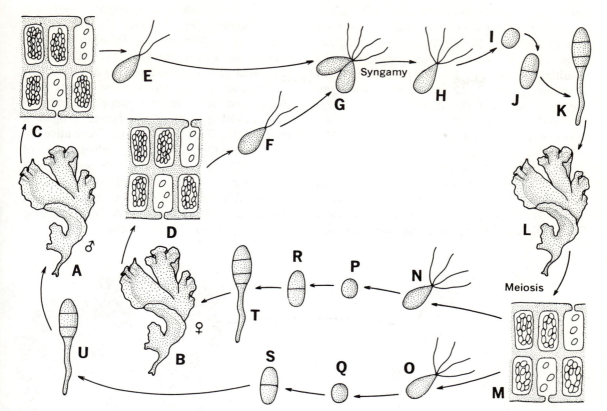

FIGURE 11–11 Sporic life history (*Ulva*) with alternation of isomorphic generations. A, B, mature gameto-phytes (pale margin indicates region of gamete discharge); C, D, gamete production; E, F, gametes; G, fusion of isogametes (syngamy); H, planozygote; I, nonmotile zygote; J, K, filamentous juvenile sporophyte; L, mature sporophyte (pale margin indicates region of meiospore discharge); M, meiospore production (meiosis); N, O, motile meiospores; P-U, filamentous juvenile gametophytes. (For magnification see Fig. 11–5A, C.)

tophytes (Fig. 11–11A, B) undergo nuclear divisions to produce 8, 16, or 32 terminally biflagellate gametes that are released through a pore in the wall (Fig. 11–11C–F). The male gametes appear orange due to an abundance of carotenoid pigments. Syngamy occurs in the water, and for a brief period the zygote may be quadriflagellate (Fig. 11–11G, H). The flagella soon disappear and the thin-walled zygote ger-minates, immediately forming by repeated mi-totic divisions a uniseriate multicellular fila-ment (Fig. 11–11J, K). Subsequently this filament gives rise to the typical flat, distromatic foliose thallus (Fig. 11–11L). Although this phase is morphologically identical to the game-

tophyte, it is cytologically different, since it has diploid cells. At maturity, all cells of the thallus, except those near the base, are potentially ca-pable of functioning as meiosporangia. Meiosis, followed by a number of mitotic divisions, pro-duces 4, 8, or 16 terminally quadriflagellate zoospores (Fig. 11–11N, O). These spores are released the same way as gametes and then settle down, losing the flagella. The spores ger-minate immediately, again forming by mitotic divisions first a uniseriate filament (Fig. 11–11P–U) and then the typical foliose game-tophyte plant (Fig. 11–11A, B).

In the marine chlorophyte *Codium* (Fig. 11–12) the gametes (Fig. 11–12A, B) are

DIVISION CHLOROPHYTA AND ALGAL ECOLOGY

produced in large numbers in clearly differentiated gametangia (Fig. 11–12H–J) as a result of meiosis followed by mitosis. Syngamy (Fig. 11–12C) occurs in the water, and the resulting zygote (Fig. 11–12D) is a thin-walled structure (Fig. 11–12E). It germinates immediately to form the diploid thallus of aggregated coenocytic filaments (Fig. 11–12F) which becomes massive (Fig. 11–12G). Development of a thallus from an unfertilized gamete has also been reported in *Codium*.

Other orders of the Chlorophyceae that are not clearly part of the three lines of evolution are the well known fresh-water Zygnematales and Oedogoniales. The Zygnematales includes filamentous forms such as *Spirogyra, Zygnema,* and *Mougeotia* (Fig. 11–13A–C) and the desmids such as *Micrasterias, Staurastrum, Cosmarium,* and *Closterium* (Fig. 11–13D–G). No flagellated cells are produced by any members of the order. Sexual reproduction results from conjugation of somewhat amoeboid gametes (Fig. 11–14A, B), and the zygote is again a resting cell (Fig. 11–14C, D). Vegetative division is by fragmentation or cell division. In the desmids the vegetative cell is composed of two halves, or semicells, which are mirror images. After nuclear division, each semicell regenerates itself (Fig. 11–15A–D), producing two new identical daughter cells.

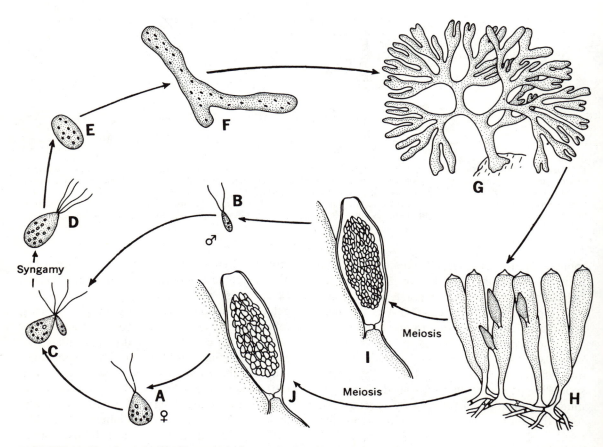

FIGURE 11–12 Gametic life history (*Codium*). A, female gamete; B, male gamete; C, fusion of anisogametes (syngamy); D, planozygote; E, zygote; F, filamentous multinucleate juvenile stage; G, mature diploid thallus; H, vesicles with gametangia; I, male gametangium (meiosis); J, female gametangium (meiosis). (For magnification see Fig. 11–7L, M.)

In the filamentous Oedogoniales (Fig. 11–16), both the zoospores (mitospores and meiospores) and sperms have many flagella, thus exhibiting stephanokont flagellation (Fig. 11–16C). In this order oogamy occurs and gametes are produced in specialized gametangia (Fig. 11–16B, D, E). A special type of intercalary cell division creates cellulosic rings, called cap cells, at the anterior end of some vegetative cells (Fig. 11–16A).

CLASS CHAROPHYCEAE
(Stoneworts)

Morphological Diversity

The Charophyceae is a relatively small group commonly known as stoneworts; they occur submerged and attached to the bottom

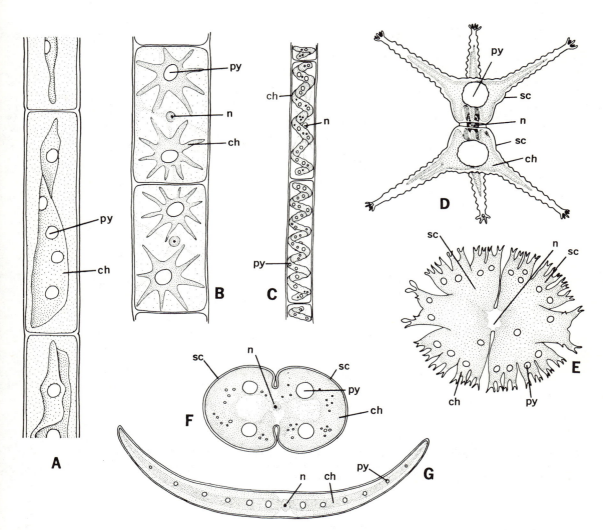

FIGURE 11–13 Morphological diversity in Zygnematales. A–C, filamentous types, showing chloroplast (*ch*), nucleus (*n*), and pyrenoid (*py*). A, *Mougeotia*, ×510; B, *Zygnema*, ×735; C, *Spirogyra*, ×215. D–G, unicellular desmids, showing the semicell (*sc*). D, *Staurastrum*, ×264; E, *Micrasterias*, ×274; F, *Cosmarium*, ×220; G, *Closterium*, ×524.

DIVISION CHLOROPHYTA AND ALGAL ECOLOGY

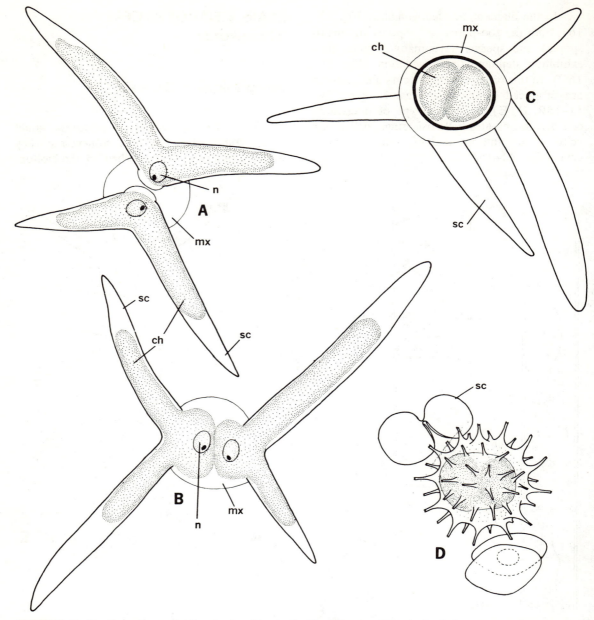

FIGURE 11–14 Sexual reproduction in desmids. A–C, *Closterium,* ×350. A, B, fusion of amoeboid gametes from semicells (*sc*), showing chloroplast (*ch*) and nuclei (*n*), within mucilaginous matrix (*mx*); C, young zygote wth empty semicells. D, resting zygote of *Cosmarium,* ×350.

primarily in fresh water. Although there are only a few genera with about 250 living species, other genera and numerous species are known from the fossil record. Most of the forms in this class have heavily calcified walls.

This group of algae is so distinctive morphologically (Fig. 11–17A) from the other green algae that some botanists place them in a separate division. The stoneworts are taxonomically remote from the other groups of green algae,

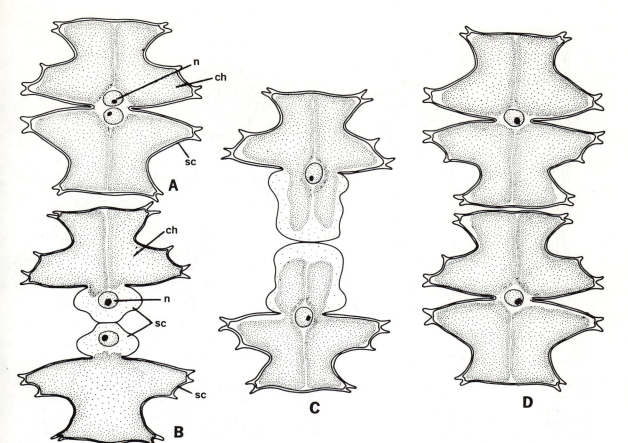

FIGURE 11–15 Asexual reproduction in desmids. A–D, stages in semicell regeneration (asexual reproduction) in *Micrasterias*, ×350. A, binucleate condition of cell; B, C, stages in regeneration of new semicells (*sc*) (note chloroplast and nucleus positions in new semicell); D, regeneration of semicells complete. *ch*, chloroplast; *n*, nucleus.

but judging from their biochemical characteristics they probably have a common evolutionary origin with the Chlorophyceae. Some botanists consider the stoneworts closer to the bryophytes than to the algae.

The Charophyceae are morphologically distinguished by an apical growth and are differentiated into nodal and internodal regions (Fig. 11–17A–E). From the nodes, whorls of branches of limited growth arise. In some genera, such as *Chara* (Fig. 11–17C), the internodal region is covered by corticating filaments of cells, which also arise from the nodes and extend up and down over the internodal cells. In *Nitella* (Fig. 11–17A, B), cortication is absent. At the base of the branched thallus in

Charophyceae there is a differentiated system of branched septate rhizoidal filaments (Fig. 11–17D). Most of the cells are uninucleate, but the large internodal cells are often multinucleate.

Reproduction and Life History

Vegetative reproduction occurs by fragmentation of specialized groups of cells, but zoospores are never produced. Oogamous sexual reproduction is the chief method of reproduction, and many species produce both male and female reproductive organs on the

DIVISION CHLOROPHYTA AND ALGAL ECOLOGY

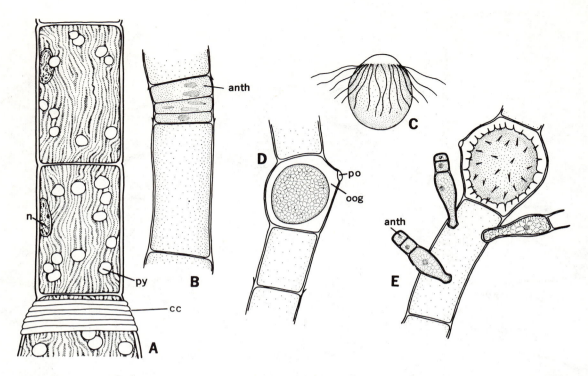

FIGURE 11–16 Morphology of *Oedogonium* (Oeodogoniales). A, part of vegetative filament showing rings comprising cellulose cap (*cc*), ×2,620; B, filament with narrow, immature antheridial cells (*anth*), ×696; C, multiflagellate sperm, ×1,598; D, filament with mature oogonium (*oog*) containing single egg, and showing subapical fertilization pore (*po*), ×696; E, filament with spiny resting zygote, showing three epiphytic dwarf male plants, two immature with two antheridia each, and one mature with antheridia discharged, ×823. *n,* nucleus; *py,* pyrenoid.

same thallus (Fig. 11–17C). The oogonia (Fig. 11–17F) may be considered unicellular; however, the male reproductive organs are multicellular and structurally complex (Fig. 11–17G).

In *Chara,* the oogonium, containing a single egg, is borne at a nodal region of the thallus on a short stalk-like cell. Five sterile vegetative sheath cells originate beneath the oogonium and grow up in a spiral fashion around the

oogonium to form a protecting sheath. At maturity the sheath cells reach to and cover the tip of the oogonium. At the end of each sheath cell one or two small cells are cut off (Fig. 11–17F). The entire female reproductive structure, including its outer protective cells, is commonly referred to as a nucule.

In contrast to the relatively simple development of the female reproductive organ, the male reproductive structure of *Chara* is the

FIGURE 11–17 Morphology of Charophyceae. A, B, *Nitella.* A, habit sketch, showing node (*n*) and internode (*in*), ×0.5; B, uncorticated axis with two nodes and one internode, ×30. C–G, *Chara.* C, corticated axis with female gametangium (above) and male gametangium (below) attached at node, ×30; D, juvenile thallus originating from germinating zygote (*z*) with protonemal basal system (*bs*), rhizoids (*rh*), and erect system (*es*) with whorls of branches at nodes (*n*), ×225; E, longitudinal section of apex of thallus showing apical cell (*ac*) and initiation of alternating node and internode regions, ×395; F, female gametangium (nucule) with twisted cover cells (*co*) and short crown cells (*cr*) protecting oogonium (*oog*); G, male gametangium (globule) with antheridial filaments (*af*) and sterile cells (*sc*), ×750. (D, after Smith with permission of McGraw-Hill Book Company.)

NONVASCULAR PLANTS

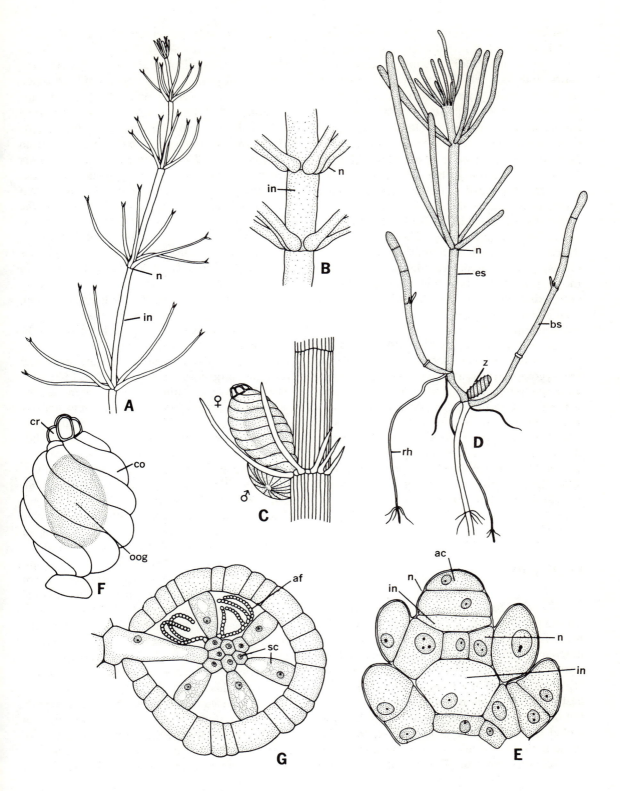

213

DIVISION CHLOROPHYTA AND ALGAL ECOLOGY

most complex in the algae. It is also borne at a nodal region of the thallus and generally appears as a spherical structure attached by a short stalk-like cell. Early in its development an outer sterile layer of cells is differentiated from an inner fertile group of cells. This is very similar in theory to the development of a bryophyte antheridium. Attached to the inner surface of the sterile cells is a small cell which forms one or more antheridial filaments (Fig. 11–17G). Each cell of the antheridial filament produces a single coiled sperm, which has two coiled flagella extending backward from the apical point of attachment. This type of sperm, which is comparable to that of some higher plants, possibly indicates the close affinity of the stoneworts and bryophytes. Each cell of the antheridial filament, or the whole structure (the globule), may be interpreted as a separate antheridium.

Syngamy occurs *in situ* after the sperm passes between the protective nucule cells and the zygote secretes a heavy wall. The zygote, with the remnant of the surrounding sheath, persists as a resting stage. At germination, the zygote nucleus divides meiotically to produce four haploid nuclei. Three of these apparently degenerate, and the functional nucleus produces first a filamentous stage, the protonema (Fig. 11–17D), which eventually gives rise to the typical thallus with apical growth.

Phylogeny

Various fossil green algae of uncertain taxonomic affinities are reported from as far back as the Pre-Cambrian Period. However, a number of groups have left an excellent record; some of these are clearly related to modern representatives of the Chlorophyceae. The earliest of these fossils is found in the Ordovician Period, but the Chlorophyta are well represented throughout the geological record up to modern times. Forms that can be unquestionably identified with the Dasycladales have been particularly well preserved because of heavy calcification of the walls. The Dasycladales are particularly abundant in Permian, Triassic, and Tertiary deposits. They apparently reached their greatest diversity and complexity in the Triassic and Jurassic Periods but have declined since then. Of some 70 genera referred to the Dasycladales, about 60 are known only from the fossil record. The remainder comprise six genera known only as living forms, and four with both living and fossil representatives, such as *Acetabularia* (Fig. 11–18B). From the Ordovician and Silurian are forms very similar to living genera, such as the fossil *Paleodasycladus* (Fig. 11–18C), which closely resembles the living *Dasycladus* (Fig. 11–18D). Certain of the Codiales, also lime-encrusted, probably occurred as far back as the Ordovician Period, but definitely occur in the Permian.

The Charophyceae have also left a substantial fossil record from the Silurian Period on, although the records are fragmentary and restricted largely to the oogonia (Fig. 11–18A). These fossil structures, which resemble the oogonia of present-day *Chara,* are particularly abundant in Lower Tertiary beds. Many genera are known only from the fossil record; but others, such as *Nitella* and *Chara,* have numerous living as well as fossil representatives.

Thus, the green algae are undoubtedly an extremely ancient group of plants. Some believe that they and all other algal groups are derived from bacteria. Most botanists agree that higher plants must have evolved from the green algae. The structure of the green algae is not as complex as that of some of the Rhodophyta or Phaeophyta. However, it must be remembered that the more highly evolved Chlorophyceae probably gave rise to land plants such as the bryophytes and vascular plants. The biochemical and morphological characteristics of the class offer support for this view. It is also apparent in this direct line of evolution that a number of significant offshoots have occurred. In some instances, these have terminated in rather complex forms that, although advanced, have features that are actually "dead ends" in an evolutionary series (see Fig. 11–3).

214

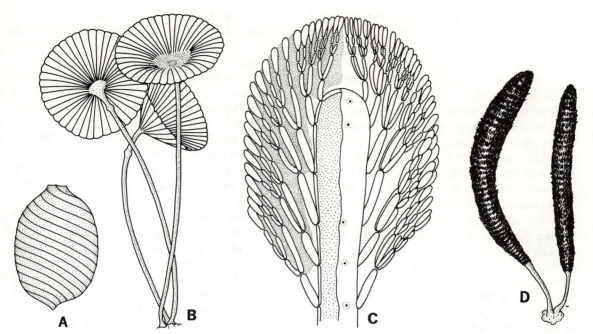

FIGURE 11–18 Living and fossil Chlorophyta. A, Charophyceae; fossil *Chara* nucule showing spirally twisted cover cells, ×30. B–D, Chlorophyceae. B, living *Acetabularia*, ×1.5; C, reconstruction of fossil *Paleodasycladus*, ×25; D, living *Dasycladus*, ×3. (C, after Pia in Hirmer's *Handbuch der Paläobotanik*, with permission of R. Oldenbourg.)

ALGAL ECOLOGY

Algae are widely distributed throughout the fresh-water and marine environments. They are planktonic (free-floating) as well as attached on other aquatic plants as epiphytes, or on other submerged solid substrates. They are also present on and in the soil, on the bark of trees, on brickwork and on roofs and rock walls; on wharf pilings, the hulls of ships, in tide pools, and in the spray zone above the intertidal region on exposed coasts. In fact, algae occur in any place where moisture can collect for even a brief period of time. Most algae occurring in temporarily moist habitats are well adapted to extended periods of drought and short periods of moisture during which reproduction occurs rapidly.

Ecology of Fresh-Water Algae

Although fresh-water algae occur in a wide range of habitats, most are encountered in standing bodies of water (lakes and ponds) and in flowing waters (rivers and streams). The distribution of these algae is correlated with environmental factors, in both space (vertically and horizontally) and in time (seasonal periodicity). Temperature plays the most important role in ultimate distribution of the fresh-water phytoplankton in standing waters of the temperate zone since there is an annual temperature cycle creating vertical stratification of the water mass. In the spring, the waters are constantly mixed due to winds and the cooling effect of lower air temperatures on the surface layers. This results in an unstratified water mass of relatively uniform temperature. When the surface waters warm, the upper layers gradually become stable, so that thorough mixing is impossible.

Although temperature is probably the most effective factor in vertical distribution of the fresh-water phytoplankton, light, oxygen, and nutrients must also be considered. For example, light intensity determines the lower limits at which photosynthesis occurs. Oxygen availability is related to temperature, since more oxygen is in solution at lower temperatures and availability of nutrients may be limiting in a lake.

Water movement is of little consequence in bodies of standing water. But in flowing waters, the bottom and shore vegetation are continuously receiving new water, whereas fresh-water plankton are carried downstream, ultimately to the sea and probable death. In slowly moving streams and rivers, the conditions are similar to those in standing water and thus the same types of algae may occur. Cascading water has been found to be important in gas exchange of the algae. More gas may go into solution because of the greater turbulence and resulting contact between air and water. In fast flowing waters, nutrient material is carried away quickly, thus limiting to some extent algal development. In slowly moving water, nutrients tend to settle, remaining available for a rich algal growth.

Seasonal changes in the fresh-water algal flora generally follow the same plan year after year. Such periodicity is best known from standing waters. Certain species that occur throughout the year may constitute as much as 40 per cent of the total population. For those forms not present at all times, a prerequisite is the ability to form resistant stages, such as auxospores, resting zygotes, akinetes, or hypnospores. Most of these species have a peak occurrence at the same time each year. The plankton forms usually have two maxima a year (spring and autumn) and two minima (winter and midsummer). The spring and autumn flora may be markedly different, since the water temperature usually changes more slowly than the light intensity. Nutrient supply is particularly important in determining seasonal abundance. In early spring, following the annual overturn and thorough mixing, nutrients from the bottom are redistributed and available in the upper layers. As summer stratification occurs and mixing is reduced, nutrients may be exhausted and become limiting. In late summer, mixing occurs and the nutrients again become available.

Some algae occur in vast numbers in the fresh-water phytoplankton. The presence of many extremely small species in the nannoplankton is of considerable significance in assessing the role of these minute organisms in primary production. Other larger plankton species may occur in such large quantities that they color a body of water a brilliant green, blue-green, or red. These dense concentrations of planktonic forms are termed blooms. Optimum conditions for blooms are the result of the interaction of many factors, such as light, temperature, and available nutrients—especially nitrogen and phosphorus. Blooms that occur in domestic drinking water supplies, such as reservoirs, tend to clog filters and often give the water a disagreeable taste or smell. In extreme conditions of algal growth the water may be unfit for human or livestock consumption, and may be toxic to fish or other aquatic organisms. This is especially true of some blue-green algae (Cyanophyceae).

Many algal species have a narrow range of tolerance to temperature, salinity, and nutrients. Their distribution and physiological requirements are thus intimately related to the physical-chemical characteristics of the water. Therefore, the algae are useful as indicators of these conditions. In fresh-water habitats, the composition of algal communities is used as an indicator of varying ecological conditions. For example, rivers free from pollution are composed of many species of diatoms (Bacillariophyceae), each present in relatively small populations. In polluted waters the number of diatom species is small, due to the many limiting factors imposed by the polluting materials. In lakes and ponds the presence of certain diatom species indicates unpolluted waters, whereas the occurrence of one or of a few species of blue-green algae in great numbers indicates pollution. A bloom of blue-green algae in certain ponds or lakes can cause death of livestock and wildlife, especially wild fowl. The

216

algal cells produce a toxin that some species excrete into the water and other species retain in the cells until they are broken. Both toxins affect the respiratory system and cause convulsions to the affected animals. No deaths among humans have been reported, although many instances of 24-hour (gastrointestinal) flu may be due to algal toxins.

Several species of blue-green algae are common inhabitants of thermal springs, tolerating high temperatures ranging from 55–85°C. At the other extreme, certain species, mainly some microscopic Chlorophyceae, have been collected growing on snow and ice as well as in lakes of the Arctic and Antarctic. Still other algae live intimately in association with other organisms. Within some colorless algae occur certain unicellular blue-green species. Similar associations exist between green algae and certain ciliates such as *Paramecium* and some invertebrate animals such as *Hydra*. Some Cyanophyceae occur within higher green plants such as bryophytes, ferns, gymnosperms, and angiosperms. Although the association is not clear, there is some suggestion of nitrogen-fixation by the blue-green algae, thus making nitrogen available to the host plants. Species of Cyanophyceae, Chlorophyceae, and Xanthophyceae are common algal symbionts of some lichens (see Chapter 7).

Some algae, considered fresh-water species, are tolerant of high concentrations of different salts. These algae occur in alkaline environments where the concentration of dissolved salts is well over 100 parts per thousand.

The diversity of fresh-water habitats is as great as the number of places that retain moisture for a short period of time. Even the deserts are inhabited by algae; sufficient moisture collects on the underside of rocks to enable several species of Cyanophyceae to occur in these arid regions.

Ecology of Marine Algae

Marine algae occur both attached to solid substrates and as plankton. The attached marine algae (seaweeds) cover a small area, primarily because of the relatively limited area of continental shelf or water shallow enough to allow sufficient light to penetrate for plant growth. Less than a tenth of the oceans, including adjacent seas, have a depth shallower than about 225 meters, and attached algae seldom grow to this depth. A much greater area of the globe and volume of water is therefore available for the support of the marine plankton algae—such as diatoms and dinoflagellates—than for the attached algae.

Seaweeds. Although the sea is often thought of as a more uniform environment than the land, the topography and substrate beneath the sea are just as varied. As on land, variety in the marine environments is reflected by a diversified flora. The greatest number of marine species and individuals live on the rocky shores. The mud flats and sandy beaches generally have few seaweeds because of the unstable bottom. The smoothness or roughness of the substrate may determine the type or size of plant that can be supported or anchored. The attached marine algae do not have true roots. However, they generally have extremely strong holdfasts, which anchor them under conditions of pounding surf and wave action.

Because of the constant ebb and flow of the tide through the intertidal region, which may cover a vertical distance of 8 meters or more in some areas, the plants in this zone are alternately submerged and exposed for varying periods of time. The seaweed collector must arrange his collecting trips to coincide with periods when the tide is low, because at this stage the greatest number and variety of seaweeds can be found and studied. In most instances, the whole plant must be bathed in water for at least the greater part of the day, since there are no true roots, stems, or leaves, and little conduction in most algae. This is the only way in which the plant can obtain directly through its surfaces inorganic materials and other substances necessary for plant growth. The physical-chemical conditions to which the intertidal algae are subjected vary greatly, sometimes over

217

rather short vertical distances. Because the physiological requirements of seaweeds differ, and because many have fairly narrow limits of tolerance to changes in temperature, light, and salinity, there is a striking vertical distribution in the intertidal region of the more conspicuous species in distinct bands. The vertical distribution of these bands is generally directly related to the tidal characteristics of a particular region. The tidal pattern varies greatly in magnitude and character from one part of the world to another and from one part of an ocean to another, and even locally from one region to another. Many factors modify the characteristic tidal pattern in any given area.

The vertical distribution of a seaweed may be controlled in part by the amount of light it requires, by wave action, by its ability to withstand freezing or desiccation, or by the amount of oxygen available. Since the sun provides energy for synthesis of food substances, the degree of penetration of sunlight into water (or the transparency of the water) is very important to marine plants. There may be specific light requirements of intensity, quality, and perhaps even duration. Both quality and intensity of light change with depth in the water. The depth at which seaweeds grow depends on available light, so their distribution may also vary with latitude. In lower latitudes light can penetrate to a greater depth than in higher latitudes. In the Mediterranean, where the water is highly transparent, seaweeds are reported at depths approaching 100 meters; but in the northeastern Pacific, where the waters are rather turbid, significant development of attached algae generally does not extend below 35 meters.

There is also a marked distributional pattern of seaweeds related to the physical-chemical changes that occur horizontally. Certain marine algae are characteristic of water of high salinity; others extend into brackish zones. On the whole, for example, there is a marked progressive depletion of genera and species in the brown algal flora as one proceeds from the cold Arctic and Antarctic regions to the warmer waters of the tropics.

Algal groups represented. The brown seaweeds (Phaeophyceae) are almost entirely marine in distribution, including brackish water and salt marshes. A number of large brown seaweeds (such as *Nereocystis* and *Macrocystis*), which grow attached in deeper water (to 35 meters or more) in the North Pacific, form dense subtidal forests. At times the distal branches of these large kelps float in dense mats along the sea surface. In tropical and semitropical regions the many species of *Sargassum* also occur in dense beds. Such forests serve as breeding and grazing areas for many marine animals. Some species (such as *Sargassum*) occur free-floating far from shore in the North Atlantic (Sargasso Sea); and in the Sea of Japan other species may occur either attached or free-floating in salt marshes and lagoons or embedded in the sand.

The brown algae occur throughout the intertidal region, and extend down to a depth of 35 meters or more (depending on the transparency of the water). However, they are more characteristic of the intertidal and shallower subtidal regions. Because of the vertical differences in the environment, certain species occur only high in the intertidal area and may form conspicuous narrow bands along the shore. Among these is the common rockweed, *Fucus*. Some of these plants may be exposed for hours or even for several consecutive days. The phycocolloids, such as algin, hold water within the plant tissues most effectively, helping such algae resist desiccation from exposure to the sun or to frost. Other species and genera are only rarely exposed. Still others occur only in the subtidal region and are never exposed to the air. Brown algae, in general, grow abundantly in the conditions suitable for most photosynthetic plants: optimum light, temperature, and a constant supply of inorganic nutrients and growth substances. These photosynthetic plants are found in the cold shallow waters of the continental shelf where drainage from the land, turbulence, and upwelling of deeper, nutrient-rich water provide the necessary constituents.

Some of the larger brown algae contribute significantly to the phytoplankton through motile stages in their life history (zoospores and gametes). For example, in dense beds of *Nereocystis,* through an average depth of about 20 meters, an estimated 3 million zoospore cells (about 5 microns in diameter) may be produced per liter per day from June to September.

The red seaweeds (Rhodophyceae) are predominantly marine and are more widely distributed than the brown algae. They are the most widely distributed geographically and vertically of all the attached algae. Although more species of red algae occur in tropical waters, they are also well represented in colder water, but seldom are as conspicuous as the larger brown seaweeds. Most of the tropical species are relatively small and inconspicuous, whereas some of the cold-water reds attain considerable size. The red algae are generally much more extensive in vertical distribution than the brown algae. Some of them, such as *Porphyra,* occur high in the intertidal region, where they may be exposed sometimes for several consecutive days and dry out until they are brittle, but without adverse effect. Other red algae occur at great depths—especially in the tropics, where they have been recorded below 120 meters.

The extreme range in red algal color follows the vertical variations in light conditions. The intertidal forms achieve the greatest diversity in color. They range from a dull green or black high in the intertidal zone to purplish-red, brown, or rosy-red lower in the intertidal zone. Those from greater depths are generally a bright rosy red, with the phycoerythrin masking and exceeding the chlorophyll present. The presence of the accessory phycobiliprotein pigments permits photosynthesis at great depths. Light of shorter wave lengths (blue light) penetrates deepest in water. The phycobiliprotein pigments absorb most of this light.

Green seaweeds (Chlorophyceae) are well represented in the sea, although they are generally less conspicuous than the larger brown algae. In colder waters, they occur more commonly in the intertidal region. Some genera have representative species in both tropical and cold-water areas. In tropical areas, members of the Codiales, Siphonocladales and Dasycladales are among the dominant elements of the marine

flora, and the latter two orders are entirely tropical. Because of the greater transparency of most tropical seas, many of the species of green algae range to much greater depths than most seaweeds attain in colder, more turbid waters.

Plankton. Although microscopic, the free-floating or free-swimming plankton are by far the most important producers of organic substances in the sea. Because most of them are photosynthetic, they occur primarily in the upper illuminated regions of the sea. However, they are represented in all seas and at all depths and are often present in great concentrations. The peaks of abundance are related to seasonal conditions and to the complex oceanographic conditions to which they are subjected horizontally and vertically. Generally they are most abundant at times of the year and in places where optimum conditions of light, temperature, and nutrients prevail.

Algal groups represented. The most conspicuous groups of marine plankton algae are the diatoms (Bacillariophyceae) and dinoflagellates (Dinophyceae). However, some of the golden algae (Chrysophyceae), such as the coccolithophores, are often predominant in marine plankton in the southern Mediterranean and warm oceans such as the Indian and tropical Atlantic. Marine plankton yellow-green algae (Xanthophyceae) and green algae (Chlorophyceae) are rare, although they may be more important than is presently apparent, since the marine nannoplankton are still not well known. A number of cryptomonads (Cryptophyceae) apparently occur as symbionts in radiolarians and corals, where they have been commonly referred to under the general term zooxanthellae.

Marine blue-greens (Cyanophyceae) are abundant and important in certain parts of the world, although as a whole they are much less conspicuous than in fresh-water habitats. A few blue-greens occur as marine plankton and have been known to occur in extensive blooms in parts of the Indian Ocean, causing mass mortality in fish populations. They are also important in certain tropical marine reef formations, resulting in characteristic calcareous incrustations. The exact mechanism is not understood, but the algae apparently secrete calcium and magnesium carbonates and build up extensive deposits of travertine in a variety of forms.

Diatoms occur free-floating in the plankton, as well as on surfaces of solid substrates, on mud-flat surfaces, in salt marshes, and attached as epiphytes to other algae and marine seed plants. They occur in vast numbers in the marine phytoplankton, and they may form extensive blooms. The presence of many extremely small species of diatoms in the nannoplankton is of considerable significance in assessing the role of these minute organisms in primary production.

In past geological ages diatom production was as important as now—if not more so. Under natural conditions, as the diatoms died, many of the empty silicified walls accumulated in great numbers as diatomaceous ooze at the bottom of the sea and to some extent in lakes. Raised above sea level by geologic activity, these vast deposits of diatomaceous earth are now mined in various places. At Lompoc, California, surface quarrying may yield more than 6 million frustules in 1 millimeter. At Lompoc, this surface accumulation of fossil diatoms, which is almost entirely composed of littoral marine species, is over 200 meters deep. In other areas, extensive subterranean marine deposits vary from 10 meters to the exceptional deposits of 1,000 meters in the Santa Maria oil fields of California.

Dinoflagellates are more numerous in the sea than in fresh water. They occur in the open sea, in coastal regions, as well as in brackish areas and in beach sand. Certain of the dinoflagellates contribute to the luminescence resulting when sea water is disturbed at night, as in the wake of a ship. The marine unarmored forms are more common in the open ocean, whereas the armored forms are more common in coastal plankton.

Because of rapid reproduction by cell division, extensive blooms of dinoflagellates can be produced in a very short time. Under optimum environmental conditions, cells may divide several times a day. Concentrations of marine species in natural waters are typically several million cells per liter. In this dense concentration they color the water green, brown, or red.

A number of dinoflagellates are responsible for so-called red water or red tide. These conditions are particularly prevalent along the coasts of North America when water temperatures are unusually high and, in northern areas, when exceptionally long hours of sunlight occur. These conditions result in tremendous numbers of dinoflagellates, which can lead to death of many marine animals.

Another phenomenon related to such blooms is known as mussel poisoning or shellfish poisoning. In this instance, filter feeding invertebrates—such as clams, mussels, and oysters—extract cells from the water. Although there is apparently no lethal effect on the shellfish, these invertebrates remove and accumulate a toxic substance in certain tissues. The toxin may remain in the tissues for several months and is only gradually eliminated. When the shellfish are eaten by man or other mammals such as cats, dogs, or rodents, paralysis can result in distal parts of the body. The amount of paralysis depends on poison concentration in the invertebrate tissues, and in severe cases may result in death. Apparently the toxic material is closely related to the curare group of poisons produced by some tropical flowering plants.

12 / Division Bryophyta

The mosses and moss allies belong to a single division, the Bryophyta. The Bryophyta are generally divided into three classes: Hepaticae (liverworts), Anthocerotae (hornworts), and Musci (mosses). This division includes the most primitive of the green land plants; in both morphology and anatomy *bryophytes* are structurally simple.

The bryophytes are archegoniate plants. Like the primitive vascular plants, bryophytes possess a peculiar multicellular female sex organ, the archegonium, in which the egg is enclosed. In bryophytes the archegonium is always flask-shaped.

The Bryophyta form an isolated group; they are not closely related to any other plant group nor have they served as ancestors to other groups of plants. Of all of the plant groups, the Psilophyta and Pterophyta appear to show closest relationships.

All Bryophyta are small: the largest erect forms are less than 60 centimeters tall; some creeping or aquatic mosses are more than a meter long and some epiphytic mosses reach lengths of more than 60 centimeters. The smallest bryophytes are nearly microscopic.

Most bryophytes are strictly terrestrial and grow in humid environments; some grow in arid sites and a few are essentially aquatic.

GAMETOPHYTE

The gametophyte, the conspicuous generation in most bryophytes, is thallose (strap-shaped) or leafy. In the latter case, the main shoot bears lateral flattened leaves. The leaves are generally a single cell thick. Usually, the stem is also structurally simple. The gametophyte is either annual or perennial.

The gametophyte is generally attached to the substrate by means of rhizoids. They are either branched or unbranched filaments of cells; or each is an elongated tube-like cell arising from either the stem or leaves and extending into or over the substrate.

In bryophytes the female sex organ, the archegonium, is microscopic, flask-shaped, and multicellular; its lower swollen portion encloses the single egg. Generally, each gametophyte produces several archegonia, which are often surrounded by a protective sleeve or an envelope of leaves.

The male sex organ, the antheridium, is generally attached to the gametophyte by a stalk, is always multicellular, and is either elongate or spherical. The outer jacket of cells is sterile, and each of the many inner cells gives rise to a single sperm. When the antheridium is mature and wet, its jacket bursts, releasing hundreds of anteriorly biflagellate, coiled sperms. One of these unites with an egg to form the zygote.

SPOROPHYTE

Although some bryophytes are not known to produce sporophytes, most develop a sporophyte by mitotic division of the zygote, differentiating to produce a morphologically distinct structure. As the sporophyte develops, portions of the archegonium also divide to form an enclosure—the calyptra—which protects the developing sporophyte. The sporophyte usually contains chlorophyll until the spores are produced. However, as the sporophyte matures, the chlorophyll disappears.

LIFE HISTORY

The basic life cycle of a bryophyte begins with the germination of the haploid spore, which generally produces a photosynthetic gametophyte (Fig. 12–1, 2). The gametophyte begins as a much-branched, filamentous protonema in most mosses; but in most liverworts and hornworts it begins as a very simple, few-celled mass that produces a more highly differentiated thallose or leafy structure that bears the sex organs. The protonema is a relatively undifferentiated multicellular structure that precedes the development of the leafy or thallose gametophyte.

The sperms, expelled from the mature antheridia, at first swim randomly in the water immersing the antheridia. But as a sperm enters the neck cell fluid diffusing from the archegonium, it moves toward the area of greater concentration of this material and ultimately reaches the egg. The fusion of sperm and egg (syngamy) results in the zygote, the first cell of the diploid ($2n$) sporophyte generation. In most bryophytes the sporophyte differentiates into a seta (or stalk), which raises the capsule

(spore case) above the gametophyte. In all bryophytes the sporophyte produces both sterile cells and spore mother cells. The jacket of the capsule is always made up of sterile cells. The spore mother cells undergo meiosis, and each produces a tetrad of meiospores, which are ultimately released from the mature capsule. In most bryophytes the spore is wind-borne and, if it lands in a suitable environment, produces a gametophyte.

Bryophytes also reproduce by vegetative means. Any young cell in the gametophyte or sporophyte of most bryophytes is capable of producing an entire gametophyte. In some bryophytes, nearly any part of a gametophyte—special branches, paraphyses, rhizoids, leaves, or stems—can produce special asexual reproductive bodies such as gemmae (Fig. 12–3). A gemma differentiates into a new gametophyte, or into a filamentous protonema, from which the gametophyte ultimately arises.

It is probable that most bryophytes increase in numbers more by vegetative reproduction than by sexual reproduction. This is highly significant in the evolution of bryophytes, because the concept of many species is based on widely distributed material that is clonal. The rare occurrence of spore-originated gametophytes in the same species would lead to populations of greater genetic diversity. Because of this diversity these populations would be considered aberrant. But it is in these more diverse populations that selection can occur, leading to evolution of different species. Since such populations are often uncommon in some bryophytes, then evolution is considerably slower than in plants that commonly reproduce sexually.

NUTRITION AND DISTRIBUTION

Bryophytes obtain much of their basic nutrient from substances dissolved in atmospheric moisture. Some substances are probably absorbed directly from the substrate by diffusion through the cells of the gametophyte. Since most bryophytes possess chlorophyll, they man-

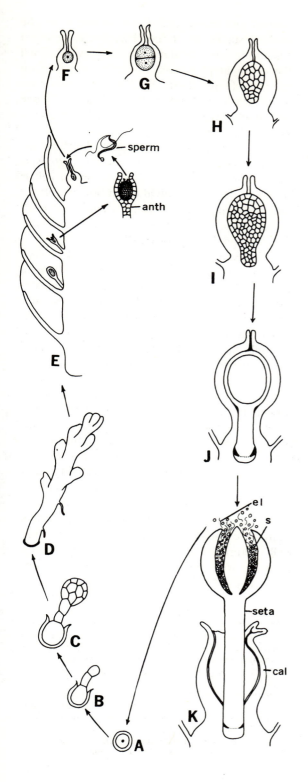

ufacture their own food by photosynthesis. As in other land plants, bryophytes store food in the form of carbohydrates, fats, and proteins.

In the tropics bryophytes reach their greatest diversity, but they occur in all parts of the world. In frigid climates mosses are more common than hepatics, and in the north temperate zone the vegetation of moist habitats is made up largely of mosses. In temperate coniferous forests the growth of moss carpets is often extensive.

ECOLOGY

Like all land plants, bryophytes vary in the climates and substrates where they can thrive. Some bryophytes grow only on a particular kind of wood in certain stage of decay; others occur only in acid bogs or alkaline fens. Some species grow either on cliffs of acidic rock or on the smooth hard acidic bark of living trees.

Many bryophytes are significant pioneers on newly exposed substrates. Many mosses and leafy liverworts colonize bare rock surfaces. By building up organic material, they produce a water- and mineral-retaining substrate on which vascular plants can grow, ultimately entirely covering a site with vegetation. In the aquatic environment bryophytes are also important pioneers.

CLASS HEPATICAE
(Liverworts)

Most hepatics possess a dorsiventrally flattened gametophyte that is either a strap-

223

FIGURE 12–1 Life cycle of typical leafy hepatic. A–D, germination of spore and development of gametophyte; E, detail of apex of fertile shoot showing antheridia, archegonium, and fertilization; F–J, development of zygote and differentiation of sporophyte; K, mature sporangium bursting to shed spores. *anth,* antheridium; *cal,* calyptra; *el,* elater; *s,* spore; *seta,* seta; *sperm,* sperm. (After Schuster with permission of *American Midland Naturalist* and Johnson Reprint Corporation.)

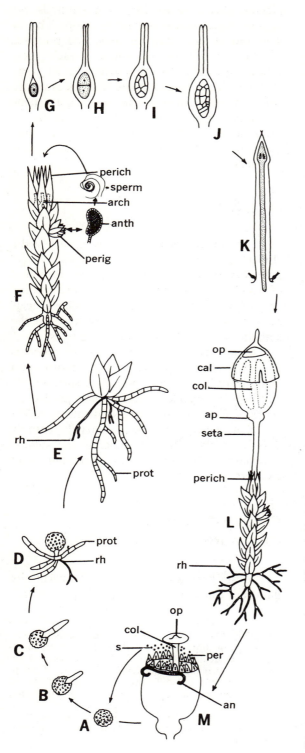

shaped branching thallus or is leafy. In the latter instance the larger leaves are arranged bilaterally on the stem; and a row of small leaves, or amphigastria, is ventrally located on the stem (Fig. 12–5E, F). Since the leaves always lack a true midrib, they are generally one cell thick throughout. Leaves are frequently notched at the tip or variously lobed.

The gametophyte generally develops directly from the spore without any extensive preliminary protonema. Thus, an apical cell is differentiated early, dividing in several planes and producing a recognizable thallose or leafy gametophyte. When present, rhizoids are unicellular and lack chlorophyll.

The sporophyte possesses little chlorophyll and has a very short maturity (generally only a few days). The archegonium sheathes the developing sporophyte until the spores are mature and the capsule is fully developed. However, when the seta elongates, the capsule is pushed through the apex of the archegonium, which has grown to produce a calyptra.

The cells of the capsule wall frequently possess transverse thickenings and stomata are absent. In the differentiation of the capsule, the outer cells produce the capsule jacket. The inner cells differentiate further into spore mother cells and sterile cells. The sterile cells, termed elaters, usually possess spiral thickenings and are hygroscopic—i.e., they coil and uncoil in response to changes in humidity. These sterile cells often effectively help to discharge spores from the capsule, usually as soon as the capsule wall ruptures. The capsule jacket usually splits open by four longitudinal slits derived from previously differentiated lines of weakness.

FIGURE 12–2 Life cycle of typical moss. A–E, germination of spore and development of gametophyte; F, mature gametophyte showing antheridium, archegonia, and fertilization; G–K, development of zygote and differentiation of sporophyte; L, gametophyte bearing mature sporophyte; M, detail of sporangium, showing spore release. *an*, annulus; *anth*, antheridium; *ap*, apophysis; *arch*, archegonium; *cal*, calyptra; *col*, columella; *op*, operculum; *per*, peristome tooth; *perich*, perichaetium; *perig*, perigonium; *prot*, protonema; *rh*, rhizoid; *s*, spore; *seta*, seta; *sperm*, sperm.

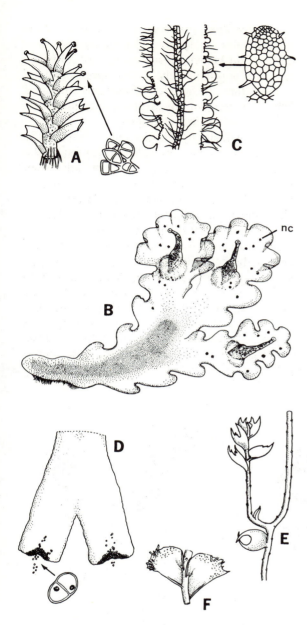

Most hepatics are relatively small, although some forms are occasionally 30 centimeters or more long. All hepatics possess apical growth. Growth continues through the favorable season, which normally coincides with the highest annual humidity and with temperatures well above freezing. During the later stages of this growth the sporophytes generally mature and release their spores.

The Hepaticae can be conveniently separated into six well-differentiated orders. The most primitive of these is generally considered to be the Calobryales and the most advanced the Marchantiales. Each of the orders represents a distinctive evolutionary line. Since fossil material of hepatics is scanty, and that which is available appears to cast little light on the interrelationships among the hepatics, all evidence concerning relationships is derived from knowledge of extant Hepaticae.

Order Calobryales. This order is generally considered the most primitive on the basis of the very simple nature of the gametophytes. Two genera, *Takakia* and *Haplomitrium,* make up the order, and each represents a well-differentiated evolutionary line (Fig. 12–4). *Takakia,* the more primitive genus, is found only locally in alpine regions of Japan, North Borneo, India, and on the north Pacific coast of North America. *Haplomitrium* is best represented in Australasia, Malaysia, and South America, but there is also one rare north temperate species.

In all Calobryales the gametophyte consists of erect leafy photosynthetic shoots arising from pale rhizomatous shoots lacking rhizoids. The leaves are at first spirally arranged in three ranks, but this arrangement is frequently distorted as the shoot elongates.

Haplomitrium has flattened leaves one cell in thickness that vary in shape from nearly round to elliptic. In *Takakia* the leaves are simply short determinate branches forming elongated cones of cells tipped by a single cell (Fig. 12–4C). The leaf cells are thin-walled and, when mature, contain many chloroplasts. The gametophyte is always small. The largest is occa-

225

FIGURE 12–3 Asexual reproduction in hepatics. A, *Lophozia ascendens,* with gemmae on apical leaf lobes, ×15; B, *Blasia pusilla* thallus with gemma "bottles," ×5. *nc, Nostoc* colonies. C, *Metzgeria* sp., with marginal gemmae on thallus, ×15; D, fragment of gemmiferous section of *Riccardia palmata* thallus, showing terminally produced gemmae, ×15; E, *Plagiochila tridenticulata* shoot showing barren stem from which propagating deciduous leaves have fallen, ×14; F, *Plagiochila virginica* shoot sector with gemma-bearing leaves, ×6.)A, C–F, after Schuster with permission of *American Midland Naturalist.*)

DIVISION BRYOPHYTA

sionally 3.5 centimeters tall; the smallest is often less than 1 centimeter tall.

The simple structure of the gametophyte emphasizes the primitive nature of the order. In *Takakia* the gametophyte shows little differentiation; structurally, the leaves are barely different from the stem. The radial arrangement of appendages is a more generalized design than the bilateral arrangement in the Jungermanniales. In most Calobryales the number of sex organs is high; this and the absence of rhizoids are considered to be primitive features.

In *Takakia* the sporophyte is unknown. In *Haplomitrium,* as the embryo develops, gametophytic stem tissue also develops and, with further growth of the archegonium, forms a protective cylindrical sleeve, the stem calyptra. The stem calyptra is left at the base of the colorless seta as the latter elongates, extending the cylindrical capsule through this sleeve and above the gametophyte. The mature capsule usually dehisces by four valves. Characteristic elaters occur among the spores.

Order Jungermanniales. The order Jungermanniales (scale mosses) contains over two-thirds of all known liverworts; at least 230 genera and approximately 8,000 species belong to more than 35 families. These are distributed from the arctic to the tropics, reaching their greatest variety in the tropics.

The gametophyte is generally dorsiventrally flattened with two rows of lateral leaves; on the ventral surface of the (normally) reclining stem is usually a row of ventral leaves termed amphigastria. If present, the amphigastria are generally simpler in outline than the lateral leaves. The leaves are unlobed or variously lobed. Leaves are usually one cell thick, and in most genera the cells are isodiametric and have the same shape throughout the leaf. Rhizoids in most Jungermanniales are smooth-walled and arise from the cortical cells of the stem. The stem is structurally very simple. The outer cells forming the cortex are generally chlorophyllose, whereas the inner cells forming the central cylinder generally lack chloroplasts.

226

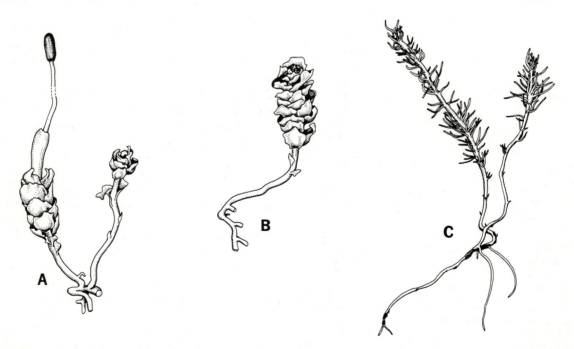

FIGURE 12–4 Morphology of Calobryales. A, B, *Haplomitrium hookeri*. A, habit showing sporophyte with elongated stem calyptra sheathing base of seta, ×4; B, habit of gametophyte showing terminal clusters of antheridia, ×4; C, *Takakia lepidozioides,* habit, ×4.

Antheridia are normally spherical or ovoid and are borne on a multicellular stalk, singly or in groups, and are surrounded by lateral leaves that differ from others of the gametophyte. Archegonia are always at the apex of the main shoot, and the apical cell is utilized in producing the archegonia. Jungermanniales are thus said to be acrogynous. The archegonia are frequently surrounded by a specialized sleeve (Fig. 12–5A, C–F), which develops while the archegonia are differentiating. Often, specialized larger leaves surround the perianth. Gametophytes are unisexual or bisexual.

Asexual reproduction is frequent. Deciduous masses of undifferentiated cells are often budded off the leaves or stem; these are gemmae

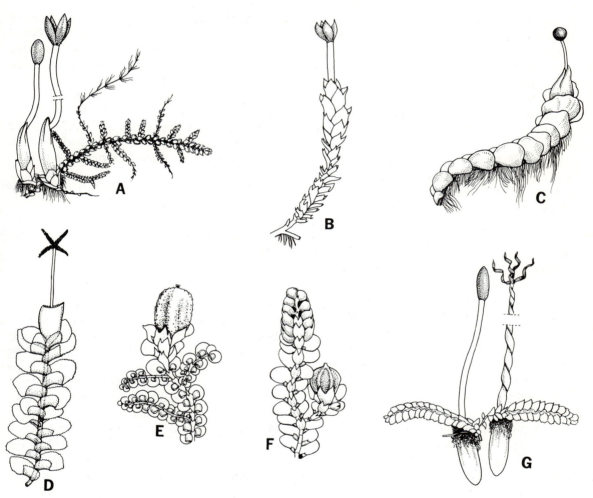

FIGURE 12–5 Morphology of Jungermanniales, showing various sporophytes and gametophytes. A, *Lepidozia reptans* shoot with ripe sporangia, ×5; B, *Marsupella sprucei* shoot with mature sporophyte, ×12; C, *Plectocolea hyalina* shoot with sporophyte, ×8; D, *Scapania nemorosa* shoot with open sporangium, ×5; E, *Frullania dilatata* shoot with perianth (note also the helmet-shaped lobules and the notched amphigastria), ×9; F, *Lejeunea flava* shoot, showing terminal perigonial branch and lateral perianth-bearing branch (note also notched amphigastria and lobules of lateral leaves), ×15; G, *Calypogeia fissa* shoot, showing fleshy subterranean perigynium and emergent sporophytes, ×4. (A, C–E, G, after Müller with permission of Akademische Verlagsgesellschaft, Geest and Portig K.–G., Leipzig; B, after Schiffner in Engler, *Die natürlichen Pflanzenfamilien*, Vol. 1, Pt. 3, p. 77, Fig. 41A, 1909; F, after Schuster with permission of *Journal of Elisha Mitchell Scientific Society* and *American Midland Naturalist*.)

DIVISION BRYOPHYTA

and can produce new gametophytes (several methods are illustrated in Fig. 12–3).

The mature sporophyte normally has a long colorless seta that carries the capsule well above the calyptra. The capsule is either spherical or cylindrical (Fig. 12–5A, C, G). The outer and generally the inner cells of the jacket of the capsule have thickenings that give it a dark brown color. The capsule jacket generally dehisces by four longitudinal slits, separating four valves, which in turn release the spores. The inner cells differentiate to form sterile cells and spore mother cells. When the sterile cells lose their chlorophyll, the walls generally develop spiral brown thickenings; these cells become hygroscopic elaters. The unicellular elaters are usually cylindrical and tapered at both ends, varying in length and in the number of spiral thickenings. Elaters are usually very numerous and scattered among the spores. Spore discharge is often aided by the nature and position of the elaters. Spores are always unicellular, although some develop precociously within the capsule and are thus multicellular when released. The walls are often variously sculptured. The spores contain chloroplasts and food reserves—oils and starch.

Within the Jungermanniales the relationships are not clear. This order, the largest and most complex in the Hepaticae, is also the least understood. Thus, attributed relationships among genera and even families continue to fluctuate as new information becomes available, particularly from the tropics.

Order Metzgeriales. The order Metzgeriales contains 24 genera and approximately 550 species in eight families. The Metzgeriales are found throughout the world but are most abundant in the humid tropics. They grow predominantly in damp shaded habitats but are also found in more exposed sites.

The gametophyte is generally thallose and is one to several cells thick (Fig. 12–6). The thallus frequently branches dichotomously in a single plane. The tissue of the thallus is almost uniform. The rhizoids are simple and unicel-

lular; they arise from epidermal cells on the lower surface of the thallus. In leafy Metzgeriales, the stems of the gametophytes have lateral leaves, but they never possess amphigastria (Fig. 12–6C). Lateral leaves are generally simple in outline. Growth of the thallus is indefinite even after the production of the sex organs, which arise behind the apical cell and are borne on the dorsal surface.

Antheridia structurally similar to those of the Jungermanniales are borne on the dorsal surface of the thallus or are on short branches in a globose sac formed from a branch, buried in a chamber, naked, or each covered by a single scale. Archegonia are also structurally similar to those in the Jungermanniales. They are borne on a special dorsal branch and enclosed in a sleeve-like chamber, are naked, or in a pocket-like cavity. Gametophytes may be unisexual or bisexual.

The sporophyte resembles that of the Jungermanniales. Asexual reproduction is usually by fragmentation of the thallus, but in some genera there are specialized asexual reproductive structures.

Order Monocleales. This order contains a single family, Monocleaceae, with one genus, *Monoclea,* and two tropical species (Fig. 12–7).

The gametophyte is thallose and may be as long as 20 centimeters and as wide as 5 centimeters, making it one of the largest thallose liverworts. The thallus of homogeneous parenchyma cells lacks air spaces. The upper cells of the thallus are chlorophyllose, whereas those lower down contain starch grains as well as chloroplasts. Some scattered cells contain a single brown oil body—a feature shared by the thallus of Marchantiales. Rhizoids occur over the entire ventral surface of the thallus and, as in Marchantiales, are of two types: some rhizoids are oriented parallel to the length of the thallus, others are vertical and anchor the thallus.

Monoclea is unisexual. Often three or four sporophytes emerge from each archegonial tube on the female thallus. The colorless seta elongates rapidly and carries the cylindrical sporan-

228

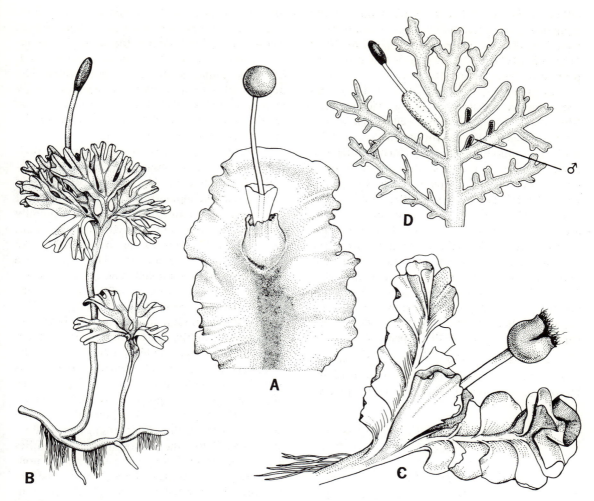

FIGURE 12–6 Metzgeriales; habits of a variety of morphological types. A, *Pellia neesiana* sporophyte-bearing thallus lobe, ×6; B, *Hymenophytum flabellatum* thallus with sporophyte, ×3; C, *Fossombronia cristata* habit showing sporophyte on gametophyte, ×25; D, *Riccardia multifida*, portion of thallus with sporophyte and antheridial lobes, ×5. C, after Schiffner in Engler, *Die natürlichen Pflanzenfamilien*, Vol. 1, Pt. 3, p. 59, Fig. 34A, 1909.)

gium high above the thallus. The capsule dehisces by a single vertical slit and opens into a spoon-like structure that releases the spores by the aid of the long hygroscopic elaters (Fig. 12–9B).

This order is primitive, showing some relationships to the Marchantiales but still others to the Calobryales and Metzgeriales. If just the gametophyte were known, this genus would undoubtedly be placed in the Marchantiales.

Order Sphaerocarpales. The order Sphaerocarpales contains three genera and approximately 20 species in two families (Fig. 12–8). They are found primarily in warm temperate to subtropical countries, where they are locally abundant. Both *Sphaerocarpos* and *Geothallus* are found on damp soil, whereas *Riella* is strictly a submerged aquatic growing on mud in shallow quiet pools or lakes. *Riella* is the only submerged aquatic liverwort now extant, although the fossil liverwort *Naiadita* (of the Triassic) was presumably also a submerged aquatic and is considered to be related to *Riella* (Fig. 12–21C–F). All genera of this order appear to be winter annuals.

In many respects the thallus of the Sphaerocarpales resembles that of the Metzgeriales. The thallus is one or more cells thick and is undifferentiated throughout its thickness. Rhizoids are smooth-walled. A basic difference from the Metzgeriales is the presence of a unistratose "bottle" around each sex organ (Fig. 12–8B–E). These bottles are on the dorsal surface of the thallus or, as in *Riella,* are lateral. Most species produce unisexual gametophytes. Within the sporophyte, the sterile cells are not elaters but are starch-rich cells that break down to supply nutritive materials for the developing spores. A seta is essentially absent; the sporangium remains within the bottle, even when mature, and dehiscence of the capsule is by decay of the capsule wall.

Order Marchantiales. This order, generally considered the most highly evolved of the Hepaticae, contains 11 families with approximately 450 species in 32 genera (Fig. 12–9, 10). Members of this order are world-wide in distribution—for example, the genus *Marchantia.* Most species grow on moist earth or mud; a few are found most commonly in water. The popular idea of a liverwort is exemplified by members of this order, probably a result of the relatively large size of the gametophytes and the abundance of some of the species.

The gametophyte is always a prostrate thallus, generally differentiated internally into several distinct tissues. The uppermost layer of cells forms the epidermis, the outer walls of which are often cutinized. These cells generally possess little or no chlorophyll. In most genera the epidermis is interrupted by special pores that lead into air chambers. These pores are surrounded by several cells and are often elaborate in structure (Fig. 12–10B). In most instances the pores remain open at all times. The air chambers contain filaments of cells rich in chloroplasts; or the cells forming the chamber walls are strongly chlorophyllose while the chambers contain no filaments; or both walls and filaments contain chloroplasts. The pattern of the air chambers gives many of the genera a distinctive appearance that immediately separates members of this order from other thallose liverworts. Below the photosynthetic region lies a region of parenchymatous tissue, mainly nonchlorophyllose and functioning as storage tissue; occasional mucilage cells and cells containing large oil bodies are often scattered among the parenchymatous cells. A ventral epidermis encloses this layer.

From some of the lower epidermal cells, colorless rhizoids of two types generally emerge —some with smooth walls and others with regular peg-like ingrowths of the wall. Rhizoids are oriented both at right angles to the thallus surface and parallel to it. The rhizoids parallel to the thallus surface are important only in capillary conduction, whereas those perpendicular to it also anchor the thallus to the substrate. On the ventral surface of the thallus, multicellular ventral scales may also be present.

Thalli may be unisexual or bisexual, depending on the species. Archegonia and anther-

230

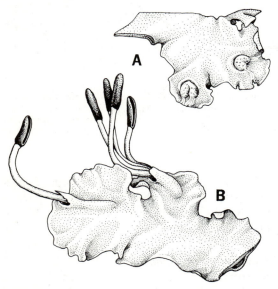

FIGURE 12–7 Monocleales; *Monoclea forsteri.* A, portion of thallus with antheridial pads, ×0.75; B, portion of thallus with sporophytes, showing longitudinal dehiscence of the capsules, ×0.75.

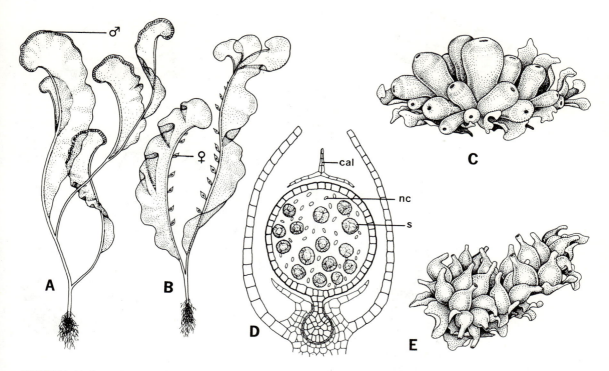

FIGURE 12–8 Sphaerocarpales. A, habit of *Riella americana* thallus with antheridia on margin, ×3; B, *R. americana* thallus with sporophytes on stem, ×3; C, *Sphaerocarpos texanus* archegoniate plant, showing bottles containing sporangia, ×15; D, longitudinal section through *Sphaerocarpos* sporangium and bottle, ×35; E, *S. texanus* antheridial plant, showing antheridium-containing bottles, ×50. *cal*, calyptra; *nc*, nurse cell; *s*, spores. (A, B, after Studhalter from *The Scientific Monthly*, Vol. 35, p. 307, fig. 2, October, 1932, with permission of *Science*.)

idia do not differ significantly in structure from those of other bryophytes. Their position on the thallus is variable throughout the order. In many genera the antheridia are borne dorsally on an elaborate, specialized, radially symmetrical perpendicular branch—the antheridiophore. The antheridia are often embedded in a flattened receptacle that surmounts the antheridiophore (Fig. 12–9A). In other genera the receptacle is simply a pad borne on the dorsal surface of the thallus near its apex (Fig. 12–9E), or the antheridia are in scattered pockets near the thickened central portion of the thallus. In most instances each pocket contains a single antheridium. The archegonia are similarly placed on the thallus. When present, the archegoniophore is often elaborately papillose, hairy, or sculptured. The archegonia are first borne

dorsally, but growth of the receptacle ultimately inverts them so that they eventually hang neck downward.

The location of the sporophytes depends on the location of the archegonia. When mature, the sporophyte usually possesses a short seta. Elaters are present in most genera but are absent in others. As in most other hepatics, the spores are generally released by four valves or by irregular rupturing of the apex of the capsule. In some genera, spores are released only upon decay of the capsule wall; in others a differentiated lid, or operculum, breaks off and releases the spores.

Special asexual reproductive structures are uncommon in the order, but a few genera, such as *Marchantia,* bear gemma cups on the dorsal surface. Stalked multicellular gemmae in these

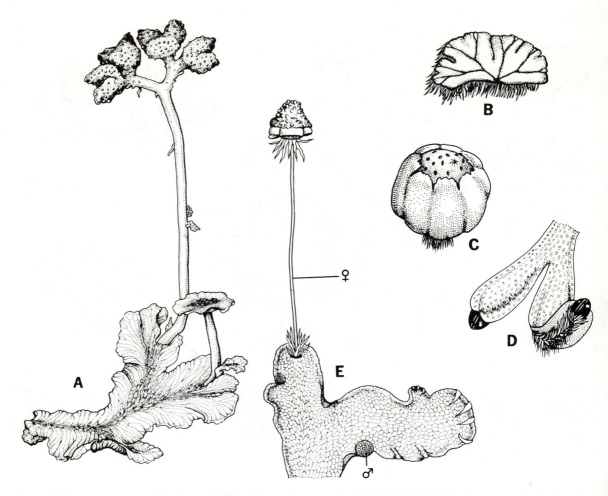

FIGURE 12–9 Marchantiales, showing variation in morphology. A, *Neohodgsonia mirabilis,* unisexual thallus with carpocephalum (left) and antheridiophore (right), ×4; B, *Ricciocarpus natans,* habit of aquatic thallus, ×6; C, *Carrpos monocarpus* thallus surrounding carpocephalum containing sporangium, ×15; D, *Targionia hypophylla,* portion of thallus with ventral sporangia, ×3; E, *Mannia siberica,* unisexual thallus with single carpocephalum (note operculum on sporangium), ×5. (C, after Carr with permission of *Australian Journal of Botany;* E, after Schuster with permission of *American Midland Naturalist* and Johnson Reprint Corporation.)

cups are released when the stalks break. On germination the gemma produces a new gametophyte.

Evolution

Evolution in hepatic gametophytes shows the following general pattern, beginning with the primitive and proceeding to highly evolved characteristics:

1. Leaves radially arranged, all similar, barely differing from the stem; rhizoids absent.
2. Leaves radially arranged, all similar, differing from the stem and leaf-like; rhizoids absent.
3. Leaves radially arranged, one rank

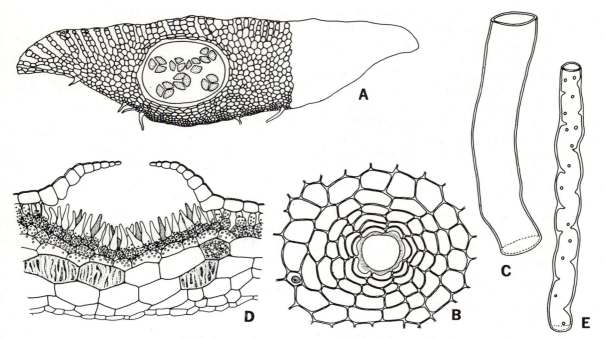

FIGURE 12–10   Anatomy of Marchantiales (cross sections through thalli). A, *Riccia beyrichiana*, showing sporangium containing spores, ×20; B, surface view of air-chamber pore of *Conocephalum conicum*, ×180; D, air chamber of *C. conicum*, showing chlorophyllose filaments and the "pitted" cells of the thallus, ×90; E, C, rhizoids of *C. conicum*, ×360. (A, B, after Schuster with permission of *American Midland Naturalist* and Johnson Reprint Corporation.)

slightly smaller and leaf-like; rhizoids absent.

4. Leaves bilaterally arranged with an additional rank forming amphigastria; rhizoids rare.

5. Leaves as in (4) but the location of rhizoids specialized: scattered over the under surface of the stem, restricted to amphigastria, or restricted to pads that replace the amphigastria.

6. Gametophyte with leaves irregular in shape and arranged bilaterally, so that the gametophyte suggests a thallus.

7. Thallose gametophyte with leafy sexual branches.

8. Thallose gametophyte with no tissue differentiation; rhizoids thin-walled.

9. Thallose gametophyte with thallus much differentiated into tissues; rhizoids of two types.

Similar evolution exists in other aspects of gametophytic structure, developmental morphology of the sex organs, and general structure of the sporophyte. However, evolutionary trends in the sporophyte are not so apparent in the Hepaticae as in the Musci.

CLASS ANTHOCEROTAE (Hornworts)

Superficially the hornworts resemble the thallose liverworts, but a number of significant features separate this class from other bryophytes. The class contains approximately 100 species in a single order, the Anthocerotales, containing a single family, the Anthocerotaceae, with five genera.

DIVISION BRYOPHYTA

Hornworts are found throughout the world, although they are uncommon in Arctic regions. Generally they grow on damp, shaded earth, but some are epiphytic.

All members of the order have a thallose gametophyte that normally forms a rosette in which the dichotomous branching is often not apparent. The thallus of parenchymatous cells is not differentiated into tissues, although cavities commonly filled with mucilaginous material (Fig. 12–11G) appear in the thallus. These cavities frequently open to the ventral surface by stomate-like pores (Fig. 12–11B) and may be invaded by the blue-green alga *Nostoc*. Each cell of the thallus generally contains a single chloroplast surrounding a central pyrenoid, as in some of the green algae.

Sex organs are sunk deeply in the upper layers of the generally bisexual thallus (Fig. 12–11G). One or several antheridia are produced in each chamber. Each antheridium is structurally similar to that of the liverworts. Rupturing of the overlying thallus cells exposes the antheridia, which shed their sperms by splitting of the antheridial wall.

Although flask-shaped in inner contour, archegonia are not clearly differentiated from the other thallus cells. The egg is thus at the bottom of a flask-shaped depression that opens to the dorsal surface of the thallus.

The sporophyte is an elongated spindle attached to the gametophyte by its swollen haustorium-like base, the foot. There is no seta. Growth of the sporophyte is by a basal intercalary meristem; thus, the sporophyte can continue to grow as long as external conditions favor it. Until mature, the sporophyte is chlorophyllose. In the epidermis of most species are stomata with characteristic guard cells (Fig. 12–11C). These stomata lead to a system of intercellular spaces.

The sporangium generally ruptures along two preformed lines of weakness, which run the length of the maturing sporangium (Fig. 12–11A). Maturation is from the apex downward, and the valves split back from the columella—a central cylinder of sterile cells—to expose the spores. The valves sometimes coil and uncoil in response to moisture changes, thus assisting in spore removal. While spores are released from the apex of the sporophyte, new growth at the base continues to differentiate new sporangial tissue, as long as the sporophyte survives. Among the spores are elongate, somewhat branched pseudoelaters, both unicellular and multicellular (Fig. 12–11F).

The evolutionary significance of Anthocerotales is frequently emphasized because of the superficial resemblance of *Anthoceros* to some fossil vascular plants, the psilophytes. It is generally agreed that the psilophytes and Anthocerotae have their origin in the same ancestral group of plants, and many botanists feel that the hornworts were derived from primitive psilophytes. Spores of some species of *Anthoceros* closely resemble those of the fossil psilophyte *Horneophyton*.

CLASS MUSCI
(Mosses)

The mosses are readily distinguished from the hepatics and hornworts by a number of distinctive features.

1. All mosses have a leafy gametophyte, and in most the leaves are in three to five ranks.
2. In many genera the leaf cells are elongate and the cells rarely have greatly thickened corners.
3. The leaves are often costate but otherwise generally one cell thick; they are rarely notched or lobed.
4. The leafy gametophyte generally arises from a filamentous protonema. It produces uniseriate, multicellular protonema-like rhizoids that are often chlorophyllose when young. As they mature, the cell walls of the protonema and rhizoids are generally oblique.
5. The sporophyte is of firm tissue and may persist for several years. However,

234

spores are produced in the capsule from sporogenous tissue that all matures at the same time; hence, spore production in a sporophyte is restricted to a short period.

6. The seta elongates well before differentiation of the capsule, which is covered by a cap (calyptra) formed from the ruptured archegonium. The capsule wall lacks transverse thickenings, and stomata are often present.

7. The parenchymatous central sterile cells of the capsule, the columella, generally form a central dome or cylinder continuous with the seta. The sporogenous layer forms an inverted cup around the columella or a cylinder that surrounds it.

8. In most genera the capsule opens by means of a small lid (operculum) that breaks off the top of the capsule. Beneath this lid the mouth (peristome) of the capsule is generally ringed by peristome teeth.

In the mosses a great array of morphological variation exists, both in the gametophyte and in the sporophyte. This is in marked contrast to the liverworts and hornworts, where, within the class, no great variation occurs in sporophyte structure.

The protonema of many mosses (including most Bryidae) consists of a reclining, much-branched system with indeterminate growth. In most mosses this prostrate system is of a single series of cells. Branches that penetrate or attach to the substrate are normally nonchlorophyllose but are otherwise structurally similar to other parts of the reclining system. Generally arising from the creeping system are perpendicular, strongly chlorophyllose branches, or protonemal flaps. In most mosses this erect system consists of much-branched, intertwined branches in which growth is determinate. This system may be intimately associated with the production of the protonemal buds that ultimately grow into leafy shoots bearing the sex organs.

Gametophyte

Individual leafy gametophytes branch in a number of common patterns; some are essentially unbranched. In mosses where the gametophyte is creeping, the branching habit varies.

Most moss leaves have a simple outline. The shape varies, but leaf shape is relatively constant for each species. As shown in Figure 12–18, leaf apices, margins, and bases show diversity.

The leaf cells exhibit a similar variation in shape. In many mosses the cell surface bears papillae that vary in number and elaborateness. These papillae are wart-like thickenings of the cell wall and are most conspicuous over the cell protoplast. The leaves are generally borne in more than three ranks and are usually arranged spirally on the stem. Anatomically the stem of mosses is far more complex than that of the leafy liverworts. It reaches highest complexity in the largest erect mosses, the Polytrichidae (Fig. 12–15G).

Rhizoids, found predominantly on the stem, are of relatively constant morphology throughout the mosses. They are brownish, uniseriate, much-branched filaments and attach most mosses to their substrate. End walls of the cells vary from transverse to irregularly oblique.

Sporophyte

The moss sporophyte shows equal diversity. The seta varies from long, to short, or essentially absent, with the capsule immersed among leaves. In the Andreaeidae and Sphagnidae, growth of leafless gametophytic tissue (called pseudopodium) below the developing capsule raises the capsule above the leafy gametophyte. The seta possesses chlorophyll when young, although in some genera chlorophyll is very scant.

The capsule shows considerable variation in shape. In most mosses, stomata most frequently lead into intercellular spaces in the lower part of the capsule. Sometimes the stomata can be important in gaseous exchange,

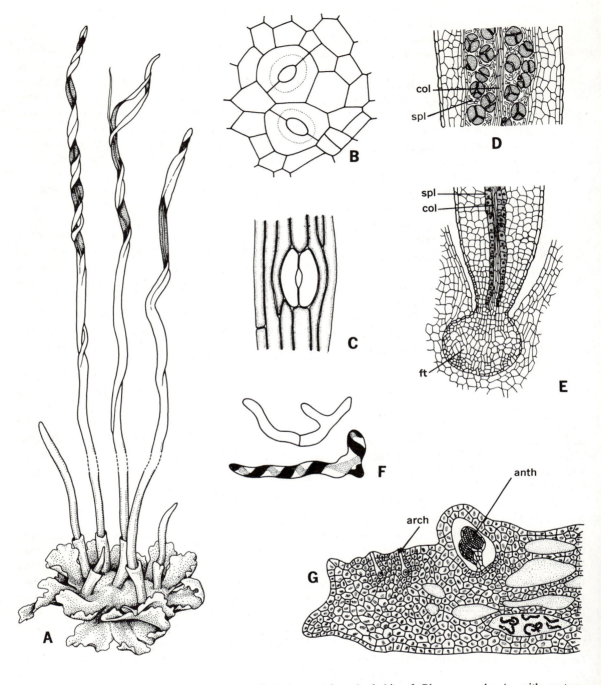

236

FIGURE 12–11 Morphology and anatomy of Anthocerotales. A, habit of *Phaeoceros laevis,* with mature sporangia, ×5; B, pores of gametophytic thallus of *Anthoceros,* ×225; C, stoma with guard cells of *Anthoceros* sporangium wall, ×150; D, longitudinal section through mature sporangium (note pseudoelaters among spore tetrads), ×100; E, base of *Anthoceros* sporangium, ×160; F, pseudoelaters of Anthocerotales (upper, *A. punctatus;* lower, *Megaceros endivaefolius*), ×500; G, cross section through fertile thallus showing mucilage chambers, one filled with *Nostoc* filaments (note single chloroplast in each cell), ×80. *anth,* antheridium; *arch,* archegonium; *col,* columella; *ft,* foot; *spl,* sporogenous layer. (F, after Proskauer with permission of *Torrey Botanical Club Bulletin;* B, after Goebel, *Organographie der Pflanzen,* with permission of G. Fischer, Jena; G, after Howe with permission of *Torrey Botanical Club Memoirs.*)

but in many genera they are probably vestigial structures.

Most mosses have a peristome. The teeth of the peristome exhibit a remarkable diversity both within orders and within genera (Fig. 12–20) but are constant within a species. Some mosses have massive and cellular peristome teeth (Fig. 12–14C). In others, there is a single ring of peristome teeth, each sculptured and formed from remnants of cell walls. Still other mosses have a peristome of two series of teeth (Fig. 12–20A, C, D). In a number of mosses the peristome is rudimentary, consisting of tiny fragments of teeth. Although they have an operculum, many mosses lack a peristome; others lack an operculum, and thus the capsule opens irregularly.

Subclasses of Mosses

The class Musci contains at least 15 orders of more than 80 families, which can be conveniently divided into six subclasses: Sphagnidae, Andreaeidae, Tetraphidae, Polytrichidae, Buxbaumiidae, and Bryidae. Each of these subclasses represents a distinct evolutionary line, and relationships among the subclasses are not clear either in the scanty fossil material or in extant species.

Subclass Sphagnidae

The genus *Sphagnum* (the peat mosses) is the sole representative of the subclass. About 150 species can be distinguished, although more than 300 have been described. Species are found throughout the world but form extensive bogs only in the Northern Hemisphere.

Gametophyte. The protonema of *Sphagnum* is an irregularly lobed thallus, one cell thick, bearing filamentous multicellular rhizoids (Fig. 12–12G). It generally produces a single leafy gametophyte that lacks rhizoids. Gametophytes are often large; some reach lengths of nearly 1 meter, although the living portion is normally less than 0.2 meters long; in compact forms the living portion is often only a few centimeters long. The main stem of the gametophyte bears widely separated leaves that generally differ from those on the branches. Branches are normally in fascicles of three to eight. If the species is submerged, all of the branches are essentially alike; but in emergent gametophytes, divergent branches usually grow outward from the stem and pendent branches lie close to the stem (Fig. 12–12A). The pendent branches normally are more slender and bear smaller leaves than the divergent branches. At the apex of the shoot all branches form a dense tuft, or capitulum.

The leaves are closely imbricated on all branches. All leaves are one cell thick and lack a costa. Mature leaves are made up of a network of elongate chlorophyllose cells surrounding large dead hyaline cells (Fig. 12–12D). The hyaline cells generally possess transverse thickenings and pores and are normally swollen and broadly circular to elliptical in cross section; they are five to ten times as wide as the chlorophyllose cells. The chlorophyllose cells vary in cross-sectional shape and position in reference to the surfaces of the leaf (see Fig. 12–12E).

The stem is often brittle and is supported by floating in water or by other stems that compact many gametophytes into a cushion or mat. The cortical cells of the stem are frequently hyaline and one to five cells thick. The cortex of the branches is always a single cell thick. Because of the presence of large dead hyaline porose cells, *Sphagnum* gametophytes can absorb great quantities of liquid, in some cases more than 20 times their own weight.

The sexual branches are generally near the apex of the plant, most often in the outer part of the capitulum. The archegonia are on a short branch and are surrounded by leaves that are generally larger than other leaves. The antheridia occur on separate divergent branches that are catkin-like in appearance. The thickened apical portion of the branch possesses a single antheridium at the axil of each leaf. Antheridia are globose, as in the hepatics, and each is borne on an elongate stalk.

Sporophyte. The sporophyte is generally ephemeral, and in some cases infrequently produced; thus *Sphagnum* is often found without it. The sporophyte consists essentially of only the capsule (Fig. 12–12I). The foot is somewhat expanded in the apex of the pseudopodium, which elongates to extend the capsule beyond the perichaetial leaves. Normally a single capsule emerges from a perichaetium.

The ripe capsule is essentially spherical, and the operculum may be somewhat flattened or convex. The capsule wall bears numerous nonfunctional stomata on the surface. The capsule jacket has two well-differentiated regions. The epidermis has thicker walled cells than the inner cell layers. The cells of the jacket are chlorophyllose while the capsule is developing, but the chloroplasts disappear when it is mature. A dome-shaped mass of spores overarches the dome-shaped columella, and the jacket closely invests the sporogenous layer.

Spore dispersal is remarkable. As the sporangium matures, the columella shrinks and is replaced by a gas-filled space. The capsule contracts in diameter as it dries, changing from spherical to cylindrical. This change causes compression of the trapped gas below the spores. When the compressed gas reaches a pressure of about five atmospheres, the operculum can no longer confine it. The operculum is then explosively thrown off, and the escaping gas carries the spores into the air.

Ecology. *Sphagnum* is a significant constituent of the vegetation in much of the glaciated portion of the Northern Hemisphere. Aquatic species growing in lake and pool margins add to the acidity of these water bodies. As a result of this acidity, as well as antiseptic substances apparently produced by *Sphagnum,* the aquatic environment becomes relatively free of decay organisms; organic material added to the water decays slowly and accumulates in the lake. The aquatic species of *Sphagnum,* at first restricted to the lake margin, form a floating mat of organic material, which expands over the lake. This quaking mat is a habitat suitable for other plants, including other *Sphagnum* species. Consequently, organic accumulation occurs both in the lake depths and on its margin. The bottom sediments are fine organic muds, but the *Sphagnum* deposits are more fibrous. In time the entire water body is completely overgrown by peat-forming vegetation, and in some areas the peat may be overgrown by forest.

Relationships. *Sphagnum* is often considered to belong to its own class, Sphagna. Apparently *Sphagnum* is in the same general evolutionary line as other Musci, although it is clearly isolated from them.

Economic Importance. In gardening, *Sphagnum* peat is added in part to increase the moisture-holding capacity of the soil. *Sphagnum* peat also has a number of other uses. For example, in Ireland peat has long been used for fuel. During the First World War, *Sphagnum* was widely used in making surgical dressings. Its great absorptive capacity and antiseptic nature make it superior to cotton in some respects.

Subclass Andreaeidae

This subclass has a single family, Andreaeceae. Three genera make up the family. *Andreaea* is found throughout the world, but is most frequent in cool temperate climates. The other genera are rare and probably restricted to temperate South America. All genera form dark brown to blackish tufts on bare siliceous rock. A few species grow in wet sites, but most species are found on exposed outcrops and boulders.

Andreaea is represented by more than 100 described species, but careful study probably would reduce the clear-cut species to fewer than 50.

Gametophyte. In *Andreaea* the spore germinates within the wall, becoming a globular multicellular mass. When the spore wall is broken, this mass gives rise to a much-branched thallose protonema. This often produces elliptic perpendicular unistratose flaps one cell in thick-

238

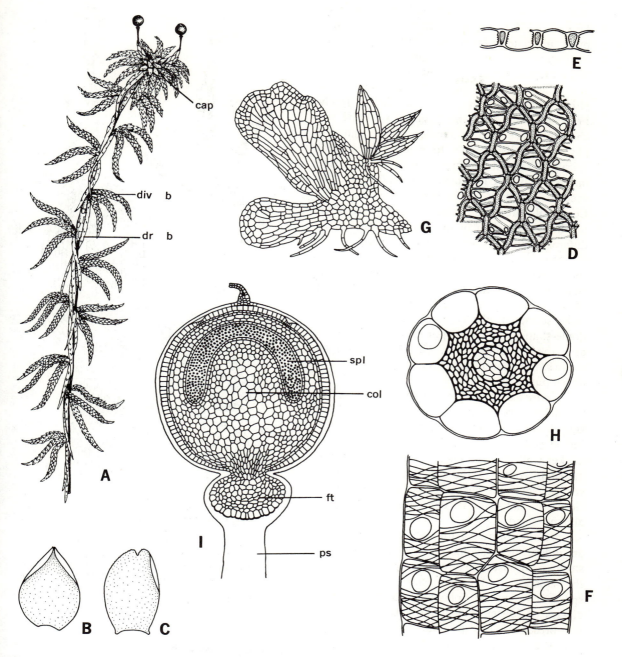

239

FIGURE 12–12 Morphology and anatomy of subclass Sphagnidae. A, habit of sporophyte-bearing shoot of *Sphagnum papillosum*, ×1; B, branch leaf of *S. papillosum*, ×12; C, stem-leaf of *S. papillosum*, ×12; D, leaf cells of *S. papillosum* (note network of chlorophyllose cells surrounding porose hyaline cells; also the fibril thickenings of walls of hyaline cells), ×165; E, cross section of *S. papillosum* leaf, showing relationship of hyaline and chlorophyllose cells, ×165; F, external view of stem of *S. papillosum*, showing hyaline porose outer cells with their fibril thickenings, ×225; G, thallose protonema of *Sphagnum* bearing young leafy shoot and rhizoids, ×75; H, cross section of branch-stem of *S. papillosum* (note hyaline outer cells and dark-walled cells of central axis), ×295; I, longitudinal section through *Sphagnum* capsule, showing anatomy, ×95. *cap,* capitulum; *col,* columella; *div b,* divergent branch; *dr b,* pendent branch; *ft,* foot; *ps,* pseudopodium; *spl,* sporogenous layer. (I, after Cavers with permission of Trustees of *New Phytologist* and Messrs. Dawsons of Pall Mall, who reprinted F. Cavers' *The Inter-Relationships of the Bryophyta* in 1964).

ness that increase the photosynthetic surface (Fig. 12–13C). From the thallose protonema, buds ultimately form that differentiate into leafy gametophytes. The gametophytes are attached to the substrate by rhizoids.

When mature, the leafy gametophyte is either unisexual or bisexual. It is freely branched, and only the younger portions are chlorophyllose; the remainder of the gametophyte is reddish brown to black. The leaves, spirally arranged and crowded (Fig. 12–13A), may or may not be costate, depending on the species. The bulk of the leaf is one cell thick. Leaf cells are small, thick-walled, and often papillose. The stem of thick-walled cells is not differentiated into any distinctive layers.

Sporophyte. As in the Sphagnidae, the sporophyte is borne on a pseudopodium. In general the capsule structure is similar to that of *Sphagnum.* The jacket is multicellular (but lacks stomata), the columella is elongate and dome-shaped, and the sporogenous cells overarch the columella (Fig. 12–13D). As in all mosses, the sporangium is chlorophyllose while developing.

Andreaea is unique among the mosses in the dehiscence of the capsule (Fig. 12–13A, B). When the capsule dries, the inner thin-walled cells of the jacket shrink and the outer thicker-walled cells do not; the capsule contracts in length, opening the four (or rarely eight) vertical slits and releasing the spores. Wetting closes the capsule. An operculum is absent in all Andreaeidae.

Relationships. Although it appears to be an independent evolutionary line showing no strong relationship to any other group of mosses, the subclass Andreaeidae stands in many respects between the Sphagnidae and other subclasses of Musci. The thallose protonema and the presence of a pseudopodium are shared with the Sphagnidae, but the closest affinity of Andreaeidae in morphology and development is with other subclasses. Additional features shared with other mosses but not with *Sphagnum* are shape of antheridia, persistence of rhizoids, and general structure of the stem.

240

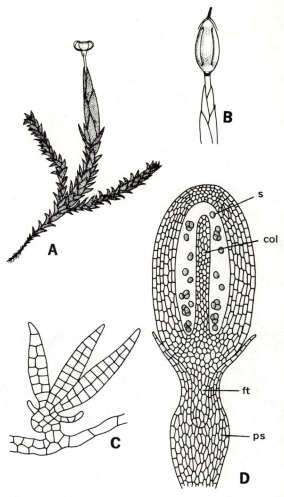

FIGURE 12–13 Morphology and anatomy of subclass Andreaeidae. A, habit sketch of *Andreaea rupestris* bearing dehiscing sporangium, × 8; B, sporangium of *A. rupestris* when moist, × 15; C, portion of straplike protonema of *Andreaea* with frondiform flaps, × 130; D, longitudinal section through sporangium of *Andreaea,* × 130. *col,* columella; *ft,* foot; *ps,* pseudopodium; *s,* spore. (C, after Ruhland in Engler, *Die natürlichen Pflanzenfamilien,* Vol. 10, p. 16, Fig. 10O, 11A, 108A, D, 1924).

Subclass Tetraphidae

This subclass contains two genera, which are essentially north temperate in distribution. *Tetraphis,* represented by two species, grows

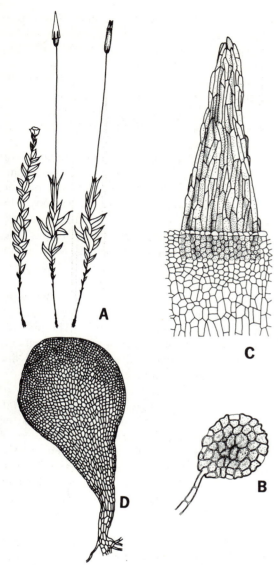

FIGURE 12–14 Morphology and anatomy of sub-class Tetraphidae: *Tetraphis pellucida.* A, habit (gemma-bearing plant at far left), ×2; B, lenticular gemma, ×225; C, multicellular peristome tooth, ×150; D, frondiform protonemal flap, ×35. (D, after Ruhland in Engler, *Die natürlichen Pflanzenfamilien,* Vol. 10, p. 19, Fig. 14, 1924.)

mainly in coniferous forests, where it is particularly luxuriant on moist rotting logs.

Gametophyte. The spore germinates to produce a normal protonema, which gives rise to frondiform flaps in much the same manner as in *Andreaea* (Fig. 12–13D). These thalloid structures often bud off a branch near the base, producing a normal leafy gametophyte. The erect leafy gametophytes form densely packed turfs in *Tetraphis.* Gametophytes are attached to the substrate by rhizoids.

The ovate to lanceolate leaves are spirally arranged in three to five ranks (Fig. 12–14A). The leaves are one cell thick except at the costa, which extends to near the leaf apex.

The plants are bisexual, and sex organs are typical for mosses. Among the sexual shoots there are also gemmiferous shoots (Fig. 12–14A), which resemble the others except that several larger leaves at the apex of the gemmiferous shoot form a cup with stalked gemmae (Fig. 12–14B). The gemmae break off readily and germinate to produce new protonemata that ultimately give rise to frondiform flaps and leafy gametophytes. The gemmae are probably dispersed by raindrops that splash into the cuplike apex of gemmiferous shoots, dislodging the gemmae.

Sporophyte. The short cylindrical sporangium is borne on an elongate seta. In all species the calyptra is pleated, bell-shaped, and covers most of the capsule (Fig. 12–14A). The operculum is conic, covering the peristome teeth.

The peristome is of four multicellular persistent teeth (Fig. 12–14C), which are attached below the mouth of the capsule. The spores are released by shaking of the capsule, which is generally raised high above the leafy gametophyte. The columella of the Tetraphidae extends up to the base of the massive peristome teeth so that the sporogenous layer forms a cylinder around the columella.

Relationships. The Tetraphidae show relationships with the Andreaeidae through *Acroschisma* on the basis of superficial similarity of the peristome. The protonemal flaps are also reminiscent of the Andreaeidae. In all subclasses other than Andreaeidae and Sphagnidae, the following are common features: the typical calyptra, the operculum, the well-differentiated stem, the erect leafy gametophyte, and the general nature of development of the peristome teeth.

241

Subclass Polytrichidae

This subclass, represented throughout the world, is relatively small, possessing a single order with two families. Eighteen genera containing nearly 370 species are recognized. Most species grow on acid soil.

Gametophyte. Gametophytes of all Polytrichidae begin as a typical chlorophyllose, much-branched protonema. In a few species the protonema persists and provides the photosynthetic surface for the growing sporophyte; in such species the gametophyte is much reduced. Most members of the subclass are unisexual.

All Polytrichidae have erect gametophytes, and the sporophytes terminate the main branch or branches. Leaves are arranged spirally and are generally in five ranks. Leaves are usually lanceolate and always costate. Normally the upper surface of the costa is covered by many longitudinal parallel lamellae (Fig. 12–15F). In many genera the lamellae are chlorophyllose, whereas the rest of the leaf possesses opaque or translucent cells without chlorophyll. In some species the lamina margin curves in over the lamellae during dry periods, thus reducing water loss in the leaf.

Gametophytes vary considerably in size. For example, in the genus *Dawsonia* some are nearly 60 centimeters tall (Fig. 12–15D), and some species of *Polytrichum* and *Pogonatum* are almost as tall. Yet in other genera the gametophyte may be less than 0.5 centimeters tall. In most genera the gametophyte is unbranched, but in some it possesses several branches and resembles a seedling spruce tree.

The stem is always wiry, indicating the large number of thick-walled cells in both the cortex and the central axis. Stem tissue is sometimes considerably differentiated. Cells that superficially resemble xylem and phloem (Fig. 12–15G) appear to be primarily supportive, although in some instances the central strand is important in transport of water and nutrients.

Sporophyte. Most gametophytes produce a single sporophyte each year, but some produce several annually. The seta is erect, wiry, and structurally similar to the stem. The cylindrical or angled capsule is usually covered by a large hairy calyptra (Fig. 12–15A, B, H). The sporogenous layer surrounds the columella. In most genera the apex of the columella is expanded to form a closure to the mouth of the capsule, the epiphragm. Spaces are present only between the peristome teeth, through which the minute spores escape.

In the capsule of most Polytrichidae there is a single row of short, multicellular peristome teeth (Fig. 12–15E, H)—usually 32, 64, or rarely 16, depending on the genus. However, in *Dawsonia* there are several irregular rows of very long intertwisted peristome teeth. The epiphragm is absent in this genus. Some other genera lack peristome teeth, but they do have an epiphragm.

Relationships. In spite of the rather complex gametophyte, the Polytrichidae exhibit a number of very primitive features. The massive peristome teeth, the mode of leaf arrangement, and the vast numbers of spores produced are all considered primitive characteristics.

The Polytrichidae are possibly related to Buxbaumiidae, through the genus *Dawsonia*. In this genus the nature of the capsule and the complex peristome suggest some features of Buxbaumiidae. The subclass has been in existence at least since the Eocene Epoch, and its present wide distribution through a diversity of habitats and climates suggests that it is likely to persist for some millennia.

Subclass Buxbaumiidae

This subclass, a small one of tiny plants, consists of predominantly Northern Hemisphere genera. Three genera and approximately 25 species have been recognized. Species grow on soil, rotten wood, humus, or acidic rock.

Gametophyte. The gametophyte of *Buxbaumia* is the simplest known among the mosses. Antheridial plants consist of a limited filamentous protonema that bears several microscopic antheridial buds. Each antheridium is surrounded by a photosynthetic clamshell-like ex-

242

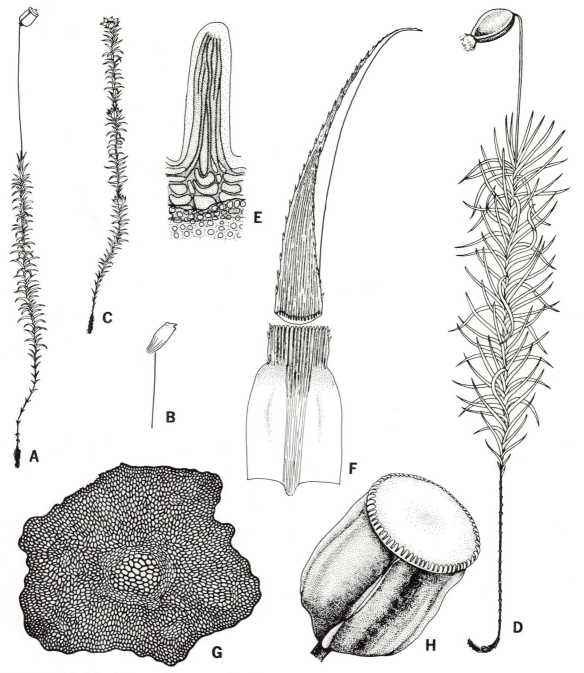

FIGURE 12–15 Morphology and anatomy of subclass Polytrichidae. A–C, E–H, *Polytrichum commune*. A, sporophyte-bearing plant after calyptra has fallen, ×1; B, sporangium with calyptra in place, ×1; C, antheridial plant, showing three successive years' crops of perigonia, ×1; E, multicellular peristome tooth, ×75; F, leaf, showing lamellae on upper surface, ×12; G, cross section of stem, showing differentiation into tissue-like areas, ×140; H, sporangium, showing peristome teeth and epiphragm, ×8; D, habit of *Dawsonia superba*, ×1.

DIVISION BRYOPHYTA

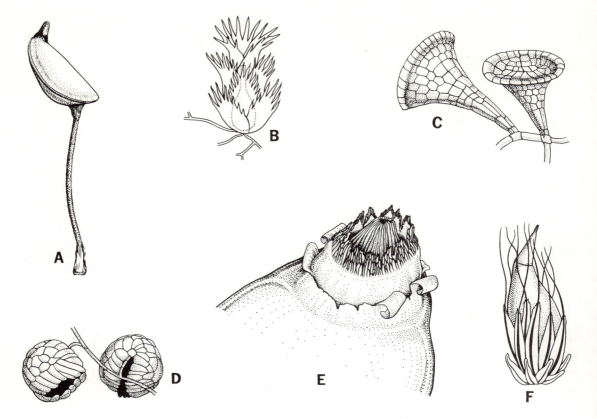

FIGURE 12–16   Morphology and anatomy of subclass Buxbaumiidae. A, B, D, E, *Buxbaumia aphylla*. A, habit, ×7; B, gametophyte with single archegonium, ×45; D, antheridial "branches," external view, ×225; E, apex of capsule showing peristome (note outer multicellular peristome and inner pleated cone), ×13.5. C, F, *Diphyscium foliosum*. C, protonemal flaps, ×25; F, habit of sporangium-bearing gametophyte, ×8. (D, after Goebel, *Organographie der Pflanzen,* with permission of G. Fischer, Jena; C, after Ruhland in Engler, *Die natürlichen Pflanzenfamilien,* Vol. 10, p. 21, Fig. 18A, 1924.)

pansion of a protonemal branch (Fig. 12–16D). The antheridium is globose, as is that of the Sphagnidae, and each is borne on a stalk. The archegonial plants have a more extensive leafy system. Each plant bears several colorless leaves, which may be ciliate on the margins (Fig. 12–16B). One or two archegonia are borne by such a plant. No paraphyses are present with the sex organs. In *Diphyscium* and *Theriotia* the gametophyte is leafy and small (Fig. 12–16F). The leaves are usually costate and dark green. In *Diphyscium,* the protonema bears peltate protonemal flaps in a manner resembling Andreaeidae and Tetraphidae (Fig. 12–16C).

Sporophyte.   The capsule of *Buxbaumia* terminates a papillose seta (Fig. 12–16A). The whole sporophyte may be about 3 centimeters tall. In both *Diphyscium* and *Theriotia* the capsule has virtually no seta and is surrounded by elongate perichaetial leaves (Fig. 12–16F). The capsule of all genera is oblique, flattened on the upper side, and tapered to the short conical operculum. When young, the sporophyte is photosynthetic. Indeed, in *Buxbaumia* the sporophyte must synthesize most of its food.

Beneath the jacket of the capsule, chlorophyllose filaments traverse an extensive area of air spaces. The spore layer forms a cylinder surrounding the columella. As in most mosses, the columella is of parenchymatous cells and ends below the operculum. When the capsule is mature, and after the operculum has fallen off, a slight pressure on the oblique upper surface of the capsule puffs out and disseminates the spores.

The peristome is formed from several cell layers, as in the *Tetraphidae,* but there are a number of distinct rows of teeth—each row formed of fragmentary, thickened cell walls, as in the Bryidae. The inner peristome is a hyaline pleated cone, open at the tip (Fig. 12–16E). Outer peristome teeth occur in several rows or they are absent or very rudimentary. When present, the outer teeth are opaque and obscurely articulate, vaguely resembling those of the Bryidae.

Relationships. In peristomial development, the Buxbaumiidae resemble both Tetraphidae and Polytrichidae, but the actual structure of the peristome teeth resembles that of the Bryidae. The Buxbaumiidae has a relatively highly developed sporophyte and considerable variation in gametophytic structure, suggesting a reduced remnant of an evolutionary line.

Subclass Bryidae

This subclass contains the bulk of the mosses. There are 12 orders, at least 75 families, 650 genera, and approximately 13,700 species. Most families are poorly studied, and few genera are well understood. Even general evolutionary lines are unclear, and inadequate information has produced a certain lack of uniformity in classification. Although general knowledge of temperate Bryidae is reasonably complete, that of tropical taxa is incomplete. Detailed morphological study has been confined to very few species.

Because of their great diversity, species of Bryidae are found nearly everywhere a plant will grow. Some species can survive extended periods of desiccation whereas others are aquatic, but most species flourish in environ-ments of high humidity. Many species have strict substrate requirements, but others can grow on diverse substrates.

Gametophyte. The morphological variety of Bryidae gametophytes is closely correlated with patterns of sporophytic variety (Fig. 12–17). In most Bryidae the gametophyte begins as a much-branched filamentous green protonema that produces buds; the buds, in turn, differentiate to produce leafy gametophytes. The protonema of a few Bryidae produces gemmae of characteristic morphology for the species. Frondiform protonemal flaps are rarely formed. The common type of protonema of the Bryidae is discussed on p. 235. In most mosses the protonema disappears soon after the leafy gametophytes arise. Under moist conditions almost any actively dividing cell of a leafy gametophyte is capable of forming a protonema which, in turn, differentiates buds in the same manner as a spore-produced protonema.

Bryidae are either acrocarpous or pleuro-carpous in general growth form. The most primitive Bryidae are conceded to be acrocarpous; the more advanced are highly elaborate, much branched, and pleurocarpous. Acrocarpous mosses have the leafy gametophyte erect, and the current year's sporophyte terminates the main shoot or a main branch (Fig. 12–17A, B). Acrocarpous mosses generally form mats or cushions of erect shoots. Pleurocarpous mosses are much branched and creeping (Fig. 12–17C); the sporophyte of the current year is borne on a special short lateral branch. Basal rhizoids attach acrocarpous mosses to the substrate, and rhizoids often attach much of the reclining stem of pleurocarpous mosses to the substrate. The leaf arrangement is generally radial.

The leaf cells in the Bryidae show considerable variation in shape and structure. The basal cells often differ from those near the apex and may be larger or smaller than those of the rest of the leaf. Most Bryidae have leaves one cell thick. If the leaf is costate—and most are —the costal region is several cells thick and cells of the costa often show a distinctive distribution of larger thin-walled and smaller thick-

245

walled cells. The costa is probably supportive; it may be solitary or multiple, prominent or obscure. The costa and the rest of the leaf are continuous with the outer cortex of the stem. Leaf margins vary in thickness and structural detail. In some genera the leaves produce gemmae. In several species the leaves are brittle and each fragment serves as a vegetative propagant.

Stem anatomy in the Bryidae is equally diverse. Differentiation of cells is never as elaborate as in the Polytrichidae, but cortical and central axis cells generally are different. The cortical cells are of one or several layers and are thick-walled or thin-walled, small or large. The central axis is usually composed of parenchymatous cells, but in many genera there is a

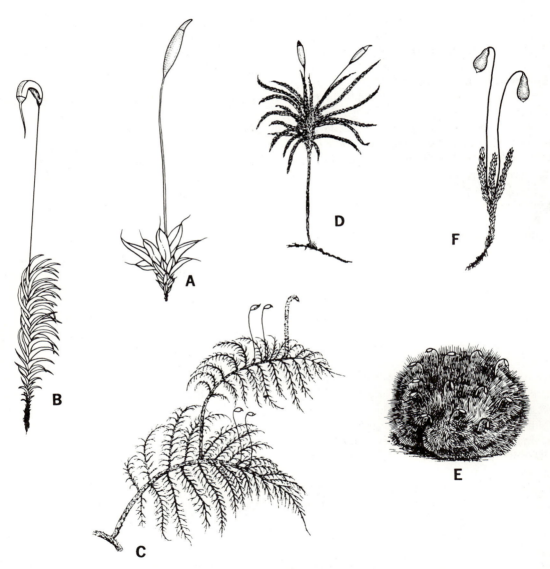

FIGURE 12–17 Variety in gametophytes and sporophytes of subclass Bryidae. A, *Tortula muralis,* ×2; B, *Dicranum scoparium,* ×1; C, *Hylocomium splendens,* ×1; D, *Climacium dendroides,* ×1; E, *Grimmia pulvinata,* ×1; F, *Bryum* sp., ×1.

central strand of thicker-walled condensed cells. When the stem is young the central strand seems to function in conduction; when the stem is old the central strand aids in support and, in a few Bryidae, also in conduction. Young stems are chlorophyllose, but as the stem ages the chlorophyll is lost. Rhizoids, present in nearly all Bryidae, are occasionally very abundant on the stem and sometimes on the leaves.

The antheridia of the Bryidae are generally banana-shaped and borne on a multicellular stalk. They are surrounded by filamentous chlorophyllose paraphyses. The archegonia are typically bryophytic, often with an extremely long neck, and surrounded by paraphyses. In bisexual species sex organs are distributed on separate branches, in the same cluster, or some mixed and others on separate branches. Many Bryidae are unisexual.

Sporophyte. In the Bryidae the sporophytic diversity parallels gametophytic variety (Fig. 12–17, 19). However, in some genera, there is great variation in peristome structure.

In most Bryidae the sporophyte is borne on a seta. All setae are chlorophyllose when young. Anatomically the seta is very like the stem, except that the cortical cells are generally thick-walled. The orientation of the capsule is diversified but is reasonably constant in a genus. In most Bryidae the capsule jacket is several cells thick and has stomata, which are generally restricted to the base of the capsule near the apophysis. The calyptra of Bryidae is generally smooth, but may be papillose or hairy.

Nearly all Bryidae have a columella of parenchymatous cells, with a surrounding sporogenous sleeve. Often a barrel-shaped series of air spaces occurs between the columella and the

247

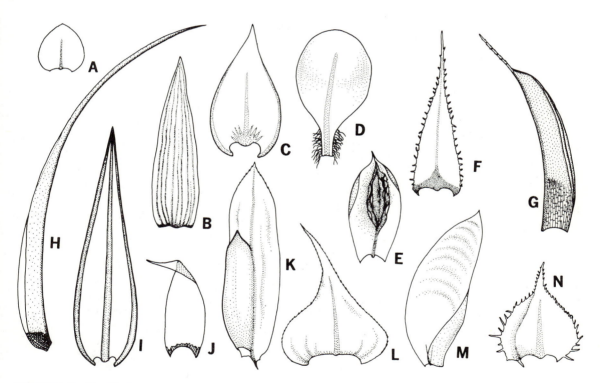

FIGURE 12–18 Variety in leaves of subclass Bryidae. A, *Hygrohypnum smithii*, ×15; B, *Orthothecium rufescens*, ×25; C, *Antitrichia curtipendula*, ×20; D, *Oedipodium griffithianum*, ×15; E, *Pterigoneurum ovatum*, ×30; F, *Leucolepis menziesii*, stem-leaf, ×25; G, *Tortula ruralis*, ×13; H, *Dicranum scoparium*, ×15; I, *Sciaromium fryei*, ×20; J, *Brotherella roellii*, ×25; K, *Fissidens adianthoides*, ×15; L, *Eurhynchium oreganum*, ×15; M, *Neckera douglasii*, ×25; N, *Thelia hirtella*, ×30.

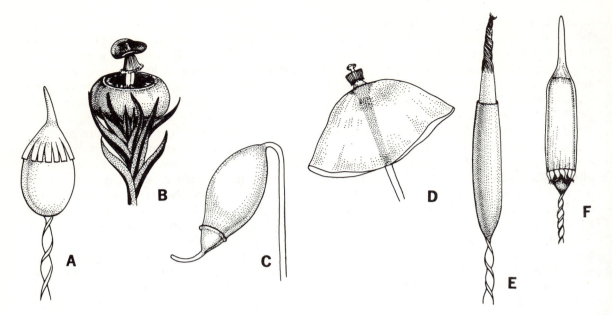

FIGURE 12–19 Variety in sporangia and calyptras of subclass Bryidae. A, *Rhacomitrium lanuginosum,* with calyptra, ×20; B, *Scouleria aquatica,* dehiscing, ×10; C, *Eurhynchium oreganum,* with operculum in place, ×10; D, *Splachnum luteum,* showing extensive hypophysis (sporangium dehiscing), ×6; E, *Tortula princeps,* dehiscing, ×7; F, *Encalypta ciliata,* with calyptra, ×10.

248

spore layer, and another between the spore layer and the jacket.

Most Bryidae possess an operculum. Often a specialized ring of hygroscopic elastic cells—the annulus—is found between the mouth of the capsule and the operculum. When the capsule is mature, this annulus aids in the release of the operculum. The operculum is generally concave and often has a central hump; or this hump often extends as a long snout (Fig. 12–17B, 19C); or the whole operculum is conical. Usually the operculum falls freely, but in some Bryidae it is fused with the columella and persists until the capsule decays (Fig. 12–19B, 20B, D). In the few Bryidae that have no operculum, the spores are shed by decay or by irregular rupturing of the capsule.

Most Bryidae that possess an operculum also have a peristome (Fig. 12–20). In the more primitive Bryidae the peristome is single and generally composed of 16 or 32 teeth formed from fragments of adjacent cell walls and derived from two cell layers. Thus, the peristome teeth consist of fragments of cell

walls. The teeth are variously sculptured and are generally brownish and opaque. In some genera the teeth are linear; in others, each tooth is forked; still others have the teeth much perforated. In nearly all Bryidae the teeth are composed of transverse plates. The teeth are hygroscopic and curl inward when slightly moist and flick outward when dry, or reverse the process in some instances. The irregular surfaces catch spores and aid in discharging them from the capsule. In some genera the peristome teeth emerge from a much-sculptured basal sleeve, or the teeth are rudimentary or even absent.

Many Bryidae, including most pleurocarpous genera, have a double peristome. The outer peristome is similar to that just described. The function of the inner peristome is not clear. It is generally translucent and often possesses a continuous basal cylinder. The teeth of the inner peristome are not hygroscopic. They tend to alternate with those of the outer peristome. The inner peristome occasionally forms a perforated dome, with the teeth supporting the

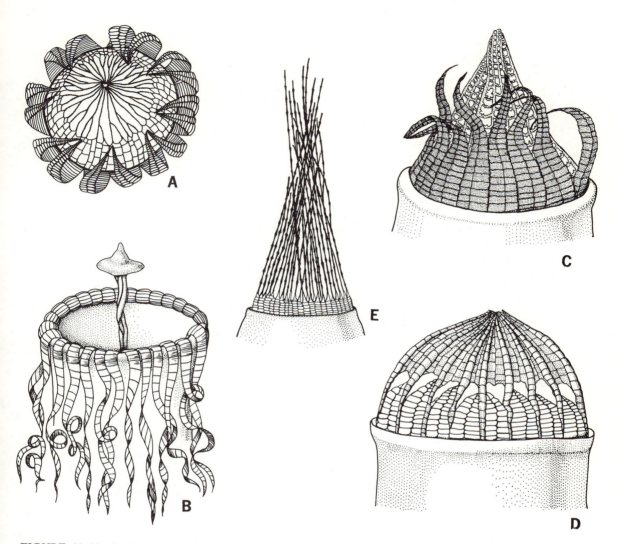

FIGURE 12–20 Variety in peristomes of subclass Bryidae. A, *Timmia bavarica,* showing endostome and exostome, ×35; B, *Tayloria splachnoides,* ×50; C, *Fontinalis antipyretica,* ×30; D, *Cinclidium stygium,* ×50; E, *Rhacomitrium canescens,* ×35. (A, after Lazarenko with permission of *The Bryologist;* B, D, after Schimper.)

dome (Fig. 12–20D). In a few genera the inner peristome is a lacy lattice of interjoined teeth (Fig. 12–20C).

The spores are generally all alike. They contain chlorophyll, oil, and generally starch.

Relationships. The Bryidae are probably most closely allied to the Buxbaumiidae, with which they share the general structure of the sporophyte. Gametophytic similarity exists as well. Whether these similarities are a result of

parallel evolution of two distinct lines is far from clear.

Within the Bryidae, evolutionary lines are just as vague. It seems probable that acrocarpous species with 16-toothed single peristomes are the most primitive, and pleurocarpous species with double peristomes are the most advanced. In the acrocarpous group the simplest gametophytic structure is present. With increase of teeth from 16 to 32, the structure and sculp-

DIVISION BRYOPHYTA

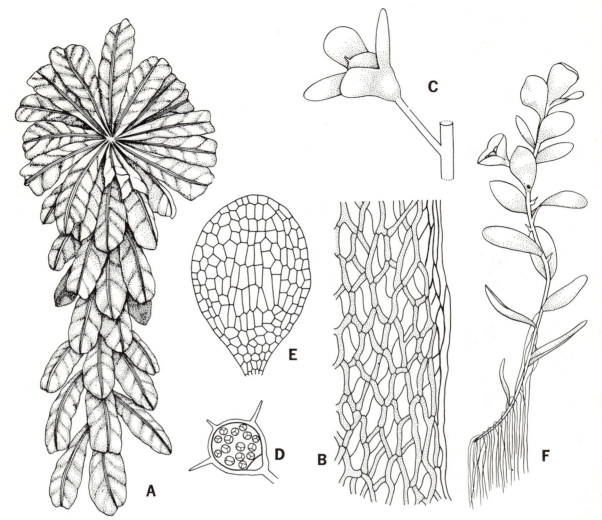

FIGURE 12–21   Fossil Bryophytes. A, reconstruction of *Vorcutannularia plicata,* moss of the Permian, ×2; B, cellular detail of leaf of *V. plicata,* showing hyaline and chlorophyllose cells as well as leaf margin, ×100; C, sporangium of *Naiadita lanceolata,* a Triassic liverwort, ×10; D, longitudinal section through sporangium of *N. lanceolata,* showing tetrads of spores, ×8; E, leaf of *N. lanceolata,* ×50; F, reconstruction of *N. lanceolata,* ×6. (A, B, after Neuberg; C–F, after Harris with permission of the Trustees of the British Museum (Natural History) and *Annales Bryologici.*)

turing of the teeth are elaborated and the pattern and sculpturing of the leaf cells are diversified. However, within these acrocarpous genera, some members are greatly reduced in structure.

Similar evolutionary lines exist in pleurocarpous Bryidae, although the greatest diversity here is in the structure of the gametophyte. Among such Bryidae it is difficult to separate some genera and even some families. Consequently, understanding of the evolutionary lines is very tenuous.

FOSSIL BRYOPHYTA

Bryophytes have made poor fossils because they are simple, delicate, and small. For a competent determination, the paleobryologist requires well-preserved material, including details of gametophyte cells and a fairly complete sporophyte. These conditions are rarely found in the fossil record. However, until recently even the small surviving fragments have often been neglected, but the work of Neuberg shows what can be done when the record is carefully studied.

Spores attributed to terrestrial plants have been found in Pre-Cambrian and Cambrian rocks in the Baltic. Whether some of these are from bryophytes is uncertain. The first apparently bryophyte fossil, from the Upper Devonian, was the gametophyte of a thallose liverwort possibly related to the Metzgeriales.

Neuberg's remarkable discovery of mosses from Permian rocks marked a milestone in fossil botany. She reported 13 species of mosses clearly of Bryidae affinities; but some representatives suggest relationships with the Sphagnidae (Fig. 12–21A, B). None can be ascribed to modern genera, but their phylogenetic implications, especially with respect to the Sphagnidae, are especially significant.

The most significant Triassic hepatic, carefully studied by Harris, is *Naiadita,* whose relationships appear to be with the genus *Riella*

in the Sphaerocarpales (Fig. 12–21C–F). It is the only fossil hepatic discovered so far with attached sporangia. The presence of gemmae, rhizoids, archegonia, and well-preserved leaves enabled Harris to reconstruct this bryophyte (Fig. 12–21F). It appears to have been aquatic, as is *Riella*—a factor that presumably favored its fossilization.

There is a great increase in fossils of the Cenozoic, and many can be compared with modern genera. A few of these fossils are of epiphytic species preserved in Baltic amber. Of the Quaternary fossils, the best represented genera are those presently common to aquatic environments. From Quaternary moss fossils it has been possible to reconstruct the floristic history of some regions, especially in Europe, but there is a low representation of hepatics in the Quaternary record.

The fragmentary nature of both the fossils and the fossil record makes it impossible to utilize them in interpreting phylogeny. The most significant discoveries have been the Permian mosses and the Triassic *Naiadita*. These were sufficiently complete to make reasonably confident interpretations about their relationships.

VASCULAR PLANTS

13 / Vascular Plants

The remaining chapters describe ten groups of vascular plants. Until recently, vascular plants were usually classified in the division Tracheophyta, because the possession of xylem and phloem conducting elements was believed to indicate close relationship. But in the last decade other morphological and anatomical differences have been recognized among some groups of vascular plants, indicating that these groups are less closely related than previously thought. Paleobotanical investigations indicate that many of the modern groups have been distinct evolutionary lines as far back in geologic time as there is a clear record of vascular plants. Thus, a system of classification like Bold's (1967), which places obviously grossly unrelated groups of vascular plants in separate divisions, appears warranted.

The earliest undoubted vascular plants are found in rocks of the early Devonian. During these times, the lycopod, arthrophyte, and psilophyte lineages were definitely established. By later Devonian times ancestors of the ferns and gymnosperms had evolved, and ancestors of all modern groups of vascular plants except the Anthophyta had appeared. (The anthophytes are first recorded from the late Lower Cretaceous but may have had a long prior evolution.) Throughout the long interval from Devonian to the present many taxa became extinct, whereas others were ancestral to new evolutionary avenues. Thus, the vascular plants of today are the net result of a very long period of evolution from at least Silurian times to the present—a span of over 400 million years.

According to three main theories, vascular plants evolved (1) from algae, probably from ancestors of the Ulotrichales of the Chlorophyta (see Chapter 11); (2) from bryophytic ancestors, possibly *Anthoceros* or closely allied plants (see Chapter 12); or (3) from an isomorphic ancestral group derived from the green algae that was presumably ancestral to both the bryophytes and vascular plants.

All theories are based on the premise that, as evolution proceeded, presumably by a series of mutations, differentiation of xylem and phloem took place in the central region of the axis. The appearance of these supportive and conducting tissues vastly increased the potential for these early plants to occupy various terrestrial habitats. The appearance of vascular plants in essentially terrestrial environments in the early Devonian is one of the most significant evolutionary developments, initiating a long evolutionary history of vascular plants on land.

If algae are considered the direct ancestors of vascular plants, it can be suggested that with evolution the algal ancestors were able to withstand increasingly longer periods of desiccation, and that these ancestors eventually gave rise to forms that could survive on dry land throughout their life history. If an *Anthoceros* or *Anthoceros*-like ancestor is assumed, the main development would appear to have been the evolution of xylem and phloem from the columella, which serves in part as an internal conducting system. Stomata, cuticle, and sporangia —all characteristic features of vascular plants— are present in the sporophyte of modern Anthocerotae as well as in many Musci.

The third hypothesis suggests that a group of extinct plants, derived from the green algae, served as an ancestral group to both bryophytes and vascular plants. This hypothesis suggests that both early vascular plants and bryophytes were derived from a common ancestor, itself an early land plant but probably not possessing a true vascular system. The bryophytes then formed an independent evolutionary line, maintaining many features that still restrict them, in their sexual reproduction, to habitats where ample water is available. Although most of the earliest vascular plants also appear to have been restricted to aquatic or very wet habitats, their immediate descendants were adapted to terrestrial conditions, almost certainly in response to the acquisition of vascular tissue in an essentially independent sporophyte.

CHARACTERISTIC FEATURES OF VASCULAR PLANTS

The only characteristics unique to vascular plants are xylem and phloem tissues, but other characteristics are common to almost all vascular plants: an external waxy covering, the cuticle (also present in some bryophytes); differentiation into true stem, leaves, and almost always roots; a distinct alternation of generations, with the sporophyte independent and structurally more complex than the gametophyte; and a high ratio of volume to surface area of the plant.

The cuticle, vascular tissue, and a high volume/surface-area ratio favor survival upon land, particularly in habitats lacking free surface water. The development of a cuticle provides for conservation of water in an aerial medium, as does a high ratio of volume to surface area. The specialized xylem cells make possible adequate conduction of water from the soil to aerial portions of the plant, and so are vital to tall herbs, perennial shrubs, and trees that extend tens of meters into the air.

MAIN EVOLUTIONARY TRENDS

In general, the fossil record supports the hypothesis that evolution in the early vascular plants progressed from herbaceous aquatic forms to woody terrestrial plants. Almost all of the vascular plants in the early Devonian were small and apparently nonwoody (see *Rhynia*, p. 261; *Baragwanathia, Drepanophycus,* and *Protolepidodendron*, pp. 266–267; and Hyeniales, p. 283). In Middle and Upper Devonian times larger and woody forms became common, and by Carboniferous times plants of tree stature were numerous (see p. 286). It is likely that during this same period the vascular plants were encroaching on more upland regions of the earth, becoming farther removed from aquatic habitats as more elaborate structures were evolved for acquiring and conserving water.

Evolutionary trends are also evident in the vascular tissue, both in the xylem and in the stelar patterns. Xylem tracheids appear to have evolved secondary wall thickenings in the series: annular–helical–scalariform–reticulate– bordered pitted (Fig. 13–1A–E). Xylem vessels apparently evolved from tracheids by the dissolution of end-plates, and seem to have evolved independently in several groups, e.g., lycopods (*Selaginella*), gnetophytes (*Gnetum*), and anthophytes. The increase in amount of secondary thickening in the tracheid series corresponds to the trend in increased woodiness. The evolution of vessels provided a much more efficient water-conducting system, and

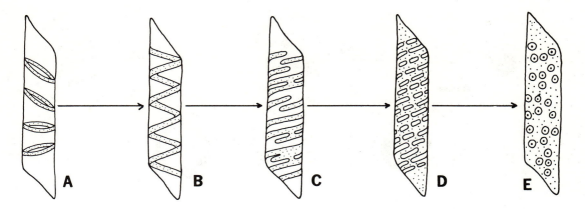

FIGURE 13–1   Evolutionary series of xylem tracheids. A, annular; B, helical; C, scalariform; D, reticulate; E, bordered pitted; ×475.

may be one factor that has allowed the anthophytes to become the dominant group of vascular plants in recent geological time.

Evolution of the stele appears to have followed two main pathways from the primitive protostele, as shown in Figure 13–2. The first (Fig. 13–2 D, G, H) is from the siphonostele–eustele–atactostele; the second (Fig. 13–2 D, E, F) is from the ectophloic siphonostele–amphiphloic siphonostele (solenostele)–dictyostele. These series, from the solid cylinder of vascular tissue in the protostele to the complex system of dispersed vascular strands represented by the atactostele, reflect the amount of dissection of the stele by leaf gaps, resulting from an increase in the complexity of vascularization of leaves.

Two of the most significant developments in the evolution of vascular plants were undoubtedly the *evolution of the seed habit,* and the *development of angiospermy.* As indicated later (see p. 324), the seed habit appears to have evolved separately in several distinct groups of vascular plants, providing a marked increase in protection and nutrition for the gametophyte, sex cells, and embryo. The attainment of angiospermy, by the complete enclosure of the seed and the introduction of double fertilization, apparently occurred only in the anthophytes, although structural modifications in several fossil taxa suggest that at

least some of the prerequisites for angiospermy may have evolved in several different groups.

Evidence from fossil and extant vascular plants shows an evolutionary trend in the reduction of the gametophyte generation. In those groups reflecting ancestral conditions, such as the ferns and arthrophytes, the gametophyte is relatively large, decidedly multicellular, and free living at least for a short time (Fig. 13–3A). With evolution, the gametophyte became reduced and developed entirely within the sporophytic tissue (Fig. 13–3B). The ultimate in gametophytic reduction occurs in the most recently evolved group, the Anthophyta (see p. 383), in which the mature gynogametophyte consists of as few as two cells (Fig. 13–3C), and the mature androgametophyte of one to three cells.

RANGE OF MORPHOLOGY AND DISTRIBUTION

Almost all present-day vascular plants possess roots, stems, and leaves. The only major exceptions are found in the Psilophyta. In *Psilotum* and *Tmesipteris,* rhizoids are borne on a rhizome, and *Psilotum* has scale-like emergences that some interpret as true leaves (Fig. 14–2, 3). In other vascular plants, one or more

257

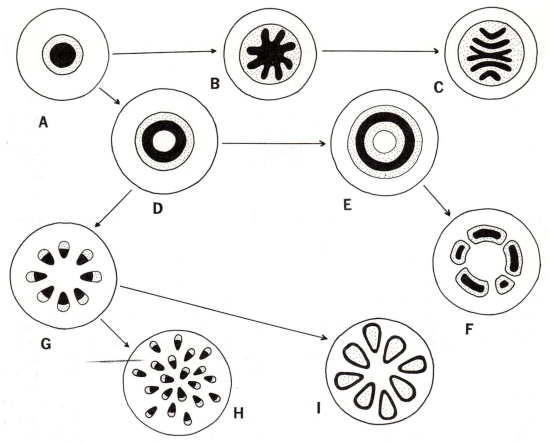

FIGURE 13–2 Probable evolutionary series of the stele. A, protostele; B, actinostele; C, plectostele; D, ecto-phloic siphonostele; E, amphiphloic siphonostele (solenostele); F, dictyostele; G, eustele; H, atactostele, collateral bundles; I, atactostele, amphivasal bundles; ×3. xylem solid; phloem stippled.

of the basic organ systems is sometimes greatly reduced. For example, the leaves of *Equisetum* are scale-like and those of most cacti are reduced to spines (Fig. 16–11). The stems of *Welwitschia* and the dandelion are also very short, barely distinguishable as narrow regions between the roots and leaves.

Vascular plants range from the tiny *Wolffia* (water-meal), with a size range of 0.7 to 1.5 millimeters, to *Sequoiadendron* (big tree of California), which grows to over 90 meters in height and over 10 meters in diameter at the base. Vascular plants include aquatics such as *Elodea,* terrestrial herbs such as some grasses and composites, woody shrubs, and trees that are predominantly woody. In general, the struc-

ture is related to the ratio of secondary to primary tissues developed in the plant. The greater the amount of secondary tissue, the woodier the plant. Most of the supporting strength in the plant is provided by the impregnated walls of secondary xylem, sclerenchyma, and periderm—all secondary tissues particularly well developed in shrubs and trees.

Vascular plants have a wide geographic distribution. Their greatest numbers in both species and individuals is in the tropics, gradually diminishing at higher latitudes. In the Northern Hemisphere vascular plants are known to occur in Greenland at 83° N. and in the Himalaya Mountains at altitudes of 6,000 meters. Vascular plants exist in virtually every

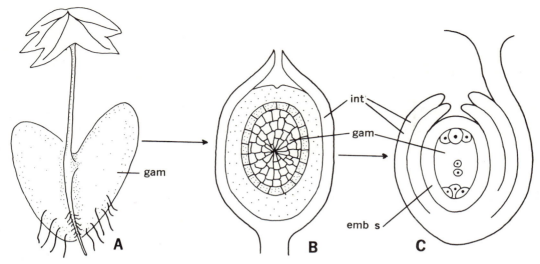

FIGURE 13–3 Hypothetical evolutionary series showing reduction of the gametophyte in vascular plants. A, gametophyte (*gam*) of fern with young sporophyte attached; B, gametophyte of a cycad enclosed by integument (*int*); C, gametophyte of an angiosperm within embryo sac (*emb s*).

type of habitat except extreme deserts and regions with permanent snow and ice. Most are essentially terrestrial, although some inhabit fresh water, and still fewer grow in brackish or marine conditions. Some species have wide ecological tolerances, whereas others are limited to very specialized conditions.

ECONOMIC IMPORTANCE

Vascular plants play an extremely important part in our economy, especially as sources of food for man and other animals and in pro-

viding building materials and fuel. Vascular plants are important also in soil conservation and wild life management. Other uses are found in the textiles industry (cotton); pharmaceuticals (atropine, digitalis, and others); and horticulture (landscaping, floral arrangements, botanical gardens). The conifers supply most timber, pulp and paper, and naval stores (chiefly resin and turpentine); several species are being widely cultivated where they are not indigenous to provide sources for these materials. The flowering plants are the main sources for food, pharmaceuticals, and horticultural plants, and are undoubtedly the most important group of plants for man.

14 / Division Psilophyta

Included in the *psilopsid* division are the Psilotales, represented only by living plants, and the Psilophytales, known only from the fossil record. Approximately 400 million years separate the occurrences of the two orders, and on this basis some botanists argue that they can hardly be closely related. However, some very close morphological and anatomical similarities exist among the plants of the two orders. Thus, the orders can conveniently be classified within the same division, with the reservation that plants of the two taxa may not be phylogenetically related.

Order Psilophytales. The plants of this order are known only from the Devonian Period. They are important components of Lower and Middle Devonian floras on several continents—particularly North America, Europe, and Northern Asia. As far as is known, the psilophytes became extinct either in the late Middle or early Upper Devonian. Until recent years, they were considered to be the simplest and most primitive of all vascular plants, and to have been the ancestral stock from which the other groups of vascular plants evolved. However, present evidence indicates that early representatives of the other groups existed along with them so that the psilophytes represent a closed evolutionary avenue. But there is no doubt that they are both simple and early vascular plants.

The most completely known psilophytes are two genera of plants discovered from the Rhynie chert in Aberdeenshire, Scotland, and reported by Kidston and Lang from 1917 to 1921. The plants were petrified in the chert and show very complete external and internal detail.

The best known of these early vascular plants is *Rhynia,* two species of which have been described (Fig. 14–1A). As reconstructed, the plant consists of a rhizome with rhizoids, and aerial stems that attain 50 centimeters in height and up to 6 millimeters in diameter. The stem branches dichotomously and is leafless. The sporangia are borne terminally on some of the dichotomies.

The aerial stem consists of an epidermis with stomata, a cortex divided into a wide inner region containing lacunae, and a narrow outer zone with larger cells (Fig. 14–1B). The stele is central, consisting of a solid cylinder of tracheids with annular thickenings and surrounded by elongate cells that probably functioned as phloem, although sieve areas have not been observed (Fig. 14–1C). No endodermis has been identified. The presence of stomata suggests that photosynthesis occurred in the stem.

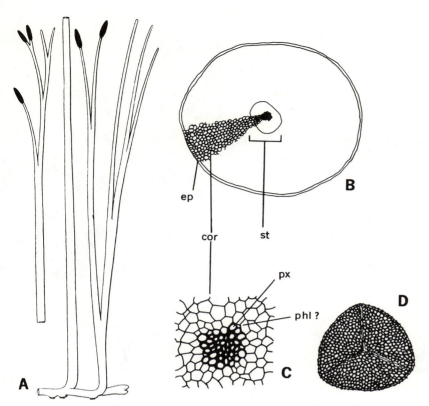

FIGURE 14–1   *Rhynia major.* A, reconstruction of habit, showing rhizome, dichotomous branching, and terminal sporangia, ×0.2; B, transverse section of stem, showing stele, cortex, and epidermis, ×9; C, transverse section of stele, showing exarch protoxylem, ×40; D, single spore with reticulate ornamentation and trilete tetrad scar, ×400. *cor,* cortex; *ep,* epidermis; *phl ?,* questionable phloem; *px,* protoxylem, *st,* stele. (After Kidston and Lang with permission of the Royal Society of Edinburgh.)

The sporangia, cylindrical and separated from the stem by a narrow constriction, range up to 12 millimeters in length and 4 millimeters in diameter. The sporangial wall consists of a cutinized epidermal layer and several inner layers of thin-walled cells. There is no structure for dehiscence. The spores vary from 35 to 65 microns in diameter and have a thick wall and a coarsely granular to reticulate ornamentation (Fig. 14–1D).

The discovery and reconstruction of *Rhynia* and several other fossil plants with similar features has suggested to botanists that the psilophyte, as exemplified by *Rhynia,* is indeed the simplest type of vascular plant. Such features as a protostelic rhizome with rhizoids,

dichotomous branching, absence of true leaves, and terminal sporangia have generally been regarded as what should be expected of simple vascular plants that evolved from aquatic ancestors. In consequence, many have accepted *Rhynia* and other psilophytes as the most primitive vascular plants, and as the stock or group from which all other vascular plants evolved. This concept has dominated evolutionary thinking on vascular plants for over 40 years, and is largely responsible for several of the proposed natural classifications. The discovery of spores and the re-evaluation of early fossils have indicated that representatives of the other major groups of vascular plants are at least as old as and probably even older than the psilophytes.

DIVISION PSILOPHYTA

FIGURE 14–2 Stems and branches of *Psilotum,* showing dichotomous branching, ×0.48.

As a result, some students of Devonian floras emphasize that while the psilophytes are admittedly simple, they are not necessarily or even probably primitive. Thus, they probably represent a group of vascular plants that evolved independently and became extinct during Devonian times.

Order Psilotales. This order comprises two genera, *Psilotum* and *Tmesipteris.* Both are known only as extant plants, although they do have some morphological and anatomical features similar to the psilophytes.

Morphology. The plant body consists of underground stems covered with rhizoids. The rhizomes extend above ground into aerial stems that are green and dichotomously branched (Fig. 14–2). In *Psilotum,* aerial stems range in length to 25 centimeters or more with numerous dichotomies. Scale-like emergences are scattered in a spiral arrangement around the stem. Since these are without veins, some botanists do not consider them true leaves. In *Tmesipteris*

FIGURE 14–3 Branch of *Tmesipteris,* showing spirally arranged leaves and several sporangia, ×1.45.

(Fig. 14–3), the stem is usually unbranched, although some stems have a single dichotomy. Leaves are arranged spirally, and inserted longitudinally rather than transversely on the stem. Each leaf is long and narrow, bears stomata, and has a single vein. Both genera have a well-defined cuticle on stem and leaves.

A transverse section of the stem of both *Psilotum* and *Tmesipteris* reveals a central stele surrounded by cortex and epidermis. The xylem of the rhizome in both genera comprises a solid core of scalariform tracheids, surrounded by elongated cells with thickened corners which apparently function as phloem. In aerial stems, the xylem occurs as separate bundles around a central pith consisting mainly of thick-walled sclerenchymatous cells. In both genera, the protoxylem consists of annular and helical tracheids, whereas all the metaxylem tracheids are scalariform.

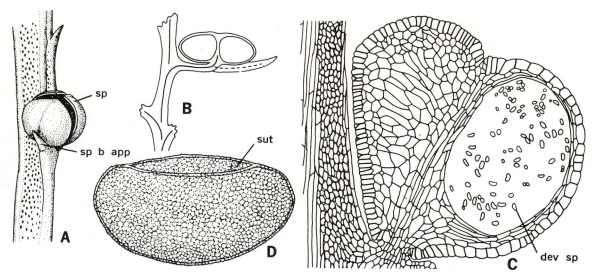

FIGURE 14–4 Reproductive organs of Psilotales. A, single sporangium of *Psilotum* subtended by sporangia-bearing appendage, ×2; B, vertical section through sporangium and appendage of *Tmesipteris*, showing vascular bundle entering sporangium, ×2; C, vertical section through sporangium of *Psilotum*, showing developing spores in one locule, ×20; D, single spore of *Psilotum*, showing a single longitudinal suture and the faint reticulate ornamentation, ×500. *dev sp*, developing spores; *sp b app*, spore-bearing appendage; *sp*, sporangia; *sut*, suture. (B, from *Morphology of Vascular Plants; Lower Groups*, by A. J. Eames, copyright © 1936, used with permission of McGraw-Hill Book Company.)

Spore-Bearing Organs. In *Psilotum,* some of the leaf-like emergences in upper regions of the stem are replaced by sporangia-bearing appendages (Fig. 14–4A). Although the exact nature of the fertile appendage is in doubt, some consider it to be a very short axis bearing two leaf-like emergences and three fused sporangia at the tip. In *Tmesipteris* the spore-bearing appendage is similar, but usually consists of only two fused sporangia at the tip of a short lateral branch with two leaves (Fig. 14–4B).

At maturity each sporangium consists of an outer wall of several layers of cells (Fig. 14–4C). The central region contains spore mother cells interspersed with parenchyma cells that act as a nutrient source for the developing spores and are completely used up by the time the sporangia split open.

Since the meiospores of *Psilotum* and *Tmesipteris* are of only one size, the plants are said to be homosporous. In both genera the spores are kidney-shaped and vary in length from 50 to 80 microns (Fig. 14–4D). The thick spore wall is faintly reticulate and has a single longitudinal suture on the concave surface where the spore attaches to the other three in the tetrad.

Prothallus. Spores germinate directly into prothallia if conditions are suitable. The young prothallus develops initially inside the spore wall but soon emerges, usually through the suture. When mature, the prothallus is cylindrical, several millimeters long, and completely infected with mycorrhizal fungal hyphae. The sex organs are antheridia and archegonia (Fig. 14–5A) that develop from superficial cells of the prothallus. Both sex organs can be observed with a hand lens, but internal detail can be noted only in microscopic section. Antheridia are globular, consisting of an outer layer of sterile jacket cells and a central mass of spermatogenous cells that eventually develop into sperms. Each sperm is coiled and covered with many flagella. Upon maturation, a single opercular cell of the antheridium splits open, and the flagellated sperms escape to swim to the archegonia.

DIVISION PSILOPHYTA

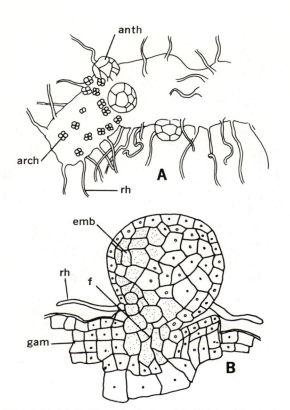

FIGURE 14–5 Gametophytes of Psilotales. A, part of prothallus of *Tmesipteris*, showing rhizoids, archegonia, and antheridia, ×12; B, embryo of *Tmesipteris*, showing foot (*f*) extending into gametophyte, and several rhizoids, ×50. *anth*, antheridia; *arch*, archegonia; *emb*, embryo; *gam*, gametophyte; *rh*, rhizoid. (A, after Lawson with permission of the Royal Society of Edinburgh; B, after Holloway with permission of the Royal Society of New Zealand.)

Embryo. The zygote divides first at right angles to the long axis of the archegonium. The upper daughter cell subsequently divides to form the juvenile stem, whereas the lower gives rise to a mass of parenchyma called the foot (Fig. 14–5B). As in the bryophytes, the foot absorbs food material from the prothallus and supplies it to the developing embryonic shoot. The first-formed branches usually develop directly into rhizomes, whereas later branches mature into aerial parts of the stem. When the young sporophyte becomes nutritionally inde-

pendent of the gametophyte, the foot degenerates.

Distribution and Ecology. The two species of *Psilotum* occur in tropical and subtropical regions of both hemispheres. One species ranges as far north as South Carolina in North America and Japan in Asia, and as far south as Australia and New Zealand. *Psilotum* normally grows on humus-rich soil in moist shaded habitats, but is sometimes epiphytic on shrubs and trees. The commoner species (*P. nudum*) is relatively easy to grow in a greenhouse if kept in a moist atmosphere.

Tmesipteris is limited to southern and eastern Australia, New Zealand, the Philippines, and some islands of Polynesia. It also thrives in damp and shaded habitats, and is epiphytic largely on tree ferns.

Relationships

Some botanists have considered *Psilotum* and *Tmesipteris* an extant group descended from the strictly fossil psilophytes. Evidence for this evolutionary relationship includes similarity of such characteristics as rhizomes with rhizoids; dichotomous branching; true leaves absent or rudimentary; sporangia terminal on branches; and protostelic vascular strands. If such a relationship is valid, it means that descendants of the Devonian psilophytes have persisted through some 400 million years without a fossil trace, a possibility that many botanists find difficult to accept.

Another interpretation is that *Psilotum* and *Tmesipteris* are the result of reduction from other groups, such as the lycopods, arthrophytes, and ferns. The most recent view is that the fertile appendage of *Psilotum* may have been derived by reduction from an ancestor bearing terminal sporangia on a dichotomously branched lateral shoot, such as in the Devonian pre-fern *Protopteridium*.

15 / Division Lycophyta

Plants in this division are usually referred to as *lycopods*. They have one of the oldest histories among vascular plants, dating certainly from the early Devonian. The fossil record indicates that several evolutionary lines existed within the group, and that in the Carboniferous the lycopods were among the largest and most numerous plants. After the Carboniferous, the large tree-like lycopods disappeared, and the group as a whole declined in relative importance among vascular plants.

With the exception of the early members of Devonian times, the lycopods can be classified in five orders. Three of these have living representatives—Lycopodiales, Selaginellales, and Isoetales. The other two, Lepidodendrales and Pleuromeiales, are known only from the fossil record.

GENERAL MORPHOLOGY

All of the extant plants in this division have true roots, stems, and leaves. Many have rhizophores with adventitious roots. Aerial portions of the stem show branching ranging from dichotomous to monopodial. Some have creeping stems.

In most lycopods, the leaves are arranged spirally and are very small. Each leaf contains a single vein that does not form a leaf gap at the point of emergence from the stele within the stem. Such leaves are microphyllous.

Sporangia are borne either in the axils or on the adaxial surfaces of more or less specialized leaves, the sporophylls. Sporophylls and sporangia of some lycopods are localized in terminal strobili or cones, whereas sporophylls of others resemble ordinary leaves. Some lycopods are homosporous, whereas others having spores of two sizes are heterosporous. In the heterosporous plants, the megaspores (large) germinate endosporally to form female gametophytes, while the microspores also develop endosporally into male gametophytes.

EARLY LYCOPODS

The earliest plant that exhibits undoubted lycopod characteristics is *Baragwanathia longifolia*, discovered in rocks of early Devonian Age in Australia (Fig. 15–1A, B). The plant consists of dichotomously branching stems closely covered by spirally arranged leaves. The leaves measure 0.5 to 1 millimeters in width

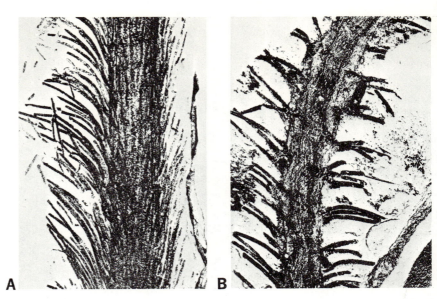

FIGURE 15–1 *Baragwanathia*. A, fragment of stem, showing crowded strap-shaped leaves, ×0.4; B, closer view of stem and leaves with several sporangia in axils, ×0.7 (After Lang and Cookson with permission of the Royal Society of London.)

and up to 4 centimeters in length. Each has a single vascular trace. On some regions of the stems, kidney-shaped sporangia are found in the axils of apparently unmodified leaves. It has not yet been determined whether the sporangia are attached to the stem or to the upper leaf surface. The vascular tissue consists of an exarch protostele, having 12 arms of primary xylem with annular tracheids.

Another genus that possesses lycopod characteristics has been found in rocks of Lower Devonian age. This is *Drepanophycus* (Fig. 15–2A). As reconstructed, it exhibits dichotomous branches arising from a rhizome. Short flattened leaves are arranged spirally around the stem. Each leaf contains a single vein. Some of the leaves bear sporangia on the upper surface, generally midway between the base and tip of the leaf.

Finally, a third plant with lycopod characteristics, *Protolepidodendron,* has been found in rocks of the Lower and Middle Devonian (Fig. 15–2B). It is similar to *Drepanophycus* but bears closely spaced leaves spirally arranged on the dichotomous stem. Each leaf is forked at the tip. Some of the leaves bear sporangia

on the upper surface, as in *Drepanophycus.* The xylem in one species is triangular, with mesarch protoxylem; but it is 16-pointed and exarch in another.

The characteristics of these three early plants are remarkably like those of some species of the modern genus *Lycopodium.* This has led some investigators to suggest that ancestors of *Lycopodium* were in existence very early in the history of vascular plants, and that there has been virtually no structural modification in this line since that time.

Order Lepidodendrales. During the Carboniferous, some of the lycopods reached tree stature. They were among the dominant elements of the forests that formed the vegetation of widespread coal swamps. These large lycopods are classified in the Lepidodendrales, an order known only from fossils of late Devonian to early Permian.

The best-known plant of this group is *Lepidodendron* (literally, scale tree). *Lepidodendron* consists of a columnar trunk with a crown of branches at the top (Fig. 15–3). In some specimens, the trunk exceeds 35 meters in

VASCULAR PLANTS

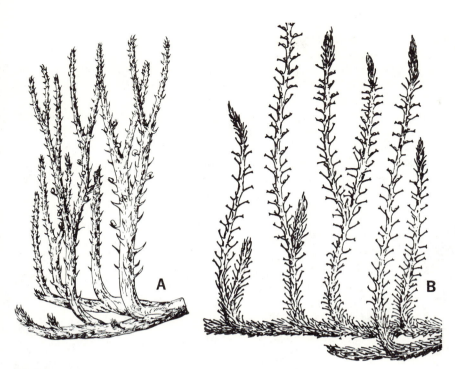

FIGURE 15–2   Early lycopods of the Devonian. A, *Drepanophycus* with dichotomous branching, flattened leaves with sharp tips, and sporangia on sporophylls in upper reaches of stem, ×1.6; B, *Protolepidodendron,* showing prostrate and upright dichotomous stems, forked leaves, and sporangia on adaxial surface of sporophylls, ×0.5. (A, after Kräusel and Weyland with permission of *Palaeontographica;* B, after Kräusel and Weyland, 1935.)

length and 1 meter in diameter. The branches of the crown are formed by dichotomous division, but the dichotomies are not always equal. Leaves are long, grass-like, and confined to the terminal regions of the end branches. Leaf cushions left behind on older regions of the stem form a very characteristic pattern on the outside of the trunk and branches. Reproductive organs consist of sporangia in cones borne on outer branches among the leaves.

Stems.   The stem consists of a relatively narrow vascular cylinder surrounded by a two-zone cortex, both contained within a relatively thick periderm that provided most of the support for the trunk. The cambium of the periderm is located on the extreme outside of the stem among the leaf bases. Periderm development was toward the inside, or centripetal, and hence did not disrupt the characteristic leaf cushions.

The rhomboidal leaf cushions (Fig. 15–4) occur in spiral rows around the stem. Each cushion contains the scars of a single vein flanked by two parichnos (Fig. 15–5). The parichnos, which may have served in aeration, are channels of parenchyma cells which connected the leaf and stem, and hence with the underground axes *Stigmaria.*

Leaves.   Each leaf contains a single vein down the center of the blade. The vein is continuous with the leaf trace of the stem and departs from the primary xylem without leaving a leaf gap. In the blade, the vein consists of a central core of xylem surrounded by cells that probably functioned as phloem. Outside the phloem is a region of tracheid-like cells, called transfusion tissue, which probably acted in transferring water and dissolved nutrients from the central vein to the outer tissues.

DIVISION LYCOPHYTA

Cones. The Lepidodendrales have sporangia and sporophylls aggregated into cones which are usually slender and cylindrical (Fig. 15–6). Some are attached by a short stalk to the stem, others are sessile. Some specimens have a length of over 30 centimeters and a width exceeding 45 millimeters but most are much smaller. The cone consists of a central axis, bearing sporophylls in a spiral arrangement. Each sporophyll is shield-shaped, turning upward at the tip. A single sporangium is attached to the upper surface of the sporophyll, and a small enation called the ligule is attached to the sporophyll a short distance distally from the sporangium. The ligule, also present on the leaves, is apparently restricted to most of the heterosporous lycopods.

Most species are heterosporous, bearing microspores and megaspores in different sporangia in the same cone. In general, microsporangia are concentrated on sporophylls toward the top of the cone, and the megasporangia toward the base.

In a related cone genus, *Lepidocarpon,* specialized structures have been compared with those of a seed (Fig. 15–7). In the cone, the sporophyll encloses the sporangium except for a narrow micropyle-like slit at one end. A single megaspore developed within the sporangium.

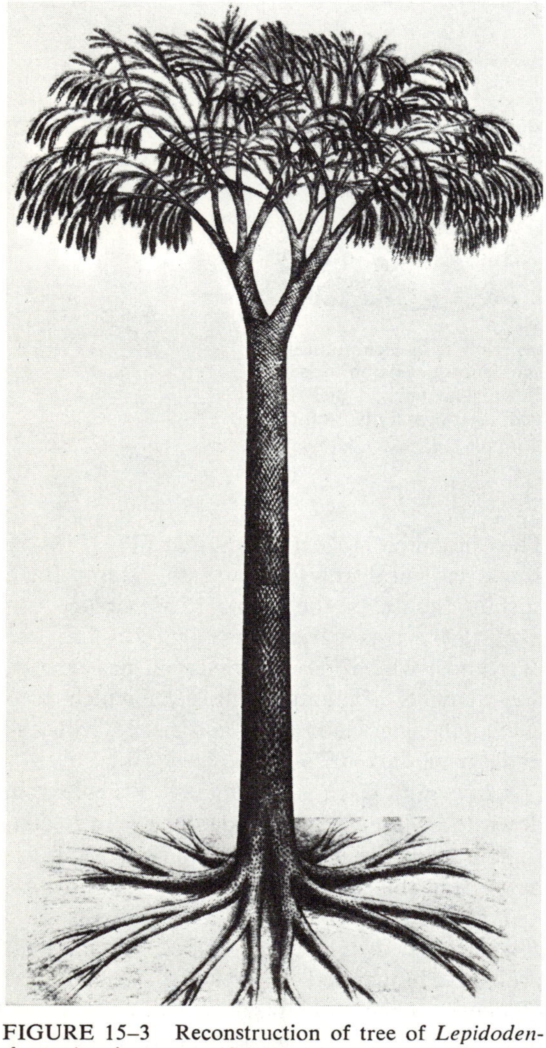

268

FIGURE 15–3 Reconstruction of tree of *Lepidodendron,* showing roots (*Stigmaria*), columnar stem, unequally dichotomous branching, and leafy twigs. (After Hirmer with permission of R. Oldenbourg.)

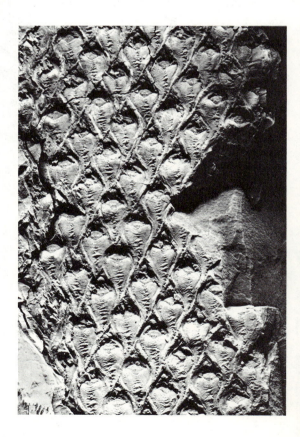

FIGURE 15–4 Part of branch of *Lepidodendron,* showing rhomboidal leaf cushions in oblique rows, ×2.

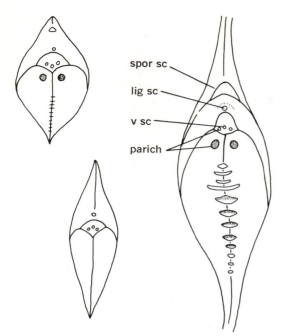

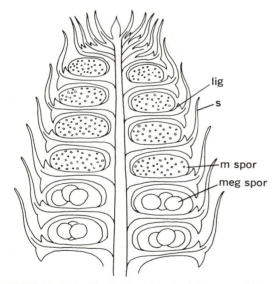

FIGURE 15–5 Leaf cushions of three different species of *Lepidodendron*, showing details of structure. *lig sc*, ligule scar; *parich*, parichnos; *spor sc*, sporangial scar; *v sc*, vascular bundle scar. (After Zeiller.)

FIGURE 15–6 Vertical section through cone of *Lepidostrobus*, showing segregation of micro- and megasporangia on different sporophylls. *lig*, ligule; *m spor*, microsporangium; *meg spor*, megasporangium; *s*, sporophyll. (After R. Zeiller, "Etudes sur le *Lepidostrobus brownii* (Unger) Schimper," *Mém. Acad. Sci.*, Tome 52, 2ème sér., 1914.)

The envelopment of the megasporangium by the sporophyll is similar to the enclosure of a female sporangium by an integument in those plants producing true seeds—e.g., the gymnosperms. Although the two organs are not truly homologous, the reproductive unit of *Lepidocarpon* probably functioned as a seed.

Another genus of tree-sized lycopods abundant during the Carboniferous is *Sigillaria*. In general habit, it is very similar to *Lepidodendron*. The main distinguishing characteristic is the pattern of leaf cushions. In *Sigillaria*, the oval or round cushions are spirally arranged around the stem but are aligned in vertical rows.

Phylogeny. The Lepidodendrales apparently arose during the latter half of the Devonian and increased in abundance and complexity during the Carboniferous. They appear to have reached a peak during the Upper Carboniferous (Pennsylvanian) and then declined very noticeably during the Permian. By the end of Permian times, the lepidodendrids were virtually extinct. It is believed that a prime factor in this dramatic decline was the profound change in world climate. Although it is generally held that the lepidodendrids represent the end of a line of lycopod evolution which culminated in an arborescent habit, a link is sometimes suggested between the Carboniferous *Sigillaria* mentioned above and a Triassic plant, *Pleuromeia*, described under the next order.

Order Pleuromeiales. This order is best represented by the genus *Pleuromeia* from Triassic rocks of Germany. *Pleuromeia* consists of a columnar and unbranched stem that reaches at least 2 meters in height and 9 centimeters in diameter (Fig. 15–8). The base of the stem expands into four or more lobes that support numerous rootlets. Leaves are attached spirally around the stem, and reach 11 centimeters in length and 1.5 centimeters in width. Each leaf bears a ligule and has two veins running full length. As in the lepidodendrids, the leaves were apparently shed from older regions as the stem grew in height.

The reproductive structures are borne in a cone at the tip of the stem. The plant is hetero-

269

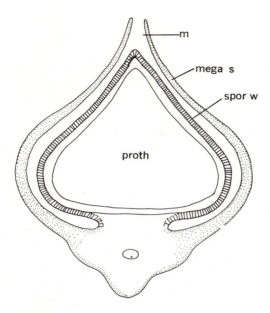

FIGURE 15–7 Vertical section through "seed" of *Lepidocarpon,* showing spore wall (*spor w*) surrounding prothallus (*proth*), megasporophyll (*mega s*), and micropyle (*m*), ×4. (From D. H. Scott, *Studies in Fossil Botany,* Adam & Charles Black, Ltd., London.)

270

sporous, with the sporangia deeply embedded in the sporophylls. The megasporangia are large and contain trilete megaspores ranging from 500 to 700 microns. The microsporangia are relatively small and carry many trilete microspores measuring between 15 and 25 microns.

Another genus, *Nathorstiana,* is often placed in this order. It has been found only in the Lower Cretaceous, and hence is younger than *Pleuromeia. Nathorstiana* is small and consists of an erect and unbranched stem up to 20 centimeters in length (Fig. 15–9). Roots occur at the bottom and emerge from ridges on the axis. No reproductive structures have been found. In size and structure *Nathorstiana* has been compared with the living *Isoetes,* and is believed by some to be a direct ancestor of the modern genus.

Order Isoetales. This order of lycopods contains two living genera, *Isoetes* and *Stylites.* The history of *Isoetes* goes back to the Lower Cretaceous, and extends through Upper Cre-

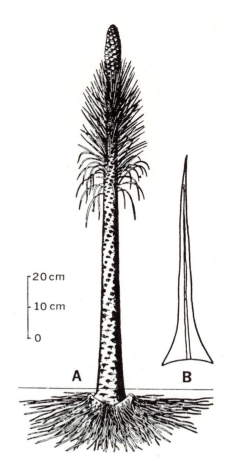

FIGURE 15–8 A, reconstruction of *Pleuromeia,* showing rootstock and roots, columnar stem, and leaves and cone toward top; B, single leaf. (A, after Hirmer with permission of *Palaeontographica;* B, after Mägdefrau, "Zur Morphologie und Phylogenetischen Bedeutung der Fossilen Pflanzengattung *Pleuromeia,*" *Beihefte Botanisches Centralblatt,* Vol. 48, 1931.)

taceous and Tertiary times to the present. *Stylites,* known only from existing plants, was first described in 1957 from specimens found growing around lake margins high in the mountains of Peru. Both genera are structurally reduced when compared with other lycopods, and are believed to represent stages of reduction in an evolutionary series *Pleuromeia–Nathorstiana–Stylites–Isoetes.*

Isoetes. One of the most distinctive vascular plants, *Isoetes* consists of a thick mass of tubular to strap-shaped leaves borne in a rosette on a very short stem (Fig. 15–10). In this habit it resembles a small onion. It grows submerged in shallow water, on the margins of ponds or lakes, on muddy river banks, or in wet meadows. Over 50 species have been described. The genus, widely distributed in temperate latitudes, is rare in the tropics.

A closer examination of *Isoetes* reveals a stem with either two or four lobes (Fig. 15–12A). The stem is very short, bears dichotomously branching roots between the lobes, and grows from both an apical and a basal meristem.

The arrangement of tissues within the stem is unique (Fig. 15–11). A core of primary xylem in the central region consists of tracheids interspersed with parenchyma. This core is surrounded by a very thin layer of primary phloem. As in other lycopods, leaf traces depart from the vascular cylinder and leave no leaf gaps.

The leaves are borne in a spiral arrangement around the top of the stem (Fig. 15–12A). Each leaf is attached by a broad base and tapers toward a point. A ligule develops on the adaxial surface (Fig. 15–12B), as in *Lepidodendron, Pleuromeia,* and most other heterosporous lycopods. A central vein runs the length of the leaf and is flanked on each side by parenchymatous canals. These have been compared with the parichnos canals of the *Lepidodendron* leaf. Air chambers characteristic of submerged aquatic plants are located in the mesophyll. These appear to function in both gas exchange and flotation.

A mature plant of *Isoetes* usually possesses three sets of leaf-like organs around the top of the stem. The outer layers of leaves normally

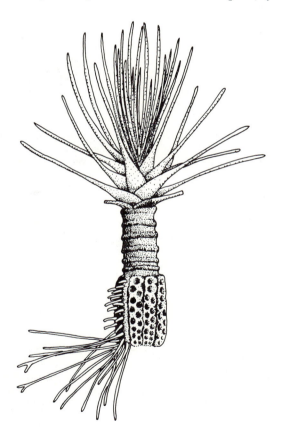

FIGURE 15–9 Reconstruction of *Nathorstiana,* showing rootstock, very short stem, and spiral collar of leaves, ×0.5. (After Mägdefrau, "Über *Nathorstiana,* eine Isoetacee aus dem Neokom von Quedinburg a. Harz," *Beihefte Botanisches Centralblatt,* Vol. 49, 1932.)

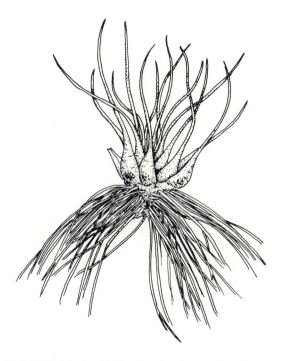

FIGURE 15–10 Habit sketch of *Isoetes,* showing leaves, stem, and roots, ×1.

DIVISION LYCOPHYTA

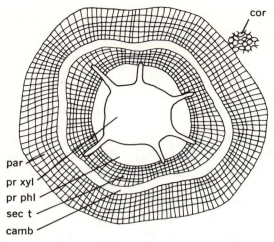

FIGURE 15–11 Transverse section of stem of *Isoetes,* showing inner core of primary xylem (*pr xyl*) surrounded by primary phloem (*pr phl*); cambium (*camb*)—the clear area— with secondary tissue (*sec.t*) on inside, secondary parenchyma (*par*) and cortex (*cor*) on outside, ×5.

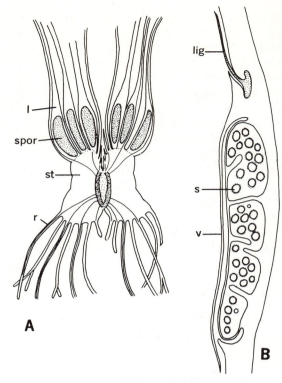

FIGURE 15–12 *Isoetes.* A, vertical section through sporophylls and stem (*st*), showing leaves (*l*), sporangia (*spor*), vascular core in stem, and attachment of roots (*r*), ×2; B, vertical section through single sporophyll, showing ligule (*lig*), velum (*v*), and spores (*s*), ×15. (A, from *Morphology of Vascular Plants; Lower Groups,* by A. J. Eames, copyright © 1936, used by permission of McGraw-Hill Book Company; B, from *Plant Morphology* by A. W. Haupt, copyright © 1953, used by permission of McGraw-Hill Book Company.

bear megasporangia and hence are megasporophylls. These in turn enclose whorls of microsporophylls. The central appendages are usually immature leaves that often bear abortive sporangia.

Stylites. This genus, with two species, closely resembles *Isoetes* (Fig. 15–13). It consists of a cylindrical stem that branches dichotomously at least three times, resembling a candelabra. Rosettes of strap-shaped leaves girdle the apex of each branch of the stem. The roots are formed around the lower end of the stem, and have trace connections with the central stele. A most remarkable feature is the attachment of the sporangia far above the base of the sporophyll. The sporangia have trabeculae similar to those of *Isoetes.*

Phylogeny. The two genera of the Isoetales are among the most distinctive of all vascular plants. Typical lycopods, they are microphyllous and have adaxial sporangia on sporophylls. The very small stems are usually interpreted as examples of extreme reduction, most likely from ancestors such as *Pleuromeia* and *Nathorstiana.* In showing some axillary extension and dichotomy, *Stylites* appears to be less reduced than *Isoetes.*

Order Selaginellales. This order of lycopods has both fossil and living representatives. The extant plants are all included in the genus *Selaginella.* The fossil genus is *Selaginellites,* a name that reflects the close relationship generally believed to exist between fossil and living plants. Indeed, apparently little evolutionary change has occurred in the *Selaginella* line from the very beginning. The ancestors to *Selaginellites* are unknown, but the line can be taken back some 300 million years to the Carboniferous.

Selaginella. This genus, with some 700

272

species, is widely distributed over the earth. Most species live in the wetter tropics, but some exist in temperate regions, and a few are found in extreme climates such as the desert or the subarctic. In general they thrive in wet and shaded sites, but some will tolerate exposed habitats such as rocky cliffs. Some species are cultivated in greenhouses and florist shops, where they are valued for their feathery appearance.

In general, *Selaginella* plants are small and delicate (Fig. 15–14). In most plants, the stems are trailing, although some species grow as erect tufts, and a few are climbers. Branching is usually dichotomous. Some stems reach several meters in length, but most range from several centimeters to several decimeters. The stems, herbaceous and thin, are densely clothed with small leaves. Thus, most *Selaginella* plants resemble mosses, with which they may be confused in the field.

The small and simple leaves vary in outline from round to lanceolate to thread-like (Fig. 15–15A–C). They are arranged spirally, in decussate pairs, or in four longitudinal rows. Most species have two rows of large leaves on the lower surface, and two rows of smaller leaves attached to the upper side. This appears to be a modification of a spiral arrangement, allowing for more efficient interception of light. This same condition is found in some fossil members. Each leaf contains a single vein, consisting of an upper band of xylem with annular and helical tracheids, and a lower column of phloem with sieve cells. The leaf trace departs from the stele of the stem without forming a leaf gap. There is a distinct epidermis, with stomata on both surfaces or sometimes restricted to only one. The mesophyll contains chloroplasts and has large intercellular spaces. In some species, a palisade layer develops beneath the upper surface. The leaves of *Selaginella* are similar to those of the Lepidodendrales, Pleuromeiales, and Isoetales in possessing a ligule. This tongue-shaped projection is formed by the adaxial epidermis near the base of the leaf. Its function is completely unknown, although it may be secretory or help to keep

the stem apex and leaf primordia from drying out during early growth.

The mature stem of *Selaginella* has a well-defined epidermis, cortex, and stele (Fig. 15–16B) which develop from either a single apical cell or a group of initials, depending on the species. The epidermis is one cell thick and does not have stomata. The cortex is composed of large parenchyma cells, and the outer layers often have thickened walls. *Selaginella* differs from most other vascular plants in having a system of air spaces traversed by elongated endodermal cells called trabeculae. These have Casparian strips on the radial wall and link the cortex and vascular tissue across the spaces.

The arrangement of the vascular tissue ranges from protostelic to siphonostelic. Some species have more than one stele and hence are polystelic (Fig. 15–16B). The polysteles extend through the central space, each being attached to the inner cortical wall by trabeculae. Each stele has exarch protoxylem, with metaxylem formed centripetally. Vessels have been reported in some species of *Selaginella*. The xylem is surrounded by several layers of parenchyma, which in turn is surrounded by sieve

273

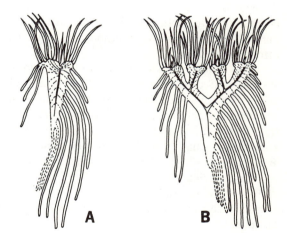

FIGURE 15–13 *Stylites*. A, side view showing disposition of roots and leaves on stem, × 1.3; B, front view showing double dichotomy of stem, × 1.3. (After W. Rauh and H. Falk, "*Stylites* Amstutz eine neue Isöetaceae aus den Hochlanden Perus," *Sitzungsberichte der Heidelberger Akademie der Wissenschaften Mathematisch-Naturwissenschaftliche Klasse*, 1959, No. 1. Abhandlung Heidelberg: Springer, 1959.)

A **B** **C**

FIGURE 15–14 Stems, leaves, and strobili of *Selaginella*, ×1. A, *Selaginella krausiana;* B, *S. wallacei;* C, *S. willdenovii.*

cells of the phloem. The stele is ensheathed by a single layer of parenchyma, from which trabeculae radiate. Both branch and leaf traces depart obliquely from the stele and pass outward through the cortex.

The primary root of the sporeling soon shrivels and dies. The functional roots are all adventitious. Some roots emanate from the underside of the stem. In other instances, the tips of structures called rhizophores—prop-like appendages that grow downward from the branch forks of ascending stems—become rootlike on entering the soil (Fig. 15–16A). Rhizophores are generally interpreted as specialized stems, since occasionally they bear both leaves and cones.

Selaginella is heterosporous, and the sporophylls bearing megasporangia and microsporangia are aggregated into strobili (Fig. 15–17A). In some, the sporophylls are compact, in others very loose. Many species have sporophylls almost identical to sterile leaves, distinguished only by sporangia. Others have sporophylls smaller than sterile leaves, often devoid of chlorophyll. Each sporophyll has a ligule identical to that of the leaf. The sporangia develop from initials that are either on the stem or on the adaxial surface of the sporophyll very near the axil (Fig. 15–17B, C). In some species, lower sporophylls bear mainly megasporangia, whereas upper ones support microsporangia. In others, each type of sporangium occurs in two vertical rows, and in still others, distribution is random.

Several hundred microspores are produced in the microsporangia (Fig. 15–17C). The microspores, subtriangular and trilete, are variously ornamented with granules, spines, and flanges (Fig. 15–17D). They range in size from 30 to 80 microns. The number of megaspores produced per megasporangium is usually four, but as few as one and as many as 40 have been reported (Fig. 15–17B). The megaspores, also subtriangular and trilete, have thick walls, various sculpturing, and range from 150 to 600 microns (Fig. 15–17E).

The gametophytes of both spores develop endosporally. In addition, the gametophytes often mature while the spores are still in their respective sporangia.

In the microspore, the nucleus divides to form a central antheridial initial and a peripheral prothallial cell (Fig. 15–18B). The antheridial initial divides many times, ultimately producing a one-cell-layer jacket that surrounds central spermatogenous cells (Fig. 15–18D). Each of the latter produces a sperm, which is disc-shaped with two anterior flagella. The jacket cells break down at maturity, and the sperms then become free swimming inside the spore wall (Fig. 15–18E). The sperms escape by the splitting of the spores along the commissures of the trilete mark.

The female gametophyte also develops endosporally while the megaspores are within the megasporangium (Fig. 15–19A). The single nucleus divides many times to produce a free nuclear stage. Wall formation around the nuclei continues until the cavity is filled with cells. Archegonia then develop on the outer regions (Fig. 15–19B, C). At this time, the megaspore wall has usually split along the trilete mark, and the prothallus of the gametophyte has protruded. Each archegonium is embedded in the prothallus and consists of four rows of neck cells, one neck canal cell, one ventral canal cell, and one egg. At maturity, the neck canal cells disintegrate, forming a canal through which the flagellated sperms have free access to the egg.

The fertilized egg divides transversely to form an upper and a lower cell. After repeated divisions, the upper cell develops into a suspensor. This is a cylindrical structure that pushes the embryo deeply into the prothallus. The

275

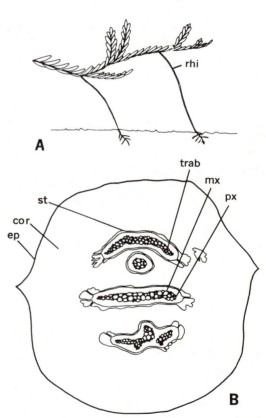

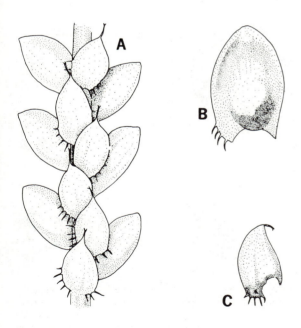

FIGURE 15–15 *Selaginella*. A, section of branch with leaves flattened into four longitudinal rows, ×100; B, single leaf from lateral row, showing broad blade with claw-like emergences, ×15; C, single leaf from upper row with narrow forked appendage at distal end of relatively narrow blade, ×15.

FIGURE 15–16 *Selaginella*. A, branch showing two rhizophores (*rhi*) extending to soil, ×1; B, diagram of transverse section of stem showing epidermis (*ep*), cortex (*cor*), metaxylem (*mx*), protoxylem (*px*), stele (*st*), and trabeculae (*trab*), ×40.

DIVISION LYCOPHYTA

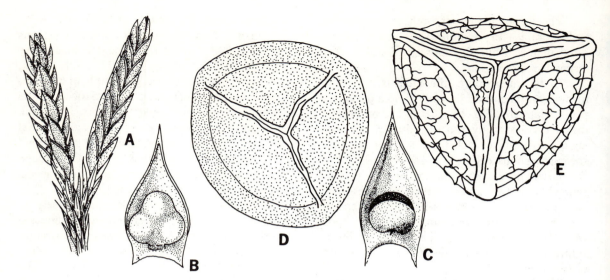

FIGURE 15–17 Reproductive organs of *Selaginella*. A, four-sided strobili at tips of two branches, ×4; B, adaxial surface of single megasporophyll, showing megasporangium with three lobes reflecting three of enclosed megaspores, ×20; C, single microsporophyll with microsporangium split open to show mass of microspores, ×20; D, microspore showing well-defined trilete mark and outer flange on wall, ×100; E, megaspore showing thick wall and thickenings along trilete tetrad scar, ×200.

lower daughter cell matures into the embryo proper. This is oriented transversely, and consists of shoot, foot, and root (Fig. 15–19D). The young sporophyte becomes independent when the developing root eventually is established in the soil, and the stems and leaves become photosynthetically active.

Selaginella is apparently related to the heterosporous lycopods through the following features: microphyllous leaves; stems with dichotomous or pseudomonopodial branching; adventitious roots; sporangia borne adaxially on sporophylls; heterospory; and ligules on both leaves and sporophylls. *Selaginella* is directly linked with the fossil *Selaginellites* by a very close similarity of structure. There appears to be no direct phylogenetic relationship to the *Lepidodendron–Isoetes* line; rather the herbaceous and heterosporous condition in *Selaginellites* appears to have persisted with little modification since at least the Carboniferous. Any ancestors to the *Selaginellites–Selaginella* line should be sought in herbaceous lycopods of the early Carboniferous or perhaps Devonian Periods. It is often assumed that the hetero-

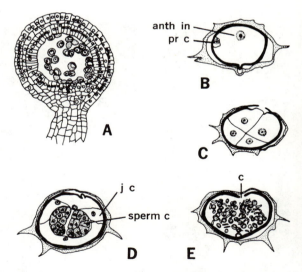

FIGURE 15–18 Male gametophyte development in *Selaginella*. A, vertical section through mature microsporangium, showing wall and developing microspores in tapetal fluid, ×50; B–E, stages in development of microspores, ×500. *anth in,* antheridial initial; *c,* commissure; *j c,* jacket cell; *pr c,* prothallial cell; *sperm c,* spermatogenous cell. (From R. A. Slagg, "The Gametophytes of Selaginella," 1932, Vol. 19, *American Journal of Botany,* with permission of *American Journal of Botany.*)

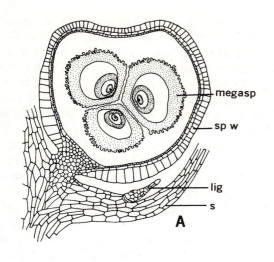

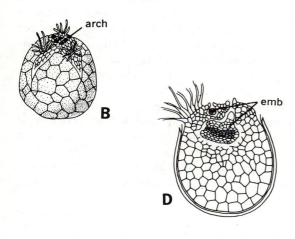

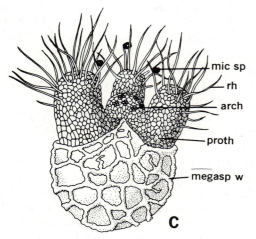

A

megasp

sp w

lig

s

B

arch

D

emb

C

mic sp

rh

arch

proth

megasp w

sporous lycopods evolved from homosporous ancestors through changes in the size of spores and segregation of the sexes. If this assumption is true—and there is no direct fossil evidence to support it—the ancestors to both of the heterosporous lycopod lines could be found in some of the herbaceous and apparently homosporous Devonian plants such as *Drepanophycus* or *Baragwanathia*.

Order Lycopodiales. This order is represented by three genera: *Lycopodium* and *Phylloglossum* are present in extant floras, whereas *Lycopodites* is reserved for fossil members. The plants of this order differ from the other lycopods mainly in being homosporous. In most other respects they are very similar to the Selaginellales, and in many of the fossil specimens, homospory and heterospory are the only criteria that can validly distinguish plants of the Lycopodiales from the Selaginellales.

Lycopodium. The common names for species of this genus are "club moss" and "ground pine," because of superficial resemblances to mosses and pines. *Lycopodium* is world-wide in distribution, but most species are found in the tropics. All are relatively small and herbaceous plants; some are erect and shrubby, whereas others are prostrate and creeping and in some cases subterranean (Fig. 15–20). All species are densely covered with small scalelike leaves. Both epiphytic and terrestrial species are known.

FIGURE 15–19 Development of female gametophyte of *Selaginella*. A, vertical section through megasporangium and three megaspores, ×250; B, single megaspore showing archegonia on slightly protruding gametophyte, ×500; C, prothallus with archegonia protruding from megaspore, showing several microspores trapped on rhizoidal appendages, ×500; D, two embryos developing in archegonia (one on left is in two-celled stage; one on right has developed primordia and foot), ×500. *arch*, archegonia; *emb*, embryo; *lig*, ligule; *megasp*, megaspore; *megasp w*, megaspore wall; *mic sp*, microspores; *proth*, prothallus; *rh*, rhizoids; *s*, sporophyll; *sp w*, megasporangial wall. (A, from *Plant Morphology*, by A. W. Haupt, copyright ©, used with permission of McGraw-Hill Book Company; B–D, after Bruchmann.)

FIGURE 15–20 *Lycopodium*. Branching stem with several cones at branch tips, ×0.8. (Courtesy Chicago Natural History Museum.)

278

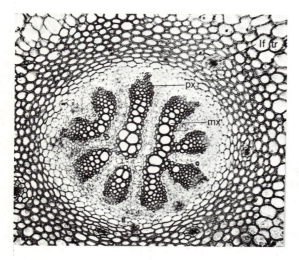

FIGURE 15–21 *Lycopodium*. Transverse sections of stem showing arrangement of xylem and phloem in plectostele, ×50. *lf tr,* leaf trace; *mx,* metaxylem; *px,* protoxylem.

The stem is usually branched dichotomously, although sympodial and pseudomonopodial branching occur in some species. Those with prostrate stems usually have a main branch

with smaller side branches and grow to several meters in length. All stems have a massive apical meristem that differentiates into a well-defined epidermis, cortex, and stele. The epidermis of the stem is one cell thick and bears stomata similar to those of the leaves. The cortex is moderately thick, with sclerenchyma bands in some species. An endodermis is usually developed on the inner face of the cortex, with Casparian strips on the radial walls. The pericycle, located inside the endodermis, varies from three to six layers of parenchyma; this is the usual site for the origin of adventitious roots.

The vascular tissue is quite variable in organization, but the different patterns are generally regarded as variations of a protostele. Furrowing of the vascular cylinder produces several patterns; the most common are the actinostele, with several radiating arms interspersed with parenchyma, and the plectostele, with xylem and phloem split into several to many plates. The xylem is all primary, and the arrangement is exarch. The protoxylem tracheids have annular and helical thickenings; those of the metaxylem are scalariform, or with circular and bordered pits. The phloem consists of sieve cells with oblique end walls and scattered sieve areas interspersed with parenchyma cells.

Leaf traces depart from the protoxylem points of the stele, without leaving a leaf gap, and pass obliquely through the pericycle and cortex into the bases of the leaves. Each leaf has only one trace, which forms the midvein. A transverse section of the stem will usually show many such leaf traces, reflecting the large number of leaves clothing the stem. The leaves of most species are small, usually lanceolate in outline, and broadly attached to the stem. The most common arrangement is spiral, but in some species they are whorled, and in a few they are of two sizes and decussate, as noted in *Selaginella*. The single vein has endarch xylem with spiral tracheids and a small amount of phloem. The whole vein is often ensheathed by an endodermis. The mesophyll contains spongy parenchyma with chloroplasts and generally

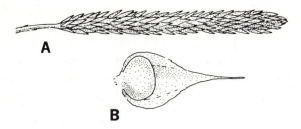

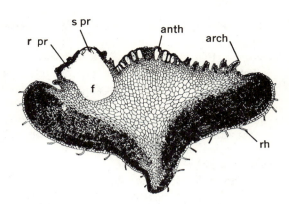

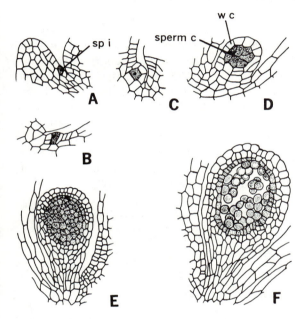

A

B

FIGURE 15–22 *Lycopodium*. A, single strobilus showing spirally arranged sporophylls, ×2; B, adaxial surface of single sporophyll showing sporangium, ×10.

FIGURE 15–24 Vertical section through prothallus of *Lycopodium*, showing rhizoids (*rh*), antheridia (*anth*), archegonia (*arch*), and a single embryo with foot (*f*), root primordium (*r pr*), and stem primordium (*s pr*), ×8. (After Bruchmann.)

FIGURE 15–23 *Lycopodium*. Stages in development of sporangium, from single-cell initial in A to mature stage with spores in F, ×50. *sp i*, sporangial initial; *sperm c*, spermatogenous cells; *w c*, wall cells. (After Bower.)

intercellular spaces. Stomata normally occur on the epidermis of both leaf surfaces, but in some species they are restricted to one side. Epidermal and guard cells usually contain chloroplasts and are covered by a cuticle.

Adventitious roots are common in *Lycopodium*. These roots arise from the pericycle and angle somewhat through the cortex before emerging. In some species, adventitious roots occur regularly on the underside of the stem.

All species of *Lycopodium* are homosporous. The relatively large and reniform sporangia are borne on the adaxial surface of sporophylls, usually close to the axil as in the other extant lycopods. In some species, the sporophylls are green and identical to vegetative leaves (Fig. 15–22B). In others, the sporophylls are pale, reduced to small scales, and aggregated into strobili. The strobili occur at the end of the main stem or on lateral branches and are either sessile or stalked (Fig. 15–22A). Each sporangium is borne on a very short stalk and opens at maturity by a narrow transverse slit (Fig. 15–23), releasing numerous triangular spores.

279

The spores germinate either on or in the soil after remaining dormant for periods ranging from several days to several years. The developing prothallus breaks through the spore along the arms of the trilete mark and becomes established in the soil. The mature gametophyte varies widely with the species but is always small and inconspicuous (Fig. 15–24).

The antheridia and archegonia are borne on the same prothallus, either on the upper surface or at the base of lobes (Fig. 15–24). Antheridia and archegonia are intermingled on the prothalli of some species but segregated into different areas on the same prothallus in others. The antheridia are globose, either completely sunken in the prothallus or slightly protruding (Fig. 15–25A). Each consists of a jacket one cell thick and a central mass of gamete mother cells that mature to produce sperms. Each sperm is fusiform or droplet-shaped and has two or sometimes three flagella at the anterior end (Fig. 15–25B). Sperms escape from the antheridium after the dissolution of a single cell of the jacket.

The archegonia are also sunken, with only the neck protruding. Each consists of three or four rows of neck cells, surrounding one to 13 neck canal cells, and a single ventral canal cell overlying a large egg (Fig. 15–25C). At maturity, the neck cells separate and the canal cells dissolve, allowing passage of the sperms directly to the egg in the venter (Fig. 15–25D).

The fertilized egg divides transversely to the long axis of the oriented archegonium, as in *Selaginella* (Fig. 15–26A). The daughter cell oriented toward the neck divides to form a several-celled suspensor, while the lower daughter cell divides to form the foot and the stem and root primordia (Fig. 15–26B). During development, the young embryo is not pushed very far into the prothallus by the suspensor. Prior to emergence, the embryo has a large foot. The root primordium is on one side; and the stem primordium, with one to several leaf primordia, arises at the opposite pole (Fig. 15–26C). Even after the young sporophyte becomes rooted in the soil, the prothallus often persists for some time before disintegrating.

Lycopodium reproduces vegetatively in several ways. In some species, bulbils or gemmae form annually on new stem tips. These appear to be flattened branch tips with enlarged lateral leaves. They fall to the ground and grow directly into new plants. In other species, the older part of the stem dies off annually, leaving the tips; these act as resting buds and take root the next growing season. In a plant with many branch endings, many new plants are established each year.

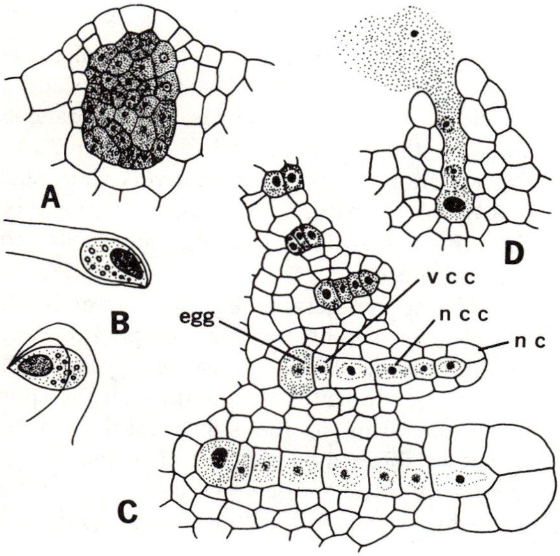

280

FIGURE 15–25 *Lycopodium*. A, immature antheridium showing central spermatogenous cells surrounded by jacket cells, ×50; B, mature sperm cells showing two flagella, ×1,000; C, stages of archegonial maturation with neck cells (*n c*), neck canal cells (*n c c*), ventral canal cells (*v c c*), and egg, ×50; D, mature archegonium which has disrupted prior to fertilization, ×50. (After Bruchmann with permission of *Flora*.)

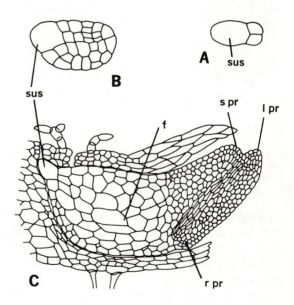

FIGURE 15–26 A–C, stages in development of embryo of *Lycopodium*, ×30. *f*, foot; *l pr*, leaf primordium; *r pr*, root primordium; *s pr*, stem primordium; *sus*, suspensor. (After Bruchmann with permission of *Flora*.)

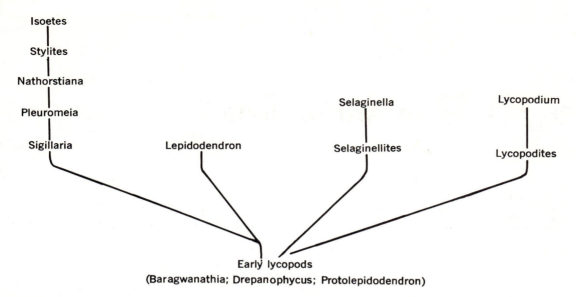

FIGURE 15–27 Graphic representation of probable evolution of three lines of descent in Lycophyta.

In most features, *Lycopodium* is similar to *Selaginella*. Both genera have herbaceous and essentially dichotomous stems, exarch xylem, microphyllous leaves, and adaxial sporangia. The fundamental differences are the homosporous condition and exosporal prothallial development exhibited by *Lycopodium*. As far as can be determined, *Lycopodium* has descended directly from *Lycopodites,* which in turn was possibly derived from some of the earliest lycopods such as *Baragwanathia* or *Drepanophycus*. There appears to have been little structural modification in this line of evolution.

PHYLOGENY

The evidence suggests that three main lines of evolutionary development have occurred in the lycopod division, as shown in Figure 15–27. No attempt is made here to select any particular early lycopod as a stock for one of the probable lines of descent, since evidence for relationships is very meager. However, in spite of this the three lines of evolution are fairly well documented from the fossil record. No doubt future research, particularly on the early lycopods, will shed much light on initial developments of the main lines in the group.

The earliest lycopods all appear to be homosporous. Heterospory probably did not evolve until sometime in the latter part of the Devonian, where megaspores are found dispersed in some plant-bearing rocks. The heterosporous condition appears to have been established independently in both the lepidodendrid–*Isoetes* and the *Selaginellites*–*Selaginella* lines of descent. Homospory, on the other hand, was probably maintained in the *Lycopodites*–*Lycopodium* line from early lycopods.

Two structural modifications would be requisite for establishing heterospory from homospory: the development of two distinct sizes of spore and the segregation of the sex cells— with the antheridia limited to the prothallus of the microspore and the archegonia restricted to the prothallus of the megaspore. It is not known how this transformation was accomplished, or how complex or lengthy it may have been. But heterospory became established in several other groups of vascular plants during their early evolution, indicating that the transformation was not unique to lycopods.

16 / Division Arthrophyta

The plants classified in this division are variously called arthrophytes, sphenopsids, or *articulates*. The last name seems to be most appropriate, because the most striking feature of these plants is the regular jointing of the stem. Together with the whorled arrangement of leaves and branches at the nodes, this jointing makes the group distinctive among vascular plants.

Arthrophyta is an ancient division of plants, with the first record in the early Devonian. As with the lycopods, the articulates were more diversified and numerous during the late Paleozoic than in later times. The division is usually subdivided into five orders: the Hyeniales, Pseudoborniales, Sphenophyllales, Calamitales, and Equisetales. Except for the Equisetales, all of the plants are known only from the fossil record. Again like the lycopods, several well-defined lines of evolution can be traced from the early Devonian representatives through the Carboniferous, where they reached a peak. This was followed by a general decline to the present time, when the genus *Equisetum* is the sole representative.

GENERAL MORPHOLOGY

With the exception of the earliest genera, plants of the Arthrophyta have true roots, stems, and leaves. As far as is known, the stem is herbaceous in all but the Calamitales of the late Devonian and Carboniferous; plants of this order have a decidedly woody habit due to the formation of secondary tissue. Again in all but the earliest genera, the stem is characterized by joints or nodes which occur at regular intervals throughout the length. The branches and leaves are arranged in whorls at the nodes. The leaves of the articulates vary from extremely small scale-like emergences to moderately large flat blades; roots are known only in a few instances and appear to be adventitious in most genera.

Reproductive organs in the early members consist of sporangia situated terminally on short lateral branches. In the later groups, the sporangia are produced on special structures called sporangiophores; these are always compacted into cones, with or without interspersed sterile bracts. Both homospory and heterospory are known in the division, but heterospory is apparently most common.

Much of our information on anatomy, gametophytes, and embryos has come from detailed investigations of the extant *Equisetum*. However, some excellent anatomical detail has also been discovered in fossil members, particularly of some genera of the Calamitales and Sphenophyllales. Together, the information obtained has given some insight into the relationships of various genera, and we have a relatively good picture of the phylogeny of the articulates.

Order Hyeniales. This order is represented by two main genera, *Hyenia* and *Calamophyton* from the early and mid-Devonian on several continents. The two are somewhat different, but show several features indicating that they represent early members of the Arthrophyta.

Hyenia. Reconstructions of *Hyenia* indicate numerous erect branches emerging from the upper surface of a rhizome (Fig. 16–1). Roots extend downward on the opposite side in at least one species. The upright shoots bear lateral branches, both sterile and fertile. The sterile branches fork dichotomously several times and terminate in narrow tips that point outward. The fertile appendages are also branched dichotomously and bear sporangia on tips bent in toward the axis. *Hyenia* lacks a jointed stem but shows a closer affiliation with other articulates in having whorled leaves and sporangia.

Calamophyton. Some extremely fine compressions of this plant have been discovered and have yielded excellent reconstructions (Fig. 16–2). The stem consists of a main axis with lower branches forming at one point in a digitate manner. Successive branchings occur dichotomously or monopodially. Some parts of the main stem bear transverse bands. Although these bands superficially resemble joints or nodes, they do not bear whorls of branches or leaves as do the joints of other orders of articulates, and hence they are not generally credited as true nodes.

Both sterile and fertile appendages are borne laterally on the stem. The sterile appendages reach up to 10 millimeters in length and branch two to four times dichotomously. Each branch terminates in notched, somewhat flattened lobes; these are generally believed to be homologous with leaves (Fig. 16–3). Each fertile branch is divided into an upper and a lower branch (Fig. 16–4). In turn, each of these bears three side branches, and each side branch terminates in two sporangia. Thus, 12

FIGURE 16–1 *Hyenia*, showing section of rhizome with three aerial branches bearing fertile appendages, ×0.5; note rhizoids, rhizome, and aerial stems bearing (at right) sterile and (at left) fertile appendages. (After Leclercq with permission of Royal Belgium Academy.)

283

sporangia could occur on every fertile appendage that has a full complement.

Except for a different arrangement of the stem and branching, *Calamophyton* is very similar to *Hyenia*. Both plants have sterile and fertile appendages in whorls and possess terminal sporangia. Although there is no clear-cut jointing of the stems, these two genera are generally believed to be among the earliest and most primitive of the articulates. Just how they may have evolved into the later representatives is not known, but continued searching in Devonian and early Carboniferous rocks will undoubtedly enhance our knowledge of the origins of the remaining four orders.

Order Sphenophyllales. This group of small herbaceous plants lived from the late Devonian to the early Triassic. The sphenophylls probably formed a considerable part of the undergrowth of forests during the Carboniferous, since they are found abundantly in rocks associated with some coal seams. From the

DIVISION ARTHROPHYTA

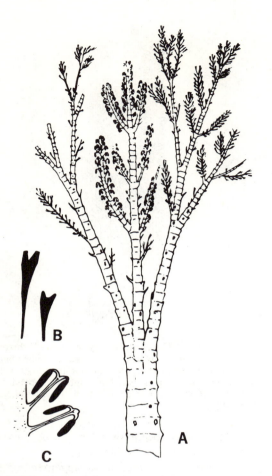

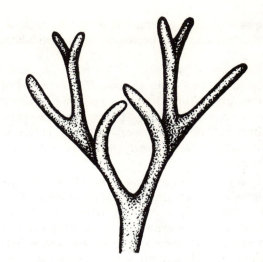

FIGURE 16–3 Sterile appendage of *Calamophyton* showing first dichotomy and three secondary branches that develop on each primary, ×10. (After Leclercq and Andrews with permission of Missouri Botanical Garden.)

284

FIGURE 16–2 *Calamophyton*. A, reconstruction of habit, ×0.3; B, leaf-like appendages; C, recurved sporangia; B, C, ×0.3. (After Kräusel and Weyland.)

general habit, several paleobotanists have suggested that the sphenophylls were creeping plants.

Sphenophyllum is the best-known genus of the group (Fig. 16–5). The stem is slender, with regularly spaced nodes and adventitious roots arising at intervals. The leaves vary in number from six to nine per whorl, and usually are not more than 2 centimeters in length. They are attached in whorls at the nodes. Each leaf is wedge-shaped, flat, and variously notched along the outer edge. Several veins arise from a single vein at the base of the leaf, then diverge and branch toward the outer edge of the leaf.

Young stems have a cortex and epidermis. Older stems have one to many layers of peri-

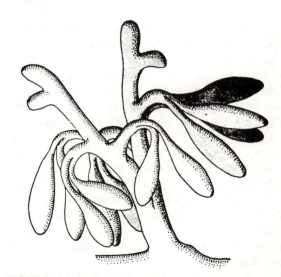

FIGURE 16–4 Fertile appendage of *Calamophyton* showing two orders of branching and six sporangia on each secondary branch. (After Leclercq and Andrews with permission of Missouri Botanical Garden.)

derm which develop within the cortex. Internally, the stem presents an interesting and unique structure. The primary vascular tissue is an exarch protostele in the shape of a triangle, with three points of protoxylem (Fig. 16–6A). In older stems, secondary xylem is formed as a

VASCULAR PLANTS

FIGURE 16–5 Several branches of *Sphenophyllum*, showing whorls of leaves at nodes and two terminal strobili on branches to left, × 0.2. (From *Cryptogamic Botany*, Vol. II, *Bryophytes and Pteridophytes*, by G. M. Smith, copyright © 1938, used by permission of McGraw-Hill Book Company.)

cylindrical zone surrounding the triangular primary xylem. In the secondary xylem, the tracheids opposite the protoxylem poles are smaller than the others. Both primary and secondary tracheids have several rows of bordered pits. Rays are conspicuous in the secondary xylem.

The reproductive units of *Sphenophyllum* are cones (Fig. 16–6B). They are thin, cylindrical, and borne at the tips of the stem. The cone consists of whorls of bracts fused to each other around the central stalk. Sporangiophores are fused to the bracts, and each bears a terminal sporangium. Both homosporous and heterosporous cones have been reported.

The jointed stems and whorled arrangement of leaves and cone bracts indicate that the sphenophylls belong to the arthrophyte division.

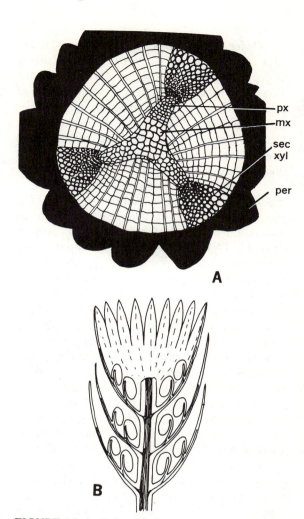

FIGURE 16–6 *Sphenophyllum*. A, transverse section of stem, showing three-armed exarch protostele, radial rows of secondary xylem and rays, and periderm, × 50; B, median longitudinal section through cone, showing fused bracts and sporangiophores, × 10; *mx*, metaxylem; *per*, periderm; *px*, protoxylem; *sec xyl*, secondary xylem. (B, from D. H. Scott, *Studies in Fossil Botany*, Adam & Charles Black, Ltd., London.)

However, they are distinct from the other orders of articulates in the structure of stem, leaf, and cone. The Sphenophyllales appear to have had a separate line of descent from their first appearance in the late Devonian, and probably arose from one of the early articulates in the Silurian or early Devonian. Following their maximum development during the Upper Carboniferous and Permian, they appear to have become extinct during the Triassic.

DIVISION ARTHROPHYTA

Order Calamitales. The order Calamitales contains several genera of plants, ranging in geologic time from the late Devonian to the Triassic. The group reached a zenith in size of plants and complexity of structure in the Upper Carboniferous. *Calamites,* the best-known genus, reached tree stature and represents in size in the Arthrophyta what *Lepidodendron* does in the Lycophyta.

As reconstructed from fossil remains of the different organs, *Calamites* consists of a large articulated stem that reaches up to 10 meters in length and 25 centimeters in diameter (Fig. 16–7A). Apparently the aerial parts were borne on rhizomes, much as in *Equisetum.* Characteristic features of the stem include well-defined nodes and vertical ribs that run the length of the internodes. Some of the fossilized stems are casts of the relatively large pith, and hence the ribs are actually imprints of the grooves of pith which lie between the proto-xylem poles. However, specimens of petrified stems show remarkably well-preserved anatomical detail, particularly of xylem.

Both leaves and branches are borne at the nodes in whorls. The leaves, found mostly on smaller branches, vary from eight to 13 in a whorl and appear to be aligned more or less parallel to the long axis of the stem. The leaves vary from oval to lanceolate in shape and have a single vein. Because they are often found detached from the stem, the leaves are usually classified in separate genera—namely, *Annularia, Asterophyllites,* and *Lobatannularia*—which differ from each other in details of morphology (Fig. 16–7B, C).

The anatomy of the stem of *Calamites* is distinctive. The vascular tissue consists of a cylinder of xylem surrounding a large central pith (Fig. 16–8). The primary xylem occurs as regular bundles around the outside of the pith. Each bundle contains a hollow canal left behind by the disintegration of the endarch protoxylem. Secondary xylem, consisting of well-defined wood rays and tracheids with bordered pits, forms a cylinder outside the primary bundles.

Roots have been found attached to the

286

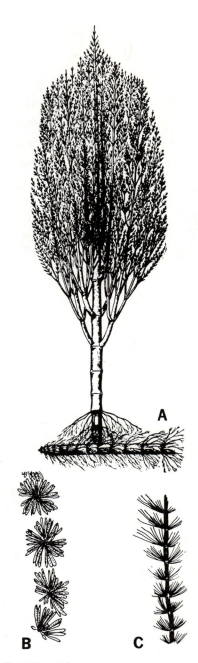

FIGURE 16–7 *Calamites.* A, reconstruction of plant showing rhizome, roots, jointed aerial stem, and side branches bearing leaves; B, leaf whorls of *Annularia,* foliage of *Calamites,* ×0.5; C, leaf whorls of *Asterophyllites* (also foliage of some species of *Calamites*), ×0.5. (A, after Hirmer with permission of R. Oldenbourg; B, C, after Andrews, copyright 1947 by Comstock Publishing Company, Inc., used by permission of Cornell University Press.)

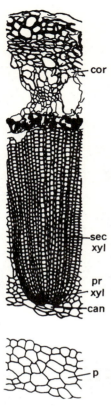

FIGURE 16–8 *Calamites.* Part of stele showing pith (*p*), canal (*can*) in the protoxylem, radiating rows of secondary xylem, cortex (*cor*), primary xylem (*pr xyl*), and secondary xylem (*sec xyl*), ×10.

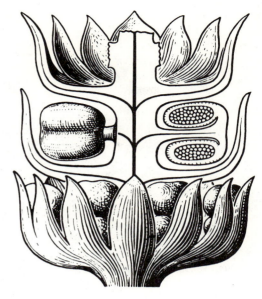

FIGURE 16–9 Reconstruction of *Calamostachys,* a cone of *Calamites,* showing sterile bracts alternating with sporangiophores, ×7. (After Zimmermann with permission of Gustav Fischer Verlag, Stuttgart.)

stems and appear to be adventitious. They have no nodes and contain exarch protoxylem. Some appear to have arisen from lower nodes of the upright stem and hence acted as prop roots.

The sporangia are grouped in cones. One of the most common genera of cones belonging to *Calamites* is *Calamostachys* (Fig. 16–9). The cones are elongate and cylindrical, measuring several centimeters in length and up to 1 centimeter in diameter. Each cone has whorls of sterile bracts alternating with whorls of sporangiophores. The peltate sporangiophores are attached at right angles to the axis halfway between the whorls of bracts; each bears sporangia directed toward the axis.

Evidence suggests that *Calamites* relates fairly closely to the extant *Equisetum,* described in the following paragraphs. The main features

in common are (1) jointed stems with whorls of leaves at the nodes, (2) canals in the protoxylem, and (3) the formation of sporangia on peltate sporangiophores. Points of difference include large leaves, secondary xylem, and whorls of sterile bracts in the cones—all of which are present in *Calamites* but absent in *Equisetum.*

Order Equisetales. This order is represented by the single extant genus *Equisetum.* The history of the order goes back to the late Carboniferous where plants very similar to the extant species are called *Equisetites.* This fossil genus, recorded through the Mesozoic and Cenozoic Eras, shows that little evolutionary change occurred during the long interval leading to the modern *Equisetum.*

In habit, a plant of *Equisetum* looks remarkably like a miniature *Calamites* of the Carboniferous. The sporophyte of *Equisetum* consists of deeply sunken rhizomes with aerial shoots (Fig. 16–10). Each upright stem consists of a central axis, with or without branches, depending on the species. If present, branches

DIVISION ARTHROPHYTA

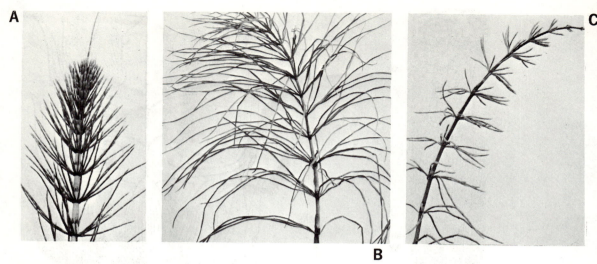

FIGURE 16–10 Habit of *Equisetum*. A, *E. sylvaticum;* B, *E. telmateia;* C, *E. arvense;* ×0.5.

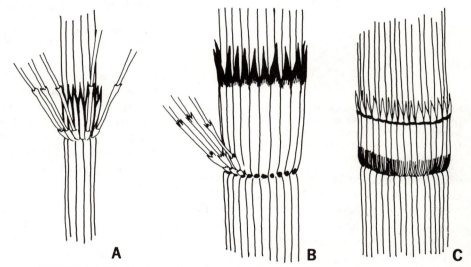

FIGURE 16–11 Sections of stems of three species of *Equisetum,* showing leaf whorls and branches, ×2. A, *E. telmateia;* B, *E. arvense,* basal segment; C, *E. hiemale.*

are arranged in whorls at regularly spaced nodes. Parallel ridges on the rhizomes, aerial shoots, and branches extend between the nodes; the ridges are formed by ribs of sclerenchyma underlying the epidermis.

The leaves, small and scale-like, are formed in whorls at the nodes (Fig. 16–11). The bases of the leaves are fused into a collar and completely encircle the stem just above the node. Each leaf has a single vein forming a midrib and bears stomata on the lower epidermis. The leaves are usually green when young, but become bleached and withered with age. Most of the photosynthetic function is performed in the stem.

The number of branches at a node is usually equal to the number of leaves. *Equisetum* is peculiar among vascular plants in having

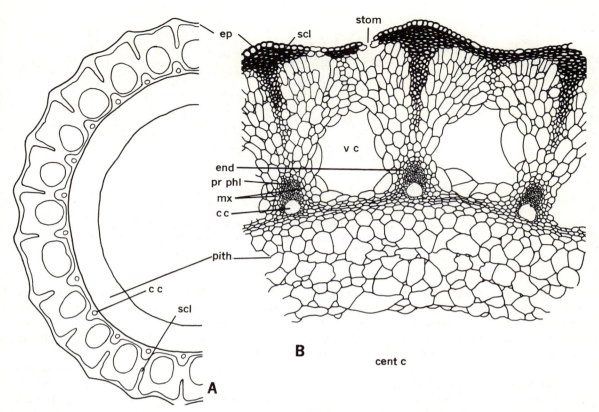

FIGURE 16–12 *Equisetum*. A, diagram of half of transverse section of stem, showing large central canal, carinal canals, vallecular canals, and bands of sclerenchyma, ×10; B, part of transverse section of *Equisetum* stem showing details of tissues, ×80. *c c,* carinal canal; *cent c,* central canal; *end,* endodermis; *ep,* epidermis; *mx,* metaxylem; *pr phl,* primary phloem; *scl,* sclerenchyma; *stom,* stoma; *v c,* vallecular canal.

branches that break through the leaf sheath. The branches arise from branch primordia hidden by the base of the sheath that is fused to the stem.

Roots are produced at nodes on the rhizome. They are adventitious and arise from the lower surfaces of branch primordia. The root primordia show active development, but the branch primordia of rhizomes are relatively dormant and only occasionally develop into aerial shoots. As the rhizome grows in length, new roots and aerial shoots form, and the colony grows. Because rhizomes are often a meter or more down in the soil and fragment easily, *Equisetum* is difficult to eradicate from gardens.

The sporangia are borne in cones at the tips of stems. In some species, cones are pro-duced on vegetative shoots; in others, on separate fertile shoots. Although structurally similar to the vegetative axes, the fertile shoots are usually without branches or chlorophyll, and they wither soon after spore maturation.

The axis of *Equisetum* comprises epidermis, cortex, and stele (Fig. 16–12A). The cortex forms a moderately narrow cylinder, as do the vascular bundles of the stele. In most species of *Equisetum*, much of the diameter of rhizomes and aerial stems consists of a relatively large pith in the center of the axis. In larger parts of aerial stems, the pith breaks down to form a cavity called the central canal.

The vascular tissue consists of bundles of primary xylem and phloem arranged in a ring on the periphery of the pith (Fig. 16–12B). Each bundle has protoxylem innermost with

DIVISION ARTHROPHYTA

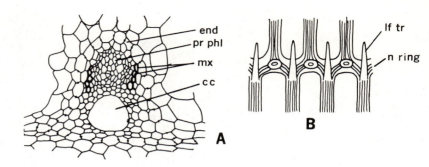

FIGURE 16–13 *Equisetum*. A, part of transverse section of stem in area immediately surrounding vascular bundle, showing endodermis (*end*), carinal canal (*c c*), metaxylem (*mx*), and primary phloem (*pr phl*), ×250; B, drawing of part of decorticated node, showing nodal ring of xylem (*n ring*) and leaf traces (*lf tr*), ×30. (B, from *Anatomy of Woody Plants* by E. C. Jeffrey by permission of The University of Chicago Press, copyright 1917.)

centrifugal metaxylem, and is hence endarch. Characteristically, most of the protoxylem cells break down to form a narrow longitudinal channel, the carinal canal (Fig. 16–13A). Usually, a few annular and helical tracheids of protoxylem remain intact on the periphery of the carinal canal. The metaxylem, with scalariform tracheids and reticulate and simple vessels, forms outside the carinal canal, usually in two lateral patches. Bounded by the carinal canal on the inside, and the two lateral islands of metaxylem on the outside, the phloem contains both sieve cells and phloem parenchyma. There is no development of secondary tissues. The individual vascular bundles fan out at the nodes to form a continuous ring of xylem and phloem called the nodal ring.

A pericycle one cell thick lies immediately outside the phloem and is continuous around the stem. In the internodes of some species, an endodermis forms a band immediately outside of the pericycle. However, in others there are two endoderms—one inside and one outside the bundles. And in still other species, an endodermis surrounds each bundle.

Immediately outside the endodermis (Fig. 16–12B) is the cortex, composed of large thinwalled parenchyma with chloroplasts in the outermost layers. Throughout the cortical parenchyma are columns of sclerenchyma that provide most of the support for the stem. The columns opposite the vascular bundles are usually larger and form the prominent ridges on the outside of the stem. Smaller columns of sclerenchyma subtend the grooves between the ridges.

A distinctive feature of the cortex is the large and regularly spaced vallecular canals that contain air and alternate with the vascular bundles. Together with the carinal and central canals, they form air channels of the type found most commonly in aquatic plants.

The epidermis is one cell thick with the wall thickened noticeably on the outer tangential surface. Silica heavily deposited on the wall surface gives a rough texture to the stem, and stomata are numerous in the grooves. Subsidiary cells are located immediately above the guard cells.

The leaf trace departs from a vascular bundle just below the nodal ring (Fig. 16–13B). It does not leave a leaf gap, and angles obliquely upward through the cortex and epidermis to form the midrib of the leaf. Each leaf trace consists of a very narrow strand of mesarch xylem and accompanying phloem. The branch traces alternate with leaf bases, and connect directly with the metaxylem of the nodal ring.

The cones consist of peltate sporangiophores (Fig. 16–14B) arranged in whorls (Fig. 16–14A). The ends of the sporangio-

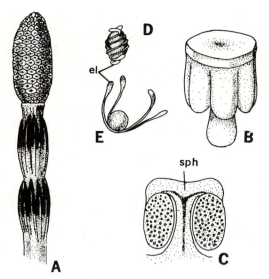

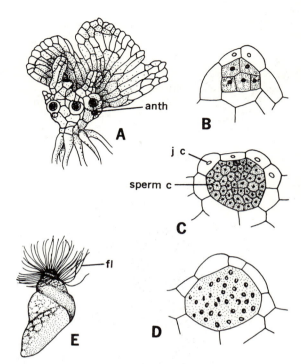

FIGURE 16–14 Reproductive organs of *Equisetum*. A, cone at tip of reproductive branch of *E. telmateia*, ×1; B, single sporangiophore, showing axis, peltate disc, and recurrent sporangia, ×12; C, vertical section through single sporangiophore (*sph*), showing masses of spores inside two sporangia, ×15; D, E, views of spores with elaters (*el*) tightly curled about endospore in D, and elaters (perispore) expanded in E, ×120. (From *Plant Morphology* by A. W. Haupt, copyright © 1953, used by permission of McGraw-Hill Book Company.)

FIGURE 16–15 *Equisetum*. A, lateral view of prothallus, showing antheridia (*anth*) toward base of lobes, ×25; B–D, stages of maturation of antheridia, showing jacket cells (*j c*) and spermatogenous cells (*sperm c*), ×200; E, single sperm with flagella (*fl*), ×1,250. (A, after Walker with permission of *Botanical Gazette*; B–D, from *Cryptogamic Botany*, Vol. II, *Bryophytes and Pteridophytes*, by G. M. Smith, copyright © 1938, used by permission of McGraw-Hill Book Company; E, after Sharp with permission of *Botanical Gazette*.)

291

phores are flattened into five- or six-sided plates, and the stalk is attached to the center of the plate (Fig. 16–14B, C). The sporangia, arranged peripherally, are directed in toward the axis; they vary in number from five to 10 per sporangiophore. The mature wall of the sporangium, only one cell thick, ruptures along a longitudinal slit to disperse the spores. The unique spores of *Equisetum* are spherical, varying in diameter from about 30 to 65 microns. The mature spores also contain numerous chloroplasts. The wall consists of an inner layer, the endospore, and an outer perispore (Fig. 16–14D, E). The elaborate perispore comprises four strap-shaped bands, called elaters, which are hygroscopic and attached at one spot. When wet, the elaters are tightly coiled in a spiral around the endospore; on drying, they expand and straighten out, assisting in the separation and dispersal of spores from the sporangium.

Measurements of spores in one instance have shown the size to be bimodal, suggesting that *Equisetum* may be heterosporous, although the size distinction is not as great as in heterosporous lycopods and ferns. Also, some spores yield unisexual prothalli bearing only antheridia, whereas others are bisexual; it is not known whether this possibly represents early stages in the evolution of heterospory, or late stages in an evolutionary reversion to homospory from heterospory.

Spores are short-lived and germinate under suitable conditions to form prothalli that are small, green, and lobed (Fig. 16–15A). Rhizoids grow from cells on the lower (ventral)

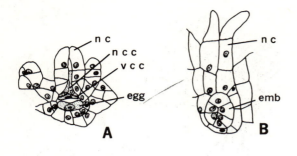

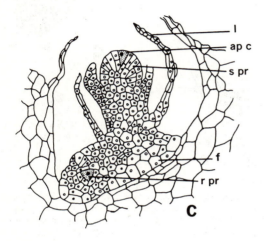

FIGURE 16–16 *Equisetum*. A, vertical section through archegonium, showing neck cells (*n c*), neck canal cells (*n c c*), ventral canal cell (*v c c*), and egg, ×210; B, vertical section through archegonium, showing early stage of embryo (*emb*) in venter, ×210; C, late embryo showing stem primordium (*s pr*) with juvenile leaves (*l*) and large apical cell (*ap c*), foot (*f*), and root primordium (*r pr*), ×120. (A, after Jeffrey; B, after Sadebeck; C, from *Cryptogamic Botany*, Vol. II, *Bryophytes and Pteridophytes*, by G. M. Smith, copyright © 1938, used by permission of McGraw-Hill Book Company.)

surface; sex organs are formed about one month following germination.

In bisexual prothalli, the archegonia form mainly on the upper surface of the cushion-like prothallus, which remains meristematic and produces upright lobes that are dark green and photosynthetic. The archegonia are similar to those of *Lycopodium* and *Selaginella*. The neck protrudes above the thallus and consists of three tiers of cells with usually four cells per tier (Fig. 16–16A). The neck contains one or two neck canal cells, and a ventral canal cell overlying a large egg in the venter.

In most species, antheridia usually form later than the archegonia on bisexual prothalli. Antheridia are similar to those of *Lycopodium*, with a jacket layer one cell thick and a central mass of spermatogenous cells (Fig. 16–15B–D). The latter develop into large, spirally twisted sperms that bear many flagella toward one end (Fig. 16–15E).

Following fertilization, the zygote divides to form four cells in a quadrant. The upper two cells develop into the stem and first leaves, the lower two into the foot and root (Fig. 16–16B, C). As in the lycopods, the embryonic root grows directly down through the prothallial tissue and into the soil. After the young stem emerges through the neck of the archegonium, secondary branches of the stem form, and one or several of these grow below the soil to become the rhizome.

Equisetum contains some 25 species. The genus is cosmopolitan except for Australia and New Zealand, with the most luxuriant species in the tropics. The plants grow well on acid soil, and are often prolific on railroad embankments, gravel bars, and sand dunes; other suitable habitats are swamps, lake margins, and moist woodlands. Although generally favored by moist climates and soils, a few species of *Equisetum* do tolerate somewhat xeric conditions.

In earlier times, *Equisetum* was used for cleaning pots and pans, and assumed the name of "scouring rush." The abrasive action was derived from the deposits of silica in the epidermis. These have also been known to cause intestinal inflammation and death in horses that browse large quantities in the spring.

PHYLOGENY

The evolutionary picture of arthrophytes is still very obscure, but present knowledge of fossil members suggests two main evolutionary offshoots from the early Hyeniales. One branch appears to have evolved into the *Sphenophyllum* group. The other suggests evolution of both *Calamites* and *Equisetum* from ancestral species but in different directions. The *Calamites* group evolved a woody habit, with relatively large leaves and sterile bracts in the cones. *Equisetum*, on the other hand, evolved in the direction of a herbaceous habit, reduced leaves, and bractless cones.

DIVISION ARTHROPHYTA

17 / Division Pterophyta

This division of vascular plants encompasses the *ferns* and several plants of the Devonian referred to as *preferns*. The ferns are distinguished from most other plants by large, feathery leaves that in most cases unroll from the tip during growth, and the possession of sporangia on the undersurface of the leaf or occasionally on special fronds.

As a group, the *pterophytes* extend in time from the mid-Devonian to the present. They have formed conspicuous elements of all major floras from the Carboniferous to modern times, but they do not appear to have been predominant plants at any one time. Because of this, it has often been suggested that the pterophytes have not been very successful as a group. However, it appears that in numbers of species and individuals they have remained relatively constant, and so have held their own from the early Mesozoic to the present.

The pterophytes are usually classified in eight orders. The preferns are Protopteridiales, Cladoxylales, and Coenopteridales. The ferns are Marattiales, Ophioglossales, Filicales, Marsileales, and Salviniales. Only the ferns have extant genera and species. The Filicales contain by far the largest number of existing ferns, with 14 families, about 170 genera, and nearly 9,000 species.

LIFE HISTORY AND MORPHOLOGY

Most extant ferns have a life history similar to the Psilotales, lycopods, and *Equisetum* (Fig. 17–1). The dominant diploid sporophyte alternates regularly with a relatively inconspicuous gametophyte, and the sporophyte develops initially on the gametophyte. Meiosis occurs in the sporangia, yielding haploid meiospores that germinate into haploid gametophytic prothalli. Syngamy results from the sperm's fertilization of the egg in the archegonium, producing the diploid sporophyte.

Two other types of life history that depart radically from the normal alternation described above are known in ferns. The first is called an obligate apogamous cycle, in which the chromosome number doubles to $4n$ in the sporangium by a process known as syndiploidy. This doubling is followed by meiosis, resulting in $2n$ meiospores. The resulting gametophyte is hence diploid instead of haploid. There is no sexual reproduction. The sporophyte grows directly from an unfertilized egg, a cell of the archegonium, a vegetative cell of the gametophyte, or from a group of gametophytic cells.

The second departure is similar to the apogamous cycle, except that meiosis does not occur. All stages in the life history possess the diploid complement of chromosomes. Spores are produced by *mitosis* from $2n$ spore mother cells in the sporangium, and germinate directly into $2n$ gametophytes. The sporophyte develops from gametophytic cells without fertilization or chromosome doubling, just as in the obligate apogamous cycle. The name given to this type of life history is "ameiotic alternation of generations."

Fern sporophytes consist of stems, roots, and leaves. In many, the stem is much reduced or exists as a creeping rhizome; in some tropical forms, it becomes columnar—the so-called "tree ferns." The main bulk of the trunk in tree ferns is made up of adventitious roots, the stem proper being relatively narrow, and considerable strength is provided by persistent leaf bases. The girth of tree ferns is due to a massive development of sclerenchyma, often accompanied by closely packed adventitious roots. The stem may be either superficial and creeping, or subterranean as a rhizome. With the exception of two genera, the ferns consist solely of primary tissues. Leaves and roots are produced from nodes, usually in clumps.

In almost all ferns the leaves are the conspicuous organs, and in some species they are large, flat, and dissected into several or many lobes. In many instances, special terms are applied to the different parts of the leaves. The whole leaf is called a frond, which includes a central stalk called the rachis. In a compound frond the subdivisions are called pinnae (singular, pinna), and the ultimate division of a pinna is usually referred to as a pinnule (Fig. 17–2).

The venation of the pinnules in ferns is either "open" or "closed" (Fig. 17–3). In the open type, the vein endings terminate very close to the margin of the pinnule or submarginally within the mesophyll, and do not link up together to form a network. This is considered to be a primitive type of venation because it is found in most of the early fossil plants. In closed venation, the smaller veins join one another to form a reticulate pattern. This is considered to be a derived condition and is possessed by most of the angiosperms as well as some ferns.

The ferns show considerable variety of internal structure (Fig. 17–4). The stele may be a protostele (*Lygodium*), a siphonostele (*Schizaea*), or a dictyostele (*Mohria*). A dictyostele is considered to be a modified siphonostele in which the ring of xylem and phloem is broken by overlapping leaf gaps into distinct units or bundles termed meristeles. The three genera listed are all members of the family Schizaeaceae (Filicales), and illustrate how different types of stele occur in one group of closely related ferns.

The primary xylem is nearly always mesarch, but in a few genera it is either exarch or endarch. The xylem consists mainly of scalariform tracheids. In at least two genera (*Pteridium* and *Marsilea*), there are true vessels, with perforated end-plates between the vessel members. The phloem usually forms a solid ring outside the xylem (ectophloic), but it is also known to occur as a ring on both sides of the xylem (amphiphloic). In ferns with dictyosteles, the phloem forms either a solid cylinder around the outside of all the bundles, or a ring around the xylem of each bundle. Leaf traces are large and conspicuous, often forming shapes such as a C or a U. The traces leave large gaps in the vascular cylinder, except in species with protosteles.

Internally, the leaves of many ferns contain mesophyll, which in some species is differentiated into palisade and spongy parenchyma (Fig. 17–5A). Intercellular air spaces are numerous, and vary in size with species. The veins are variously branched, with adaxial xylem and abaxial phloem, and are often surrounded by bands of sclerenchyma. The epidermis is lightly cutinized. Virtually all of the epidermal cells contain chloroplasts, including the guard cells. The stomata are usually confined to the lower surface.

REPRODUCTION

In extant ferns, the reproductive structures either consist of individual sporangia or synangia (fused sporangia). Sporangia may occur

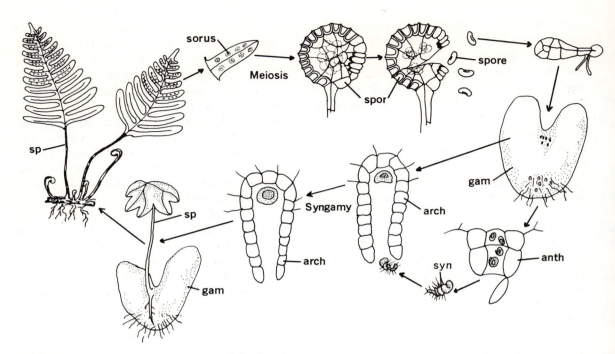

FIGURE 17–1 Life history of a fern. *anth,* antheridium; *arch,* archegonium; *gam,* gametophyte; *s,* sperm; *sp,* sporophyte; *spor,* sporangium. (From *Introductory Botany* by Arthur Cronquist, Harper & Row, 1961, Fig. 20–15, "Life Cycle of a Fern.")

296

either singly or clustered into sori (singular, sorus). In some genera the sori are covered by an outgrowth of the leaf tissue, the indusium, or they may be naked (Fig. 17–5B–F). Sporangia and synangia usually occur on the abaxial surface of the pinnules, but they are marginal in some ferns, and in a few genera they are borne on specialized stalks believed to be much-reduced fronds. Sporangia are never on sporangiophores as in the articulates, or on the adaxial surface as in lycopods.

Most ferns are homosporous, but some fossil representatives and the extant genera of the water ferns (Marsileales and Salviniales) are heterosporous.

The two ontogenetic types of sporangial development in the ferns are eusporangiate and leptosporangiate (Fig. 17–6). In eusporangiate development, the sporangium arises from one or several superficial initials on the abaxial surface of the lamina. Following periclinal divisions of the initials, the inner derivatives form the sporogenous cells, and the outer cells form the sporangial wall. At maturity, the sporangium is relatively large, has a wall of several layers, and contains a large number of spores. In leptosporangiate development, the sporangium originates from a single superficial initial on the lamina. This divides periclinally, but both the sporogenous and the wall cells are formed by the outer daughter cell. At maturity, the sporangium is small, has a single-layered wall and contains a small number of spores.

Fern gametophytes consist of a prothallus that produces gametangia and sex cells. Gametophyte development is exosporal. In some ferns, the prothallus is massive and several to many cells thick. In others, it may be heart-shaped and only one cell thick. The prothalli of homosporous ferns are generally bisexual, but as a rule the antheridia mature before the archegonia, reducing the likelihood of self-fertilization. The archegonia are flask-shaped, with the venter sunken in the tissue of the prothallus (Fig. 17–7A). The protruding neck consists of several to many tiers of cells. As a rule there is one binucleate neck canal cell, a ventral canal cell, and a large egg in the venter. The archegonia are thus very similar to those of *Equisetum* and the extant lycopods. Antheridia are globose structures either sunken into or projecting from the prothallus (Fig. 17–7B). Antheridia consist of an outside layer of sterile wall cells with a cap cell at the top that opens to release sperms. The sperms are large, spirally coiled, and multiflagellate. In many ferns, sperms apparently move toward an archegonium because they are chemically attracted by malic acid or other substances secreted from the archegonium.

As usual, fertilization results in the development of an embryo (Fig. 17–8A). At an advanced stage, the embryo consists of the primordia of root, stem, and a leaf, together with a conspicuous foot that serves as an haustorial organ transmitting food materials from the prothallus to the embryo. A suspensor develops in only a few genera. Soon after the young sporophyte becomes established in the soil, the prothallus and primary root shrivel and die (Fig.

297

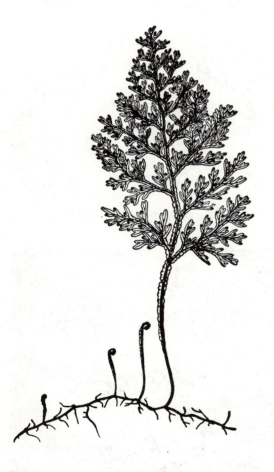

FIGURE 17–2 Habit view of filmy fern *Hymenophyllum*, showing roots on rhizome, circinate leaves, and mature frond with sporangia at tips of pinnules, ×0.5. (From *Cryptogamic Botany*, Vol. II, *Bryophytes and Pteridophytes*, by G. M. Smith, copyright © 1938, used by permission of McGraw-Hill Book Company.)

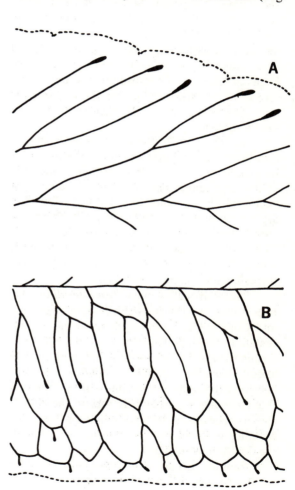

FIGURE 17–3 Fern venation. A, part of cleared pinnule of *Microlepia*, showing open venation, ×20; B, part of cleared pinna of *Polypodium*, showing net or reticulate venation, ×20.

DIVISION PTEROPHYTA

17–8B). The root function is taken over by the development of adventitious roots that arise in the pericycle of the young stem.

PREFERNS

Order Protopteridiales. The six genera of plants in this order may not be closely inter-related, but they exhibit primitive fern-like characteristics. The plants are from the Middle and Upper Devonian. Some believe that the genera of the. Protopteridiales are stocks from which later groups of ferns evolved, although the exact relationships are obscure. Most of these preferns possess characteristics similar or identical to those of the psilophytes, and there-fore some investigators believe the preferns are more closely related to the Psilophyta than to the Pterophyta.

The plants in Protopteridiales are generally fern-like in habit but show little differentiation into stems and leaves. In most plants, the ends of the appendages are somewhat flattened and expanded into pinnule-like laminae, but they are not broad as in a true frond. The sporangia are all terminal and usually grouped in clusters. They lack a special dehiscent layer, the annulus, and are all believed to have shed their spores through an apical pore or fissure.

The classical genus *Protopteridium* has been found in eastern North America, Europe, and China (Fig. 17–9). The stem has a sym-podial to monopodial type of branching with terminal branches divided dichotomously. The lateral branches support flattened append-ages that resemble a very simple frond. Some of the appendages, particularly toward the ends of the branches, bear oval sporangia on their tips. Nothing is known of the internal structure of the axis or appendages.

Another genus, *Aneurophyton*, is note-worthy because it has well-developed secondary

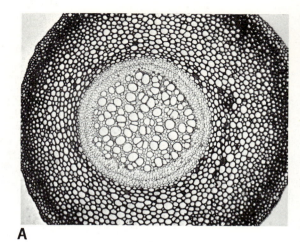

A

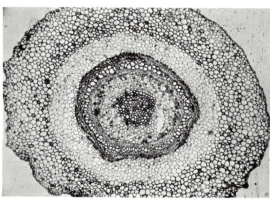

B

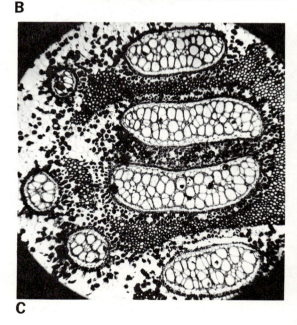

C

FIGURE 17–4 Fern steles. A, transverse section of *Gleichenia* stem, showing protostele, cortex, and epi-dermis, ×3.2; B, solenostele of stem of *Dicksonia*, ×3; C, dictyostele of rhizome of *Davallia*, ×8.

298

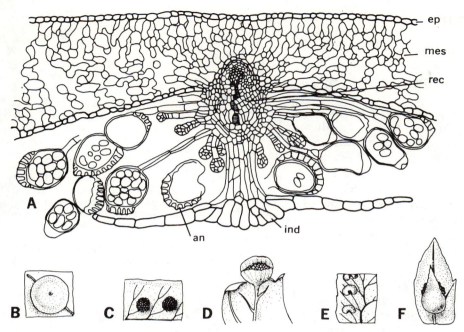

FIGURE 17–5 Fern sori. A, vertical section through fern sorus, showing receptacle (*rec*) containing scalariform tracheids, indusium (*ind*) emanating from receptacle, and stalked sporangia with annuli (*an*); mesophyll (*mes*) and epidermis (*ep*) of leaf are shown above, ×25; B–F, sori from different species, showing various shapes of indusia, ×10. C, exindusiate sori, ×10.

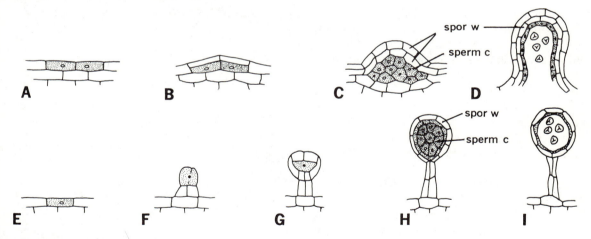

FIGURE 17–6 Two types of sporangial development. A–D, eusporangiate development, with several wall layers (*spor w*) surrounding spermatogenous cells (*sperm c*), ×120; E–I, leptosporangiate development in which outer initials form both wall and spermatogenous tissues on stalk. ×120.

wood, and apparently reached shrub or small-tree dimensions (Fig. 17–10A, B). The branching is monopodial, with the side branches supporting rows of dichotomously divided struc-tures interpreted as fronds. Sporangia borne in clusters on the tips of branches resemble modi-fied leaves. In the stem, the solid protostele is three-rayed (triarch) and is completely sur-

DIVISION PTEROPHYTA

rounded by secondary xylem. Some of the smaller specimens have a cortex with scattered strands of sclerenchyma. Some consider *Aneurophyton* to be ancestral to the conifers, and group it in the Progymnospermopsida (see p. 342).

The remaining genera, which show similar development of very rudimentary pinnule-like structures and terminal sporangia, provide support for the general belief that the Protopteridiales represent the early ancestral stock of the ferns. Whether these preferns were actually derived from the Psilophyta or evolved from an earlier stock is an unsolved problem being actively pursued by paleobotanists who search for Silurian and Devonian fossils.

Order Cladoxylales. This order of preferns ranges from the Middle Devonian through the Carboniferous. Some plants of the order occur as early in geologic time as the Protopteridiales, but some noteworthy differences in the Cladoxylales suggest that they represent a specialized line of descent which ended during the late Carboniferous.

300

The best known of several genera is *Pseudosporochnus* from the Middle Devonian (Fig. 17–11). As reconstructed, the plant appears to have the habit of a small tree with many branches. The main stem or trunk reaches a length of at least 25 centimeters and a diameter of 3 centimeters, bears roots at the bottom, and forms a crown of first-order branches at the top. The first branches re-branch into crowns of second-order branches, which in turn branch dichotomously into terminal branches. The last two orders of branches support delicate, spirally arranged fronds. Each frond consists of thin, flattened appendages that divide dichotomously several times. Some fronds are entirely sterile, whereas others bear both sterile and fertile parts. In fertile segments, oval and sessile sporangia are borne in pairs at the tips of the appendages. Nothing is known about the spores.

The arrangement of vascular tissue is peculiar but appears to be similar to that in other genera of Cladoxylales (Fig. 17–11B, C). The

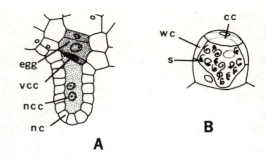

FIGURE 17–7 A, mature archegonium with neck cells (*n c*), neck canal cells (*n c c*), ventral canal cell (*v c c*), and egg; B, mature fern antheridium, showing cap cell (*c c*), wall cell (*w c*), and sperms (*s*), × 420. (A, after Stokey with permission of *Botanical Gazette;* B, from J. H. Davie, *"The Development of the Antheridium in Polypodiaceae,"* 1951, Vol. 38, *American Journal of Botany,* with permission of *American Journal of Botany.*)

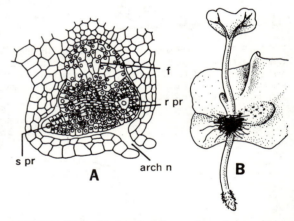

FIGURE 17–8 Embryo of ferns. A, embryo within confines of archegonial venter, showing foot (*f*), root primordium (*r pr*), stem primordium (*s pr*), and archegonial neck (*arch n*), × 100; B, young fern sporophyte with root, stem, and first leaf (still attached to prothallus), × 2. (A, from *Plant Morphology* by A. W. Haupt, copyright © 1953, used by permission of McGraw-Hill Book Company; B, after Campbell.)

xylem of the branches consists of 16 to 21 columns, which are linear, U-, or V-shaped in cross section. The protoxylem is located slightly toward the outside of each column, and development is mesarch. Most tracheids have scalariform thickenings. Apparently, the columns of xylem anastomose to varying degrees throughout the length of the axis. Very similar patterns

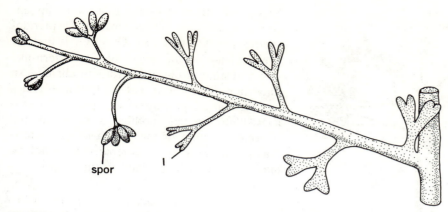

FIGURE 17–9 Side branch of *Protopteridium* with sterile leaf-like appendages (*l*), and sporangia at tips of stalks (*spor*), ×3. (After Halle with permission of *Paleontologica Sinica*.)

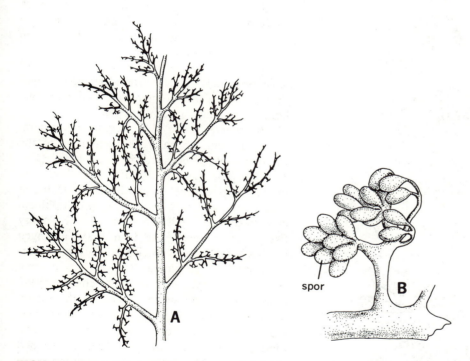

FIGURE 17–10 *Aneurophyton*. A, several branches on axis, each with terminal bifurcating appendages that probably served as leaves, ×0.5; B, single fertile stalk with sporangia (*spor*), ×20. (After Kräusel and Weyland, 1923.)

of xylem arrangement are found in *Cladoxylon,* another Devonian and Carboniferous genus.

The tissue surrounding the xylem columns is parenchyma, with circular to elliptical nests of sclereids forming a circle outside the arms of

xylem. The cortex appears to be parenchymatous. Epidermal details are lacking.

The exact relationships of the Cladoxylales to other groups are problematical. Most investigators regard the order as a specialized line of

DIVISION PTEROPHYTA

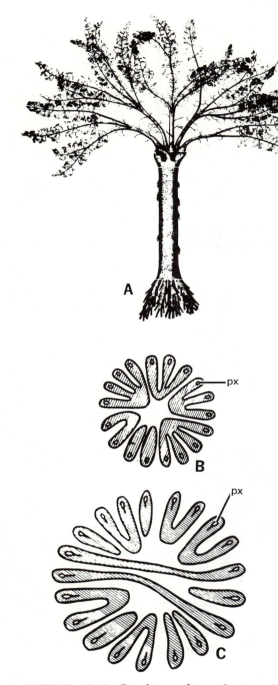

FIGURE 17–11 *Pseudosporochnus*. A, reconstruction of whole plant, showing roots, columnar stem, digitate first-order branches, and leafy appendages; B, C, two patterns of vascular bundles as found in a third-order branch B and a first-order branch C, showing the location of protoxylem (*px*). (After Leclercq and Banks with permission of *Palaeontographica*.)

ferns, but others consider it as a group ancestral to the seed plants through the pteridosperms (see Chapter 18). One view is that the Cladoxylales is an order of early fern-like plants distinct from the Protopteridiales. An important difference is that the Protopteridiales have sporangia in clusters on special appendages. Unfortunately, nothing is known of the internal structure of the genera of Protopteridiales, and so a direct comparison cannot be made with the Cladoxylales in this respect.

Order Coenopteridales. The plants of this order are known chiefly from investigations of petrified remains ranging from the late Devonian to the Permian. Many of the features of the coenopterids are primitive, and very likely many of the plants of this order are the same that are classified as Protopteridiales when found as compressions.

Four families are generally recognized. All have protostelic stems, frond-like appendages that branch in three dimensions, and sporangia borne terminally on fertile appendages.

Botryopteris, one of the best-known genera, is found from the early Carboniferous to the Permian—often petrified in coal balls (Fig. 17–12). The stem is slender, branched, and only a few millimeters in diameter. It has a cylindrical mesarch protostele, in which phloem completely surrounds the xylem. No secondary tissues are known. The fronds are arranged spirally, and in one species at least have flattened pinnules on pinnae. The petioles of some species of *Botryopteris* are quite characteristic, having the xylem in the shape of the Greek letter omega (ω) (Fig. 17–13). In one species, the sporangia are borne in clusters of several thousand on stalks having the same ω-shaped xylem trace. The homosporous sporangia are terminal on short pedicels. In some of the genera in other families of the order, the much-modified vascular strands of petioles form shapes such as two opposed anchors, a cross, or a dumbbell.

The Coenopteridales are generally fern-like because they possess mesarch protosteles, fronds, and sporangia with annuli. Some students have suggested that this group is ancestral to more modern fern groups; others consider the Coenopteridales a specialized group that ended in the Permian. Although they are often suggested as descendants of the Psilophyta, the coenopterids had clearly evolved fern-like structures and hence appear to be more closely allied with the Pterophyta. Whether the coenopterids—and indeed the other primitive preferns—evolved directly from the psilophytes or from an earlier stock is presently unknown.

TRUE FERNS

Order Marattiales. This order, with both extant and fossil genera, extends from the middle Carboniferous to the present. As far as can be ascertained, the early representatives have structures very similar to some extant genera, indicating a direct line of descent since Carboniferous times.

In the seven extant genera only one genus, *Marattia,* is distributed in both hemispheres. Most genera are found in the wetter tropics, particularly in the East Indian islands and adjacent mainland regions.

General Morphology and Anatomy. The stems of most marattiaceous ferns are short, stout, and erect—although at least one fossil attained the stature of a tree fern, and one modern genus has a creeping stem (Fig. 17–14). Branching does not occur except in some species of a single modern genus, and leaf bases are persistent except in one fossil genus.

The fronds are usually very large, oval, and once or several times pinnate, except for one genus (*Christensenia*) with a frond palmately divided into five lobes. Venation is dichotomous and open in six of the genera, and reticulate in the other (*Christensenia*, Fig. 17–15C). As in the Ophioglossales among the ferns, two fleshy stipules occur at the base of the frond petiole.

The root system generally consists of a series of adventitious roots, with one root

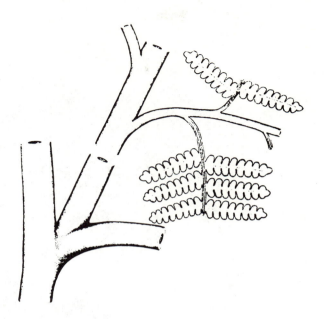

FIGURE 17–12 Reconstruction of petiole and pinnae of *Botryopteris* (note characteristic ω-shaped vascular bundle in petiole), ×4. (After Delevoryas and Morgan with permission of *American Midland Naturalist* and Johnson Reprint Corporation.)

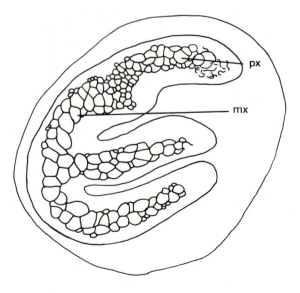

FIGURE 17–13 *Botryopteris.* A, transverse section of vascular bundle from petiole, showing positions of protoxylem (*px*) and metaxylem (*mx*), ×8.

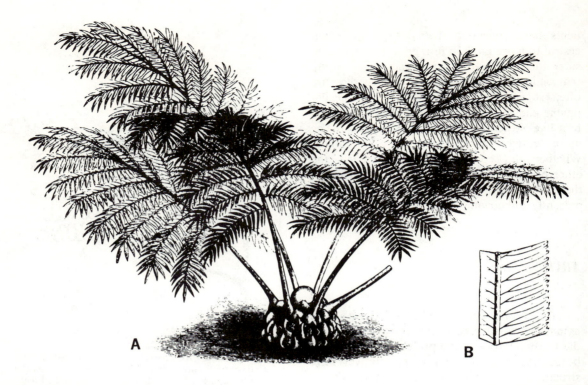

FIGURE 17–14   *Angiopteris.* Habit view (left) showing rootstock and fronds, and (right) detailed section of pinnule with venation. (After Bitter in Engler, *Die natürlichen Pflanzenfamilien,* Vol. 1, Pt. 4, p. 437, Fig. 240, 1902.)

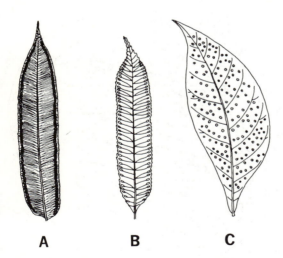

FIGURE 17–15   Pinnae of marattiaceous ferns showing outline, venation, and arrangement of sporangia. A, *Angiopteris,* ×0.5; B, *Marattia,* ×0.5; C, *Christensenia,* ×0.5 (After Bitter in Engler, *Die natürlichen Pflanzenfamilien,* Vol. 1, Pt. 4, p. 433, Fig. 238A,C,D, 1902.)

emerging from the base of each frond. The roots, thick and fleshy, branch several times.

Reproduction. Sporangia are borne in sori on the abaxial surface of the pinnules. The sori are usually arranged in two rows on the pinnule, often superimposed over a vein. They lack indusia. The sessile sporangia are large and eusporangiate in origin, and are either free or fused into synangia (Fig. 17–16A). Dehiscence of sporangia occurs by a slit or a terminal pore. All of the Marattiales are homosporous and display a wide variety of spore shapes and ornamentation. Each sporangium produces from 1,500 to 7,000 spores.

The gametophytes of marattiaceous ferns are relatively large, consisting of a flat green prothallus often irregular in shape and containing an endophytic fungus. The prothalli grow on the surface of the soil and are anchored by rhizoids. The antheridia occur on both surfaces, and produce up to several hundred coiled

VASCULAR PLANTS

sperms with many flagella. Archegonia are also sunken, with two to three tiers of neck cells, one large neck canal cell, and (except in one genus) a large ventral canal cell overlying the egg (Fig. 17–16B).

The first division of the fertilized egg is transverse. Successive divisions form a massive embryo with a weakly developed foot but with no distinct primordia for leaf, shoot, and root. A suspensor forms only in certain genera, and even then not regularly in all individuals. The long axis of the embryo is parallel to the long axis of the archegonium, and the stem and leaf primordia grow through the prothallus before emerging (Fig. 17–16C).

Fossil Genera. The first record of marattiaceous ferns has been found in the Carbonif-

erous, usually in rocks associated with coal seams. The fossils consist largely of petrified remains of stems, or petioles, and of fronds, and compressions of pinnules with sporangia and synangia attached.

The best-known genus showing vegetative structures is *Psaronius*. Judging from reconstructions based on petrified remains, this plant attained the stature of a tree fern, with a columnar tapering trunk and a crown of fronds at the top (Fig. 17–17). Close inspection has shown that the trunk consists of a central stem surrounded by a thick and compact region of adventitious roots. Toward the top, the true stem thickens and the cylinder of adventitious roots becomes thinner. It has been postulated that the main support for *Psaronius* was derived from this thick mantle of roots, as in many extant tree ferns such as *Cyathea*.

The fronds believed to belong to *Psaronius* are large and twice-pinnate. The pinnules are

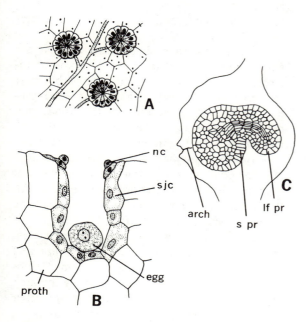

FIGURE 17–16 A, synangia of the marattiaceous fern *Christensenia*, ×1; B, vertical section through archegonium showing prothallus (*proth*), neck cells (*n c*), sterile jacket cells (*s j c*), and large egg, ×350; C, vertical section through embryo showing leaf primordia (*lf pr*), stem primordia (*s pr*), and archegonial remnants (*arch*), ×400. (A, after Bitter in Engler, *Die natürlichen Pflanzenfamilien,* Vol. 1, Pt. 4, p. 434, Fig. 239A,B,E–H, 1902; B, from *Plant Morphology,* by A. W. Haupt, copyright © 1953, used with permission of McGraw-Hill Book Company; C, after Campbell with permission of Carnegie Institution of Washington.)

FIGURE 17–17 *Psaronius.* Reconstruction of plant showing tapering trunk and crown of fronds at top, ×0.02. (After Morgan with permission of the University of Illinois Press.)

DIVISION PTEROPHYTA

usually attached by the whole width of the base, have parallel sides, and are rounded at the tips. Some fronds of this type have been found bearing sporangia and synangia very similar to those of the extant marattiaceous genera.

Phylogeny. On the basis of similarities in gross morphology, vascular anatomy, and reproductive structures, there are good grounds for referring Carboniferous and Mesozoic genera to the Marattiales. It appears that few structural changes have occurred in the order since the Carboniferous. Although nothing is known about the ancestors, the fossil evidence suggests that marattiaceous ferns were relatively important and widespread elements of the flora of the Carboniferous. However, in more recent geological times the number of individuals may have declined—and possibly the number of species as well. This hypothesis finds support in the relatively narrow geographic and ecologic distribution of six of the seven existing genera, and the small number of species in three of the genera. Unfortunately, the fossil record of the Marattiales in the Mesozoic and Tertiary is meager, and it is not known when this apparent decline occurred or how extensive it may have been.

The extant genera of the Marattiales possess characteristics that have prompted some investigators to suggest a relationship with the Ophioglossales. The common characteristics include eusporangiate development, presence of stipules, stomata on sporangial walls, similar antheridia and archegonia, and embryogeny.

An evolutionary series is sometimes erected for the reproductive structures of the Marattiales. The most generally accepted view is that the free-sporangial condition is more primitive than that of the synangium with fused sporangia. This concept is based on the fact that the early ferns and other early vascular plants all have free sporangia, and synangia could only have been derived through a fusion process from free-sporangial ancestors. However, both free and fused sporangia occur in the Carboniferous marattiaceous ferns, and there is no clue

of evolutionary links with earlier ferns from the Devonian.

Order Ophioglossales. To date, there are no authentic records of fossil ferns of this group, and the order is represented entirely by three living genera. Two of these, *Botrychium* and *Ophioglossum,* are world-wide in distribution, and each comprises about 40 species. The third genus, *Helminthostachys,* has only a single species, and is restricted to parts of tropical Asia and Polynesia.

Habit and Morphology. The ferns of this order are all herbaceous perennials, and most—particularly in the tropics and subtropics—are evergreen. Both terrestrial and epiphytic species are known. The plants are small to moderately large—with several less than 8 centimeters in height, and others about 2 meters (Fig. 17–18).

The plants have short rhizomes that are either erect or creeping. Fronds, borne at intervals, may consist of a simple single blade or they may be variously divided. The three genera are distinct in the form of the frond: that of *Botrychium* is divided pinnately, that of *Helminthostachys* ternately, and that of *Ophioglossum* is a simple blade. Venation is reticulate in *Ophioglossum,* but dichotomous and open in the leaves of the other two genera. All the leaves have erect vernation, rather than the circinate type of other ferns.

The vascular tissue of the stem ranges from an ectophloic siphonostele in *Botrychium* and *Helminthostachys* to a dictyostele in *Ophioglossum* (Fig. 17–19). The xylem is mesarch in *Helminthostachys,* and endarch in the other two genera. The pitting of the tracheids is reticulate in *Ophioglossum;* in the other two genera the pitting is bordered (the type characteristic of gymnosperm tracheids), not scalariform as in other ferns. Also of interest is the development in *Botrychium* of secondary xylem in radial tracheid rows interspersed with rays one cell wide. The primary xylem occurs as small groups on the inner edge of the secondary xylem next to the pith. Leaf traces form large

A

B

FIGURE 17–18 Habit photographs of ferns of the Ophioglossaceae. A, habit of *Ophioglossum,* showing leaf and fertile spike, × 0.96 B, *Botrychium* showing dissected pinnules and sporangial spike in center, ×0.36. (A, courtesy J. A. Herrick; B, courtesy Chicago Natural History Museum.)

gaps in the stele. Each petiole usually receives one trace, but some species of *Ophioglossum* have two. The stems contain an endodermis just outside the vascular tissue, and in some species a second endodermal layer occurs on the inside as well. The cortex is thin-walled parenchyma without sclerenchyma strands or other supporting tissue.

Reproduction.   The sporangia in the three genera are borne on stalked spikes attached to the petiole near the base of the lamina. The

spikes of *Botrychium* and *Helminthostachys* are branched, that of *Ophioglossum* unbranched. In the branched spikes, the sporangia are globular and arranged in two rows on the outside of the sterile tissue of the spike (Fig. 17–20B, C). In *Ophioglossum,* the sporangia are embedded in two lateral rows (Fig. 17–20A) and dehisce by a horizontal slit. These sporangia are thick-walled and eusporangiate, thus resembling those of the Marattiales, articulates, and lycopods.

DIVISION PTEROPHYTA

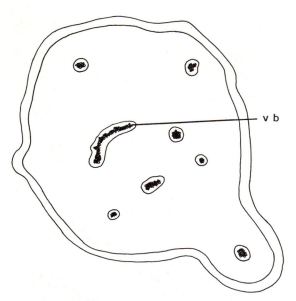

FIGURE 17–19   Transverse section of stem of *Ophioglossum,* showing dictyostelic arrangement of vascular bundles (*v b*),   ×100. (Note bundle in lobe to lower right which would eventually emerge as trace either to leaf or to sporangial spike.)

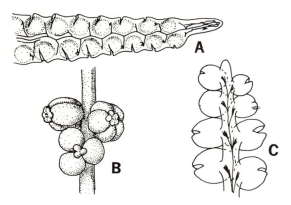

FIGURE 17–20   Sporangia of ophioglossaceous ferns. A, *Ophioglossum,* ×0.3; B, *Helminthostachys,* ×0.3; C, *Botrychium,* ×0.3. (A, C, after Goebel, *Organographie der Pflanzen,* with permission of G. Fischer, Jena; B, after Emberger with permission of Masson et Cie.)

The spores are trilete, variously ornamented, and all of one size. They are produced in large numbers (1,500–15,000). If conditions are suitable following dispersal, they germinate into prothalli. The prothalli are small, usually

resembling a cylindrical tuber, but they may be flat or irregular in shape; they are usually pale yellow or brown, and bear varying numbers of rhizoids (Fig. 17–21A). All prothalli are infected with a mycorrhizal fungus that assists in supplying nutrient material from the humus.

The antheridia and archegonia are almost identical to those of the Marattiales, the articulates, and the lycopods (Fig. 17–21B, D). The sperms are coiled and multiflagellate as in these groups (Fig. 17–21C).

The development of the embryo is similar to that in the marattiaceous ferns; some species have a suspensor, and others do not. Development of the embryo and the primordia of the main organs is slow, often taking a year or longer.

Phylogeny and Structural Series.   The complete lack of fossil representatives prevents any conclusion about the origin or phylogenetic relationships of the Ophioglossales. Mainly because the sporangia are arranged laterally on a fertile spike, some suggest that the Ophioglossales could have been derived from an ancestral group of ferns such as the Coenopteridales. While this may well be true, the case for derivation is weak without fossil evidence. Some morphologists believe the Ophioglossales exhibit primitive characteristics. Others regard these characteristics as advanced, having evolved by reduction from more complex ancestors. The latter view is favored in this text.

Order Filicales.   The ferns of this order are generally classified into some 14 or more families, with about 200 genera and some 8,000 species. They constitute the largest part of the total fern flora of the world, with their greatest development in the tropics.

The earliest record of the order is from the Carboniferous, where plants of two or three families have been discovered. All of the other families apparently evolved during the Mesozoic, and by mid-Mesozoic times the Filicales constituted one of the major elements of the world's flora. Although several families are

308

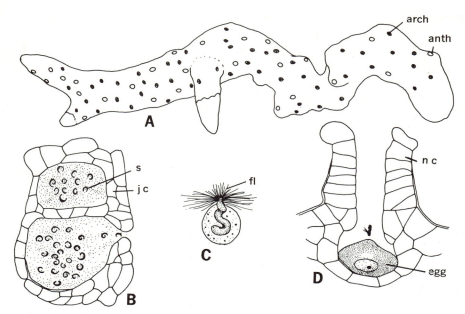

FIGURE 17–21   Sex organs of ophioglossaceous ferns. A, prothallus of *Ophioglossum* showing positions of archegonia (*arch*) and antheridia (*anth*), ×30; B, mature antheridia of *Botrychium* containing motile sperms (*s*) within jacket cells (*j c*), ×140; C, single sperm of *Ophioglossum* showing tuft of flagella (*fl*) at one end, ×1,000; D, vertical section through archegonium, showing neck cells (*n c*) and egg, ×300. (A, C, after Bruchmann; B, D, after Jeffrey.)

probably moving toward extinction, evolution of others is still progressing, and it appears probable that the order will retain a significant place among vascular plants for a considerable time.

The ferns of the Filicales differ from those of the other orders mainly in the structure and development of the sporangia. Whereas the Marattiales and Ophioglossales have large, thick-walled sporangia that develop in the eusporangiate manner, the sporangia of the Filicales and the Marsileales and Salviniales are small, thin-walled, and have leptosporangiate development. Some investigators consider that this distinction warrants dividing the Pterophyta into two classes: the Eusporangiopsida and the Leptosporangiopsida. However, a taxonomic distinction based only on this one characteristic tends to overshadow the other characteristics that distinguish the various orders of both eusporangiate and leptosporangiate ferns from each other. Furthermore, sporangial develop-

ment in the Osmundaceae shows characteristics of both types, and hence this family cannot conveniently be grouped with either of the sporangial classes.

Habit.   The habits of the ferns of this order are quite diverse. Some are very small with moss-like fronds; others are moderate in size and herbaceous; still others attain the stature of shrubs and trees. Both terrestrial and epiphytic habits are common. Some are climbers, others creepers, and many form relatively dense thickets or carpets on the forest floor or in fields.

Most ferns inhabit wet regions, but some are mesophytic, and a few exist in extremely dry sites. In the warmer latitudes most of the ferns are evergreen, whereas in colder regions the fronds die back in the winter months. However, most are perennial and the rhizome remains alive during adverse climatic conditions.

Stems.   The stems of filicalean ferns are variable, but three main types are found. Some stems are quite short, and either erect or horizontal; this is usually called a rootstock. The most common ferns have long slender rhizomes, usually creeping, and branched or unbranched. The third type of stem, that of the tree fern, ranges from short and stocky to tall and columnar. Branching is weakly developed, but is usually dichotomous. Most rhizomes are covered by a thick mat of hairs or scales that covers the growing points but often falls off from older regions. The scales are usually flat and elongated, and in many cases are diagnostic for species.

The stems of Filicales possess well-defined epidermis, cortex, and stele. The cortex almost always contains one or more bands of sclerenchyma interspersed in the cortical parenchyma. An endodermis is usually present on the inner surface of the cortex and also occurs on the inside of the vascular tissue in all species with an amphiphloic siphonostele. A pericycle of one to several layers of parenchyma lies between the endodermis and the vascular tissues. Four main types of stele are recognized in the Filicales: protostele; ectophloic siphonostele, amphiphloic siphonostele (solenostele); and dictyostele. The latter two types are most common, and the dictyostele predominates.

The protoxylem, nearly always mesarch, has helical tracheids. Metaxylem is largely composed of scalariform tracheids. Secondary xylem has not been reported in any of the Filicales. Vessels have been reported in several genera.

The phloem comprises sieve cells and parenchyma. It forms a continuous layer outside the xylem in the ectophloic siphonostele, a layer on either side of the xylem in the amphiphloic siphonostele (solenostele), and usually completely surrounds the xylem (amphicribral) in the vascular bundles of the dictyostele.

Leaves. The leaves of the Filicales range in length from a few millimeters to large fronds of several meters. The fronds are usually divided pinnately once, twice, or three times (Fig. 17–22A), but some are palmate (Fig. 17–22B).

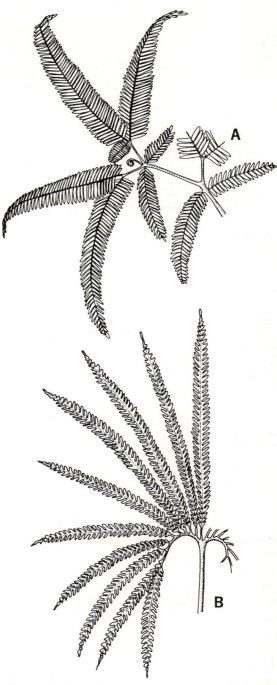

FIGURE 17–22 A, dichotomous branching of rachis and pinnae in *Gleichenia,* ×0.2; B, part of frond of *Matonia* showing two primary lateral branches, and petiolate pinnae arising from one lateral, ×0.2. (After Holttum with permission of Government Printing Office, Singapore.)

310

The lamina of the frond varies widely in shape and amount of dissection. Similarly, there is wide variation in the outline of ultimate divisions, or pinnules. Venation is open in most genera and species, with dichotomous branching of the terminal veins. However, reticulate venation is not uncommon. The fronds of all species exhibit circinate vernation, and uncoil from the base of the frond toward the tip and from the rachis to the margin (Fig. 17–22A). The coiled tips, known also as fiddleheads, are considered a culinary delicacy.

Sori and Sporangia. The sporangia of many genera of the Filicales are grouped into sori. The sori vary in size, shape, and position (Fig. 17–5). In most genera, the sori are circular, linear, or kidney-shaped; in a few, the sporangia are spread out in longitudinal rows, thus forming an extended sorus. In most families, the sori are covered by membranous indusia, although some families have naked sori (exindusiate). The indusium is attached in a variety of ways, and generally conforms in outline to the sorus.

Sori are either marginal or abaxial on the fronds. There is good evidence that during evolution from the preferns with terminal sporangia (e.g., Protopteridiales) the sporangia formed later along the margins (e.g., several Carboniferous ferns of uncertain alliance), and that in still later descendants, the sporangia shifted inward to an abaxial position (e.g., Filicales). This evolutionary trend is termed the phyletic slide (Fig. 17–23) and has led to a general acceptance of the hypothesis that genera of Filicales with marginal sporangia are primitive, whereas those with abaxial sporangia are derived.

The sori in most families lie at the vein endings or immediately under the veins. In some families, they are arranged in two rows, one on either side of the midrib. In others, the margin of the lamina curls over the sori, thus providing protection.

Three main types of sporangial development within sori have been recognized in the Filicales (Fig. 17–24). In the first, called simple, all the sporangia in a sorus mature at the same time. The second is gradate, in which the sporangia in the central region of the sorus mature before those toward the outside. In the third type, the mixed, the sporangia appear to mature in no particular sequence. This is generally accepted as an evolutionary series, with the simple type primitive, the mixed the most advanced, and the gradate intermediate.

The sporangial wall is one cell thick and has an annulus that functions in dehiscence. The annulus is quite variable in form and consists of specialized cells with all the walls but the outer thickened (Fig. 17–25). In several families, the annulus is composed of a group of cells at the apex of the sporangium. In other families, it forms as a row of cells obliquely across the wall and, in still others, as a vertical row. This series is also regarded as an evolutionary one, with the apical development primitive, the vertical advanced, and the oblique intermediate.

Both monolete and trilete spores are produced in the Filicales, with the trilete predominating in the geologically older families (Fig. 17–26). Perispores are present in some genera, particularly on the monolete spores of the Dennstaedtiaceae. The ornamentation of the spore wall is quite variable, ranging from granular to spiny, and from reticulate to coarsely striate. The number of spores produced in a

311

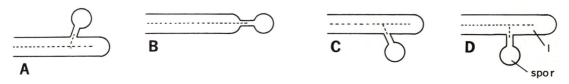

FIGURE 17–23 Sketches of "phyletic slide," depicting change in position of sporangia (*spor*) on leaf (*l*) which appears to have occurred during evolution of ferns.

DIVISION PTEROPHYTA

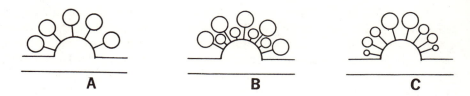

FIGURE 17–24 Three types of sporangial maturation on sori of ferns. A, simple; B, mixed; C, gradate.

FIGURE 17–25 Four types of annulus in filicalean ferns. A, *Osmunda*, with small patch of annular cells, ×230; B, *Anemia* showing annular cap characteristic of Schizaeaceae, ×230; C, oblique annulus found in Cyatheaceae, Dicksoniaceae, and Hymenophyllaceae, ×230; D, vertical annulus characteristic of Polypodiaceae and Dennstaedtiaceae, ×230. (After Bower with permission of Sir Roger Bower.)

312

sporangium varies from as low as 16 to as high as 512, the primitive families having larger numbers.

Gametophytes. In most Filicales, the spores develop into flat, heart-shaped prothalli that contain chlorophyll and grow on the surface of the soil or in moist vegetation or humus. The prothalli vary from 2 to 12 millimeters in length. Growth occurs first in the notch from an apical cell, and later from a group of meristematic cells. In several genera, the prothallus is filamentous, resembling an algal filament or moss protonema. Rhizoids develop from the lower surface, and help to anchor the prothallus to the substrate.

The antheridia and archegonia usually develop on the lower, or ventral, surface of the same prothallus. The antheridia are generally formed first, often in the central region among the rhizoids. Archegonia develop later, and usually occur in the thicker portion of the prothallus near the meristematic cells of the notch. The development of antheridia, arche-

gonia, and the embryo is essentially the same as described for the other ferns on p. 296.

Classification and Phylogeny. A good deal of revision is still taking place in the classification of the Filicales, with as few as 14 and as many as 44 families proposed by different specialists. Adopting the system outlined by Holttum, we recognize 14 distinct families in this text. Nine of these are better known, and are listed in Table 17–1 together with their known geological ranges and main characteristics.

These nine families have fossil records dating back to various geological times, and evidence suggests that at least the earliest families were descendants of Devonian and early Carboniferous ferns such as Coenopteridales, Cladoxylales, and Protopteridiales. The earliest family recognized is the Schizaeaceae in the Carboniferous; other early families are Osmundaceae and Gleicheniaceae. The remaining families appear to have evolved at later times in the Mesozoic, and most have fossil repre-

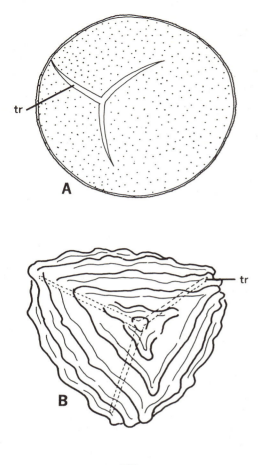

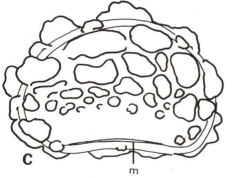

FIGURE 17–26 Filicalean spores, ×1,000. A, *Osmunda,* showing trilete mark (*tr*), thin wall, and granulose ornamentation; B, *Anemia,* with sinuate ridges on distal surface, and trilete mark (*tr*) of proximal surface indicated by broken lines; C, *Polypodium,* showing characteristic bean-shaped outline, monolete mark (*m*), and heavy razorback thickenings on wall.

sentatives showing the general evolutionary patterns that have led up to extant genera.

Many of the earlier evolved families appear to have passed their evolutionary zenith, and are likely headed toward extinction. Others appear to be actively and progressively evolving, e.g., the Dennstaedtiaceae. In this family, difficulties in classification are probably the result of active evolution in which variations in structure and cytology have not become sufficiently distinct to allow for a clear-cut delimitation of genera and species.

The recognition of primitive characteristics from early fossil members has enabled botanists to draw up schemes of classification which approach a true phylogeny of the Filicales. Such a scheme is shown in Figure 17–27. The more primitive families are in the center, and the more advanced range outward along a scale of 0 to 100. The broken lines indicate areas of affinity, in which families or subfamilies are most likely closely related. Such a diagram does not indicate the fossil ancestry of the families; to do this would require a third dimension below the diagram (see Fig. 23–1).

Several of the primitive and advanced characteristics used to determine filicalean phylogeny appear in Table 17–2. The characteristics generally used for classification are the sori and sporangia, but other criteria are often used as corroborating evidence.

Order Marsileales. Until recently the plants of this order were usually combined with those of the Salviniales into a single order, Hydropteridales. This common classification was based on heterospory and the fact that the plants are usually aquatic. However, structural differences among the genera are sufficiently great to warrant splitting the complex into at least two orders.

The three genera in the Marsileales are *Pilularia, Regnellidium,* and *Marsilea.* The last two are more closely related, and are often placed in a separate family, Marsileaceae. The history of the order is meager. The only evidence is provided by the discovery of spores identical with *Pilularia* in Jurassic rocks from

TABLE 17–1

FAMILY	GEOLOGIC RANGE	MAIN GENERA AND MORPHOLOGICAL FEATURES
Osmundaceae	Permian to present	*Osmunda*—cosmopolitan, 12 species; *Todea* and *Leptopteris*—Southern Hemisphere only; small tree ferns; lack 'sori; sporangia large; rudimentary annulus
Schizaeaceae	Carboniferous to present	4 genera—mainly tropical; *Anemia*—tropical and subtropical; *Schizaea* and *Lygodium*—extend to eastern North America and south to Australia and New Zealand; *Mohria*—limited to South Africa and Indian Ocean islands; lack sori; sporangia large; annulus an apical cap
Gleicheniaceae	Carboniferous to present; *Oligocarpia*—Carboniferous; *Gleichenites*—Mesozoic	*Gleichenia*—mainly tropical and subtropical; oblique annulus; indusia lacking; protostele
Matoniaceae	Triassic to present; *Phlebopteris*—Triassic to early Cretaceous	*Matonia* and *Phanerosorus*—mountains of Indo-Malaysian region; fan-shaped frond in *Matonia;* polycyclic stele; sori with indusia
Polypodiaceae (*sensu* Holttum)	Triassic to present; *Clathropteris* with palmate lobing	*Dipteris* and *Polypodium;* reticulate venation; no indusium; vertical annulus
Hymenophyllaceae	Carboniferous(?) to present	*Hymenophyllum* and *Trichomanes*—moist to wet areas, mainly tropical; some epiphytic; sori terminal on leaf margins; leaf flaps form indusia; oblique annulus; protostele
Dicksoniaceae	Jurassic to recent; *Coniopteris*—Jurassic and Cretaceous	*Dicksonia* and *Cibotium*—mostly tree ferns; tropics and warm-temperate Australasia; marginal and terminal sori covered by leaf flaps; oblique annulus
Cyatheaceae	Jurassic to present; *Protopteris*—early Cretaceous	*Cyathea*—tree ferns; widespread in Southern Hemisphere; abundant scales on stem apex; large fronds; cup-shaped abaxial sori; oblique annulus
Dennstaedtiaceae (*sensu* Holttum)	Jurassic to present	Diverse group—11 subfamilies; possibly derived from Dicksoniaceae; primitive characteristics shown by *Dennstaedtia;* three main types of sori: fusion, circular, and elongate

314

New Zealand. However, the vegetative remains are delicate, and the other two genera may have a fossil history as yet undiscovered.

Morphology. All three genera are small and have creeping branched rhizomes (Fig. 17–28). Adventitious roots arise from the lower surface, usually at the nodes. The leaves are borne on the upper surface, in some instances in two rows; those of *Marsilea* and *Regnellidium* have lobed leaflets, whereas the leaves of *Pilularia* are without laminae. The veins of *Marsilea* anastomose to form a network; those of *Regnellidium* are finely dichotomous. When the plants are aquatic, the leaflets float on the surface of the water; in terrestrial specimens, they are erect or somewhat spreading.

The rhizomes of all species have amphiphloic arrangements of the vascular tissue (Fig. 17–29). The xylem is exarch or mesarch, with scalariform tracheids. Leaf gaps are large, with simple traces extending into the petioles. Both an internal and an external endodermis are usually present, although *Pilularia* often lacks the internal layer. The cortex contains air cavities within the parenchyma; such a

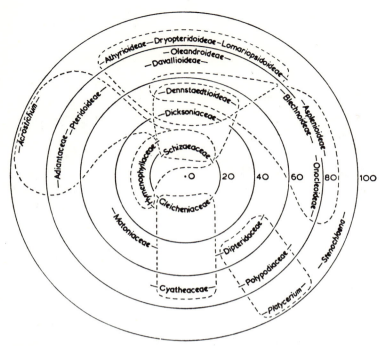

FIGURE 17–27 Classification of Filicales in which families are grouped together by broken lines according to their presumed phylogenetic relationships. Numbers represent successive grades of relative advancement expressed as percentage. (After Sporne with permission of Hutchinson & Co., Ltd.)

TABLE 17–2

Primitive and Advanced Characteristics in the Filicales *

	PRIMITIVE	DERIVED
stem	slender creeping rhizomes with two rows of fronds on upper surface; protostelic; covered with hairs	upright columnar trunk; polycyclic dictyostele; scales instead of hairs
fronds	large and much branched; dichotomous branching; venation open and dichotomous	small and unbranched; pinnate branching; venation closed and reticulate
sori	simple	gradate, leading to mixed
sporangia	terminal or marginal; large and thick-walled; stout stalk; annulus an unspecialized cluster of cells; large number of spores	superficial on abaxial surface; small and thin-walled; narrow stalk; single row of cells in annulus; small numbers of spores
gametophytes	large; flat dorsiventral thallus and thick cushion area; slow in growth and maturation	small; delicate with no cushion area; unbranched; rapid growth and maturation
antheridia	large; more than four wall cells; several hundred sperms	small; one to four wall cells; small numbers of sperms
archegonia	long and straight neck with several to many neck cells	short and recurved neck with small number of neck cells

* Compiled from Bower, Eames, Holttum, and Sporne.

DIVISION PTEROPHYTA

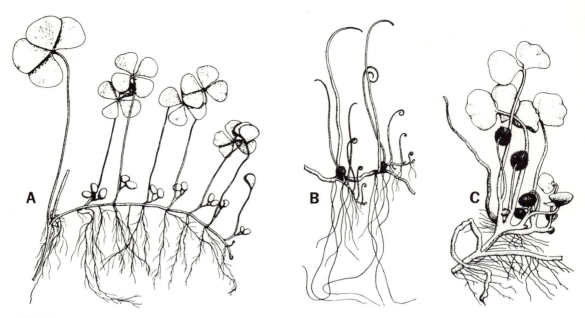

FIGURE 17–28 Marsileales. A, habit view of plant of *Marsilea* showing rhizome, roots, leaves, and sporocarps, ×1; B, habit view of *Pilularia* showing coiled leaves, sporocarps, and roots, ×1; C, habit view of *Regnellidium*, ×1. (A, after Eames; B, after Meunier in Eames; C, after Lindman in Eames; from *Morphology of Vascular Plants, Lower Groups*, by A. J. Eames, copyright © 1936, used by permission of McGraw-Hill Book Company.)

316

tissue, termed aerenchyma, is very common in aquatic plants. Presumably, it functions in gas exchange and in providing buoyancy for submerged organs.

Sporangia. The sporangia of the Marsileales are borne in a special structure called a sporocarp (Fig. 17–30). This is a hard, nut-like receptacle that varies from round to bean-shaped. It is usually interpreted as originating from a fertile pinnate leaf that has been folded inward and subsequently fused along the edges. The sporocarps are attached either in the axils of the leaves or directly to the petioles.

Within the sporocarp, the sporangia of *Marsilea* are borne on receptacles enclosed within sori. The sori are arranged in two lateral rows on the inner walls. Each sorus is elliptical, covered by an indusium, and has an elongated receptacle with a single vascular trace. The receptacle bears megasporangia along the apical ridge and microsporangia toward the base. The arrangement in *Pilularia* and *Regnellidium* is essentially the same as in *Marsilea*.

When submerged, the sporocarp splits open into two halves and the sori are extruded in a very unique manner. A gelatinous ring lying inside the sporocarp swells and emerges through the split in the wall, dragging the sori outside.

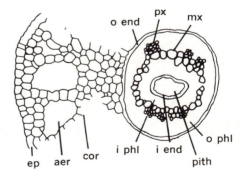

FIGURE 17–29 Transverse section of stem of *Marsilea* showing stele, and cortex with aerenchyma, ×100. *aer,* aerenchyma with large cavities; *cor,* cortex; *ep,* epidermis; *i end,* inner endodermis; *i phl,* inner phloem; *mx,* metaxylem; *o end,* outer endodermis; *o phl,* outer phloem; *px,* protoxylem. (From *Cryptogamic Botany,* Vol. II, *Bryophytes and Pteridophytes,* by G. M. Smith, copyright © 1938, used by permission of McGraw-Hill Book Company.)

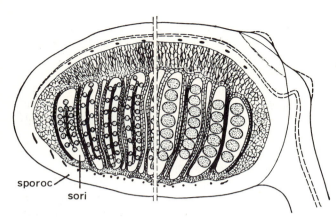

sporoc

sori

FIGURE 17–30 Vertical sections through *Marsilea* sporocarp (*sporoc*), showing sori containing microsporangia on left, and sori with megasporangia on right, ×15. (From *Morphology of Vascular Plants; Lower Groups,* by A. J. Eames, copyright © 1936, used by permission of McGraw-Hill Book Company.)

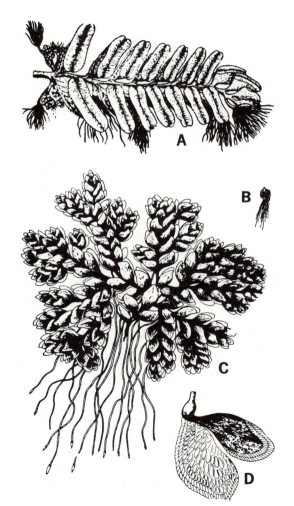

The indusium of each sorus soon disintegrates, and the spores are either shed directly or germinate inside the sorus.

Both megasporangia and microsporangia produce 32 or 64 spores, but all except one of the megaspores degenerate. The microspores are about 50 microns in diameter, trilete, and in *Pilularia* invested with a perispore. The megaspores are several hundred microns in diameter, trilete, and usually ellipsoidal. In *Marsilea,* the trilete ridge of the megaspores is elevated into a papilla, and the outer cell layer becomes gelatinous when wet. If environmental conditions are right, both types of spore germinate into small gametophytes almost immediately after shedding.

Phylogeny. Several specialists suggest that the Marsileales is related to the Filicales, particularly to the families Schizaeaceae, Hymenophyllaceae, and Cyatheaceae. This is based on similarities in structure—especially in sporangia, leaves, epidermal hairs, and anatomy. However, there are no direct links be-

317

FIGURE 17–31 Habit views showing roots, leaves, and sporocarps. A, *Salvinia,* ×10; B–D, *Azolla;* B, C, ×10; D, sporocarp, ×25. (After Martius, from *Morphology of Vascular Plants; Lower Groups,* by A. J. Eames, copyright © 1936, used by permission of McGraw-Hill Book Company.)

DIVISION PTEROPHYTA

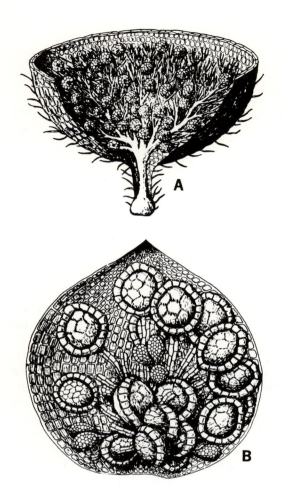

318

FIGURE 17–32 Sporocarps of Salviniales. A, *Salvinia*, ×80; B, *Azolla*, ×100. (After Martius, from *Morphology of Vascular Plants; Lower Groups,* by A. J. Eames, copyright © 1936, used by permission of McGraw-Hill Book Company.)

tween the Marsileales and any other group, and so relationships, if any, must be remote. Although the spores of *Pilularia* from the Jurassic of New Zealand indicate a history at least from the Mesozoic, a clear picture of phylogeny must await future fossil discoveries.

Order Salviniales. The ferns of this order are small and aquatic, and occur free-floating in fresh-water ponds and lakes. There are only two genera: *Azolla* with some five species, and *Salvinia* with 13 (Fig. 17–31A, B). Both are heterosporous and bear sporangia in sporo-

carps. The species of the two genera differ markedly in structural details, and are usually classified in two separate families.

The history of the Salviniales is relatively short. *Salvinia* has been reported from the Upper Cretaceous, and *Azolla* has been found in abundance in Tertiary rocks from some localities in North America, Europe, and Asia.

Morphology. Plants of both genera have very delicate branched stems that lie flat on the water. In *Salvinia,* there are whorls of three leaves, two occurring laterally, the third submerged and dissected into many hair-like filaments. These filaments are multicellular and rigid, and apparently function as roots. In *Azolla,* the leaves are spatulate, and arranged alternately in two rows. Each leaf is divided into two lobes. The upper is photosynthetic with stomata and remains exposed to the air. The lower lobe is colorless. *Azolla* differs from *Salvinia* in having true roots extending into the water from the junctions of the branches. As well as deriving nutrient material, the roots probably help to maintain the orientation of the plant in moving water.

Unlike those of the Marsileales, a sporocarp of *Azolla* and *Salvinia* represents a single sorus, and the sporocarp wall is a modified indusium. Both genera normally produce megasporangia and microsporangia in separate sporocarps on the same plant. The sporocarps of *Azolla* are borne on the first leaf of a lateral branch (Fig. 17–32B). Those producing microsporangia are large and round, whereas those containing a single megasporangium are small and somewhat elongate. In both sporocarps, the sporangia develop on elongated receptacles. Although both micro- and megasporangia begin to differentiate on each receptacle, one type usually aborts, so that the mature sporangia are of a single kind.

The sporangia of *Azolla* develop a unique structure known as the periplasmodium. This is a multinucleate, mucilaginous mass that originates from the tapetum of the sporangial wall. In the megasporangia, the periplasmodium separates into four sectors known as massulae. One of these surrounds the single functional megaspore, while the remaining three sit as a cap on top. The megaspore germinates to form a small protruding prothallus that contains one to several archegonia. The periplasmodium of the microsporangium also breaks up into a variable number of massulae. Near the outer edge of each massula are embedded trilete microspores that range from 15 to 25 microns in diameter. In some species, the units of the massulae terminate in anchor-like filaments. These become readily enmeshed with the massulae of the megaspores, thus facilitating fertilization. The male gametophyte develops into a single antheridium that ultimately produces eight sperms.

The sporocarps of *Salvinia* are similar to those of *Azolla,* except that many megasporangia develop instead of only one, and a single massula is produced in the microsporangium (Fig. 17–32A). The megagametophyte develops essentially inside the megaspore, although it protrudes slightly at maturity and exposes several archegonia for fertilization.

Phylogeny. The relationships of the Salviniales to the other ferns are completely unknown, and the order is generally considered to be a specialized group among the ferns. Some investigators have suggested a connection to the Hymenophyllaceae, based on supposed similarities in sporangial structure. However, this link appears very tenuous, and any relationship in this direction is remote.

319

18 / Division Pteridospermophyta

The plants of this division are known only as fossils. They range from the early Carboniferous to the Cretaceous and appear to have reached maximum numbers and structural diversity in the late Carboniferous.

The *pteridosperms,* or seed ferns as they are often called, are characterized by fern-like fronds that bear both seeds and pollen-producing organs. The seeds show structural similarities to those of modern cycads, whereas many of the pollen organs are synangia consisting of sporangia without annuli.

Prior to 1903, many of the fronds in Carboniferous rocks were generally believed to be those of true ferns, and the Carboniferous was referred to generally as the "Age of Ferns." In 1903, it was demonstrated that a seed belonged to the same plant as a genus with fern-like fronds. This initiated the concept of pteridosperms. Since that time, many seeds and pollen organs have been discovered attached to fronds, and there is now a fairly good concept of the pteridosperms. However, there is little doubt that additional fossil discoveries will further enhance our knowledge.

The pteridosperms are usually classified into five families. Two of these are limited to the Paleozoic, and the other three occur in the Mesozoic. Although all the families are generally considered to be true pteridosperms, they have a great diversity in structure, and the exact phylogenetic relationships are not well known.

PALEOZOIC PTERIDOSPERMS

Family Lyginopteridaceae. This Carboniferous family contains the classical *Lyginopteris oldhamia,* the first plant shown to bear both fern-like fronds and seeds (Fig. 18–1). The stem, which reaches a diameter of 3 centimeters, contains a central pith, surrounded by mesarch bundles of xylem and phloem (Fig. 18–2). Secondary xylem and phloem form a narrow cylinder outside the primary bundle. The secondary xylem has large tracheids with bordered pits and numerous rays. Outside the secondary phloem is a parenchymatous inner cortex, and an outer cortex consisting of anastomosing fiber cells with interspersed parenchyma. Stalked glands with globular heads cover the outer surface of smaller stems. A periderm, found in larger stems, appears to have differentiated from cells of the inner cortex.

FIGURE 18–1 Reconstruction of part of *Lyginopteris oldhamia,* showing roots, trunk, and fronds, ×0.5. (After Emberger with permission of Masson et Cie.)

The leaves of *Lyginopteris* are up to half a meter long and fern-like with pinnate branching. The pinnules have several lobes and are constricted at the base. The seeds of *Lyginopteris* occur on the tips of fronds (Fig. 18–3A). Each seed, barrel-shaped and approximately 5 millimeters long, consists of an innermost gametophyte enclosed by the sporangial wall, or nucellus. This in turn is enclosed by a single integument, except for a narrow opening, the micropyle, at the tip of the seed. Here, the nucellus projects as a beak into a flask-shaped chamber, the pollen chamber, which is formed between the beak and the overarching integument. It has been surmised that pollen grains found in the pollen chamber produced sperms that fertilized the egg in the archegonium directly, as in extant cycads. The whole seed is enclosed in a cupule, consisting of segments with globular glands that completely covered the seed at maturity. These glands, identical to those on the stems and frond petioles, provide important evidence for linking isolated fragments of seeds, leaves, and stems.

Although pollen organs have never been found attached to *Lyginopteris,* they are believed to be similar to those named *Crossotheca* (Fig. 18–3B). Pollen organs of *Crossotheca* consist of a central axis with lateral branches terminating in slightly flattened appendages. The sporangia hang from the margin of the lower surface of each appendage. In at least one species the spores are trilete, smooth-walled, and measure from 43 to 58 microns.

Other stems, leaves, and seeds found in Carboniferous rocks are very similar to *Lygin-*

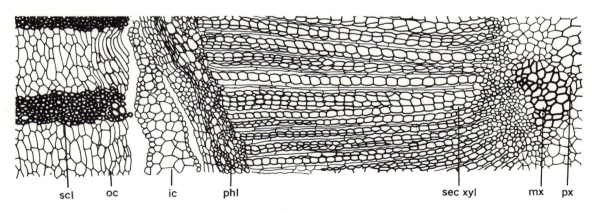

FIGURE 18–2 Strip from pith to outer cortex of transverse section of stem of *Lyginopteris,* ×30. *ic,* inner cortex; *mx,* metaxylem; *oc,* outer cortex; *phl,* phloem; *px,* protoxylem; *scl,* sclerenchyma fibers; *sec xyl,* secondary xylem.

DIVISION PTERIDOSPERMOPHYTA

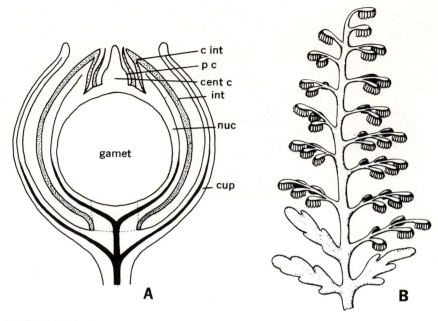

FIGURE 18–3 *Lyginopteris.* A, seed and cupule, showing vascular strands in black, ×1; B, *Crossotheca,* probable pollen organ of *Lyginopteris,* showing sporangia hanging from lower surfaces of flattened appendages, ×2. *c int,* canopy of integument; *cent c,* central column; *cup,* cupule; *gamet,* gametophyte; *int,* integument; *nuc,* nucellus; *p c,* pollen chamber. (A, after Oliver and Scott; B, from Andrews with permission of John Wiley & Sons, Inc.)

opteris, and are classified in the same family.

Family Medullosaceae. This is another family of Carboniferous pteridosperms distinguished by polystelic stems. Most of the stems are classified in a single genus, *Medullosa,* of which *M. noei* is a good example.

As reconstructed, *Medullosa noei* consists of a trunk about 5 meters in height, with prop roots around the base and spirally arranged fronds toward the top (Fig. 18–4). Numerous leaf bases cover the central regions of the stem. The fronds are dichotomously branched and have a pinnate arrangement of both secondary pinnae and pinnules.

The anatomy of the stem is very characteristic (Fig. 18–5A). The vascular tissue is in the form of a polystele, and the number of steles varies from a few in young stems to many in older stems. Each stele contains a central core of primary xylem with mesarch protoxylem, and is surrounded by a cylinder of secondary xylem and phloem. The steles, embedded in parenchyma containing secretory cells, are bounded on the outside by a parenchymatous cortex. Periderm is found on the inner face of the cortex. In older stems, the cortex sloughs off during development, and the periderm forms the outer limits of the stem.

Numerous leaf traces occur at different levels in the cortex. Each trace departs from the outside of a stele as a concentric bundle with secondary xylem. As it passes through the cortex it loses the secondary xylem and splits into several collateral bundles before entering the petiole of the frond.

Seeds named *Pachytesta* have been found closely associated with *Medullosa noei* (Fig. 18–5B). *Pachytesta* has a nucellus containing a vascular strand and possesses a somewhat flattened pollen chamber at the distal end of the nucellus. The integument consists of several layers and, except at the base, is com-

VASCULAR PLANTS

FIGURE 18–4 Reconstruction of *Medullosa* showing roots, leaf bases, and fronds, ×0.03. (After Stewart and Delevoryas with permission of The New York Botanical Garden.)

pletely free from the nucellus; it arches over the pollen chamber, forming the micropyle. Seeds of the general form of *Pachytesta* have been found in place of a terminal or lateral pinnule on some fern-like fronds.

A pollen-bearing organ believed to belong to *Medullosa* is named *Dolerotheca* (Fig. 18–6). This shallow, cup-shaped organ consists of many elongate sporangia fused together. The pollen grains have a single furrow, or sulcus, thereby resembling the grains of cycads.

PHYLOGENY

There is no direct evidence for the evolutionary ancestry of the Paleozoic pteridosperms. The early pteridosperms may have de-

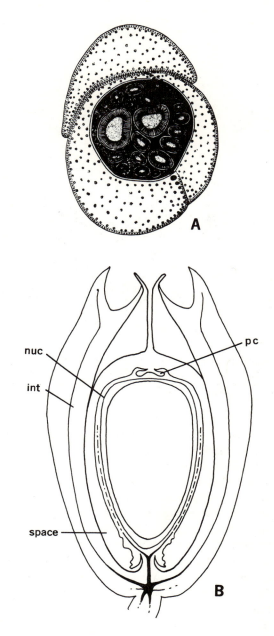

323

FIGURE 18–5 A, transverse section of *Medullosa* stem showing polystelic arrangement of vascular tissue, and secretory cells in outer parenchyma, ×1; B, vertical section through *Pachytesta* showing nucellus (*nuc*), integument (*int*), and pollen chamber (*p c*), ×1. (A, after Stewart and Delevoryas with permission of The New York Botanical Garden; B, from W. N. Stewart, "The Structure and Affinities of *Pachytesta illinoense* comb. nov.," 1954, Vol. 41, *American Journal of Botany*, with permission of *American Journal of Botany*.)

DIVISION PTERIDOSPERMOPHYTA

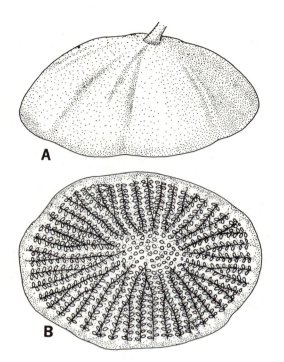

FIGURE 18–6 *Dolerotheca.* A, view of top of organ, ×2; B, view of underside showing numerous pollen sacs opening to outside, ×2. (After Schopf with permission of *Journal of Paleontology.*)

scended from such fern-like plants as *Cladoxylon,* species of which are polystelic and have secondary development of tissues. It has also been suggested that plants of the Upper Devonian progymnosperms, discussed in Chapter 20, were ancestral to the pteridosperms. According to this hypothesis, the pteridosperms probably evolved as one line from progymnosperms, and the coniferophytes along a separate line. However, the progymnosperms possess only a pteridophyte type of reproduction. There is no suggestion of an attainment of the seed habit, but they exhibit vegetative characteristics allied with both the pteridosperms and coniferophytes.

Before considering Mesozoic pteridosperms, we will digress briefly to consider the origin of the seed habit, and to introduce some terms that will be used throughout later chapters. These topics follow naturally from the discussion of Paleozoic pteridosperms, and

will provide a common background for tracing the evolution of the seed habit in other groups of seed plants.

THE SEED HABIT

The pteridosperms of the early Carboniferous are among the first plants to have true ovules and seeds. The ovule, which can be best defined as "an integumented female sporangium," is generally considered a major structural achievement in the evolution of vascular plants. The enclosure of the sporangial wall by an integument makes possible both better protection and a nutrient supply for the developing female gametophyte—features almost certainly giving seed plants an advantage over plants with uncoated sporangia. Thus, it is of great interest that plants with seeds had evolved as early as the early Carboniferous. It is even more significant that this marked the beginning of a long series of evolutionary developments among several major groups of vascular plants with seeds, including the various taxa of gymnosperms and angiosperms to be described in the following chapters.

Botanists generally accept the idea that the seed evolved by the integumentation of a megasporangium of some ancestral heterosporous stock. Because sex differentiation accompanies heterospory in some present-day plants, it is implied that the sexes were differentiated in early seed plants and their ancestors. Evolution most likely progressed from homosporous vascular plants of the early and middle Devonian to heterosporous plants of the late Devonian, and to seed plants of the early Carboniferous (Fig. 18–7A–D). This would include the reduction of megaspores from many in heterosporous ancestors to only one in the seed.

Paleobotanical evidence from seeds attributed to pteridosperms from the early Carboniferous suggests strongly that the seed evolved by enclosure of a megasporangium by vegetative lobes or filaments (Fig. 18–8A, B).

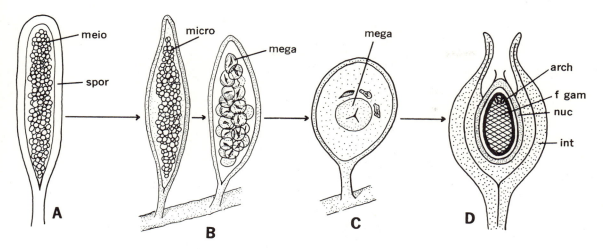

FIGURE 18–7 Probable evolution of a seed (D) from a heterosporous ancestor (B, C), which in turn likely evolved from a homosporous ancestor (A). C shows a single functional megaspore surrounded by three aborted megaspores. *arch,* archegonia; *f gam,* female gametophyte; *int,* integument; *mega,* megaspores; *meio,* meiospores; *micro,* microspores; *nuc,* nucellus (= megasporangial wall); *spor,* sporangium. (After Andrews, with permission of *Science,* Vol. 142, p. 926, copyright 1963 by the American Association for the Advancement of Science.)

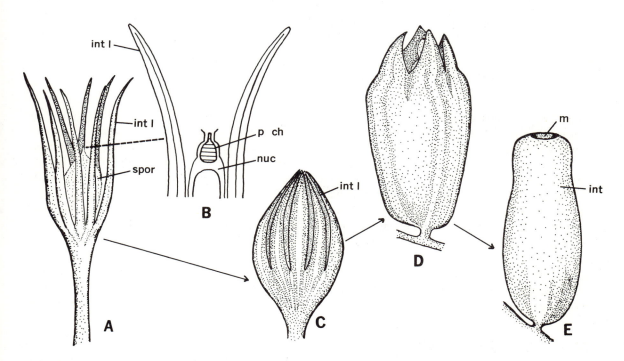

FIGURE 18–8 Series of early Carboniferous seeds attributed to pteridosperms, showing degrees of fusion of integumentary lobes leading to a true micropyle in E. B shows the development of the pollen chamber in the nucellus of the seed in A. *int,* integument; *int l,* integumentary lobe; *m,* micropyle; *nuc,* nucellus; *p ch,* pollen chamber; *spor,* sporangial wall. (A, C–E, after Andrews, Vol. 142, pp. 927–928, copyright 1963 by the American Association for the Advancement of Science; B, after Long with permission of the Royal Society of Edinburgh.)

DIVISION PTERIDOSPERMOPHYTA

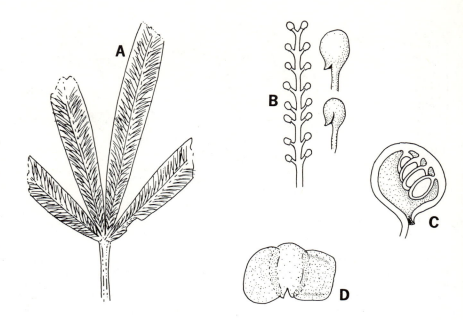

FIGURE 18–9   Caytoniaceae. A, *Sagenopteris,* leaf of plant bearing *Caytonia* seeds, ×0.3; B, *Caytonia,* seed-bearing axis, with two helmet-shaped cupules, ×0.6: C, vertical section through cupule of *Caytonia* showing four seeds attached to inner wall, ×5; D, pollen grain isolated from pollen sacs of *Caytonanthus,* ×1,000. (A, after Seward from *Fossil Plants,* Vol. II, with permission of Cambridge University Press; B, C, after Harris with permission of Meddelelser om Grønland; D, after Townrow with permission of *Grana Palynologica.*)

One of these seeds suggests the primitive condition, in which separate integumentary filaments flank the nucellus (sporangial wall); the filaments spread out at the top, so that no micropyle was formed (Fig. 18–8A). In others, the integumentary filaments are fused part way toward the distal end (Fig. 18–8C), and in at least one species, there is complete fusion of the lobes at the distal end (Fig. 18–8E). This series probably reflects the evolution of the seed habit by a progressive fusion of filaments, with the eventual enclosure of the nucellus by the integument.

MESOZOIC PTERIDOSPERMS

Plants believed to be affiliated with the seed ferns are known from Triassic and Jurassic rocks of both the Northern and Southern Hemispheres. These plants are usually classified into three distinct families, which show no apparent relationship to each other except for the possession of seeds and fern-like foliage. The families are described fully in paleobotanical texts, but can be mentioned only briefly here.

Because of their possession of seeds and their position in time, the chief significance of these plants is the possibility that they offer clues to the origin of angiospermy. This is particularly true of the plants of the Caytoniaceae, which have characteristics so close to angiospermy that they were once considered to be actual forerunners of the angiosperms.

Family Caytoniaceae.   This family is represented by leaves, seed-bearing organs, and pollen-producing organs in rocks ranging in age from Triassic to Lower Cretaceous (Fig. 18–9). Although they were originally believed to be angiospermous, later investigations indicated that the plants were not truly angiosperms; they are now generally considered to be a specialized offshoot of the pteridosperms.

The most significant fossil is the seed-bearing organ called *Caytonia*. This consists of a central axis with two lateral rows of circular sacs (Fig. 18–9B). Each of these is a cupule that opens by a lip near the base (Fig. 18–9C). Seeds are attached inside the wall of the cupule and project into the cavity. The resemblance of this cupule to the carpel of an angiosperm prompted botanists to assign *Caytonia* originally to the angiosperms. Later work, however, disclosed pollen grains not only inside the cupule, but also inside the micropyle of the seed, indicating that pollination took place in each ovule rather than on the lip of the cupule—not a true angiospermous condition. However, *Caytonia* is an example of evolutionary development close to angiospermy, and suggests how the process may have occurred in other lines.

19 / Divisions Cycadophyta and Ginkgophyta

The divisions Cycadophyta and Ginkgophyta are unrelated phylogenetically as far as is known. Both groups first appeared in the late Paleozoic, and both were probably derived from seed-bearing ancestors of the Carboniferous.

DIVISION CYCADOPHYTA

The *cycadophytes* are classified into two distinct orders, the Bennettitales (sometimes called Cycadoideales) and the Cycadales. The Bennettitales are known only from fossil remains, ranging from the early to late Mesozoic. The Cycadales are also recorded as fossils from the early Mesozoic but persist to the present, with nine genera scattered in subtropical and tropical latitudes. Both groups reached maximum development in mid-Mesozoic times, when they formed a conspicuous and dominant part of the flora. It is almost certain that both lines had their origin in the Paleozoic pteridosperms.

Order Bennettitales (Cycadoideales). The plants of this order form one of the strik-ing and dominant elements of Mesozoic floras, leading some investigators to call the Mesozoic Era the "Age of Cycads." The Bennettitales apparently evolved in the late Carboniferous or Permian, reached a zenith of development in the Jurassic, and declined dramatically to extinction in the late Cretaceous. Thus, in general evolutionary pattern, they appear to parallel the rise and fall of the dinosaurs.

The Bennettitales comprise two families, the Cycadeoideaceae and Williamsoniaceae. Although obviously related, plants of the two families show distinct differences in habit, anatomy, and reproductive structures.

Cycadeoidea is the best-known genus of the Cycadeoideaceae (Fig. 19–1). It has been found in many parts of the world but especially in the Black Hills of South Dakota. The stems consist of short, often barrel-shaped trunks that superficially resemble pineapple fruits. Some species have branched trunks, but many are unbranched. A close examination reveals a dense covering of leaf bases arranged spirally around the stem. These bases are surrounded by a thick mat of long, flat multicellular hairs or scales. No mature leaves have been found attached to the stems, but young leaves indicate a pinnate arrangement of leaflets. From this it

FIGURE 19–1   Petrified trunk of *Cycadeoidea* showing rhomboidal leaf bases and embedded strobili, ×0.33. (After Wieland with permission of Carnegie Institution of Washington.)

is generally interpreted that mature leaves were pinnate fronds arranged in a crown at the top of the trunk.

The stems have a large pith and cortex, and a narrow cylinder of xylem. In this arrangement, they resemble the stems of the extant species of the Cycadales. The primary xylem is endarch, with tracheids and rays of secondary xylem arranged in radial rows. The tracheids have bordered pitting of a circular or scalariform pattern. Leaf traces are numerous, and they are usually conspicuously C-shaped with the concave side pointing inward.

The reproductive organs of *Cycadeoidea* are most interesting and have received much critical attention. They are sessile on the trunk, closely surrounded by the leaf bases, often in large numbers. Each unit is a bisporangiate fructification, consisting of a central cone-shaped receptacle. In some species, the receptacle is surrounded by fleshy segments containing embedded pollen sacs (Fig. 19–2A, B). The seeds are surrounded by closely packed interseminal scales on the same receptacle; each has a single integument, and so is similar to the seeds of extant cycads.

The bisporangiate structure has been called a strobilus, cone, or flower, but its exact nature is unknown. Recent studies of the vascular bundle arrangement have indicated that the reproductive stalk has connections with the leaf traces instead of directly with the stele as in normal axillary branches. Although similar in general arrangement to a flower such as that of *Magnolia* (see Chapter 22), the seeds are entirely without development of an ovary. Thus, there is no homology with the angiosperm flower, and the term "flower" should be abandoned or used with reservations in any group but the Anthophyta (see Chapter 22). The whole structure appears closer to a compound strobilus or cone, and such a designation avoids any suggestion of homology or relationship with anthophytes.

The well known genus *Williamsonia* is found in Jurassic rocks on several continents. The plants differ from *Cycadeoidea* in having elongated, branched, and somewhat columnar trunks with the characteristic spirally arranged leaf bases, and whorls of leaves at the branch endings (Fig. 19–3). The leaves are frond-like, with one row of pinnate leaflets arranged along each side of the rachis.

DIVISIONS CYCADOPHYTA AND GINKGOPHYTA

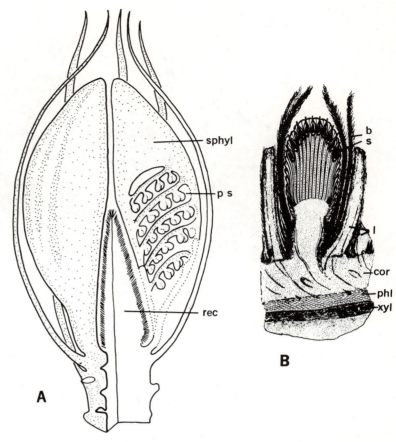

FIGURE 19–2 A, simplified reconstruction of a cycadeoid bisporangiate cone. A vertical section through a sporophyll (*sphyl*) on the right shows attachment of pollen sacs (*p s*). Note the central receptacle (*rec*) surrounded by sporophylls, ×1. B, vertical section through strobilus of *Cycadeoidea* showing numerous seeds embedded in receptacle, ×1. *b*, bract; *cor*, cortex; *l*, leaf base; *phl*, phloem; *s*, seed; *xyl*, xylem. (A, after Delevoryas, with permission of *Palaeontographica*; B, after Wieland.)

Phylogeny. The Bennettitales are generally believed to have originated from the pteridosperms. The structure of stem and leaf are evidence of such a derivation, but the relationships of the reproductive organs are obscure.

The Bennettitales also apparently have a somewhat remote relationship to the Cycadales. Although they share general anatomical and morphological similarities, the Cycadales differ markedly from the bennettites in having unisexual cones and a different type of development of stomatal apparatus. It is generally believed that the Bennettitales and Cycadales evolved from the pteridosperms, but along different paths from an early time. The bennettite avenue, which led to the development of a flower-like organ, ended in extinction at the end of the Cretaceous. In contrast, the cycads evolved unisexual cones and have persisted to the present as nine genera.

Order Cycadales. This order of cycadophytes forms one of the smallest, yet most interesting groups of living vascular plants. From Mesozoic times, when they were widespread

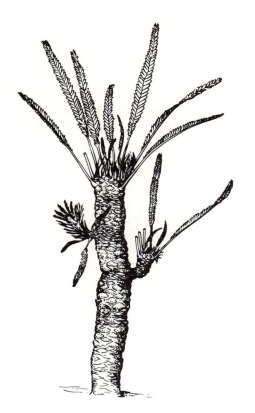

FIGURE 19–3 Reconstruction of *Williamsonia* showing branches, leaf bases, and leaves, × 0.03. (After B. Sahni with permission of Geological Survey of India.)

and relatively abundant, they declined in numbers of species and individuals during the Cretaceous and Tertiary Periods. Today, the nine extant genera are found in relatively limited regions of the tropics and subtropics (Table 19–1). The restricted ranges suggest that the cycads are heading toward extinction.

Morphology. In general habit, the extant cycads most closely resemble palm trees and tree ferns (Fig. 19–4). The forms of stem range from very short and bulbous to tall and columnar. In nearly all, the leaves are large pinnate fronds borne in a crown at the apex of the stem. Cycads range from very small forms, with mainly subterranean stems (*Bowenia* and *Stangeria*), to arborescent plants at least 18 meters in height (*Macro-*

zamia). Most genera and species are arborescent and range in height between the extremes but seldom reach over 2 meters.

The outside of the trunk in all arborescent species is covered by a conspicuous armor of leaf bases (Fig. 19–5). The leaves are cut off by an abscission layer that develops in the petiole several centimeters out from the stem. The number of leaf bases on a stem has been used to calculate the age in several genera. For example, in *Dioon,* some plants are estimated to be as much as 1,000 years old.

The leaves resemble fern fronds and are pinnate in all but *Bowenia,* which is bipinnate. The leaflets are aligned in two lateral rows, one on each side of the rachis. Leaflets are usually entire, tough, and xeromorphic with a thick cuticle and sunken stomata. Most species show well-marked palisade and spongy mesophyll (Fig. 19–6). The venation appears at first glance to be parallel but is definitely dichotomous; the branch veins depart obliquely and quickly assume a parallel orientation. Leaflets of *Cycas* have only one vein, which forms a prominent midrib.

TABLE 19–1

Distribution of Extant Cycads

GENUS	DISTRIBUTION	
Cycas	Australia; East Indian Islands; India; China; southern Japan	EASTERN HEMISPHERE
Macrozamia *Bowenia*	Australia	
Encephalartos *Stangeria*	South Africa	
Zamia	Florida; West Indies; Mexico; Central America; northern South America; Andes Mountains south to Chile	WESTERN HEMISPHERE
Microcycas	Western Cuba	
Ceratozamia *Dioon*	Mexico	

DIVISIONS CYCADOPHYTA AND GINKGOPHYTA

FIGURE 19–4 Habit view of *Cycas,* ×0.005. (Used with permission of Blaisdell Publishing Company, from *The Plant Kingdom* by William H. Brown.)

FIGURE 19–5 Trunk of *Dioon spinulosum* showing thick covering of sharp leaf bases, ×0.3. (Courtesy Chicago Natural History Museum.)

Anatomy. The internal structure of the cycads is somewhat similar to that of the Bennettitales (Fig. 19–7). The pith and cortex are relatively thick, and the vascular cylinder relatively thin. A small amount of secondary wood develops centrifugally in radial rows but without forming well-defined growth rings. The pitting of the tracheids is generally bordered. Rays vary from one to several cells in width, and up to 20 cells in depth; they often contain starch grains or crystals of calcium oxalate. Both the pith and cortex contain prominent mucilaginous canals and large amounts of starch. The cortex is bounded on the outside by a well-marked but thin periderm.

One of the most interesting features of cycad anatomy is the arrangement of leaf traces. The number of traces varies with the species but always shows a pattern called girdling (Fig. 19–8). Individual traces arise from leaf gaps which are located some distance around the stele from the leaf insertion. Thus, in passing to the leaf base, the traces girdle the stele. Each trace passes upward slightly through the cortex, approaching closer to other traces before entering the leaf base. This process is also found in many angiosperms, particularly monocotyledons with parallel venation. However, it is not present in the bennettites, which have traces passing directly from the stele to the leaf base.

The primary root of cycads is large, especially in the seedling. Adult roots attain great lengths; in one example, a *Dioon* root 12 meters from the stem has a diameter of 3 centimeters. The primary vascular tissue is an exarch protostele, ranging from diarch to tetrarch. Secondary growth is common. A noteworthy feature is the negative geotropism exhibited widely in the roots. On reaching the surface of the soil, many roots develop clusters of nodules. At first these contain bacteria and later the cyanophyte *Anabaena.* Whether the nodules function in nitrogen fixation and assist in assimilation has not been determined.

Reproduction. In all extant cycads except seed-bearing plants of *Cycas,* reproductive

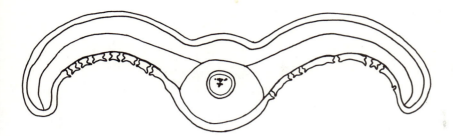

FIGURE 19–6 *Cycas revoluta*. Vertical section of leaf, showing vascular bundle and stomata, ×35.

units are compacted into either strobili or cones. The seed cones (gynostrobili) of *Cycas* and *Dioon* are similar to true strobili, whereas those of the other genera are compact cones. All genera are completely dioecious.

Most of the cycads bear the strobili at the apex of the stem, but in at least two genera they are borne laterally and in the axils of the leaves. Many of the strobili are extremely large and heavy; seed cones (gynostrobili) exceeding 70 centimeters in length and weighing over 30 kilograms are typical for *Macrozamia denisonii*. In most cycads, the seed cones are conspicuously larger than the pollen cones (androstrobili).

The pollen cones are borne singly or in small groups at the stem tip (Fig. 19–9). Each cone consists of many androsporophylls spirally arranged on a central axis. The sporophylls are narrow at the point of insertion and flare out distally; they are usually oriented in vertical rows (Fig. 19–9A). Each sporophyll has clusters of androsporangia congregated on both sides of a median keel. These clusters have been called sori and contain from one to five sporangia, depending on the genus. The total number of sporangia per sporophyll varies from 28 in *Zamia* to over 1,000 in *Cycas*.

Each androsporangium is essentially sessile and develops eusporangiately. After repeated divisions of initials, several layers of cells are produced. Inner cells become the spore mother cells, whereas the outer layers develop into the tapetum and the sporangial wall. During development of the androspore

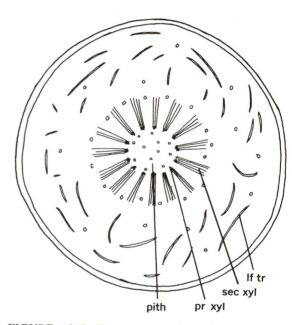

FIGURE 19–7 Transverse section of cycad stem showing pith, primary xylem (*pr xyl*), secondary xylem (*sec xyl*), and oblique leaf traces (*lf tr*) in cortex, ×1. (From *Morphology of Gymnosperms* by J. M. Coulter and C. J. Chamberlain by permission of The University of Chicago Press, copyright 1910 and 1917.)

mother cells, the tapetum and inner wall cells break down, forming a multinucleate protoplasm that serves as a source of food for the maturing androspores.

Following meiosis in the spore mother cells, the androspores differentiate endosporally into the gametophyte (Fig. 19–10). The androsporal cell divides into a small prothallial cell and the large central antheridial

DIVISIONS CYCADOPHYTA AND GINKGOPHYTA

initial. The antheridial initial then divides to form a small generative cell that lies against the prothallial cell, and a larger tube cell that is centrally located.

At this stage of maturation, the immature androgametophytes are shed from the sporangia as pollen grains. The pollen grains of most cycads are circular or elliptical, with a single furrow on one surface. They are produced in large numbers and are generally dispersed by wind.

When a pollen grain lands on the pollen drop at the micropyle of an ovule, further elaboration of the gametophyte takes place. A pollen tube begins to evaginate from the furrow of the grain; it gradually grows into the nucellus of the ovule, serving an haustorial function. At the same time, the tube nucleus

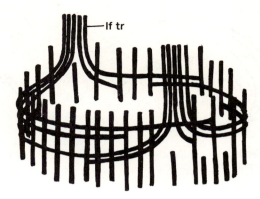

FIGURE 19–8 Vascular pattern of cycad stem, showing "girdling" of leaf traces (*lf tr*), ×0.3. (After Dorety with permission of *The Botanical Gazette*.)

334

A

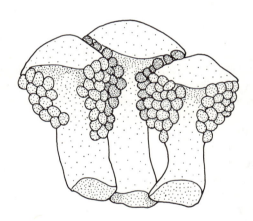

B

FIGURE 19–9 A, androstrobilus of *Zamia* showing vertical rows of androsporophylls, ×1; B, three androsporophylls of *Zamia,* showing closely packed pollen sacs on abaxial surfaces, ×5. (A, courtesy Chicago Natural History Museum.)

migrates out into the basal part of the pollen tube. The swollen base extends into the pollen chamber formed from the dissolution of nucellar cells. The generative cell also divides to form two cells—a sterile cell that develops next to the prothallial cell, and an androgenous cell (spermatogenous cell) near the base of the pollen tube (Fig. 19–10C). Finally, the androgeneous cell undergoes a single division to form two androgametes, or sperm cells.

All but two genera of cycads have compact seed cones consisting of spirally arranged gynosporophylls (Fig. 19–11). *Cycas* has a rosette of sporophylls that resembles reduced pinnate leaves. In *Dioon,* the gynostrobilus contains loosely compacted sporophylls that are entire. This lessening in complexity of gynosporophylls is accompanied by a reduction in ovule number from six to eight in *Cycas* to two in most other genera. This is generally considered to represent a reduction series that reflects an evolutionary trend.

The ovules are usually sessile or are borne on very short stalks on the adaxial surface of the gynosporophylls. In most instances the ovules are oriented with the micropyle toward the central axis (Fig. 19–12A, D). Ovules vary in size from 6 centimeters in some species of *Cycas* and *Macrozamia* to as small as 5 millimeters in *Zamia pygmaea.*

The essential structures of an ovule can best be observed in a median longitudinal section (Fig. 19–13). Initially, the white central mass is the nucellus (gynosporangium). This is surrounded by an integument that comprises three distinct layers—a middle stony layer with a fleshy layer on either side. The inner fleshy tissue is largely resorbed during development of the gametophyte, but part remains as a thin papery layer. Two vascular strands enter the base of the integument; each branches to send strands into both outer and inner fleshy layers.

Within the central region of the gynosporangium, a gynospore mother cell undergoes meiosis to form four gynospores that initiate the gametophyte generation (Fig. 19–14A). The four gynospores are normally arranged in a linear tetrad within the gynosporangium.

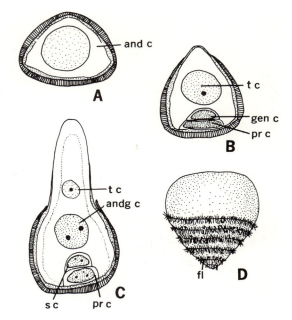

FIGURE 19–10 Androgametophyte of cycads. A, single-celled pollen grain with androsporal cell (*and c*), ×900; B, pollen grain with prothallial cell (*pr c*), generative cell (*gen c*), and tube cell (*t c*), and with pollen tube just beginning to form (top), ×900; C, late stage of maturation of androgametophyte with prothallial cell, sterile cell (*s c*), androgenous cell (*andg c*), and tube cell, ×900; D, single androgamete showing spirally arranged flagella, ×1,000. (A–C, after Chamberlain with permission of *The Botanical Gazette;* D, after Webber.)

335

Usually only the basal gynospore remains functional and the other three degenerate. In their germination, the gynospores follow stages very similar to those in a free-sporing plant such as *Selaginella.* The functional gynospore enlarges markedly, undergoing many nuclear divisions (Fig. 19–14D). At the same time, the cells of the surrounding gynosporangium are digested, providing both space and nutrient for the enlarging gynospore. At maximum development, the free-nucleate gametophyte fills most of the original gynosporangium. The many free nuclei are suspended in watery cytoplasm, and are congregated at the periphery of the gametophyte.

Following the completion of free-nuclear division, cell walls begin to form around the nuclei. Wall formation starts at the periphery

DIVISIONS CYCADOPHYTA AND GINKGOPHYTA

FIGURE 19–11 Gynostrobilus of cycads. Gyno-strobilus of *Encephalartos* attached to top of stem, ×0.15.

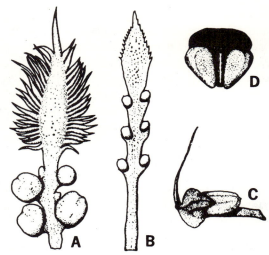

FIGURE 19–12 Gynosporophylls of cycads. A, seeds attached below leaf-like blade of *Cycas revoluta* sporophyll, ×0.2; B, seeds and sporophyll of *Cycas circinalis,* ×0.2; C, single gynosporophyll of *Macrozamia* with short spike-like protuberance, ×0.2; D, sporophyll of *Zamia* showing nonelaborated peltate sporophyll, ×0.6. (From *Plant Morphology* by A. W. Haupt, copyright ©, used by permission of McGraw-Hill Book Company.)

and continues centripetally until all the nuclei are involved. The resulting tissue is the gyno-gametophyte, which produces archegonia toward the micropylar end and later acts as a nutritive tissue for the developing embryo (Fig. 19–13).

In most genera, archegonia develop from superficial archegonial initials at the micropylar end of the gametophyte; from one to four large archegonia mature. At maturity, each archegonium has two neck cells (a characteristic of all cycads), a ventral canal nucleus, and an egg nucleus (Fig. 19–14B). In most instances, no wall forms between the ventral canal and egg nuclei. The layer of gametophytic cells enclosing the egg forms a jacket and functions in transferring nutrients from the gametophyte to the egg. This is facilitated by haustorial threads that extend from the egg cytoplasm through plasmodesmata into the cells

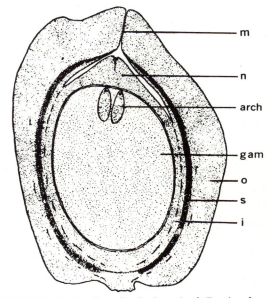

FIGURE 19–13 Longitudinal seed of *Zamia,* showing gametophyte (*gam*), archegonia (*arch*), nucellus (*n*), integument (*i*), middle stony layer of integument (*s*), outer fleshy integumentary layer (*o*), and micropyle (*m*), ×4. (From *Plant Morphology* by A. W. Haupt, copyright ©, used by permission of McGraw-Hill Book Company.)

VASCULAR PLANTS

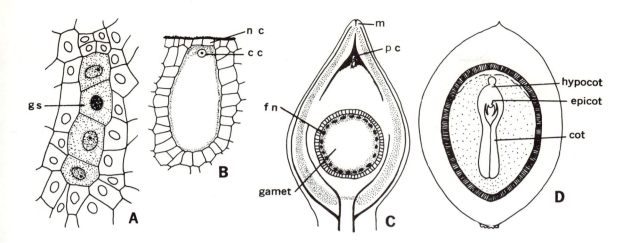

FIGURE 19–14 Development of gynogametophyte of cycads. A, tetrad of gynospores, ×900; B, single arche-gonium showing large central cell, two small neck cells, and surrounding gametophytic tissue, ×50; C, free nuclei around periphery of gametophyte, ×4; D, simple embryo showing two cotyledons, two leaf primordia, epicotyl, and hypocotyl, ×4. *c c*, central cell; *cot*, cotyledon; *epicot*, epicotyl; *f n*, free nuclei; *gamet*, gynogame-tophyte; *gs*, gynospore; *hypocot*, hypocotyl; *m*, micropyle; *n c*, neck cell; *p c*, pollen chamber. (A, after Smith with permission of *Botanical Gazette;* B–D, from *The Living Cycads* by C. J. Chamberlain by permission of The University of Chicago Press, copyright 1919.)

of the jacket. When fully expanded, the egg measures up to 3 millimeters long and is ex-tremely turgid.

The ventral canal nucleus is short-lived and begins to disintegrate soon after formation. The egg nucleus then moves to a central posi-tion and expands to 0.5 millimeter in some instances. At fertilization the swollen pollen tube bursts, discharging the two androgametes and their fluid cytoplasm. This process is some-times sufficiently violent to tear the band of flagella from the androgamete. The andro-gamete nucleus then moves through the cyto-plasm of the egg and fuses with the egg nu-cleus, forming the zygote.

In most genera, the embryo consists of two large cotyledons; these encompass a short axis comprising hypocotyl and epicotyl (Fig. 19–14C). At germination, the bases of the cotyle-dons elongate, forming a "new" hypocotyl and pushing the radicle out through the micropyle. The cotyledons remain for several weeks or longer in contact with the gynogametophyte, ab-

sorbing food for the developing shoot. Even-tually, the young sporophyte anchors in the soil and becomes independent of the food sup-ply in the seed.

Phylogeny. The cycads, with a fossil rec-ord from the early Triassic, appear to have evolved from the pteridosperms. The two groups have similar pinnately compound leaves, the same stomatal pattern, and closely comparable seeds. Furthermore, in *Cycas* and to a lesser extent in *Dioon* the seeds are borne on gynosporophylls that obviously represent reduced leaves—probably a reduction from the condition in pteridosperms, where seeds are borne on the terminal segments of fronds. Among the extant cycads, a noteworthy reduc-tion series includes several species of *Cycas* through to *Dioon* to *Zamia* and others with much-reduced gynosporophylls. However, the cycads show less relationship to the pterido-sperms in the anatomy of the stem, the girdling of leaf traces, and the arrangement of andro-sporangia in the androstrobili.

DIVISIONS CYCADOPHYTA AND GINKGOPHYTA

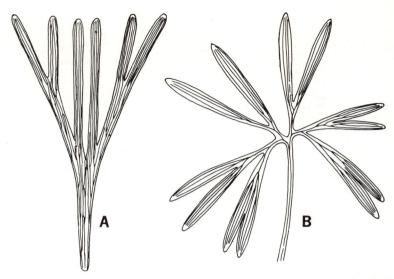

FIGURE 19–15   Leaves of fossil ginkgophytes. A, *Baiera,* with long dichotomous leaf segments, ×0.5; B, *Ginkgoites,* with primary, secondary, and tertiary dichotomies of blade from petiole, ×0.5. (B, after Heer.)

338

FIGURE 19–16   *Ginkgo biloba.* A, young tree showing characteristic pyramidal branching; B, mature tree with rounded crown. (Photographs courtesy Chicago Natural History Museum.)

VASCULAR PLANTS

DIVISION GINKGOPHYTA

This division of vascular plants is represented in the extant flora by a single species, *Ginkgo biloba.* It is the sole survivor of a group of plants that probably originated in the late Paleozoic, and became very widespread and moderately abundant during mid-Mesozoic times. In company with the other groups such as the cycadophytes that flourished during the Mesozoic, the *ginkgophytes* diminished in both numbers of taxa and individuals during the Tertiary (Fig. 19–15).

Although the ancestors of the ginkgophytes are not known, the plants appear to share characteristics with both the cycadophytes and the conifers. However, the general structure is quite distinctive, and it is very possible that the ginkgophytes evolved from seed-bearing ancestors different from those that evolved into either cycads or conifers. Practically the only remains of ginkgophytes in rocks of the Mesozoic are leaf compressions. Although other ginkgophyte organs are rarely found, the abundance of different leaf forms indicates much diversity in the group during the Mesozoic.

Ginkgo biloba. This species is popularly called the "maidenhair tree" because its leaf resembles that of *Adiantum,* the maidenhair fern. *Ginkgo biloba,* sole surviving member of an ancient lineage, is often referred to as a "living fossil." Originally known only from gardens in eastern Asia, particularly China and Japan, it has been found in recent times in what appear to be wild stands in a small mountainous area of southeastern China. These may be indigenous populations or they may have escaped from gardens.

Ginkgo trees have been cultivated in various countries since the nineteenth century and are becoming increasingly popular as shade trees and ornamentals. The species is dioecious, and staminate trees are preferred in cultivation because the outer fleshy layer of the seeds decays and produces butyric acid, which pollutes the air with the smell of rancid butter. It was formerly impossible to tell whether a seedling was staminate or ovulate, and horticulturists had to wait for a plant to mature before segregating the staminate trees. Now sex is determined by the presence of X and Y chromosomes.

Morphology and Anatomy. Younger trees of *Ginkgo* have monopodial growth, giving them a marked pyramidal shape (Fig. 19–16A). However, as they mature, the main trunk loses its prominence, and the side branches grow relatively larger and longer to form a rounded crown (Fig. 19–16B). Some trees reach a height approaching 30 meters and a trunk diameter of over 1 meter. The tree is deciduous, and the leaves appear very late in the spring and persist well into the autumn in mid-latitudes.

As in many of the conifers, *Ginkgo* has two kinds of branches, the long shoot and the spur (or short) shoot. Long shoots have indeterminate growth with scattered leaves and form the main branches of the tree (Fig. 19–17). Spur shoots have limited growth, increasing only a few millimeters in length each year; they form on the long branches during the second year of growth and bear a cluster of leaves at the tip. Scars of former petioles form a prominent spiral around them. Although spurs usually remain short and leaf-bearing, in some instances a spur suddenly develops into a long shoot with scattered leaves, often as the result of an injury to a neighboring long shoot. Similarly, long shoots can become retarded, changing to spur shoots. There is a marked difference in the relative amounts of tissues produced by long and spur shoots of the same age. Long shoots have a narrow pith, wide vascular cylinder, and thin cortex. In contrast, spur shoots have a wide pith, very narrow xylem cylinder, and wide cortex. The secondary xylem forms a thick cylinder of irregular radial rows of tracheids, rays, and weakly defined growth rings.

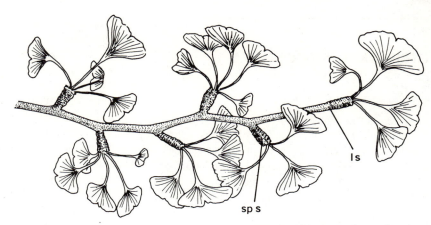

FIGURE 19–17 *Ginkgo biloba*. Section of long shoot with spur shoots bearing spirally arranged leaves, × 0.3. *l s*, long shoot; *sp s*, spur shoot.

The distinctive leaves of *Ginkgo biloba* have a long petiole that fans out into a broad blade (Fig. 19–18). In leaves of long shoots, the blades are usually notched in the middle; hence, the specific epithet *"biloba."* In contrast, leaves of spur shoots are mainly entire. The petiole contains two leaf traces that divide dichotomously in the base of the blade. Additional dichotomies occur in the blade as far as the margin, giving a fan-like appearance to the leaf. Although most vein branchings are open and dichotomous, some veins have anastomoses.

Reproduction. Like the cycads, *Ginkgo biloba* is consistently dioecious. Interspersed with leaves at the tips of spur shoots, androsporangia are borne on loose strobili; ovules are borne singly at the ends of forked peduncles.

An androstrobilus of *Ginkgo* is a lax catkin-like structure bearing sporophylls spirally arranged around the axis (Fig. 19–19). Each androsporophyll is a curved stalk bearing two androsporangia at the tip. An androsporangium has four to seven wall layers, a tapetum, and a number of central sporo-

FIGURE 19–18 Leaf structure of *Ginkgo biloba*, showing petiole, dichotomous venation, and central notch in blade, × 1.

FIGURE 19–19 Reproductive organs of *Ginkgo*. A, catkin-like androstrobili (*and s*) emerging from tip of spur shoot, × 1.

VASCULAR PLANTS

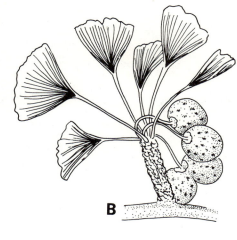

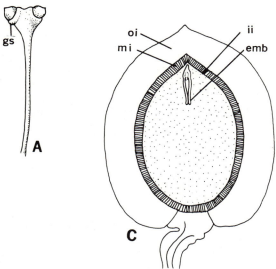

FIGURE 19–20 Reproductive organs of *Ginkgo biloba*. A, single peduncle supporting two young ovules that are subtended by collar representing gynosporophyll, × 1; B, several mature seeds borne at tip of spur shoot, × 1; C, longitudinal median section of seed with young embryo, × 2. *emb*, embryo; *gs*, gynosporophyll; *ii*, inner layer of integument; *mi*, middle layer of integument; *oi*, outer layer of integument. (C, from *Morphology of Gymnosperms* by J. M. Coulter and C. J. Chamberlain by permission of The University of Chicago Press, copyright 1910 and 1917.)

genous cells that function as androspore mother cells and undergo meiosis to form tetrads of spores. Before they are shed, spores begin to develop into pollen grains containing the immature androgametophytes. Development of the androgametophyte is similar to that of cycads.

Two ovules are borne on each peduncle— one at the tip of each dichotomous branch (Fig. 19–20A, B). Beneath each ovule is a collar which some botanists believe to be homologous to a leaf because occasional freaks occur in which the ovules are associated with leaf-like structures. As in cycads, each ovule has a single integument with three distinct tissue regions. Following pollination, the three layers mature into an inner fleshy layer that dries out to a papery skin, a central stony layer, and an outer fleshy layer. The outer layer contains the butyric acid that causes the foul odor of the seeds in autumn. The development of the gyno-gametophyte in the ovule is similar to that in cycads.

Following fertilization, the embryo develops cotyledons, an epicotyl, and a hypocotyl, resorbing the cells of the gynogametophyte. Eventually, the young radicle grows through the micropyle and makes contact with the soil. The cotyledons remain attached to the seed and continue to absorb nutrient material from it.

Phylogeny. The ancestors of the ginkgos are unknown. *Ginkgo* is similar to cycads in many respects, especially in the sex organs and gametophyte development. However, the leaves are distinctive and generally unlike the pinnate leaves of cycads and pteridosperms. In addition, the stem, with extensive wood, small pith and cortex, and bordered pitting, is similar to that of the coniferophytes (see Chapter 20); the ginkgos are usually aligned with this group. The most reasonable hypotheses are that the ginkgophytes evolved either from the same stock as the Cordaitales, most likely the progymnosperms, or that they evolved from unknown ancestors, presumably pterophytes, into a separate line of seed plants. Future research on Devonian and Carboniferous plants offers the main hope for determining the phylogeny of the ginkgophytes.

341

20 / Division Coniferophyta

The *coniferophytes* encompass two main orders of plants, the fossil Cordaitales, and the Coniferales which are represented by both fossil and extant families and genera. Also included is a group of Upper Devonian plants referred to as *progymnosperms*. Beck has suggested that the progymnosperms were ancestral to both the pteridosperm and coniferophyte lines. They are considered together in this chapter for convenience, rather than because they show closer relationship to the coniferophytes than to the pteridosperms.

If we accept the derivation of coniferophytes from progymnosperms, the most likely evolutionary link is between the progymnosperms of the Upper Devonian and the Cordaitales of the Carboniferous (see Fig. 20–25). The Cordaitales are most abundant in the later Carboniferous Period, where they overlap with the early conifers. The Coniferales extend from the late Carboniferous to the present. Athough they appear to have reached a maximum in the mid-Mesozoic, the conifers are still major elements of the world's floras.

In spite of gaps to be filled, there is good evidence for believing that the Coniferales evolved from the Cordaitales through intermediate stages represented by the Lebachi-aceae, an early Mesozoic family of conifers. The evolutionary progression is best documented from investigations of ovule-bearing appendages, as stressed in the descriptions and discussion in the succeeding pages.

PROGYMNOSPERMS

Three separate orders containing eight genera have been described for this group; undoubtedly the best known is the genus *Archaeopteris*. Originally, this plant was known from leaf compressions found rather widely in Upper Devonian rocks. On the basis of leaf form and sporangia, *Archaeopteris* was usually considered an early fern, and classified with the Protopteridiales. However, in 1960 a leaf of *Archaeopteris* was found attached to a stem called *Callixylon,* a genus that had previously been allied with the Cordaitales. This discovery initiated the concept of progymnosperms and prompted the hypothesis that *Archaeopteris* and related forms were ancestral to both the coniferophytes and pteridosperms.

As reconstructed, *Archaeopteris* is clearly an arborescent plant that reached a height of

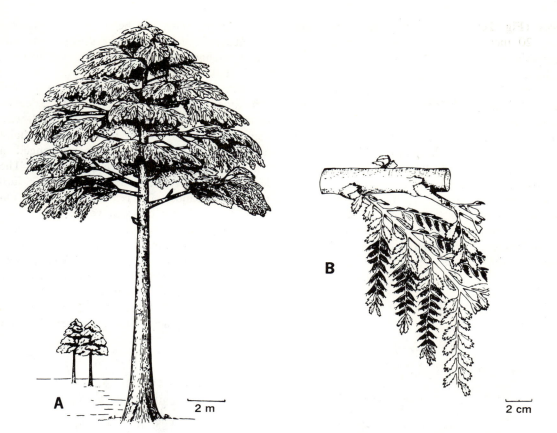

FIGURE 20–1 *Archaeopteris.* A, reconstruction of complete plant; B, branch bearing two fronds, with both sterile and fertile pinnules on lower frond. (From C. B. Beck, "Reconstruction of *Archeopteris,* and further consideration of its phylogenetic position," 1962, Vol. 49, *American Journal of Botany,* with permission of *American Journal of Botany.*)

at least 20 meters (Fig. 20–1A). The largest trunk known is over 1.5 meters in diameter, and most trunks taper up to a crown of branches. The main branches appear to be horizontal or only slightly angled upward. The leaves range from less than 60 centimeters to over 1.5 meters in length and are frond-like (Fig. 20–1B). In most species, some of the leaf pinnae contain both sterile and fertile pinnules, whereas others appear completely sterile. The sporangia are aligned on the leading edges of fertile pinnules, and have yielded spores that are round to deltoid, trilete, and unornamented. Although several species are reported to be heterosporous, others have only one size of spore and are presumably homosporous.

The stem contains a narrow pith, mesarch primary xylem strands, and secondary xylem. The tracheids of the secondary xylem have a unique pattern of round bordered pits that occur in patches on the radial walls in groups of six to 20, and in two to three vertical rows.

Order Cordaitales. Three families are generally assigned to the Cordaitales. Two of these comprise mainly genera of petrified wood, and their relationships are somewhat obscure. The best-known genus is *Cordaites,* in which both leaves and compound strobili have been found attached to stems.

Cordaites is a large arborescent plant that was probably the tallest of the Carboniferous

DIVISION CONIFEROPHYTA

trees (Fig. 20–2). Petrified stems measuring over 20 meters long have been found; some probably reached a height of at least 30 meters.

The anatomy of the stem is known in detail. The pith has a diameter up to 1.5 centimeters and consists of lens-shaped cavities within the parenchyma tissue. Primary xylem lies immediately outside the pith. The tracheids show a progression outward from helical to scalariform to bordered. The primary xylem grades into secondary xylem, which has tracheids with one to three rows of alternating and hexagonal bordered pits. The secondary xylem forms a thick cylinder of wood which in most Carboniferous specimens shows no growth rings. This has been cited as suggesting absence of well-defined seasonal or climatic changes during formation of Carboniferous coal swamps.

The leaves are thin, strap-shaped, and sometimes over a meter long and 15 centimeters wide (Fig. 20–3). Many length-wise veins that appear to be parallel are actually acutely dichotomous. Stomata are arranged in bands on the under surface of the leaf. The leaves apparently derived much of their support from bands of sclerenchyma which extend longitudinally between veins.

The reproductive organs of *Cordaites* consist of loose compound strobili in the axils of some leaves on outer branches. Both pollen-bearing and seed-bearing strobili are placed in the same genus, *Cordaianthus* (Fig. 20–4A). The compound strobilus consists of two rows of awl-shaped bracts—one on either side of a

344

FIGURE 20–2 Reconstruction of *Cordaites*. Note compound strobili interspersed among leaves of side branches, × 0.003. (From D. H. Scott, *Studies in Fossil Botany,* Adam & Charles Black, Ltd., London.)

FIGURE 20–3 Twig of *Cordaites,* showing strap-shaped leaves and compound strobili, × 10. (After Grand' Eury from D. H. Scott, *Studies in Fossil Botany,* Adam & Charles Black, Ltd., London.)

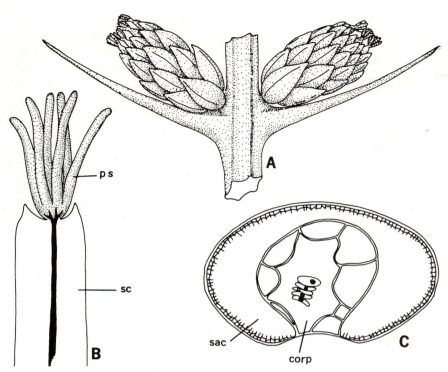

FIGURE 20–4 Reproductive organs of *Cordaites*. A, androstrobili in axils of bracts on primary strobilar axis, ×6; B, single scale (*sc*) on androstrobilus, showing attachment of pollen sacs (*p s*) at tip, ×25; C, pollen grain of *Cordaites* with several gametophytic cells in corpus (*corp*), surrounded by single saccus (*sac*), ×800. (A, from T. Delevoryas, "A New Male Cordaitean fructification from Kansas Carboniferous," 1953, Vol. 40, *American Journal of Botany,* with permission of *American Journal of Botany;* B, C, from Florin with permission of *Palaeontographica* and *Svensk Botanisk Tidskrift.*)

central axis. In the axil of each bract is a short shoot bearing spirally arranged appendages, or scales. Some of the scales bear pollen sacs (Fig. 20–4B). Several have yielded pollen grains that show a central body, or corpus, presumably of gametophytic tissue, which is surrounded by a single bladder, or saccus (Fig. 20–4C).

As mentioned previously, the ovule-bearing strobilus forms the first stage in an evolutionary series of such organs in the Coniferophyta. The ovule-bearing strobili are similar to those bearing pollen but are known in more detail (Fig. 20–5). A long axis supports two lateral rows of bracts, each with a dwarf shoot in the axil. The dwarf shoot has spirally arranged scales—some fertile, others sterile. The

fertile scales are somewhat elongate and bear one or more terminal ovules. Ovules in some species extend well beyond the end of the dwarf shoot but are virtually hidden in other species.

The seeds of the Cordaitales are small and heart-shaped, with the integument expanded into a wing. The integument is free from the nucellus except at the base, and the nucellus often projects into a nucellar beak. In general morphology, the seeds of the Cordaitales are very similar to those of the pteridosperms.

The work of Florin and others has suggested that the seed cone of the Coniferales was probably derived by reduction and elaboration of an inflorescence such as *Cordaianthus*. This will be considered in some detail

DIVISION CONIFEROPHYTA

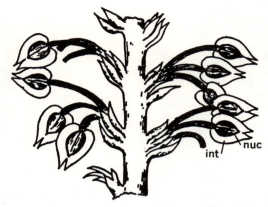

FIGURE 20–5 Part of compound gynostrobilus of *Cordaites* showing dwarf shoots in axils of bracts, and both sterile and fertile scales emanating from dwarf shoot. Seeds are heart-shaped, with wing-like integument (*int*) surrounding nucellus (*nuc*), ×2. (After Carruthers.)

under the extant conifers; probable intermediate stages can be noted in the ovule-bearing shoots of the family Lebachiaceae described below.

Order Coniferales. This is a large order with eight families, seven of which have extant genera, and one of which, the Lebachiaceae, is represented only by fossil members. The family Lebachiaceae, ranging from the late Carboniferous to the Jurassic, comprises plants that appear to be the immediate ancestors of all the families of extant conifers except the Taxaceae.

Family Lebachiaceae. This family consists of a few genera found on several continents of the Northern Hemisphere; the best-known genus is *Lebachia* from the late Carboniferous and early Permian (Fig. 20–6A). It was a tree of uncertain size, consisting of a main axis with pinnately arranged side branches. Leaves on the small ultimate twigs are needle- or scale-like, entire, and have a single unbranched vein. Each leaf has four bands of irregularly arranged stomata—two long bands on the abaxial surface and two shorter bands on the adaxial surface. *Lebachia* has single-celled epidermal hairs on both sides of the leaf—a characteristic shared with many extant conifers.

Both seed-bearing and pollen-bearing cones are attached terminally on some of the side branches of *Lebachia.* The pollen-bearing cones consist of an axis with spirally arranged and scale-like androsporophylls. On the abaxial surface of each androsporophyll, two pollen sacs are partly covered by an outgrowth of the sporophyll itself.

Pollen grains of *Lebachia* have a single saccus surrounding a central corpus (Fig. 20–6B). The bladder is interrupted on the distal surface by the germinal furrow. In several related genera, two sacci are attached to a corpus—a disaccate condition occurring in the modern conifer families Pinaceae and Podocarpaceae.

Doyle has suggested that the disaccate condition evolved from the monosaccate of *Lebachia* (Fig. 20–7A) by a suppression of the single saccus along the proximal surface of the grain. The evolution of the disaccate condition has been linked with the inversion of the ovules, which occurred in several genera of Lebachiaceae found somewhat later in the geologic record than *Lebachia* itself. According to this hypothesis, the evolution of the disaccate condition resulted in the grains floating *upward* through the pollination fluid in the micropyle of *inverted* ovules, thus bringing the germinal area of the pollen in close proximity to the nucellus. The pollen tube would have had only a short distance to traverse to the nucellus, thereby increasing the chances for fertilization. In genera with *upright* ovules such as *Lebachia,* the single bladder would have allowed the grain to float in the pollination fluid but with the germinal surface *down,* i.e., facing the nucellus.

As in other genera with spiral sporophylls and two abaxial sporangia, the pollen-bearing cones of *Lebachia* are essentially simple cones or strobili and almost identical in structure to their counterparts in extant conifers. But the cones of *Lebachia* differ markedly from the pollen-bearing organs of *Cordaites,* which are compound strobili. Furthermore, androsporangia in *Cordaites* are terminal rather than abaxial on sporophylls. Thus, the marked

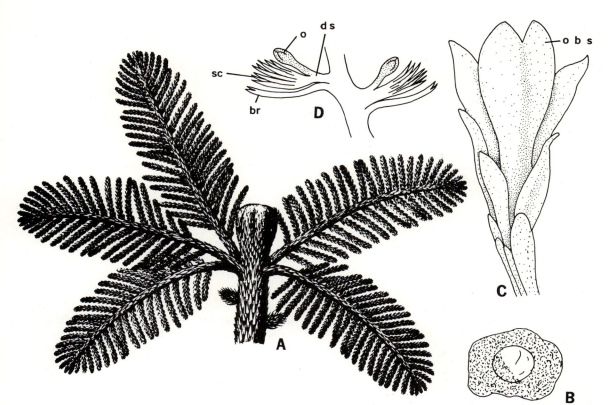

FIGURE 20–6   A, sterile branch of *Lebachia* with five twigs, showing pinnate arrangement of ultimate branches, ×0.33; B, single pollen grain showing central corpus and surrounding saccus, ×185; C, dwarf shoot of seed-bearing cone showing spirally arranged scales and single ovule-bearing scale (*o b s*) at top, ×10; D, longitudinal section of seed-bearing cone showing bracts (*br*), sterile scales (*sc*), and single ovule (*o*) attached to dwarf shoot (*d s*), ×4. (After Florin with permission of *Palaeontographica*.)

difference in structure of the pollen-bearing cone between *Cordaites* and the Lebachiaceae so far has not been bridged by fossil discoveries.

The seed-bearing strobilus of *Lebachia* is elliptical to circular in outline, with many compact bracts spirally arranged on the central axis (Fig. 20–6D). Each bract is two-forked, with a single vein that divides to provide one vein for each of the two lobes. In its axil, each bract contains a dwarf shoot with spirally arranged appendages or decurrent and upright scales. Usually only one scale is fertile and bears a single ovule at the tip (Fig. 20–6C, D). The seed-bearing scale occurs next to the main axis of the cone, in the same spiral sequence as the sterile scales. The micropyle of

the ovule is directed outward. The integument appears to be a continuation of the tissue of the seed scale that overarches the nucellus, forming a relatively deep micropyle.

In a closely related genus of seed organs, *Ernestiodendron,* the dwarf shoot also arises in the axil of a bract. The somewhat flattened dwarf shoots have only a few sterile scales, or sometimes none. From three to seven spirally arranged gynosporophylls occur in central or terminal regions of the dwarf shoot. Each bears a single ovule, with the sporophyll grading into the integument as in *Lebachia*. Some of the ovules are erect; others are inverted with the micropyles directed toward the axis.

The over-all structure of the compound gynostrobili in genera of the Lebachiaceae is

DIVISION CONIFEROPHYTA

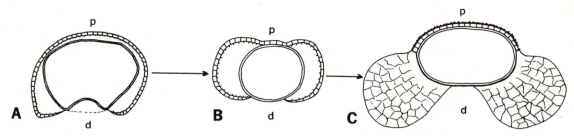

FIGURE 20–7   Apparent evolution of saccate pollen grains. A, *Lebachia piniformis* (Lower Permian); B, *Ullmannia bronnii* (Upper Permian); C, extant grain of *Pinus. d,* distal pole and surface; *p,* proximal pole and surface. (A, B, after Florin with permission of *Palaeontographica.*)

similar to that of *Cordaites*. In the Lebachiaceae, there is a general reduction in the length of the dwarf shoot and in the numbers of sterile scales and ovules. This may represent an early stage in the evolution of Mesozoic and Cenozoic conifers which resulted in further reduction of parts in several directions. The final arrangements of seed-cone structures are found in the seven extant families.

Extant Conifers.   During early and middle Mesozoic times, the conifers underwent marked and apparently rapid evolution. As a result, they became a predominant part of the floras of the Jurassic and early Cretaceous. During this time, most of the modern families were differentiated. However, in rocks older than the Upper Cretaceous, most conifers appear in several generalized forms that cannot be distinguished in terms of extant genera. These earlier indistinct forms, referred to as the transition conifers, have been given a series of form- or organ-genus names, based largely on morphology, which sometimes suggest natural affiliation—for example, *Prepinus* and *Araucarioxylon*.

During the Upper Cretaceous and Tertiary, almost all of the extant genera became differentiated but apparently at different times. During this interval, many of the genera also began to appear in regions of present distribution, which in some instances entailed a retreat from a more widespread distribution. Such restrictions are almost certainly an indication of senescence or even of impending extinction. Some of the most dramatic examples are found in the family Taxodiaceae,

where genera such as *Metasequoia* (dawn redwood), *Sequoia* (California redwood), and *Taxodium* (bald cypress) were widespread across the Northern Hemisphere during the earlier Tertiary. Today, the same genera are restricted to very narrow geographical and ecological ranges, and are almost certainly facing extinction. A main factor leading to extinction appears to be competition, particularly from angiosperms; another factor is genetic senescence, which prevents speciation in diverse ecological niches.

General Distribution of Families.   The seven extant families are distributed in both hemispheres. Several, such as the Pinaceae, are more characteristic of the Northern Hemisphere, whereas others, such as the Araucariaceae, are more widespread in the Southern Hemisphere (Table 20–1).

Although some genera are declining, others appear to have evolved fairly recently—for example, *Pseudotsuga*. In terms of absolute number of extant species, there are only about one-twentieth as many conifers as ferns, and only about one-sixtieth as many conifers as monocotyledons. Although the number of genera and species is relatively low, some conifers, such as *Pinus,* are conspicuous because of the large numbers of individuals which occur in certain regions. As a group, therefore, the conifers are still among the dominant forest trees of the world, particularly in the boreal forests of the Northern Hemisphere. They are adapted for mesic or xeric conditions and occupy most ecological niches, except areas such as extreme deserts and the tundra. They pro-

348

TABLE 20–1

Main Morphological Characteristics and Distribution of Coniferales

FAMILY (NUMBER OF GENERA IN PARENTHESES)	RANGE	GENERAL CHARACTERISTICS
Pinaceae (10)	Almost entirely Northern Hemisphere	Leaves needle-like; leaves and cone scales spirally arranged; bract and ovuliferous scale distinct; pollen grains mostly saccate
Taxodiaceae (10)	China, Japan, Formosa, Tasmania, California, southern United States, and Mexico	Leaves and cone scales spirally arranged; bract and ovuliferous scale almost completely fused; pollen small with a papilla
Cupressaceae (16)	Widespread in both hemispheres	Leaves and cone scales cyclic; bract and ovuliferous scale strongly fused; pollen small with a small pore
Araucariaceae (2)	Almost completely Southern Hemisphere	Leaves and cone scales spirally arranged; bract and ovuliferous scale completely fused; ovules solitary; pollen large and nonsaccate
Podocarpaceae (7)	Mostly Southern Hemisphere, Central America, and West Indies	Leaves flat and broad with either a single vein or many veins; ovules terminal and single; pollen saccate
Taxaceae (5)	Mostly Northern Hemisphere	Leaves flat and pointed; spiral; ovules terminal and solitary, with fleshy aril; pollen round and nonsaccate
Cephalotaxaceae (1)	China, Japan, tropical Himalayas	Leaves flat and narrow; spiral; cone scales decussate; 2 ovules on ovuliferous scale; pollen circular and nonsaccate

349

vide our main source of lumber and wood products, including pulp and paper.

Life History. The conifers have a life history essentially similar to that of the ferns, with the sporophyte dominant and the gametophyte reduced and completely dependent on the sporophyte (Fig. 20–8). The androgametophyte at maturity consists of from none to many prothallial cells, and develops within the spore wall or pollen grain. As in cycads and *Ginkgo,* the gynogametophyte consists of a mass of cells embedded in the nucellus. In most conifers, the sporophyte grows for several to many years before gametophytes are produced, but under normal conditions, the sporophyte continues to produce pollen and ovules for the rest of its life.

Morphology. In habit, the conifers are nearly all trees, some reaching gigantic proportions. The largest is *Sequoiadendron giganteum,* the "big tree" of California, with some specimens over 10 meters in diameter, 90 meters in height, and possibly 4,000 years old. A few genera, such as *Juniperus,* are characteristically shrubby. None is herbaceous.

Most of the conifers are monopodial, with excurrent and whorled or spiral branching (Fig. 20–9). Some conifers, such as the Pinaceae, lose the leaves on older branch regions, whereas others, such as the Araucariaceae, retain the leaves on all but the oldest branches. Several genera—such as *Pinus, Larix,* and *Cedrus*—have both long and spur shoots as in *Ginkgo.* In *Pinus,* one to eight leaves are ar-

DIVISION CONIFEROPHYTA

350

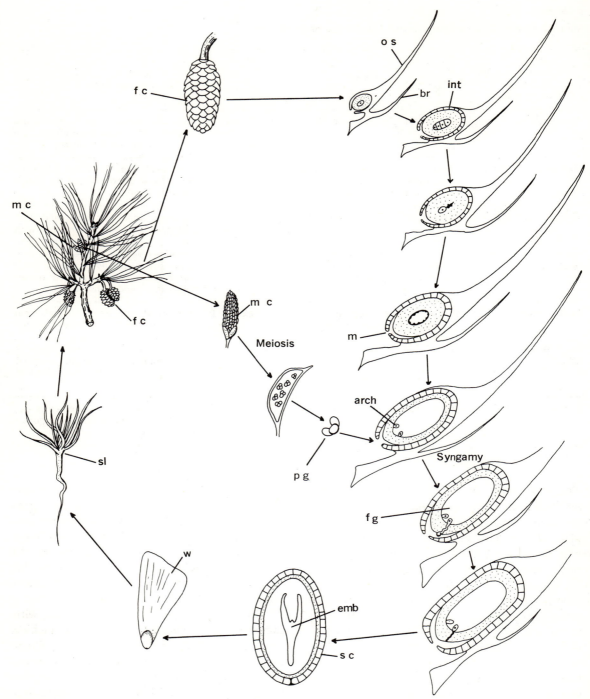

FIGURE 20–8 Life history of a pine. *arch*, archegonium; *br*, bract; *emb*, embryo; *f c*, female cone; *f g*, female gametophyte; *int*, integument; *m*, micropyle; *m c*, male cone; *o s*, ovuliferous scale; *p g*, pollen grain; *s c*, seed coat; *sl*, seedling; *w*, wing. (From *Introductory Botany* by Arthur Cronquist; Harper & Row, 1961, Fig. 20–16, "Life Cycle of *Pinus*.")

FIGURE 20–9 Habit views of extant conifers. A, *Cedrus deodara* (note hanging branches with clusters of evergreen leaves on dwarf shoots), ×0.027; B, *Araucaria araucana* (leaves are persistent and very sharp on regularly whorled branches), ×0.03.

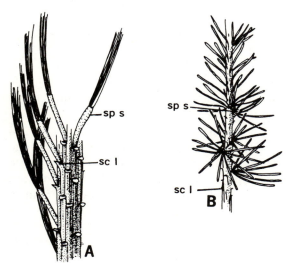

FIGURE 20–10 Leaf arrangement in conifers. A, twig of *Pinus* with spur shoots (*sp s*) emanating from axils of scale leaves (*sc l*), and bearing needles at tips, ×4; B, *Cedrus* showing both spur shoots and green leaves arising from axils of scale leaves, ×1.

ranged spirally at the tip of the spur, which occurs in the axil of a nonphotosynthetic scale leaf of the long shoot (Fig. 20–10A). The spurs fall off after several years, leaving a scaly long shoot. In *Larix* and *Cedrus,* the leaves vary in number and are spirally arranged on the spur shoot (Fig. 20–10B).

The leaves of conifers are widely variable in shape, texture, and size. In general, four main morphological groups can be recognized (Fig. 20–11). (1) The first group includes needle leaves that are distinctly tetragonal in cross section and have a single vein (Fig. 20–11A); examples are found in *Picea, Cedrus, Cryptomeria,* and some species of *Araucaria, Dacrydium,* and *Podocarpus.* (2) Leaves of the second group are linear to lanceolate in outline, and usually distinctly flattened; examples are *Sequoia, Taxodium,* and *Metasequoia* (Fig. 20–11B) in the Taxodiaceae;

DIVISION CONIFEROPHYTA

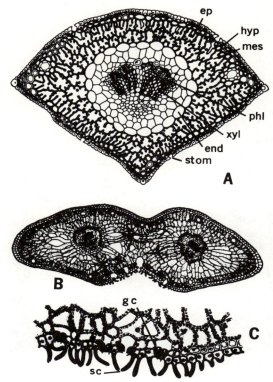

FIGURE 20–12 Anatomy of conifer leaves. A, transverse section of *Pinus* leaf, ×60; B, transverse section of leaf of *Sciadopitys,* ×25; C, enlarged view of B, with subsidiary cells over-arching stomata, ×250. *end,* endodermis; *ep,* epidermis; *g c,* guard cell; *hyp,* hypodermis; *mes,* mesophyll; *phl,* phloem; *s c,* subsidiary cell; *stom,* stoma; *xyl,* xylem. (A, with permission of Blaisdell Publishing Company, from *The Plant Kingdom* by William H. Brown; B, C, from *Gymnosperms* by C. J. Chamberlain.)

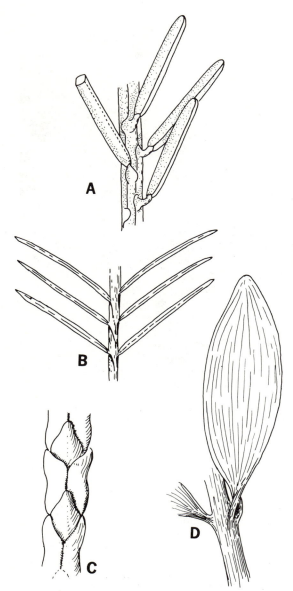

352

FIGURE 20–11 Leaf types of conifers. A, leaves of *Picea* showing single vein, ×4; B, leaves of *Metasequoia* showing flattened blade and opposite arrangement on twig, ×2; C, reduced leaves of *Cupressus* in two rows on twig, ×4; D, leaf of *Agathis* showing expanded blade and steeply dichotomizing veins, ×0.75.

Tsuga, Abies, and *Pseudotsuga* in the Pinaceae; and some species of *Araucaria, Dacrydium,* and *Podocarpus.* The linear to lanceolate leaf form is the commonest in living conifers. (3) Leaves of the third group are much reduced, scale-like, and usually closely appressed to the stem; they are found most often in genera of the Cupressaceae (Fig. 20–11C), and in *Sequoiadendron, Taxodium,* and some species of *Podocarpus.* (4) The fourth leaf type is the least common in the conifers; leaves are flat, broad, usually ovate in outline, and many-veined (Fig. 20–11D). Venation appears to be parallel but is actually acutely dichotomous. This fourth type is found almost exclusively in conifers of the Southern Hemisphere, especially in *Agathis* and some species of *Araucaria* and *Podocarpus.*

Most of the conifers are evergreen, but several genera are deciduous (*Larix, Tax-*

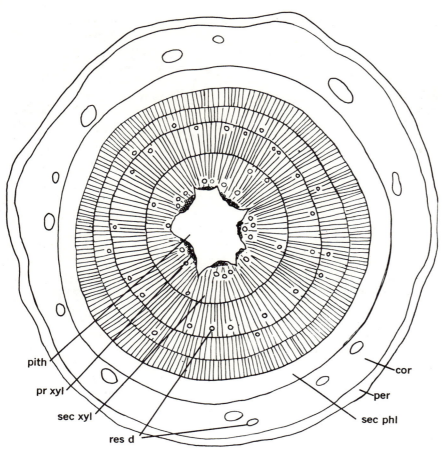

pith

pr xyl

sec xyl

res d

cor

per

sec phl

FIGURE 20–13   Transverse section of four-year-old twig of *Pinus,* ×30. *cor,* cortex; *per,* periderm; *pr xyl,* primary xylem; *res d,* resin ducts; *sec phl,* secondary phloem; *sec xyl,* secondary xylem.

odium, and *Metasequoia*). In *Larix,* the needles fall from spur shoots; in *Taxodium* and *Metasequoia,* complete leafy twigs fall each autumn. Almost all conifer leaves are adapted for xeric conditions. Typically, there is a heavy cuticle on a thick epidermis with sunken stomata (Fig. 20–12C). The stomata have prominent subsidiary cells that sometimes overarch the stomatal opening, thereby providing a constricted aperture. The stomata occur in longitudinal bands on the leaves of many conifers.

Immediately inside the epidermis is a hypodermis of one to three layers of thick-walled cells. This surrounds the mesophyll tissue, which consists of convoluted cells in the needle and scale leaves, but is differentiated into palisade and spongy layers in many of the broad flat leaves. The vascular bundles vary from one to many—usually one or two in the needle and scale leaves, and many in the broad-leaf forms. In most leaves the bundle or bundles are surrounded by a well-defined endodermis. Often, cells with secondary walls and bordered pits extend from the vascular bundles to the endodermis, presumably functioning in conduction between the mesophyll and vascular bundle; hence, this is referred to as transfusion tissue.

Stem Anatomy.   The stems of all conifers have a narrow pith, primary vascular cylinder, and cortex (Fig. 20–13). In contrast, many

DIVISION CONIFEROPHYTA

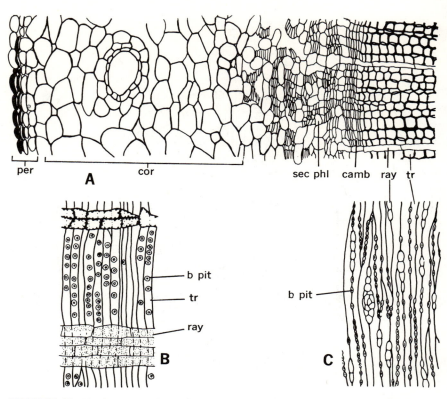

per | A | cor | sec phl | camb | ray | tr

b pit
tr
ray
B

b pit
C

FIGURE 20–14 Anatomy of *Pinus* stem. A, transverse section through secondary xylem to outside of bark, ×110; B, radial section of secondary xylem, ×100; C, tangential section of secondary xylem, ×100. *b pit,* bordered pit; *camb,* cambium; *cor,* cortex; *per,* periderm; *sec phl,* secondary phloem; *tr,* tracheid.

have a very wide cylinder of secondary xylem. The bark may be as thick as 10 centimeters and in *Sequoiadendron* has been reported to reach 100 centimeters. The bark includes both secondary phloem and periderm, with large resin ducts in many genera. Growth rings in the secondary xylem are prominent and vary in thickness depending on the ecological conditions of the particular year. Reconstructions of climatic fluctuations and dates of certain past events can be made from growth-ring analyses. Rings are extremely narrow in areas where periods of growth are restricted by climate or soil factors, such as the muskeg regions of the subarctic. In these areas, over 200 rings within a diameter of 10 centimeters are common.

In some genera the secondary xylem consists of tracheids, ray parenchyma, and xylem parenchyma (Fig. 20–14). The tracheids have bordered pitting, with a single row of pits in most conifers except the araucarians, which have two or three alternate rows (Fig. 20–14B). As in *Ginkgo,* the tracheids contain crassulae between the bordered pits. These are common in all families except the Araucariaceae, where they appear sporadically. No function or significance is attached to the crassulae. In *Taxus, Cephalotaxus,* and *Pseudotsuga* a tertiary thickening is arranged spirally on the inside of the secondary wall. This has been credited with providing the elasticity that has made the wood of yew popular for archery bows.

The xylem rays vary in length, width, and depth; they are only a single cell wide in many genera (Fig. 20–14A). In addition to having ray parenchyma cells with simple pits,

354

xylem rays of most genera of the Pinaceae have one to three rows of cells called ray tracheids, with bordered pits and without protoplasts at the bottom and top of the ray. In wounded tissue, gradational series have been noted between ordinary and ray tracheids, suggesting that the latter originate from regular tracheids. Ray parenchyma cells stay alive for varying periods and apparently function in both conduction and food storage. Some rays are several cells wide and contain resin ducts. These develop from the separation of resin-producing cells, forming a central duct (Fig. 20–14C). The resin-producing cells are called epithelial cells; they often enlarge to close the duct and are then termed tylosoids.

Resin ducts form also in the vertical plane among the tracheids. In conifers such as *Pinus,* resin ducts appear to be an integral feature of the wood. However, in many other conifers, resin ducts are apparently produced in the wood largely in response to injury. Resin ducts, or resin canals, are also common features in the leaves and bark of many conifers. Resin is highly antiseptic and prevents invasion by certain microorganisms. It is very effective in sealing wounds in the tree. The presence of abundant resin is also credited with helping to preserve coniferous wood in sediments.

Each year all of the secondary phloem is incorporated as an inner layer of the bark (Fig. 20–15). The secondary phloem contains sieve cells, parenchyma, and phloem fibers. The elongated sieve cells form sieve areas on the radial walls and particularly on the overlapping end walls. Certain of the phloem parenchyma cells are often filled with dense, deeply stained cytoplasm. These are called albuminous cells (Fig. 20–15A). Although the phloem of conifers contains no companion cells, the albuminous cells appear to function like companion cells when they are associated with sieve cells.

In addition to secondary phloem, the bark of conifers contains small amounts of crushed primary phloem and extensive periderm (Fig. 20–15B). The periderm and tissues outside of it are usually referred to as outer bark or

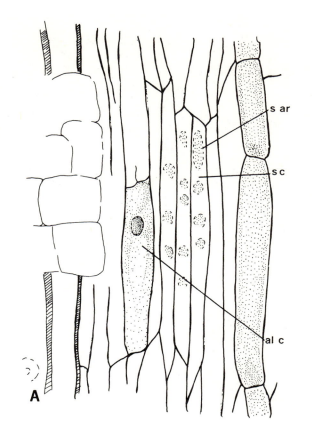

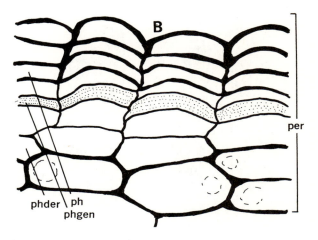

FIGURE 20–15 Anatomy of *Pinus* stem. A, longitudinal section through cambium and secondary phloem, showing sieve cells (*s c*), with sieve areas (*s ar*), and single albuminous cell (*al c*), ×1,000; B, transverse section of periderm (*per*) showing cork cambium or phellogen (*phgen*), cork cells or phellem (*ph*), and inner phelloderm cells (*phder*), ×800.

DIVISION CONIFEROPHYTA

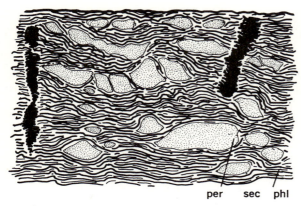

FIGURE 20–16 Transverse section of bark of *Pseudotsuga,* showing lenses of periderm (*per*) embedded in secondary phloem (*sec phl*), ×1.

356

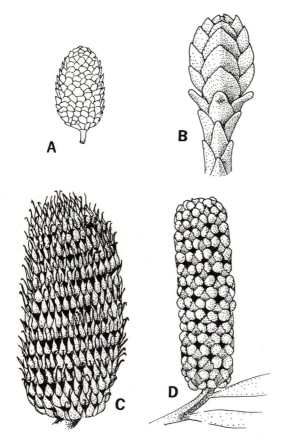

FIGURE 20–17 Habit views of androstrobili of conifers. A, *Picea,* ×3; B, *Cupressus,* ×5; C, *Araucaria,* ×2; D, *Podocarpus,* ×2.

rhytidome. In many conifers, the periderm forms as lenticular or conchoidal plates in successively deeper layers, and the older and outer layers split off and fall away (Fig. 20–16). The inner bark consists of phloem containing distorted and crushed fibers.

Reproduction. Pollen sacs and ovules are borne in strobili, or cones, in all families except the Taxaceae, which have terminal ovules and no strobili. Most genera are monoecious, but several are reported to be dioecious. Some families, such as the Cupressaceae, have both monoecious and dioecious genera. Although there is no direct evidence, it is generally believed that the dioecious condition was derived from the monoecious—mainly because in most plant groups from the algae to the angiosperms, evolution has apparently tended toward the separation of the sexes.

In all families, the pollen-bearing organs are androstrobili clustered on smaller branches, often in lower reaches of the tree (Fig. 20–17). The androstrobili vary in length from 2 millimeters in *Juniperus communis* to over 12 centimeters in some species of *Araucaria.* In all families except the Cupressaceae, the androsporophylls are arranged spirally on the axis; in the Cupressaceae they are cyclic. The sporophylls are so regularly disposed that they appear to be aligned in vertical rows (Fig. 20–17C, D). The androsporophylls are quite variable in size and shape. In some species, such as *Araucaria cunninghamii,* the sporophyll is virtually indistinguishable from a leaf. However, in most the androsporophyll is reduced and modified in shape. Several different types are shown in Figure 20–18. In most of the conifers, androsporangia are borne on the abaxial surface of the sporophyll. The number of sporangia varies from two to over 15, the largest numbers occurring in the Araucariaceae.

The pollen grains of the conifers are variable in morphology (Fig. 20–19). In size, they range from approximately 20 to 150 microns. All grains have a wall composed of two main layers—an inner thin layer called the intine, and an outer, thicker layer, the exine. In almost all grains, the exine itself is stratified into one or more distinct layers. The outer layer of the exine is often sculptured with pits, granules, reticulate markings, or other types of ornamentation. In general, the ornamentation is not particularly distinctive for genera or species, but in some cases it can be used in identification. As mentioned before, in most genera of the Pinaceae and Podocarpaceae the exine of pollen grains extends into sacci. These sacci range in number from one to several and are variable in size, ornamentation, and method of attachment to the corpus of the grain. Most of the extant genera have two sacci attached to the distal surface of the corpus.

Most conifer pollen grains have a thin specialized layer of exine that develops at the distal pole of the grain. This is called the leptoma (Fig. 20–19B). In saccate grains, the leptoma lies between the sacci; in bladderless grains, it variously forms a short papilla (Taxodiaceae), a small aperture (some genera of Cupressaceae), or simply a weakly defined area (*Tsuga, Athrotaxis, Callitris*). In almost all instances the pollen tube forms by an evagination of the intine at the leptoma.

All of the conifers are anemophilous, or wind-pollinated. The grains are shed at different times of the year, depending on latitude, altitude, and climate. Some travel over several hundred miles from the producing trees, but most appear to settle within shorter distances. Production is often prodigious, with an estimated several million grains from a single cone of *Araucaria*. In general only a few of the millions of grains shed ever reach a micropyle to effect pollination and fertilization.

The amount of gametophytic tissue developed in the pollen varies according to the genus and, to a lesser extent, the family. In the Araucariaceae and Podocarpaceae, the first two or three prothallial cells continue to divide to form several to many cells. The Pinaceae have two prothallial cells, whereas most genera of the Taxodiaceae and Cupres-

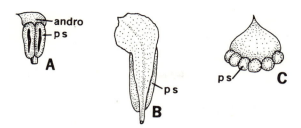

FIGURE 20–18 Androsporophylls (*andro*) and pollen sacs (*p s*) of conifers, × 8. A, *Pinus*; B, *Picea*; C, *Cryptomeria*. (From *Gymnosperms* by C. J. Chamberlain.)

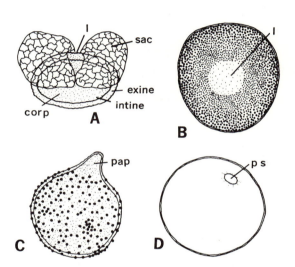

FIGURE 20–19 Pollen grains of conifers. A, *Pinus*, lateral view; B, *Araucaria*; C, *Sequoia*; D, *Chamaecyparis*. A,B, × 500; C,D, × 1,000. *corp*, corpus; *l*, leptoma; *pap*, papilla; *p s*, pseudospore; *sac*, saccus.

357

saceae have none. The stages following the development of the prothallial cells and antheridial initial from the androsporal cell are almost identical to those in the cycads and *Ginkgo* (Fig. 20–20). At first the antheridial initial divides to form a generative cell and a tube cell. In many conifers, the pollen is shed at this stage. If a grain lands on a micropyle and conditions are favorable, development of the androgametophyte continues. As the tube nucleus migrates toward the tip of the pollen tube, the generative cell divides to form a

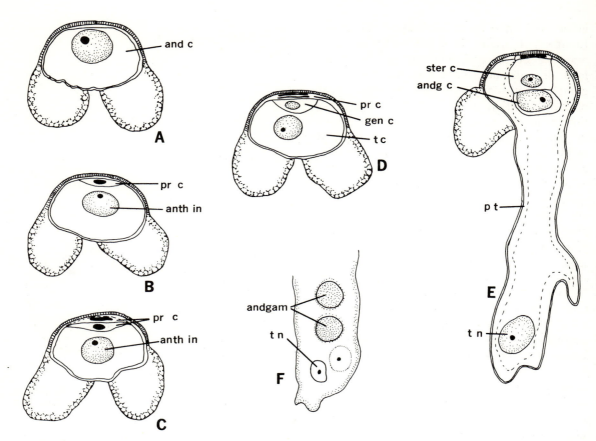

FIGURE 20–20   Development of androgametophyte of *Pinus,* ×500. A, pollen grain with androsporal cell (*and c*); B, first prothallial cell (*pr c*) and antheridial initial (*anth in*) formed from division of androsporal cell; C, second prothallial cell has formed; D, antheridial initial has produced generative cell (*gen c*) and tube cell (*t c*); E, tube nucleus (*t n*) has migrated to tip of pollen tube (*p t*) and generative cell has divided to form sterile cell (*ster c*) and androgenous cell (*andg c*); F, androgenous cell has divided to produce two androgametes (*andgam*), while tube nucleus remains at tip of pollen tube. (A–E, from *Morphology of Gymnosperms* by J. M. Coulter and C. J. Chamberlain, by permission of The University of Chicago Press, copyright 1910 and 1917; F, after Coulter.)

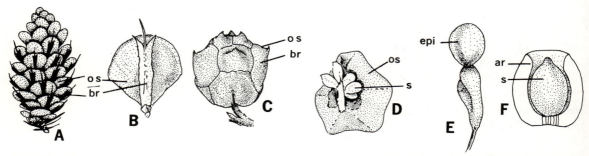

FIGURE 20–21   Gynostrobili of conifers. A,B, *Pseudotsuga;* note elongated bracts (*br*) protruding beyond ovuliferous scales (*o s*) (A, ×0.5; B, ×1); C,D, *Cupressus* (bract and ovuliferous scales are almost completely fused, and several seeds (*s*) are borne on each scale), (C, ×0.5; D, ×1); E, *Podocarpus,* with epimatium (*epi*) enclosing a single seed, ×0.5; F, *Taxus,* with fleshy aril (*ar*) surrounding single seed, ×2.

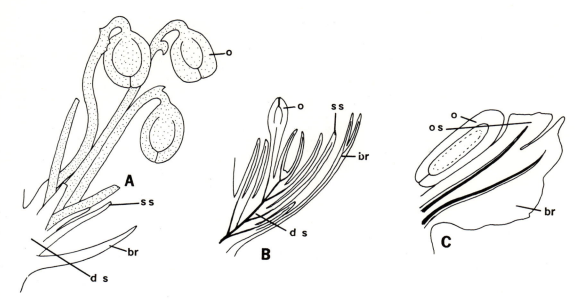

FIGURE 20-22 Probable evolution of gynostrobilus in coniferophytes. A, *Cordaites,* with several ovules (*o*) and sterile scales (*s s*) attached to dwarf shoot (*d s*) in axil of bract (*br*), ×2; B, *Lebachia,* in which ovules are reduced to one on dwarf shoot with sterile scales, again in axil of bract, ×4; C, *Pinus,* with two ovules attached to ovuliferous scale (*o s*), which almost certainly is homologue of dwarf shoot of *Lebachia,* ×5. (A, B, after Florin with permission of *Palaeontographica.*)

sterile cell and an androgenous cell (Fig. 20–20E). In most instances, the androgenous cell lies between the tube nucleus and the sterile cell. As the tube lengthens, the sterile cell loses its wall and, together with the androgenous cell, begins to move into the pollen tube. Just before fertilization, the androgenous cell divides to form two androgametes (Fig. 20–20F). Two types of androgametes are found in the conifers—one highly organized, with a nucleus and a definite wall, the other with no wall and a thin covering of cytoplasm. In both groups, the androgametes completely lack flagella or other appendages for locomotion.

In almost all conifers, the pollen tube grows through the nucellus until the tip of the tube reaches an archegonium. Then the tip of the pollen tube ruptures, and the androgametes are discharged into the archegonium. One gamete fuses with the egg, and the other aborts. The cytoplasm of the androgamete persists after its union with the egg, forming a dense coating on the zygote. In *Pinus* and some other conifers there is no fusion or blending

of nuclei. Instead, the two sets of chromosomes remain side by side until they are incorporated into a group on a single spindle during the first mitosis of the fertilized egg.

In most conifers, ovules are borne in cones that are compound structures as in the Cordaitales and Lebachiaceae. They consist of bracts with an ovuliferous scale attached to the basal part of the adaxial surface of each bract (Fig. 20–21). The bracts are whorled in the Cupressaceae but are spirally arranged in the Pinaceae, Taxodiaceae, and Araucariaceae. The bracts and ovuliferous scales are virtually free from each other in the Pinaceae but are coalesced to greater or lesser extent in the Cupressaceae, Taxodiaceae, and Araucariaceae (Fig. 20–21C). Although the bract is usually much smaller than the ovuliferous scale, it reaches well beyond the scale in *Pseudotsuga* (Fig. 20–21B), *Larix,* and *Abies.* Both bract and scale have a variety of shapes and sizes which are distinctive for genera and even species in all families.

Much controversy has centered around

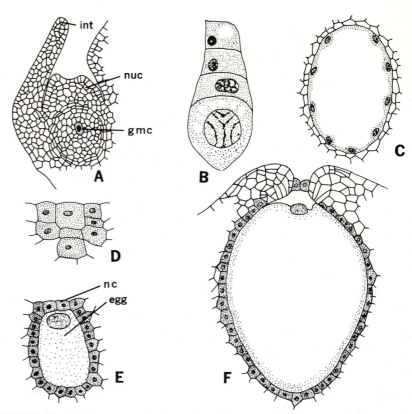

FIGURE 20–23 Development of gynogametophyte of conifers. A, longitudinal section of young ovule, showing integument (*int*) partly fused to nucellus (*nuc*) and a single gynospore mother cell (*g m c*) in central part of nucellus, ×40; B, linear tetrad of gynospores, with lowest enlarging and other three beginning to abort, ×485; C, free-nuclear stage with nuclei arranged around periphery of gynospore; D, archegonial initials at micropylar edge of gametophyte; E, immature archegonium showing two necks cells (*n c*) and large egg; F, mature archegonium with fully expanded egg and egg nucleus sitting just below neck (C–F, ×55). (A–C, after Ferguson; D–F, from *Morphology of Gymnosperms* by J. M. Coulter and C. J. Chamberlain by permission of The University of Chicago Press, copyright 1910 and 1917.)

the origin and structure of the bract and scale of coniferous gynostrobili. In early stages of evolution, the bract was most likely derived from a leaf. However, the ovuliferous scale has been equated to many structures, including a flattened branch in the axil of a leaf (the bract), a ligule, an open carpel, a placenta, the blended integuments of two ovules, a leaf of an axillary shoot, and the first two leaves of an axillary shoot fused along one margin. A clue to the probable origin and evolution of the ovuliferous scale can be found in the op-

posite orientation of the xylem and phloem in the bract and ovuliferous scale of extant conifers (Fig. 20–22C). In the bract, the phloem of the vascular bundles is on the lower (abaxial) side of the xylem in the normal arrangement for a leaf on a stem. By contrast, in the ovuliferous scale the phloem is on the upper (adaxial) side of the xylem. The most likely explanation for this opposite orientation is that the ovuliferous scale is a much-reduced homologue of the dwarf shoot of *Lebachia,* with fused sporophylls and scales. The inverted

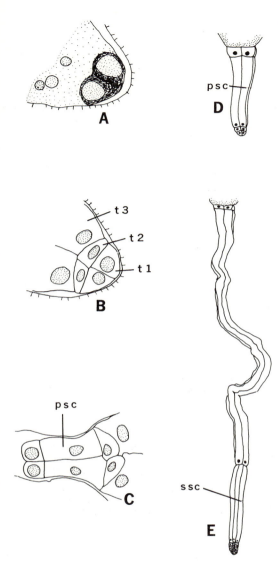

FIGURE 20–24 Embryonic development in conifers. A, free-nuclear stage with two proembryonic nuclei at chalazal end, × 100; B, longitudinal section of proembryo showing three tiers of cells (t1, t2, t3), each with four cells, × 100; C, cells on central tier elongated to form primary suspensor cells (p s c), × 100; D, primary suspensor cells further elongated, and cells of first tier divided to form several tiers of embryonic initials, × 40; E, primary suspensors greatly elongated, and secondary suspensor cells (s s c) have formed to push embryonic cap even deeper into gametophytic tissue, × 50. (A–C, adapted from Donald Alexander Johansen, *Plant Embryology—Embryogeny of the Spermatophyta*, copyright 1950, The Ronald Press Company, New York; D,E, after Buchholz with permission of Illinois State Academy of Science.)

xylem-phloem of the ovuliferous scale possibly represents reduced sporophylls and scales which were present on the adaxial surface of the axillary shoot of *Lebachia* (Fig. 20–22).

The ovules are attached to the adaxial surface of the ovuliferous scale, varying in number from one to seven. They are oriented in two main ways. In the Pinaceae, Araucariaceae, and many of the Podocarpaceae, the micropyle is directed toward the cone axis. In the Cupressaceae, Taxaceae, and most genera of the Taxodiaceae, the micropyle is directed away from the axis.

All ovules have only one integument, free or partly fused to the nucellus (Fig. 20–23A). Unlike the cycads or *Ginkgo*, there is no pollen chamber or nucellar beak. The integument is divided into an outer fleshy, a middle stony, and an inner fleshy layer. The outer layer is thin and usually sloughs off. The ovules of most conifers lack vascular tissue, but some have bundles at the base. Only *Podocarpus* has vascular bundles extending to the tip of the integument.

In some species of conifers, the seed has an attached wing. In *Pinus,* it is long and flat, and assists in wind dispersal of the seed. The wing, not actually a part of the seed, is the upper surface of the ovuliferous scale that abscises at seed maturation.

Ovules of the Taxaceae, Cephalotaxaceae, and Podocarpaceae are covered by a fleshy outgrowth of the stalk. In plants of the first two families this is called an aril; in the Podocarpaceae this is called an epimatium (Fig. 20–21E, F). The origin of the aril is uncertain, but the epimatium probably represents a modified ovuliferous scale.

The development of the gynogametophyte of conifers is very similar to that in the cycads and *Ginkgo*. The spore mother cell develops hypodermally, sometimes deeply within the nucellus (Fig. 20–23A). Four gynospores are formed at meiosis, nearly always in a linear tetrad (Fig. 20–23B). As a rule only one develops, but several are known to function up to the free-nuclear stage in *Taxus*. The gynospore expands greatly, undergoing free-

361

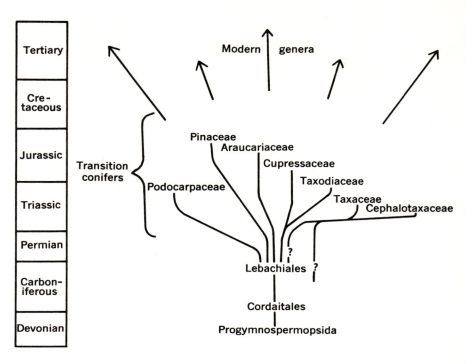

FIGURE 20–25 Flow chart depicting probable evolutionary pattern of conifers. Note questionable origins of the Taxaceae and Cephalotaxaceae and long period during which transition conifers were evolving.

nuclear division (Fig. 20–23C). Walls then form centripetally, producing a central mass of gametophytic cells, with the cells toward the chalazal end charged with nutrient materials.

In all conifers, the archegonia arise from the differentiation of superficial cells at the micropylar end or along the flanks of the nucellus (Fig. 20–23D). The archegonia usually develop two tiers of neck cells, each tier with four cells (Fig. 20–23E, F). Occasionally there are eight cells in each tier, and sometimes as few as two.

Following fertilization, the zygote undergoes a period of free-nuclear division in all conifers except *Sequoia* (Fig. 20–24A). In most families, four to eight nuclei are formed, but as many as 64 are reported in the Araucariaceae. Again, except in the Araucariaceae, the nuclei migrate to the basal end of the egg cell, where they form into a single plane. The nuclei undergo several additional divisions ac-

companied by wall formation, resulting in three or four tiers of cells (Fig. 20–24B–E).

In all the conifers, a greatly elongated suspensor develops. In *Pinus* and most of the Pinaceae, the suspensors originate from cells of the second tier which were formed by division of cells of the basal tier (Fig. 20–24C, D). These cells, called primary suspensors, elongate rather quickly to shove the basal tier down into the gametophyte. At the same time, the basal tier divides to produce one, two, or three additional tiers of cells called secondary suspensor cells or embryonal tubes. These cells elongate to variable extents and push the embryonic cells deeper into the gametophyte (Fig. 20–24E).

EVOLUTION OF CONIFERS

There is good evidence from investigations of both fossil and modern representatives that

VASCULAR PLANTS

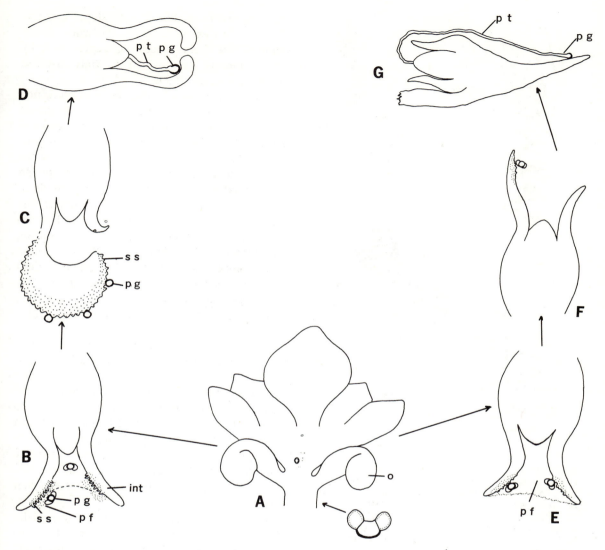

FIGURE 20–26 Probable evolution of pollination mechanisms in conifers. One pathway is shown in the series *Pseudovoltzia*-type (A) to *Pinus* (B) to *Larix* (C) to *Pseudotsuga* (D); a second pathway is shown from the *Pseudovoltzia*-type (A) to the *Abies* (E) to the *Cedrus* (F) to the *Tsuga* (G). *p f*, pollination fluid; *p g*, pollen grain; *p t*, pollen tube; *o*, ovule; *int*, integument; *s s*, stigmatic surface. (After Doyle with permission of Royal Dublin Society.)

evolution proceeded from the late Devonian progymnosperms to the Cordaitales of the Carboniferous, and hence through the Leba-chiaceae of the Permian to modern families (Fig. 20–25). During the early and middle Mesozoic, the conifers evolved rapidly and all of the extant families became differentiated. In the later Mesozoic, many of the modern conifer genera became distinct. Although these have persisted down to the present, many have become reduced in number and areal distribution. Some genera seem to be heading toward extinction, whereas others still appear to be evolving.

The most significant evolutionary trends are found in the evolution of the seed cones

DIVISION CONIFEROPHYTA

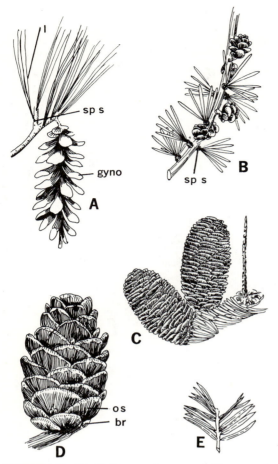

FIGURE 20–27 Foliage and cones of Pinaceae. A, *Pinus*, showing fascicles of needles (*l*) on spur shoots (*sp s*) and one pendulous gynostrobilus (*gyno*), ×0.5; B, *Larix*, with spurs, needles, and gynostrobili, ×0.5; C, *Abies*, with erect gynostrobili, ×0.5; D, *Keteleeria*, showing bracts (*br*) and ovuliferous scales (*o s*), ×0.5; E, foliage shoot of *Keteleeria* showing flattened and pointed needle leaves, ×0.3.

and pollination mechanism. In the seed cone, Florin has suggested that the fertile dwarf shoot of the Cordaitales and the Lebachiaceae appears to have been reduced with evolution,

accompanied by fusion of both sterile and fertile scales. In extant conifers, the whole dwarf shoot of the Lebachiaceae is represented by the ovuliferous scale, which is firmly fused to the bract (see p. 359).

Doyle has developed several interesting evolutionary series linking pollen structures with pollination mechanisms in three coniferous families. The basic type is shown in genera of the Lebachiaceae with inverted ovules and disaccate pollen, in which the pollen grains floated upward in the pollination fluid, orienting the germinal area toward the nucellus (see p. 346). In the Pinaceae, Doyle has derived two evolutionary series, each showing four major modifications (Fig. 20–26). These four modifications are loss of pollination fluid exudate; development of stigmatic surfaces on the integument; reduction and loss of air sacs; pollen germination other than on the nucellus. The most specialized mechanisms are found in *Larix* and *Pseudotsuga* (first series), which have well-developed stigmatic surfaces and bladderless pollen; and in species of *Tsuga* (second series) with bladderless pollen and vigorous pollen-tube growth. According to Doyle, the most specialized mechanism in conifers is possessed by *Araucaria*, in which the apex of the nucellus protrudes from the micropyle, and the completely bladderless pollen produces a very active and elongate pollen tube.

In some vegetative structures, especially the leaves, major gaps occur between the progymnosperms and the Cordaitales, and again between the Cordaitales and the Lebachiaceae. However, at the same time, anatomical similarities exist among the three groups, especially in the bordered pitting on the tracheids of the secondary xylem.

21 / Division Gnetophyta

This division comprises three orders of vascular plants: the Ephedrales, Welwitschiales, and Gnetales. Each order of *gnetophytes* has one family and one genus. The genera are *Ephedra, Welwitschia,* and *Gnetum* —the second monotypic and the other two with several species each. Although the three orders are allied with the gymnosperms, they actually have little in common with one another or with other gymnosperm taxa. Features shared among the three genera are the following: vessels in the secondary xylem; compound androstrobili and gynostrobili; a second structure surrounding the integument of the ovule, variously referred to as sporophyll, second integument, or small bracts; opposite or whorled leaves; and absence of resin canals.

The Ephedrales and Welwitschiales can be traced to the Permian, where fossil pollen grains have been found. Confirmed fossils of *Gnetum* have not been discovered to date. Although they are generally classified as gymnosperms, the three orders are of unknown origin and ancestry, and they stand apart from all other living and fossil taxa.

Order Ephedrales. The genus *Ephedra* has about 40 species. It is distributed sporad- ically in warm-temperate latitudes, occurring in the Mediterranean region, east to Persia, India, and China; in the southwestern United States; and in the mountainous regions of western South America. *Ephedra,* truly xerophytic, grows best on sandy or rocky sites such as deserts and mountains. The alkaloid ephedrine obtained from one Asiatic species is widely used to contract blood vessels and to alleviate asthma.

In habit, *Ephedra* is shrubby, some species reaching a height of 2 meters. It is much-branched, and bears two to four leaves that are opposite or whorled at nodes (Fig. 21–1A). The leaves are deciduous, much reduced, and seldom reach a length of over 1 centimeter. Photosynthesis takes place chiefly in the main stem and branches.

Ephedra is usually dioecious or rarely monoecious. The androstrobili are borne on stalks that arise at the nodes. Each androstrobilus bears two to eight opposite pairs of cone bracts on a central axis (Fig. 21–1B). Except for the basal pair, each cone bract subtends a short secondary shoot that arises from the axis and extends beyond the bract pair. At its base, the secondary shoot bears two membranous scales, the bracteoles (Fig. 21–1C); at the tip of the shoot, from one to eight

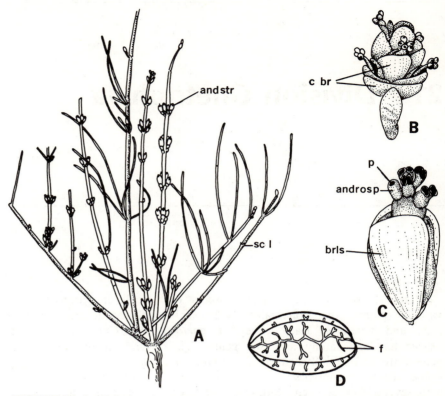

FIGURE 21–1 *Ephedra.* A, several branches bearing very tiny scale leaves (*sc l*) and whorls of androstrobili (*andstr*) at nodes, ×1; B, single androstrobilus showing whorls of cone bracts (*c br*) and protruding clusters of androsporangia, ×5; C, single secondary strobilar axis with two bracteoles (*brls*) subtending androsporangia (*androsp*) with pores (*p*), ×5; D, pollen grain in lateral view showing sinuous branched furrows (*f*), ×500. (A–C, after Métro and Sauvage with permission of Société des Sciences Naturelles et Physiques du Maroc.)

androsporangia are grouped—each of which dehisces by a terminal pore. The pollen grains are fusiform, with several longitudinal furrows extending from pole to pole (Fig. 21–1D).

Gynostrobili are similar in construction to the androstrobili and are also borne on stalks at the nodes. Each gynostrobilus consists of four to seven pairs of opposite cone bracts on a central axis. A short secondary shoot in the axil of the upper bracts bears a single terminal ovule. The ovule is subtended by a cup-shaped disc called an involucre. Although this has been related to a second integument, it appears to be homologous to the bracteoles of the secondary shoot in the androstrobilus. The true integument of the ovule is elongated into a micropylar tube and is chlorophyllous at pollination.

The androgametophytes and gynogametophytes develop essentially as in the coniferophytes. Inside the pollen grain are formed two prothallial cells, a tube cell, androgenous cells, and sterile cells. The tube nucleus and two androgametes migrate into the pollen tube. Wind pollination occurs about the time archegonia are formed in the ovule.

One gynospore enlarges and undergoes free-nuclear division. Prothallial cells form centripetally, and archegonia are formed on the edge of the micropylar end. A unique feature

FIGURE 21–2 *Welwitschia*. A, habit view of single plant showing two large spreading leaves and bowl-like stem supporting strobili, ×0.05; B, close-up of strobili (*str*) attached to stem (*st*), ×0.1.

is the development of 40 or more neck cells in the archegonium of *Ephedra*—the highest number in all gymnosperms.

A complete breakdown of the nucellar cells at the micropyle results in a large pollen chamber with no nucellar beak. The pollen tube extends directly through the neck of the archegonium, ruptures, and discharges the two androgametes into the egg. Following fertilization, the cells of the archegonial wall generally disintegrate and fuse with the cytoplasm of the zygote.

Order Welwitschiales. The single species of *Welwitschia* is the most bizarre of all gymnosperms. It is restricted to a small region near the southwestern coast of Africa, between latitudes 14° and 23° S. and from the coast to about 100 miles inland. It is an extreme xerophyte and inhabits rocky benches or dried stream beds where the precipitation rarely exceeds 5 centimeters a year.

The plant consists of a very short, yet massive, bowl-shaped stem only a few centimeters high (Fig. 21–2A). It is elliptical in plane view, and ranges to over 1 meter in diameter. It has only two leaves; these are very large, strap-shaped, and grow from the rim of the stem outward over the surface of the soil. Below the surface, the stem tapers quickly and merges with a large tap root reported to extend several meters down to the water table.

The two leaves are broad, flat, and coriaceous. They reach a width of over 20 centimeters and a length of approximately 2 meters. The tips become split and tattered mainly by the action of the wind. A basal meristem adds new growth that compensates for terminal abrasion—a unique feature of *Welwitschia*. The coriaceous texture of leaves and stem results from numerous sclereids in the parenchyma tissue.

The reproductive organs consist of compound strobili that arise by stalks from the cortex of the upper tip of the stem (Fig. 21–2B). The stalks are branched at nodes, and each node bears two nodal bracts. In the androstrobili, each terminal branch bears a primary androstrobilus that is elongate and terete in outline, with four vertical rows of overlapping axillary bracts (Fig. 21–3A, B). Each axillary bract subtends a structure that has been called a flower because of its superficial resemblance to an angiosperm flower. The flower consists of a short stalk with an inner and outer pair of bracts. The bracts surround six androsporangia and a central ovule (Fig. 21–3B). Each androsporangium is stalked and three-lobed, thus forming a synandrium. The central ovule is always sterile, and the androstrobilus is therefore unisexual.

The androgametophyte in the pollen grain is extremely reduced, approaching a typical angiosperm in development. The first division

367

results in a single prothallial cell and an antheridial initial; the latter then divides to form a generative cell and a tube cell. The pollen is discharged at this stage. Upon germination, the generative cell divides directly to give two androgametes, and the prothallial cell degenerates. Thus, the androgametophyte consists at all times of only three nuclei.

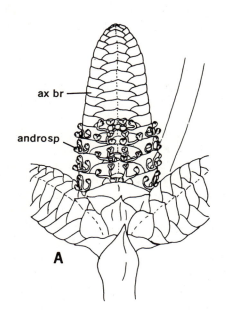

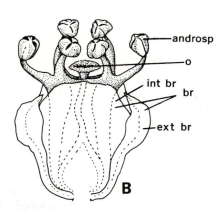

FIGURE 21–3 *Welwitschia.* A, androstrobilus showing four rows of overlapping axillary bracts (*ax br*) and protruding androsporangia (*androsp*), ×5; B, single secondary strobilus showing three of four bracts (*br*), central sterile ovule (*o*), and six androsporangia, ×12. (After Church with permission of Royal Society of London.)

The gynostrobili are borne on separate plants on similar branched stalks subtended by nodal bracts (Fig. 21–4A). The gynostrobilus is also terete, with four vertical rows of wings. The wing is closely surrounded by a pair of bracts (Fig. 21–4B, C). The integument of the ovule is much elongated and protrudes well above the wing.

Order Gnetales. This order is represented by the genus *Gnetum,* which has about 30 species inhabiting the more luxuriant tropics. Most of the species are native to Indonesia and tropical Asia, two occur in tropical Africa, and 12 in Central and South America. None of the species is common to both Western and Eastern Hemispheres.

Most species of *Gnetum* are lianas that climb and twine or trail on other plants. Several are shrubs, and a few are trees. They have both long and short shoots. In lianas, leaves are borne only on short shoots. The leaves are opposite, with flat blades and pinnate secondary venation. Thus, the leaves resemble closely those of some dicotyledons and, without comparing reproductive organs, can easily be mistaken for members of that group of angiosperms.

In some species secondary wood on the outside of the primary bundles consists of vessels, tracheids, and ray parenchyma. The perforations in the vessels resulted during evolution from the loss of circular bordered pits in end walls of tracheids. In this respect they differ fundamentally from vessels of angiosperms, which appear to have developed by the dissolution of elongated bordered pits to produce first a scalariform perforation plate and later a single opening in the end wall. The phloem contains sieve cells and cells functioning as companion cells that arise directly from the cambium instead of from a common mother initial as in angiosperms. As in *Welwitschia,* the cortex consists of parenchyma, fibers, and sclereids.

The pollen-bearing organ is a compound strobilus consisting of whorls of cone bracts on a central axis (Fig. 21–5B). In its axil each

368

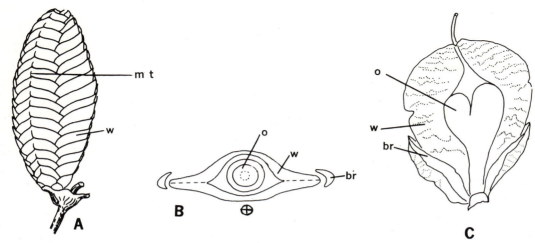

FIGURE 21-4 *Welwitschia.* A, single inflorescence showing rows of overlapping wings (*w*), and micropylar tubes (*m t*), ×5; B, single female flower from inflorescence in A, showing relationships of verticil, wing, and integument, ×12; C, diagrammatic view of flower showing bract (*br*), wing (*w*), ×12. *o*, ovule. (After Martens with permission of *La Cellule*.)

369

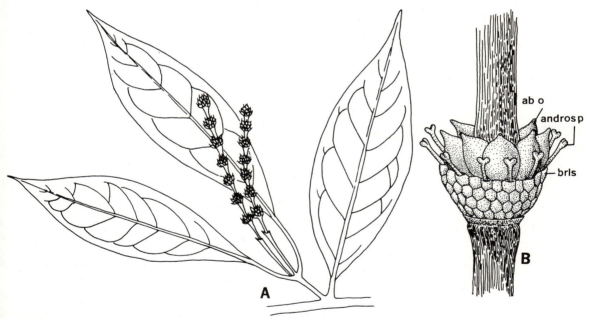

FIGURE 21-5 *Gnetum.* A, several leaves and compound androsporangia, ×0.5; B, single whorl of androsporangia (*androsp*), attendant bracteoles (*brls*), and ring of abortive ovules (*ab o*) at node of fertile stalk, ×15. (Used with permission of Blaisdell Publishing Company, from *The Plant Kingdom* by William H. Brown.)

cone bract contains a structure referred to as a secondary androstrobilus. It consists of a collar of almost completely fused bracteoles surrounding a central androsporangium, which in turn encircles a ring of abortive ovules. The androsporangium is a synandrium with two to four locules.

The ovules are borne in compound gyno-

DIVISION GNETOPHYTA

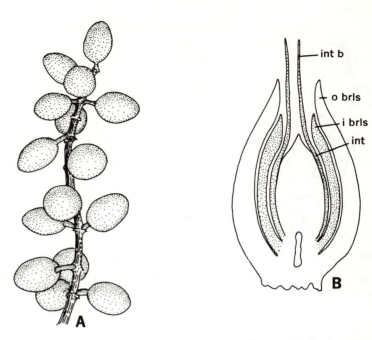

FIGURE 21–6 *Gnetum.* A, twig with seeds, ×0.4; B, median longitudinal section of single ovule, showing integument (*int*) extended into integumentary beak (*int b*), inner bracteoles (*i brls*), and outer bracteoles (*o brls*), ×40. (A, used wth permission of Blaisdell Publishing Company, from *The Plant Kingdom* by William H. Brown; B, after Lotsy.)

370

strobili (Fig. 21–6A). The primary gyno-strobili are arranged in whorls on small tertiary branches. Each primary strobilus occurs in the axil of a bract that is joined to the others of the whorl. The secondary strobilus has a pair of outer bracteoles and a pair of inner bracteoles that are often called an outer integument (Fig. 21–6B). The actual integument (inner integument) is prolonged into a beak that protrudes beyond the bracteoles.

The gynogametophyte of *Gnetum* differs from that of other gymnosperms in remaining free-nucleate at its micropylar end until after fertilization. *Gnetum* also is unique among gymnosperms in not forming archegonia. Instead, one (or more) of the free nuclei acts directly as an egg, uniting with an androgamete nucleus to form a zygote. In this respect, *Gnetum* is somewhat closer to the condition in some angiosperms, in which no gametophytic tissue is formed and free nuclei combine di-rectly with androgamete nuclei to form the zygote and endosperm.

PHYLOGENY

The origin and relationships of these three very distinct genera are obscure. Pollen grains similar to *Ephedra* and *Welwitschia* have been found as early as the Permian, whereas pollen assigned to *Gnetum* has been reported only from the Tertiary. On the basis of fossil pollen, *Ephedra* and *Welwitschia* appear to have had more species in former times than they do now, suggesting that they have declined in numbers of species since the early Mesozoic. Also, some pollen grains in Mesozoic and Tertiary rocks are associated with mesophytic plants, suggesting that *Ephedra* and *Wel-*

witschia may not always have been restricted to xeric environments.

The gnetophytes have been cited as a transitional group between gymnosperms and angiosperms, and some have considered them to be the immediate forerunners of angiosperms. The angiosperm characteristics include vessels in the xylem, compound strobili that resemble flowers, bracteoles that are often compared with a second integument, and the type of fertilization in *Gnetum*. However, the free-nucleate gametophyte is a typically gymnospermous characteristic, as is the absence of carpels; and the gnetophytes are almost certainly more closely allied to gymnosperm ancestors than to any angiosperm stock.

22 / Division Anthophyta

The Anthophyta includes all that are commonly known as *flowering plants,* and as such it is the largest and most conspicuous group in the modern flora. About 300 families are recognized, including about 275,000 species. If for no other reason, we should be interested in learning something about Anthophyta because our economy is largely based upon them. From various species we get wood (for construction, cabinet work, and flooring), fibres, condiments, spices, essential oils, and the raw material for certain medicines. Most of our food comes directly or indirectly from them.

Characterizing the Anthophyta is difficult. The only single characteristic that distinguishes this division is double fertilization and the consequent development of endosperm. In most instances, the possession of a closed carpel, and the fruit arising from it, are distinctive. Other features held to be characteristic of the flowering plants are to be found to a greater or lesser extent in other divisions of vascular plants. Nevertheless, anthophytes in general have the following: vessels in the xylem; companion cells in the phloem; flowers with some of the floral parts sterile and others functioning as reproductive structures; and carpels enclosing one or more ovules that may mature into seeds and, together with the carpel wall, form a fruit. The Anthophyta can be separated only by a combination of characteristics, and since the most significant of these are apparently hidden in the ovule, the chance of detecting their initial evolutionary stages in fossils is most improbable.

Unfortunately, the fossil record of the anthophytes gives us few clues to their origin. There is general agreement that sufficient evidence to formulate a satisfactory phylogenetic arrangement of flowering plants is not yet available. But we know that by the mid-Cretaceous the anthophytes were very highly developed morphologically, that many modern families were clearly differentiated, and that a number of modern genera are recognizable. Axelrod concludes that evidence favors an origin for anthophytes long before the Cretaceous, back even into Triassic and Permian times. According to this view, a fossil record may be lacking because the early flowering plants evolved and existed on upland sites where fossilization was unlikely. Scott, Barghoorn, and Leopold believe that angiosperms evolved rapidly during the early part of the Cretaceous from pre-angiosperm stock and flourished in response to their newly acquired characteristics; according to these investigators, the lack of any bona fide anthophyte pollen grains and other fossils from rocks earlier than Cretaceous strongly indicates that anthophytes had not evolved up to that time. Probably the most widely held view is that anthophytes were derived from seed ferns of the Pteridospermophyta.

The modern anthophyte flora is primarily terrestrial, but representatives are found in practically all habitats. Some are hydrophytes, immersed like *Elodea* or floating like *Lemna;* at the other extreme, they can be found growing under most xeric conditions. They are found in the tropics, as well as in the Arctic and Antarctic to the highest latitudes at which vegetation exists. Some lacking chlorophyll are obligate saprophytes, others are parasites. Among the latter are the mistletoes and dodders. Morphologically anthophytes are tremendously varied, ranging in size from the little aquatic *Wolffia,* which is like a green pinhead floating on the surface of small ponds, to a giant species of *Eucalyptus* (*E. regnans*) that has been recorded at a height of over 100 meters and a diameter of almost 3 meters.

A few general characteristics are ordinarily used to separate the two classes of Anthophyta. In the Dicotyledonae, two cotyledons (seed leaves) are present in the seed, and the stem has a functioning cambium in most species; in the Monocotyledonae, a single cotyledon is generally present, and the stem is polystelic without a functional cambium. Dicotyledonous leaves ordinarily have a special type of venation described as net-veined; leaves of monocotyledons are parallel-veined. Finally, in dicotyledons the floral parts are generally in fours, fives, or multiples of these; floral parts of monocotyledons are typically in threes or multiples of three.

However, the boundary between these two classes is actually rather blurred. Exceptions to the above generalizations suggest that the systematic position of a plant must be determined from all characteristics. Simple "key" characteristics have their place as aids to identification, but other characteristics may be more important morphologically and phylogenetically. For example, *Maianthemum,* with floral parts in fours, may appear out of place in the monocotyledons, but it is actually closely linked to them in all other features.

Leaves are conspicuous on most flowering plants. Because these organs usually persist for some time and are subjected to continued environmental stresses, they must be well adapted to their surroundings. In most instances it is not difficult to see the adaptive value of a particular leaf morphology as the outcome of continued selection operating over long periods of time. Therefore, it is not surprising to find leaves of all sizes and shapes: some are thin, some thick; some scale-like, others many meters long; some with petioles, others sessile; some hairy, others smooth. Despite these differences, all generally facilitate photosynthesis. In particular instances leaves may be highly modified for other functions, such as storage in many desert species; for vegetative reproduction, as in the development of plantlets from adventitious buds in *Kalanchoe;* as brightly colored floral bracts in poinsettia (*Euphorbia pulcherrima*) and the flowering dogwood (*Cornus nuttallii*); as tendrils in many Leguminosae; and as specialized insect traps in *Drosera, Dionaea, Sarracenia,* and several other genera. Another general type of leaf, the small scale-like cataphyll, is found on certain rhizomes and as protective scales enclosing buds.

In many dicotyledonous genera a pair of appendages, called stipules, develop at the base of the petiole. These occur in a variety of forms (Fig. 22–1, 2), some of which at least are obviously adaptive. They may be free or adnate to the petiole, evanescent or persistent, relatively large or small. In some cases (*Pisum, Lathyrus, Galium, Viola*) the stipules are foliaceous and undoubtedly make a significant photosynthetic contribution; in *Smilax* they develop as tendrils; in *Robinia, Acacia,* and many other legumes the stipules become thorns; in instances such as the tulip tree (*Liriodendron*) they have the role of bud scales.

FLORAL MORPHOLOGY

It seems proper to limit the use of the term *flower* to the sexually reproductive organs of the Anthophyta, although this is not always done. In the past botanists have referred to flowers in some gymnosperms particularly. There is much speculation and debate about how flowers evolved; particularly controversial are the origins of stamens and carpels. Unfortunately, there is little paleobotanical evidence to help in interpreting early stages in flower evolution; however, a number of genera in the Ranales that are considered primitive on other grounds probably offer valid clues to the general nature of the ancestral flower.

The literature dealing with floral morphology and its interpretations is very extensive. Space does not permit a presentation of the current points of view, but these can be found in Esau and Lam. Along with bibliographic references, Esau gives a critical summary and points out that in the oldest and still most popular concept, the flower is a shortened determinate shoot and the parts are modified leaves. Opposing this classical view are a number of modern botanical philosophers whose arguments are summarized by Lam. However, Foster and Gifford state that "marked resemblances can be demonstrated between vegetative leaves and floral appendages with respect to their initiation, early ontogeny, and basic plan of vasculation." The degree of resemblance to foliage leaves varies considerably with both the genus and the organ—for example, sepals and petals are basically more leaf-like than are some extremely specialized stamens and carpels.

Flowers

Perianths range in size from 1 millimeter or even less in diameter in the case of some tiny annuals to nearly 1 meter across in species of *Rafflesia*. The primary function of the perianth is to attract pollinating insects, and secondarily to protect the pollen and attractant nectar from rain and from depredation by nonpollinating organisms. The extent to which floral morphology is related to pollinating mechanisms and agencies will be dealt with later.

The conventional flower is made up of both sterile and fertile parts. The sterile parts comprise the calyx, made up of sepals, and the corolla, made up of petals. In certain instances it is convenient to combine calyx and corolla under the term perianth, particularly if it is difficult to distinguish between the calyx and the corolla. The fertile organs of the flower are the androecium, made up of stamens, and the gynoecium, made up of carpels.

Perianth

If the parts of the perianth resemble one another closely, as in the tulip (*Tulipa*), the units are referred to as tepals. If the perianth contains only one whorl, by convention the whorl is regarded as the calyx—unless there is good evidence to the contrary as in the Valerianaceae and the Compositae, where the calyx is much reduced and in some instances fails to develop at all. If there is no corolla or if the petals are inconspicuous, the calyx may be petaloid, as in such genera as *Anemone*, *Clematis* and *Helleborus*. Ordinarily, sepals are quite leaf-like in appearance and have three major vascular bundles, which is the general case for leaves. As a rule sepals are green and photosynthetic but not differentiated to the extent of having a palisade layer.

Petals are much more varied in shape and size than sepals, and can usually be distinguished from them by color. Color is due either to chromoplasts or to dissolved pigments in the cells. Despite certain superficial resemblances to sepals, petals are anatomically—and in some instances even morphologically—more like sterile stamens. As in the stamen, a single trace usually enters the base of the petal. In certain instances, the close relationship is shown by "double" flowers in such genera as *Paeonia, Rosa, Pelargonium,* and

374

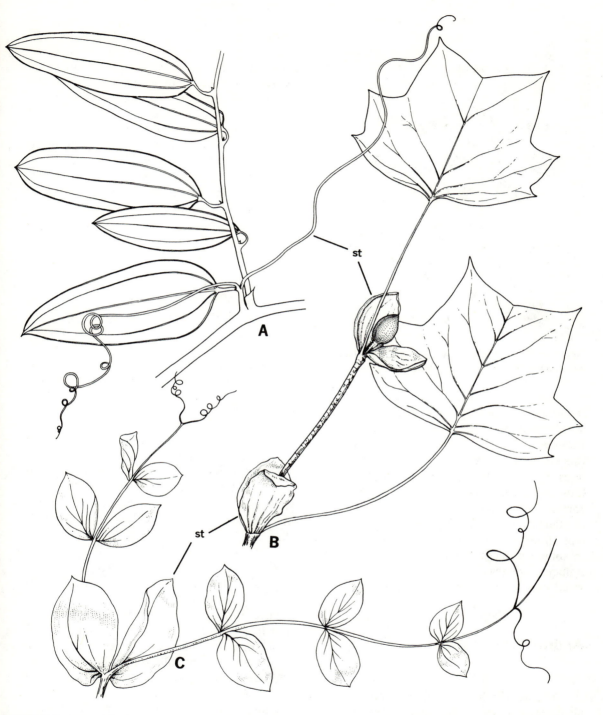

FIGURE 22–1   Stipules. A, *Smilax laurifolia* with stipular tendrils, ×0.5; B, *Liriodendron tulipifera* with stipules functioning as bud scales, ×0.5; C, *Pisum sativum* with foliaceous stipules, ×1. *st*, stipule.

DIVISION ANTHOPHYTA

FIGURE 22–2 Stipules. A, *Robinia pseudoacacia* with stipular thorns, ×1. *st,* stipule.

Dianthus, in which the extra petals are clearly transformed stamens. However, genera like *Trillium* often show partial or complete reversion of the petals to green sepal-like structures. In certain members of the Magnoliaceae, Calycanthaceae, and Nymphaeaceae there is a continuous transition from sepals though petals to stamens (Fig. 22–3). This probably means that through convergent evolution the corolla in some instances is derived secondarily from stamens, whereas in other instances it is derived directly from modification of leaves.

Androecium

The androecium is the aggregation of stamens in a flower. The stamens range from many to one depending on the species and are indefinite or definite in number, also depending on the species. The stamens develop on the receptacle above (inside) the corolla. In arrangement they may be spiral, whorled, or fasciculate—the fascicles usually occurring in whorls. Studies in dicotyledonous families such as the Winteraceae, Dilleniaceae, Magnoliaceae, Nymphaeaceae, and even some genera of the Ranunculaceae, show the primitive androecium to consist of many spirally arranged stamens, or androsporophylls.

In its commonest form the stamen is composed of a thread-like filament supporting on its upper end an anther that contains two pairs of androsporangia. It is a fair assumption that a stamen of this type is in a relatively advanced stage of evolution. According to Goethe's theory, stamens are the homologues of leaves. Until fairly recently morphological resemblances between stamens and leaves were not recognized. Furthermore, most flowering plants have stamens with a single vascular bundle—not three as in leaves. However, we now know that some reduced leaves have only a single bundle and that stamens of primitive genera may have three. A number of investigators studying primitive members of ranalian stock have shown that here at least the stamen is undoubtedly a sporophyll. In *Degeneria,* which Canright considers to be the closest of all known types to a primitive angiosperm stamen, the stamen is a broad leaf-like organ with very little distinction between the fertile and sterile parts and with three vascular bundles.

The connective, the tissue lying between the pairs of sporangia, is a strip not distinguishable histologically from the tissues of the wall of the anther. In some families the connective is reduced to a slender median axis, and in others it is reduced only to a point of attachment for the anther lobes. However, in some relatively specialized families, such as the Violaceae, the connective may be prominent; this is generally regarded as a secondary development related to pollination. The connective forms a nectary in *Viola* (Fig. 22–4).

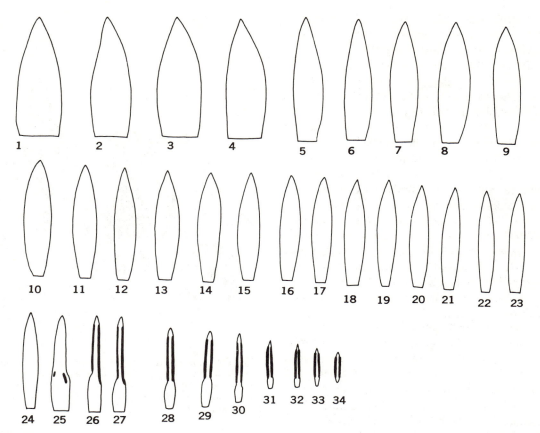

FIGURE 22–3 Floral parts of water lily showing transitions. 1–4, sepaloid; 5–24, petaloid; 25–34, stamens. (After Gibbs.)

Departures from the conventional stamen morphology can nearly always be related to some special pollinating mechanism. This is also generally true for the method of dehiscence of the anthers. Dehiscence is introrse when the opening is toward the center of the flower, extrorse when outward. In most genera, anthers shed their pollen through narrow, lengthwise slits (longitudinal dehiscence). Transverse dehiscence (through transverse slits) occurs very infrequently, while porose dehiscence (through small, rounded openings) is characteristic of a few families such as the Ericaceae. In some instances the slit is shaped to free a valve-like flap of tissue (valvular dehiscence), characteristic of the Berberidaceae and Lauraceae in particular.

Gynoecium

The gynoecium is made up of the ovule-bearing organs, the carpels or gynosporophylls. As with stamens, the carpels range in number from many in primitive flowers, to one in more advanced cases; in arrangement they vary from spiraled to whorled.

Like the stamen, the carpel is an elongate organ, primitively flattened laterally. Also similar to the stamen, the carpel is leaf-like in all its relationships to the stem. However, the carpel differs by developing gynosporangia only on the adaxial side, whereas the androsporangia develop on either the adaxial or the abaxial side of the stamen. In the course of evolution the margins of the carpel blade have

DIVISION ANTHOPHYTA

apparently been folded adaxially toward the midrib, thereby enclosing the gynosporangia in a cavity known as the locule (Fig. 22–5).

Evolutionary developments have apparently resulted in the complete closure of the carpel, a reduction in the number of ovules, and a restriction of ovules to the lower part of the carpel (ovary); the sterile upper part became the style, with the stigma localized at its apex. Bailey and Swamy point out that, in more primitive flowers, the style is clearly conduplicate and is commonly vascularized by both the dorsal and the two ventral veins.

According to Bailey and Swamy, the least modified form of contemporary carpel appears to be that of *Drimys piperita*. At flowering, this carpel is stipitate with a relatively thin, conduplicately folded blade that encloses a number of ovules attached to its adaxial surface. These ovules are in a more or less linear series between the dorsal and the lateral veins. The placentation is clearly laminal and somewhat medial, rather than marginal. The margins of this carpel are not coherent (Bailey and Swamy refer to them as being "unsealed"), and there is no localized stigmatic surface. Instead, stigmatic hairs are extensively developed on the inner surfaces, and on the free margins of the carpel the hairs form a pair of stigmatic crests extending from top to bottom on the open ventral side. The space between the closely opposed ventral surfaces of the carpel becomes filled with a felt-like development of these hairs. Pollen grains are held by the external glandular hairs, and the pollen tubes grow inward among the hairs to the ovules. In another section of the genus *Drimys*, the opposed ventral surfaces of the carpel are partly, or even completely, grown together

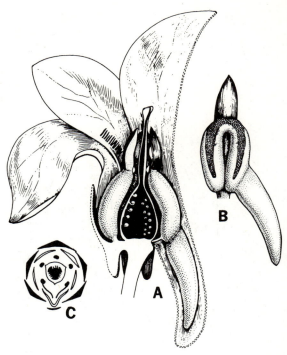

FIGURE 22–4 *Viola* flower, ×5. A, median section showing lateral view of stamen with basal part of connective extending into spur as nectary; B, stamen in adaxial view; C, floral diagram. (After Jones with permission of Blackie and Sons, Ltd.)

except toward the top of the carpel. The much-reduced, paired stigmatic crests are limited to this unsealed part.

Gynoecia may be made up of one or more free carpels (apocarpy) or two or more fused carpels (syncarpy). As pointed out above, the ovules are borne on the adaxial surface of the carpel. Their arrangement is referred to as the placentation; the tissue from which the ovules are developed, often somewhat enlarged or swollen, is the placenta. Free carpels mainly

---

FIGURE 22–5 A–D, primitive carpels. A, side view, showing paired stigmatic crests; B, transverse section, showing pollen grains and penetration of pollen tube; C, unfolded lamina, showing placentation, distribution of glandular hairs, and course of pollen tubes; D, cleared unfolded lamina, showing vasculature. E–H, trends of modification of primitive carpels. E, primitive form of conduplicate carpel; F, lateral and terminal closure, with stigmatic crests restricted to projecting unsealed part; G, laterally sealed carpel with capitate stigma; H, laterally sealed carpel, with expanded, terminal, stigmatic crests. (After I. W. Bailey and B. G. L. Swamy, "The Conduplicate Carpel and its initial trends of specialization," 1951, Vol. 38, *American Journal of Botany*, with permission of *American Journal of Botany*; and adapted from Irving W. Bailey and B. G. L. Swamy, "The Conduplicate Carpel of Dicotyledons and Its Initial Trends of Specialization," in *Contributions to Plant Anatomy*, by Irving W. Bailey, 1954, The Ronald Press Company, New York.)

378

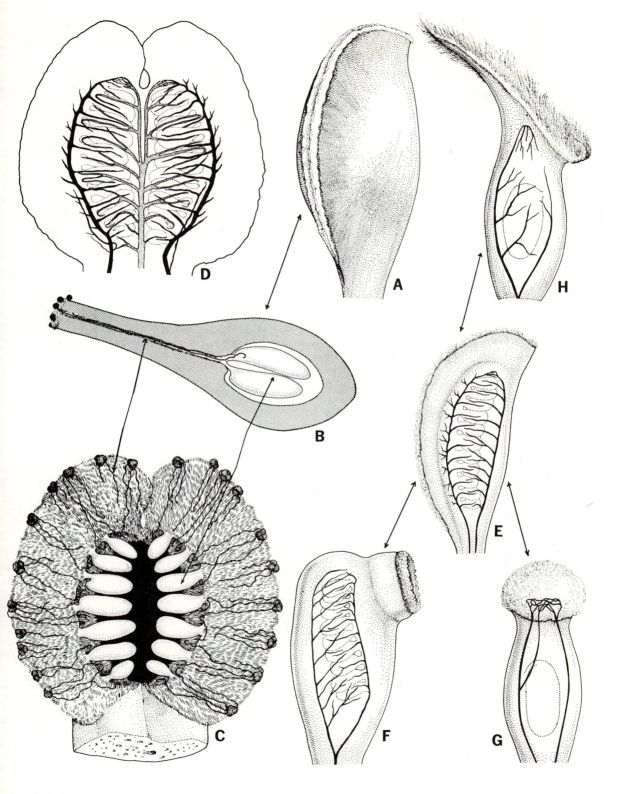

DIVISION ANTHOPHYTA

show two types of placentation; most commonly the ovules occur in rows near margins of the carpels (submarginal placentation), but in a few instances the ovules occur irregularly over the surface of the lamina (laminar placentation). There is good evidence that the laminar type is primitive and is probably found only in families generally accepted as primitive —e.g., Nymphaeaceae, Cabombaceae, Butomaceae, and Lardizabalaceae. Certain families show a series in which the number of ovules is reduced in the more advanced genera.

Syncarpy is a common feature associated with the specialization of the gynoecium. There is general agreement that syncarpy has arisen independently in many unrelated taxa, and variation in the extent of fusion may be found even within a single genus. Commonly carpels

380

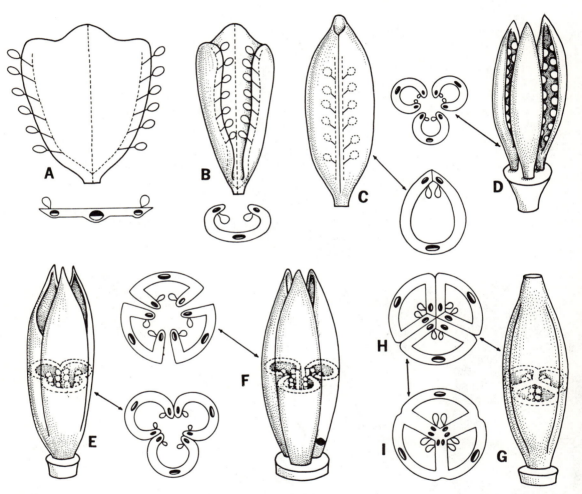

FIGURE 22–6 Hypothetical evolution of simple and compound ovary (vascular strands shown with xylem elements blackened). A, three-lobed carpel with submarginal ovules; B, same as A, somewhat involute; C, simple ovary derived from B by infolding of ovules and fusing of ventral margins; D, axis bearing three involute, open carpels; E, compound ovary derived from D by fusion of edges of adjoining carpels; F, axis with three open carpels, adjoining sides more or less parallel; G, compound ovary derived from F by fusion of adjoining sides and margins; H, cross section of G (hypothetical); I, transverse section of G (actual). (After Lawrence, with permission of The Macmillan Company from *Taxonomy of Vascular Plants,* by G. H. Lawrence, copyright 1951 by The Macmillan Company.)

become connate by the fusion of the dorsal surface of folded or inrolled laminae, and much less commonly by the ventral margins (Fig. 22–6). Where the fusion occurs along the whole length of the carpels, the ovaries, styles, and stigmas will be involved; if fusion is only in the basal part of the carpel, the styles and stigmas will be free. When closed, or nearly closed, carpels are laterally connate and the ovules are submarginal. The placentae will lie close together around the vertical center of the gynoecium. This is axile placentation, considered a primitive type of syncarpous gynoecium and one from which free-central and some kinds of basal placentation have been derived. Parietal placentation in all probability had a different origin. In a syncarpous, unilocular gynoecium with parietal placentation, the ovules are developed in longitudinal rows on the wall of the cavity. Free-central placentation exists when the ovules are borne on a central column in a unilocular, syncarpous ovary and free from carpel walls.

The last type of placentation to be discussed is basal, i.e., when the ovules develop at the base of the locule. It is derived most commonly from free-central placentation through reduction of the size of the fused placentae and a decrease in the number of ovules.

In the past century morphologists have probably given more attention to the morphology of the inferior ovary than to any other problem. Under the appendicular theory, the outer whorls of the flower are considered to be concrescent around the ovary and adnate to it. The axial theory supposes that the whole of the inferior ovary consists of receptacular tissue bearing ovules, and that the walls of the carpels are reduced to a sterile covering including little more than the styles and stigmas.

In support of the appendicular theory it should be pointed out that there is a general ontogenetic tendency for fusion between floral parts that are close together, both horizontally and vertically. This results in the cohesion and adhesion so frequently present in flowers where the parts develop in close whorls. Flowers with their parts in spiral arrangements show little fusion. In many instances where coherence and adherence are not superficially obvious, they are often revealed by careful anatomical study.

The anthophyte ovule consists of a central mass of archesporial cells, of which most are sterile while one or more function as gynospore mother cells. The functional gynospore is enclosed by one or, more commonly, two integuments. It is borne on a basal stalk, the funiculus, which arises from the placenta. The central mass of cells consists of a distal part, the nucellus, and a basal part, the chalaza (Fig. 22–7). The ovule primordium arises from the placenta as a conical protuberance with a rounded apex.

The first, and usually the only, gynospore mother cell can be recognized by its size and the density of its cytoplasm. The inner integument arises from a collar-like ring of meristematic cells slightly below the apex of the protuberance. It grows faster than the nucellus and partially encloses it, leaving a little canal-like micropyle. If the outer integument develops, it arises slightly below the inner integument and grows in the same way.

Several types of ovules are distinguished by variations in general form and in the position of the micropyle. All ovules are fundamentally much alike and are probably evolutionary modifications of a basic type, and transitional forms are common. The ovule is said to be orthotropous when it is straight and upright on the placenta, with the micropyle distal and the funiculus short or wanting. If the ovule is completely inverted so that the micropyle faces the placenta, it is said to be anatropous; in such instances the ovule is usually appressed or adnate to the funiculus. Other names are applied to intermediate conditions (Fig. 22–8).

Many morphological interpretations have been given to the angiosperm ovule. It was long considered a bud because it seemed to resemble an axis with a growing point and leaves. It has more commonly and recently been interpreted as a modified leaf or portion of a leaf. The exclusive application of either of these theories resulted in such inconsisten-

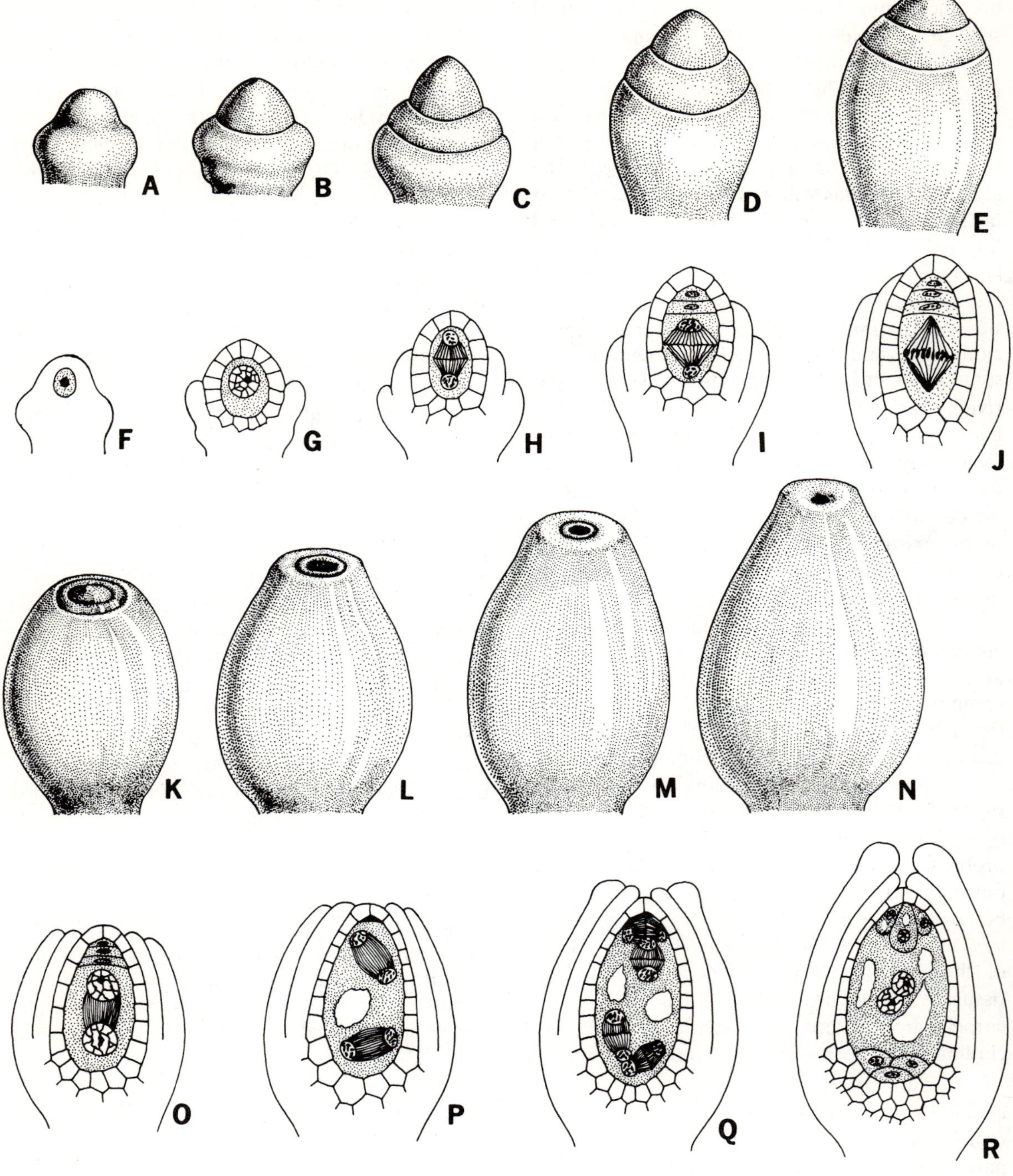

FIGURE 22–7 Development of ovule. A–E, K–N, growth of integuments; F, G, gynospore mother cell; H, I, meiosis; J, O, three gynospores degenerating, nucleus of remaining one dividing; P–R, development of female gametophyte (at micropylar end, two synergids and egg nucleus; at chalazal end, three antipodal cells; at center, two polar nuclei fusing to form primary endosperm nucleus). (Used with permission of Blaisdell Publishing Co., from *The Plant Kingdom* by William H. Brown.)

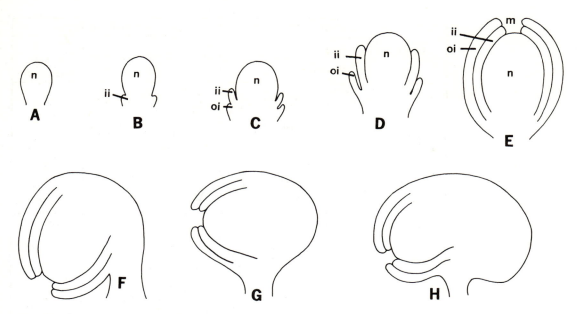

FIGURE 22–8 A–E, development of orthotropous ovule (*ii,* inner integument; *m,* micropyle; *n,* nucellus; *oi,* outer integument). F–H, anatropous, amphitropous, and campylotropous ovules, respectively. (After Gibbs.)

cies and strained interpretations that many morphologists were led to the conclusion that ovules might have had both origins. The fact that this state of affairs might imply different origins in even closely related anthophyte taxa has apparently not been seriously considered. According to a third interpretation, it is an independent structure borne on either axial or foliar organs, the integuments being new structures.

Increasing knowledge of the gymnosperms, and particularly of the pteridosperms, has led twentieth-century morphologists away from stressing the carpel altogether and has directed their attention to much earlier stages of evolution. This has given added strength and significance to the fourth, or *sui generis,* theory in which the ovule is primarily a gynosporangium —the nucellus being the wall of the sporangium and the integuments protective structures. Although fossil evidence supports this theory, some investigators are critical of this comparatively simple and perhaps too facile explanation and suggest that the stage is now set for new avenues of search for ancestral forms.

GYNOGAMETOPHYTE

In the majority of anthophytes only a single gynospore mother cell is differentiated. As in the gymnosperms, this mother cell undergoes a meiotic division to produce a linear tetrad of gynospores oriented parallel to the long axis of the ovule. In most instances only the gynospore toward the chalaza functions to produce the gynogametophyte (embryo sac) whereas the other three degenerate. The development of the gynogametophyte begins with the endosporal germination of the gynospore. Mitotic division of the gynospore nucleus is followed by two simultaneous divisions of the daughter nuclei, producing eight free nuclei within the now somewhat distended wall of the gynospore. Of these eight nuclei, three are at the micropylar end, three at the chalazal end, and the remaining two (termed the polar nuclei) migrate to the center of the gametophyte. The three micropylar nuclei enclosed by delicate walls constitute the egg apparatus, which includes the egg (the female gamete) and two synergids. The three nuclei (termed the antipodals) at the

DIVISION ANTHOPHYTA

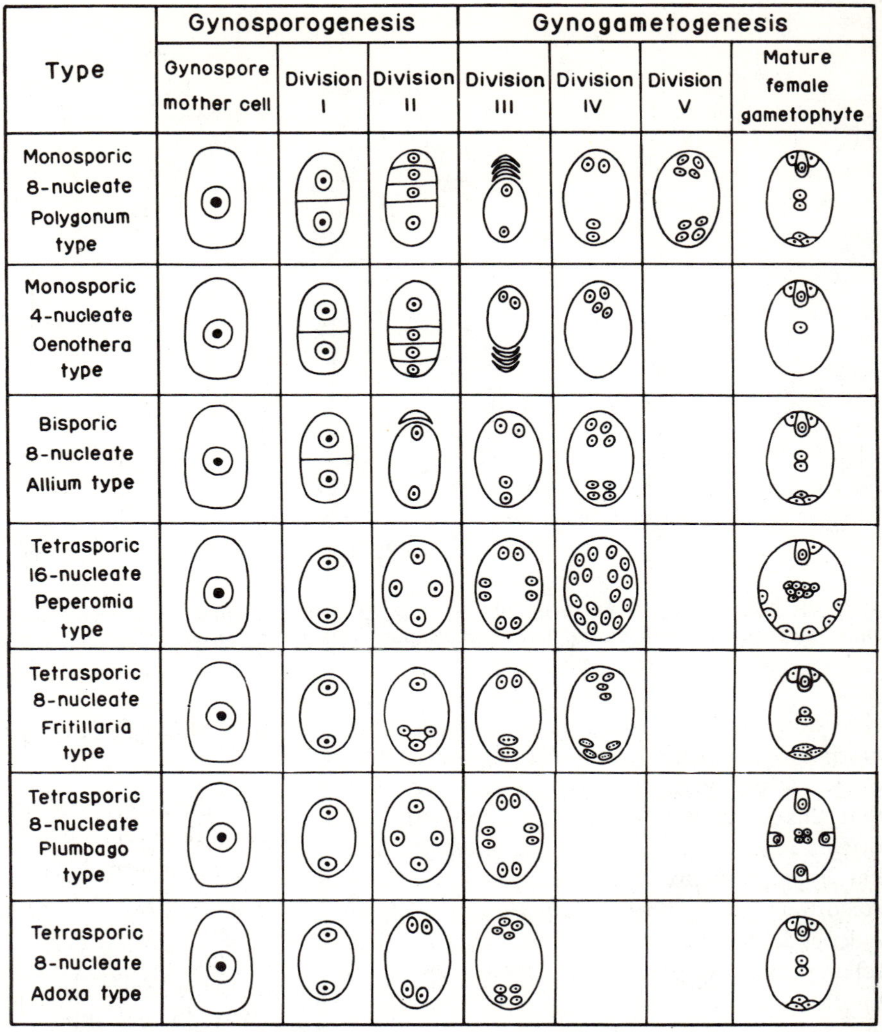

Type	Gynosporogenesis			Gynogametogenesis			
	Gynospore mother cell	Division I	Division II	Division III	Division IV	Division V	Mature female gametophyte
Monosporic 8-nucleate Polygonum type							
Monosporic 4-nucleate Oenothera type							
Bisporic 8-nucleate Allium type							
Tetrasporic 16-nucleate Peperomia type							
Tetrasporic 8-nucleate Fritillaria type							
Tetrasporic 8-nucleate Plumbago type							
Tetrasporic 8-nucleate Adoxa type							

FIGURE 22–9 Some important types of female gametophytes in angiosperms. (From *An Introduction to the Embryology of Angiosperms*, by P. Maheshwari, copyright © 1950, used by permission of McGraw-Hill Book Company.)

chalazal end usually become walled also, but the polar nuclei remain unwalled (Fig. 22–7O–R).

An eight-nucleate female gametophyte with this ontogeny and arrangement of nuclei is characteristic of the great majority of flowering plants that have been examined critically. Many deviations from this so-called "normal" pattern are now known and are discussed in detail by Maheshwari and summarized by Eames. Maheshwari recognizes ten types of gametophyte based on the number of nuclear divisions intervening between the gynospore mother cell and the mature gametophyte, and on the number and arrangement of the gametophyte nuclei. The distinguishing features of the most interesting or frequently encountered of these types are best shown in Figure 22–9. Each type has been given the name of the genus in which it was first clearly described.

The number of antipodals ranges from zero in the *Oenothera* type to 11 in the *Drusa* type; the central nucleus ranges from haploid in the *Oenothera* type to octoploid in *Peperomia;* and the egg apparatus has only a single nucleus in *Plumbago* in contrast to the normal three. In the *Plumbago* and *Adoxa* types the female gamete (egg) nucleus is produced by a single division of a meiospore.

ANDROGAMETOPHYTE

In anthophytes, androspores are typically produced in large numbers in the four androsporangia (pollen sacs) of the anther. In most instances, meiosis of the androspore mother cells takes place at an early stage in the development of the flower, even when the flower bud is quite small. Meiosis is followed by endosporal germination of the androspore to the extent of one of two divisions, following which the immature androgametophyte becomes dormant until shed as a pollen grain. As in other seed plants, a pollen grain is an immature androgametophyte consisting of the androspore wall containing one, two, or three cells—or nuclei if the cell walls fail to develop. Pollination, the transfer of pollen from the anther to a stigma, will be considered later.

The tetrads of pollen grains show various grouping arrangements, resulting in differences in shape and certain surface features of the individual grains. Some of this variety in size, shape, and sculpturing of the outer wall (the exine) is shown in Figure 22–10.

The monocolpate type of pollen grain appears to be primitive, with its single colpus on the distal side—i.e., the side away from the point of contact of the grain in the tetrad. Monocolpate grains are characteristic of the monocotyledons, most of the Ranales, and a few other families in other orders. Essentially the same type is also found in the cycads, bennettites, and pteridosperms.

The distinguishing characteristics of pollen grains are the number and position of the apertures and the nature and pattern of sculpturing. These features provide important diagnostic criteria for the identification of pollen grains. Fortunately, because it contains a cutin-like substance very resistant to decay, the exine persists in peat, in sedimentary rocks, and especially in coal and oil shales of all ages. The study of such microfossils and modern spores and pollen is now included in the comparatively new science of palynology. Results of palynological studies are shedding much light on phylogenetic relationships and also on climatological conditions in the past.

When pollen grains arrive on a compatible stigma, they germinate by developing a pollen tube. This tube begins as an extension of the inner wall (intine) of the grain, swelling out through a germinal aperture. However, the tube soon acquires growth of its own. The contents of the grain, including the nuclei, move out into the tube, and the vegetative nucleus, now known as the tube nucleus, takes the apical position.

In most instances investigated, germination of the pollen grain takes place with very little delay. The tube penetrates the tissue of the stigma, follows the course of the style, and then passes through a placenta into the cavity of the ovary. Here it may take a short aerial course to the micropyle of an ovule; in other instances, it grows on the surface of the placenta, along the funiculus and integuments, to the micropyle. What directs the course of the pollen tube is not known. Generally the tube is regarded as chemotactic, with the attracting substance called a pollen tube factor.

Sometimes when the pollen grain is shed —although usually before this stage—the meiospore nucleus divides into a generative nucleus and a vegetative nucleus (later known as the tube nucleus). In other instances, the generative nucleus divides again before shedding to form two male gamete nuclei, and so the pollen grain is shed in a three-nucleate stage. In either case, two gamete nuclei are present in the tip of the pollen tube when it reaches the vicinity of the egg apparatus. The fertilization that follows is unique to the An-

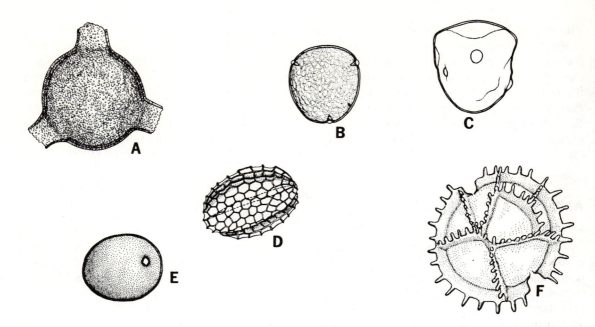

FIGURE 22–10 Angiosperm pollen grains. A, *Epilobium angustifolium* (Onagraceae), with three large pores, ×400; B, *Fagus sylvatica* (Fagaceae), three colporate with scabrate exine about 2.5 microns thick, ×600; C, *Carex* sp. (Cyperaceae), having smooth wall with one large central pore and two faint lateral pores, ×800; D, *Salix sitchensis* (Salicaceae), tricolpate with fine but distinct reticulum, ×1,600; E, *Bromus inermis* (Graminae), with single pore characteristic of grass pollen (pore is covered by operculum, which is usually lost in grains processed for microscopic examination), ×500; F, *Taraxacum* sp. (Compositae), tricolpate having elaborate branching ridges with echinate projections on crests (ridges enclose lacunae with very thin exine-forming floor; surrounding ridges restrict opening of pore-like colpae, ×1,200).

thophyta. One male nucleus fuses with the egg nucleus, resulting in a zygote from which the embryo plant will develop. The other male nucleus fuses with the centrally situated fusion nucleus (made up from the two polar nuclei), producing the primary endosperm nucleus from which will develop the cellular food reserve known as the endosperm. This special type of fertilization in which both male gamete nuclei take part is called double fertilization.

EMBRYOLOGY

Plant embryology for a long time was eclipsed by other botanical studies that seemed likely to throw more light on problems of evolution and phylogeny. There seemed to be little prospect that embryology could contribute to the history of plant evolution as it has so notably in the vertebrates. However, in the last half-century, plant embryology has begun to come into its own. Numerous investigations have shown that it is not possible to speak of a "typical" dicotyledonous or monocotyledonous embryo. There is too much diversity in ontogeny and even in the basic pattern of development. Maheshwari and Johansen summarize the immense amount of detailed comparative information now available, and their writings should be consulted for details that cannot be included here. Johansen recognizes six types of embryonic development and has further divided each main type into a number of variations. However, in practically all instances the differences are found to be in the earliest ontogenic stages—

i.e., in the proembryo. Moreover, the various embryological types show very little taxonomic affiliation, and so in themselves are of limited value as phylogenetic criteria.

In the flowering plants, as in many of the lower plants (particularly the ferns), embryos are sometimes produced without fertilization, despite the presence of a mechanism for sexual reproduction. The term apomixis is applied to all types of asexual reproduction which tend to replace or act as substitutes for sexual methods. Those interested in learning the extent and numerous methods of apomictic development known in the plant kingdom should consult the monographic reviews and analysis of Gustafsson. The generally accepted classification of apomixis is based on two principal types; vegetative reproduction and agamospermy. The former is only considered as apomixis where it assumes the role of sexual reproduction, in whole or in considerable part. In agamospermy, embryos and seeds are formed asexually. As a result, the embryo is genetically identical to its maternal parent. The simplest method of agamospermy is known as adventive embryony. For example, in various species of *Citrus,* embryos may arise directly from diploid sporophytic tissue of the nucellus or integument. A small group of cells usually divides actively and pushes its way into the embryo sac, eventually forming a true embryo.

Diploid gametophytes may produce embryos either parthenogenetically (directly from an unfertilized egg) or apogamously from some other cell. The former method is more common in seed plants, whereas the latter is frequent in ferns. Apomixis may have any one of several origins and may be facultative or obligate in different groups. Many of the larger families of Anthophyta have genera and species that reproduce by apomixis. In the Compositae, *Antennaria, Taraxacum,* and *Hieracium* are classical examples; in the Rosaceae, *Prunus, Sorbus, Rubus,* and *Crataegus;* and in the Gramineae, *Poa* and *Calamagrostis.*

The causes of sexual sterility in the Anthophyta are so numerous and varied that no simple theory can account for the origin of apomixis. It has been well established that a high correlation exists between polyploidy and apomixis, and between apomixis and the perennial habit to which vegetative reproduction is also correlated. However, all apomicts are not polyploids and vice versa, nor are all polyploids perennials.

POLLINATION

An interesting evolutionary study in the anthophytes is the relationship between floral morphology and pollination. Pollination in the flowering plants can be defined as the transfer of pollen from an anther to a stigma. This is brought about in a great variety of ways, many of which show a high degree of adaptation and specialization. There is a vast literature on the subject, and only some of the highlights can be sketched here. For further details and a selected bibliography, consult Meeuse's recent *The Story of Pollination.*

A mystical relationship between pollen and the formation of fruit was apparently known to the ancient Mesopotamians in the ninth century B.C. Bas-reliefs of this period illustrate a ceremonial dusting of the fruit-bearing date palms with the inflorescences from pollen-producing plants. However, this practical folklore was without any scientific basis until toward the end of the seventeenth century A.D. when Nehemiah Grew wrote that the grains within the stamens represented male parts, and the seed-producing parts were female. The first recorded experiments on sex in plants are those of Camerarius in 1694. He discovered that unless pollen came in contact with a stigma, fruit would not develop.

Now we have very precise information on pollination in many instances. Pollination can be carried out by a number of agencies. The most important are wind (anemophily), insects (entomophily), and birds (ornithophily); pollination by bats (chiropterophily) and water (hydrophily) occur, but are relatively uncommon.

Anemophily

The earliest seed plants probably were wind-pollinated, as are most modern gymnosperms. However, in many angiosperms there is good evidence that wind pollination has been acquired and that the flowers probably have been derived from entomophilous ancestors. A case in point is the meadow rue (*Thalictrum*). This genus belongs to a family (Ranunculaceae) noted for brilliant flowers and considerable specialization for insect visits, yet it lacks a corolla and is wind-pollinated.

In general, anemophilous flowers are marked by negative characteristics. They have no nectar, scent, or brilliantly colored perianth parts. On the positive side, we find special features of the stamens, stigmas, and pollen grains. The anthers are often suspended from long filaments hanging free from the flower. In catkin inflorescences whole flowers are swayed by the wind, and the dislodged pollen is caught up in air currents (Fig. 22–11). The stigmas, like the stamens, are freely exposed; they are often branched, feathery, or provided with brush-like outgrowths suitable for intercepting air-borne pollen (Fig. 22–12). The pollen grains are generally small, smooth, and produced in very large quantities.

Entomophily

Although the first seed plants probably were wind-pollinated, irregular insect visits to flowers may have occurred even in the seed ferns. The insects of the Carboniferous had biting jaws, rather than mouth parts adapted for sucking nectar. Part of their food may have been fleshy sporophylls and possibly even spores. It was not until the Tertiary, when flowering plants predominated and most modern families became differentiated, that most contemporary orders of insects also appeared. It is almost certain that the intimate association between particular flowers and their insect visitors began during the Tertiary.

An insect visits a flower to obtain food, either in the form of nectar or sometimes of pollen. Nectar is a watery fluid containing sugar secreted by special glands known as nectaries. Floral nectaries can be associated with a variety of organs and may occupy a number of positions. In fact, almost any part of the flower may secrete nectar (Fig. 22–13).

Insects are attracted to flowers chiefly by color and scent, and the appeal of the two attractants varies with the type of insect visitor. Much experimental work has been done on the color perception of different kinds of insects. We know that bees, for example, can see yellows, blues, and purples—which explains why bee flowers characteristically have these colors. However, bees do not necessarily prefer these colors because they are attracted by them. Rather, bees distinguish these colors and associate them with nectar. In different species of flowers, different means of guiding the way to the nectar have evolved (Fig. 22–14, 15D). Sometimes it is a vivid patch of color in sharp contrast to the background color of the corolla, as in forget-me-not (*Myosotis*), certain irises (*Iris*), and toadflax (*Linaria*); some flowers have a set of darker stripes or streaks of dots—e.g., nasturtium (*Tropaeolum*), broom (*Sarothamnus*), violet (*Viola*), foxglove (*Digitalis*), and monkey flower (*Mimulus*).

Many details of floral structure can be related to the morphology, size, and habits of particular insects and the way they visit a flower. Entomophilous flowers have been divided into a number of classes, partly on the basis of their structure and partly according to their insect visitors. Only some of these types of flowers will be discussed briefly below.

Hymenoptera Flowers. These are visited almost exclusively by bees. The specialized morphology of the flowers permits the visit of only one particular insect or of a limited group of about the same size. In some of these flowers the nectar is so deeply located in a tube that only an insect with a long tongue or proboscis can reach it. A good example is red

FIGURE 22–11   Anemophilous flowers. *Garrya elliptica,* ×1. Male catkin is shown; female flowers are in similarly pendant catkins.

clover (*Trifolium,* Fig. 22–15H, I), where the nectar is situated about 9 millimeters from the mouth of the flower and is available only to bumble bees. In others, the parts of the corolla are so firm that only a heavy insect can open the flower—e.g., snapdragon (*Antirrhinum*) and broom (*Sarothamnus,* Fig. 22– 15A–C). In markedly zygomorphic flowers a landing stage for the insect is combined with nectar at the base of a long corolla tube, or at the base of spurs. Examples include sage (*Salvia,* Fig. 22–15E–G), monkshood (*Aconitum,* Fig. 22–13), violet (*Viola,* Fig. 22–4), and many Orchidaceae. In many such flowers,

DIVISION ANTHOPHYTA

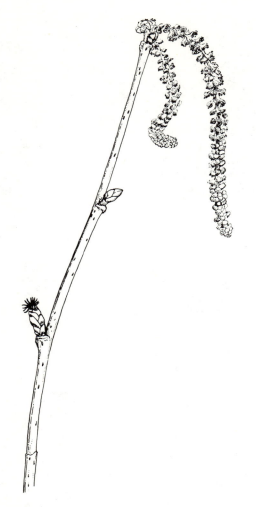

FIGURE 22–12 Anemophilous flowers. *Corylus avellana,* × 2. Male flowers are in pendant catkins, female in short bud-like spike with conspicuous stigmas.

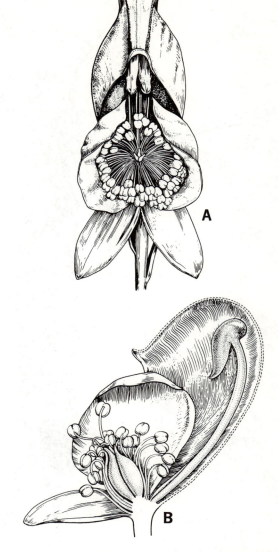

FIGURE 22–13 Flower of *Aconitum napellus,* × 2. A, front elevation; B, median section showing in hood one of the two posterior petals modified to nectary.

small flies and beetles may be prevented from entering by hairs or scales at the throat of the corolla.

Lepidoptera Flowers. Most of these flowers are actinomorphic, and their insect visitors hover while feeding (Fig. 22–16B). A rather usual characteristic is a somewhat pungent but aromatic scent. In flowers such as tobacco (*Nicotiana*), night-scented stock (*Matthiola*), and night-blooming cacti (Fig. 22–16C)—which are pollinated by night-flying moths—the scent is much stronger in the eve-

ning. This type of flower is usually relatively large and pale, and presumably can be distinguished better by insects as a result.

Many lepidopterous flowers have nectar concealed in spurs. A classical case is a Madagascar orchid (*Anagraecum sesquipedale*), which carries its nectar at the bottom of a slender spur nearly 30 centimeters long (Fig. 22–16A). Charles Darwin predicted that an insect would some day be discovered with a tongue long enough to reach the nectar. After many years a moth with such a tongue was found and Darwin's prediction justified.

Diptera Flowers. These are visited largely by flies and are generally less specialized than the last two types. Floral morphology in itself is probably only important in such cases as the speedwell (*Veronica*), pollinated by hover flies (Fig. 22–17C–E). The corolla is slightly zygomorphic, with the somewhat posterior petal formed by the cohesion of two petals. There are only two stamens with long, widely divergent filaments. A long slender style with a small capitate stigma is positioned over the anterior petal. A nectary located at the base of the corolla tube is protected by hairs. In pollination the lower (posterior) petal acts as a landing platform on which a fly alights and comes in contact with the style. If the fly is carrying pollen on its ventral surface, pollination is effected. In trying to reach the nectar, the fly grasps the filaments of the two stamens, draws them under its body, and is dusted with pollen.

The starflowers (*Stapelia*) of South African deserts may be taken as an example of another class of dipterous flowers—those that attract flies by a somewhat nauseous odor reminiscent of rotting meat (Fig. 22–18C). In many *Stapelia* the flowers not only smell but also look like rotten meat. The female carrion flies are attracted to the blossoms, pollinate them, and are so completely fooled that they lay their eggs (or deposit the larvae) on the perianth; finding no food, the larvae perish. Carrion flies are also attracted by the odor of the small European spotted arum lily (*Arum maculatum*, Fig. 22–17A, B). What is often referred to as the flower of this species is an inflorescence of a spadix, bearing numerous flowers enveloped by a large bract, the spathe. There are two sets of flowers, female at the bottom and male above; the topmost flowers are sterile and modified into a set of bristles. The upper part of the inflorescence is a naked reddish-brown appendix, the source of a very unpleasant smell. Small flies attracted to the appendix slide down the smooth surface of the spathe past the male flowers to the female flowers below. Their attempts to escape up the spadix are thwarted by the bristly palisade of the sterile male flowers, and they become trapped for a day. During this time they crawl over the stigmas, dusting them with any pollen

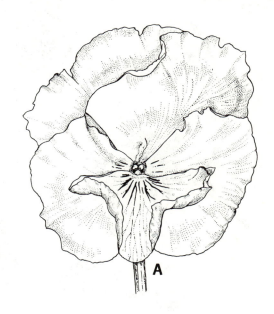

391

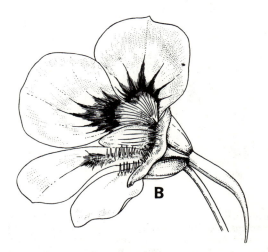

FIGURE 22–14 Honey guides. A, *Viola*, ×1; B, *Tropolaeum*, ×1.

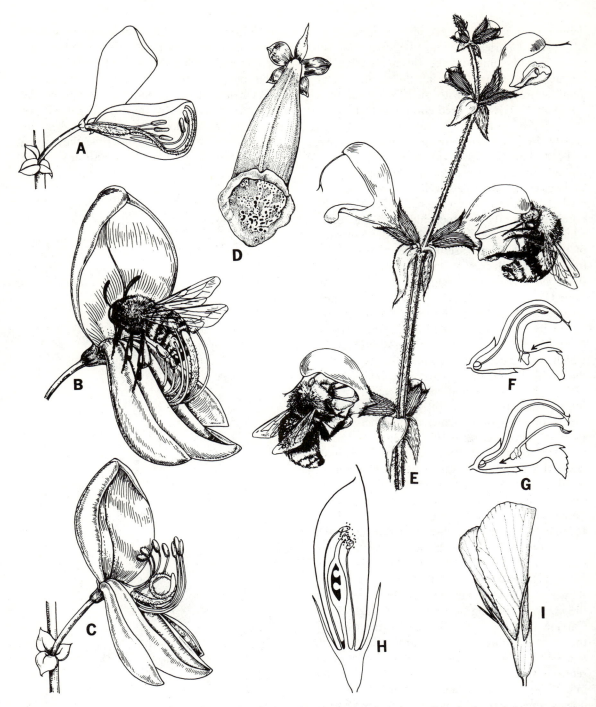

FIGURE 22–15 Hymenopterous flowers. A–C, *Sarothamnus scoparius*. A, median section of flower showing stamens and style concealed within the keel, ×1; B, visit of heavy insect depresses keel and triggers explosive upward movement of stamens so they come in contact with belly and back of visitor, with stigma touching back, ×2; C, a "tripped" flower showing further coiling of style, ×1. D, *Digitalis purpurea*, ×1. E–G, *Salvia pratensis*, ×1. E, bumblebees visiting flowers; F, G, median sections of flowers, showing pivot mechanism at base of filament which brings anther down on back of bee, ×1. H, I, *Trifolium*-type flower in section and side views, nectary shown at base of carpel, ×5. (A–G, adapted from *The Story of Pollination*, by B. J. D. Meeuse, copyright © 1961, The Ronald Press Company, New York; H–I, after Hagerup and Petersson with permission of Ejnar Munksgaard.)

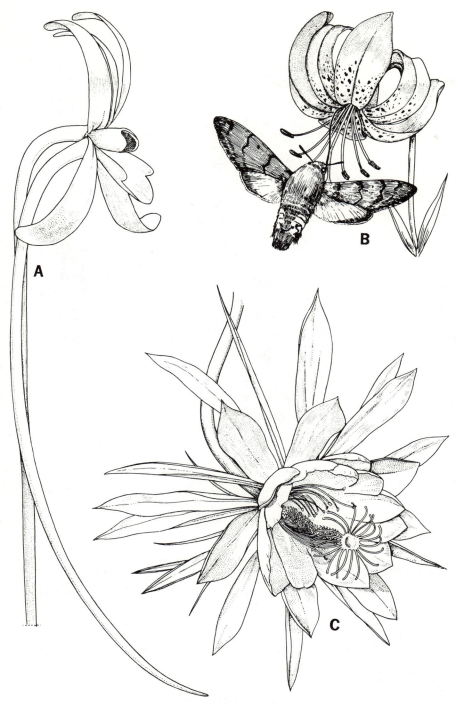

FIGURE 22–16 Lepidopterous flowers. A, *Anagraecum sesquipedale,* showing long slender spur, ×1; B, *Lilium martagon,* showing hawk moth taking nectar from petal pouch, ×1; C, *Phyllanthus,* night-blooming cactus, ×1. (B, after Ross and Morin.)

DIVISION ANTHOPHYTA

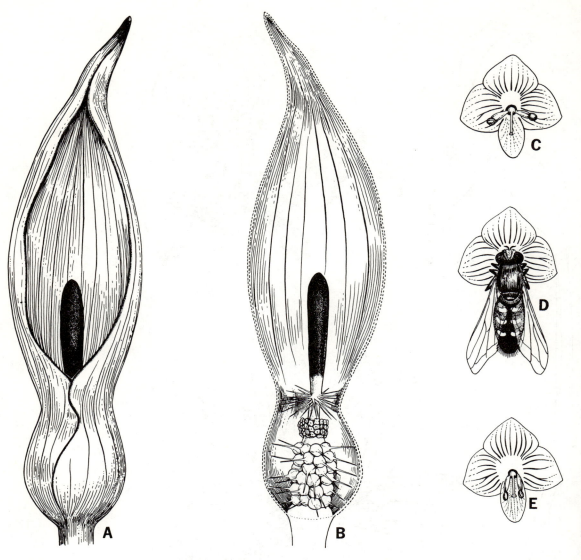

FIGURE 22–17 Dipterous flowers. A, B, *Arum maculatum.* A, inflorescence enclosed by spathe, upper part of spadix visible, ×2; B, portion of spathe removed to show sterile male flowers at constriction of spathe, functional male flowers immediately below them, and female flowers at base of spadix, ×2. C–E, *Veronica,* flowers before (C), during (D), and after (E) visit of crescent fly, ×2. (C–E, adapted from *The Story of Pollination,* by B. J. D. Meeuse, copyright © 1961, The Ronald Press Company, New York.)

adhering to their lower surfaces. On the second day the anthers of the male flowers dehisce, the bristles wilt, and the flies are freed to visit another inflorescence and continue their role of pollinators. The Dutchman's pipe (*Aristolochia*) has a somewhat similar gnat trap, although in this instance only a single flower is involved rather than an inflorescence (Fig. 22–18A, B).

Ornithophily

Birds of various kinds are important pollinating agents for a number of tropical and

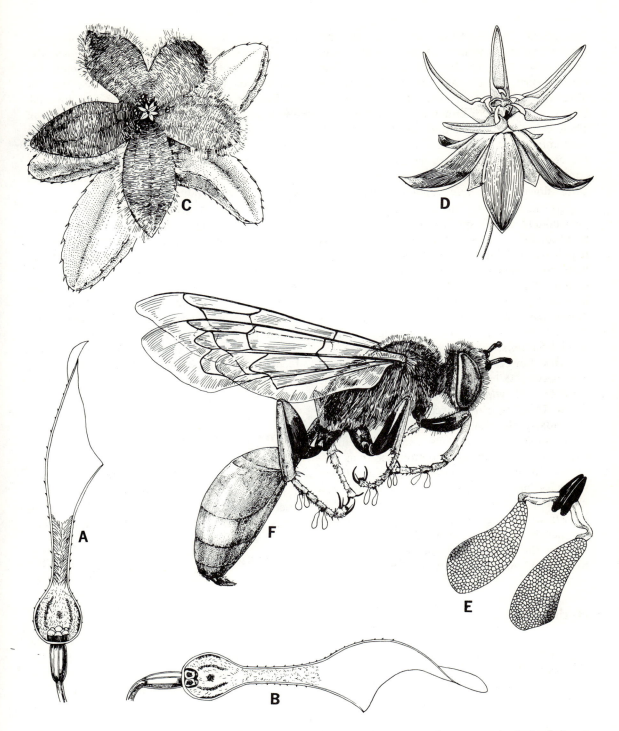

FIGURE 22–18 A, B, Dutchman's pipe (*Aristolochia sipho*). A, flower erect (stiff downward-pointing hairs on inner wall prevent escape of trapped small flies), ×2; B, flower limp and hairs wilted so that flies can escape, ×2. C, *Stapelia grandiflora,* with flower showing small masses of larvae near base of petals, ×0.5. D–F, milk-weed (*Asclepias speciosa*). D, flower with five scoop-shaped nectaries and translator as dark spot between two, ×2; E, pair of pollinia suspended from translator, ×15; F, dead insect with pollinia caught on its legs, ×5. (A, B, adapted from *The Story of Pollination,* by B. J. D. Meeuse, copyright © 1961, The Ronald Press Company, New York.)

subtropical species. Birds active in this respect are sunbirds, honeysuckers, and hummingbirds—some of which are no larger than moths. Bird flowers and insect flowers are often much alike, and certainly more similar to one another than either is to wind flowers. Their colors are bright and intense, with reds predominating to the extent of more than 80 per cent in 159 species studied. Brilliant color contrasts are common, as in the bird-of-paradise flower (*Strelitzia reginae*). Most bird flowers lack scent. Meeuse states that approximately 2,000 species of birds belonging to about 50 families visit flowers more or less regularly, with about two-thirds of these relying on flowers as their most important source of food. Since these bird visitors vary so much in size and feeding habits, no one type of flower particularly adapted to bird visits has evolved. However, individually some do show special features.

Bird flowers often secrete an abundance of thin nectar. It is said that each flower of the coral tree (*Erythrina*) contains about a thimbleful. In some bird flowers the floral parts—particularly the filaments, styles, and stigmas—are quite rigid, perhaps enabling them to withstand the vigorous attentions of their visitors. Some birds, such as hummingbirds, hover while feeding on the nectar; for others a perch may be provided by a modified bract, as in *Strelitzia*. Although birds generally visit flowers for nectar, it seems likely that in some instances the purpose of the visit is actually to feed on small insects attracted by the nectar.

Hydrophily

Certain immersed hydrophytes (e.g., *Ceratophyllum*) are monoecious; the ovulate flowers remain below the water level, and the staminate flowers shed their pollen into the water. The pollen is of the same specific gravity as the water and so is dispersed through it; eventually some of the pollen comes into contact with the stigmas. A more ingenious arrangement has evolved in the ribbon grass (*Vallisneria*, Fig. 22–19). It is dioecious; the ovulate flower buds start out well below the surface of the water. As these mature, the pedicel becomes much elongated and spiraled, eventually raising the flower to the surface of the water, where it floats. The flower then opens and lies, with its stigmas recurved, in a dimple on the water surface. The minute staminate flowers, only about 1 millimeter in diameter, are produced by the hundreds from a single inflorescence. Each flower consists of two stamens enclosed by a perianth of two large segments and one small one. The whole flower is shed under water and gradually floats to the surface. Here it opens and the perianth recurves to form a little tripod support for the flower. The staminate flowers drift about on the surface of the water until they come close to an ovulate flower and are drawn into the dimple by surface tension. Pollination is effected when the staminate flowers are tipped over so that the anthers touch the stigmas.

Some Special Cases

To show the high degree of specialization for pollination achieved by some plants, four special cases will be described. All involve insects as agents, but the mechanisms are very different in each case.

Milkweeds (Asclepiadaceae). In this family (Fig. 22–18D–F) the five anthers are fused into a ring around the gynoecium of two carpels. Each anther bears a cup-like nectary in the shape of a horn. There is a narrow vertical slit between adjacent anthers, but the pollen masses (pollinia) of these adjacent anthers are fastened together by a little horny clip that can usually be seen quite readily as a dark dot. When an insect crawls over the flower seeking nectar, its legs are likely to slip into the slit between the anthers. As the insect tries to withdraw, bristles on its leg catch on the clip, pulling the clip and the

396

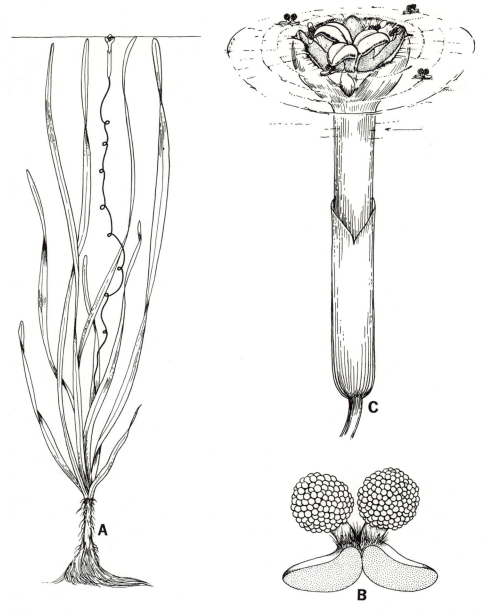

FIGURE 22–19 *Vallisneria americana.* A, female plant showing flower floating on surface of water, ×0.2; B, male flower, ×5; C, boat-like male flowers coming in contact with stigmas, ×15. (B, after Gleason with permission of The New York Botanical Garden.)

securely attached pollinia free from the pollen sacs. The insect then departs with one or more of these little saddlebags of pollen suspended from bristles on its legs. If the insect visits another flower of the same species, a funnel-shaped cavity guides the pollinia down to the stigma, thus pollinating the flower. Sometimes the pollinia do not break away from the clip,

DIVISION ANTHOPHYTA

and the insect is trapped. It is not unusual to find in an inflorescence a number of dead flies and even bees caught in this way.

Spanish Bayonet (*Yucca*). A completely obligate relationship seems to exist between the Spanish bayonet and a small moth (*Tegiticula,* formerly known as *Pronuba*). Yuccas grown beyond the range of the moth will produce flowers but never set seed. The moth in turn appears to be quite dependent on the yucca flowers as an egg-laying site. The flowers of all species of *Yucca* are borne in large panicles; the flowers are pendent, pale creamy in color, and somewhat bell-shaped. When the buds open in the evening, they are visited by *Tegiticula* females that creep into the flowers and gather pollen from the small anthers. The pollen is somewhat sticky and is rolled into a tight little ball and held by the specialized mouthparts of the insect. After collecting all the pollen it can carry, the moth pierces the ovary wall (of the same or another flower) with its long ovipositor, and lays a batch of eggs among the young ovules. It then crawls down the style and pushes its ball of pollen into the cavity between the lobes of the stigma. The moth larvae hatch out in a few days and live on the developing seeds; eventually they gnaw their way through the ovary wall, lower themselves to the ground, and pupate until the yuccas bloom again. Although about 20 per cent of the yucca seeds are destroyed in this fashion, this is a small price to pay for such efficient pollinating service.

Figs (*Ficus*). As far as is known, all species of the extremely large tropical and subtropical genus *Ficus* are pollinated by small chalcid wasps, and several genera are involved. Here, too, the relationship is obligatory and sometimes very complex. The wild fig (*Ficus carica*) of southern Europe is pollinated by a single species of wasp (*Blastophaga grossorum*) with a very complicated life history (Fig. 22–20). The fruits (syconia) of *Ficus* are compound structures made up of the flattened axis of the inflorescence which becomes a hollow inverted urn with a small apical pore

opening to the outside. Flowers line the inside of this urn. *Ficus carica* is monoecious and bears three generations of flowers and fruits in a year. The first develops in February and contains staminate flowers formed chiefly around the pore, with abortive ovulate "gall flowers" lower down. The gall flower has a rudimentary ovary, a short style with an open canal, and a single rudimentary ovule incapable of forming a seed. Female wasps enter the syconium and deposit a single egg in the ovule of each gall flower. Here the larvae hatch out, feed, grow, and undergo metamorphosis. The male wasps gnaw their way out, locate the gall flowers containing females, pierce the wall of the ovary, and fertilize the females within. The male wasps then die without leaving the syconium. By this time the fruit is ripe, though tough and bitter, and the staminate flowers are shedding their pollen. The gravid female wasps leave the gall flowers and crawl out through the pore of the syconium, becoming dusted with pollen on the way. This generation of wasps is very sedentary and flies very little. The wasps crawl about on the tree in search of young syconia in which to lay their eggs. These they find in the second generation of figs, which develops toward the end of May. These syconia, however, contain only normal ovulate flowers with long styles; the wasps try in vain to lay their eggs, and in so doing deposit pollen on the stigmas. These syconia ripen to become fleshy and edible. In the meantime the third generation of fruits is developing. Females finally make their way into these and lay their eggs in the gall flowers, which are the only kind present. Here the larvae pass the winter, emerging in the spring to repeat the cycle.

The cultivated fig, with its numerous varieties, is derived from the wild *Ficus carica*. It exists in two races, the fig and the caprifig, and it has been known since very early times that for many varieties of cultivated fig both races must be present in order to produce a crop of fruits. Although both races produce three generations of syconia each year, the caprifig bears staminate flowers and gall flowers; the

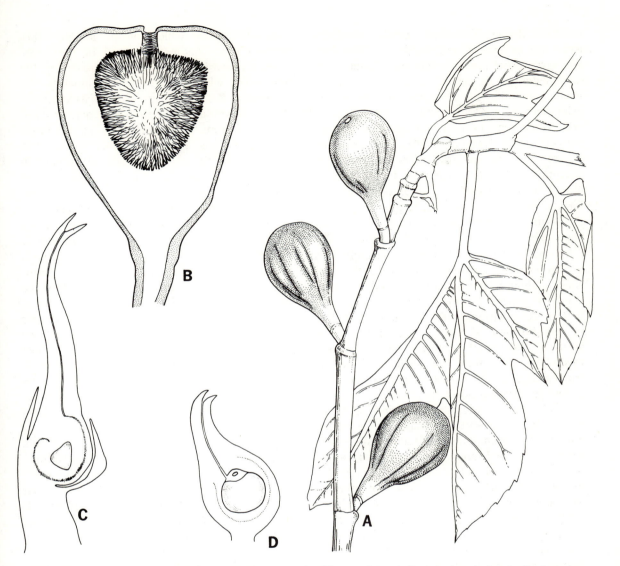

FIGURE 22–20 Fig (*Ficus carica*). A, fruiting branch with syconia, ×1; B, syconium in longitudinal section, showing apical pore (flowers line the urn-shaped interior), ×2; C, normal female flower, ×10; D, gall flower (sterile female flower), ×10. (B, after LeMaout and Decaisne; C, D, after Condit with permission of *Hilgardia*.)

fig only ovulate flowers. This means that the caprifig is essentially male, the fig female. In this very unusual instance, a monoecious wild plant has been changed by selection into a dioecious cultivated form. When the Smyrna variety of fig was first introduced into California, it was found necessary to introduce the caprifig as well as the *Blastophaga* in order to obtain a crop. Certain varieties of fig develop edible, fleshy fruits parthenocarpically. However, these do not keep well and cannot be dried; the dried figs of commerce always contain aborted "seeds."

SEEDS AND FRUITS

The term seed, like so many other morphological terms of wide application, is difficult to define. However, certain characteristics are associated with seeds, whether they are gymnospermous, monocotyledonous, or dicotyledonous in origin. A seed is a mature ovule containing an embryo plant whose development is generally arrested for a period, and which may or may not have an accompanying food reserve. While this definition covers the great majority of cases, there are exceptions that differ in degree. In the cycadophytes and *Ginkgo* no embryo may have formed at the time the seeds are "ripe" and shed—in fact, fertilization frequently takes place when the ovule is on the ground. The Orchidaceae have seeds that consistently lack a differentiated embryo at the time they are shed, although fertilization has taken place. While in general a period of dormancy occurs before germination, there is great variation in the duration of the dormant period. The seeds of the poplar (*Populus*) germinate immediately after they are shed, and certain tropical genera (*Myristica, Durio*) are also reported to have no dormant period.

Seeds with endosperm are said to be albuminous, while those lacking it are exalbuminous. In albuminous seeds the embryo frequently is small and undifferentiated, as in many ranalian families; this is perhaps the primitive condition among the anthophytes. Monocotyledons commonly have albuminous seeds with the endosperm bulking quite large compared to the embryo. Exalbuminous seeds are characteristic of many families, such as Aceraceae, Cruciferae, Geraniaceae, Cucurbitaceae, and Compositae; other families have genera with endosperm and others without, such as Araceae, Rosaceae, Papilionaceae, and Betulaceae. A variety of substances are stored in endosperm, including proteins, fats, oil, and starch (the principal carbohydrate). In the absence of endosperm, the cotyledons usually assume the storage and nutritive roles; but sometimes, as in the Brazil nut (*Bertholletia excelsa*), these roles are assumed by the hypocotyl.

Seeds vary greatly in size and weight—from the minute, dust-like seeds of orchids and some Ericaceae which weigh about 0.001 milligram, to the massive seed of the *coco-de-mer* (*Lodoicea*), the double coconut of the Seychelles, which may weigh as much as 20 kilograms. Seeds also vary in details of structure, although as a rule the seed coat, or testa, is formed from the integuments; the micropyle can be seen as a small opening in the testa close to the tip of the radicle. Especially in anatropous ovules the place of abscission of the funiculus is evident as a scar, the hilum. Some seeds have fleshy coats or appendages of various origins commonly referred to as arils—a loose morphological term referring to any fleshy external part of the seed. The term is applied to outgrowths of the chalaza or integuments which more or less envelop the ovule, also to the fleshy funiculus as in *Magnolia* and species of *Acacia*. In general, arils are associated with tropical seeds and are rare in plants of temperate regions. While arillate developments are particularly common among primitive angiosperms, they cannot be regarded as indications of primitiveness, because fleshy outgrowths occur in such a variety of families, including gymnosperms that they must have arisen independently during evolution. In fact, fleshy outgrowths offer good examples of so-called "parallel evolution"—a widespread phenomenon that results in similar structures in unrelated groups of plants. It seems likely that arils are an ecological modification related to dissemination.

The longevity of seeds is another topic of both biological and practical interest. The time that seeds remain viable varies from a very brief period in such genera as *Quercus, Acer, Populus, Salix, Citrus,* and some grasses to hundreds of years in other cases. It is reported that seeds of *Nelumbo* and *Albizia julibrissin* that had been in the British Museum for 150 years germinated after becoming wet during the "Battle of Britain." Viable seeds of lotus (*Nelumbo nucifera*) found by a Japanese botanist in a peat deposit in Manchuria have been carbon dated at 2,000 years old. Even this great age is trifling compared with that of some arctic lupine (*Lupinus arcticus*) seeds reported recently by Porsild of the National Museum of Canada as germinating after a radiocarbon-established age of 10,000 years. They had survived in permafrost soil in Yukon. An investigation to determine the differential viability of a number of common Michigan weed seeds was started in 1879 by Professor Beal of what was then Michigan State College. The seeds of 20 species were mixed with sand and buried in the ground in inverted open-mouthed bottles. At first samples were removed at five-year intervals to test viability; later this was increased to ten-year intervals. After 80 years three species still had viable seeds. The experiment is planned to continue for 160 years.

In addition to functioning as reproductive structures, seeds show very considerable adaptation to the environment. For example, Went discusses in some detail the adaptation of seeds of certain species to desert conditions. He describes three groups of annuals: winter annuals, summer annuals, and an intermediate group. Germination in each group requires some rainfall but is actually triggered by temperature; summer annuals will only germinate at 26–30° C, whereas winter annuals remain dormant at these temperatures but do germinate at 10° C. Furthermore, observations in nature show that the germination of seeds of certain desert plants is not related to moisture as such, but to a sufficient amount and duration of rain. Went describes a number of different mechanisms that have been evolved to permit germination only under very favorable conditions. The first group of seeds mentioned by Went (from *Euphorbia* spp. and *Pectis papposa*) contain water-soluble germination inhibitors. Germination will take place only after these inhibitors have been completely leached from the seeds. In the second group, germination is inhibited by salt concentrations in the soil somewhat higher than those tolerated by the growing plants of the same species. A heavy rainfall will leach the salts out of the upper layers of soil and so permit germination. In the third group, delay in germination is probably due to the presence of encasing structures,

such as husks in certain grasses. Heavy precipitation causes sand and gravel to scarify these structures, making germination possible. Went discusses other mechanisms, but the foregoing are sufficient to indicate one aspect of evolution where the origin of certain structures is related closely to the environment.

The term fruit is often very loosely used and is difficult to define precisely. It has been called a "mature flower," which is a good definition if all the implications are appreciated. In all cases a flower (or flowers) precedes the development of a fruit; and flowers at anthesis have immature parts, at least in the gynoecium. In general, a fruit consists of a matured gynoecium and may include accessory parts of the flower—even the axis of the inflorescence, pedicel, or peduncle in particular cases. Pollination followed by fertilization is the usual prelude to fruit development; but in many instances, parthenocarpy occurs—that is, a complete fruit is formed without fertilization. Such parthenocarpic fruits do not contain seeds. A well-known example is the banana (*Musa*); others with fleshy fruits are seedless varieties of oranges (*Citrus*), cucumber (*Cucumis*), and grapes (*Vitis*). It should be noted that the development of parthenocarpic fruits can be induced by the plant hormone indoleacetic acid.

The ripened ovary wall in a fruit is the pericarp, which may be dry or fleshy, fibrous or stony. Three distinct layers can often be recognized in the pericarp: the outer (exocarp), the middle (mesocarp), and the inner layer (endocarp) (Fig. 22–21). Pericarp features are used considerably in classifying fruits —a process often artificial but very useful for taxonomic purposes.

In classifying fruits, three main types are recognized (see Table 22–1). The first group is comprised of simple fruits formed from a single simple or compound ovary. The second type includes aggregate fruits formed from a single flower but with separate unfused carpels, each actually forming a fruit but the whole aggregating as a unit—e.g., raspberry (*Rubus*), strawberry (*Fragaria*), and *Magnolia*.

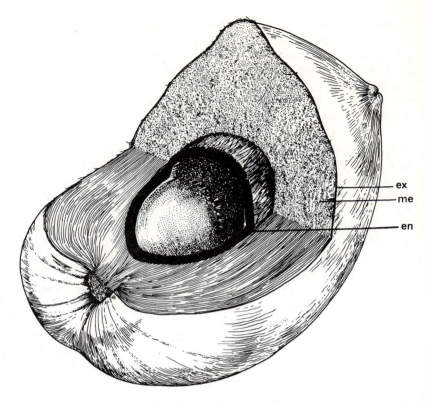

ex
me
en

FIGURE 22–21   Coconut fruit (*Cocos nucifera*) cut to show three layers of pericarp, ×0.5. *ex,* thin hard exocarp; *me,* fibrous mesocarp; *en,* stony endocarp.

In the third type, multiple fruits, several flowers are involved—as in the flowering dogwood (*Cornus nuttallii*), plane tree (*Platanus*), mulberry (*Morus*), and pineapple (*Ananas*).

As fruits mature, they become either dry or fleshy. Dry fruits may remain closed (indehiscent) when ripe or they may open in one of several ways (dehiscent, Fig. 22–22). Fleshy fruits as a rule are indehiscent (Fig. 22–23).

In both aggregate and multiple fruits, the individual elements are described in the same terms as for simple fruits—e.g., in the strawberry the actual fruits are achenes borne on a fleshy receptacle, whereas in the raspberry the fruits are druplets. The pineapple (*Ananas*) is a special type of multiple fruit in which the axis of the inflorescence enlarges to become

part of the fruit. In the syconium of the fig we find a multiple fruit; the actual fruits are achene-like inside the hollow urn-shaped structure, which is the expanded, deeply concave axis of the inflorescence.

In the array of fruit types, the plant biologist is likely to see adaptations that protect the embryo plant from desiccation or, what is more general, a series of devices to assist and promote the spread of species into new areas. Fruits may be agents in the dissemination of seeds or may themselves act as disseminules.

Of prime importance to worldwide occurrence is the dispersal of plants—i.e., their transportation from place to place—whether as fruits, seeds, or specialized vegetative structures. It can be argued that dispersal is a more important factor in the evolution of

TABLE 22–1
A Classification of Fruits

(For illustrations of fruits see Figures 22–24, 25, 26, 27)

I. Fruits dry, pericarp dry when fruit is mature.

  A. Indehiscent fruits in which the pericarp remains closed at maturity.

    a. *Achene*—a small single-seeded fruit with a relatively thin pericarp; except for its attachment by the funiculus, the seed lies free in the cavity of the ovary: buttercup (*Ranunculus*), crowfoot (*Potentilla*), water plantain (*Alisma*), buckwheat (*Fagopyrum*).

    b. *Caryopsis*—achene-like except that it is derived from a compound ovary and the seed coat is firmly united to the pericarp: characteristic fruit of the Gramineae.

    c. *Cypsela*—achene-like but derived from an inferior, compound ovary: characteristic fruit of the Compositae.

    d. *Nut*—like an achene but derived from two or more carpels, and with a hard or stony pericarp: hazel nut (*Corylus*), basswood (*Tilia*), acorn (*Quercus*).

    e. *Samara*—a winged achene: elm (*Ulmus*), ash (*Fraxinus*), tree-of-heaven (*Ailanthus*), hop tree (*Ptelea*).

    f. *Schizocarp*—the product of a compound ovary that splits apart at maturity into a number of one-seeded portions termed mericarps: maple (*Acer*), many Umbelliferae, Labiatae, Malvaceae, Geraniaceae.

  B. Dehiscent fruits in which the fruit splits, or opens in some manner to release the seeds.

    a. *Follicle*—derived from a single carpel that splits at maturity down one side, usually along the ventral suture: columbine (*Aquilegia*), peony (*Paeonia*), larkspur (*Delphinium*), milkweed (*Asclepias*).

    b. *Legume*—also from a single carpel, but dehiscing down both the dorsal and ventral sutures to form two valves: characteristic fruit of Papilionaceae.

    c. *Silique*—the product of a superior compound ovary of two carpels, the pericarp separating as two halves leaving a persistent central portion with the seed or seeds attached to it: characteristic fruit of Cruciferae.

    d. *Capsule*—from a compound ovary; various types of dehiscence are found—e.g., longitudinal, porous, or circumscissile; in general the dehiscence is from top downward and the separated portions (valves or teeth) remain attached: characteristic of numerous families.

II. Fruits fleshy, pericarp partly or wholly fleshy or fibrous.

    a. *Drupe*—carpels one or more but usually single-seeded; mesocarp fleshy but the endocarp hard and stony: cherry, peach, plum (*Prunus*), coconut (*Cocos*), olive (*Olea*).

    b. *Berry*—one to several carpels, usually many-seeded; both mesocarp and endocarp are fleshy: one-seeded, nutmeg (*Myristica*), date (*Phoenix*); single carpel and several seeds, baneberry (*Actaea*), barberry (*Berberis*), *Mahonia*; others with more than one carpel, grape (*Vitis*), tomato and potato (*Solanum*), *Asparagus*.

    c. *Pome*—derived from a compound inferior ovary; much of the fleshy portion is the enlarged base of the perianth tube with only the central part composing the pericarp; both the exocarp and mesocarp are fleshy while the endocarp (the core) is stony or cartilaginous: characteristic fruit of the Pomoideae, apple (*Malus*), pear (*Pyrus*), quince (*Cydonia*), mountain ash (*Sorbus*).

403

flowering plants than their many and ingenious adaptations for pollination. Apparently few species suffer from lack of pollination due to the absence of an essential pollinator; on the other hand, the migration of plants to new areas very closely depends on modifications for dispersal. In view of the undoubted biological importance of dispersal and of the variety of related adaptations that have evolved in the flowering plants, it is surprising that this study has not caught the attention of more investigators. The encyclopedic work of Ridley, which provides the basis for the following account, should be consulted by any who wish to pursue this topic further.

Dissemination by Wind

Tumble-weeds. The whole plant, or the fruiting portion, breaks off and is blown by wind across open country, scattering seeds as it goes. Such plants are always herbaceous and usually annuals. They include Russian thistle (*Salsola kali*), pigweeds (*Amaranthus*), certain Gramineae, and tumbling mustard (*Sisymbrium*).

Light Fruits and Seeds. These are blown about by the wind and owe dispersal to their lightness—e.g., Orchidaceae and many Ericaceae.

Winged Fruits. Wings are usually formed by persistent bracts or perianth parts, or the whole pericarp may develop as a wing. Winged fruits, commonest in trees and shrubs, include the tropical dipterocarps (*Dipterocarpus*), maple (*Acer*), ash (*Fraxinus*), elm (*Ulmus*), dock (*Rumex*), and Betulaceae (Fig. 22–24).

Winged Seeds. The fruit is usually a capsule that dehisces to release seeds in which the testa has developed into a thin wing. This is common in trees and shrubs, and particularly climbers—e.g., jacaranda (*Jacaranda*), trumpet vine (*Tecoma*), catalpa (*Catalpa*), and many other genera of Bignoniaceae, butter-

and-eggs (*Linaria*), and yam (*Dioscorea*). (See Fig. 22–25E, G, H.)

Plumed Fruits. Plumes develop from the pappus in some Compositae, from the perianth in various Cyperaceae, from the persistent style (*Geum, Anemone, Clematis*), or from the pedicels of spikelets in certain Gramineae (Fig. 22–25A–D).

Plumed Seeds. Tufts of light silky hairs may develop at one (rarely both) end of the seed, as in fireweed (*Epilobium*), milkweed (*Asclepias*), dogbane (*Apocynum*), and epiphytes such as some Bromeliaceae (Fig. 22–25F).

Woolly Fruits or Seeds. The pericarp or the seed coat may be covered with woolly hairs, as in willows and poplars (Salicaceae),

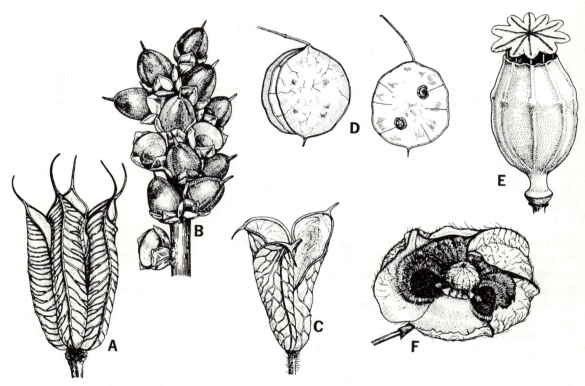

FIGURE 22–22 Dry dehiscent fruits. A, follicles (*Aquilegia*), ×3; B, pyxis (*Plantago major*), capsular fruit with circumscissile dehiscence, ×7; C, follicles (*Delphinium*), ×2; D, silicle (*Lunaria annua*), short silique, showing replum, ×1; E, capsule (*Papaver somniferum* with porous dehiscence, ×1.5; F, schizocarp (*Malva moschatus*) showing numerous, coarsely hairy mericarps, ×3.5.

cotton (*Gossypium*), kapok (*Ceiba*), and *Anemone*.

Dispersal by Water

Rain. Rainwash in the plains, both in temperate and tropical regions, is of very great importance in the dispersal of seeds. The action of rain is accentuated in the mountain forests of the tropical rain zone. Periodically the rush of water from mountains is tremendous. At such times vast numbers of seeds are brought down and spread, some in suitable places for growing in the plains below. In general these occurrences are fortuitous, and the seeds show no special adaptation. In a few cases—e.g., pearlwort (*Sagina*) and mitrewort (*Mitella*)—the opened capsule with seeds lying in it strongly suggests a "splashcup" mechanism so common in the fungi (Fig. 22–26).

Streams. The fruits and seeds of many streamside and aquatic plants are adapted for floating for short periods of time, usually by reason of air trapped in some part of the disseminule—e.g., marsh marigold (*Caltha*) and several aquatic Umbelliferae with corky mericarps. In some cases, seedlings are buoyant or so small that surface tension keeps them up and they are carried by water—e.g., loosestrife (*Lythrum*), monkey flower (*Mimulus*). Immersed and floating aquatics are also dispersed by streams through the transport of winter buds or other fragments of the plants themselves.

Sudd. This is the name given to dense masses of vegetation growing out from the banks of rivers and often blocking the channel. The whole mass, or a portion of it, may be torn away by a sudden flood and carried down the stream, often ending up in adjacent lakes or pools. Sudd usually occurs in slow-moving rivers in flat open country, such as the Nile or Ganges. Good examples of sudd plants are papyrus (*Cyperus papyrus*), water hyacinth

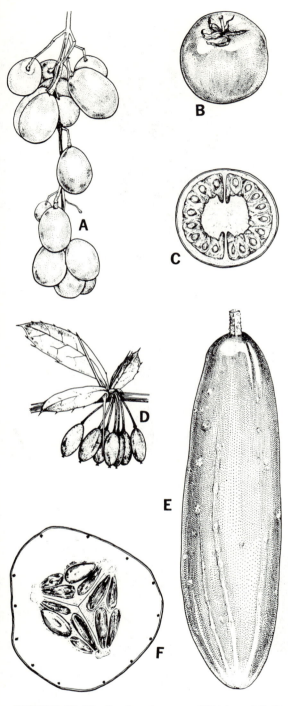

FIGURE 22–23 Berries. A, grape (*Vitis*), ×0.5; B, C, tomato (*Lycopersicum esculentum*), ×0.5; D, barberry (*Berberis*), ×0.5; E, F, cucumber (*Cucumis sativus*), a special type of berry known as pepo, ×1.

406

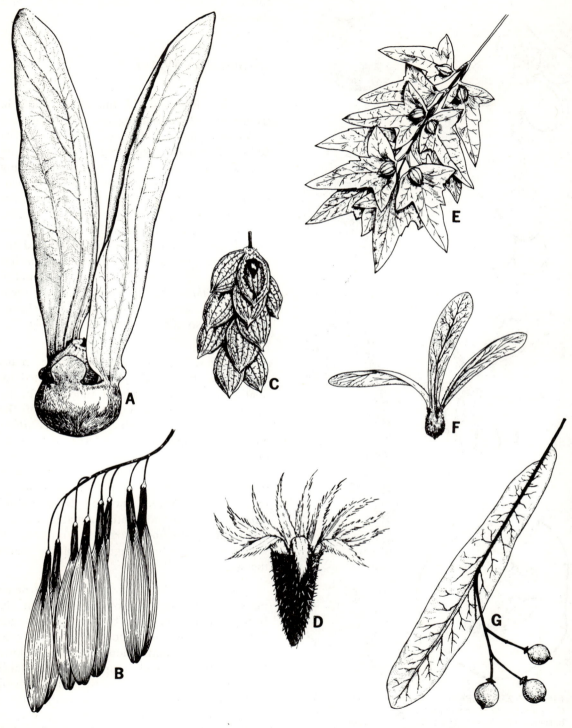

FIGURE 22–24 Winged fruits. A, *Dipterocarpus retusus* (the two wings are part of persistent calyx), ×0.5; B, *Fraxinus,* samara, ×1; C, *Ostrya virginiana,* with each fruit contained in inflated, involucral sac, ×1; D, *Galinsoga,* with cypsela fruit and wings of pappus scales, ×50; E, *Carpinus caroliniana,* with nut-like fruit subtended by single involucral bract, ×1; F, *Triplaris,* with wings of elongated perianth lobes, ×1; G, *Tilia,* with petiole adnate to a large, strap-shaped bract, ×2.

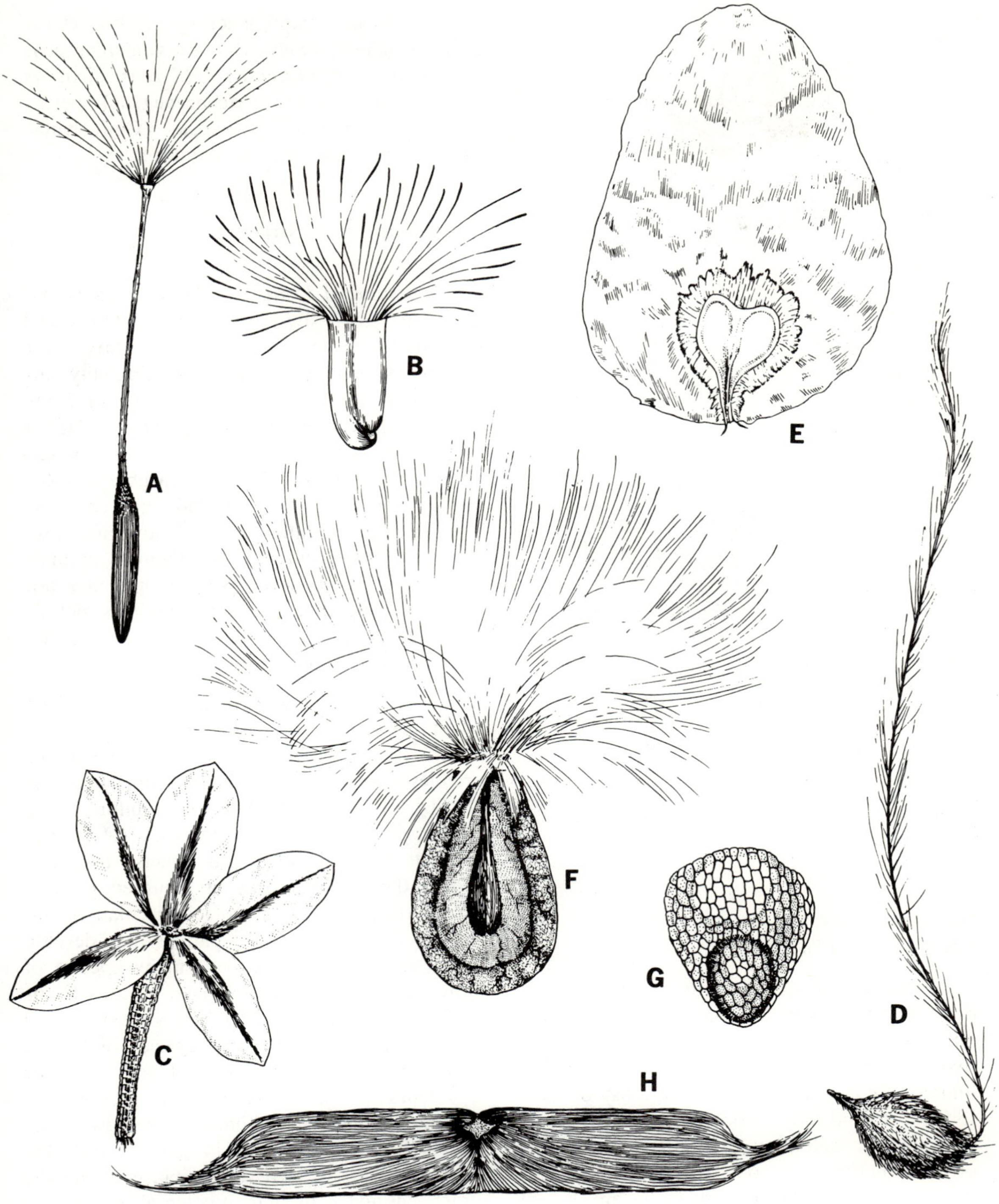

FIGURE 22–25 Airborne fruits and seeds. A–D, fruits. A, *Hypochaeris*, ×5; B, *Centaurea*, ×5; C, *Ursinia*, ×5; D, *Clematis*, ×5. E–H, seeds. E, *Spathodea*, ×5; F, *Asclepias*, ×5; G, *Castilleja*, ×20; H, *Catalpa*, ×2.

DIVISION ANTHOPHYTA

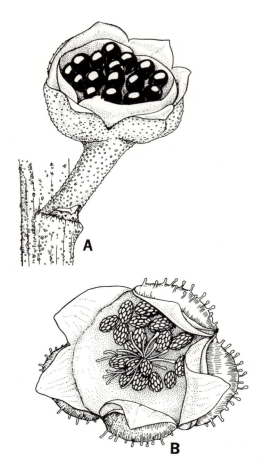

FIGURE 22–26 "Splash-cups." A, mitrewort (*Mitella*), ×5; B, pearlwort (*Sagina*), ×5. Under damp conditions, seeds are splashed out of capsules by rain. (B, after Gibbs.)

(*Eichornia*), water chestnut (*Trapa*), and water lettuce (*Pistia*).

Oceans. Ocean currents disperse plants over very long distances, certainly over 1,000 miles. For two reasons the number of species that can travel effectively in this manner is limited. First, the seed or fruit must be able to float for a long period without becoming waterlogged, killed by exposure to seawater, or germinating too soon. Second, the seeds must be ecologically adapted to establishment on the littoral conditions of a sand or mud bank. Species in many genera are so adapted—

e.g., *Erythrina* (Papilionaceae), *Cakile* (Cruciferae), *Arenaria peploides* (Caryophyllaceae), *Calophyllum* (Guttiferae), *Hibiscus tileaceus* (Malvaceae), *Carapa* (Meliaceae), all species of Rhizophoraceae, *Ipomoea* (Convolvulaceae), and *Cocos nucifera* (Palmae).

Dispersal by Animals

Ingestion of Fruits and Seeds. Birds and mammals eat fleshy fruits of many kinds and pass the seeds through the alimentary tract unharmed, and even with germinability increased. It appears that the majority of fruits with a fleshy pericarp are specially adapted for this mode of dissemination; common examples are cherry (*Prunus*), raspberry (*Rubus*), currants (*Ribes*) and gooseberries, Oregon grape (*Mahonia*), and flowering dogwood (*Cornus nuttallii*). Herbivorous animals may ingest small seeds with foliage and not harm them by chewing; good examples include seeds of some of the Papilionaceae, and the small dry fruits of Gramineae.

Adhesion to Fur and Feathers. The adaptations in these cases are generally well known and consist of the development of prickles, hooks, spines, hairs, and sticky or viscid fruits and seeds. The whole inflorescence may be involved as in the burdock (*Arctium*) with its hooked involucral bracts; in *Agrimonia* there is a crown of incurved prickles on the outside of the receptacle; in many Compositae (e.g., *Bidens*) the pappus may develop awns that are often barbed; many species of Boraginaceae and *Galium* have various forms of hooks on the exocarp; the style too may become hooked as in some species of *Geum*; many grass fruits are provided with awns or stiff hairs on the florets; in some plants, such as the twinflower (*Linnaea borealis*), the bracts bear adhesive viscid glands, with the abscission of the fruit taking place below the bract; viscid, glandular involucral bracts are not uncommon in Compositae (e.g., *Adenocaulon*); viscid hairs on the calyx are found

VASCULAR PLANTS

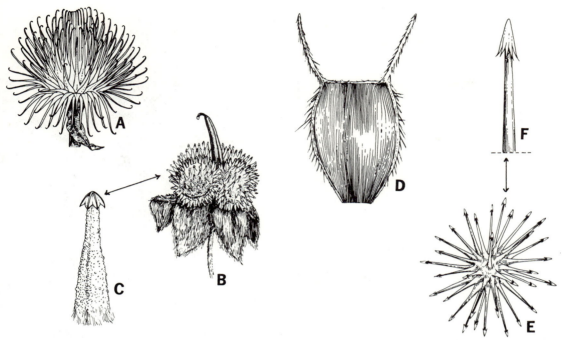

FIGURE 22–27 Animal-dispersed fruits. A, *Arctium minus,* involucral bracts with stiff hooked tips, ×2; B, *Cynoglossum officinale,* nutlets covered with short barbed spines, ×2; C, single spine of *Cynoglossum,* ×20; D, *Bidens,* pappus represented by two stiff barbed awns, ×10; E, *Acaena,* with sepals sharp and spiny, ×7.5; F, showing grapnel-like tips of sepaline spines in *Acaena,* ×25.

in *Plumbago;* and in certain species of Gramineae, *Juncus,* and *Plantago* a very adhesive, mucilaginous secretion is evident on wetting the fruits or seeds (Fig. 22–27).

The fruits of one family, the Pedaliaceae, are characterized by highly specialized and most formidable hooks in almost all genera. In the mule-grab (*Proboscidea*) the woody fusiform capsules are about 8 centimeters long, ending in two curved sharp claws 15 centimeters long. The fruit lies on the ground with the claws upward; if an animal steps on it, the fruit tips up and the claws clasp the fetlock. The seeds are shed from the capsule as the animal moves about. In the South African genus *Harpagophytum* (grapple plant) the woody fruit has four wings, each cut into a number of very stout linear arms with many strong hooks chiefly on the tips of the arms. The fruits become attached, almost irremovably, to the feet or tail of any large animal unfortunate enough to come in contact with them. Again the seeds are dislodged from the capsule as the animal moves about (Fig. 22–28).

The tropical and subtropical genus *Pisonia* (Nyctaginaceae) has one-seeded fruits covered by an extremely sticky perianth tube. So viscid and glutinous are the fruits that they sometimes trap small birds that cannot disentangle themselves. It is said that the ancient Hawaiians used gum from a species of *Pisonia* for catching birds. There can be no question that this exudate causes the fruits to adhere firmly to the feathers of birds, with consequent dispersal. The missel thrush has long been associated with the European mistletoe (*Viscum album*) because the birds feed on the berries. The flesh of the berries contains an abundance of a glutinous material which is only partially digested by passage through the alimentary tract. The excreted seeds and skins of the fruit

DIVISION ANTHOPHYTA

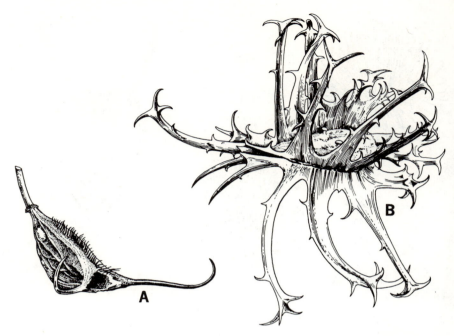

FIGURE 22–28 Fruits highly specialized for animal dispersal. A, *Proboscidea*, ×0.5; B, *Harpagophytum*, ×0.5. Both are capsular fruits.

are stuck together by the gluten, and the mass frequently becomes securely fastened to the branches of trees. Also, seeds may become attached to the bills of missel thrushes after berries are eaten. Such seeds may be removed when the bill is rubbed against the bark of a branch and so placed in position for germination.

Adhesion of Small Disseminules. A large number of plants probably owe their distribution to the adherence of disseminules to the fur, feathers, or feet of passing mammals and birds. These disseminules are mostly picked up in mud and show no particular adaptations except their small size. This form of dispersal is especially likely for the seeds and fruits of water and marsh plants. In the *Origin of Species,* Darwin reports an examination and study he made of about half a pound of dried mud. He wet it and kept it covered under conditions suitable for germination. In the course of six months 537 seedlings of various species appeared. He also took a ball of mud from the leg of a partridge, and from this raised 84 plants of three species. Man himself has been an active agent in dispersal when mud becomes attached to boots and vehicles.

Mechanical Dispersal

In some species—mostly herbaceous—the mature fruit explodes and throws its seeds a considerable distance from the parent plant. Such fruits are found in many families. Best known is perhaps the touch-me-not (*Impatiens,* Fig. 22–29D). Its fleshy capsules are often somewhat dilated at the upper end where the seeds are borne. The pericarp develops a high turgor pressure and elastic cell walls. As the fruit matures the valves become only very slightly coherent. When ripe, the valves separate suddenly, either spontaneously or when touched. Each valve curls inward with considerable force and throws the seeds for some distance. Certain species of *Oxalis* have developed a similar mechanism.

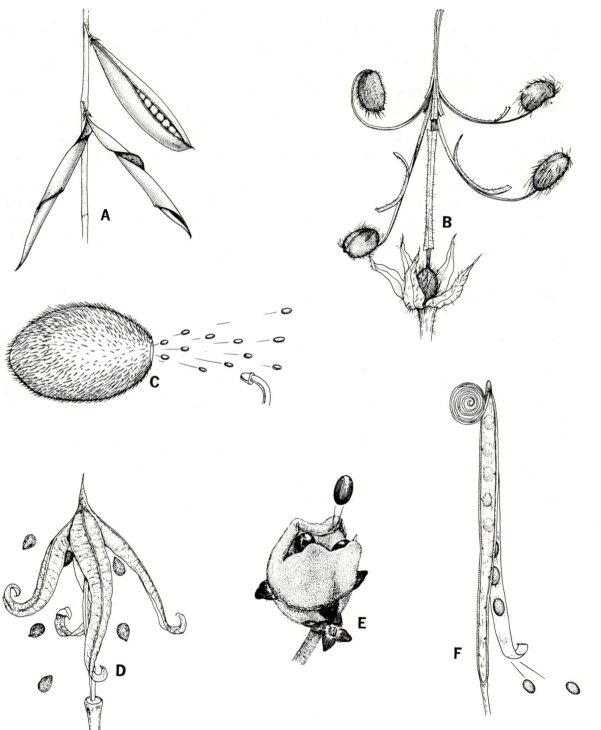

411

FIGURE 22–29 Examples of mechanically dispersed seeds. A, *Vicia gigantea* (Leguminosae), ×1; B, *Geranium bicknellii* (Geraniaceae), ×4; C, *Ecballium elaterium* (Cucurbitaceae), ×0.5; D, *Impatiens aurella* (Balsaminaceae), ×6; E, *Hamamelis virginiana* (Hamamelidaceae), ×3; F, *Cardamine hirsuta* (Cruciferae), ×4. (C, after Kerner v. Marilaun and Oliver.)

Species of *Geranium* have evolved a very ingenious sort of sling mechanism that is remarkably efficient (Fig. 22–29B). The fruit is a schizocarp consisting of five carpels, each containing a single seed. The seeds are each in a pouch at the base of a somewhat elongated beak-like stylar column. As the fruit ripens, the outer tissues of this column split suddenly into five springs that curve up and out, slinging out the seeds for a meter or more. In the witch hazel (*Hamamelis*) the fruit is a woody capsule with two valves that split apart at the top when dry, exposing two black seeds in each valve. As the fruit dries further, the endocarp contracts, discharging the seeds with great force as far as 14 meters (Fig. 22–29E).

The dehiscence of the fruits of many legumes is related to a hygroscopic mechanism. The layers of the pericarp contract to different extents as they dry out, so that considerable tensions are set up among them. When these tensions overcome the cohesion of the cell walls, the walls suddenly separate. In many instances the valves of the legume flick into a spiral and forcibly eject the seeds (Fig. 22–29A). It is usual for the separation to be both violent and rapid, so that the seeds are discharged for a distance of a meter or more.

Quite a different kind of dehiscing mechanism is found in the squirting cucumber (*Ecballium elaterium*), a trailing herb of dry Mediterranean regions (Fig. 22–29C). The fruit is an oblong berry about 5 centimeters in length borne on a stout pedicel. The apex of the pedicel projects into the base of the fruit like a stopper. When the fruit is ripe, the tissues around the stopper break down and its connection with the fruit becomes loosened. The seeds by this time are surrounded by a mass of semi-liquid mucilage. A considerable turgor pressure builds up inside the fruit, distending the outer layers and putting them in a state of tension. Finally, the wall of the fruit contracts, the tissue at the base of the pedicel breaks, the pedicel is blown out like a cork, and the juicy contents are discharged, including the seeds, which travel some distance.

TAXONOMY

During the 150 million years or so that the Anthophyta have been evolving, they have diverged tremendously. Nearly every possible combination of morphological and anatomical feature is represented in present-day flowering plants. The orderly classification of this great array is the special field of taxonomists. Results of their activities are not presented here, since they may be found in a number of the publications listed among the references for this chapter at the end of the book.

412

23 / Phylogeny and Evolution

Biologists have often said that the ultimate goal in the study of plants and animals is the establishment of natural relationships. Indeed, botanists and zoologists continually try to relate taxa to each other at all taxonomic levels. Because all taxa except the earliest have been derived from previously existing organisms, it is impossible to deal with origins without considering the mutual relationships of taxa in an evolutionary series. Such relationships are termed phylogenetic relationships (see Chapter 2).

It is axiomatic that because evolution is the key to phylogeny, a complete picture of phylogenetic relationships above the species level can be realized only through the fossil record. The exception to this is where new species have been created experimentally—as in the bacteria, mosses, and flowering plants—and their immediate ancestry is known. If sufficiently complete, the fossil record will reflect the actual morphological, anatomical, and biochemical changes that have occurred during the evolution of a particular lineage. Examples of well-documented evolutionary series include the horse in the animal kingdom and the ovule-bearing organs of the coniferophytes in the plant kingdom. Unfortunately, good examples of evolutionary series in the plant kingdom are

rare. This is mainly because plants have an open system of growth and possess structural elements that are more delicate than the skeletal parts of many animals. In addition, plants tended to fragment and decay before the opportunity for fossilization occurred, so that chiefly organs or mere fragments rather than whole plants are found.

As might be expected, the lack of information on evolutionary stages in plants is most apparent in the bacteria, fungi, algae, and bryophytes. Being structurally more resistant, and generally larger, the vascular plants have a much better fossil record, and there is a fairly good picture of evolution and phylogeny in most of the main groups. However, significant evolutionary gaps occur, especially concerning the origins and relationships of the divisions, and the immediate ancestors of the earliest members of the divisions. These gaps in the record are popularly referred to as "missing links."

Two main reasons are usually advanced to explain the "missing links" in the fossil record. First, there are undoubtedly many gaps in the geological record for which we can scarcely expect fossils of the characteristic plants or animals, particularly in terrestrial organisms. Plants and animals living and dying on upland regions would be lost as a result of forces of erosion and disintegration. Furthermore, some evidence suggests that much of the evolution of terrestrial organisms actually occurred in such upland regions. If this is true, the early products of mutation, interbreeding, and natural selection would be largely and permanently lost from the record. A second explanation relates to the phenomenon that the earliest stages of evolution in any line are likely to be both rapid and of short duration. Hence, because of the odds against fossilization taking place, the evolutionary stages most critical for establishing phylogeny are probably often lost. As a result, what we find are, in general, the longer lasting stages of evolution—stages showing the least evidence of their derivation from an ancestral group.

As a result of the general lack of fossil information, botanists dealing with the fungi, algae, bryophytes, and angiosperms have depended heavily on structural and biochemical features of extant organisms when attempting to determine phylogeny. From evidence of fossils of nonangiospermous vascular plants, it has been shown that certain trends of morphological and anatomical change have occurred. Some of the more important are reduction in numbers of parts, fusion of parts, and simplification of structure. Good examples of such trends are found in the fossil history of the leaf of the ginkgophyte line and in the ovule-bearing organs of the coniferophytes. These trends have been applied to related taxa of extant plants in order to establish phylogenetic series. Thus, even though direct evidence of ancestry is lacking, some approximation to the evolutionary series can be made.

EVOLUTIONARY RELATIONSHIPS

The distinction between phylogenetic relationships based on fossil evidence and phenetic relationships derived from modern comparative studies has been dramatically illustrated by Sporne. As shown in Figure 23–1, Sporne's concept can best be expressed in a three-dimensional figure. The fossil representatives of two related groups, X and Y, are shown along the radii of a circle, with probable relationships indicated as branches of different lengths. The extant members are disposed on rectangular areas of the circumference, on which probable relationships are shown as plot points on concentric circles. In taxa having no fossil representation, only the surface rectangular areas would be applicable for determining relationships. Obviously, without fossil representation, it would be difficult to establish a real phylogenetic link between X and Y; the relationship would then be phenetic.

A large number of systematic botanists are interested in trying to establish phenetic and phylogenetic classifications. The basic concepts followed and methods employed are discussed thoroughly by Sokal and Sneath. They make a clear distinction between phenetic and phylogenetic classifications, and point out that special care is necessary in attempting to change a phenetic into a phylogenetic classification in the absence of a fossil record.

In establishing a phenetic series, it is important for the investigator to assess and use as many *different* characteristics and lines of evidence as possible to show similarities or differences between taxa. These include morphological characteristics such as number of parts, size, shape, color, sculpturing, and appendages; anatomical characteristics such as xylem, phloem, leaf traces, and petiole structure; leaf anatomy, including the structure and pattern of epidermal cells, stomatal cells, and trichomes; the anatomy of floral parts; pollen and spore morphology; embryological characteristics and processes; cytological and cytogenetical characteristics; and biochemical and physiological factors such as pigments, aminoacid sequences, storage products, and metabolic pathways.

In recent years, the study of cytogenetics has contributed much to an understanding of relationships. Of particular value are the numbers and shapes of chromosomes. In general, the results of chromosome studies have supported conclusions previously arrived at by

414

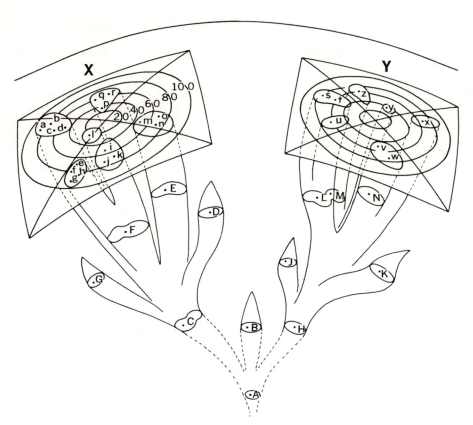

FIGURE 23–1 Two types of relationships of taxa. Finger projections along radii of circle represent evolutionary or *phylogenetical* relationships. Concentric rings along circumference represent series of criteria ranging from 0 to 100, and extant taxa fall within rings in groups, depending on similarity of characteristics—e.g., *m, n,* and *o.* Such groupings of taxa either alone or in multiples form *phenetic* series. (After K. R. Sporne, "On the Phylogenetic Classification of Plants," 1959, Vol. 46, *American Journal of Botany.*)

morphological and anatomical studies. The scope of these studies is steadily increasing, and will undoubtedly be of even greater assistance in the future.

Comparative phytochemistry is a recent field of study that has already revealed some interesting series of chemical compounds and promises to play an ever increasing role in understanding evolution, phylogeny, and classification. Although most phytochemical studies are shedding light on phenetic series of compounds in plants, at least one attempt (in the flavenoid pigments, Fig. 23–2) has been made to establish a phylogenetic series.

In the study of all characteristics, the application of statistical methods is of great assistance in showing correlations and in establishing the degree of similarity or dissimilarity among members of a phenetic series. This is the basis for the doctrine of correlation. The doctrine holds that primitive characteristics should be expected to show positive correlation, because their distribution in any taxon is not random. Thus, primitive species should have a higher number of primitive characteristics. In attempting to assess advanced characteristics, the correlation depends on how much convergence, parallelism, or divergence has occurred

PHYLOGENY AND EVOLUTION

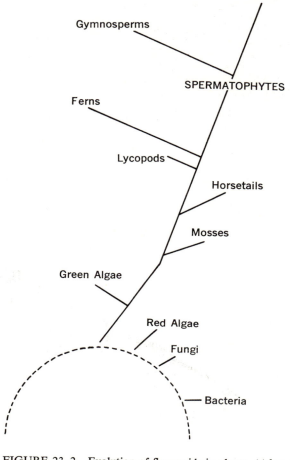

PHYLOGENETIC TREE

Angiosperms

Gymnosperms

SPERMATOPHYTES

Ferns

Lycopods

Horsetails

Mosses

Green Algae

Red Algae

Fungi

Bacteria

FLAVONOID COMPLEMENT

} Complete range of flavonoids (Biflavonyls rare)

Most flavonoids, but usually structurally simple types. Biflavonyls characteristic.

Structurally simple flavonoids:
  3-Deoxyanthocyanins
  Flavones
  Flavonols
  Leucoanthocyanins
  Chalcones
  Flavanones

Few flavonoid types: only 3-deoxyanthocyanins, flavonols, and glycoflavones

Flavonoids completely absent

416

FIGURE 23–2   Evolution of flavonoids in plants. (After Harborne with permission of Academic Press, Inc.)

with evolution of a characteristic. Convergent and parallel evolution will give relatively high correlations, whereas divergence will give a low correlation. In applying the doctrine to dicotyledons, Sporne concluded on the basis of chi square significance tests that the following characteristics were primitive: woody habit, glandular leaves, alternate leaves, stipulate leaves, unisexual flowers, actinomorphic flowers, free petals, many stamens, many carpels, arillate seeds, seeds with two integuments, integuments with vascular bundles, nucleate endosperm, free carpels, and axile placentation. On this basis,

and assuming that all characteristics are of equal importance, Sporne attempted to assess the relative primitiveness of families of dicotyledons.

GEOLOGIC TIME AND THE EVOLUTION OF PLANT DIVISIONS

Recent estimates of the age of the earth ranges from 4×10^9 to 6×10^9 years. The earliest fossils, resembling bacillar bacteria, have been dated by radiometric methods at approximately 3 billion years. Also the alkanes pristane and phytane, as well as porphyrins, possibly chlorophyll derivatives, have been identified from rocks approximately 1×10^9 years old. Although there must have been a long period of evolution of living matter before then, the record of plants (and animals) does not become prominent until the Paleozoic Era. The main record of algae and invertebrates starts approximately with the Pre-Cambrian–Cambrian boundary. In contrast, land plants do not appear until the late Silurian and early Devonian; but proceeding from that time there is a record of progressive evolution of most major groups of land plants. The general picture of distribution of the major divisions of plants in geologic time is given in Figures 23–3 and 23–4. The figures show clearly that the prokaryotes were among the earliest, if not the first, organisms to appear on earth. This supports the hypothesis that the characteristics displayed by extant prokaryotes, such as mucopeptide walls, lack of membrane-bounded organelles, and enzymes dispersed in the cytoplasm, are truly primitive. It also suggests that a great deal of *intracellular* evolution occurred between the early stages of organic evolution (ca. $3-4 \times 10^9$ years), and the earliest record of the eukaryotes (ca. 2×10^9 years). It also seems reasonable that the main groups of organisms in existence today—prokaryotes and eukaryotes (fungi, photosynthetic plants, and animals)—became differentiated in this early interval, i.e., between 3 and 2×10^9 years. To date the record is sparse, but we are beginning to catch glimpses of the early stages of evolution, largely through the application of the electron microscope and biochemical analyses to the very early rocks.

An approach to the general picture of evolution of the eukaryotic photosynthetic plants is shown in Figure 23–5. Although in many instances the fossil record supports the suggested relationships, it should be emphasized that some taxa are necessarily grouped as phenetic series based on similarities of extant members. This is particularly true in the algae, fungi, and bryophytes, where the fossil

record in most instances is too fragmentary to provide phylogenetic series. Exceptions are found in some families of red algae (Rhodophyceae) and green algae (Chlorophyceae) in which fossil reconstructions demonstrate evolutionary series from the Paleozoic to the present.

From the late Pre-Cambrian until the early Devonian, the fossil record shows the presence of bacteria, fungi, and algae, particularly the cyanophytes (Cyanophyceae), red (Rhodophyceae) and green (Chlorophyceae) algae. As shown in Figure 23–3, other algal groups appear to have evolved at various later times, although our knowledge of some groups is admittedly poor, and hence the evolutionary pattern is biased in favor of those groups with better fossil records. Particularly noteworthy, however, is the relatively late appearance of the diatoms (Bacillariophyceae) in the early Jurassic, and their marked increase from the Cretaceous to the present. Also, the origins of the dinoflagellates (Dinophyceae) and golden algae (Chrysophyceae) may well antedate the times shown in Figure 23–3; they may be as yet unrecognized within a large group of unicellular fossils called acritarchs that range from the Pre-Cambrian to the present but are especially common in the Paleozoic.

The fungi have a sporadic occurrence in the fossil record from the Pre-Cambrian to the present. Hyphae and reproductive structures are often associated with petrified tissues of vascular plants. Fungal lesions are common on Cretaceous and Tertiary leaves, and fungal spores are often abundant in shales and coals from the Mesozoic to the present. The origins of the three main fungal groups are obscure, although the phycomycetes appear to antedate both the ascomycetes and basidiomycetes by a long time span.

Modern bryophytes occupy nearly all terrestrial environments and are tolerant, as a group, of greater environmental extremes than most other groups of land plants. Their extremely wide distribution and great diversity suggests that they have existed for a long period of time. It is impossible to make an unequivocal statement concerning the first ap-

418

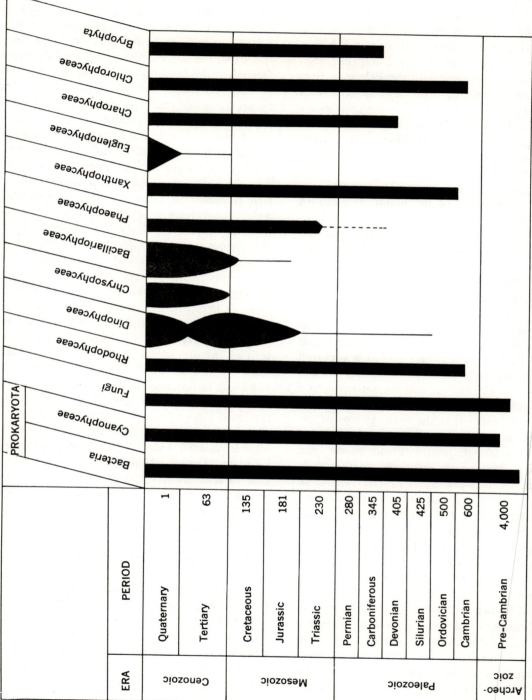

FIGURE 23–3 Fossil record of main groups of nonvascular plants. Numerals opposite each geological period indicate the beginning of the period in millions of years. Relative abundances of taxa, where known, are shown by the width of the bar.

VASCULAR PLANTS

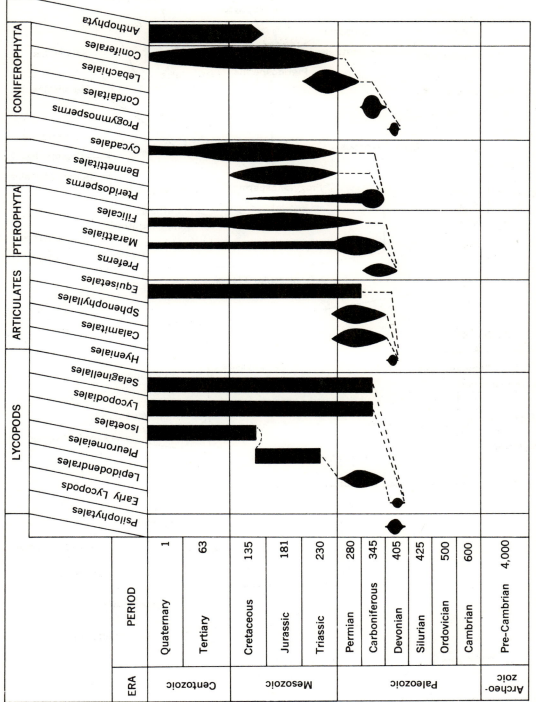

FIGURE 23-4 Fossil record of main groups of vascular plants. Numerals opposite each geological period indicate the beginning of the period in millions of years. Relative abundances of taxa, where known, are shown by the width of the bar. Dotted lines indicate assumed evolutionary relationships.

419

PHYLOGENY AND EVOLUTION

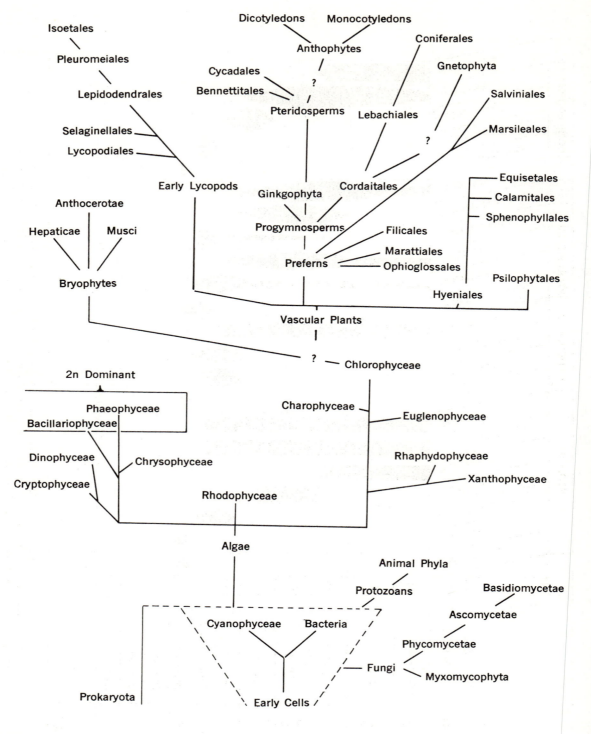

FIGURE 23–5   Flow diagram of probable evolutionary relationships among main groups of plants.

pearance of the bryophytes in geological times, or to judge their abundance or significance. The evolutionary history of the bryophytes is poorly documented. The earliest fossils interpreted as hepatics are found in the late Devonian. Since no sporophytes are attached to the fossils (presumed to be gametophytes) they could as reasonably be interpreted as belonging to psilophytes. The fossils determined as hepatics from the Carboniferous are equally enigmatic, although they show very strong resemblances to gametophytes of modern genera, and some botanists have placed them in very close relationship with specific orders of the Hepaticae. A number of Permian fossils interpreted to be gametophytes of mosses are more promising. These show no absolute affinity to any modern genera, but again the absence of sporophytes greatly hampers an adequate understanding of the phylogenetic significance of the fossils. The leaf cell structure and arrangement clearly indicate that the fossils are mosses. Triassic fossils of undoubted bryophytes clearly belong to orders still in existence.

Evolution of vascular plants is first recorded by spores in the Silurian. By early Devonian times, at least several main groups (psilophytes, lycopods, articulates, and preferns) had appeared in terrestrial habitats. Derived presumably from some ancestral stock (or stocks) of the green algae, vascular plants became adapted for a terrestrial existence by evolving xylem and phloem for conduction, a cuticle and stomata for control of water loss, and either rhizoids or roots for anchorage and obtaining a water supply. As far as is known, the sporophyte was the dominant generation in the earliest vascular plants, a condition maintained throughout the evolutionary history of the group.

Early evolution of vascular plants in the Devonian progressed from an herbaceous to woody habit, a trend which culminated in the Carboniferous with the development of large woody trees in the lycopod, articulate, and coniferophyte groups. In response to desiccation and cooling during the Permian and early

Triassic Periods, the conifers and cycadophytes underwent extensive evolution to become dominant groups of Jurassic and early Cretaceous floras. The unexplained sudden explosion in the evolution of the anthophytes in the Upper Cretaceous heralded the dominance of this group to the present. This process appears to be continuing, as evidenced by the relatively recent appearance of such large groups as the composites and grasses in the Tertiary Period.

MORPHOLOGICAL EVOLUTION

The processes of genetic change and natural selection acting through more than 3×10^9 years produced a multiplicity of variations in plant form and function. The genetic variants that persisted in their environment over prolonged periods have given us, through the fossil record, at least a glimpse of morphological changes that have occurred. The number of morphological variations is as great as the number of species (and even of individuals) that have lived and are living. Nevertheless, evolution has generally progressed along paths that can be recognized in retrospect as morphological trends. Several of these have been discussed in previous chapters, but two important major trends have been purposefully left until now— namely, the *differentiation of the plant body* and *alternation of generations*. Many of the concepts discussed here are elaborated in the *Telome Theory* of Zimmermann and *Evolution of Genetic Systems* by Darlington.

Differentiation of the Plant Body

We have already indicated that the earliest forms of life recognizable to date appear to be exemplified in the prokaryotic cells of the cyanophytes and bacteria. Logically, the next evolutionary development would have been a single-celled eukaryote. Evolutionary developments from the single cell probably re-

421

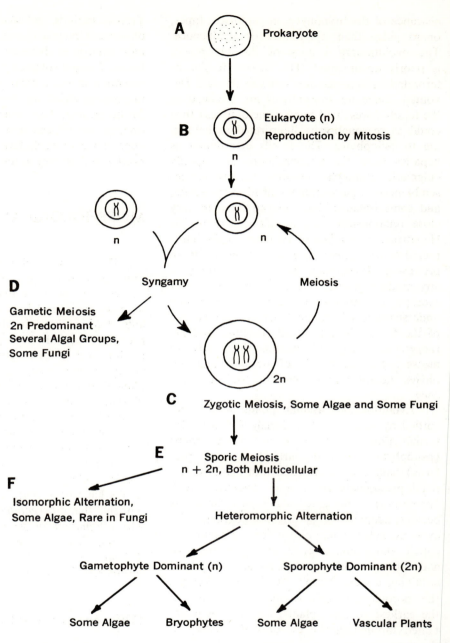

FIGURE 23–6   Probable evolutionary pathways of the main types of alternation of generations in plants.

A   Prokaryote

B   Eukaryote (n)
Reproduction by Mitosis

n

n

n

Syngamy

Meiosis

D

Gametic Meiosis
2n Predominant
Several Algal Groups,
Some Fungi

2n

C   Zygotic Meiosis, Some Algae and Some Fungi

E   Sporic Meiosis
n + 2n, Both Multicellular

F

Isomorphic Alternation,
Some Algae, Rare in Fungi

Heteromorphic Alternation

Gametophyte Dominant (n)

Sporophyte Dominant (2n)

Some Algae

Bryophytes

Some Algae

Vascular Plants

sulted in a progression from loose colonies—simple filaments–branched filaments–branched filaments with differentiation of parenchyma. Further division and differentiation of cells in several planes eventually led to relatively complex tissue zoning, exemplified in more complex algae such as Dasycladales of the green algae or Laminariales of the brown algae. The types of branching and differentiation of filaments appears to have resulted from different types of rotation of the meristematic cells, providing a wide variety of forms.

In the evolution of the vascular plants, the form of the axis appears to have progressed essentially from dichotomous (early vascular plants)–pseudomonopodial (early ferns)–monopodial (later vascular plants). Again, different types of rotation of either an apical cell or cells of the apical meristem appear to account for the different types of branching. The evolution of leaf form in the vascular plants provides an interesting example of evolutionary adaptation. As far as we know, the earliest vascular plants lacked differentiated leaves of any kind; photosynthesis must have taken place in the branch tips or even in the main axis. Evolution of the leaf in later vascular plants, such as *Protopteridium*, involved an expansion of a branch in the *vertical* plane. Later, leaves evolved in the *horizontal* plane. The leaf form became larger in plants that evolved during the Carboniferous, possibly in response to the warm, humid, and equable conditions. In contrast, one of the dominant conifer families of the Permian and Triassic Periods, the Lebachiaceae, had needle leaves modified for xerophytic conditions that prevailed during that interval. This type of leaf form has persisted in many of the modern conifers, even through periods when conditions were more humid and equable. This is almost certainly an example of an evolutionary adaptation that became genetically entrenched and did not respond to forces of natural selection in later times.

Alternation of Generations

The alternation of generations is a characteristic of plants, and four main types are recognized (Fig. 3–8, 3–9). Excluding the *dikaryon* life cycle (Fig. 3–9B) that is unique to some fungi, it is interesting to speculate on the origin, significance, and probable evolutionary development of the other three types: *zy-gotic meiosis* (Fig. 3–8A); *gametic meiosis* (Fig. 3–8B); and *sporic meiosis* (Fig. 3–9A). All three types occur in various algal and fungal groups, whereas both bryophytes and vascular plants exhibit only sporic meiosis. In the bryophytes, the gametophyte (n) generation is predominant, with the sporophyte ($2n$) at least partly dependent on the gametophyte for nutrients. All vascular plants have a dominant sporophyte, and show an evolutionary trend of decreasing size and increasing dependency of the gametophyte generation, culminating in complete dependency in the seed plants.

Accepting the hypothesis that the algae evolved initially from prokaryotic cells (such as Cyanophyceae), and that the bryophytes and vascular plants probably evolved from ancestral members of the Chlorophyceae, the probable evolutionary pathway of alternation of generations can be postulated as in Figure 23–6.

The two prerequisites to the evolution of alternation of generations were the initiation of sexual reproduction, meiosis, and syngamy, allowing for more variability than could be derived solely from mutations; and the increased potential for variability introduced by the doubling of the chromosome number to $2n$. Although genetic recombination occurs in prokaryotic cells, sexual reproduction appears to have evolved concurrently with the evolution of eukaryotic from prokaryotic cells, and the accompanying formation of discrete nuclei and chromosomes. Hence, the primitive eukaryotes would have had a single chromosome complement (n) (Fig. 23–6B). The next evolutionary step probably involved the mating of two similar eukaryotic cells (likely by chance, and many different times) to form a $2n$ zygote, thereby initiating diploidy and making possible the process of zygotic meiosis (Fig. 23–6C). Meiosis might have resulted from a single mutation, causing the $2n$ complement of the zygote to reduce to n. Whether or not meiosis resulted from a single mutation, succeeding evolution involved the elaboration of both the n (gametophytic) and the $2n$ (sporophytic) generations in many algal groups. The main evolutionary

423

trend was toward alternation involving sporic meiosis, in which both generations are multicellular (Fig. 23–6E). In some taxa, alternation resulted in isomorphic generations; in others heteromorphic generations, with either the gametophyte or sporophyte predominating (Fig. 23–6F).

The inception of diploidy was an important step in evolution because it increased the reservoir of genetic variability within natural populations. This, together with the meiotic process, permitted the production of genetic recombinations, thus giving species much greater genetic plasticity, and enabling them to respond to pressures of natural selection. The doubling of the chromosome number also appears to have been associated with elaboration of relatively complex tissues and organs of the sporophyte, as in some algae and the vascular plants. This may have resulted from an increase in the quantitative biochemical expression of a larger number of interacting genes.

Throughout geologic time, many groups of algae and the bryophytes retained a dominant gametophytic generation. In contrast, other algal groups and vascular plants developed a dominant sporophytic generation. In general, the evolutionary trend has been toward greater complexity of the sporophyte. This trend has been most dramatically expressed in the vascular plants, in which complex and elaborate sporophytes have evolved, accompanied by a marked simplification of the gametophyte. The reduction of the gametophyte appears to have been an evolutionary trend resulting from increased retention of the gametophyte, first within the spore wall as in some ferns and *Selaginella,* and later within the gynosporangium. The evolution of the seed habit (see p. 325, Figs. 18–7, 8) resulted in even greater reduction of the gametophyte, probably in response to a direct supply of nutrients from the enclosing sporophytic tissue. The ultimate in this trend is shown by the angiosperms, where the gametophyte is reduced to a few cells (see Fig. 22–9) and nutrition of the embryo is provided by endosperm formed by double fertilization. The evidence of gametophytic reduction leads to speculation that future evolutionary developments in angiosperms or their descendants might see further reduction or even elimination of the gametophyte, resulting in a condition exemplified by *Fucus* (see p. 170) and animals, in which gametes are produced directly from meiosis of diploid initials.

It is also interesting to speculate on why animals apparently evolved initially into diploid dominant organisms, whereas the early plants developed a dominant haploid multicellular body. The only basic factor appears to be differences in the mode of nutrition. Animals, which are heterotrophic, require outside sources of energy and more elaborate structures for obtaining nutrients than plants, most of which are autotrophic. The double set of chromosomes in animals would provide the genetic reservoir for the development of elaborate tissues required of the heterotrophic habit. Early plants, manufacturing their nutrients through photosynthesis, were apparently well adapted to the aquatic environments and hence had little pressure from natural selection to assume a multicellular diploid generation. The evolution of a dominant and elaborate sporophyte resulted in certain algae becoming adapted to particular ecological niches (e.g., *Codium, Nereocystis, Ectocarpus*) and in the vascular plants conquering terrestrial habitats.

424

REFERENCES, GLOSSARY, INDEX

References

CHAPTER 1 / INTRODUCTION

Dobzhansky, T., *Genetics and the Origin of Species,* 2nd ed. New York: Columbia University Press (1941).

Huxley, J. S., *Evolution: The Modern Synthesis.* New York: Harper & Row, Publishers, Inc. (1942).

McDougal, W. B., "The Classification of Symbiotic Phenomena." *Plant World,* 21: 250–256 (1918).

Stebbins, G. L., Jr., *Variation and Evolution in Plants.* New York: Columbia University Press (1950).

Stebbins, G. L., Jr., *Processes of Organic Evolution.* Englewood Cliffs, N.J.: Prentice-Hall, Inc. (1966).

CHAPTER 2 / CLASSIFICATION

Benson, L., *Plant Classification.* Boston: D. C. Heath & Company (1957).

Bold, H. C., "Some Aspects of the Classification of the Plant Kingdom." *Bull. Assoc. Southeastern Biol.,* 3:35–51 (1956).

Cronquist, A., "The Divisions and Classes of Plants." *Bot. Rev.,* 26(4): 425–482 (1960).

Lawrence, G. H. M., *Taxonomy of Vascular Plants.* New York: The Macmillan Company (1951).

Stebbins, G. L., Jr., *Variation and Evolution in Plants.* New York: Columbia University Press (1950).

Stebbins, G. L., Jr., *Processes of Organic Evolution.* Englewood Cliffs, N.J.: Prentice-Hall, Inc. (1966).

CHAPTER 3 / NONVASCULAR PLANTS

Bold, H. C., *Morphology of Plants,* 2nd ed. New York: Harper & Row, Publishers, Inc. (1967).

Brown, W. H., *The Plant Kingdom.* Boston: Ginn and Company (1935).

Chadefaud, M., and Emberger, L., *Traité de Botanique (Systématique).* Tome I: *Les Végétaux Non Vasculaires (Cryptogamie).* Paris: Masson et Cie (1960).

Coombe, D. E., and Bell, P. R. (translators), *Strasburger's Textbook of Botany.* London: Longmans, Green and Co., Ltd. (1965).

Cronquist, A., *Introductory Botany.* New York: Harper & Row, Publishers, Inc. (1961).

Dittmer, H. C., *Phylogeny and Form in the Plant Kingdom.* Princeton, N.J.: D. Van Nostrand Company, Inc. (1964).

Dodd, J. D., *Form and Function in Plants.* Ames, Iowa: The Iowa State University Press (1962).

McLean, R. C., and Ivimey-Cook, W. R., *Textbook of Theoretical Botany.* Vol. 1. London: Longmans, Green & Co., Ltd. (1951).

Scagel, R. F., Bandoni, R. J., Rouse, G. E., Schofield, W. B., Stein, J. R., and Taylor, T. M. C.,
An Evolutionary Survey of the Plant Kingdom.
Belmont, Calif.: Wadsworth Publishing Company, Inc. (1965).

Smith, G. M., *Cryptogamic Botany,* 2nd ed. Vol.
1: *Algae and Fungi.* New York: McGraw-Hill
Book Company, Inc. (1955).

Weisz, P. B., and Fuller, M. S., *The Science of
Botany.* New York: McGraw-Hill Book Company, Inc. (1962).

CHAPTER 4 / DIVISION SCHIZOMYCOPHYTA

Breed, R. S., Murray, E. G. D., and Smith, N. R.,
Bergey's Manual of Determinative Bacteriology,
7th ed. London: Bailliere, Tindall & Cox, Limited; Baltimore: Williams and Wilkins Co.
(1957).

Brock, T. D., *Principles of Microbial Ecology.*
Englewood Cliffs, N.J.: Prentice-Hall, Inc.
(1966).

Gunsalus, I. C., and Stanier, R. Y. (eds.), *The
Bacteria.* Vol. 1: *Structure.* New York: Academic Press, Inc. (1960).

Pelczar, M. J., and Reid, R. D., *Microbiology,*
2nd ed. New York: McGraw-Hill Book Company, Inc. (1965).

Skerman, V. D. B., *A Guide to the Identification
of the Genera of Bacteria.* Baltimore: Williams
and Wilkins Co. (1959).

Stanier, R. Y., Doudoroff, M., and Adelberg,
E. A., *The Microbial World,* 2nd ed. Englewood Cliffs, N.J.: Prentice-Hall, Inc. (1962).

CHAPTER 5 / DIVISION CYANOPHYTA

Drouet, F., "Cyanophyta." In Smith, G. M. (ed.),
Manual of Phycology. Waltham, Mass.: Chronica Botanica (1951). Pp. 157–166.

Drouet, F., "Myxophyceae." In Edmondson, W. T.
(ed.), *Freshwater Biology.* New York: John
Wiley & Sons, Inc. (1959). Pp. 95–114.

Echlin, P., "The Blue-green Algae." *Scientific
American,* 214: 74–81 (1966).

CHAPTER 6 / DIVISION MYXOMYCOTA

Alexopoulos, C. J., *Introductory Mycology,* 2nd
ed. New York: John Wiley & Sons, Inc. (1962).

Alexopoulos, C. J., "Morphogenesis in the Myxomycetes." In *The Fungi,* Vol. II: *The Fungal
Organism,* edited by G. C. Ainsworth and A. S.
Sussman. New York: Academic Press, Inc.
(1966).

Bonner, J. T., *The Cellular Slime Molds.* Princeton, N.J.: Princeton University Press (1959).

Gregg, J. H., "Organization and Synthesis in the
Cellular Slime Molds." In *The Fungi,* Vol. II:
The Fungal Organism, edited by G. C. Ains-
worth and A. S. Sussman. New York: Academic
Press, Inc. (1966).

Lister, A., *A Monograph of the Mycetozoa,* 3rd
ed. (revised by G. Lister). London: Trustees
of The British Museum (1925).

Martin, G. W., "The Myxomycetes." *North American Flora* 1 (i): 1–151. With bibliography, pp.
153–178, by H. W. Rickett and index, pp.
179–190, by G. M. Miller (1949).

CHAPTER 7 / DIVISION EUMYCOTA

Ainsworth, G. C., *Dictionary of the Fungi.* Kew:
Commonwealth Mycological Institute (1961).

Ainsworth, G. C., and Sussman, A. S. (eds.),
The Fungi, Vols. I–III. New York: Academic
Press, Inc. (1965, 1966).

Alexopoulos, C. J., *Introductory Mycology,* 2nd
ed. New York: John Wiley & Sons, Inc. (1962).

Brock, T. D., *Principles of Microbial Ecology.*
Englewood Cliffs, N.J.: Prentice-Hall, Inc.
(1966).

Cochrane, V. W., "Physiology of Fungi." New
York: John Wiley & Sons, Inc. (1958).

Ingold, C. T., *The Biology of Fungi.* London:
Hutchinson Educational, Ltd. (1961).

Ingold, C. T., *Spore Liberation.* Oxford: Claren-
don Press (1965).

Lichens

Ahmadjian, V., *The Lichen Symbiosis.* Waltham,
Mass.: Blaisdell Publishing Company (1967).

Brightman, F. H., "Neglected Plants—Lichens."
New Biol., 29: 75–94. Middlesex: Penguin
Books, Ltd. (1959).

Hale, M. E., *Lichen Handbook: A Guide to the
Lichens of Eastern North America.* Washington,
D.C.: Smithsonian Institution (1961).

Hale, M. E., *The Biology of Lichens.* London:
Edward Arnold, Ltd. (1967).

Smith, A. L., *Lichens.* Cambridge: Cambridge
University Press (1921).

426

CHAPTER 8 / DIVISION RHODOPHYTA

Dixon, P. S., "The Rhodophyta: Some Aspects of Their Biology." *Oceanogr. Mar. Biol. Ann. Rev.,* 1: 177–196 (1963).

Drew, K. M., "Rhodophyta." In Smith, G. M. (ed.), *Manual of Phycology.* Waltham, Mass.: Chronica Botanica (1951). Pp. 167–191.

Kylin, H., *Die Gattungen der Rhodophyceen.* Lund, Sweden: Gleerup Förlag (1956).

CHAPTER 9 / DIVISION PHAEOPHYTA

Papenfuss, G. F., "Phaeophyta." In Smith, G. M. (ed.), *Manual of Phycology.* Waltham, Mass.: Chronica Botanica (1951). Pp. 117–158.

Scagel, R. F., "The Phaeophyceae in Perspective." *Oceanogr. Mar. Biol. Ann. Rev.,* 4: 123–194 (1966).

CHAPTER 10 / DIVISIONS CHRYSOPHYTA, XANTHOPHYTA, PYRROPHYTA, EUGLENOPHYTA

Chrysophyceae

Fritsch, F. E., "Chrysophyta." In Smith, G. M. (ed.), *Manual of Phycology.* Waltham, Mass.: Chronica Botanica (1951). Pp. 86–92.

Bacillariophyceae

Fritsch, F. E., "Chrysophyta." In Smith, G. M. (ed.), *Manual of Phycology.* Waltham, Mass.: Chronica Botanica (1951). Pp. 92–101.

Lewin, J. C., and Guillard, R. L., "Diatoms." *Ann. Rev. Microbiol.,* 17: 373–414 (1963).

Patrick, R. L., and Reimer, C. W., *The Diatoms of the United States.* Vol. I. Philadelphia: Academy of Natural Sciences (1966).

Xanthophyceae

Fritsch, F. E., "Chrysophyta." In Smith, G. M. (ed.), *Manual of Phycology.* Waltham, Mass.: Chronica Botanica (1951). Pp. 84–86.

Dinophyceae

Graham, H. W., "Pyrrophyta." In Smith, G. M. (ed.), *Manual of Phycology.* Waltham, Mass.: Chronica Botanica (1951). Pp. 105–118.

Kofoid, C., and Swezy, O., "The Free-living Unarmoured Dinoflagellata." *Univ. Calif. Memoirs,* 5: 1–562 (1921).

Cryptophyceae

Graham, H. W., *Cryptophyceae.* In Smith, G. M. (ed.), *Manual of Phycology.* Waltham, Mass.: Chronica Botanica (1951). Pp. 117–118.

Pringsheim, E. G., "Some Aspects of Taxonomy in the Cryptophyceae." *New Phytologist,* 43(2): 143–150 (1944).

Euglenophyceae

Gojdics, M., *The Genus* Euglena. Madison,: The University of Wisconsin Press (1953).

Leedale, G. F., *Euglenoid Flagellates.* Englewood Cliffs, N.J.: Prentice-Hall, Inc. (1967).

Wolken, J. J., *Euglena, an Experimental Organism for Biochemical and Biophysical Studies,* 2nd ed. New York: Appleton-Century-Crofts, Inc. (1967).

CHAPTER 11 / DIVISION CHLOROPHYTA AND ALGAL ECOLOGY

Chapman, V. J., "The Chlorophyta." *Oceanogr. Mar. Biol. Ann. Rev.,* 2: 193–228 (1964).

Iyengar, M. O. P., "Chlorophyta." In Smith, G. M. (ed.), *Manual of Phycology.* Waltham, Mass.: Chronica Botanica (1951). Pp. 21–67.

Algal Ecology

Blum, J. L., "The Ecology of River Algae." *Bot. Rev.,* 22: 291–341 (1956).

Boney, A. D., *A Biology of Marine Algae.* London: Hutchinson Educational (1966).

Chapman, V. J., *Seaweeds and Their Uses.* London: Methuen & Co., Ltd. (1950).

Chapman, V. J., *The Algae.* London: Macmillan & Co., Ltd. (1962).

Dawson, E. Y., *Marine Botany, an Introduction.* New York: Holt, Rinehart and Winston, Inc. (1966).

Edmondson, W. T. (ed.), *Freshwater Biology,* 2nd ed. New York: John Wiley & Sons, Inc. (1959). ("Myxophyceae," by F. Drouet, pp. 95–114, figs. 5.1–5.43; "Algae," by R. H. Thompson, pp. 115–170, figs. 6.1–6.428; "Bacillariophyceae," by R. Patrick, pp. 171–189, figs. 7.1–7.57.)

REFERENCES

Fogg, G. E., *Algal Cultures and Phytoplankton Ecology*. Madison, Wis.: The University of Wisconsin Press (1965).

Lewis, J. R., *The Ecology of Rocky Shores*. London: The English Universities Press, Ltd. (1964).

Macan, T. T., *Freshwater Ecology*. London: Longmans, Green & Co., Ltd. (1963).

Moore, H. B., *Marine Ecology*. New York: John Wiley & Sons, Inc. (1958).

Prescott, G. W., *Algae of the Western Great Lakes Area*, rev. ed. Dubuque, Iowa: William C. Brown & Co. (1962).

Round, F. E., *The Biology of the Algae*. London: Edward Arnold (Publishers), Ltd. (1965).

Smith, G. M., *Freshwater Algae of the United States*, 2nd ed. New York: McGraw-Hill Book Company, Inc. (1950).

Smith, G. M. (ed.), *Manual of Phycology*. Waltham, Mass.: Chronica Botanica (1951).

Tiffany, L. H., *Algae, the Grass of Many Waters*, 2nd ed. Springfield, Mo.: Charles C. Thomas, Publisher (1958).

Wood, E. J. F., *Marine Microbial Ecology*. Modern Biological Studies. London: Chapman and Hall, Ltd. (1965).

428

CHAPTER 12 / DIVISION BRYOPHYTA

Anderson, L. E., "Modern Species Concepts: Mosses." *Bryologist*, 66: 107–119 (1963).

Bower, F. O., *Primitive Land Plants*. London: Macmillan & Co., Ltd. (1935).

Fulford, M., "Modern Species Concepts: Liverworts." *Bryologist*, 66: 101–106 (1963).

Fulford, M., "Evolutionary Trends and Convergence in the Hepaticae." *Bryologist*, 68: 1–31 (1965).

Goebel, K., *Organographie der Pflanzen*. Part 2: *Bryophyten-Pteridophyten*. Jena: G. Fischer (1930).

Grout, A. J., *Mosses with a Hand-lens and Microscope*. New York: Mt. Pleasant Press (1903–1908).

Grout, A. J., *Moss Flora of North America, North of Mexico*. 3 vols. Newfane, Vt.: Published by the Author (1928–1940).

Harris, T. M., "*Naiadita*, a Fossil Bryophyte with Reproductive Organs." *Ann. Bryol.*, 12: 57–70 (1939).

Herzog, T., *Geographie der Moose*. Jena: G. Fischer (1926).

Schuster, R. M., "The Hepaticae and Anthocerotae of North America East of the Hundredth Meridian." Vol. 1. New York: Columbia University Press (1966).

Smith, G. M., *Cryptogamic Botany*. Vol. 2: *Bryophytes and Pteridophytes*, 2nd ed. New York: McGraw-Hill Book Company, Inc. (1955). Pp. 1–130.

CHAPTER 13 / VASCULAR PLANTS

Andrews, H. N., Jr., *Studies in Paleobotany*. New York: John Wiley & Sons, Inc. (1961).

Bold, H. C., *Morphology of Plants*, 2nd. ed. New York: Harper & Row, Publishers, Inc. (1967). Pp. 250–503.

Delevoryas, T., *Morphology and Evolution of Fossil Plants*. New York: Holt, Rinehart and Winston, Inc. (1962).

Foster, A. S., and Gifford, E. M., *Comparative Morphology of Vascular Plants*. San Francisco: W. H. Freeman & Company, Publishers (1959).

Sporne, K. R., *The Morphology of Pteridophytes*. London: Hutchinson & Co. (Publishers), Ltd. (1962).

CHAPTER 14 / DIVISION PSILOPHYTA

Andrews, H. N., Jr., "Evolutionary Trends in Early Vascular Plants." *Cold Spr. Harb. Symp. Quant. Biol.*, 24: 217–234 (1960).

Bierhorst, D. W., "Observations on the Aerial Appendages in the Psilotaceae." *Phytomorphology*, 6: 176–184 (1956).

Holloway, J. E., "The Prothallus and Young Plant of *Tmesipteris*." *Trans. Proc. N. Z. Inst.*, 50: 1–44 (1918).

Leclercq, S., "Are the Psilophytales a Starting or a Resulting Point?" *Svensk. Bot. Tidsskr.*, 48(2): 301–315 (1954).

McLean, R. C., and Ivimey-Cook, W. R., *Textbook of Theoretical Botany*. Vol. 1. London: Longmans, Green & Co., Ltd. (1951).

Rouffa, A. S., "Induced *Psilotum* Fertile-Appendage Aberrations, Morphogenetic and Evolutionary Implications." *Can. J. Bot.*, 45(6): 855–861 (1967).

CHAPTER 15 / DIVISION LYCOPHYTA

Boureau, E. (ed.), *Traité de Paléobotanique*. Tome II: *Bryophyta, Psilophyta, Lycophyta*. Paris: Masson et Cie (1967). Pp. 436–845.

Foster, A. S., and Gifford, E. M., *Comparative Morphology of Vascular Plants.* San Francisco: W. H. Freeman & Company, Publishers (1959). Pp. 130–190.

Sporne, K. R., *The Morphology of Pteridophytes.* London: Hutchinson & Co. (Publishers), Ltd. (1962). Pp. 50–93.

Stewart, W. N., "More about the Origin of Vascular Plants." *Plant Sci. Bull.,* 6(5): 1–5 (1960).

CHAPTER 16 / DIVISION ARTHROPHYTA

Bierhorst, D. W., "Vessels in *Equisetum.*" *Am. J. Bot.,* 45: 534–537 (1958).

Bierhorst, D. W., "Symmetry in *Equisetum.*" *Am. J. Bot.,* 46: 170–179 (1959).

Bonamo, P. M., and Banks, H. P., "*Calamophyton* in the Middle Devonian of New York State." *Am. J. Bot.,* 53(8): 778–791 (1966).

Boureau, E. (ed.), *Traité de Paléobotanique.* Tome III; *Sphenophyta Noeggerathiophyta.* Paris: Masson et Cie (1964).

Foster, A. S., and Gifford, E. M., *Comparative Morphology of Vascular Plants.* San Francisco: W. H. Freeman & Company, Publishers (1959). Pp. 191–219.

Golub, S. J., and Wetmore, R. H., "Studies of Development in the Vegetative Shoot of *Equisetum arvense.* L., II: The Mature Shoot." *Am. J. Bot.,* 35: 767–781 (1948).

Sporne, K. R., *The Morphology of Pteridophytes.* London: Hutchinson & Co. (Publishers), Ltd. (1962). Pp. 91–113.

CHAPTER 17 / DIVISION PTEROPHYTA

Bower, F. O., *The Ferns.* Vols. 1–3. London: Cambridge University Press (1923, 1926, 1928).

Copeland, E. B., *Genera Filicum.* Waltham, Mass.: Chronica Botanica (1947).

Evans, A. M., "Ameiotic Alternation of Generations: A New Life Cycle in the Ferns." *Science,* 143: 261–263 (1964).

Holttum, R. E., "A Revised Classification of Leptosporangiate Ferns." *J. Linn. Soc. (Bot.) London,* 53: 123–158 (1947).

Sporne, K. R., *The Morphology of Pteridophytes.* London: Hutchinson & Co. (Publishers), Ltd. (1962). Pp. 114–174.

White, R. A., "Tracheary Elements of the Ferns, II." *Am. J. Bot.,* 50: 514–522 (1963).

CHAPTER 18 / DIVISION PTERIDOSPERMOPHYTA

Andrews, H. N., Jr., *Studies in Paleobotany.* New York: John Wiley & Sons, Inc. (1961). Pp. 129–166.

Andrews, H. N., Jr., "Early Seed Plants." *Science,* 142: 925–931 (1963).

Delevoryas, T., *Morphology and Evolution of Fossil Plants.* New York: Holt, Rinehart and Winston, Inc. (1962). Pp. 103–128.

Thomson, R. B., "Evolution of the Seed Habit in Plants." *Trans. Roy. Soc. Canada,* Ser. 3, 21(5): 229–272 (1927).

CHAPTER 19 / DIVISIONS CYCADOPHYTA AND GINKGOPHYTA

Division Cycadophyta

Arnold, C. A., "Origin and Relationships of the Cycads." *Phytomorphology,* 3: 51–65 (1953).

Chamberlain, C. J., *The Living Cycads.* Chicago: University of Chicago Press (1919).

Chamberlain, C. J., *Gymnosperms: Structure and Evolution.* Chicago: University of Chicago Press (1935). Pp. 1–164.

Delevoryas, T., "Investigations of North American Cycadeoids: Cones of *Cycadeoidea.*" *Am. J. Bot.,* 50: 45–58 (1963).

Delevoryas, T., "Investigations of North American Cycadeoids: Structure, Ontogeny and Phylogenetic Considerations of Cones of *Cycadeoidea.*" *Palaeontographica,* 121B, 122–143 (1968).

Division Ginkgophyta

Arnott, H. J., "Anastomoses in the Venation of *Ginkgo biloba.*" *Am. J. Bot.,* 46: 405–411 (1959).

Dorf, E., "The Geological Distribution of the *Ginkgo* Family." *Bull. Wagner Free Inst. Sci.,* 33(1): 1–10 (1958).

Gunckel, J. E., and Wetmore, R. H., "Studies of Development in Long Shoots and Short Shoots of *Ginkgo biloba* L. II. Phyllotaxis and the Organization of the Primary Vascular Tissue: Primary Phloem and Primary Xylem." *Am. J. Bot.,* 33: 532–543 (1946).

Pollock, E. G., "The Sex Chromosomes of the Maidenhair Tree." *J. Heredity,* 48: 290–294 (1957).

REFERENCES

CHAPTER 20 / DIVISION CONIFEROPHYTA

Arnold, C. A., *An Introduction to Paleobotany.* New York: McGraw-Hill Book Company, Inc. (1947). Pp. 280–332.

Beck, C. B., "Reconstructions of *Archaeopteris* and Further Consideration of Its Phylogenetic Position." *Am. J. Bot.,* 49: 373–382 (1962).

Chamberlain, C. J., *Gymnosperms: Structure and Evolution.* Chicago: University of Chicago Press (1935). Pp. 165–360.

Johansen, D. A., *Plant Embryology.* Waltham, Mass.: Chronica Botanica (1950). Pp. 22–78.

Laubenfels, D. J., "The External Morphology of Coniferous Leaves." *Phytomorphology,* 3: 1–12 (1953).

Sterling, C., "Structure of the Male Gametophyte in Gymnosperms." *Biol. Rev.,* 38: 167–203 (1963).

CHAPTER 21 / DIVISION GNETOPHYTA

Chamberlain, C. J., *Gymnosperms: Structure and Evolution.* Chicago: University of Chicago Press (1935). Pp. 361–426.

Eames, A. J., "Relationships of the Ephedrales." *Phytomorphology,* 2: 79–100 (1952).

Negi, V., and Lata, M., "Male Gametophyte and Megasporogenesis in *Gnetum.*" *Phytomorphology,* 7: 230–236 (1957).

Pearson, H. H. W., *Gnetales.* London: Cambridge University Press (1929).

Rodin, R. J., "Anatomy of the Reproductive Bracts in *Welwitschia.*" *Am. J. Bot.,* 50: 641–648 (1963).

Thompson, W. P., "Independent Evolution of Vessels in Gnetales and Angiosperms." *Bot. Gaz.,* 65: 83–90 (1918).

Wilson, L. R., "Geological History of the Gnetales." *Oklahoma Geol. Surv. Notes,* 19(2): 35–40 (1959).

CHAPTER 22 / DIVISION ANTHOPHYTA

Bailey, I. V., and Swamy, B. G. L., *Contribution to Plant Anatomy.* Waltham, Mass.: Chronica Botanica (1954).

Canright, J. E., "The Comparative Morphology and Relationships of the Magnoliaceae, I: Trends of Specialization in the Stamens." *Am. J. Bot.,* 39: 484–497 (1952).

Constance, L., "The Systematics of the Angiosperms." In *A Century of Progress in the Natural Sciences, 1853–1954.* San Francisco: California Academy of Sciences (1955). Pp. 405–483.

Cronquist, A., *The Evolution and Classification of Flowering Plants.* New York: Houghton-Mifflin Co. (1968).

Esau, K., *Plant Anatomy.* New York: John Wiley & Sons, Inc. (1953).

Foster, A. S., and Gifford, E. M., Jr., *Comparative Morphology of Vascular Plants.* San Francisco: W. H. Freeman & Company, Publishers (1959). Pp. 443–539.

Gleason, H. A., *Illustrated Flora of Northeastern States.* New York: New York Botanical Garden (1952).

Hutchinson, J., *The Families of Flowering Plants,* 2nd ed. Vols. 1 and 2. London: Oxford University Press (1959).

Johansen, A., *Plant Embryology.* Waltham, Mass.: Chronica Botanica (1950).

Lam, H. J., "Taxonomy: General Principles—Angiosperms." In Turrill, W. B. (ed.), *Vistas in Botany.* London: Pergamon Press, Ltd. (1963). Pp. 3–75.

Lawrence, G. H. M., *Taxonomy of Vascular Plants.* New York: The Macmillan Company (1951).

Maheshwari, P., *An Introduction to the Embryology of the Angiosperms.* New York: McGraw-Hill Book Company, Inc. (1950).

Meeuse, B. J. D., *The Story of Pollination.* New York: The Ronald Press Company (1961).

Puri, V., "Floral Anatomy and Inferior Ovary." *Phytomorphology,* 2: 122–129 (1952).

Scott, R. A., Barghoorn, E. S., and Leopold, E. B., "How Old Are the Angiosperms?" *Am. J. Sci.,* 258: 284–299 (1960).

Stebbins, G. L., Jr., "Apomixis in Angiosperms." *Bot. Rev.,* 7: 507–542 (1941).

CHAPTER 23 / PHYLOGENY AND EVOLUTION

Barghoorn, E. S., and Schopf, J. W., "Microorganisms Three Billion Years Old from the Precambrian of South Africa." *Science,* 152: 758–763 (1966).

Barghoorn, E. S., and Tyler, S. A., "Microorganisms from the Gunflint Chert." *Science,* 147: 563–577 (1965).

430

Bower, F. O., *The Origin of a Land Flora*. London: Macmillan & Co., Ltd. (1908).

Darlington, C. D., *Evolution of Genetic Systems*, 2nd ed. Edinburgh and London: Oliver and Boyd, Ltd. (1958).

Davis, P. H., and Heywood, V. H., *Principles of Angiosperm Taxonomy*. Edinburgh: Oliver and Boyd, Ltd. (1963).

Engel, A. E. J., et al, "Alga-like Forms in Onverwacht Series, South Africa: Oldest Recognized Lifelike Forms on Earth." *Science,* 161: 1005–1008 (1968).

Harborne, J. B., *Comparative Biochemistry of Flavonoids*. New York and London: Academic Press, Inc. (1967).

Kulp, J. L., "Geological Time Scale." *Science,* 133: 1105–1114 (1961).

Margulis, L., "Evolutionary Criteria in Thallophytes: A Radical Alternative." *Science,* 161: 1020–1022 (1968).

Sokal, R. R., and Sneath, P. H. A., *Principles of Numerical Taxonomy*. San Francisco: W. H. Freeman & Company, Publishers (1963).

Sporne, K. R., "Statistics and the Evolution of Dicotyledons. *Ecology,* 8: 55–64 (1954).

Sporne, K. R., "The Phylogenetic Classification of the Angiosperms." *Biol. Rev.,* 31: 1–29 (1956).

Sporne, K. R., "On the Phylogenetic Classification of Plants." *Am. J. Bot.,* 46: 385–394 (1959).

Stebbins, G. L., *Variation and Evolution in Plants.* New York: Columbia University Press (1950).

Swain, T. (ed.), *Comparative Phytochemistry.* London and New York: Academic Press, Inc. (1966).

REFERENCES

Glossary

abaxial Facing away from the axis of the plant.

abscission layer Cell layer that breaks down or forms cork so that one part of a plant separates from remainder of plant (usually refers to leaves or fertile organs).

acervulus (plural, **acervuli**) Discoid or pillow-shaped fungal structure in which conidia and conidiophores are formed.

acrasins Substances which are secreted by myxamoebae and which regulate streaming together during the aggregation stage of Acrasiales.

acritarchs Name applied to microfossils whose affiliations are unknown; many acritarchs are probably fossil algae.

acrocarpous In Bryidae, a growth form in which the gametophyte is erect and the sporophyte terminates the main axis.

acrogynous In Jungermanniales, a condition in which the apical cell produces the gametangia, thus bearing the sporophyte terminally.

actinomorphic In flowers, radially symmetrical—i.e., symmetrical about more than one plane.

actinostele Protostele with vascular tissue arranged in radiating arms interspersed with parenchyma.

adaxial Situated toward the axis of the plant.

adnate Condition in which unlike parts are fused.

adventitious Applied to a structure not arising in its usual place (such as adventitious roots emanating from a stem rather than a root).

aeciospore Dikaryotic spore produced in an aecium of the Uredinales (Heterobasidiomycetes).

aecium (plural, **aecia**) Structure (often cup-shaped) in which aeciospores are formed.

aerenchyma Cortical tissue containing air spaces within the parenchyma.

aerobic Requiring the presence of oxygen.

aerola (plural, **aerolae**) Wall markings in the Bacillariophyceae consisting of thin areas bounded by ridges of siliceous material and having an aggregation of many fine pores.

aethalium A sessile, rounded, or pillow-shaped fructification formed by a massing of all or part of the plasmodium in the Myxomycetes.

agamospermy Asexual formation of embryo and subsequent development of a seed.

agar Complex phycocolloid substance occurring in cell wall of some Rhodophyta; also prepared as a commercial product and used to solidify culture media.

aggregate fruit A fruit formed by the fusion of many separate carpels from a single flower.

aggregation Movement of amoebae in Acrasiomycetes toward one point prior to pseudoplasmodium formation.

akinete Thick-walled resting spore in the algae, generally incorporating original vegetative cell wall.

alar region Cells in the basal corner of a moss leaf.

albuminous Applies to seeds containing endosperm at maturity.

albuminous cells Parenchyma cells in gymnosperm phloem morphologically and physiologically associated with sieve cells but not derived from the same initials.

algin Phycocolloid substance occurring in cell walls and intercellular spaces of Phaeophyta (commercially marketed).

alternation of generations Alternation of a sexual gamete-producing phase with a meiospore-producing stage; usually the alternation of a haploid with a diploid generation.

ameiotic Division of nuclear material by cleavage or splitting without visible chromosome formation.

amitotic Division of nuclear material by cleavage or splitting without visible chromosome formation.

amoeboid Resembling an amoeba.

amphibious Adapted to live both on land and in water.

amphicribral Type of vascular arrangement with the phloem surrounding the xylem.

amphigastria Ventrally located row of generally smaller leaves in some Hepaticae, especially Jungermanniales.

amphiphloic Arrangement of phloem on both sides of xylem.

amylopectin Storage polysaccharide composed of α, 1–6, 1–4 glucoside linkages; also known as "branching factor" of starch.

anacrogynous Condition in some Hepaticae in which the gametangia are lateral in position, having been formed from subapical cells—thus, the sporophyte is borne laterally.

anaerobe Organism able to grow without free oxygen.

anastomosis (plural, **anastomoses**) Parts joined or coming together, as in the veins of certain leaves.

anatropous Ovule position in carpel, with micropyle facing the placenta (Anthophyta).

androecium Collective term for the stamens of a flower.

434

androgamete In seed plants, the sex cells (or nuclei) produced by the division of the androgametophyte within the pollen grain.

androgametophyte In seed plants, gametophyte within the wall of the pollen grain which produces the androgametes.

androgenous cell Cell in pollen grain that gives rise directly to male gametes.

androsporangium In seed plants, meiosporangium that produces androspores.

androspore In seed plants, a meiospore that produces the male gametophyte (androgametophyte); in the Oedogoniales (Chlorophyta), a haploid mitospore that produces a dwarf male filament.

androsporophyll In seed plants, an appendage that bears the androsporangium.

androstrobilus A strobilus bearing microsporangia or pollen sacs.

anemophily Pollination by wind.

angiosperm Any vascular plant with seeds covered and protected by a carpel; also termed an anthophyte or a flowering plant.

anisogamy Fusion of gametes of similar form but differing in size; generally the larger gamete is considered the female and the smaller the male.

annular thickening Rings of secondary wall thickening of vessel elements and tracheids.

annulus A ring; in the Basidiomycetes, remnants of the partial veil on the stipe; in the Bryophyta and Pterophyta, a specialized ring of cells on the sporangium indirectly involved in spore release.

antheridial initial A cell in a pollen grain resulting from the division of the androsporal cell; the antheridial initial then divides to form a generative cell and a tube cell.

antheriodiophore Specialized branch bearing antheridia in members of the Marchantiales (Hepaticae).

antheridium (plural, **antheridia**) Gametangium producing male gametes; in fungi and algae, a single cell; in bryophytes and vascular plants, many cells, including sterile jacket cells.

anthesis Time (maturation) of flowering.

antipodal Vegetative cell in mature gynogametophyte of Anthophyta, usually located away from micropyle.

aplanospore Nonmotile spore.

apocarpy Condition in which carpels are separate or unfused.

apogamy Condition in which embryo develops without fusion of gametes.

apomixis Type of asexual reproduction replacing or acting as a substitute for sexual reproduction.

apothecium (plural, **apothecia**) Ascocarp (often cupulate or discoid) in which the hymenium is exposed at maturity of the ascospores.

appendix Specialized upper part of inflorescence axis not bearing flowers; characteristic of the Araceae (Anthophyta).

archegoniophore Specialized branch bearing archegonia in members of the Marchantiales (Hepaticae).

archegonium (plural, **archegonia**) Multicellular gametangium producing female gamete; generally flask-shaped with elongate neck and swollen portion containing single egg.

archesporium Mass of cells from which sporogenous cells originate.

aril Fleshy covering around seeds; in Coniferophyta, formed as a fleshy outgrowth of the stalk; in Anthophyta, of diverse origin and generally associated with tropical plants.

armored Possessing articulated plates covering the cell surface, as in some Dinophyceae.

ascocarp Ascus-bearing structure, or "fruiting body" of Euascomycetes.

ascogenous hypha Hypha that develops from the ascogonial surface after plasmogamy and gives rise to asci.

ascogonium (plural, **ascogonia**) In Euascomycetes, female cell that receives nuclei from the antheridium.

ascospore Spore formed within an ascus, typically the result of a meiotic and mitotic division.

ascostroma (plural, **ascostromata**) A stroma within which locules and asci develop.

ascus (plural, **asci**) A sac-like cell in which ascospores are produced; in most ascomycetes, the cell in which both karyogamy and meiosis occur.

GLOSSARY

asexual reproduction   Production of more individuals identical to the parent without syngamy and meiosis.

assimilative   Growing and absorbing food; vegetative or nonreproductive.

atactostele   The stele of monocotyledons consisting of vascular bundles dispersed throughout parenchyma tissue of the stem.

ATP   Adenosine triphosphate—a substance containing energy in the form of high energy phosphate bonds (this bond energy directly or indirectly drives all energy-requiring processes of life).

autotroph   Plant that requires only inorganic substances and light as an energy source for growth.

auxiliary cell   In some Rhodophyta, a cell to which the diploid zygote nucleus is transferred and where growth of the carposporophyte is initiated.

auxospore   Cell in the Bacillariophyceae generally resulting from syngamy.

auxotroph   Photosynthetic alga that needs an external supply of some organic substance.

awn   A bristle-like appendage.

axile   Central in position; as in some algae, where the chloroplast is centrally located in the cell.

axile placentation   Attachment of ovules in central area of gynoecium in Anthophyta.

bacillus (plural, **bacilli**)   Straight rod-shaped bacteria.

bacteriochlorophyll   Photosynthetic pigment occurring in purple photosynthetic bacteria.

basal body   Structure at base of flagellum to which are anchored the flagellar rootlets.

basal placentation   Attachment of ovules at base of the locule in Anthophyta.

basidiocarp   Basidium-bearing structure or "fruiting body" of Basidiomycetes.

basidiospore   Spore formed exogenously on a basidium, generally following karyogamy and meiosis.

basidium (plural, **basidia**)   Cell in which karyogamy and meiosis occur and upon which basidiospores are borne.

benthonic (benthic)   Living on and generally attached to the bottom of aquatic habitats.

binary fission   Reproduction occurring when a single cell divides into two theoretically equal parts.

bisexual   Having both sexual reproductive structures (male and female) produced by any one individual.

bordered pit   Pit in which secondary wall overarches the pit membrane (typical of gymnosperm tracheids).

bract   Leaf-like structure subtending one or more flowers or other reproductive organs.

bracteole   A small bract.

budding   Type of asexual reproduction in which a small protuberance develops and is separated from the parent cell.

bulbil   Special bud, often with thickened leaves, which serves as a means of vegetative propagation.

calcareous   Limy; consisting of, or containing calcite, or calcium or magnesium carbonate.

callose   Cell wall constituent in Laminariales (Phaeophyceae).

calyptra   The enlarged archegonium that surrounds and protects the developing sporophyte in Bryophyta, forming a sheathing cap over the capsule in most mosses.

calyx   Sterile outer whorl of flower parts composed of sepals.

cambium   Lateral meristem in vascular plants which produces secondary xylem, secondary phloem, and parenchyma, usually in radial rows.

capillitium   In some fungi and myxomycetes, thread-like strands (often forming a network) interspersed with spores.

capitulum   Small head; in Sphagnidae (Musci), dense tufts of branches at apex of gametophyte; in Anthophyta, an inflorescence composed of a dense aggregation of sessile flowers.

capsule   A case; in the Schizomycophyta, an encasing layer of slime material outside the cell wall; in the Bryophyta, the spore case containing meiospores and sterile tissue; in the Anthophyta, a type of dry dehiscent fruit formed from more than one carpel.

carinal canal   Long narrow channel in stems of some Arthrophyta apparently resulting from breakdown of protoxylem cells.

carotene   General name for group of orange hydrocarbon carotenoid pigments.

carotenoid   Class of yellow or orange fat-soluble pigments; includes carotene and xanthophyll pigments.

carpel   An ovule-bearing locule of the ovary, characteristic of the Anthophyta.

carpogonium   Female gametangium in the Rhodophyta.

carposporangium   Sporangium produced directly or indirectly as a result of division of the zygote nucleus in the Rhodophyta.

carpospore   Spore (may be haploid or diploid) produced by a carposporangium in the Rhodophyta.

carposporophyte   Collection of carposporangia occurring in chains (on the gonimoblast filaments) in the Rhodophyta; also referred to as the gonimoblast.

carrageenin   Complex phycocolloid occurring in the cell wall of some Rhodophyta (commercially marketed).

Casparian strip   A thickening of suberin occurring as a band on the primary cell wall of some vascular plant cells, especially typical of endodermal cells.

cataphyll   Small scale-like leaf often serving for protection.

cauline   Belonging to or arising from a stem.

cellulose   Main polysaccharide cell wall material of plants; composed of β, 1–4, 1–6 glucoside linkages.

central canal   The central cavity in aerial stems of Arthrophyta formed by breakdown of the pith.

centric   Cylindrical; common name for diatoms (Bacillariophyceae) with markings centrally arranged.

cephalodium   Epiphytic lichen growing as wart-like protuberance on upper surface of host lichen.

435

chalaza Basal part of ovule, adjacent to the stalk and opposite the micropylar end.

chalazal With reference to the basal part of ovule, adjacent to the stalk and opposite the micropylar end.

chemoautotroph Autotrophic plant that derives energy from chemical reactions such as oxidation-reduction reactions of inorganic compounds.

chemotactic The attraction by certain chemical substances.

chemotroph Organism deriving energy from chemical reactions; *see* Chemoautotroph.

chiropterophily Pollination by bats.

chitin Polysaccharide cell wall material composed of glucoside units and nitrogen.

chlamydospore Thick-walled, nondeciduous spore produced by rounding up of hyphal cells.

chlorobium chlorophyll Photosynthetic pigment occurring in the green sulfur bacteria.

chlorococcine line Evolutionary series in the green algae.(Chlorophyceae) including uninucleate, nonmotile, nonfilamentous unicellular or colonial forms; usually considered part of tetrasporine line.

chlorophyll General name of green fat-soluble photosynthetic pigments.

chloroplast Cell organelle with lamellar structure containing chlorophyll and carotenoid pigments.

chromatophore Nonlamellar pigment-bearing cell organelles occurring in photosynthetic Schizomycophyta and in animals.

chromoplast A colored plastid; a plastid containing only carotenoid pigments, as distinguished from a chloroplast, which contains green pigments as well.

chromosome Nuclear rod-shaped body containing genes in a linear order.

circadian rhythm Natural rhythm, e.g., as in the maturation and firing of sporangia in *Pilobolus*, in which patterns are repeated over 24-hour cycles.

circinate vernation Characteristic coiling of young leaves (fronds) of the Filicales (Pterophyta).

clamp connection Outgrowth of one hyphal cell to an adjacent one at time of cell division in dikaryotic hyphae of the Basidiomycetes.

cleistothecium Ascocarp in which the hymenium is completely enclosed at maturity of ascospores.

clonal With reference to a clone—a group of individuals (in which all individuals are of the same biotype) propagated vegetatively by mitosis from a single ancestor.

coccoid Round, spherical cell type and growth form or morphological type.

coccus (plural, **cocci**) Spherical bacterial cell.

coenobium (plural, **coenobia**) Colony of algal cells of a definite cell arrangement and number not increasing at maturity.

coenocyte Multinucleate cell or thallus lacking cross walls; generally tubular or thread-like.

coenozygote Multinucleate zygote in some Zygomycetidae (Phycomycetes).

colony In bacteria, yeasts, and algae, a mass of individuals of one species living together; in some instances consisting of a few individuals that may be attached to one another in a definite or regular pattern.

colpa (plural, **colpae**) In the exine of pollen grain, a furrow running from one pole to another.

columella Small column; in Myxomycetes, often a continuation of stipe into sporangium and may be capillitial in nature; in Phycomycetes, bulbous septum of sporangiophore; in Anthocerotae and Musci, central column of sterile cells in the sporangium surrounded by the sporogenous layer.

columellate Possessing a columella.

commissure Narrow slit-like opening in the tetrad scar of spores of most land plants.

companion cell Specialized phloem parenchyma cell in the Anthophyta derived from the same initial cell as sieve tube element.

conceptacle In some Phaeophyta, a cavity in thallus in which gametangia are formed.

conchoidal Having the form of half of a bivalve shell.

concrescent Growing together of parts originally separate.

cone A compact strobilus containing sporophylls and sometimes thickened bracts.

conidiophore Specialized hypha bearing conidia.

conidium (plural, **conidia**) Type of asexual spore not produced in a sporangium; actually a separable portion of a hypha.

conjugation Copulation, especially of isogametes or isogametangia; in the Schizomycophyta, transfer of genetic material from a donor to a recipient; in Phycomycetes and some Chlorophyceae, fusion of gametangial protoplasts; in yeasts and others, fusion of cell protoplasts following development of a conjugation tube.

connate Fusion of like parts.

connective tissue Sterile tissue lying between pairs of androsporangia in stamen of Anthophyta.

context Sterile inner part of the cap or pileus in most Basidiomycetes.

corolla Sterile whorl of flower parts composed of petals (interior to calyx).

corpus (plural, **corpi**) The body of a bladdered pollen grain—e.g., in Coniferophyta.

cortex Tissue located internal to the epidermis but not in a central position.

corticate Having a cortex; parenchymatous.

costa (plural, **costae**) Ridge; in the Bacillariophyceae, wall marking formed by two well-defined ridges and containing fine pores (striae); in the Bryophyta, midrib area of leaf or thallus.

cotyledon First leaf produced by embryo of seed plants; also termed seed leaf.

crozier formation In ascogenous hyphae, formation of a hook in which conjugate nuclear division occurs and is followed by cytokinesis; crozier formation may or may not immediately precede ascus formation.

crustose Lichen growth form in which the thallus adheres tightly to the substrate.

culm The hollow stem or "straw" of grasses.

cuticle The external waxy layer covering the outer walls of epidermal cells of vascular plants and some bryophytes, consisting of an almost impermeable fatty compound called cutin.

cutin Waxy material covering external cell surfaces of vascular plants and some Bryophyta (the layer is referred to as cuticle).

cyst Resistant spore-like body (often thick-walled), developing by the rounding up of reproductive cells (Eumycota and Myxomycota) or vegetative cells (Schizomycophyta and some algae).

cystidium Sterile structure produced in the hymenium of some Basidiomycetes.

cytokinesis Cytoplasmic division, usually following nuclear division.

cytological With reference to the structure of the cell.

decussate Pairs of appendages occurring alternately at right angles to one another (usually used with leaves, sporophylls, or branches).

deoxyribonucleic acid *See* DNA

diarch Having two protoxylem poles.

dichotomous Branching in which the two arms are more or less equal.

dicotyledon Group of anthophytes characterized by having two seed leaves, dictyostelic stem with cambium, floral parts in fours or fives or multiples of these.

dictyostele Stele with cylindrical arrangement of xylem and phloem in separate vascular bundles; a modified siphonostele.

diffuse growth Cell division and elongation occurring throughout the plant.

digitate Finger-like.

dikaryon Nuclear pair—i.e., conjugate nuclei—found in ascogenous hyphae and in secondary hyphae of basidiomycetes.

dioecious Refers to seed plants in which pollen-bearing and ovule-bearing strobili, or flowers, are borne on two separate plants.

diploid Having a single set of paired chromosomes (twice the number of chromosomes as in the gametes); $2n$.

discoid Round and/or flattened with rounded margins.

disseminule Plant part that gives rise to new plant.

distromatic Having thallus two cells thick.

DNA (deoxyribonucleic acid) Main (genetic) component of chromosomes; involved in transmission of heredity.

double fertilization Phenomenon characteristic of the Anthophyta in which one sperm nucleus fuses with the egg nucleus to form the zygote, while the second sperm nucleus fuses with the fusion nucleus to form the primary endosperm nucleus.

ectophloic Arrangement of phloem external to the xylem.

effused Referring to type of basidiocarp that is spread out or flattened.

egg apparatus Egg and two synergid nuclei located at the micropylar end of the gynogametophyte in Anthophyta.

ejectosome In the Chloromonadophyceae, the cytoplasmic organelle ejected when the organism is disturbed; *see also* trichocyst.

elater Sterile hygroscopic cell or structure; a cell among the spores in the capsule of many Hepaticae; outer part of the meiospore in *Equisetum*.

elliptic Shaped like an ellipse.

embryo sac. Gynogametophyte of Anthophyta.

embryogeny Formation of the embryo.

embryonal tube Tier of cells produced by basal tier of suspensor cells in the embryo of vascular plants; also termed secondary suspensor.

endarch A type of xylem maturation in which the oldest xylem elements (protoxylem) are closer to the center of the axis.

endocarp Innermost layer of the carpel wall, or pericarp, of fruit (Anthophyta).

endodermal cells Inner cell layer of root cortex that controls water intake into xylem cells (cells have thickened walls on the periclinal surface).

endodermis Inner layer of cortex tissue in vascular plants; often contains cells with thickened walls on the periclinal surface, with or without Casparian strips, and often surrounds individual vascular bundles.

endophyte Plant growing within another plant.

endosperm Cellular food reserve of Anthophyta resulting from double fertilization.

endosporal Referring to the development of a gametophyte within the confines of the spore wall.

endospore Spore formed within parent cell; in the Schizomycophyta, a thick-walled resistant spore; in the Cyanophyta, a thin-walled spore; the term is also used for inner layer of spore wall.

entomophily Pollination by insects.

epicotyl Portion of seedling above the cotyledons which will develop into the shoot (includes stems, leaves, etc.).

epimatium Fleshy outgrowth covering ovule in Podocarpaceae (Coniferophyta).

epiphragm In most Polytrichidae (Musci), a multicellular parchment-like membrane closing the mouth of the capsule after the operculum has fallen; consists of the expanded apex of the columella.

epitheca Outer cell half, or frustule, of Bacillariophyceae cell.

eukaryotic Cells containing membrane-bounded organelles (having a nucleus with nuclear membrane, chromosomes, and a nucleolus).

437

eusporangiate sporangium Type of sporangial development in which there are several wall layers, and in which several sporogenous initials develop from the inner side of the first initial; such sporangia are generally large and produce a large number of spores.

eustele Cylindrical stele composed of anastomosing vascular bundles.

evagination An outgrowth; or unsheathing.

exalbuminous Referring to seeds lacking endosperm at maturity.

exarch A type of maturation of the primary xylem in which the oldest xylem elements (protoxylem) are located closest to the outside of the axis.

exindusiate Without an indusium.

exine Outer thick layer of spores and pollen grains, usually divided into two main layers: an outer ectexine and an inner endexine.

exocarp Outermost layer of carpel wall, or pericarp.

exoenzyme An enzyme secreted or formed externally to the protoplast of a cell and functioning outside the cell proper.

exosporal The development of the gametophyte outside the confines of the spore wall.

exospore Type of spore formed basipetally, and one at a time, in some Cyanophyta.

extrorse Opening of the anther toward outside of flower.

eyespot Red to orange carotenoid-containing organelle in motile cells of many algae.

facultative Parasite having the ability to exist either saprobically or parasitically.

false branching In some Cyanophyta, breakage of filament with one or both ends protruding from the sheath.

fasciculate In clusters.

fertilization tube Branch from male gametangium which transfers male nuclei to female gametangium in some Phycomycetes.

fibril Submicroscopic thread-like structure; in *Sphagnum*, thickening of the hyaline walls.

filament Thread-like process, structure, or growth form; in the Anthophyta, the stalk of the stamen supporting the anther.

filamentous Elongate, thread-like cellular growth form or morphological type.

fimbriae Bacterial appendages that are flagellum-like in appearance but do not function in motility.

fission Splitting in two; characteristic especially of Schizomycophyta, Myxomycota, and Cyanophyta; also termed binary fission.

flagellate Referring to cells that possess organelles for motility; also a growth form or morphological type.

flagellin A muscle-like protein composing the flagella of bacteria.

flagellum (plural, **flagella**) Long whip-like cell organelle controlling movement of motile cell; distinguished from cilium by type of movement.

floret One of the small individual flowers of a composite flower.

foliose Leaf-like; in lichens, a growth form in which the flattened prostrate thallus may be easily removed from the substrate; in algae, a flattened, usually erect blade-like thallus.

form genus In fungi, genus name based on morphology of asexual structures; in fossil plants, a name for parts with the same form or morphology.

fragmentation Breaking apart.

free-central placentation Attachment of ovules around central column and free from carpel wall except at base.

free nuclear stage A stage in the development of the gynogametophyte of some vascular plants, in which many unwalled nuclei result from repeated division of the gynospore nucleus.

frond Fern leaf, or similar leaf-like structure.

fruit Mature gynoecium including associated accessory floral parts.

fruiting The production of fruits and, by analogy, the formation of spore-bearing bodies of fungi and other organisms.

frustule One-half of cell wall in Bacillariophyceae.

fruticose Lichen growth form in which the thallus is shrub-like and generally branched.

funiculus Basal stalk of ovule arising from the placenta in Anthophyta.

gametangial contact Sexual reproduction in which, following contact of gametangia, nuclei are transferred from the antheridium to the eggs through a fertilization tube (Phycomycetes).

gametangium (plural, **gametangia**) Structure producing gametes; in fungi and algae, generally a single cell; in Bryophyta and vascular plants, a multicellular structure with an outer sterile protective layer.

gamete Sex cell; capable of fusion with another gamete to form a zygote.

gametogenesis Formation of gametes.

gametophyte Gamete-producing plant; generally haploid and producing gametes by mitosis.

gemma (plural, **gemmae**) Specialized group of cells for vegetative reproduction; in Bryophyta, produced on the gametophyte; in Lycophyta, produced on the sporophyte.

gene Unit of inheritance, arranged in a linear sequence on the chromosome.

generative cell In the pollen grain, cell of androgametophyte that produces sperm nuclei.

genotype The genetic make-up of an organism, determined by the assemblage of genes it possesses.

geotropism The response to gravitational pull.

girdle Encircling, or middle; in Dinophyceae, transverse groove containing flagellum; in Bacillariophyceae, region where frustules overlap.

gleba Spore-producing zone in basidiocarp of some Gasteromycetes.

globule In Charophyceae, male reproductive structure, including sterile and fertile cells.

438

glycogen Complex polysaccharide similar to starch, but probably with more amylopectin; does not give blue-black color with iodine solution.

gradate sorus Sorus in which sporangia mature from the center toward the outside.

granum (plural, **grana**) A stack of closely appressed (or fused) photosynthetic lamellae.

guard cells Specialized epidermal cells forming a stoma.

gullet Longitudinal groove present in some Cryptophyceae and Euglenophyceae.

gymnosperm Vascular plant having an integumented seed not protected by carpel tissue; includes Pteridospermophyta, Cycadophyta, Ginkgophyta, Coniferophyta, and Gnetophyta.

gynoecium (plural, **gynoecia**) Collective term for carpels of a flower.

gynogametophyte In seed plants, gametophyte within the ovule which produces archegonia and female gametes (eggs).

gynosporangium Meiosporangium within the ovule of seed plants which produces gynospores; also termed the nucellus.

gynospore Meiospore in the ovule of seed plants which produces the gynogametophyte.

gynosporophyll A leaf-like appendage bearing gynosporangia in seed plants.

gynostrobilus A strobilus bearing megasporangia, ovules, or seeds.

haploid Having a single set of unpaired chromosomes; the chromosome complement present in the gametes; $1n$.

haptonema Coiled cell organelle for attachment, occurring in some Chrysophyceae.

haustorium (plural, **haustoria**) An absorptive structure that derives food from host by penetrating the cells.

helical thickening Secondary walls of vessel elements and tracheids in the form of a helix or coil.

hematochrome Red pigment granules, probably xanthophyll in nature, occurring in some Chlorophyceae and Euglenophyta.

herbaceous Having characteristics of an herb; with little, if any, secondary growth (and thus not woody).

heterocyst Spore-like structure produced by some Cyanophyta; may be a spore or a degenerate cell.

heterogeneous Differing or unlike; heterozygous.

heterokaryotic Refers to mycelium in which there are two or more genetically distinct types of nuclei.

heterokont Having flagella of unequal length on a motile cell.

heteromorphic Morphologically unlike.

heterosporous Producing meiospores of two different sizes, one of which develops into a female gametophyte and the other into a male gametophyte.

heterothallism In Zygomycetidae (Phycomycetes) and Basidiomycetes, having thalli separable into two or more morphologically similar sexual strains, with conjugation occurring only when compatible mating types are paired; in Euascomycetidae (Ascomycetes), the term has been used for hermaphroditic, self-sterile species.

heterotrichy Occurrence of erect filaments arising from prostrate portion in some algae and bryophytes.

heterotroph Plant that requires an external source of one or more organic compounds as an energy source.

heterozygous Having two different genes (or alleles) at same locus of homologous chromosomes.

hilum Scar resulting from abscission of funiculus from the seed.

holdfast Attaching discoid or root-like structure of some algae.

homogeneous Having the same nature or consistency.

homothallism In Zygomycetidae (Phycomycetes) and Basidiomycetes lacking distinguishable male and female gametangia, condition in which a single thallus is able to reproduce sexually without the interaction of two differing thalli; in Ascomycetes, sometimes used for species that are hermaphroditic and self-fertile.

homozygous Having identical genes (not alleles) at same locus on homologous chromosomes.

hormogonium (plural **hormogonia**) Multicellular segment capable of gliding motion, in the filamentous Cyanophyta.

host Living organism serving as substrate and/or energy source for another.

439

hydrophily Pollination by water.

hydrophyte An aquatic plant.

hygroscopic Readily absorbing and retaining moisture; refers to certain cells or structures that respond to changes in humidity.

hymenium Aggregation of asci or basidia and related sterile structures in a continuous layer; also termed fertile or fruiting layer.

hypha (plural, **hyphae**) One of the tubular filaments composing mycelium.

hypnospore Spore formed inside parental cell and secreting new wall.

hypocotyl Part of seedling below the cotyledons (may include the root).

hypodermis Layer of cells immediately internal to epidermis.

hypogeous Developing below soil surface.

hypogynous In Anthophyta, below the gynoecium; in some Rhodophyta, beneath the carpogonium.

hypophysis Expanded apophysis.

hypothallus Thin, shiny, membranous adherent film at base of fructification of Myxomycota.

hypotheca Inner cell half, or frustule, of Bacillariophyceae cell.

imbricated Having parts overlying each other like shingles on a roof.

indusium (plural, **indusia**) Outgrowth of leaf tissue covering sorus in Pterophyta.

integument Outer cell layer (or layers) of the ovule which covers the gynosporangium.

intercalary Inserted or between two cells or tissues.

intercalary meristem Meristem in a position some distance from the apex.

internode Portion of axis between two nodes.

intertidal region Portion of sea floor exposed between the highest and lowest tide levels.

intine Innermost, thin wall layer of spores or pollen grain.

introrse Opening of the anther toward inside of flower.

invagination An ingrowth; or ensheathed.

inversion Mutation in which there is a reversal of a segment of a chromosome or sequence of genes in relation to the rest of the chromosome.

involucre Covering; in Gnetophyta, cup-shaped disc subtending the ovule; in Anthophyta, bracts subtending an inflorescence.

isidium (plural, **isidia**) Rigid protuberance of upper part of lichen thallus which may break off and serve in vegetative reproduction.

isodiametric Having equal diameters; used to describe cell shape where length and width are essentially equal.

isogamy Fusion of gametes that are the same size and are morphologically alike.

isokont Having flagella of same length.

isomorphic Morphologically alike.

karyogamy Fusion of two sex nuclei following fusion of protoplasts (plasmogamy).

lacuna (plural, **lacunae**) Any space within a cell or tissue; usually refers to the large cavity inside the cell, or air spaces in leaf, stem, or root parenchyma.

lamella (plural, **lamellae**) Plate, or layer; submicroscopic structure of chloroplast indicates the pigments are in lamellae; in Bryophyta, refers to thin sheets or flap-like plates of tissue on the dorsal surface of the thallus or leaves; in Basidiomycetes, the gills of a mushroom.

lamina Leaf or blade; in Phaeophyta, expanded leaf-like part of thallus; in vascular plants, expanded part of leaf.

laminarin Storage polysaccharide composed of β, 1–3, 1–6 glucoside linkages, characteristic of the Phaeophyta.

leaf cushion Rhomboidal to circular area where a leaf abutted on the stem in the Lepidodendrales (Lycophyta).

leaf gap Region of parenchyma tissue where a leaf trace departs from the vascular tissue of the stem.

leaf trace Vascular bundle in stem extending from the vascular system of the stem into the base of the leaf.

lenticular Lens shaped (a double convex).

leptoma A thin region of exine at distal pole of a pollen grain which usually functions as the point of emergence of pollen tube.

leptosporangiate sporangium Type of sporangial development in which a single initial cell develops into a sporangium; such sporangia are generally small, with a single wall layer, and produce a small number of spores.

lichenic acid Water-insoluble organic acid produced by some lichens; often accumulates as crystals.

lichenin Storage polysaccharide in lichens; gives negative reaction to iodine solution.

ligule A tongue-like outgrowth on the adaxial surface of leaves and sporophylls in heterosporous Lycophyta.

lipid Any group of compounds comprising fats.

locule Compartment, cavity, or chamber; in Ascomycetes, stromatic chamber containing asci; in Anthophyta, cavity in ovary containing ovules.

lorica Surrounding case that is separate from protoplast in some algae.

mannan Polysaccharide material occurring in cell walls of some Rhodophyta, Chlorophyceae, and yeasts.

massula (plural, **massulae**) Refers to a segment of the periplasmodium which is derived from the sporangia of *Azolla* (Pterophyta); the individual massula contains many androspores, or in the megaspore one massula surrounds the megaspore and the other three sit on top of the megaspore as a cap.

mastigoneme Hair-like thread or process occurring along the length of some flagella.

mating type In algae and fungi, the term used to designate a particular genotype with respect to compatibility in sexual reproduction.

medulla Innermost region of thallus in lichens, and in some Phaeophyta and Rhodophyta.

megasporangium Meiosporangium producing usually one to four megaspores.

megaspore Large meiospore of some Lycophyta and Pterophyta which forms the female gametophyte.

megasporophyll Leaf-like appendage bearing megasporangia.

meiocyte Meiospore mother cell, or cell in which meiospores are produced.

meiosis Reduction division in which the number of chromosomes is reduced from the diploid ($2n$) to the haploid (n) state.

meiosporangium Structure in which spores are produced by meiosis (reduction division).

meiospore Spore produced by meiosis, with a reduction in chromosome number from diploid to haploid (spores usually produced in fours).

meristele Individual vascular unit of a dictyostele.

meristem Tissue concerned with formation of new cells.

meristoderm Outer meristematic cell layer (epidermis) of some Phaeophyta.

mesarch A type of maturation of the primary xylem from a central point outward; that is, the oldest xylem elements (protoxylem) are surrounded by the later-formed metaxylem.

440

mesic Characterized by a temperate moist climate.

mesocarp Middle layer of pericarp or carpel wall.

mesome Portion of axis between successive branches of telome.

mesophyte Plant growing in conditions of moderate moisture.

metaxylem Primary xylem formed secondarily after the protoxylem; generally cell elongation is complete or almost so.

microfossil Microscopic fossil particle, including spores, pollen grains, tracheids, pieces of cuticle, small algae, fungi, etc.

microphyllous Having small leaves with one vein and leaf trace as in Psilophyta and Lycophyta.

micropyle Small thread-like opening of ovule formed by incomplete fusion of the integuments.

microsporangium Meiosporangium of heterosporous plants producing many microspores.

microspore The smaller of the two types of meiospores of some heterosporous Lycophyta and Pterophyta that forms the male gametophyte.

microsporophyll Leaf-like appendage bearing microsporangia.

midrib Central vein of leaf.

mitochondrion (plural, **mitochondria**) Cell organelle in which cellular respiration occurs.

mitosporangium Structure producing spores by mitosis (equational division).

mitospore Spore produced by mitosis and having same chromosome number as spore mother cell.

mixotroph Photoautotroph capable of utilizing organic compounds in environment; may also be termed facultative heterotroph.

monocotyledon Group of flowering plants (Anthophyta) lacking functional cambium and having one seed leaf, a polystelic stem, and floral parts in threes or multiples thereof.

monoecious Refers to seed plants in which separate pollen-bearing and ovule-bearing strobili (or flowers) are both borne on the same plant.

monokaryotic Hyphal condition in which the compartments contain a single haploid nucleus—e.g., the primary mycelium of Basidiomycetes.

monopodial Having one main axis of growth.

monosporangium Vegetative cell that metamorphoses to produce a single spore; characteristic of some Rhodophyta.

monospore Single spore produced by metamorphosis of single vegetative cell, the monosporangium; characteristic of some Rhodophyta.

monostromatic Having thallus one cell thick.

mucocomplex The heteropolymer constituting the rigid component in prokaryotic cell walls.

mucopeptide Complex polymer giving the bacterial wall its rigidity.

multiaxial Main (central) axis composed of many parallel or almost parallel filaments.

multiple fruit A fruit formed by the fusion of carpels of several flowers on a common receptacle.

multiseriate Having many rows of cells.

mutation Change in genetic composition.

mutualistic Symbiotic associations in which both partners benefit.

mycelium (plural, **mycelia**) Mass of hyphae; the thallus of a fungus.

mycobiont Fungal partner, or component, of a lichen.

mycorrhiza Symbiotic relationship of fungus and root or root-like structure.

myxamoeba (plural, **myxamoebae**) Naked amoeboid cell characteristic of some Myxomycota.

nannoplankton Plankton with dimensions less than 70 to 75 microns.

neck Slender part of archegonium through which male gamete travels to reach the female gamete.

neck canal cells Inner row of cells in neck region of archegonium; at maturity these cells disintegrate.

neck cells Cells comprising the narrow tube or neck of the archegonium.

nectary The organ in which nectar is secreted.

nitrogen fixation Conversion of free atmospheric nitrogen to combined forms.

nodal ring Continuous ring of xylem and phloem at the nodes of the stem of *Equisetum* (Arthrophyta).

node Point on an axis where one or more parts are attached.

441

nucellus Meiosporangium, or sporangial, wall enclosing the gynogametophyte in the ovule of seed plants.

nuclear body Structure in bacterial or cyanophyte cell containing nuclear material and embedded in a matrix distinct from cytoplasm.

nucleus DNA-containing organelle in eukaryotic cells.

nucule In Charophyceae, female reproductive structure including oogonium and outer protective cells.

obligate Generally used for an organism that must be a parasite.

ontogenetic With reference to the life history or development of an individual organism.

ontogeny Development of an organism in its various stages from initiation to maturity.

oogamy Production of gametes in which the female is large and nonmotile with the male small and either motile or nonmotile.

oogonium Female gametangium consisting of a single cell (occurring in fungi and algae).

oosphere Egg or female gamete produced in an oogonium (Phycomycetes).

oospore Thick-walled resting spore of some Phycomycetes developing from a fertilized oosphere.

open system of growth Manner of growth typical of plants in which new cells are formed at the apices.

opercular cell A cell which forms a lid or cover.

operculum Lid or cover; in the fungi, part of a cell wall; in the Bryidae, a multicellular tissue in the capsule.

organ Distinct and differentiated plant part composed of tissues.

organ-genus A genus name used for parts of fossil plants which can be classified in a family.

organelle Part of cell (such as a flagellum or chloroplast).

ornithophily Pollination by birds.

orthotropous Upright ovule position in carpel with micropyle away from placenta and on short funiculus (Anthophyta).

ostiole Opening or pore.

ovule A sporangium surrounded by an integument and maturing into a seed following fertilization.

paleobotanist One who studies fossil plants and their relationships to environment and age of rocks.

palmelloid Growth form or morphological type, in which single cells are embedded in a gelatinous matrix.

palynology Study of pollen grains and spores.

panicle A tuft or branch of flowers or seeds, close or scattered.

papilla (plural, **papillae**) Blunt projection or protuberance.

pappus Bristle or scale-like calyx.

paraphysis (plural, **paraphyses**) Sterile hair or thread; in the Ascomycetes, sterile hypha in the hymenium; in Phaeophyta and Bryophyta, unicellular or multicellular hair associated with the sporangia or gametangia.

parasite Organism that derives its nutrients and energy from a living host.

parenchymatous Composed of living, thin-walled, randomly arranged cells.

parichnos Scar on leaf cushion representing parenchyma strands adjacent to leaf vein of *Lepidodendron* (Lycophyta).

parietal Peripheral in position; as in some algae, the chloroplast is located near the periphery of the cell.

parietal placentation Attachment of ovules in longitudinal rows on carpel wall.

parthenocarpy Fruit development without fertilization.

partial veil Membranous layer covering the developing hymenium in some Basidiomycetes.

pectic With reference to the polysaccharide material (pectin) in the cell wall and middle lamella.

pectin Polysaccharide material in cell wall and middle lamella.

peduncle Stalk bearing a strobilus or an inflorescence.

pellicle Thin membrane or covering around protoplast in the Euglenophyta.

peltate Shield-shaped.

pennate Common name for diatoms (Bacillariophyceae) generally of rectangular shape with markings in parallel rows.

perianth Protective organs around reproductive structure; in Jungermanniales (Hepaticae), sheath of leaves surrounding archegonia and developing sporophyte; in Anthophyta, calyx and corolla of the flower.

pericarp Around fruit; in Rhodophyta, urn-shaped gametophyte tissue surrounding the carposporophyte (sometimes collectively referred to as cystocarp); in Anthophyta, the mature ovary wall.

pericentral Around the central axis.

periclinal Parallel to the circumference or the surface.

pericycle Stelar tissue located between endodermis and vascular tissue in many vascular plants.

periderm Outer protective and supportive secondary tissue of some vascular plants, formed by cork cambium.

peridiole Lenticular body in which basidiospores are formed in the Nidulariales (Basidiomycetes).

peridium Membranous covering or outer sterile layer of sporangium of Myxomycota, and some Basidiomycetes.

periplasmodium Multinucleate, mucilaginous mass derived from sporangium wall of *Azolla* (Pterophyta).

periplast Differentiated membrane surrounding the protoplast of some algae.

perispore A wrinkled outer covering of some vascular plant spores, especially ferns of the Polypodiaceae and Dennstaedtiaceae (Pterophyta).

peristome teeth Tooth-like structures ringing mouth (peristome) of capsule of Musci.

perithecium Ascocarp in which the hymenium is completely enclosed at maturity of the ascospores except for a small opening or ostiole; generally urn-shaped.

phagotroph Organism that ingests solid food particles.

phenetic system Classification of extant taxa arranged according to morphological, anatomical, physiological, or biochemical criteria; the arrangement does not reflect phylogeny, because the evolutionary history is unknown.

phenotype The external visible appearance of an organism.

phloem Food-conducting tissue of vascular plants.

photoautotroph Autotrophic plant that derives energy for metabolism from sunlight.

phycobiliprotein Water-soluble pigment, similar to bile pigment, occurring in Cyanophyta, Rhodophyta, and Cryptophyceae.

phycobiont Algal partner or component of a lichen.

phycocolloid Complex colloidal substance produced by algae, especially some Phaeophyta and Rhodophyta.

442

phycocyanin Blue phycobiliprotein pigment occurring in Cyanophyta, Rhodophyta, and Cryptophyceae.

phycoerythrin Red phycobiliprotein pigment occurring in Cyanophyta, Rhodophyta, and Cryptophyceae.

phyletic slide Apparent evolutionary shift of fern sporangia from terminal to marginal to abaxial position on the leaf.

phylogenetic With reference to the evolutionary history of a group of organisms.

phylogeny Relationships of groups of organisms as reflected by their evolutionary history.

phytoplankton Free-floating, or weakly swimming, aquatic plant life.

pileus Cap or structure bearing hymenium on lower surface in some Ascomycetes and Basidiomycetes.

pinna (plural, **pinnae**) Subdivision of compound leaf or frond.

pinnule The ultimate subdivision of a pinna of a compound leaf or frond.

pit connection Protoplasmic connection between cells.

placenta Carpel tissue to which ovules are attached in the Anthophyta.

placentation Arrangement of ovules in an ovary.

plankton Aquatic organisms that are microscopic and free-floating or weakly swimming.

planospore Motile spore with one or more flagella; also termed zoospore.

plasma membrane Double-layered membrane external to protoplast of cell.

plasmodiocarp Sessile sporangium developing from main plasmodial branches in Myxomycetes.

plasmodium Naked, acellular, assimilative stage in Myxomycetes.

plasmogamy Fusion of protoplasts of two haploid cells, without fusion of nuclei (characteristic of Ascomycetes and Basidiomycetes).

plastid Organelle occurring in the cytoplasm of a cell.

plectostele A protostele split into many plate-like units.

pleomorphism Having more than one shape or form.

pleurocarpous Growth form in Bryidae in which gametophyte is much branched and creeping (sporophyte is borne on short lateral branch).

polar nucleus One of two nuclei which migrates to the center of an anthophyte gynogametophyte, ultimately fusing with other nuclei to form the endosperm.

pollen chamber Flask-shaped chamber at the top of the nucellus in the ovule, where pollen lands in seed-producing plants other than Anthophyta.

pollinium (plural, **pollinia**) Mass of pollen grains.

polysiphonous Composed of several filaments in tiers of parallel, vertically elongate cells.

polystelic Having more than one stele.

primary suspensor Cells derived from second tier of proembryonal cells.

primary tissue Tissue originating from primary meristems which are responsible for growth in elongation (generally not offering much support).

primary xylem formed by procambium; consists of protoxylem and metaxylem.

progametangium (plural, **progametangia**) In Mucorales (Phycomycetes), the fertile branch top in conjugation (the gametangium develops by deposition of a wall in the progametangium).

prokaryotic With reference to cells that have nuclear bodies, lack chromosomes, nucleoli, and nuclear membranes (other membrane-bounded bodies typically are absent from such a cell).

propagule The part of a plant that propagates it; either a vegetative structure, a seed, or a spore.

prothallial cell Sterile cells formed during development of pollen grain of seed plants other than Anthophyta.

prothallial development The growth and differentiation of the female gametophyte (gynogametophyte) of vascular plants.

prothallus (plural, **prothallia**) Gametophyte of a vascular plant.

protonema (plural, **protonemata**) Filamentous gametophyte stage of Charophyceae and many Bryophyta; usually results from spore germination.

protostele Stele having solid column of vascular tissue.

protoxylem Primary xylem that is the first formed before elongation is completed.

protozoa Unicellular microscopic animals.

pseudoelater Sterile structures among meiospores in sporangium of Anthocerotae.

pseudomonopodial Appearing monopodial; refers to branching in which the main leader or branch is not completely dominant (mainly in Psilophyta and Lycophyta).

pseudoparenchymatous Mass of densely packed filaments which have lost their individuality and are randomly arranged, resembling parenchyma tissue.

pseudoplasmodium Structure formed from aggregation of myxamoebae in Acrasiomycetes.

pseudopodium False foot; in Andreaeidae and Sphagnidae (Musci), leafless gametophytic tissue acting as a seta, raising the capsule above the main part of the gametophyte.

punctum (plural, **puncta**) Wall marking in the Bacillariophyceae; actually containing finer pores, but not as complicated as an aerola.

pycnidium (plural, **pycnidia**) Flask-shaped structure in which conidia are formed in some Ascomycetes and Fungi Imperfecti.

pyrenoid Organelle associated with chloroplasts of some algae and the Anthocerotae; often a center for starch formation, especially in Chlorophyta.

443

rachis Axis of a compound leaf, or inflorescence.

raphe Vertical unsilicified groove or cleft in valve of some Pennales (Bacillariophyceae).

ray Tissue initiated by cambium and extending radially in secondary xylem and phloem; consists mainly of parenchyma but may include tracheids in the xylem.

reciprocal parasitism Partnership between two dissimilar organisms in which both benefit; also referred to as symbiosis.

refractile Capable of reflecting.

reservoir Enlarged posterior part of gullet in some motile cells such as Cryptophyceae.

reticulate Net-like.

reticulate thickening In tracheids and vessels, secondary wall thickening in the form of a network.

rhizoid Unicellular or multicellular root-like filament that attaches some nonvascular plants and gametophytes of some vascular plants to the substrate.

rhizome Underground stem.

rhizophore Prop-like organ produced at a node and forming roots at its tip; present in some Lycophyta.

rhytidome Outer tissues of bark.

rootstock Short erect or horizontal stem bearing roots.

saccus (plural, **sacci**) Wing-like extensions of the exine in conifer pollen giving buoyancy to the pollen grains.

saprobe Heterotrophic organism deriving its source of energy from dead organisms; also termed saprophyte.

saprophyte *See* Saprobe.

scalariform thickening Secondary wall material deposited in a ladder-like pattern in vessel elements and tracheids.

scarify To scratch or cut the seed coat as an aid in germination.

schizocarp A pericarp which splits into one-seeded portions.

sclereid A sclerenchyma cell that is not elongated, but somewhat isodiametric, and often much ramified.

sclerenchyma Tissue composed of cells with thick lignified walls; generally dead at maturity.

sclerenchymatous With reference to sclerenchyma.

sclerotium (plural, **sclerotia**) In Myxomycota, a hard plasmodial resting stage; in Eumycota, a resting body composed of a hardened mass of hyphae and frequently rounded in shape.

secondary suspensor Elongated cells derived from divisions of the basal tier of proembryonal cells, after the formation of the primary suspensor.

secondary tissue Tissue produced by lateral or secondary meristems; results in growth in diameter and generally provides support.

secondary xylem Tissue produced by vascular cambium providing conducting and supporting tissues; also referred to as wood.

444

seed Mature ovule containing an embryo, generally in arrested stage of development; a food reserve may or may not be included.

segregation Separation of homologous chromosomes and hence linkage groups of genes at meiosis.

septate Divided by a partition.

septum (plural, **septa**) A crosswall, generally perpendicular to length of filament.

serological With reference to a reaction of substances (antibodies) formed in the body with foreign substances (antigens), e.g., components of bacterial cells.

sessile Without a stalk.

seta Sporophyte stalk in the Bryophyta.

sieve element One cell in a series constituting a sieve tube.

sieve plate area Area in wall of sieve tube element or sieve cell with fine pores and occupied by connecting protoplasmic strands, also termed sieve plate or sieve area.

sieve tube In Anthophyta and some Phaeophyta, a phloem-conducting structure composed of tube-like series of sieve tube elements with sieve plate areas in common end walls.

simple fruit A fruit derived from a single carpel or compound ovary of one flower.

siphonostele Stele having vascular tissue in form of hollow cylinder, surrounding a central pith.

siphonous Morphological type of growth form which is nonseptate and multinucleate, and often elongate.

siphonous line Line of evolution in the green algae (Chlorophyceae) containing organisms with multinucleate thalli.

sirenin A substance produced by female gametes that attracts the male gametes in *Allomyces*.

solenostele An amphiphloic siphonostele.

soredia Mass of algal cells surrounded by fungus hyphae, extruded through upper or outer cortex of lichen.

sorocarp The simple fruiting body of Acrasiomycetes; lacks a containing membrane and often is of irregular shape.

sorophore Stalk holding the sorus in the Acrasiomycetes.

sorus (plural, **sori**) Cluster of spores or spores together with sporangia; may include associated sterile elements.

spadix Spike with a fleshy or succulent axis, supporting inflorescence of Arales (Anthophyta).

spathe Leaf-like, often colored bract, investing the inflorescence of Arales (Anthophyta).

speciation The creation of new species in natural habitats by mutation, genetic recombination, and natural selection.

species Taxonomic unit in which the organisms included possess one or more distinctive characteristics and generally interbreed freely.

spermatangium   Structure that produces one or more spermatia in Rhodophyta.

spermatium (plural, **spermatia**)   Nonmotile cell functioning as male gamete in some Ascomycetes, Uredinales (Basidiomycetes), and the Rhodophyta.

spermatogenous cell   Synonym for androgenous cell.

spheroidal   Approaching the form of a sphere.

spirillum (plural, **spirilla**)   Helical or coiled morphological form of bacterial cell; also termed spiril.

sporangiophore   Special branch bearing sporangia.

sporangiospore   Spore produced in sporangium.

sporangium   Structure in which spores are produced; unicellular in algae, fungi, and bacteria; in Bryophyta and vascular plants, multicellular with outer sterile layer of protective cells.

spore   General name for reproductive structure, usually unicellular, but multicellular in some Eumycota and rarely in Bryophyta.

sporocarp   Many-celled structure bearing spores; a fruiting body.

sporophyll   Leaf-like appendage bearing sporangia.

sporophyte   Spore-producing plant (generally diploid and producing meiospores).

squamule   Small, loosely attached lobe in squamulose lichen.

squamulose   Lichen growth form similar to foliose type but with numerous, small, loosely attached thallus lobes, or squamules.

starch   The common carbohydrate formed by most plants.

statospore   Type of resting cell formed within a cell and often ornamented, in some Chrysophyta and Xanthophyceae.

stelar   With reference to the stele.

stele   Vascular cylinder composed of pith, xylem, phloem, and pericycle.

stephanokont   Having an anterior ring of flagella.

sterigma (plural, **sterigmata**)   Minute spore-bearing process (Basidiomycetes).

sterol   Type of organic compound present in some plants, possibly as a storage product; includes ergosterol, fucosterol, and sitosterol.

stigma   Receptive surface of carpel.

stipe   Stalk lacking vascular tissue; may be unicellular or multicellular.

stipule   One of a pair of appendages at base of petiole.

stolon   Aerial runner; in Eumycota, aerial hyphae, usually bearing rhizoids and sporangiophores at points of contact with the substrate; in vascular plants, aerial stem, usually prostrate.

stoma (plural, **stomata**)   Pore in epidermis formed by two generally kidney-shaped guard cells.

stria (plural, **striae**)   Linear row of punctae in some Bacillariophyceae.

strobilus (plural, **strobili**)   Collection or lax aggregation of sporophylls and associated bracts.

stroma (plural, **stromata**)   A compact mass of fungus cells, or of mixed host and fungal cells, in or on which spores or sporocarps are formed.

submarginal   Near the margin.

subsidiary cell   Epidermal cell associated with guard cells of stomata, often assisting in the stomatal function.

substrate   Foundation; underlying surface providing point of attachment or host for plant.

subtidal   With reference to that portion of sea floor below the lowest low-tide level (never exposed).

sulcus   Longitudinal furrow; in pollen grains, a relatively broad longitudinal leptoma; in Dinophyceae, longitudinal posterior groove containing the trailing flagellum.

supporting cell   Specialized cell from which carpogonial branch arises in some Florideophycidae (Rhodophyta).

suspensor   Multicellular filamentous structure produced by the first divisions of the embryo in seed plants.

suture   Line formed by fusion of two adjacent margins; also line of dehiscence or splitting.

swarm cell   Flagellated cell resulting from spore germination in Myxomycota (also called swarmer).

syconium   Special type of multiple fruit with superior ovaries.

symbiosis   Partnership between two dissimilar organisms in which both benefit; also referred to as reciprocal parasitism.

sympodial   Axis formed of successive dichotomous branches in which one branch is shorter or suppressed.

synandrium (plural, **synandria**)   United androsporangia.

synangium (plural, **synangia**)   United sporangia.

syncarpy   United carpels.

syndiploidy   Meiosis without syngamy; results from doubling of chromosome number immediately prior to meiosis.

synergids   Micropylar nuclei associated with the egg in Anthophyta; part of the egg apparatus.

syngamy   Fusion of gametes; fertilization.

tapetum   Nutritive layer of cells within a sporangium.

taxon (plural, **taxa**)   Term applied to any taxonomic grouping.

teliospore   Thick-walled resting spore that bears the basidium in some rusts and smuts (Basidiomycetes).

telium (plural, **telia**)   Structure producing teliospores in some rusts and smuts (Basidiomycetes).

tepals   Units of an undifferentiated perianth.

ternate   Arranged in threes.

testa   Seed coat.

tetrasporangium   Meiosporangium in Florideophycidae (Rhodophyta) in which four spores are produced.

tetraspore   Meiospore produced in Florideophycidae (Rhodophyta).

tetrasporine line Evolutionary series in the green algae (Chlorophyceae) ranging from the palmelloid type to filamentous growth form.

tetrasporophyte Plant producing tetraspores, usually free-living diploid plant (Rhodophyta).

tinsel flagellum Flagellum with many fine hairs, or mastigonemes, in one or two rows along the length of the flagellum.

trabecula (plural, **trabeculae**) Row of cells bridging an intercellular space.

tracheid A xylem conducting element in vascular plants that has no perforations in end wall, although pits are abundant throughout the wall; several kinds of secondary thickenings occur, such as annular, bordered, helical, reticulate, or scalariform.

transduction Transfer of genetic material from one bacterial cell to another by bacterial viruses (bacteriophages).

transformation The incorporation of genetic material of dead cells from the medium into the genetic make-up of living cell, as in some bacteria.

transfusion tissue A tissue in the leaves of some gymnosperms, consisting of tracheids and parenchyma cells, and occurring between the vascular bundles and the mesophyll.

transition zone Intercalary meristem between lamina and stipe in some Phaeophyta.

triarch Protostele with three protoxylem poles.

trichocyst Cytoplasmic organelle in some Cryptophyceae and Chloromonadophyceae; those released upon being disturbed also known as ejectosomes.

trichogyne Receptive hair-like extension of female gametangium in Rhodophyta and Ascomycetes.

trichome Linear row of cells within the sheath in the Cyanophyta.

trichothallic Intercalary growth at base of hair-like, uniseriate filament in Phaeophyta.

tube cell Cell of the androgametophyte believed to control the production of the pollen tube.

turbinate Shaped like a top.

tylosoid Resin-producing cell often closing the resin duct in some Coniferophyta.

unarmored Lacking specific articulated plates or armor, as in some Dinophyceae.

uniaxial Main (central) axis consisting of a single filament of usually large cells.

uniseriate Having a single row of cells.

unisexual Having only one type of sexual structure (either male or female) produced by any one individual.

universal veil Membrane covering the developing basidiocarp in the Agaricales (Basidiomycetes).

uredium (plural, **uredia**) Structure producing uredospores in some rusts (Basidiomycetes).

uredospore Dikaryotic repeating spore in some rusts (Basidiomycetes).

vacuole A cavity in the protoplasm of a cell containing cell sap.

vallecular canals Air-containing canals alternating with the vascular bundles in stem of some Arthrophyta.

valve In diatoms, each half of the silicified portion of the cell; in hepatics, parts resulting from bending outward of capsule wall when capsule opens by means of regular longitudinal splits.

valve view Surface view of cell in Bacillariophyceae.

vascular system A plant conductive system composed of xylem and phloem.

vector Organism that transmits a disease from one plant or animal to another, e.g., transmission of malaria by mosquito.

vegetative With reference to the nonreproductive or fertile phase of plant structure and growth.

venter Lower swollen, egg-containing portion of archegonium.

ventral canal cell In lycopods, arthrophytes, and ferns, the cell at the base of the archegonial neck, immediately overlying the egg.

vernation The arrangement of leaves within a bud.

vessel Xylem-conducting structure of some vascular plants composed of tube-like series of vessel members with perforations in common end walls; several kinds of secondary thickenings occur, such as annular, bordered, helical, reticulate, or scalariform.

vibrio Short, curved, rod-shaped bacterial cell.

volutin Stored food substance in bacteria, often appearing as granules.

volva Cup-like fragment of universal veil at base of stipe of some Agaricales (Basidiomycetes).

volvocine line Evolutionary series in the green algae (Chlorophyceae) exemplified by a series of colonial forms with cells not arranged in a filament.

whiplash flagellum Smooth-surfaced flagellum (without mastigonemes); may have distal thinner region.

xanthophyll General name for group of yellow, carotenoid pigments composed of oxygenated hydrocarbons.

xeric Characterized by a scanty supply of moisture.

xeromorphic Having a form that is structurally adapted for growth with a limited supply of water.

xerophyte Plant tolerant to a dry habitat.

xylem Water-conducting tissue of vascular plants; constitutes the major portion of wood.

zoospore A spore motile by means of one or more flagella; also termed planospore.

zygomorphic Bilateral symmetry—i.e., symmetrical only about a single axis.

zygospore Thick-walled resting spore resulting from the fusion of gametangia (conjugation) in Zygomycetidae (Phycomycetes).

zygote Product of syngamy; diploid cell resulting from fusion of two haploid gametes.

Index

447

---

*A boldface number indicates that an illustration of the index entry appears on that page.

449

450

453

454

456

458

460